Psychology of Retention

Melinde Coetzee · Ingrid L. Potgieter
Nadia Ferreira
Editors

Psychology of Retention

Theory, Research and Practice

Springer

Editors
Melinde Coetzee
Department of Industrial and Organisational Psychology
University of South Africa
Pretoria, Gauteng, South Africa

Nadia Ferreira
Department of Human Resource Management
University of South Africa
Pretoria, Gauteng, South Africa

Ingrid L. Potgieter
Department of Human Resource Management
University of South Africa
Pretoria, Gauteng, South Africa

ISBN 978-3-030-07547-7 ISBN 978-3-319-98920-4 (eBook)
https://doi.org/10.1007/978-3-319-98920-4

This Springer imprint is published by the registered company Springer Nature Switzerland AG
The registered company address is: Gewerbestrasse 11, 6330 Cham, Switzerland

This book is dedicated to all retention researchers, scholars and practitioners worldwide

Preface

Introduction and Overview of the Book

Psychology of Retention: Theory, Research and Practice covers up-to-date theory and research that inform retention practices in the contemporary volatile, uncertain, complex, ambiguous (VUCA) landscape. The various chapters, written by professional scholars, subject matter experts and practitioners in the field of retention, contain much rich information about the psychology of retention as manifested in real-life contexts across the globe. Presented from an integrated conceptual framework for the psychology of retention, the book is novel in exploring retention from both classical (e.g. Job Demands-Resources Model, Self-Determination Theory, Conservation of Resources Theory, Broaden-and-Build Theory and Expectancy Theory) and new models and conceptual frameworks relevant to the contemporary work context. Apart from being anchored in sound theoretical frameworks and research evidence, the various chapters provide practical guidelines for retention practice and recommendations for future research. The book is timely when considering the continuing "war for talent" in times of skills scarcity demands globally. Losing talented employees can be a costly exercise for organisations because of severe losses in terms of productivity, creativity, efficiency and profit. Talent retention is also important for business competitive advantage and sustainability and, therefore, as highlighted by the various chapters, remains a topic of high interest and challenge for most organisations and practitioners.

Generally, the scholars in this book describe retention as a systematic attempt by an organisation to develop and nurture an encouraging environment that promotes employees' decision to remain in the organisation through policies that consider various needs. The various chapters refer to the concept of retention ("retain") as meaning (1) "to hold or keep in possession" and (2) "to engage the services of". The psychological focus of this book emphasises practices relevant to the digital era brought about by the Fourth Industrial Revolution's rapid technological advancements. Contemporary retention practices are focused on engaging employees fully in the organisation as a continuous contemporary theme. To this end, the book focuses especially on deepening the reader's understanding of the role of various psychological and job/career factors in retention. The chapters also point to differing needs of a multigenerational and diverse workforce for which retention practices should cater. The chapters also evaluate the role of organisational practices such as work ethics, mentoring and rewards in contemporary retention practice.

The book is divided into six major parts as illustrated below. The six parts represent the elements of an integrated conceptual framework for understanding the psychology of retention.

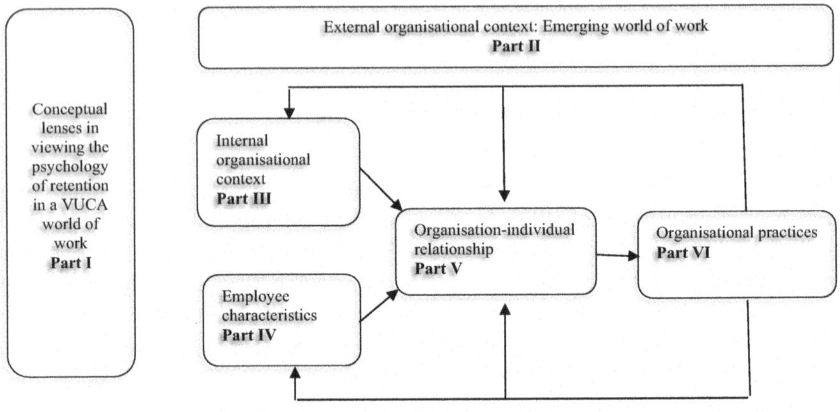

Towards an integrated conceptual framework for the psychology of retention

Part I of the book, *Conceptual Lenses in Viewing the Psychology of Retention in a VUCA World of Work*, comprises two chapters that illustrate the psychology of retention from the perspective of two conceptual lenses, namely the Job Demands-Resources dual process model (Chap. 1) and the Flow@Work Model (Chap. 2) which is relevant for not only retaining employees, but also to improve business performance in the contemporary world of work.

Part II of the book (Chaps. 3 and 4), *External Organisational Context: Emerging World of Work*, positions the psychology of retention within the pervasive influencing context of the VUCA and digital landscape which demands innovative thinking regarding retention practices that promote employee engagement over the long term. The authors make a compelling case for retention practices that address the needs of a fast-evolving digital era employee. Articulating an appealing employee value proposition (EVP) and mapping and surveying employee experiences in terms of meaningfulness and engagement across various areas of the employee journey within the organisation are emphasised.

Part III of the book, *Internal Organisational Context*, comprises four chapters (Chaps. 5–8) that illustrate the dynamics of the psychology of retention within the internal organisational context. The dynamics of personal and organisational resources, factors influencing person–job fit and embeddedness, and the creation of need supportive environments and practices are highlighted. The basic premise is that employee behaviour is a function of personal and environmental factors that manifest within a specific organisational context. The interplay between these factors should be considered in understanding the reasons why employees decide to stay in or leave an organisation. The authors highlight key insights that inform retention practices.

Part IV of the book, *Employee Characteristics*, comprises five chapters (Chaps. 9–13) that explore the role of employee characteristics in the psychology of retention. The various chapters extend on the basic premise of Part III and demonstrate how socio-demographic diversity impacts on retention by examining how person–organisational factors interact with individuals' socio-demographic characteristics.

Part V of the book, *Organisational-Individual Relationship: Psychological Contract*, comprises three chapters (Chaps. 14–16) that illustrate the role of the psychological contract in the psychology of retention. Linking back to the external organisational context (VUCA and digital landscape see Part II) influencing the psychology of retention, Part V contributes to a better understanding of especially Millennials' expectations at work and their retention.

Part VI of the book, *Organisational Practices*, comprises four chapters (Chaps. 17–20) that address work ethics, mentoring and reward solutions as important practices in the psychology of retention. The authors reiterate that retention practices should address the total rewards elements of compensation, benefits, performance management, work-life balance, recognition, and talent development and career opportunities.

In a nutshell, the various sections of the conceptual framework illustrate that retention strategies and practices should be aligned to the changing nature of work and jobs which is influenced by the technological advancements of the digital era and knowledge economy. Retention practices should take cognisance of the psychological contract expectations and career development needs of a diverse workforce and especially those of young talent (e.g. Millennials). In this regard, the employee value proposition (EVP) is a critical element of a retention strategy. Employee engagement continues to be a pervasive theme for retention. Retention strategies should include fostering a conducive and supportive environment for enhancing employees' engagement, intrinsic motivation and commitment. Managers and practitioners need a sound understanding of the psychological and job/career factors, and job demands and job resources that contribute to engaging or disengaging (withdrawal) behaviours. A holistic approach, including a total rewards strategy which focuses on retention-related policies and practices relevant to compensation and benefits, performance management, work-life balance, reward and recognition, talent development and career advancement opportunities, training and development, supervisor support and employee wellness/well-being, is seen as essential for staff retention. The book advocates the notion of design thinking relevant to the digital era to map actual employee experience throughout the employee journey in the organisation. Assessing and monitoring employees' experiences of the organisation across the various areas of a total rewards strategy, including sourcing and recruiting, pre-boarding, onboarding (orientation and initial training), communication, and community involvement, job embeddedness, person–job fit, organisational culture, performance and development mentoring and feedback, continuous learning and growth feedback, retirement, termination or resignation, will ultimately help to foster employee engagement.

We acknowledge that retention is a complex theme and that the chapter contributions only provide a snapshot of the themes and practices of relevance and interest in the contemporary work context. Although the book generally presents retention, low turnover rates and low turnover intentions as the hallmark of a healthy organisation, we also acknowledge that not all staying or retaining is necessarily good and to the benefit of the organisation. As Holtom and colleagues (Chap. 5) so eloquently point out, with turnover comes an influx of potentially new and creative energy and talent to fuel an organisation forward. However, we trust that the readers of this book will find the theory, research findings and practical retention guidelines helpful to their own understanding of the psychological principles underpinning retention. We also hope that the thoughts and suggestions presented in the various chapters will stimulate further research endeavours that will contribute to much-needed innovative evidence-based retention practices that benefit both employees and their organisations.

Enjoy reading the book!

Pretoria, South Africa

Melinde Coetzee
Ingrid L. Potgieter
Nadia Ferreira

Acknowledgements

As authors, we acknowledge that our understanding of the psychological underpinnings of retention and supportive enabling retention practices relevant to the contemporary work context has been shaped by many research scholars, practitioners, colleagues, clients and students, past and present, in the international and multicultural workplace and educational contexts. We are truly grateful for these wonderful people who have shared their practices, wisdom and insights with us in person and through the professional scholarly literature. As editors, we would also like to offer our profound gratitude to the team of authors we worked with on this book for their quality contributions, hard work and their forbearance.

Note: The manuscript and chapters in this book have been independently peer reviewed before publication. A blind peer review process was followed. The authors would also like to offer their gratitude to the reviewers for their feedback and suggestions for improving the quality of the chapter contributions and the book in general.

Contents

Part I Conceptual Lenses in Viewing the Psychology of Retention in the VUCA World of Work

1 **A Job Demands—Resources Framework for Explaining Turnover Intentions** 5
Gerhard (Gert) Roodt

2 **The Flow@Work Model as a Talent Retention Framework for the Knowledge Economy** 35
Dieter Veldsman

Part II External Organisational Context: Emerging World of Work

3 **Digital Employee Experience Engagement Paradox: Futureproofing Retention Practice** 55
John Ludike

4 **The Relevance of the Employee Value Proposition for Retention in the VUCA World of Work** 75
Dieter Veldsman and Desiré Pauw

Part III Internal Organisational Context

5 **Job Embeddedness Theory as a Tool for Improving Employee Retention** 95
Brooks C. Holtom and Tiffany Darabi

6 **Job Demands-Resources, Person-Job Fit and the Impact on Turnover Intention: Similar Across Professional and Administrative Job-Types?** 119
Leon T. de Beer, Salomé Elizabeth Scholtz and Johanna Christina Rothmann

7 **School Principal Support, and Teachers' Work Engagement and Intention to Leave: The Role of Psychological Need Satisfaction** . . . 137
Sebastiaan Rothmann and Elmari Fouché

8 **Capitalising on Employee's Psychological Wellbeing Attributes in Managing Their Retention: The Adverse Influence of Workplace Bullying and Turnover Intention** . . . 157
Melinde Coetzee and Jeannette van Dyk

Part IV Employee Characteristics

9 **Personal Attributes Framework for Talent Retention** . . . 183
Ingrid L. Potgieter

10 **Multi-generational Workforce and Its Implication for Talent Retention Strategies** . . . 203
Edyta Kostanek and Violetta Khoreva

11 **Talent Retention Strategies: The Role of Self-regulatory Career Behaviour Among Working Adults** . . . 223
Nadia Ferreira

12 **Career Development of Professional Women: The Role of Person—Centered Characteristics on Career Satisfaction** . . . 243
Ndayiziveyi Takawira

13 **Encouraging Older People to Continue Participating in Civil Society Organizations: A Systematic Review and Conceptual Framework** . . . 263
Rodrigo Serrat, Feliciano Villar and Montserrat Celdrán

Part V Organisational–Individual Relationship: Psychological Contract

14 **Millennial and Psychological Contract: Social Constructivist Approach** . . . 287
Ade Irma Anggraeni

15 **Knowing Me is the Key: Implications of Anticipatory Psychological Contract for Millennials' Retention** . . . 307
Nada Zupan, Katarina Katja Mihelič and Darija Aleksić

16 **Managing Diversity in Talent Retention: Implications of Psychological Contract, Career Preoccupations and Retention Factors** . . . 331
Alda Deas

Part VI Organisational Practices

17 Ethical Context in Relation to Employee Commitment in a Developing Country Setting 357
Jeremy Mitonga-Monga

18 Tap the Experienced to Care for the Inexperienced: Millennial Employees' Retention Challenge? Mentoring is the Solution 379
Mohammad Faraz Naim

19 Reward Solutions to Retention Questions 395
Mark Bussin

20 Total Rewards as a Psychosocial Factor Influencing Talent Retention 415
Calvin Mzwenhlanhla Mabaso

Conclusion: Theory, Practices and Research in Support of an Integrated Conceptual Framework for the Psychology of Retention 435

Index 437

Editors and Contributors

About the Editors

Melinde Coetzee (DLitt et Phil) is a Professor in the Department of Industrial and Organisational Psychology at the University of South Africa, Pretoria, South Africa. She has extensive experience in the corporate environment on psychological interventions pertaining to organisational development, human capacity and career development and talent retention. Her research interests include issues of employability and career and retention psychology in multicultural work contexts. She is Chief Editor of the *South African Journal of Industrial Psychology* and also the author, co-author and editor of a number of academic books. She has published in numerous accredited academic journals. She has also co-authored and contributed chapters to books nationally and internationally. She has presented numerous academic papers and posters at national and international conferences. She is a professionally registered psychologist (cat. industrial) with the Health Professions Council of South Africa (HPCSA) and a master human resource practitioner with the South African Board for People Practice (SABPP). She is a member of SIOPSA and IAAP.

Ingrid L. Potgieter (DCom) is an Associate Professor in Human Resource Management in the Department of Human Resource Management at the University of South Africa (UNISA), South Africa. She is a registered psychologist (cat. industrial) at the Health Professions Council of South Africa (HPCSA) since 2009 and also a registered human resource practitioner and the South African Board for People Practices (SABPP). She is also an author and co-author of several published articles in local and international journals. In addition, she presented several papers at national and international conferences.

Nadia Ferreira (DCom) is an Associate Professor in Human Resource Management in the Department of Human Resource Management at the University of South Africa (UNISA), South Africa. She is a registered human resource practitioner with the South African Board for People Practices (SABPP). She is also an author and co-author of several published articles in local and international journals. In addition, she presented several papers at national and international conferences.

Contributors

Darija Aleksić Faculty of Economics, University of Ljubljana, Ljubljana, Slovenia

Ade Irma Anggraeni Jenderal Soedirman University, Purwokerto, Indonesia

Mark Bussin Gordon Institute of Business Science, University of Pretoria, Pretoria, South Africa

Montserrat Celdrán University of Barcelona, Barcelona, Spain

Melinde Coetzee Department of Industrial and Organisational Psychology, University of South Africa, Pretoria, South Africa

Tiffany Darabi ILR School, Cornell University, Ithaca, NY, USA

Leon T. de Beer WorkWell Research Unit, North-West University, Potchefstroom, South Africa

Alda Deas Department of Human Resource Management, University of South Africa, Pretoria, South Africa

Nadia Ferreira Department of Human Resource Management, University of South Africa, Pretoria, South Africa

Elmari Fouché North-West University, Vanderbijlpark, South Africa

Brooks C. Holtom McDonough School of Business at Georgetown University, Washington, DC, USA

Violetta Khoreva Department of Management and Organization, Hanken School of Economics, Vaasa, Finland

Edyta Kostanek Faculty of Business and Law, School of Strategy and Leadership, Coventry University, Coventry, UK

John Ludike Independent Management Consultant, London, UK

Calvin Mzwenhlanhla Mabaso College of Business and Economics, University of Johannesburg, Johannesburg, South Africa

Katarina Katja Mihelič Faculty of Economics, University of Ljubljana, Ljubljana, Slovenia

Jeremy Mitonga-Monga University of Johannesburg, Johannesburg, South Africa

Mohammad Faraz Naim School of Business, University of Petroleum & Energy Studies, Dehradun, India

Desiré Pauw MMI Holdings Limited, Centurion, South Africa

Ingrid L. Potgieter Department of Human Resource Management, University of South Africa, Pretoria, South Africa

Gerhard (Gert) Roodt Department of Industrial Psychology and People Management Johannesburg Business School, University of Johannesburg, Johannesburg, South Africa

Johanna Christina Rothmann WorkWell Research Unit, North-West University, Potchefstroom, South Africa

Sebastiaan Rothmann North-West University, Vanderbijlpark, South Africa

Salomé Elizabeth Scholtz WorkWell Research Unit, North-West University, Potchefstroom, South Africa

Rodrigo Serrat University of Barcelona, Barcelona, Spain

Ndayiziveyi Takawira Department of Human Resource Management, University of South Africa, Pretoria, South Africa

Jeannette van Dyk Department of Industrial and Organisational Psychology, University of South Africa, Pretoria, South Africa

Dieter Veldsman Mindset Management, Pretoria, South Africa

Feliciano Villar University of Barcelona, Barcelona, Spain

Nada Zupan Faculty of Economics, University of Ljubljana, Ljubljana, Slovenia

Part I
Conceptual Lenses in Viewing the Psychology of Retention in the VUCA World of Work

Overview and Insights

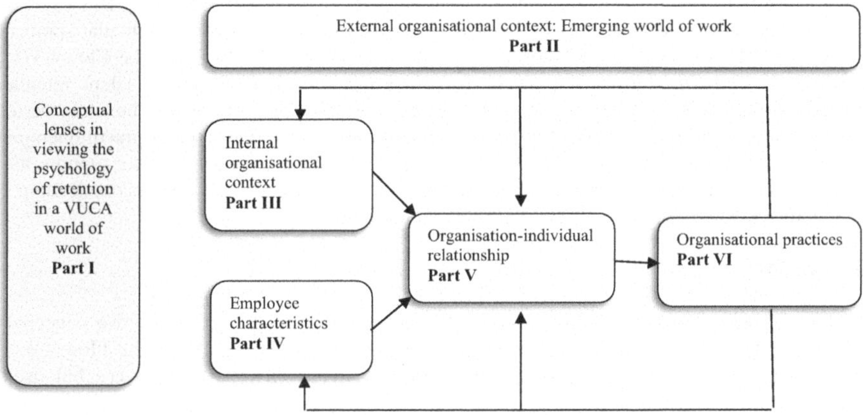

Towards an integrated conceptual framework for the psychology of retention

Part I, *Conceptual Lenses in Viewing the Psychology of Retention in a VUCA World of Work*, comprises two chapters that provide useful conceptual foundations for understanding the psychology of retention.

Overview

In Chap. 1, *A Job Demands—Resources Framework for Explaining Turnover Intentions*, Gerhard Roodt posits that talent loss and talent retention are respectively associated with the intention to leave or to stay in the organisation. Based on a sound review of the research literature, the author argues that talent retention is dependent on how engaging or disengaging employees view their working conditions and job characteristics in their organisations. The author uses the well-known job demands-resources (JD-R) model as theoretical lens to critically review the dynamic interaction between resources (JR: pull factors) and demands (JD: push factors), on the one hand, and outcomes (engaging and withdrawal behaviours), on the other hand, as mediated by personal dispositional factors (i.e. sense-making and meaning of work; personal resources; self-regulation/self-determination; and personal agency). The author discusses a number of distal contextual push and pull factors that are related to engaging or disengaging work behaviours (i.e. organisational support; quality of supervisor relationship; workload; task identity; perceived external prestige; perceived team climate; and contract breach as distal factors and advancement opportunities; growth opportunities; work–family conflict/balance; and job insecurity as proximate factors). The author describes how the intermediate outcomes (engagement or disengagement) influence individuals' final decision to stay or leave the organisation. Based on the latter finding, some suggestions are made for practitioners and for researchers to foster a healthy workplace for talent retention.

Chapter 2 by Dieter Veldsman, *The Flow@Work Model as a Talent Retention Framework for the Knowledge Economy*, makes a compelling case for new talent retention frameworks that address the unique challenges posed by the knowledge economy of the volatile, uncertain, complex and ambiguous (VUCA) world of work. The author emphasises that the world of work has entered the Fourth Industrial Revolution, with technological innovation, a multi-generational workforce that is distributed across the globe, and the rise of on-demand talent changing the way in which organisations operate. Talent has become a scarce commodity, with organisations having to compete for this global and mobile workforce. The chapter makes a novel contribution to the retention literature by presenting the Flow@Work model as a talent retention framework for knowledge economy organisations. The model is built upon the theoretical concept of psychological work immersion, which refers to a pervasive state of profound emotional, cognitive and physical identification with, and enjoyment of, the work experience within a particular sociocultural context. This chapter contributes on a practical level by indicating that the Flow@Work model has been utilised as a framework for the implementation of various talent retention strategies within South African organisations as a method to drive sustainable business performance. In the retention space, the Flow@Work model provides organisational practitioners and leaders with a simple framework that can be applied to their environments to support their employees to continuously achieve higher states of psychological work immersion, leading to benefits for both the organisation and the individual employee.

Key Insights

Part I of the book illustrates the psychology of retention from the perspective of two conceptual lenses, namely the job demands-resources dual process model (Chap. 1) and the Flow@Work model (Chap. 2), which is relevant for new world of work to not only retain employees, but also to improve business performance.

Practice Guidelines

The job demands-resources dual process model (Chap. 1) is especially useful to help managers and practitioners understand, address, and measure the psychological factors that either promote engaging or disengaging behaviours and attitudes. Practice guidelines include inter alia surveys to assess how engaging or disengaging employees view their working conditions and job characteristics in their organisations in terms of JRs and JDs. HR practices should focus on interventions to grow and develop those personal dispositional factors that will result in optimally functioning individuals who possess competencies and skills to effectively and systematically deal with job challenges and hindrances (JDs).

The author of Chap. 2 presents the concept of creating an enabling environment for the retention of employees by means of the Flow@Work model. The model is built upon the theoretical concept of psychological work immersion, which refers to a pervasive state of profound emotional, cognitive, and physical identification with, and enjoyment of, the work experience within a particular sociocultural context, all of which allude to the psychology of retention. The model is operationalised in terms of an empirically tested scale (the psychological work immersion scale: PWIS) which serves as a reliable and valid diagnostic framework to identify critical areas of focus to drive talent retention over the longer term. The author illustrates by means of two real-life case studies how the PWIS was applied to identify key areas of focus for targeted long-term OD interventions. The usefulness of the PWIS lies in its measurement of impact of the people component on the business performance/profit side.

Research Gaps
Some of the research gaps highlighted by the author of Chap. 1 include research on an organisational level (i) to determine which JDs and JRs are active and dominant for different organisations, (ii) on which levels in these organisations these JRs and JDs are active, and (iii) also for which job families or communities of practice in these organisations it is the case. The author views the information as a prerequisite for designing and developing effective interventions to promote engagement levels for specific work roles on the various organisational levels. The author (Chap. 1) also makes a case for evaluation research to test the effectiveness of different interventions with the aim to grow and develop particular JRs and also to reduce the negative impact of JDs that will result in positive gain spirals.

In Chap. 2, the author recommends further testing of the PWIS in terms of its applicability to other contexts globally, with specific reference to non-Westernised working environments. Continuous research regarding the longitudinal impact of the model by means of the PWIS on employee retention and business performance should also be explored.

Chapter 1
A Job Demands—Resources Framework for Explaining Turnover Intentions

Gerhard (Gert) Roodt

Abstract This chapter is based on the well-known and widely used premise that B = f (P X E) (where B = behaviour; f = function of; P = Person and E = Environment). The chapter will first introduce a number of distal contextual (environmental) factors that may have an impact on individuals' levels of engaging work behaviours and consequently their intention to stay or leave the organisation. Second, a number of proximate contextual factors will be introduced that may influence individuals' decision to leave or stay in the organisation. Third, are unique individual dispositional factors that may mediate/moderate the relationship between environmental factors and intermediate outcomes. Fourth, a framework based on the well-known Job Demands—Resources (JD-R) Model will be introduced. This model provides a perspective on the dynamic interactions of the contextual factors (viewed either as resources or demands from a JD-R perspective) and personal factors as well as how these are related to outcomes such as engagement or withdrawal behaviours. Fifth, these outcomes will influence the decision to stay or leave the organisation. Finally, some practical implications for retention are pointed out and suggestions for research are made.

Keywords Job demands-resources · Turnover intention · Distal factors
Proximate factors · Dispositional factors · Retention · Engagenment

Introduction

The retention of personnel remains one of the most important topics in Human Resource Management and Industrial Psychology literature today. It therefore comes as no surprise that some authors (e.g. Michaels et al. 2001) use military terminology to describe this continuous and severe struggle to retain talent as the

---

G. (Gert) Roodt (✉)
Department of Industrial Psychology and People Management Johannesburg Business School, University of Johannesburg, Johannesburg, South Africa
e-mail: groodt@uj.ac.za

M. Coetzee et al. (eds.), *Psychology of Retention*,
https://doi.org/10.1007/978-3-319-98920-4_1

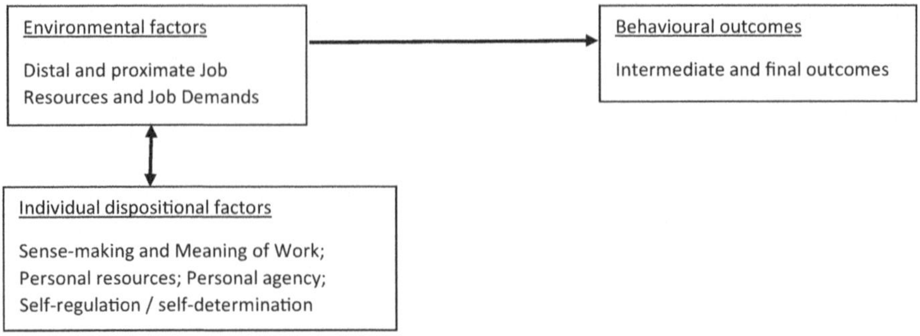

Fig. 1.1 A graphical depiction of the behaviour equation (own compilation)

'war for talent'. This chapter is focused on talent retention and its structure is based on the well-known and widely used premise that B = f (P X E), (where B = Behaviour; f = function of; P = Person and E = Environment). This equation is graphically depicted in Fig. 1.1 as:

Flowing from Fig. 1.1, this chapter will first introduce a range of distal contextual (environmental) factors that may have an impact on an individual's level of work engagement (or disengagement) and consequently their intention to stay or leave the organisation. Second, the number of proximate contextual factors will be introduced that may influence individuals' intermediate outcomes such as work engagement (or disengagement) and consequently their final decision to leave or stay in the organisation. Third, are unique individual (personal) dispositions such as personal resources as well as personal agency that contribute to optimal individual functioning. Fourth, a dual process framework based on the well-known Job Demands—Resources (JD-R) Model will be introduced. This model provides a dynamic perspective on the dual process interaction of contextual (viewed either as resources or demands from a JD-R Model perspective) and personal dispositional factors that either facilitate or inhibit individual engagement levels as intermediate outcomes. The proposed framework suggests that the relationship between the dynamic interaction between resources (pull factors) and demands (push factors) on the one hand and outcomes (engagement and withdrawal behaviours) on the other hand are mediated by individual dispositional factors. Fifth, the intermediate outcomes (engagement or disengagement) will influence individuals' final decision to stay or leave the organisation. Finally, some suggestions are made for practitioners and for researchers.

Contextual (Environmental) Factors

Referring back to Fig. 1.1, the contextual (environmental) factors can be divided into distal and proximate contextual factors (job resources and demands). Based on their prominence in published empirical research, a selection of the distal contextual factors will be presented first.

(i) Distal contextual (environmental) factors

A range of different distal contextual factors may contribute to an individual's engagement or disengagement in the work place. Several publications have shed light on factors that promote engagement (or disengagement) in the workplace (Bakker and Demerouti 2007, 2008; Bakker et al. 2008, 2014; Demerouti et al. 2001; Rothmann and Rothmann 2010; Schaufeli and Bakker 2004). Schaufeli and Taris (2014) also listed a range of such factors on an individual level whilst Joubert (2010) listed not less than 57 management practices on different levels in organisations that contribute to work engagement on an individual, team, organisational and a managerial level. According to Hakanen and Roodt (2015: 86) JDs and JRs may be located on the following levels in organisations, namely on the *organizational* (e.g. salary and career opportunities), *interpersonal and social relationships* (e.g. supervisor and co-worker support), *organization of work* (e.g. role clarity, participation in decision-making), and *task* levels (e.g. performance feedback, skill variety, autonomy).

Perhaps the most significant attempt to date to create a framework or a taxonomy for organising the different demand (push) and resource (pull) factors is the study of Demerouti et al. (2001) that resulted in the Job Demands—Resources (JD-R) Model. The JD-R Model suggests that if JRs weigh proportionally more than the JDs, then engaging work behaviours (such as work engagement) will follow. Again, if JDs weigh proportionally more than the JRs, then disengaging work behaviours (also referred to as withdrawal behaviours) will follow. There is also empirical support for the premise that JRs buffer the negative effects of JDs in promoting work engagement (Bakker et al. 2007). The JD-R Model seems to have wider applicability then only the prediction of work engagement, because it can also be extended to the prediction of work identity (i.e. the identification with work and all its related facets) as was established by the De Braine (2012) study (also see De Braine and Roodt 2011). But not all these pull and push factors mentioned by Joubert (2010) or by Schaufeli and Taris (2014) are linked to or included in the JD-R Model (which is too limited or restrictive). There are other engagement facilitating factors or inhibiting factors also respectively referred to as pull and push factors. In view of this, JDs may also be referred to as inhibiting or push factors and JRs can also be named facilitators or pull factors.

More specifically, *job resources* (JRs) are "…Those physical, psychological, social or organizational aspects of a job that either/or (1) reduce job demands and the associated physiological and psychological costs; (2) are functional in achieving work goals; and (3) stimulate personal growth, learning and development" (Demerouti et al. 2001: 501). According to De Braine and Roodt (2015) these JRs can be grouped into proximate and distal JRs, where the proximate JRs are closer to the individual and include factors such as the relationship with the supervisor, peers and role clarity. Distal (contextual) JRs are moved further away from the individual and may include aspects such as the perceived team climate, perceived external prestige of the organisation and information/communication flow. It should be noted at this point in time that the absence of any job resource may turn into a job demand. For instance, the absence of a good relationship with a supervisor may become a job demand.

Bakker et al. (2007: 275) are of the opinion that *job demands* (JDs) "represent characteristics of the job that potentially evoke strain, in case they exceed the employee's adaptive capability". JDs are more precisely defined as "…those physical, social, psychological, or organizational aspects of a job that require sustained physical and/or psychological (i.e. cognitive and emotional) effort on the part of the employee and are therefore associated with certain physiological and/or psychological costs" (Demerouti et al. 2001: 501). JDs can also be grouped into proximate and distal JDs where proximate JDs include emotional demands, role ambiguity, role conflict and lack of social support from supervisors and peers as well as work overload to name a few. Distal (contextual) JDs on the other hand may include unfavorable working conditions as well as an unsupportive work climate. Van den Broeck et al. (2010) argue that all job demands are not equal and that one should distinguish between job hindrances (which are more severe) and job challenges.

An important premise the JD-R Model is working on, is that two sets of working conditions prevail (see Hakanen and Roodt 2010) that provide the basis for referring to this model as a dual process model. Two different, but related processes according to Bakker and Demerouti (2007: 313) and Schaufeli and Bakker (2004: 296) are: "(1) an energy sapping, health impairment process in which high job demands exhaust employees' mental and physical resources leading to burnout, and eventually to ill-health; and (2) a positive motivational process in which job resources foster engagement and organizational commitment" (Hakanen and Roodt 2010: 87). The health impairment process results in constant overload and eventually to exhaustion and employee withdrawal (disengaging) work behaviours. On the other hand, the motivational process leads to increased extrinsic motivational levels to cope with job demands and for achieving work goals. This results in increased engagement levels and other forms of engaging work behaviours.

It should also be noted that sufficiently decreased job demands may turn these demands into job resources. For instance, the absence of role conflict may become a job resource. A selection of these distal contextual factors will be discussed next.

Perceived Organisational Support

De Braine and Roodt (2015) view *perceived organisational support* (POS) as an umbrella term that contains a number of sub-dimensions. These sub-dimensions are employees' relationships with their supervisors (to be discussed under the next heading); flow of information and communication; role clarity; and participation in decision-making. The term *perceived organisational support* was coined by Eisenberger et al. (1986: 501) as employees' "…global beliefs concerning the extent to which the organization values their contributions and cares about their wellbeing". In view of this definition, perceived organisational support is classified as a JR.

Empirical research that links POS and different forms of engaging behaviours (e.g. attachment; job involvement; work engagement; organisational commitment; organisational citizenship behaviours (OCBs); organisational identification; work identity; and others) are amongst those reported by Anthun and Innstrand (2016), Campbell et al. (2013), Christian et al. (2011), Cheung and Wu (2013), De Braine (2012), Fuller et al. (2006a), Rothmann and Joubert (2007), and Rothmann and Rothmann (2010). Research by Sundin et al. (2006) reported on factors that contribute to perceived social and supervisory support. These listed studies suggest that POS is an antecedent for work engagement or other forms of engaging workplace behaviours that may eventually lead to the decision to stay with the organisation.

Quality of Supervisor Relationship

The saying "people leave because of their supervisor" has nearly become general knowledge now. Employees assess the quality of their relationship with their supervisor. *Supervisory support* is defined as "…the degree to which employees perceive that supervisors offer employees support, encouragement, and concern" (Babin and Boles 1996: 60). In short, it all boils down to the fact that if the supervisor is supportive, considerate and caring it would make the employees wish to stay. Supervisory support can therefore be classified as a JR.

Studies that link the quality of the supervisor relationship and different forms of engaging behaviours are Barkhuizen et al. (2013), Collins et al. (2014), Friede et al. (2008), Geertshuis et al. (2015), Menguc et al. (2016), O'Connor and Srinivasan (2010), Paglis and Green (2002), Schermuly and Meyer (2016), Sollitto et al. (2016), Stringer (2006), Volmer et al. (2012), Yee et al. (2015) and Yuan and Woodman (2010). On the other hand Liao et al. (2010), and Zhao et al. (2013) reported improved employee creativity levels where LMX quality is considered to be high. These listed studies suggest that quality of the supervisor relationship is an antecedent for work engagement and/or other forms of engaging workplace behaviours that may eventually lead to the decision to stay with the organisation.

Work Load (Overload and Underload)

Work load is a neutral term, whilst *work overload* is regarded as anything that places high attentional demands on an employee over an extended period of time

(Berry 1998). Overload can be described in qualitative and quantitative terms. Quantitative overload suggests that there is too much work to do in the available time space. Qualitative overload on the other hand is considered to be work that exceeds the skills level or concentration level of an employee (De Braine and Roodt 2015). Work overload is clearly a JD, and two types of work overload are where demands exceed the employees' mental or emotional capacities to deal with these types of demands. Continuous mental and emotional demands may eventually lead to different types of withdrawal behaviours and ultimately to stress and burnout. *Work underload* can also be classified as a JD where the mental and emotional capacities of an employee are not sufficiently challenged.

Empirical research where work overload is connected to different forms of disengaging behaviours (e.g. work alienation; withdrawal; lethargy; burnout; organisational estrangement; counter-productive behaviours (CPBs); organisational de-identification; and others) are amongst others those reported by Buys and Rothmann (2010), Friedemann and Buckwalter (2014), Hakanen et al. (2017), Jensenet al. (2011), Karatepe (2013), Lackritz (2004), Rothmann and Joubert (2007), Schaufeli et al. (2009), and Xanthopoulou et al. (2007). These listed studies suggest that workload (either overload or underload) is an antecedent for burnout and/or other forms of disengaging workplace behaviours that may eventually lead to the decision to leave the organisation.

Task Identity

Task variety has been included previously in JD-R research, but research on task identity in this context is limited. Hackman and Oldham (1975: 161) define task identity as "…the degree to which the job requires completion of a 'whole' and identifiable piece of work—that is, doing a job from beginning to end with a visible outcome". According to De Braine and Roodt (2015) task identity also positively influences the experience of meaning at work. Task identity can be classified as a JR, but if a clear task identity is lacking at work it can easily turn into a JD.

Studies that reported on the link between task identity and engaging work behaviours are limited and only those of De Braine (2012), and Rothmann and Jordaan (2006) could be found.

Perceived External Prestige (PEP)

Employees' willingness to identify with an organisation is dependent on an organisation's corporate reputation, its organisational identity, and perceived external prestige (De Braine and Roodt 2015). *Perceived external prestige* (PEP) is defined as "…the judgment or evaluation about an organization's status regarding some kind of evaluative criteria, and refers to the employee's personal beliefs about how other people outside the organization such as customers, competitors and suppliers judge its status and prestige" (Carmeli et al. 2006: 93). When employees assess PEP as being positive, then PEP is considered to be a JR. But when PEP is evaluated as being negative, then PEP can turn into a JD.

Reported research on the link between PEP and engaging work behaviours are Carmeli (2004, 2005), Carmeli and Freund (2009), Ciftcioglu (2011), De Braine (2012), Fuller et al. (2006a, b), Guerrero and Challiol-Jeanblanc (2017), Kang et al. (2011), and Smidts et al. (2001). These listed studies suggest that PEP is an antecedent for different forms of engaging workplace behaviours that may eventually lead to the decision to stay with the organisation.

Perceived Team Climate

Team climate can be viewed as a team's shared perception of organisational policies, practices and procedures. Anderson and West (1998) further propose that *perceived team climate* comprise of four broad factors: (a) shared vision and objectives; (b) participative safety; (c) commitment to excellence, involving a shared concern for the quality of task performance; and (d) support for innovation which includes expressed and practical support. Team climate also refers to a shared commitment to teamwork, high standards and systemic support for cooperation (De Braine and Roodt 2015). Based on this description, perceived team climate can be classified as a JR if rated positively, but if rated negatively, it can turn into a JD.

Empirical research on the relationship between perceived team climate and engaging team behaviours are Anderson and West (1998), De Braine (2012), Joubert and Roodt (in review); and Torrente et al. (2012). Only a few studies were conducted that considered perceived team climate as an antecedent of team level engagement. These listed studies suggest that team climate is an antecedent for different engaging workplace behaviours that may eventually lead to the decision to stay with the organisation.

Contract Breach

As opposed to the explicit employment contract, the implicit psychological contract is a set of subjective expectations and obligations that employees and employers hold of one another in respect of a range of work-related conditions, such as development opportunities, advancement, compensation, performance management as well as justice and fairness. If the conditions and principles of the psychological contract are honoured, it can be classified as a JR, but if the conditions and principles are violated (also termed psychological contract breach), it can easily turn into a JD. In the case where contract breach is a JD, it leads to feelings of resentment and consequently to organisational estrangement and also to organisational de-identification (De Braine and Roodt 2015).

Research studies that report on the relationship between contract breach and disengaging work behaviours are Bester (2012), and Suazo et al. (2008). Empirical research on contract breach as a JD is sparse. These listed studies suggest that contract breach is an antecedent for disengaging workplace behaviours that may eventually lead to the decision to leave the organisation.

A selection of proximate contextual factors that may have an impact on work engagement (or disengagement) which ultimately results in the decision to leave or stay with the organisation will be discussed next.

(ii) Proximate contextual (environmental) factors

Proximate contextual factors are a set of environmental factors that are more closely related to an employees' job and to him/her as a person. These factors can also be classified as either a JR or as a JD. Based on their prominence in published empirical research, a selection of the most important proximate (contextual) JRs and JDs of this model or taxonomy will be discussed next in more detail.

Advancement Opportunities

Opportunities for advancement or progress in the workplace is an umbrella term that includes a number of sub-dimensions. De Braine and Roodt (2015) have included remuneration, career progression possibilities, and training opportunities under this category. This means that employees would assess advancement opportunities in an organisation as the opportunity to progress and increase income, status, and career progression. Advancement opportunities will be viewed as a JR if this aspect is rated positively by employees, but if absent this aspect will turn into a JD.

Several studies reported on the relationship between advancement opportunities and engaging work behaviours such as those reported by Amiri et al. (2016), Cho and Huang (2012), De Braine (2012), Ezzedeen and Ritchey (2009), Inandi (2009), Rothmann and Joubert (2007), Rothmann and Rothmann (2010), and Tharshini et al. (2016). On the other hand a study by Meddour et al. (2016) did not find any relationship between career advancement opportunities and turnover intentions in Malaysia.

These listed studies suggest that advancement opportunities is an antecedent for different forms of engaging workplace behaviours that may eventually lead to the decision to stay with the organisation.

Growth Opportunities

Growth opportunities is also an umbrella term that refers to two sub-dimensions, (1) the opportunity to grow and develop a variety of work-related skills, and (2) providing the opportunity to learn and to develop. According to De Braine and Roodt (2015) the latter refers to providing opportunities that will enable employees to grow and development knowledge, skills and attitudes in the workplace. If growth opportunities are rated positively by employees it will be considered to be a JR, but if rated negatively this aspect will turn into a JD.

A number of studies reported on the relationship between growth opportunities and engaging work behaviours such as those reported by Altunel et al. (2015), Buys and Rothmann (2010), De Braine (2012), Kira et al. (2010), Park et al. (2014), Rothmann and Rothmann (2010), Van Wingerden et al. (2017), and Weer and Greenhaus (2017). These listed studies suggest that growth opportunities is an antecedent for different forms of engaging workplace behaviours that may eventually lead to the decision to stay with the organisation.

Work—Family Conflict/Balance

Owing to the fact that in recent times there is a better representation of both males and females in the workplace and the fact that dual career couples (where both partners are working) is a general phenomenon in modern economies as well as in the current economic climate, resulted in the emergence of the work—family conflict phenomenon. This phenomenon can have several dimensions or facets where for instance a working individual is experiencing difficulty to balance the workplace demands with family demands or vice versa. Closely related, are spill-over effects between work and family life for an individual where events in one sphere have an impact (either positive or negative) in another sphere. It may also happen that partners of dual career couples are experiencing difficulty to balance work and/or family events and to juggle priorities between them. Crossover effects again refer to the conditions where experiences of one partner are carried over to the other partner in the relationship. Against this backdrop Greenhaus and Beutell (1985: 77) define *work—family conflict* as "…a form of inter-role conflict in which the role pressures from the work and family domains are mutually incompatible in some respect". From this definition's point of view work—family conflict/balance can be viewed as a JD, but in the case of the absence of any conflict it may become a JR.

Empirical research that reported on the effects between work—family conflict and different types of engaging work behaviours are those reported by Baer et al. (2016), Bakker et al. (2009), Brotheridge and Lee (2005), Byrne and Canato (2017), Chen and Huang (2016), Chernyak-Hai and Tziner (2016), De Braine (2012), Ezzedeen and Ritchey (2009), Fiksenbaum (2014), Friedemann and

Buckwalter (2014), Halbesleben et al. (2009), Hall et al. (2010), Karatepe (2013), Karatepe and Karadas (2013), Mache et al. (2016), Mauno et al. (2015), Medina-Garridoet al. (2017), Nielson et al. (2001), Robinson et al. (2016), Schaufeli et al. (2009), Straub (2007), Thanacoody et al. (2009), Tement and Korunka (2015), Watanabe and Falci (2016), and Yamaguchi et al. (2016).

These listed studies suggest that the presence of work-family conflict is an antecedent for different forms of disengaging workplace behaviours that may eventually lead to the decision to leave the organisation.

Job Insecurity

Experiencing a sense of security (feeling protected from fear and threat) in the workplace has emerged as an important research variable in more recent Industrial Psychological research. Rothmann et al. (2006) describe *job insecurity* as "feeling insecure in the current job and level with regard to the future thereof". Greenhalgh and Rosenblatt (1984: 438) take a sociological view of job insecurity as "…a sense of powerlessness to maintain desired continuity in a threatened job situation". In view of these definitions it is evident that job insecurity is considered to be a JD, but in the case of job security (the absence of insecurity), it is a JR.

Several studies reported on the empirical link between job insecurity and disengaging work behaviours. Amongst others are the studies reported by Bosman et al. (2005), De Braine (2012), Moshoeu and Geldenhuys (2015), Rothmann and Jordaan (2006), Rothmann and Joubert (2007), Rothmann et al. (2006), Stander and Rothmann (2010), Sverke and Hellgren (2002), and Van Zyl et al. (2013). Van Schalkwyk et al. (2010) however reported no significant relationships between job security and employee engagement in the case of a petrochemical firm. These listed studies suggest that job insecurity is an antecedent for different forms of disengaging workplace behaviours that may eventually lead to the decision to leave the organisation.

It is evident form the discussion above that the proximate and distal JRs and JDs may present themselves on different organisation levels (i.e. individual, team, organisational or management levels) and Joubert and Roodt (in review) consequently argue that the roles individuals occupy on these different levels in organisations, may result in different degrees of engaging behaviours on the said levels. Stated differently, an individual may be engaged based on his own contextual JRs and JDs on an individual level, but be disengaged as a team member because of the unfavourable ratio between JRs and JDs on a team level. Based on the different organisation levels and the multiple roles phenomena, it is argued that employee engagement should rather be viewed as a multi-level construct. Proximate and distal JRs and JDs should therefore be considered for each role and on each level in the organisation if one wishes to establish the degree of engagement on a particular level. It is furthermore argued that different higher level contexts may have an influence on lower level contexts and vice versa. For instance, poor management/

leadership engagement may result in poor team and individual engagement levels or vice versa (also see Schaufeli 2015; Tuckey et al. 2012; Van Schalkwyk et al. 2010).

Individual Dispositions

Referring back to Fig. 1.1, there are a number of individual dispositional factors that are unique to any individual that may moderate or mediate the relationship between the contextual factors and the intermediate and final outcomes. The basic assumption on which these factors are presented, is that individuals' own unique dispositions may capitalise on the contextual (environmental) factors in order to attain goals more effectively. Individuals who possess these dispositional factors or who display such behaviours are often referred to as optimally functioning individuals. Personality, locus of control, self-confidence and self-esteem are some dispositions often reported on in research. The four dispositional variables that are selected for purposes of this discussion that contribute to optimal human functioning, but that are not so frequently used, will be presented next.

Sense-Making and the Meaning of Work

The personal interpretation and meaning an individual may attach to work and to the work-role in the creation of their own identity formation is unique to every individual. Sense-making and meaning are two inseparable terms. *Sense-making* precedes the creation of meaning in the sense that it "retrospectively ascribes meaning" to events. "…it is an aid that serves individuals to deal with the complexity and uncertainty of their environment, by creating a reasonable account of the world" (Asik-Dizdar and Esen 2016: 2). *Meaning of work* on the other hand is defined as "… as sense of coherence, direction, significance, and belonging in the working life" (Schnell et al. 2013: 543). The Meaning of Working (MoW)—International Research Team (1987) was conceptually defined in five major domains with a brief explanation by Harpaz and Fu (2002) of each below:

Work centrality as a life role. Work in modern society is considered to be one of the most important activities for people that is central to their being. Work role centrality is based on the assumption that work plays a central and fundamental role in the lives of individuals (also see Bothma et al. 2015).

Societal norms regarding work: **entitlement and obligation**. The two societal norms *entitlement* and *obligation* were developed based on the premise that on the one hand one can expect certain rights and responsibilities from society in return for work and on the other hand one has a duty to contribute to society by working and to serve society.

Valued work outcomes. This domain investigates the general outcomes achieved by working and their relative importance. Six general meanings of work as developed by Kaplan and Tausky (1974) are covered in this domain that were classified by Wiltshire (2016) into expressive and instrumental meanings (shown in brackets):

(a) status and prestige (status and prestige bestowing activity)
(b) needed income (an economic activity, a means of survival)
(c) time absorption (a scheduled or routinized activity)
(d) interesting contacts (satisfying interpersonal experiences)
(e) service to society (morally correct activity)
(f) interest and satisfaction (intrinsically satisfying activity).

Importance of work goals. This domain focuses on the relative importance of work goals and values that individuals wish to attain through work. This aspect is also closely related to the self-regulation aspect to be discussed further down under this personal resources heading.

Work-role identification. This aspect covers the extent that people evaluate and identify working in terms of the various life roles and functions that they are involved in (also see Bothma et al. 2015).

It is argued that the meaning attached to work (psychological meaningfulness) by an individual is unique and serves as the foundation for becoming engaged and for developing a work identity (see Anthun and Innstrand 2016; Beukes and Botha 2013; Ghadi et al. 2013; Krok 2016; Leunissen et al. 2016; Olivier and Rothmann 2007; Petro et al. 2017). However, Steger et al. (2012) found that other dispositional factors may contribute to work engagement even when the work is meaningless. Flowing from a well-developed work identity is a growing attachment to work and work involvement.

Personal Resources (Hope; Efficacy; Resilience; Optimism)

Another variable that contributes to the unique interpretation of a person's environment is what is termed *personal resources* or *PsyCap*, (The term *PsyCap* is derived from psychological capital). Personal resources or PsyCap consists of four sub-dimensions, namely Hope, Efficacy, Resilience, and Optimism. In terms of these four dimensions PsyCap is defined by Luthans et al. (2007: 3) as:

> An individual's positive psychological state of development characterized by: (1) having confidence (self efficacy) to take on and put in the necessary effort to succeed at challenging tasks; (2) making a positive attribution (optimism) about succeeding now and in the future; (3) persevering towards goals, and when necessary, redirecting paths to goals (hope) in order to succeed; and (4) when beset by problems and adversity, sustaining and bouncing back and even beyond (resilience) to attain success.

It is argued that these four personal resources positively contribute towards an individual's interpretation of a situation and to the development of personal capacities to effectively deal with a situation. Research publications by Avey et al. (2009), (2010), Luthans and Youssef (2004), and Luthans et al. (2007) has shown that this collection of personal resources (PsyCap) is a powerful variable that is contributing to optimal human functioning, to personal well-being and to individual performance. Furthermore Sweetman and Luthans (2010) build a strong argument that PsyCap is a prerequisite condition for work engagement to occur.

Some of the studies that show the moderating role of personal resources between job characteristics and engaging behaviours are those of Barbier et al. (2013), Bermejo-Toro et al. (2016), De Stasio et al. (2017), Lorente et al. (2014), Temblay and Messervey (2011), Wang et al. (2016), Xanthopoulou et al. (2007, 2009).

It is against this backdrop that personal resources (PsyCap) provide the unique set of competencies and skills to effectively engage with workplace challenges and to cope with workplace conflicts and demands.

Self-regulation Theory/Self-determination Theory

Self-regulation and self-determination are two closely related processes and skills. Where self-regulation is more externally focused on goal setting and processes of goal attainment, self-determination is more internally focused on the degree of autonomy a person has in choosing one's own actions.

Orehek et al. (2017: 365) describe *self-regulation* as a process where "…a person monitors the current status of his/her own action in comparison with a reference value". When a discrepancy between his or her current and desired state is observed, he/she engages in actions to reduce the discrepancy. According to Orehek et al. (2017: 365) self-regulation consists of two basic processes: "A person must (a) make comparisons *(i.e. evaluate)* through a process of assessment, and (b) engage in the action necessary to move forward by locomoting" (i.e. *action initiation*) (sections in italics and in brackets is the author's own insertion).

According to Nielsen (2017) the first component of self-regulation relates to goal setting. Goal setting involves determining which goals to pursue and establishing the criteria against which progress can be monitored. The second and third components relate to goal striving and refer to the planning and implementation of actions that promote goal attainment and the protection of the goals against distraction and disruption.

It is argued that self-regulation can mediate the relationship between job characteristics and engaging job behaviours (see Diestel and Schmidt 2009; and Koole et al. 2012).

Self-determination theory is a human motivation approach that focuses the facilitation of self-motivation and healthy psychological development through understanding innate psychological needs (Deci and Ryan 2000; Ryan and Deci 2000). *Self-determination* is described as the degree of freedom a person has in choosing to initiate actions. *Autonomy* is considered to be the central premise of self-determination as it is a "…sense of choice in initiating and regulating one's own actions" (Deci et al. 1989: 580).

As in the case with self-regulation it is also argued that self-determination can mediate the relationship between job characteristics and engaging job behaviours (see Roche and Haar 2013; Rockmann and Ballinger 2017; Shih 2015; and Trépanier et al. 2015).

It is argued that individuals with well-developed self-regulatory and self-determination skills will function more optimally, and will consequently have a more crystalized personal and work identity and will therefore be more successful in attaining work-related goals and objectives (also see Friede et al. 2008).

Personal Agency

According to Crafford et al. (2015) *individual agency* is a means of expressing personal identity (as opposed to following established social practice) in such a way that it negotiates and addresses challenges in the immediate context. "It is through this active expression of identity that people define themselves as unique beings, and individual agency as an expression of subjective identity is a means of self-determination that includes a degree of intentionality and personal influence" (Crafford et al. 2015: 62).

This process of establishing a unique identity also suggests that a person should sufficiently differentiate him/herself within a group without alienating him/herself in the process. In essence, identity formation involves identity negotiations on two dimensions, namely (1) on a unique personal identity (agency) versus an accepted social practice dimension, and (2) on a uniqueness (me-ness) versus a social membership (we-ness) dimension.

Against this background it is argued that personal agency is one of the drivers of providing unique interpretations to contextual factors and for providing unique solutions to workplace challenges.

Optimally functioning individuals are the ones that possess the capabilities and skills to effectively deal with challenges in their (work) lives. It is argued that individuals who understand the meaning of work in their lives; who possess the necessary personal resources (PsyCap); who are self-regulated and self-determined (who purposefully strive towards achieving their goals); and finally who through personal agency can successfully establish and negotiate their work identities will be able to deal more effectively with job demands (specifically the hindrances).

The JD-R Model as Basis for the Dynamic Dual Process Framework

In view of the discussion thus far, a dynamic dual process framework will be presented that will connect the different components presented above into the proposed model. This model is a more detailed model then the one presented in Fig. 1.1, but contains in essence the same environmental factors, individual dispositional factors and behavioural (intermediate and final) outcomes, but in a more detailed dual-process format. The dual process entails a positive engaging behaviour outcome process on the one hand, and a negative disengaging behaviour process on the other hand. These two processes are not mutually exclusive, but should be viewed as a kind of double helix process that continuously develops in reciprocal, intertwined and in a cyclical way. One cannot fully understand or explain JRs and engaging behaviours without knowing what the JDs and the disengaging behaviours are—they should be considered both at the same time.

The proposed model in Fig. 1.2 consists of four columns, where the first column introduces environmental factors in the form of different distal and proximate JRs and JDs. The second column presents personal resources that can potentially act as moderators or mediators between the environmental factors and the intermediate outcomes. The third column presents the intermediate outcomes that can either be engaging or disengaging behaviours. The fourth column presents the final outcomes in the form of intentions to stay or leave that will ultimately result in employee loss or employee retention.

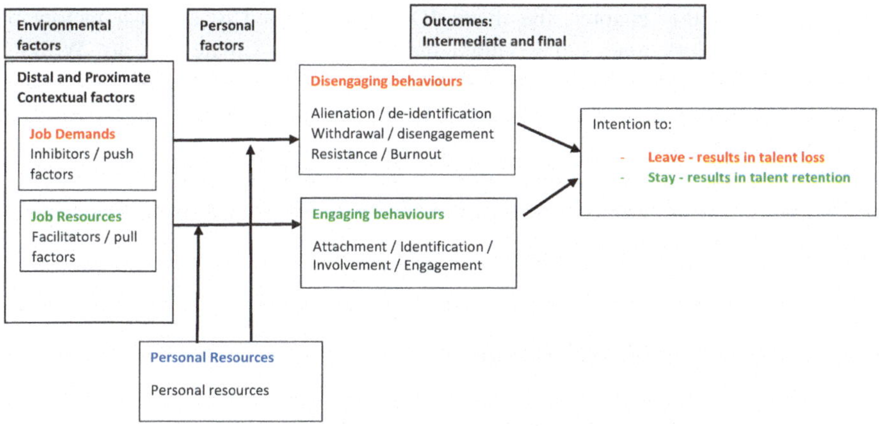

Fig. 1.2 The dynamic dual process framework (own compilation)

Proximate and Distal Job Resources (Pull Factors/ Facilitators)

A range of different distal and proximate contextual factors were introduced in this chapter that may have an impact on intermediate outcomes such as engaging behaviours. These factors were categorized as potential JRs (or also referred to as pull factors or facilitators).

The distal JRs identified for purposes of this model are Perceived organisational support (POS); Quality of supervisor relationships; Task identity; Perceived external prestige (PEP); and Team climate. The proximate JRs are Advancement opportunities; and Growth opportunities. The underlying thesis is that if JRs proportionally outweigh the JDs, then it would most likely result in engaged employees.

These listed JRs may also serve as buffers for the potential negative effects of the JDs. In order to promote the likelihood of engaged employees, the mentioned JRs should be supported, strengthened and expanded. Research reported by Van Wingerden et al. (2015) shows that such interventions to strengthen and expand JRs, lead to increased engagement levels. Leiter and Maslach (2010) made suggestions on how these interventions can be structured and what they can potentially be focusing on (the dependent variables) in order to track (or evaluate) the impact and/or effectiveness of these interventions.

Proximate and Distal Job Demands (Push Factors/Inhibitors)

For purposes of this chapter, the distal JDs (also referred to as push factors or inhibitors) are Work load and Contract breach. The proximate JDs are Work—Family Conflict/balance (WFC) and Job insecurity. The underlying premise is that when these JDs proportionally outweigh the JRs, then it would most likely result in disengaged employees.

In order to reduce the likelihood of disengaged employees, the negative effects of JDs should be reduced and the positive effects of JRs increased, so that JRs can proportionally out-weigh the JDs.

Individual Dispositional Factors

For the purposes of this chapter, four personal dispositional factors that are associated with optimal functioning of individuals were listed, namely sense-making and meaning of work; personal resources or PsyCap; self-regulation/ self-determination; and personal agency that could possibly mediate or moderate the relationship between JRs and JDs on the one hand and the intermediate outcomes on the other hand. These unique capabilities (abilities and skills) of individuals with respect to these four personal dispositional factors are not innate, but learned or acquired behaviours. Sweetman and Luthans (2010) are of the opinion that these behaviours could be taught or developed by means of learning interventions. These dispositional factors can enable individuals to deal effectively with contextual factors that will result in enhanced engagement levels and performance and thereby reduce the probability of leaving the organisation.

Dual Intermediate Outcomes (Work Engagement—Disengagement)

As explained earlier the basic premise that the JD-R model works on, is that the weight of the JRs are proportionally weighed against the JDs. If the JRs proportionally out-weigh the JDs, then the intermediate outcomes will be positive and will result in some form of engaging behaviours such as attachment, work identification and/or job involvement and ultimately the desire to stay on in the organisation. Hobfoll's (1998, 2002) Conservation of Resources (COR) Theory (also see Chen and Huang 2016) suggests that the access to resources will result into positive gain spirals (see Hakanen et al. 2008; Salanova et al. 2010) where the current resource base is broadened and expanded on—in short, access to resources will lead to gaining more resources.

However, if the JDs proportionally out-weigh the JRs, then the intermediate outcomes will be negative and will result in some form of disengaging behaviours such as withdrawal, alienation, or under some conditions even resistance. If these conditions persist it will ultimately lead to burnout and the desire to leave the organisation. This state of affairs may result in negative loss spirals if the current resource base is reduced and it may result in the future loss of resources.

Dual Final Outcomes: Intentions and Decisions to Finally Leave or Stay

Empirical research thus far has indicated that there is a strong link between engagement and intentions to stay (or in the case of the inverse, between disengagement and intentions to leave). Bothma and Roodt (2013) in their longitudinal study, have established that turnover intentions are strong predictors of actual turnover over a four month and a four year period.

In the case where JRs proportionally out-weigh the JDs, there is a high probability that committed and engaged employees would develop and emerge from this type of scenario (also see Schaufeli 2015; Tuckey et al. 2012; Van Schalkwyk et al. 2010 on how leadership empowerment behaviour improves work engagement and reduces employee turnover intentions). In the case where JRs outweigh JDs, there will be a strong link between different engaging behaviours (e.g. work identity and work engagement) and the intention to stay (compare Bothma and Roodt 2013), which would ultimately lead to talent retention. This proposition is also supported by a meta-analysis conducted by Halbesleben (2010).

However, the opposite is also true. In the case where JDs proportionally out-weigh the JRs, there is a high probability that alienated employees would develop and emerge from this type of scenario. In this case there will be a strong link between different disengaging behaviours (e.g. personal alienation and burn-out) and the intention to leave (compare Bothma and Roodt 2013), which would ultimately lead to talent loss.

Conclusions and Implications for Retention Practice and Research

It is evident from this overview of the research literature on the JD-R Model above suggests the following in respect of promoting engagement and the likelihood to stay on in the organisation:

1. Talent loss and talent retention is respectively associated with the intention to leave or to stay in the organisation and is in the final instance dependent on how engaging or disengaging employees view their working conditions and job characteristics in their organisations (also referred to as JRs and JDs) to be. Positive conditions or characteristics are associated with positive emotions and experiences that trigger the desire to stay. Negative conditions or characteristics on the other hand are viewed as being stressful that trigger the desire to leave. A research question that needs to be addressed is how much of these conditions have to be present to create an 'identity threat' and how many and which conditions then trigger what is termed an 'identity exit'?
2. Job characteristics (labelled as proximate and distal JRs and JDs in this chapter) are important antecedents for explaining either engaging or disengaging work behaviours that are respectively associated with a positive motivational process or with a negative de-energising process that is ultimately associated with stress and ill-health. HRM practitioners and immediate line managers should be aware of what these job characteristics on different organisational levels are.
3. If JRs proportionally out-weigh the JDs, a positive motivational process is triggered which results in positive gain spirals where the resource base is grown and expanded. This positive motivational process is also associated with different types of engaging workplace behaviours that are in turn linked with the desire to stay with the organisation—an important precursor to talent retention.

4. If JDs on the other hand proportionally out-weigh the JRs, then the negative energy sapping process is activated which results in turn in negative loss spirals where the resource base is diminished or reduced. This negative de-motivational process is also associated with different types of disengaging workplace behaviours that ultimately leads to the desire to leave or escape from the stress-inducing context or organisation. In this case, it is an important pre-condition for talent loss.
5. Both the JRs and the JDs should be considered simultaneously in an attempt to understand and to explain their impact on (dis)engaging workplace behaviours. It should also be mentioned that the work-roles and organisational levels individuals are functioning in, should also be taken into account when trying to promote engaging behaviours in the workplace. Roles on different organisational levels may each have a unique set of push and pull factors that result in either engaging or in disengaging behaviours.
6. In order to retain talent in organisations, the challenge for HRM practitioners and immediate line managers therefore is to know which JRs and JDs are predominantly active on which organisational levels and/or for which job families or communities of practice. This knowledge is a prerequisite for designing interventions that will strengthen and grow JRs and to simultaneously reduce the JDs and/or their negative impact for a given work-role and/or job family.
7. Industrial Psychologists in collaboration with HRM practitioners can also design interventions to grow and develop those personal dispositional factors that will result in optimally functioning individuals who possess competencies and skills to effectively and systematically deal with job challenges and hindrances. It is known that these dispositional factors positively mediate the relationship between job characteristics and engaging workplace behaviours that result in the desire to stay on in organisations.
8. Research challenges on an organisational level are (i) to determine which JDs and JRs are active and dominant for different organisations, (ii) on which levels in these organisations these JRs and JDs are active, and (iii) also for which job families or communities of practice in these organisations it is the case. This information is a prerequisite for designing and developing effective interventions to promote engagement levels for specific work-roles on the said organisational levels.
9. Evaluation research to test the effectiveness of different interventions with the aim to grow and develop particular JRs and also to reduce the negative impact of JDs that will result in positive gain spirals is urgently needed. Little empirical research has been conducted in this space.
10. Another research agenda point, is to develop and to assess the impact of interventions aimed at developing the personal competencies (personal resources) of individuals that will finally result in optimally functioning individuals.

Summary

Based on a systematic literature review, this chapter is structured on a well-known premise that behaviour is a function of personal and environmental factors. This chapter first provided a number of distal contextual push and pull factors that are related to engaging or disengaging work behaviours. These factors are perceived organisational support; quality of supervisor relationship; work-load; task identity; perceived external prestige; perceived team climate; and contract breach. Second, a number of proximate contextual push and pull factors were identified, namely advancement opportunities; growth opportunities; work—family conflict/balance; and job insecurity. Third, personal dispositional factors were identified that may mediate the relationship between contextual factors and engaging or disengaging work behaviours, namely sense-making and meaning of work; personal resources; self-regulation/self determination; and personal agency. Fourth, a dual process framework based on the well-known Job Demands—Resources (JD-R) Model was introduced. The proposed framework suggested that the dynamic interaction between resources (pull factors) and demands (push factors) on the one hand and outcomes (engaging and withdrawal behaviours) on the other hand are mediated by personal dispositional factors. Fifth, the intermediate outcomes (engagement or disengagement) do influence individuals' final decision to stay or leave the organisation. Based on the latter finding, some suggestions were made for practitioners and for researchers to promote a more healthy work-place and talent retention.

References

Altunel, M. C., Kocak, O. E., & Cankir, B. (2015). The effect of job resources on work engagement: a study on academicians in Turkey. *Educational Sciences: Theory and Practice, 15*(2), 409–417.

Amiri, M. et al. (2016). Burnout and its influencing factors among primary health care providers in the North East of Iran. *Plos ONE, 11*(12), 11 p. https://doi.org/10.1371/journal.pone.0167648.

Anderson, N. R., & West, M. A. (1998). Measuring climate for work group innovation: Development and validation of the team climate inventory. *Journal of Organisational Behavior, 19*(3), 235–258.

Anthun, K. S., & Innstrand, S. T. (2016). The predictive value of job demands and resources on the meaning of work and organizational commitment across different age groups in the higher education groups in the higher education sector. *Journal of Higher Education Policy and Management, 38*(1), 53–67. https://doi.org/10.1080/1360080x.2015.1126890.

Asik-Dizdar, O., & Esen, A. (2016). Sensemaking at work: meaningful work experience for individuals and organizations. *International Journal of Organizational Analysis, 24*(1), 2–17. https://doi.org/10.1108/ijoa-12-2013-0728.

Avey, J. B., Luthans, F. L., & Jensen, S. M. (2009). Psychological capital: A positive resource for combating employee stress and turnover. *Human Resource Management, 48*(5), 677–693. https://doi.org/10.1002/hrm.20294.

Avey, J. B., Luthans, F. L., Smith, R. M., & Palmer, N. F. (2010). Impact of positive psychological capital on employee well-being over time. *Journal of Occupational Health Psychology, 15*(1), 17–28. https://doi.org/10.1037/a0016998.

Babin, B. J., & Boles, J. S. (1996). The effects of perceived co-worker involvement satisfaction. *Journal of Retailing, 72*(1), 57–75. https://doi.org/10.1016/s0022-4359(96)90005-6.

Baer, S. M., Jenkins, J. S., & Barber, L. K. (2016). Home is private… Do not enter! Introversion and sensitivity to work-home conflict. *Stress and Health, 32,* 441–445.

Bakker, A. B., Hakanen, J. J., Demerouti, E., & Xanthopoulou, D. (2007). Job resources boost work engagement, particularly when job demands are high. *Journal of Educational Psychology, 99*(2), 274–284. https://doi.org/10.1037/0022-0663.99.2.274.

Bakker, A. B., & Demerouti, E. (2007). The job demands-resources model: State of the art. *Journal of Managerial Psychology, 22*(3), 309–328. https://doi.org/10.1108/02683940710733115.

Bakker, A. B., & Demerouti, E. (2008). Towards a model of work engagement. *Career Development International, 13*(3), 209–223.

Bakker, A. B., Demerouti, E., & Sanz-Vergel, A. I. (2014). Burnout and work engagement: The JD-R approach. *Annual Review of Organizational Psychology and Organizational Behavior, 1,* 389–411.

Bakker, A. B., Schaufeli, W. B., Leiter, M. P., & Taris, T. W. (2008). Work engagement: An emerging concept in occupational health psychology. *Work & Stress: An International Journal of Work, Health and Organisations, 22*(3), 187–200.

Bakker, A. B., Westman, M., & Van Emmerik, I. J. H. (2009). Advancements in crossover theory. *Journal of Managerial Psychology, 24*(3), 206–219. https://doi.org/10.1108/020683940910939304.

Barbier, M., Hansez, I., Chmiel, N., & Demerouti, E. (2013). Performance expectations, personal resources, and job resources: How do they predict work engagement? *European Journal of Work and Organizational Psychology, 22*(6), 750–762. https://doi.org/10.1080/1359432X.2012.704675.

Barkhuizen, N., Rothmann, S., & Van de Vijver, F. J. R. (2013). Burnout and work engagement of academics in higher education institutions: Effects of dispositional optimism. *Stress & Health, 30,* 322–332.

Bermejo-Toro, L., Prieto-Ursúa, M., & Hernández, V. (2016). Towards a model of teacher well-being: Personal and job resources involved in teacher burnout and engagement. *Educational Psychology, 36*(3), 481–501. https://doi.org/10.1080/01443410.2015.1005006.

Berry, L. M. (1998). *Psychology at work: An introduction to industrial and organisational psychology* (2nd ed.). New York: McGraw-Hill.

Beukes, I., & Botha, E. (2013). Organisational commitment, work engagement and meaning of work of nursing staff in hospitals. *SA Journal of Industrial Psychology, 39*(2), 10 p. https://doi.org/10.4102/sajip.v39i2.1144.

Bosman, J., Rothmann, S., & Buitendach, J. (2005). Job insecurity, burnout and work engagement: The impact of positive and negative affectivity. *SA Journal of Industrial Psychology, 31*(4), 48–56.

Bothma, F. C., & Roodt, G. (2013). The validation of the turnover intention scale. *SA Journal of Human Resource Management, 11*(1). https://doi.org/10.4102/sajhrm.v11i1.507. Art #507, 12 pages.

Bothma, F. C., Lloyd, S., & Khapova, S. (2015). Work identity: Clarifying the concept. In P. G. W. Jansen & G. Roodt (Eds.), *Conceptualising and measuring work identity: South-African perspectives and findings* (pp. 87–116). Dordrecht: Springer Science and Business Media.

Brotheridge, C. M., & Lee, R. T. (2005). Impact of work-family interference on general well-being: A replication and extension. *International Journal of Stress Management, 12*(3), 203–221.

Buys, C., & Rothmann, S. (2010). Burnout and engagement of reformed church ministers. *SA Journal of Industrial Psychology, 36*(1). https://doi.org/10.4102/sajipv36i1.825.

Byrne, J. M., & Canato, A. (2017). It's been a hard day's night: Work family interference and employee engagement. *Organizational Dynamics, 46,* 104–112.

Campbell, N. S., Perry, S. J., Maertz, C. P., Allen, D. G., & Griffeth, R. W. (2013). All you need is… resources: The effects of justice and support on burnout and turnover. *Human Relations, 66*(6), 759–782. https://doi.org/10.1177/0018726712462614.

Carmeli, A. (2005). Perceived external prestige, affective commitment, and citizenship behaviors. *Organization Studies, 26*(3), 443–464. https://doi.org/10.1177/0170840605050875.

Carmeli, A. (2004). The link between organizational elements, perceived external prestige, and performance. *Corporate Reputation Review, 6*(4), 314–331.

Carmeli, A., & Freund, A. (2009). Linking perceived external prestige and intentions to leave the organization: The mediating role of job satisfaction and affective commitment. *Journal of Social Service Research, 35,* 236–250. https://doi.org/10.1080/01488370900873.

Carmeli, A., Gilat, G., & Weisberg, J. (2006). Perceived external prestige, organisational identification and affective commitment: A stakeholder approach. *Corporate Reputation Review, 9*(2), 92–104.

Chen, Y., & Huang, S. Y. J. (2016). A conservation of resources view of personal engagement in the development of innovative behaviour and work-family conflict. *Journal of Organizational Change Management, 29*(6), 1310–1040. https://doi.org/10.1108/jocm-11-2015-0213.

Chernyak-Hai, L., & Tziner, A. (2016). The "I believe" and the "I invest" of work-family.

Balance: The indirect influences of personal values and work engagement via perceived organizational climate and workplace burnout. *Journal of Work and Organizational Psychology, 32,* 1–10.

Cheung, F., & Wu, A. M. S. (2013). Older workers' successful aging and intention to stay. *Journal of Managerial Psychology, 28*(6), 645–660. https://doi.org/10.1108/JPM-09-2011-0062.

Christian, M. S., Garza, A. S., & Slaughter, J. E. (2011). Work engagement: A quantitative review and test of its relationships with task and contextual performance. *Personnel Psychology, 64,* 89–136.

Cho, V., & Huang, X. (2012). Professional commitment, organizational commitment, and the intention to leave for professional advancement: An empirical study on IT professionals. *Information Technology & People, 25*(1), 31–54.

Ciftcioglu, A. (2011). The relationship between perceived external prestige and turnover intention: An empirical investigation. *Corporate Reputation Review, 13*(4), 248–263.

Collins, B. J., Burrus, C. J., & Meyer, R. D. (2014). Gender differences in the impact of leadership styles on subordinate embeddedness and job satisfaction. *The Leadership Quarterly, 25,* 660–671.

Crafford, A., Adams, B. G., Saayman, T., & Vinkenburg, C. (2015). The process of identity work: Negotiating a work identity. In P. G. W. Jansen & G. Roodt (Eds.), *Conceptualising and measuring work identity: South-African perspectives and findings* (pp. 87–116). Dordrecht: Springer Science and Business Media.

De Braine, R. (2012). *Predictors of work-based identity*. Unpublished doctoral thesis. University of Johannesburg, Johannesburg.

De Braine, R., & Roodt, G. (2011). The job demands—resources model as predictor of work identity and work engagement: A comparative analysis. *SA Journal of Industrial Psychology, 37*(2). Art. # 889, 11 p https://doi.org/10.4102/sajip.v37i2.889.

De Braine, R., & Roodt, G. (2015). Personal and situational work-based identity antecedents. In P. G. W. Jansen & G. Roodt (Eds.), *Conceptualising and measuring work identity: South-African perspectives and findings* (pp. 87–116). Dordrecht: Springer Science and Business Media.

Deci, E. L., Connell, J. P., & Ryan, R. M. (1989). Self-determination in a work organization. *Journal of Applied Psychology, 74*(4), 580–590.

Deci, E. L., & Ryan, R. M. (2000). The 'what' and 'why' of goal pursuits: Human needs and the self-determination of behaviour. *Psychological Inquiry, 11*(4), 227–268.

Demerouti, E., Bakker, A. B., Nachreiner, F., & Schaufeli, W. B. (2001). The job demands-resources model of burnout. *Journal of Applied Psychology, 86,* 499–512.

De Stasio, S., Fiorilli, C., Benevene, P., Uusitalo-Mamivaara, L., & Di Chiacchio, C. (2017). Burnout in special needs teachers at kindergarten and primary school: Investigating the role of personal resources and work wellbeing. *Psychology in the Schools, 54*(5), 472–486.

Diestel, S., & Schmidt, K.-H. (2009). Mediator and moderator effects of demands on self-control in the relationship between work load and indicators or job strain. *Work & Stress, 23*(1), 60–79.

Eisenberger, R., Huntington, R., Hutchinson, S., & Sowa, D. (1986). Perceived organisational support. *Journal of Applied Psychology, 71*(3), 500–507. https://doi.org/10.1037/0021-9010.71.3.500.

Ezzedeen, S. R., & Ritchey, K. G. (2009). Career advancement and family balance strategies of executive women. *Gender in Management: An International Journal, 24*(6), 388–411. https://doi.org/10.1108/17542410910980388.

Fiksenbaum, L. M. (2014). Supportive work-family environments: Implications for work-family conflict and well-being. *International Journal of Human Resource Management, 25*(5), 653–672. https://doi.org/10.1080/09585192.796314.

Friede, A., Kossek, E. E., Lee, M. D., & MacDermid, S. (2008). Human Resource Manager insights on creating and sustaining successful reduced-load work arrangements. *Human Resource Management, 47*(4), 707–727.

Friedemann, M.-L., & Buckwalter, K. C. (2014). Family caregiver role and burden related to gender and family relationships. *Journal of Family Nursing, 20*(2), 313–336. https://doi.org/10.1177/1074840714532715.

Fuller, J. B., Hester, K., Barnett, T., Frey, L., & Relyea, C. (2006a). Perceived organizational support and perceived external prestige: Predicting organizational attachment for university faculty, staff, and administrators. *The Journal of Social Psychology, 146*(3), 327–347.

Fuller, J. B., Hester, K., Barnett, T., Frey, L., Relyea, C., & Beu, D. (2006b). Perceived external prestige and internal respect: New insight into the organizational identification process. *Human Relations, 59*(6), 815–846. https://doi.org/10.1177/0018726706067148.

Geertshuis, S. A., Morrison, R. L., & Cooper-Thomas, H. D. (2015). It's not what you say, It's the way that you say it: The mediating effect of upward influencing communications on the relationship between leader-member exchange and performance ratings. *International Journal of Business Communication, 52*(2), 228–245. https://doi.org/10.1177/2329488415572784.

Ghadi, M. Y., Fernando, M., & Caputi, P. (2013). Transformational leadership and work engagement: The mediating effect of meaning in work. *Leadership & Organization Development Journal, 34*(6), 532–550. https://doi.org/10.1108/LODJ-10-2011-0110.

Greenhalgh, L., & Rosenblatt, Z. (1984). Job insecurity: Towards conceptual clarity. *Academy of Management Review, 9,* 438–448.

Greenhaus, J. H., & Beutell, N. J. (1985). Sources of conflict between work and family roles. *Academy of Management Review, 10*(1), 76–88.

Guerrero, S., & Challiol-Jeanblanc, H. (2017). Ex ante i-deals, perceived external prestige and turnover intentions. *Personnel Review, 46*(6), 1199–1212.

Halbesleben, J. R. B. (2010). A meta-analysis of work engagement: Relationships with burnout, demands, resources, and consequences. In A. B. Bakker & M. P. Leiter (Eds.), *Work engagement: A handbook of essential theory and research* (pp. 102–117). New York: Psychology Press.

Halbesleben, J. R. B., Harvey, J., & Bolino, M. C. (2009). Too engaged? A conservation of resources view of the relationship between work engagement and work interference with family. *Journal of Applied Psychology, 94*(6), 1452–1465. https://doi.org/10.1037/a0017595.

Hall, G. B., Dollard, M. F., Tuckey, M. R., Winefield, A. H., & Thompson, B. M. (2010). Job demands, work-family conflict, and emotional exhaustion in police officers: A longitudinal test of competing theories. *Journal of Occupational and Organizational Psychology, 83,* 237–250.

Hackman, J. R., & Oldham, G. R. (1975). Development of the job diagnostic survey. *Journal of Applied Psychology, 60*(2), 159–170. https://doi.org/10.1037/h0076546.

Hakanen, J. J., Perhoniemi, R., & Toppinen-Tanner, S. (2008). Positive gain spirals at work: From job resources to work engagement, personal initiative and work-unit innovativeness. *Journal of Vocational Behaviour, 73*(1), 78–91.

Hakanen, J. J., & Roodt, G. (2010). Using the job demands-resources model to predict engagement: Analysing a conceptual model. In A. B. Bakker & M. P. Leiter (Eds.), *Work engagement: A handbook of essential theory and research* (pp. 85–101). New York: Psychology Press.

Hakanen, J. J., Seppälä, P., & Peeters, C. W. (2017). High job demands, still engaged and not burned out? The role of job crafting. *International Journal of Behavioral Medicine, 24,* 619–627. https://doi.org/10.1007/s12529-017-9638-3.

Harpaz, I., & Fu, X. (2002). The structure of the meaning of work: A relative stability amidst change. *Human Relations, 55*(6), 639–667.

Hobfoll, S. E. (1998). *Stress, culture and community: The psychology and philosophy of stress.* New York: Plenum Press.

Hobfoll, S. E. (2002). Social and psychological resources and adaptation. *Review of General Psychology, 6,* 307–324.

Inandi, Y. (2009). The barriers to career advancement of female teachers in Turkey and their levels of burnout. *Social Behavior and Personality, 37*(8), 1143–1152. https://doi.org/10.2224/sbp.2009.37.8.1143.

Jensen, J. N., Holten, A.-L., Karpatschof, B., & Albertsen, K. (2011). Does collective efficacy moderate the associations between physical work load and intention to leave or sickness absence? *Journal of Advanced Nursing, 67*(11), 2425–2434. https://doi.org/10.1111/j.1365-2648.2011.05674.x.

Joubert, M. (2010). *Identifying enabling management practices for employee engagement.* Unpublished Master's thesis, University of Johannesburg, Johannesburg, South Africa.

Joubert, M., & Roodt, G. (in review). Conceptualizing and measuring employee engagement as a role-related, multi-level construct. *Acta Commercii.*

Kang, D., Stewart, J., & Kim, H. (2011). The effects of perceived external prestige, ethical organizational climate, and leader-member exchange (LMX) quality on employees' commitments and their subsequent attitudes. *Personnel Review, 40*(6), 761–784. https://doi.org/10.1108/00483481111169670.

Karatepe, O. M. (2013). The effects of work overload and work-family conflict on job embeddedness and job-performance: The mediation of emotional exhaustion. *International Journal of Contemporary Hospitality Management, 25*(4), 614–634. https://doi.org/10.1108/09596111311322952.

Karatepe, O. M., & Karadas, G. (2013). Service employees' fit, work-family conflict, and work engagement. *Journal of Services Marketing, 30*(5), 554–566. https://doi.org/10.1108/JSM-02-2015-0066.

Kaplan, H., & Tausky, C. (1974). The meaning of work for the hard-core unemployed. *The Pacific Sociological Review, 17*(2), 185–198.

Kira, M., Van Eijnatten, F. M., & Balkin, D. B. (2010). Crafting sustainable work: Development of personal resources. *Journal of Organizational Change Management, 23*(5), 616–632. https://doi.org/10.1108/09534811011071315.

Koole, S. L., Jostmann, N. B., & Baumann, N. (2012). Do demanding conditions help or hurt self-regulation? *Social and Personality Psychology Compass, 6*(4), 328–346. https://doi.org/10.1111/j.1751.9004.2012.00425.x.

Krok, D. (2016). Can meaning buffer work pressure? An exploratory study on styles of meaning in life and burnout in firefighters. *Archives of Psychiatry and Psychotherapy, 1,* 31–42. https://doi.org/10.12740/APP/62154.

Lackritz, J. R. (2004). Exploring burnout among university faculty: Incidence, performance, and demographic issues. *Teaching and Teacher Education, 20,* 713–729.

Leiter, M. P., & Maslach, C. (2010). Building engagement: The design and evaluation of interventions. In A. B. Bakker & M. P. Leiter (Eds.), *Work engagement: A handbook of essential theory and research* (pp. 164–180). New York: Psychology Press.

Leunissen, J. M., Sedikides, C., Wildschut, T., & Cohen, T. R. (2016—online). Organizational nostalgia lowers turnover intentions by increasing work meaning: The moderating role of Burnout. *Journal of Occupational Health Psychology.* https://doi.org/10.1037/ocp0000059.

Liao, H., Liu, D., & Loi, R. (2010). Looking at both sides of the social exchange coin: A social cognitive perspective on the joint effects of relationship quality and differentiation on creativity. *Academy of Management Journal, 53*(5), 1090–1109.

Lorente, L., Salanova, M., Martínez, I. M., & Vera, M. (2014). How personal resources predict work engagement and self-rated performance among construction workers: A social cognitive perspective. *International Journal of Psychology, 49*(3), 200–207. https://doi.org/10.1002/ijop.12049.

Luthans, F., & Youssef, C. M. (2004). Human, social and now positive psychological capital management. *Organisational Dynamics, 33,* 143–160.

Luthans, F., Youssef, C. M., & Avolio, B. J. (2007). *Psychological capital: Developing the human competitive edge*. Oxford: Oxford University Press.

Mache, S., Bernburg, M., Groneberg, D. A., Klapp, B. F., & Danzer, G. (2016). Work-family conflict in its relations to perceived working situation and work engagement. *Work, 53,* 859–869. https://doi.org/10.3233/WOR-162257.

Mauno, S., Ruokolainen, M., & Kinnunen, U. (2015). Work-family conflict and enrichment from the perspective of psychosocial resources: Comparing Finnish healthcare workers by working schedules. *Applied Ergonomics, 48,* 86–94.

Meddour, H., Rosli, M. A. B. M., Majid, A. H. A., Auf, M. A. A., & Aman, A. M. (2016). Intention to leave manufacturing organisation: A study of the automotive industry in Malaysia. *International Journal of Economic Perspectives, 10*(4), 484–499.

Medina-Garrido, J. A., Biedma-Ferrer, J. M., & Ramos-Rodriquez, A. R. (2017). Relationship between work-family balance, employee well-being, and job performance. *Academica Revista Latinoamericana de Administración, 30*(1), 40–58. https://doi.org/10.1108/ARLA-08-2015-0202.

Menguc, B., Auh, S., Katsikeas, C. S., & Jung, Y. S. (2016). When does (mis)fit in customer orientation matter for frontline employees' job satisfaction and performance? *Journal of Marketing, 80,* 65–83. https://doi.org/10.1509/jm.15.0327.

Michaels, E., Handfield-Jones, H., & Axelrod, B. (2001). *The war for talent*. Boston: Harvard Business Press.

Moshoeu, A. N., & Geldenhuys, D. J. (2015). Job insecurity, organisational commitment, and work engagement among staff in an open distance learning institution. *Southern African Business Review, 19*(1), 22–43.

MOW-International Research Team. (1987). *The meaning of working*. London: Academic Press.

Nielsen, K. S. (2017). From prediction to process: A self-regulation account of environmental behaviour change. *Journal of Environmental Psychology, 51,* 189–198. https://doi.org/10.1016/j.jenvp.2017.04.002.

Nielson, T. R., Carlson, D. S., & Lankau, M. J. (2001). The supportive mentor as a means of reducing work-family conflict. *Journal of Vocational Behavior, 59,* 364–381. https://doi.org/10.1006/jvbe.2001.1806.

O'Connor, C., & Srinivasan, S. (2010). Influence of employment type on LMX, organisational commitment and job satisfaction. *Employment Relations Record, 10*(2), 75–93.

Olivier, A. L., & Rothmann, S. (2007). Antecedents of work engagement in a multi-national oil company. *SA Journal of Industrial Psychology, 33*(3), 49–56.

Orehek, E., Vazeou-Niewenhuis, A., Quick, E., & Weaverling, G. C. (2017). Attachment and self-regulation. *Personality and Social Psychology Bulletin, 43*(3), 365–380. https://doi.org/10.1177/0146167216685292.

Paglis, L. L., & Green, S. G. (2002). Both sides now: Supervisor and subordinate perspectives on relationships quality. *Journal of Applied Social Psychology, 32*(2), 250–276.

Park, Y. K., Song, J. H., Yoon, S. W., & Kim, J. (2014). Learning organization and innovative behavior: The mediating effect of work engagement. *European Journal of Training and Development, 38*(1/2), 75–94. https://doi.org/10.1108/EJTD-04-2013-0040.

Petro, P., Bakker, A. B., & Van den Heuvel, M. (2017). Weekly job crafting and leisure crafting: Implications for meaning-making and work engagement. *Journal of Occupational and Organizational Psychology, 90,* 129–152.

Robinson, L. D., Magee, C., & Caputi, P. (2016). Burnout and the work-family interference: A two-wave study of sole and partnered working mothers. *Career Development International, 21* (1), 31–44. https://doi.org/10.1108/CDI-06-2015-0085.
Roche, M., & Haar, J. M. (2013). Leaders' life aspirations and job burnout: a self-determination theory approach. *Leadership & Organization Development Journal, 34*(6), 515–531. https://doi.org/10.1108/LODJ-10-2011-0103.
Rockmann, K. W., & Ballinger, G. A. (2017). Intrinsic motivation and organizational identification among on-demand workers. *Journal of Applied Psychology, 102*(9), 1305–1317. https://doi.org/10.1037/apl0000224.
Rothmann, S., Mostert, K., & Strydom, M. (2006). A psychometric evaluation of the Job demands-resources scale in South Africa. *SA Journal of Industrial Psychology, 32*(4), 76–86.
Rothmann, S., & Jordaan, G. M. E. (2006). Job demands, job resources and work engagement of academic staff in South African higher education institutions. *SA Journal of Industrial Psychology, 32*(4), 87–96.
Rothmann, S., & Joubert, J. H. M. (2007). Job demands, job resources, burnout and work engagement of managers at a platinum mine in the North West Province. *South African Journal of Business Management, 38*(3), 49–61.
Rothmann, S., & Rothmann, S. (2010). Factors associated with employee engagement in South Africa. *SA Journal of Industrial Psychology, 36*(2), 27–38. https://doi.org/10.4102/sajip.v36i2.925.
Ryan, R. M., & Deci, E. L. (2000). Self-determination theory and the facilitation of intrinsic motivation, social development, and well-being. *American Psychologist, 55*(1), 68–78.
Salanova, M., Schaufeli, W. B., Xanthopoulou, D., & Bakker, A. B. (2010). The gain spiral of resources and work engagement: Sustaining a positive worklife. In A. B. Bakker & M. P. Leiter (Eds.), *Work engagement: A handbook of essential theory and research* (pp. 118–131). New York: Psychology Press.
Schaufeli, W. B. (2015). Engaging leadership in the job demands-resources model. *Career Development International, 20*(5), 446–463. https://doi.org/10.1108/CDI-02-2015-0025.
Schaufeli, W. B., & Bakker, A. B. (2004). Job demands, job resources and their relationship with burnout and engagement: A multi-sample study. *Journal of Organizational Behavior, 25,* 293–315.
Schaufeli, W. B., Bakker, A. B., & Van Rhenen, W. (2009). How changes in job demands and resources predict burnout, work engagement, and sickness absenteeism. *Journal of Organizational Behavior, 30,* 893–917. https://doi.org/10.1002/job.595.
Schaufeli, W. B., & Taris, T. W. (2014). A critical review of the Job Demands-Resources model: Implications for improving work and health. In G. F. Bauer & O. Hämmig (Eds.), *Bridging occupational, organizational and public health: A transdisciplinary approach* (pp. 43–68). Dordrecht: Springer Science+Business Media. https://doi.org/10.1007/978-94-007-5640-3_4.
Schermuly, C. C., & Meyer, B. (2016). Good relationships at work: The effects of leader-member exchange and team-member exchange on psychological empowerment, emotional exhaustion, and depression. *Journal of Organizational Behavior, 37,* 673–691. https://doi.org/10.1002/job.2060.
Schnell, T., Höge, T., & Pollet, E. (2013). Predicting meaning in work: Theory, data, implications. *The Journal of Positive Psychology, 8*(6), 543–554. https://doi.org/10.1080/17439760.2013.830763.
Shih, S.-S. (2015). An investigation into academic burnout among Taiwanese adolescents from the self-determination theory perspective. *Social Psychology Education, 18,* 201–219. https://doi.org/10.1007/s11218-013-9214-x.
Smidts, A. L. E., Pruyn, A. D. T. H., & Van Riel, C. B. M. (2001). The impact of employee communication and perceived external prestige on organizational identification. *Academy of Management Journal, 49*(5), 1051–1062.
Sollitto, M., Martin, M. M., Dusic, S., Gibbons, K. E., & Wagenhouser, A. (2016). Assessing the supervisor-subordinate relationship involving part-time employees. *International Journal of Business Communication, 53*(1), 74–96. https://doi.org/10.1177/2329488414525462.

Stander, M. W., & Rothmann, S. (2010). Psychological empowerment, job insecurity, and employee engagement. *SA Journal of Industrial Psychology, 36*(1), 1–8. https://doi.org/10.4102/sajip.v36i1.849.

Steger, M. F., Littman-Ovadia, H., Miller, M., Menger, L., & Rothmann, S. (2012). Engaging in work even when it is meaningless: Positive affective predisposition and meaningful work interact in relation to work engagement. *Journal of Career Assessment, 21*(2), 348–361. https://doi.org/10.1177/1069072712471517.

Straub, C. (2007). A comparative analysis of the use of work-life balance practices in Europe: Do practices enhance females' career advancement? *Women in Management Review, 22*(4), 289–304. https://doi.org/10.1108/09649420710754246.

Stringer, L. (2006). The link between the quality of the supervisor-employee relationship and the level of the employee's satisfaction. *Public Organization Review, 6,* 125–142. https://doi.org/10.1007/s11115-006-0005-0.

Suazo, M. M., Turnley, W. H., & Mai-Dalton, R. R. (2008). Characteristics of the supervisor-subordinate relationship as predictors of psychological contract breach. *Journal of Managerial Issues, 20*(3), 295–312.

Sundin, L., Bildt, C., Lisspers, J., Hochwaelder, J., & Setterlind, S. (2006). Organisational factors, individual characteristics and social support: What determines the level of social support? *Work, 27,* 45–55.

Sverke, M., & Hellgren, J. (2002). The nature of job insecurity: Understanding employment uncertainty on the brink of a new millennium. *Applied Psychology: An International Review, 51,* 23–42.

Sweetman, D., & Luthans, F. (2010). The power of positive psychology: Psychological capital and work engagement. In A. B. Bakker & M. P. Leiter (Eds.), *Work engagement: A handbook of essential theory and research* (pp. 54–68). New York: Psychology Press.

Thanacoody, P. R., Bartram, T., & Casimir, G. (2009). The effects of burnout and supervisory social support on the relationship between work-family conflict and intention to leave: A study of Australian cancer workers. *Journal of Health Organization and Management, 23*(1), 53–69. https://doi.org/10.1108/14777260910942551.

Tharshini, U., Kumar, S., & Rathnasekara, H. (2016). Climbing ladders of success: Perceptions of barriers to public sector career advancement in Jaffna District, Sri Lanka. *South Asian Journal of Human Resource Management, 3*(1), 1–24. https://doi.org/10.1177/2322093716631089.

Temblay, M. A., & Messervey, D. (2011). The job demands-resources model: Further evidence for the buffering effect of personal resources. *SA Journal of Industrial Psychology, 37*(2), 1–19. https://doi.org/10.4102/sajip.v37i2.876.

Tement, S., & Korunka, C. (2015). The moderating impact of types of caregiving on job demands, resources, and their relation to work-to-family conflict and enrichment. *Journal of Family Issues, 36*(1), 31–55. https://doi.org/10.1177/019251.

Torrente, P., Salanova, M., Llorens, S., & Schaufeli, W. B. (2012). From I to we: The factorial validity of a team work engagement scale. In J. Neves & S. P. Gonçalves (Eds.), *Occupational health psychology: From burnout to well-being*. Edições Sílabo: Lisboa.

Trépanier, S.-G., Forest, J., Fernet, C., & Austin, S. (2015). On the psychological and motivational processes linking job characteristics to employee functioning: Insight from self-determination theory. *Work & Stress, 29*(3), 286–305. https://doi.org/10.1080/02678373.2015.1074957.

Tuckey, M. R., Bakker, A. B., & Dollard, M. F. (2012). Empowering leaders optimize working conditions for engagement: A multilevel study. *Journal of Occupational Health Psychology, 17*(1), 15–27. https://doi.org/10.1037/60025942.

Van den Broeck, A., De Cuyper, N., De Witte, H., & Vansteenkiste, M. (2010). Not all job demands are equal: Differentiating job hindrances and job challenges in the job demands-resources model. *European Journal of Work and Organizational Psychology, 19*(6), 735–759.

Van Schalkwyk, S., Du Toit, D. H., Bothma, A. S., & Rothmann, S. (2010). Job insecurity, leadership empowerment behaviour, employee engagement and intention to leave in a petrochemical laboratory. *SA Journal of Human Resource Management, 8*(1), 1–7. https://doi.org/10.4102/sajhrmv8i1.234.

Van Wingerden, J., Bakker, A. B., & Derks, D. (2015). A test of job demands-resources intervention. *Journal of Managerial Psychology, 31*(3), 686–701. https://doi.org/10.1108/JMP-03-2014-0086.b.

Van Wingerden, J., Derks, D., & Bakker, A. B. (2017). The impact of personal resources and job crafting interventions on work engagement and performance. *Human Resource Management, 56*(1), 51–67.

Van Zyl, L., Van Eeden, C., & Rothmann, S. (2013). Job insecurity and the emotional and behavioural consequences thereof. *South African Journal of Business Management, 44*(1), 75–86.

Volmer, J., Spurk, D., & Niessen, C. (2012). Leader-member exchange (LMX), job autonomy, and creative involvement. *The Leadership Quarterly, 23,* 456–465.

Wang, Y., Huang, J., & You, X. (2016). Personal resources influence job demands, resources, and burnout: A one-year, three-wave longitudinal study. *Social Behavior and Personality, 44*(2), 247–258. https://doi.org/10.2224/sbp.2016.44.2.247.

Watanabe, M., & Falci, C. D. (2016). A demands and resources approach to understanding faculty turnover intentions due to work-family balance. *Journal of Family Issues, 37*(3), 393–415. https://doi.org/10.1177/0192513X14530972.

Weer, C. H., & Greenhaus, J. H. (2017—online). Managers' assessment of employees' organizational career growth opportunities: The role of extra-role performance, work engagement, and perceived organizational commitment. *Journal of Career Development*, 1–16. https://doi.org/10.1177/0894845317714892.

Wiltshire, A. H. (2016). The meanings of work in a public work scheme in South Africa. *International Journal of Sociology and Social Policy, 36*(1/2), 2–17. https://doi.org/10.1108/IJSSP-02-2015-0014.

Xanthopoulou, D., Bakker, A. B., Demerouti, E., & Schaufeli, W. B. (2007a). The role of personal resources in the job demands-resources model. *International Journal of Stress Management, 14*(2), 121–141. https://doi.org/10.1037/1072-5245.14.2.121.

Xanthopoulou, D., Bakker, A. B., Demerouti, E., & Schaufeli, W. B. (2009). Work engagement and financial returns: A diary study on the role of job and personal resources. *Journal of Occupational and Organizational Psychology, 82,* 183–200.

Xanthopoulou, D., Bakker, A. B., Dollard, M. F., Demerouti, E., Schaufeli, W. B., Taris, T. W., et al. (2007b). When do job demands particularly predict burnout? The moderating role of job resources. *Journal of Managerial Psychology, 22*(8), 766–786. https://doi.org/10.1108/02683940710837714.

Yamaguchi, Y., Inoue, T., Harada, H., & Oike, M. (2016). Job control, work-family balance, and nurses' intention to leave their profession and organization: A comparative cross-sectional survey. *International Journal of Nursing Studies, 64,* 52–62.

Yee, R. W. Y., Guo, Y., & Yeung, A. C. L. (2015). Being close or being happy? The relative impact of work relationship and job satisfaction on service quality. *International Journal of Production Economics, 169,* 391–400.

Yuan, F., & Woodman, R. W. (2010). Innovative behaviour in the workplace: The role of performance and image outcome expectations. *Academy of Management Journal, 53*(2), 323–342.

Zhao, H., Kessel, M., & Kratzer, J. (2013). Supervisor-subordinate relationship, differentiation, and employee creativity: A self-categorization perspective. *The Journal of Creative Behavior, 48*(3), 165–184. https://doi.org/10.1002/jocb.46.

Gerhard (Gert) Roodt (DAdmin) is a licensed psychologist and a registered personnel practitioner. He is author/co-author of more than 100 peer-reviewed journal articles and about 60 conference proceeding papers; 15 technical reports; and co-editor/co-author of 11 books; author/co-author of 60 book chapters; and several articles in non-research based journals. He is also presenter/co-presenter of approximately 135 peer-reviewed papers at national and international academic conferences. Gert was the Vice Dean: Research in the Faculty of Management at the University of Johannesburg, South Africa. He was the former head of the Centre for Work Performance in the Department of Industrial Psychology and People Management. He is a former chair of the Society for Industrial Psychology (1995–1997). He serves on review/editorial boards of nine local and international scholarly journals.

Chapter 2
The Flow@Work Model as a Talent Retention Framework for the Knowledge Economy

Dieter Veldsman

Abstract The world of work has entered the fourth Industrial Revolution. Technological innovation, a multi-generational workforce that is distributed across the globe, and the rise of on-demand talent have changed the way in which organisations operate. Talent has become a scarce commodity, with organisations having to compete for this global and mobile workforce. The ability to attract and retain top talent has become a critical organisational capability, yet organisations are battling to retain employees, with talent attrition rates reaching alarming levels. The changing psycho-social contract, employees wanting to work for multiple employers at the same time, and a workforce that views loyalty as an outdated concept have resulted in organisations having to redefine their talent strategies to remain competitive. Concepts such as purpose, meaningful work, lifelong learning, and growth have become key priorities as organisations are redefining their internal brands to become employers of choice. This chapter discusses the Flow@Work Model as a talent retention framework for knowledge-economy organisations. The model is built upon the theoretical concept of psychological work immersion, which refers to a pervasive state of profound emotional, cognitive, and physical identification with, and enjoyment of, the work experience within a particular socio-cultural context. The Flow@Work Model has been utilised as a framework for the implementation of various talent retention strategies within South African organisations as a means to drive sustainable business performance.

Keywords Psychological work immersion · People-effective enablers
Talent retention practices · Employee retention · Flow@Work model

---

D. Veldsman (✉)
Mindset Management, Pretoria, South Africa
e-mail: dieter.veldsman@mmiholdings.co.za

M. Coetzee et al. (eds.), *Psychology of Retention*,
https://doi.org/10.1007/978-3-319-98920-4_2

Introduction

The world of work has entered the fourth Industrial Revolution. Technological innovation, a multi-generational workforce that is distributed across the globe, and the rise of on-demand talent have changed the way in which organisations operate. Talent has become a scarce commodity, with organisations having to compete for this global and mobile workforce. The ability to attract and retain top talent has become a critical organisational capability, yet organisations are battling to retain employees, with talent attrition rates reaching alarming levels. The changing psycho-social contract, employees wanting to work for multiple employers at the same time, and a workforce that views loyalty as an outdated concept have resulted in organisations having to redefine their talent strategies and approaches to remain competitive. Concepts such as purpose, meaningful work, lifelong learning, and growth have become key priorities as organisations are redefining their internal brands to become employers of choice.

For organisations to be successful in this ever-changing environment, a revised approach is required with regard to how talent is attracted and retained. Traditional talent retention mechanisms have yielded limited success, and organisations need new approaches that go beyond monetary and tangible benefits if they are to attract and, more importantly, retain the required talent to build sustainable organisations.

This chapter discusses the Flow@Work Model as a talent retention framework for knowledge-economy organisations. The model is built upon the theoretical concept of psychological work immersion, and has been successfully utilised in numerous knowledge economy organisations as a framework to develop and measure talent retention mechanisms and strategies. The chapter discusses psychological work immersion in terms of its underpinning theoretical foundation. The Flow@Work Model as an empirical method and its application in practice is examined, and the discussion concludes with a reflection on the relevance of the Model to current organisational development perspectives.

Defining the Concept of Psychological Work Immersion

Psychological work immersion is defined by Coetzee and Veldsman (2013) as a deep state of physical, emotional, and cognitive identification with the work experience, within a particular social-cultural context, that flows from positive perceptions of people-effectiveness enablers. Enhanced levels of psychological work immersion have been connected with higher levels of employee productivity, retention, and positive association with employer brands. While related to concepts such as work engagement, job involvement, and flow, psychological work immersion can be distinguished by its focus on psychological presence. Kahn (1990, 1992) describes psychological presence as a feeling of being connected, fully attentive, and focused on one's work role. Veldsman (2013) built on this concept by stating that individuals should not only draw upon their inner self in order to express their thoughts and feelings regarding their job roles, but that the socio-cultural context should also play a role in fostering psychological attachment to or engagement in the organisation, and not just the task itself. As such, there is a need for organisations to create environments where psychological presence can occur and employees can feel connected to both the task and, by implication, the broader organisation through the presence of people-effectiveness enablers.

People-effectiveness enablers such as manager effectiveness, appreciative feedback, intra-team relations, and individual congruence are important socio-cultural factors that influence individuals' level of psychological attachment or engagement. Psychological work immersion allows for the channelling of energy as influenced by socio-cultural (people) performance enablers from an individual into physical, cognitive, and emotional labours within a particular setting at a particular time, and further refers to the cognitive and emotional attachment that the individual experiences with regard to the identity of the organisation. This perspective positions psychological work immersion as a state of connection to the organisation, the individual contribution to the organisational purpose within a particular context, and a deep involvement in the individual job role and task.

Given the changing nature of the knowledge-economy work environment, psychological work immersion describes the connection that individual employees have to the organisation's identity, which transcends the requirement of a physical presence in a particular work environment. Through this broader approach, psychological work immersion encapsulates the requirements of a knowledge-economy workplace that is characterised by a diversified workforce, virtual teams, and geographical distribution, by positioning the state of work immersion, not just in terms of the psychological presence of the self, but also in terms of the attachment to the broader organisational purpose (Coetzee and Veldsman 2013). In this perspective, psychological work immersion acts as a critical mechanism and enabler of talent retention.

Theoretical Foundation of the Flow@Work Model

The construct of psychological work immersion has its origins in the positive psychology movement of the early 2000s (Seligman 2012). Historically, psychology focused predominantly on understanding human behaviour to address a lack of optimal functioning. Such an understanding was heavily influenced by behaviouristic and psychoanalytical paradigms of thought (Snyder and Lopez 2014). Although valuable, these perspectives, from an organisational point of view, drove an approach to organisational development practices that focused predominantly on understanding the barriers to effective functioning, understanding the sum of its parts, and then proposing a method for achieving effectiveness (Seligman and Csikszentmihalyi 2014).

During the 1950s, the humanistic movement started to influence thinking patterns about how psychology is applied in the workplace (Csikszentmihalyi 1975). This approach, often referred to as the third force, was conceptualised by theorists, including Maslow, and focused on understanding the individual experiences of human beings in order to understand what drives us towards self-actualisation (Pedersen 2015). This school of thought shifted psychology towards a more existentialist and phenomenological approach, yet was often criticised for the research methods associated with the paradigm (Hergenhahn and Henley 2013). From an organisational development perspective, however, this paradigm started to view the individual not as an element that needed to be fixed, but rather as an opportunity to create meaning that would lead to higher levels of functioning and, in the organisational context, performance. This movement provided the basis for the development of other branches of psychology that were more focused, not only on understanding barriers to effective functioning, but also the enablers that could create effectiveness (Meyers et al. 2013).

Positive psychology focuses on creating environments and experiences for individuals to thrive and perform at an optimal level (Seligman and Csikszentmihalyi 2014). Positive psychology can be defined as the scientific study of positive experiences and positive individual traits in the workplace in order to leverage them to create effective and optimal functioning (Seligman 2012). This movement does not aim to ignore developmental areas of thought as conceptualised by traditional psychological paradigms, but rather to complement the manner in which we view human development (Seligman 2012). This movement has given rise to numerous fields of research, including values, strengths, virtues, and talents, and, within the context of the Flow@Work Model, the ways in which social systems and institutions can foster environments that are conducive to optimal and effective functioning (Seligman and Csikszentmihalyi 2014).

The knowledge-economy workplace has called for an environment that optimises organisational effectiveness, with a focus on people effectiveness as a critical component. Traditional schools of thought in psychology can only provide a limited view of organisational effectiveness, owing to their key focus on the barriers to effectiveness, as suggested by their focus on understanding shortcomings in the environment and providing reactive solutions to existing problems. The positive psychology movement, however, allows for a broader perspective. While not ignoring the factors that are inhibiting optimal functioning in organisations, it also provides a perspective on the use of areas of strength in order to neutralise areas for development, to enable optimal functioning (Meyers et al. 2013). This approach has become popular in the modern organisational effectiveness literature, because of its solid grounding in motivational theory, self-actualisation, self-determination theory, goal attainment, and the possibilities that it provides in terms of proactive organisational interventions to enable effectiveness (Seligman et al. 2005). This is in contrast to previous approaches, which focused on understanding existing problems, providing interventions aimed at addressing the identified barriers, and re-measuring the effectiveness of the solutions. Positive psychology provides a perspective in terms of which organisations can enable working environments that proactively facilitate effective functioning and, as such, enable effectiveness, as opposed to fixing the barriers that inhibit optimal functioning (Seligman and Csikszentmihalyi 2014).

The theoretical framework underpinning the Flow@Work Model is embedded in the positive psychology movement towards optimising people effectiveness and functioning in the workplace. The Model was conceptualised on the basis of an understanding of the barriers that inhibit optimal functioning in the organisation, and subsequently builds on areas of strength. The approach conceptualised by Coetzee and Veldsman (2013) acknowledges the organisation as a living system that needs to develop over time, and focuses on characterising the organisation in terms of areas of optimal functioning and learning how to neutralise areas of development (Wheatley 2006). This approach is in line with the shift in thinking towards open system theories, which view the organisation as a holistic and living entity that needs to be understood in terms of all of its interrelated parts and environmental influences (Wheatley 2006). Optimal functioning, on the other hand, was conceptualised in terms of the prevalent states of psychological work immersion present in the environment (Coetzee and Veldsman 2013). The states of psychological work immersion are measured through people-effectiveness enablers, referring to areas of development and strength that lead to experiences of psychological attachment (commitment, absorption, and employee motivation), which, in turn, lead to enabling of an effective workforce that contributes to the achievement of business performance (Coetzee and Veldsman 2013).

Veldsman (2013) stated that psychological work immersion is dependent on three conditions, namely (1) the alignment between employee expectations, the work environment, and organisational practices, (2) a significant relationship between the employee's job activities and his or her contribution to organisational goals, and (3) the espoused conventions, practices, and values of the organisation and consistency in terms of how employees are experiencing these.

The Model was conceptualised on the basis of three major influencing theories. Work engagement was conceptualised according to the original work of Kahn (1990), the Job Demands–Resources Model of Demerouti (1999), and the research related to psychological states of flow. Each of these foundational theories provided insight into the development of the Flow@Work Model and its applicability to knowledge-economy organisations, as summarised by the Table 2.1.

The Flow@Work Model

Figure 2.1 provides an overview of the Flow@Work Model, which will be discussed in terms of the people-effectiveness enablers and psychological attachment variables.

Table 2.1 Influencing theories on psychological work immersion and the Flow@Work Model

Influencing theory	Reference	Key criteria influencing the Flow@Work Model
Work engagement	Kahn (1990)	Incorporation of enablers that will lead to psychological engagement Theoretical view of psychological attachment as being characterised by the constructs of commitment, absorption, and intrinsic motivation as descriptors of engagement The relationship between engagement, individual task performance, and business performance Psychological attachment as a key component of people effectiveness Relevance of psychological attachment in knowledge economy organisations
Job resources and demands model	Demerouti (1999) Bakker et al. (2003)	People effectiveness enablers act as job resources at both an organisational and an individual level to create levels of psychological engagement The absence of people-effectiveness enablers will lead to increased levels of stress, burnout, and disengagement The relationship between people-effectiveness enablers and psychological attachment in terms of a reciprocal relationship Psychological attachment can be seen as a personal resource
Flow	Csikszentmihalyi (1975)	Utilisation of a self-awareness scale to measure states of immersion Led to the acknowledgement that flow occurs within a specific socio-cultural context, which makes the flow concept applicable to modern knowledge economy organisations Inclusion of certain people-effectiveness enablers related to the required conditions for flow to occur Item development of the scale, also assessing the skills–challenge balance required for the state of flow to occur Inclusion of intrinsic motivation as a key measure of psychological engagement

People-Effectiveness Enablers

People-effectiveness enablers can be described in terms of the psychological behavioural state of attachment to the organisational identity resulting from the employee's emotional-cognitive identification with or psychological attachment to the work and the organisation (Veldsman 2013). A number of constructs have been identified that will influence this particular state, and these should be seen as drivers that create an environment for psychological work immersion to occur. From an organisational development perspective, these drivers should be used as a key focus

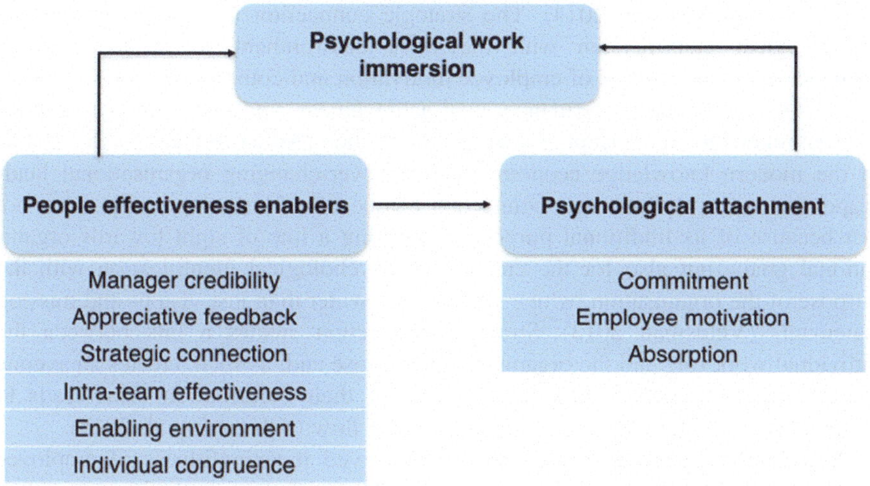

Fig. 2.1 The Flow@Work model

in interventions aimed at improving levels of psychological work immersion, owing to their influence on psychological attachment variables (Coetzee and Veldsman 2013).

Manager effectiveness relates to the extent to which managerial practices are perceived as fair, respectful, and consistent, creating a relationship of trust between employees and their direct managers (Veldsman and Coetzee 2014). The concept further refers to the ability of managers to connect employees to the organisational purpose from a psychological point of view, which, in turn, influences the level of psychological attachment to the organisational identity that the employees experience. Research has shown that a trusting relationship between managers and employees has positive implications for job performance, retention, job satisfaction, and organisational citizenship behaviours (Roussin and Webber 2012). Employees' perceptions are shaped by the way they are treated by their managers, which then influence the organisational climate and culture and set the tone for creating a psychologically safe environment where employees can flourish (Jiang et al. 2010).

Individual congruence relates to the perception of employees that there is a fit between their strengths, competencies, and skills and the requirements of the job, articulated in their day-to-day roles (Veldsman et al. 2014). The construct has shown a strong relationship with factors such as positive work experiences, feelings of significance, and the ability to master personal goals and objectives (Swann et al. 2015). Individual congruence has also shown a relationship with goal achievement and levels of commitment and motivation within the organisational context, and is often seen as a key contributing factor to work engagement (Tims et al. 2013).

Strategic connection refers to the connection between individual contribution and broader organisational goal achievement, and is underpinned by enabling employees to feel that they are making a significant contribution to the organisation

(Veldsman and Coetzee 2014). The strategic connection is crucial for enabling psychological identification with the work environment, as well as a key influencing factor in terms of employee motivation and commitment (Barrick et al. 2015). Organisational performance, goal achievement, and task significance have all been related to the concept of strategic connection (Armstrong and Taylor 2014). In the modern knowledge economy with its ever-changing organisational landscape, the concept of strategic connection has become increasingly important, not just because of its traditional purpose of creating a line of sight towards organisational goals, but also for the creation of psychological identification with the purpose of the organisation, which stretches far wider than just vision- and mission statements (Veldsman 2013). Strategic connection creates a link between the individual work role and the organisational purpose and, as such, creates an avenue for employees to create meaning in terms of their contribution. This leads to feelings of self-efficacy, work engagement, and flow (Albrecht et al. 2015).

Appreciative feedback refers to the perceived meaningfulness of employee feedback related to individual performance and areas of strength (Veldsman and Coetzee 2014). Appreciative feedback shows a clear relationship with enhanced employee self-efficacy, motivation, and the prevalence of problem-solving behaviour (Jordan and Audia 2012). Appreciative feedback has been shown to have a significant influence on employee commitment, feelings of significance, and the ability of employees to grow and develop (Shahid and Azhar 2013). From a performance perspective, appreciative feedback also relates to the perceived effectiveness of processes, such as performance feedback, and is a clear influencing factor in whether employees feel that they can grow and develop in the organisation (Mone and London 2014). The construct of appreciation refers to far more than just tangible rewards, also encompassing the intangible perceived benefits that employees obtain in exchange for their contributions to and membership of the organisation. Recent research conducted by Mone and London (2014) found that feelings of appreciation lead to higher psychological identification with the organisation and its purpose, and result in higher levels of productivity.

An enabling environment refers to the extent to which the employee perceives the policies, procedures, and physical work environment as helpful in achieving organisational goals (Veldsman and Coetzee 2014). In the modern knowledge economy, the rise of virtual work teams, distributed geographical models, and fluid organisational designs and practices have introduced this concept as a key contributing factor to employees' connection with the organisation and its ability to remain relevant (Iorio and Taylor 2014). Flexible work practices, often in contrast to traditional organisational policies, have demanded a shift in the way in which working environments are governed and managed, so as to allow innovative ways of enabling employees to work (Lohikoski et al. 2016). With the millennial generation entering the workforce, many traditional hierarchical and policy-driven structures and practices have become irrelevant and obsolete (Veldsman 2015). The modern knowledge economy, therefore, has key implications for workplace design, and calls for a shift from traditional command-and-control management principles to a focus on issues such as collaboration, shared working spaces, and innovation hubs (Richmond 2015). The enabling environment also refers to the perception of safety regarding the physical environment, which has major implications for where organisations are located, where employees are based, and how workplaces are managed.

Intra-team effectiveness refers to the perception of individuals regarding the competence of their team members, how team members treat each other in terms of the principles of dignity and respect, and whether they feel supported by their team members to be able to achieve organisational goals (Veldsman and Coetzee 2014). The concept of teams has become a prominent feature of knowledge-economy organisations (McGurrin 2015). Recent research on teams has shown that perceptions of competence will influence the openness of individuals to collaborate, trust one another, and work together in a productive and effective manner (Du et al. 2015). Dignity and respect have been highlighted as the basis of a trusting team relationship; however, these behaviours are only built up over time as a result of perceived competence shared by team members, team benevolence, and integrity in their dealings with one another (Prooijen and Ellemers 2015). The knowledge economy has broadened the concept of teams to the virtual workplace, with team members often not interacting face to face with one another at all, yet being expected to work together in a way that drives organisational performance (Gilson et al. 2015). Rothmann (2014) stated that positive team interactions can lead to stronger psychological identification with the workplace, commitment to other team members, and loyalty towards the organisation.

The people effectiveness enablers as antecedents of engagement will influence psychological attachment in terms of levels of commitment, absorption, and employee motivation present in the organisation (Veldsman and Coetzee 2014). Psychological attachment as a measure of engagement refers to the variables that influence the levels of psychological work immersion. Commitment, absorption, and employee motivation have been identified as three consequences of positive perceptions of people-effectiveness enablers, and can be seen as a measure of the levels of psychological work immersion present in the organisation (Veldsman and Coetzee 2014).

Commitment is the extent that the individual identifies with the organisation's purpose and the underlying value system present within the organisation (Veldsman and Coetzee 2014). Oyewobi et al. (2012) stated that commitment entails a readiness to exert effort to achieve organisational goals and a drive to remain associated with and retain membership of the collective organisation. The construct of commitment has been shown to have a strong relationship with retention and productivity, making it a relevant construct within the context of organisational effectiveness measures (Dhar 2012). Commitment also implies an alignment of the individual to the organisational value system and an identification with the organisational identity. This has been shown to lead to low turnover intentions and enhanced loyalty towards the organisation (Aggarwal and D'Souza 2012).

Absorption refers to the levels of attachment that an individual feel towards his/her work (Veldsman and Coetzee 2014). Schaufeli et al. (2002) conceptualised absorption as a key component of work engagement, which describes employees' sense of energetic involvement in and connection to their work activities. Absorption is influenced by factors such as perceived organisational support, opportunities for growth, job resources provided, and environmental factors such as psychological safety (Jeve et al. 2015). Coetzer and Rothmann (2007) further stated that higher levels of absorption lead to work engagement and a willingness on the part of employees to involve themselves and push towards new levels of achievement. As such, the concept of absorption is relevant within the domain of organisational effectiveness, owing to its influence on factors such as goal achievement, productivity, work engagement, and commitment (Eldor et al. 2015).

Motivation is a well-researched concept that underpins a number of modern organisational effectiveness theories (Milner 2015). Employee motivation refers to an intrinsic drive that results in individual energy, and influences the levels of enjoyment experienced by employees in the work environment (Veldsman and Coetzee 2014). In their seminal work, Hackman and Oldman (1980) demonstrated that factors such as employees feeling challenged in their work environment, experiencing autonomy in terms of making decisions in their own work, and seeing how their individual contribution makes a difference in the broader organisation will influence their levels of motivation. Employee motivation is also characterised by feelings of personal mastery in relation to the achievement of both personal and organisational goals, and, as such, ties in with the modern organisational practices of reward and recognition prevalent in many knowledge-economy organisations (Shields 2007). Boredom, disengagement, and feelings of insignificance are often mentioned as the antithesis of employee motivation, yet, despite motivational practises, a rise in these factors in modern organisations has become a reality, with Gallup (2013) stating that 70% of the knowledge-economy workforce is experiencing a lack of motivation. Studies on burnout have become increasingly important as the modern employee struggles to remain engaged, motivated, and healthy in a turbulent environment that is forever demanding more (Sulea et al. 2015).

The Flow@Work Model can be applied as a framework for measuring people effectiveness, psychological attachment, and psychological work immersion levels within the organisation. Higher levels of psychological work immersion lead to higher levels of employee retention through the availability of people-effectiveness enablers, which lead to higher levels of psychological attachment.

Applying the Model in Practice

The Psychological Work Immersion Scale (PWIS) (Veldsman 2013) was developed as a modern measure of people effectiveness, and provides an understanding of people-effectiveness enablers (manager credibility, appreciative feedback, strategic connection, intra-team effectiveness, enabling environment, and individual congruence) that lead to psychological attachment (commitment, absorption, and employee motivation). The scale provides insight into the people practices prevalent in the organisation, as well as the alignment between individual employee expectations pertaining to the work environment and the lived practices in the organisation. The PWIS has undergone rigorous statistical validation (Veldsman and Coetzee 2014), and has shown acceptable validity and reliability in measuring the underlying constructs that can be described as people-effectiveness enablers and psychological attachment. The PWIS (Veldsman 2013) has been applied in various industries, such as manufacturing, information technology, the not-for-profit sector, the services, research, financial sectors, and fast-moving consumer goods, and has been shown to be a valuable and reliable measure of people effectiveness in knowledge-economy organisations (Veldsman and Coetzee 2014). From a practical perspective, the PWIS (Veldsman 2013) has also been used to identify organisational development interventions aimed at improving the levels of psychological attachment by addressing people-effectiveness enablers and creating an environment conducive to high performance.

Table 2.2 provides an overview of the theoretical framework that underpins the relationship between people-effectiveness enablers and organisational development interventions aimed at the individual, team, and organisational levels.

Table 2.2 People-effectiveness enablers and relationship to OD interventions

People-effectiveness enablers	*Level of organisational development interventions*			References
	Organisational	Team	Individual	
Manager effectiveness	Leadership competency model design Culture interventions Leadership development Training	Team coaching Leadership development	Individual coaching Individual development	Jiang et al. (2010) Roussin and Webber (2012)
Individual congruence	Organisational design	Functional design	Work design Job rotation Personal development	Swann et al. (2015) Tims et al. (2013)
Strategic connection	Vision- and value interventions Performance management Communication practices	Cascading of performance goals Communication forums	Individual feedback to employees regarding performance One-on-one communication mechanisms	Barrick et al. (2015) Armstrong and Taylor (2014)
Appreciative feedback	Total rewards practices Recognition and incentive programmes	Team recognition processes	Performance feedback Individual recognition practices	Jordan and Audia (2012) Shahid and Azhar (2013)
Enabling environment	Talent management Policy reviews Process optimisation Ergonomic design	Ergonomic design	Personal development Career pathing	Iorio and Taylor (2014) Lohikoski et al. (2016) Richmond (2015)
Intra-team effectiveness	Culture interventions	Team effectiveness	Team effectiveness Role clarification	Gilson et al. (2015) Prooijen and Ellemers (2015)

The following section demonstrates how the Flow@Work Model has been applied empirically by discussing two case studies. Each case study is discussed in terms of context, key business challenge, application of the Flow@Work Model through the PWIS, key organisational development (OD) interventions, and the impact on organisational practices. The case studies indicate the relevance of the Flow@Work Model, as well as the applicability of the PWIS as a mechanism and measure to monitor people effectiveness and talent retention levels in knowledge-economy organisations. The model serves as a diagnostic framework to understand critical areas of focus to drive talent retention over the longer term.

Case study 1: Applying the model to retain millennial talent in a creative agency

Organisational context	Company A is a small boutique creative agency that services a number of corporate organisations by supporting them in realising their brand ambition. The organisation positions its offering as "the ability to tell compelling brand stories that lead to realising potential" The organisation had grown from a small entrepreneurial business, started by four founders, to an organisation that employs more than 80 people, in the space of six years. The organisation aimed to grow its own talent, and employees, with the exception of the founding members, were in their early twenties
Key business challenge	The organisation started to experience the need to formalise practices in order to be able to realise their future growth ambition. The challenge, however, was that the perception was that they were starting to lose touch with the organisational identity—what had made employees want to join the business originally—and, given the average age of the workforce, they started to lose key talent because they were getting frustrated with the lack of supporting resources, given the demands set for them regarding performance and growth
Application of the PWIS	The PWIS was utilised across all levels of the organisation to explore employees' current levels of psychological work immersion, as well as the factors that were either enabling or inhibiting these levels. The PWIS reported low levels of strategic connection and individual congruence, which indicated that employees were losing sight of what the organisation was, what the goals were for the future, and the part they had to play in helping the organisation succeed. Employees also reported low levels of feedback, and that they did not feel as if they were growing their own skill sets whilst helping the organisation to achieve its ambitions
OD interventions	Based on the identified areas of strength and development, as measured by the PWIS, the following interventions were implemented: 1. Creating a compelling strategic narrative and value system The founders crafted and articulated a compelling narrative that told the story of why the organisation was started, the dream that had led the organisation to this point, and what their dream for the future was. The narrative was told as a story, with designated chapters, each with different characters (individuals who played a key role during that phase of the organisation), including villains (key challenges that were faced

(continued)

(continued)

	and had to be overcome) and milestones (key achievements that were celebrated and which formed the fabric of their identity) The founders each took ownership of a component of the story, and translated it into a narrative that was authentic, meaningful, and relevant to the employees. As a next phase, the narrative was made visual through a photo-and-story wall that was created in the main offices. This told the story according to a timeline, with visual artefacts reinforcing key elements of the story 2. Relooking the organisational design An open-space workshop was held with all employees, to gather collaborative contributions towards a new organisational model. The model was crafted based on a compelling question: *If this is who we want to become, how should we work?* The following significant changes were effected: • The formal hierarchy was abolished and replaced with feature teams that were formed around projects, skills, and clients Employees were pooled and assigned roles and responsibilities depending on the scope of the work per project • 'Rules of engagement' were created to guide how they worked with, talked to, and related to one another • Formal coaching structures were introduced to guide project- and team leaders to be able to manage employees in line with the newly crafted rules of engagement • An end-to-end work process was defined that allowed employees to always understand how and where they would be able to contribute to any particular project 3. There would be a focus on employee development and recognition An informal, continuous 360° feedback process was developed, which tied into the main work processes and allowed employees to receive feedback on a regular basis regarding their own progress, areas of development, and successes. This was utilised to further reinforce a culture of celebration and transparency, and also to allow them to continuously have information upon which to draw when focusing on their own individual development plans. This process was supported by the creation of a recognition system that used gamification principles; employees were rewarded according to a leaderboard that was visibly displayed in the office. Employees earned points by being recognised by the leadership team or other team members for their contributions on projects, living the rules of engagement, or for certain achievements. Points were later converted into designated rewards as part of their annual recognition process, e.g., the top five employees were allowed to attend the Design Indaba, which is a very prestigious industry awards ceremony where the best of the best are celebrated
Impact	The focus on these key elements enabled the organisation to not only significantly reduce employee turnover, but to set the tone for the future growth culture of the organisation. Three years later, the organisation is still growing strong—it has grown by almost 30% in terms headcount whilst retaining 80% of its workforce—and was recently acquired by a global agency as part of their international expansion strategy

Case study 2: Applying the model to measure people effectiveness during a turnaround strategy

Organisational context	Bank ABC focuses on providing credit solutions to the lower income market across Southern Africa. The organisation operates from a call centre environment, with regional and local branches distributed across all provinces in South Africa. The organisation had run into difficult times, and a new leadership team had taken the reins after the organisation had been put under curatorship by the Reserve Bank. The task of the new leadership team was to implement a focused turnaround strategy to guide the organisation back to profitability
Key business challenge	Given the focused turnaround strategy, the organisation was faced with the challenge of having to keep levels of psychological work immersion at the desired levels to ensure the sustainability of the organisation, as well as retain key talent during this transition process, which was marked by uncertainty
Application of the PWIS	The organisation utilised the PWIS every six months to monitor areas of psychological work immersion and to identify which areas they should focus on every quarter to create an environment for psychological work immersion to occur. This was important, as they had identified that lower levels of psychological work immersion led to higher levels of talent attrition, and they utilised this metric at an executive level to ensure that they retained the critical talent required to implement the turnaround strategy
OD interventions	A variety of OD interventions were implemented over a three-year period in the key areas of focus identified through various iterations of the PWIS measurement. At a high level, the following themes were evident across all three years: 1. Creating a strategic narrative of the future Given the turbulent period, the PWIS indicated that a key focus was required on helping employees understand what the future state of the organisation should look like, as well as the roadmap to get there. This roadmap was broadly and regularly communicated to employees across all levels and used as an artefact for all leaders to tell a compelling story of hardship, progress, and ambition 2. Focusing on manager intent at all levels The new leadership team was integrated into the organisation through various interventions, with a key focus on building trust between the new leadership team and the rest of the organisation. A leadership philosophy was defined, leaders were assessed against this framework, and relevant interventions such as coaching, external development actions, etc. were implemented for all senior leaders. With each PWIS measurement, data were further explored to identify pockets of excellence within the organisation, where leaders were able to build trust with their employees and create conditions conducive to high levels of psychological work immersion. These were studied, and the practices were duplicated in other areas of the organisation 3. Creating a people committee Given the importance of people as part of the turnaround strategy, a people committee was created, with a focus on discussing the health of human capital in the organisation. The committee was chaired by the

(continued)

(continued)

	CEO, and the PWIS was used on a six-monthly basis to identify, prioritise, and monitor people interventions for the coming period, based upon the PWIS measurement dashboard that had been created as a monitoring mechanism
Impact	Four years after the inception of the turnaround strategy, the organisation declared a profit. During this time, they also managed, year-on-year, to improve the levels of psychological work immersion in the organisation, whilst also growing the business in terms of its footprint, financial achievements, and stakeholder confidence

Implications of the Model for Future Research and Talent Retention Practices

As can be seen from the discussion above, the concept of psychological work immersion and the underpinning Flow@Work Model are relevant in the new world of work to not only retain employees, but also to improve business performance. The Model, however, does have certain limitations, which need to be addressed by future research:

- The model should be tested in terms of applicability to other contexts globally, with specific reference to non-westernised working environments.
- Continuous research regarding the longitudinal impact of the Model on employee retention and business performance should be explored.
- Even though research has been done in terms of the applicability of the model in terms of demographic factors, further research is required in a global context.

Employee retention is a critical success factor for organisations that want to compete in the knowledge economy. The Flow@Work Model has been proven to be a useful framework and measure to identify areas of strength and development that need to be addressed for organisations to achieve their potential. The Model provides organisational practitioners and leaders with a simple framework that can be applied to their environments to support their employees to continuously achieve higher states of psychological work immersion, leading to benefits for both the organisation and individual employees.

Summary

This chapter positioned the Flow@Work Model as useful framework for talent retention in knowledge economy organisations. The chapter explored the theoretical basis and influencing theories applicable to the conceptualisation of the

Flow@Work Model whilst also positioning its usefulness as a diagnostic framework for modern organisational development practices. The chapter concluded by positioning potential future avenues for research and how the Flow@Work Model could be applied within the domain of employee retention.

References

Aggarwal, U., & D'Souza, K. C. (2012). Transformational leadership: The link between P-O fit, psychological contract and signature experiences. *The Indian Journal of Labour Relations, 47,* 485–497.

Albrecht, S. L., Bakker, A. B., Gruman, J. A., Macey, W. H., & Saks, A. M. (2015). Employee engagement, human resource management practices and competitive advantage: An integrated approach. *Journal of Organizational Effectiveness: People and Performance, 2*(1), 7–35.

Armstrong, M., & Taylor, S. (2014). *Armstrong's handbook of human resource management practice* (13th ed.). London: Kogan Page.

Bakker, A., Demerouti, E., & Schaufeli, W. (2003). Dual processes at work in a call centre: An application of the Job Demands-Resources model. *European Journal of Work and Organizational Psychology, 12*(4), 393–417.

Barrick, M. R., Thurgood, G. R., Smith, T. A., & Courtright, S. H. (2015). Collective organizational engagement: Linking motivational antecedents, strategic implementation, and firm performance. *Academy of Management Journal, 58*(1), 111–135.

Coetzee, M., & Veldsman, D. (2013). Exploring espoused organizational values in relation to lived values experiences in the South African financial sector. *African Journal of Business Management, 7,* 480–489.

Coetzer, C. F., & Rothmann, S. (2007). Job demands, job resources and work engagement of employees in a manufacturing organisation. *Southern African Business Review, 11*(1), 17–32.

Csikszentmihalyi, M. (1975). *Beyond boredom and anxiety.* San Francisco, CA: Jossey-Bass.

Demerouti, E. (1999). *Burnout: Eine Folge konkreter Arbeitsbedingungen bei Dienstleistungs-und Produktionstätigkeiten.* Lang.

Dhar, R. L. (2012). Employees' perception of organizational support: A qualitative investigation in the Indian information technology (IT) industry. *Work, 43*(2), 211–222.

Du, J., Shin, Y., & Choi, J. N. (2015). Convergent perceptions of organizational efficacy among team members and positive work outcomes in organizational teams. *Journal of Occupational and Organizational Psychology, 88,* 178–202.

Eldor, L., & Vigoda-Gadot, E. (2015). The nature of employee engagement: Rethinking the employee-organization relationship. *Academy of Management Proceedings, 1,* 10650.

Gallup (2013). *The global state of the workforce.* Retrieved from Gallup website. http://www.gallup.com/services/178517/state-global-workplace.aspx.

Gilson, L. L., Maynard, M. T., Young, N. C. J., Vartiainen, M., & Hakonen, M. (2015). Virtual teams research: 10 years, 10 themes, and 10 opportunities. *Journal of Management, 41*(5), 1313–1337.

Hackman, J. R., & Oldham, G. R. (1980). *Work redesign.* Reading: Addison-Wesley.

Hergenhahn, B., & Henley, T. (2013). *An introduction to the history of psychology.* Belmont: Wadsworth Cengage Learning.

Iorio, J., & Taylor, J. E. (2014). Boundary object efficacy: The mediating role of boundary objects on task conflict in global virtual project networks. *International Journal of Project Management, 32*(1), 7–17.

Jeve, Y. B., Oppenheimer, C., & Konje, J. (2015). Employee engagement within the NHS: A cross-sectional study. *International Journal of Health Policy and Management, 4*(2), 85.

Jiang, D., Lin, Y., & Lin, L. (2010). Business moral values of supervisors and subordinates and their effect on employee effectiveness. *Journal of Business Ethics, 100,* 239–252.

Jordan, A. H., & Audia, P. G. (2012). Self-enhancement and learning from performance feedback. *Academy of Management Review, 37*(2), 211–231.

Kahn, W. A. (1990). Psychological conditions of personal engagement and disengagement at work. *Academy of Management Journal, 33,* 692–724.

Kahn, W. A. (1992). To be fully there: Psychological presence at work. *Human Relations, 45*(4), 321–349.

Lohikoski, P., Kujala, J., Haapasalo, H., Aaltonen, K., & Ala-Mursula, L. (2016). Impact of trust on communication in global virtual teams. *International Journal of Knowledge-Based Organizations (IJKBO), 6*(1), 1–19.

McGurrin, D. P. (2015). *Investigating shared norms in multicultural teams: Exploring how team member scripts and cognitive adjustment strategies impact the norm formation process* (Unpublished dissertation). NC State University.

Meyers, M. C., Van Woerkom, M., & Bakker, A. B. (2013). The added value of the positive: A literature review of positive psychology interventions in organizations. *European Journal of Work and Organizational Psychology, 22*(5), 618–632.

Milner, J. B. (2015). *Organizational behavior 1: Essential theories of motivation and leadership.* New York: Routledge.

Mone, E. M., & London, M. (2014). *Employee engagement through effective performance management: A practical guide for managers.* New York: Routledge.

Oyewobi, L. O., Suleiman, B., & Muhammad-Jamil, A. (2012). Job satisfaction and job commitment: A study of quantity surveyors in Nigerian public service. *International Journal of Business and Management, 7*(5), 179–192.

Pedersen, M. J. (2015). Activating the forces of public service motivation: Evidence from a low-intensity randomized survey experiment. *Public Administration Review, 75*(5), 734–746.

Prooijen, A. M., & Ellemers, N. (2015). Does it pay to be moral? How indicators of morality and competence enhance organizational and work team attractiveness. *British Journal of Management, 26*(2), 225–236.

Richmond, O. P. (2015). The dilemmas of a hybrid peace: Negative or positive? *Cooperation and Conflict, 50*(1), 50–68.

Rothmann, S. (2014). Flourishing in work and careers. In M. Coetzee (Ed.), *Psycho-social career metacapacities: Dynamics of contemporary career development* (pp. 203–220). Dordrecht: Springer.

Roussin, C. J., & Webber, S. S. (2012). Impact of organizational identification and psychological safety on initial perceptions of co-worker trustworthiness. *Journal of Business and Psychology, 27,* 317–329.

Schaufeli, W. B., Salanova, M., Gonzáles-Romá, V., & Bakker, A. B. (2002). The measurement of engagement and burnout: A confirmative analytic approach. *Journal of Happiness Studies, 3,* 71–92.

Seligman, M. E. (2012). *Flourish: A visionary new understanding of happiness and well-being.* New York: Simon and Schuster.

Seligman, M. E., & Csikszentmihalyi, M. (2014). *Positive psychology: An introduction.* Dordrecht: Springer.

Seligman, M. E., Steen, T. A., Park, N., & Peterson, C. (2005). Positive psychology progress: Empirical validation of interventions. *American Psychologist, 60*(5), 410.

Shahid, A., & Azhar, S. M. (2013). Gaining employee commitment: Linking to organizational effectiveness. *Journal of Management Research, 5*(1), 250.

Shields, J. (2007). *Managing employee performance and reward.* Cambridge: Cambridge University Press.

Snyder, C. R., & Lopez, S. (2014). *Handbook of positive psychology.* Virginia: Crossmark.

Sulea, C., Van Beek, I., Sarbescu, P., Virga, D., & Schaufeli, W. B. (2015). Engagement, boredom, and burnout among students: Basic need satisfaction matters more than personality traits. *Learning and Individual Differences, 42,* 132–138.

Swann, C., Crust, L., Keegan, R., Piggott, D., & Hemmings, B. (2015). An inductive exploration into the flow experiences of European Tour golfers. *Qualitative Research in Sport, Exercise and Health, 7*(2), 210–234.

Tims, M., Bakker, A. B., Derks, D., & Van Rhenen, W. (2013). Job crafting at the team and individual level: Implication for work engagement and performance. *Group and Organizational Management, 38*(4), 427–454.

Veldsman, D. (2013). *Moving towards a strategic human capital return on investment model: An exploratory study of the psychological work immersion scale (Unpublished research report).* Randburg, South Africa: Rocketfuel Consulting.

Veldsman, D., & Coetzee, M. (2014). People effectiveness enablers in relation to employees' psychological attachment to the organization. *Journal of Psychology in Africa, 24*(6), 480–486.

Wheatley, M. J. (2006). *Leadership and the new science*. San Francisco: Berrett-Koehler.

Dieter Veldsman (DCom) is a registered Psychologist (cat. Industrial) with the HPCSA with a key focus on organisational development, people analytics, people effectiveness and organisational design. He is currently the Head of Research and Development at Mindset Management, a people analytics software business that specialises in the development of human capital measurement models and supporting software. He has consulted across various industries and has completed numerous global consulting assignments across Africa, Europe and Asia. He is a regular speaker at international conferences on the topics of employee engagement, human capital metrics and organisational development. He lectures part-time at the University of Johannesburg and is involved in a variety of other academic institutions as lecturer and moderator.

Part II
External Organisational Context: Emerging World of Work

Overview and Insights

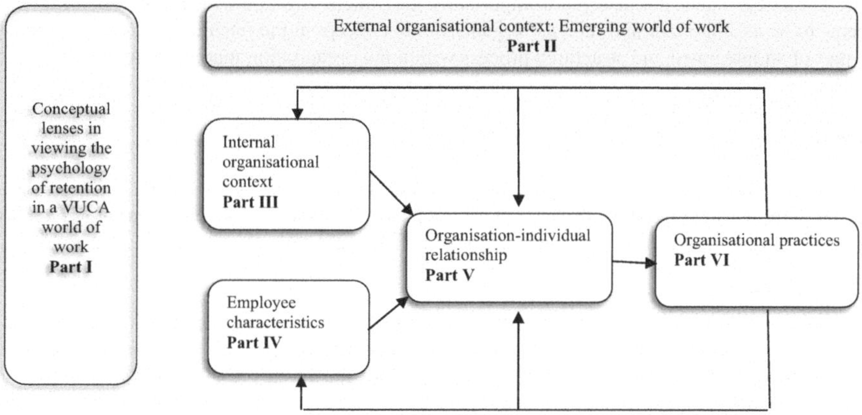

Towards an integrated conceptual framework for the psychology of retention

Part II, *External Organisational Context: Emerging World of Work*, comprises two chapters that illustrate the impact of the characteristics of the volatile, uncertain, complex and ambiguous (VUCA) and digital landscape of the Fourth Industrial Revolution on the psychology of retention.

Overview

Chapter 3 by John Ludike, *Digital Employee Experience Engagement Paradox: Futureproofing Retention Practice,* explores how digital disruption is impacting the future of work and what work in the future is likely to look like with obvious implications for retention practices. The author poses the question whether future digital technology work processes or digital workforce contexts will enable sustainability despite massive automation and deskilling of knowledge work. The chapter contributes to retention practice by providing recommendations for futureproofing retention and engagement via the (re)-design of next-generation employee experience. The author argues that it is ever increasingly pervasive that the current era of disengaged, transient talent affects every aspect of the business, and makes a case for the need to reignite purpose at work for talent. The author proposes practices such as organisational network analysis and establishing next-generation engagement platforms involving measuring digital engagement and identifying areas of communication to futureproof employee retention and sculpting a more meaningful employee experience.

Chapter 4 by Dieter Veldsman and Desiré Pauw, *The Relevance of the Employee Value Proposition for Retention in the VUCA World of Work*, contributes to the retention literature by exploring the employee value proposition (EVP) as a mechanism for retaining talent within the contemporary volatile, uncertain, complex, ambiguous (VUCA) landscape. The authors argue that the VUCA and digital landscape poses unique challenges which make traditional retention mechanisms obsolete. With critical talent being able to determine how, when, and where they want to work, organisations increasingly battle to attract, engage, and retain talent. The authors argue for a shift towards crafting a holistic employee experience through an attractive, realistic, and coherent employee value proposition (EVP). The chapter focuses on defining the concept, different approaches associated with crafting a compelling EVP, and the challenges faced during EVP implementation. The chapter concludes with the discussion of a real-life EVP implementation case study in the South African environment. The chapter contributes to the retention literature by showing that the EVP is important in terms of attracting and retaining top talent as well as being able to differentiate the organisation from its competitors. Talent retention is a critical challenge for organisational success, and it seems as if a well-articulated EVP can support organisations to not only attract top talent but also more importantly keep them engaged over the longer term. EVP seems to be an important and relevant organisational concept in the retention space when utilised as part of an integrated and structured process within the organisation that is aligned to the culture and values.

Key Insights

Part II of the book positions the psychology of retention within the pervasive influencing context of the VUCA and digital landscape which demands innovative thinking regarding retention practices that promote employee engagement over the long-term.

Practice Guidelines
The author of Chap. 3 makes a compelling case for retention practices that address the needs of a fast-evolving digital era employee. Mapping and surveying employee experiences in terms of meaningfulness and engagement across various areas of the employee journey within the organisation are emphasised. This involves surveying the engagement experiences of employees in the processes of sourcing and recruiting, pre-boarding, onboarding (orientation and initial training), compensation and benefits, ongoing learning and development, ongoing engagement, communication, and community involvement, rewards and recognition, performance planning, feedback, and review, career advancement, and retirement, termination, or resignation.

The authors of Chap. 4 illustrate by means of a real-life case study how utilising a well-articulated and appealing EVP as part of an integrated and structured process which is aligned to the culture and values of the organisation promotes the attraction of top talent and keep them engaged over the longer term. Employees' perceptions of the EVP are important as current employees will continuously weigh the perceived value of their relationship with the employer against the perceived value of other employers in the market.

Research Gaps
The pervasive influence of the VUCA rapid-evolving digital landscape on the psychology of retention needs further research. Chapters 3 and 4 illustrate the influence of the external context (digital disruption and evolution; volatile, uncertain, complex, and ambiguous business markets) on the psychology of retention. However, more empirical evidence is required and it is recommended that retention research should further explore how the external environmental factors influence the experiences, perceptions, and engagement of employees.

Chapter 3
Digital Employee Experience Engagement Paradox: Futureproofing Retention Practice

John Ludike

> *The human spirit must prevail over technology.*
>
> —Albert Einstein

Abstract The digital disruption of everything technology, society, business models is impacting the future of work inclusive of the evolution of the role of both the generalist and specialist human capital practitioner. Futureproofing the employee experience through design thinking, robust workplace people analytics and agile transformation ways of working is the new normal for evidence based human resource practitioners. This chapter explores how specifically digital disruption is impacting future of work and what work in the future is likely to look like. Possible answers to which digital capabilities, competencies and business culture might enable not a race and battle against the smart machines but rather a constructive collaborative augmentation. Which of these future digital technology work processes or digital workforce contexts will enable sustainability despite massive automation and deskilling of knowledge work? The chapter makes recommendations for futureproofing retention and engagement via the (re) design of next generation employee experience.

Keywords Digital disruption · Employee experience · Design thinking
Workforce analytics · Agile transformation · Engagement · Retention

Introduction

The digital transformation of work and or the future of work and with it the workplace and its workforce have been enormously contemporary if not popular themes amongst futurists, technologists, human capital practitioners of all makes and descriptions as well as corporate executives. Amongst several others this digital transformation has been described as a renaissance by Miller and Marsh (2014),

J. Ludike (✉)
Independent Management Consultant, London, UK
e-mail: jludike@hotmail.com

M. Coetzee et al. (eds.), *Psychology of Retention*,
https://doi.org/10.1007/978-3-319-98920-4_3

a digital tsunami by Bhaduri (2016) and Brynjolfsson and McAfee (2012) describe it as a race against the machine. Kaplan (2016) even argues rather apocalyptically that humans need not apply only to be cheekily contradicted by Davenport and Kirby (2016) concretely stating that there are winners and losers in the age of smart machines and that actually only humans need apply.

It is well known that business models and contexts are rapidly being ravished by wide array of not just exponentially evolving technologies but highly disruptive technologies that will according to a recent McKinsey Global Institute report literally "transform life, business and the global economy". These include but are not limited to artificial machine intelligence, cognitive and quantum computing, as well as stellar advances in automation, robotics and, block chain and the so called internet of things. Social, mobile, analytics and cloud computing are already considered passé. These all ambiguously impact the future of work, the workplace context and future digital workforce.

This chapter explores how specifically digital disruption is impacting future of work and what work in the future is likely to look like. Possible answers to which digital capabilities, competencies and business culture might enable not a race and battle against the smart machines but rather a constructive collaborative augmentation. Which of these future digital technology work processes or digital workforce contexts will enable sustainability despite massive automation and deskilling of knowledge work? Where possible examples to illustrate these will be provided.

Human resource (HR) practitioners of every ilk be it scientifically inspired occupational psychologists or generalist HR practitioners are all scrambling around for an elixir or alchemy of agile methodologies and/or human centered design thinking which will revitalize what is now popularly and poignantly emerging as the employee experience. The practical implications of these given future digital work and workforce will further be elaborated on in this chapter and accordingly contextualized.

As the overall focus of this publication centres on the 21st century industrial psychologist and HR practitioner need to continually psychologically struggle with enigma of how best to define, frame, focus, mobilise and sustain employee engagement and retention in measureable and tangible terms, importantly however for this chapter albeit digitally so.

The Digital Disruption of Everything

Two recent stories of major even iconic businesses and their leaders having not mastered the disruptive transformational realities of new digital economy namely Nokia and General Electric aptly demonstrates Brynjolfson and McAfee's (2014) and Surdak's (2014) notions that digital technological advances have engendered the greatest changes in human history and has not just generated change on a par with the Industrial Revolution but that exponentially speaking most of the changes being wrought by digital technologies have yet to appear.

Following on Brynjolfson and McAfee's (2014) further argue that given the ever-increasing pervasive connectedness, and data enablement of digital context for example of Smartphones and their apps—25 billion apps have been downloaded from Apple alone machines will produce the majority of mobile data traffic, not humans. Workforces create and consume vast amounts of data. In the future they believe social media's revolution in communications will define society's evolution.

We all recall some of us even fondly how Nokia was dominant leading player and game changer in the cellular market given how it innovated and introduced countless revolutionary models. Ironically its leadership didn't have foresight like Apple of a platform based hand held device like the iPhone and like the Sony Walkman before it was less responsive to its customers and more importantly ignorant of exponentially evolving digital communications ecosystem (mobile, music, photo's camera, messaging, and video). The final result being that Nokia was sold to Microsoft by the then CEO, Stephen Elop, who at the press conference announcing the acquisition commented, "We didn't do anything wrong, but somehow, we lost."

Similarly, General Electric (GE) recently announced that Jeffrey Immelt has resigned from this iconic conglomerate following 16 years as director and CEO having famously succeeded the legendary Jack Welch after not being able to engender and sustain investors' confidence specifically related to speed and impact of its digital transformation efforts. Accordingly, digital business researchers Raskino and Waller (2015) report that the latest seminal wave of innovation in social, mobile, data analytics and cloud as well as machine learning technology further erodes the boundaries between the physical and digital worlds and more importantly that it is advisable keeping in mind that all enterprise's now are digital companies as technology keeps opening opportunities.

The realities of these so termed platform (Parker et al. 2017) and gig economy (McGovern 2017) type enterprises are often further described by mentioning that Uber, the world's largest taxi company, owns no vehicles. Facebook, the world's most contemporary media owner, creates little if any content and Amazon the most valuable retailer, noticeably has no inventory and further that the world's largest accommodation provider, Airbnb owns no property.

New sources of value innovation and progressive business models and players are radically transforming entire industries true to the notion that software and artificial intelligence is eating the world given its central role in creating so much lower cost based service value innovation and distinctive customer experiences we thrive on. It is there for unashamedly vital for HR and other more scientifically driven practitioners to acknowledge that both the speed and nature of business and technology evolution is accelerating and maintaining the status quo is not an option.

Notoriously Kurzweil (2005) in explaining his law of accelerating returns he predicts an exponential increase in technologies like computers, genetics, nanotechnology, robotics and artificial intelligence further famously pronouncing that machine intelligence will be infinitely more powerful than all human intelligence combined. Maybe not such a profound proposition given that already, artificial intelligence is all around us, from self-driving cars and drones delivering Amazon package's and fertilising crops to virtual assistants and software enabled chatbots that translate, invest and even control lighting of premises remotely, all voice activated off course. Regrettably business as usual as Kodak discovered is no longer a feasible option and many a well-known organization will not see the light of day over next decade. Digital innovation is driving new generation of agile innovative organizations e.g. As mentioned the likes of Netflix, Instagram, Amazon, Airbnb, and Uber have used exponential technologies to completely disrupt the entertainment, photography, publishing, retail, hotel, and transportation industries. Organizations intuitively sense and know that to remain relevant in the new economy they need to be more innovative, more often.

Needless to say Raskino and Waller (2015) further maintain that in addition this unsurmounted technological innovation will in addition lead to a supply-side economic gains with further long-term improvements in both efficiency and productivity. Consequently, transportation and communication costs will drop, with logistics and global supply chains becoming more effective, impacting the cost of trade progressively liberating new markets which propel economic growth.

Although while all this might well be true and exponentially evolving so to speak the current contradiction is that there remains a significant chasm between radical new technology(ies) and the slower pace of both human skill and organization development. The increasing effect of digitization on society and the economy however is not to be underestimated. Quintessentially in addition to being the custodians of human cooperation, compassion and creativity the optimum rather grand challenge of our time for all human capital practitioners is inventing effective organizations worthy of the human spirit and equally if not more so the boundary less potential of the human species.

The transformative effects of digitalization have upended entire industries—publishing, music, movies, retail, gaming, and others. Sensors, artificial intelligence, micropayments, driverless vehicles, and tools such as virtual reality and 4D printing are changing every dimension of business. Evolving as an exponential organization as termed by Ismail et al. (2014) is as much a necessity as it is a choice. They believe that countless industries will digitize and that the so called digital revolution so far is just the tip of the iceberg given that every company is or will evolve into an information-based entity and thrive on abundance, not scarcity as they have propensity to rather than owning assets, exponential driven organizations borrow or lease them at little or no cost—like Uber, Airbnb and Google, remaining agile, through renting employees and leveraging cloud computing.

In order to rise to this challenge and the pivotal leadership role of HR practitioners we need to focus on how digital disruption is impacting the future of work and work of the future with its workforce capabilities inclusive of culture and context. Thereafter we can well proceed to reflect on implications of all and how HR practitioner's might go about futureproofing their organizations meaning move faster or face oblivion.

Future of Work and Work of the Future

Given this exponentially networked, digital platform based and gig experience driven economy it is necessary for us to proceed to further briefly explore some of the realities of the future of work and the future workforce. Many HR practitioners can well find this unnerving especially if they have not transitioned to what Prensky (2012) terms either a digital native or digital immigrant needing to familiarise themselves with how everyday devices becoming smarter and smarter and constantly connected to and via internet of things e.g. Wearable Fitbit, Garmin and or Netflix, Showmax, U Tube mobile and screen-based downloads in data, knowledge rich world. Meister and Willyerd (2010) in describing the Workplace of 2020 elaborate on various changes relating to the future of work and work of the future as follows:

1. Employees, will be hired and promoted based upon their individual reputation or personal brand capital hence for employees to advance, workers will need extensive, high-quality social networks, strong personal brands and demonstrated expertise and accomplishments. These components comprise reputation capital.
2. Contract and assignment or project based jobs will be the path to permanent full-time employment to let firms test potential employee's capabilities before hiring them full time but also given emphasis and preference of new generation workforce relating to agile, flexible as well as remote and virtual working.
3. Employee's mobile device of choice will become their office, their classroom and their concierge as smart phones and tablets are replacing personal computers as the internet connection devices of choice. Easy to use, superb connectivity and great versatility, these as well as wide range of platform Apps enable employees to work anywhere, any time.
4. CEO's job requirement's will include need for a digital 2020 mind-set in order for them to thrive in a networked always on world where there is pressing need to communicate, connect and collaborate 24/7 be it via Blogging, Twitter, Instagram or Facebook all preferred channels of the 21st century workforce and consumer. Digital fluency and social media literacy and in many cases advanced analytics if not coding will be as basic a requirement as reading.
5. Lifelong learning will be a business requirement and the corporate curriculum will use "video games." Alternate reality games and simulations to engage young people.
6. Corporate social responsibility programs will increasingly be designed to attract and retain employees as employment branding becomes more prominent. New generation high potential employees focus on the "triple bottom line: people, planet and profits" where diversity and gender equality will be a critical business issue rather than an HR issue.

It seems therefore that digital technology enables real time employee engagement at scale. Video Blogs (vlogs), Twitter and digital video are assisting pioneering leaders to connect, communicate and more importantly collaborate with their organizations.

Enterprise social platforms further elevates progressive, open and inclusive two-way communication where employees share, collaborate and co-design their respective futures in real time. Digital technology ushers in new era in which leaders engage with employees in unprecedented authentic manner which makes transformative change happen. As such it empowers employees by giving them a voice to make organization vision a reality. The digital tools encourage conversation and provide all opportunity to participate in sculpting of organizations destiny.

In digital economy's parlance employees are crowdsourced to co-create and co-design and as such accelerate creation of and adoption of agile fit for strategic purpose solutions. Culturally it embeds transparency and reduces potential for digital divide.

The Workforce of the Future Index which is published by the Economist Intelligence Unit quantifies the technological aptitude of national workforces in 56 countries, across the following six dimensions which can easily be integrated into future digital workforce planning and most importantly deployment efforts:

1. Technology and connectivity infrastructure which focuses measures relating to access toreliable electricity and high-speed Internet inclusive of the number of secure Internet servers as well as quality of information and communication technology (ICT). Interestingly the top-ranking nations include South Korea, the Netherlands and Switzerland.
2. Technology and society similarly this element measures the prevalence of technology in the everyday lives of a nation's citizens, including affordability, number of active Internetusers, e-commerce sales and local hosting of web content. The top-ranking nations are the United States of America, the United Kingdom and Norway.
3. Labour markets education and technology skills as can be expected this dimension focus and evaluates the prevalence of skilled workers and the quality of their skills. Factors affecting this category include the general state of education (including tertiary education), students' mathematics and programming skills, and prevalence of the Internet in schools. The top-ranking nations are the United States of America, the United Kingdom and Germany.
4. Government environment regulations and legislation laws contribute to the accessibility of technology. Indicators here include a nation's cyber laws, protection of intellectual property, online services and general commitment to both privacy and security of ICT related information. Not surprisingly top-ranking nations in this category are France, the United States of America and the Netherlands.

5. Business environment—equally important is measurement of a market's ability to adopt new technologies, and the quality of the political and economic environment in a country which enables and scrutinises countries local start-up culture. The top-ranking nations are the United States of America, Germany and United Kingdom.

It must therefore follow that a so called digital workforce constitutes more than the merging of technology and business it's about the cultivation and optimisation even leveraging of entire new generation of digital mind-set employee all who can to explore, connect, socialize, and in turn sculpt differentiating consumer experiences. Ingham (2017) argues that by organizations optimising on delivering capabilities of innovation, talent, change, and collaboration they shift their focus from developing individuals to enabling networks and relationships between employees. Accordingly, at work it would seem that, good relationships correlate to higher engagement and productivity. It further enables employees to cope with the rapid pace of change. People are the core differentiator today, and to enable people, organizations must empower them digitally with the necessary resources and support a mind-set shift given that an inherent curiosity combined with social driven learning and collaboration capabilities are definitive digital competencies of the future workforce. In an increasingly digital world, said digital transformation is not just about more and better, faster as well as different technologies. It entails what is known as digital congruence—aligning your company's culture, people, structure, and tasks. That's why it's crucial to embrace the diversity of generations and technological advances, and to realize that improving leadership skills and fostering an environment of continuous learning is paramount. Both agility and collaboration are going to be ever prevalent and inherent job requirement's whilst organization's will continuously need to create type of environments to optimize and leverage workforce and people's capacity for growth, learning and innovation.

Essential that HR practitioners understand, appreciate and value the complex relationship between meaning people attach to their work experiences as its integral component of their personal and social identity. In many ways the drastic impact of ecosystem of cognitive, social, cloud and analytic chatbots, virtual assistants etc. is not fully apparent yet however more than plausible to argue that it could represent gigantic socio-cultural workplace transformation.

Fortuitously McKinsey (2017) during time of writing has published a report on the impact of automation on jobs and estimate 400–800 million workers will be displaced due to the emergence of robots and automation by the year 2030. The 400 million figure is a midpoint; dependent on the pace of adoption of the technology, there could be 800 million people who could be displaced. Fortunately, technology will also lead to the creation of jobs that would offset the job loss. The caveat here being that organizations and countries will have to be adept at ensuring the smooth transition of the displaced workers towards the sectors and areas of strong job creation.

The report also states that around 75–375 million people would have to switch occupation by 2030. Here too, 75 million is the midpoint, while 375 million is when the adoption of technology will be fastest.

It mentions that the impact of automation will also vary:

- By the country's income level.
- Demographics.
- Industry structure.

Mancini (2015) in his interpretation of collaborative work spaces states that the gap is widening between individual workers making use of new collaborative technologies and organizations' ability to control these tools. He argues compellingly that work culture and traditional hierarchies are evolving in response to collaborative technology, however emphasises that organizational structures must facilitate this evolution if businesses wish to take full advantage of technical innovations and people's ability to use its advantages to augment productivity. Ingram's (2017) views that the organization of the future will need to be social and connected, and postulates further that the technologies and structures to facilitate this will be increasingly important.

According to previous mentioned McKinsey report, the following factors will serve as a catalyst in the creation of work for both the developed and the developing economies:

- **Rising incomes and consumption, especially in emerging economies**: The report estimates that global consumption would grow $23 trillion between 2015 and 2030. And as income will rise, the consumption pattern will also change with consumers spending more on all categories. The sectors which will be affected by the same leading to greater job creation are as follows: consumer durables, leisure activities, financial and telecommunication, housing, healthcare, and education.
- **Healthcare of aging population**: The report estimates that there will be an addition of 300 million to the population above 65 years of age as compared to 2014. This will lead to increased spending on healthcare and personal services. Potentially, this could result in the creation of 80 million jobs globally in the healthcare and related sector.
- **Investment in infrastructure and building**: The report estimates on an average $3.3 trillion per year will need to be invested per year to fill the infrastructure gap. This could lead to the creation of 80–200 million jobs by 2030.
- **Investment in renewable energy, energy efficiency, and climate adaption**: In case of a step scenario, which is organizations and nations proactively working towards meeting the commitment of the Paris climate accord, there could be a potential creation of 10 million jobs in manufacturing, construction, and installation.
- **Technology development**: The report estimates that investment in technology will increase by more than 50% between 2015 and 2030. The investment would be largely focused on technology services and technology consultation.

The resultant would be the rise in jobs related to the developing and deploying technology. The jobs which will be impacted would include the following profile: computer scientists, IT administrators, and engineers. Approx., 25–50 million jobs will be created globally.
- **Marketization for previously unpaid work**: As per the report, 75% of the unpaid work falls in women's domain there could well be a shift with individual households either investing in paid work, or the government providing universal childcare and other services. The shift could lead to the marketization of 50–90 million unpaid jobs by 2030 which would be constructive.

So in summary 60% of occupations could have up to 30% of their activities automated including radiologists, design engineers, market researchers and well wide array of HR professionals including occupational psychologist given mammoth rate of automation and cognitive (AI) technologies impacting entire HR value chain of attraction, assessment, development engagement and deployment. They are being replaced by big data analysts, social media experts, cloud builders, app developers, and other types of information specialists. Software engineering jobs will grow at a rate of 18.8% by 2024 which is triple the rate of overall job growth rate.

As challenging and profound as to comprehend Davenport and Kirby (2016) further convincingly elaborate on the use of smart machines and how it encroaches on knowledge work and threatens professionals, including lawyers, doctors, accountants, professors, pilots, and more. They do however argue that it is possible and necessary to prepare employees to augment machines given that machines streamline tasks and people supplement that work with variable, complex thought. Machines and humans produce better results than either could alone. Augmentation finds ways for humans and machines to form partnerships. They argue in order for humans to remain relevant and make meaningful impact people in organizations need to adopt following approaches or steps:

- **Step up**—Humans have "big-picture" perspectives. They can focus on more generalized and large-scale strategic thinking to remain relevant. Automation does not excel in that area.
- **Step aside**—Personal interaction is important but beyond the scope of computers.
- For example, salespeople, motivational coaches and therapists perform work that may benefit from machine analyses but requires human engagement.
- **Step in**—Companies must have a few people who can "understand, monitor, and improve" the functionality of computers and information systems.
- **Step narrowly**—Jobs with a limited purview may not be worth automating. Finding these niche fields is a path for career growth.
- "**Step forward**"—Those who understand computer systems will have jobs in modifying and designing technology to meet the changing needs of businesses and industries.

Amidst this general malaise relating to the digital workplace and it's even more digitally enhanced, augmented and/or deskilled workforce it increasingly will be about HR practitioners and the wider HR community's employees' ability to re-envision, reimagine if not reposition and reinvigorate their roles. Given the apparent lower levels of trust and engagement in and with leadership practitioner's emphasis is increasingly going to center on futureproofing via collaborating, communicating, and connecting with the wider human network of things.

Burning questions, which remain after reflecting on how digital disruption is impacting future of work, the workforce and organizational culture are:

- How to define, frame, focus, mobilise and sustain, meaning futureproof employee engagement and retention in measureable terms?
- How relevant are either of these (engagement and retention) given increasing temporary and transient nature of digital work context e.g. Half-life of knowledge and skills and average tenure of C Suite Executive down to less than 4 years with organizations now around 15 years before obsolescence?
- Which processes, methodologies and practices, e.g. design thinking, agile organizational design, talent analytics etc., will optimise employee experience to ensure human potential fully leveraged throughout individual and organization lifecycle?
- How is organizations and work to be redesigned to leverage the digital workforce and sculpt breakthrough employee experience?
- How must practitioners reinvent themselves and HR evolve to ensure relevance and meaningful impact on optimum productivity and retention of employees on one hand and competitive innovative driven organization culture on the other?

Futureproofing Retention and Engagement via the (Re) Design of Next Generation Employee Experience

Amidst this sea change in digital workplace context, with its rapid continuing technological advancement with unprecedented volatility and tormenting ubiquity. Both Adams (2017) and Morgan (2017) argue for radical change meaning to either disrupt or be disrupted. They implicitly imply in their work that only true certainty is needed for humanising the workplace employee experience. Their respective yet mutually reinforcing positions are that by treating employees as adults not children as well as handling employees as consumers or customers (not a one-size-fits-all approach) and more importantly by valuing employees as humans, HR practitioners can contribute to the creation of a workplace context in which employees are able to invest more of their whole selves into the workplace.

They remain perplexed by the fact that given fact that we can buy online with one click from Amazon, Takealot make video calls with Skype and What's App connect to our social networks via Facebook, Instagram etc. and share knowledge and ideas through Twitter and Pinterest it is hard to comprehend why our corporate procurement systems, teleconferencing, directory and collaborative workgroup services, and corporate communications platforms are at times lagging and so incredibly cumbersome by comparison, leading to sense of disillusionment and disenfranchisement and this all amidst what Pine and Gillmore (2011) termed an experience economy.

Morgan (2017) through his research into 17 attributes of the Employee Experience Index (EEI) focusing on technology, physical spaces and organizational culture argues that organizations which progressively invest and devote resources to sculpting workplace experiences are:

- included 11.5 times as often in Glassdoor's Best Places to Work.
- listed 4.4 times as often in LinkedIn's list of North America's Most In-Demand Employers.
- 28 times more often listed among Fast Company's Most Innovative Companies.
- listed 2.1 times as often on the Forbes list of the World's Most Innovative Companies.
- twice as often found in the American Customer Satisfaction Index.

In addition, what these cutting-edge companies like General Electric, Cisco, International Business Machines (IBM) and Marriott International were found doing to create environments that are helpful and stimulating, instead of taxing and draining lead them to having more than 4 times the average profit and more than 2 times the average revenue. They were also almost 25% smaller, which suggests higher levels of productivity and innovation. As such these findings would suggest the need for clear conceptualization of the employee experience as the new frontier of competitive value innovation.

For retention purposes, the employee experience needs to be clearly differentiated and Patterson et al. (2017) are adamant that it encapsulates the entire relationship and journey that an employee experiences while interacting with an organization and as such human capital practitioners would be well advised to:

- Make the employee experience a core part strategy.
- Understand employee expectations and bridge the "Expectation Gap".
- Establish rock-solid Brand, Transactional, and Psychological Contracts that breed trust and confidence.
- Build an employee-employer partnership in creating something extraordinary.
- Leverage employee engagement into to propel customer satisfaction, loyalty, profit, and growth.

It is therefore clear that employee experience is total sum of everything an employee experiences throughout his or her connection to the organization—every employee interaction, from the first contact as a potential recruit to the last interaction after the end of employment. It is as such further distinguishable from:

- New and automated or "transformed HR"—While human resource and occupational psychologist practitioners shape and transform some of the most critical processes within (recruiting, assessment and selection, on-boarding, performance reviews and talent management planning), employee experience involves so much more. It needs to be considered as the intersection of employee expectations, needs, and wants and the organizational design of those expectations, needs, and wants.
- Employee engagement—Often used interchangeably with employee experience represents an employees' commitment to a company and its jobs and is the end goal while actual realized employee experience is considered the means to that end. The now momentous battle for hearts and minds of employees however is played out daily and constitutes far more than the results from annual employee engagement survey. In many ways these once off isolated engagement initiatives serve more to impact leader's credibility and further erode trust as organizations and their leadership are perceived by new generation workforce as inept and even clumsy as they not proactively designing and leading meaningful employee experiences to produce measureable employee retention and engagement.
- Employer or employment branding—Again far to regularly in order to improve rankings in various Best or most admired and innovative Places to Work type surveys and under the guise of competing in the war for talent, many companies try to develop an external reputation to help improve their digital, high potential talent attraction and retention efforts. Many of these however are "paid to participate" type surveys and employees increasingly growing weary of them as doesn't truthfully reflect and or ultimately represent human—experience of for example either belonging as feeling part of a team, group or organization or purpose meaning understanding why one's work matters. Practitioners are often asked to work with Marketing, Communications and Corporate Affairs functions to develop a brand. Many organizations e.g. Kentucky Fried Chicken (KFC), Mc Donald's, Pizza Hut as example notorious for positioning iconic external brands yet internally employee experiences lack any happiness or vigour which IBM describes respectively as the pleasant feeling arising in and around work as well as the presence of energy, enthusiasm and excitement at work. All which are valuable attributes to consider for employee retention and sculpting experience which drives it.
- Benefits, compensation or events—Normally shortly following one of many surveys already mentioned be it culture, engagement, retention, trust on annual basis people practitioners of every description called upon to assist with wish list of what benefits, compensation, parties and events can be arranged to better ensure retention and engagement. The more scientific and evidence orientated practitioners have even termed these the EVP or employee value proposition. Although practitioners might include such tactics which as with previously mentioned employee branding is then normally cascaded throughout organization as means to pacify response and or rectify results from various surveys and although the EVP could in part impact an employee's decision to join, stay, remain etc. it's not synonymous therewith. Employee experience design goes

well beyond making employment more fun and enjoyable it involves designing and delivering distinctive experiences for employees that are strategically aligned with and fosters increasing digital capable organizational culture.

True to Patterson et al. (2017) definition practitioners in their quest to address the psychology of employee retention and engagement need to deeply scrutinize and appreciate that the Employee Experience is the sum of the various perceptions employees have about their interactions with the organization in which they work throughout their employment journey. Morgan (2017) suggest practitioners continue to focus their abilities on technology, physical spaces and organizational culture as accordingly the experiences organizations design are ultimately what shape the actions that employees take and the relationships or associations that they want to have with a specific organization. It is easy for HR practitioners to be lulled into sense of comfort that themes related to digital future of work is decades away however Meister and Willyerd (2010) already proposed that by 2020 employees will expect the following five principles to resonate strongly in their workplaces:

- "Collaboration"—This calls for interwoven work, internally and externally.
- "Authenticity"—Core values and transparency demonstrate genuineness.
- "Personalization"—Employees want tailor-made personalised career paths.
- "Innovation"—In a changing world, new thinking enables sustainability.
- "Social connection"—Workplaces will be based on sharing and forming a community.

Continuing Meister and Willyerd (2010), further argued that by 2020, HR teams would grow and/or evolve to include new specialists such as the following:

- "Capability planners" who ensure that the company develops much-needed skills.
- "Chief technologists" who serve as HR's IT experts.
- "Community gardeners" who help to create and nurture online communities.
- "Futurists" who work with companies to anticipate their future needs.
- "People capability planners" who map out employees' career path and/or route for development.
- "Place planners" who ensure that site-specific features work well at presentations and at 'virtual and collaboration sites', professional career paths and/or routes of development.
- "Social connectors" who provide expertise in using social networks and social media.
- "Talent scouts" who spot emerging talent and approach experienced professionals for hiring.
- "Talent development agents" who help to plan and create accelerated as well as enriched learning experiences, if not widened opportunities for employees.

So both these principles as well as new HR practitioner specialisms can easily collaborate in order to sculpt and renew and align employee experience to purpose of hyper connected exponential organization of the 21st century where agility and value innovation are drivers of accelerated double digit growth and sustainability (Ismail et al. 2014).

Design Thinking, Robust Workplace Analytics and an Agile Mind-Set are Enabling Centrepieces of Digital Transformation Roadmap

Having reflected on digital disruption which is dramatically impacting the future of work and work of the future as well as ubiquitous morphing of employee experience inclusive of retention and engagement, the following reality emerges: Human capital practitioners will often be faced with having to reinvent, reimagine and future proof impact of these digital changes to business and operating models by answering questions from the CEO and Board like:

- What is our digital transformation roadmap for our people?
- How do we align our people culture to simultaneously enhance agility and lower cost?
- What does optimal differentiated employee experience look like across the different stages of an employee journey for a digital ready increasingly contingent, virtual and mobile segmented workforce?
- How do we align our people attraction, engagement and retention strategies with our organizations ideals of being value innovators in social, mobile, analytics and cloud space?
- How do we accelerate organizational and cultural change via data driven and predictive analytic based decision-making?
- How do we both simplify and scale structure of HR people management function to ensure that it delivers global solutions to managers and workforce?

New generation employees value creative jobs that enable them to make positive social impact on their communities and society as a whole as well as having huge expectations relating to how they experience their working lives all which were alluded to previously as it relates to optimising and designing meaningful employee experiences on one hand and organizations having to out innovate their competitors in order to avoid going the same way as the Dodo hence need to articulate a digital transformation roadmap to address various challenges as presented.

Kolko (2015) eloquently stated that people need their interactions with technologies and other complex systems to be simple, intuitive, and pleasurable. He further proposed that empathic human cantered design enhances the user experience at every touch point, and as such fuels the creation of products and services that deeply resonate with people be they employees and/or customers.

Adopting a human centred design thinking approach to employee experience would therefore make huge sense in order to shift focus away from merely developing programs, processes etc. but co-creating and co-designing meaningful employee experience that are compelling, enjoyable, and simple. It as such enables HR practitioners to transform from process developers to experience architects. This approach to thinking could further create empowering environment that fosters fresh, innovative ways to continuously search for new ways to communicate, collaborate and explore new purposeful social nuances and connections related to employee and organizational digital transformation journey. As thinking is highly collaborative co-design across disciplines and functions it is deeply engaging and as such contributes and enables to creating a narrative which humanizes and simplifies all and as such could accelerate change.

Brown (2009) describes the need to establish choices as it relates to innovation as a set of principles relating to design thinking that balance the needs of individuals and of society as a whole; new ideas that tackle the global challenges which design thinking can be applied to by diverse people to a wide range of problems. Implying and meaning new strategies that result in differences that matter and a sense of purpose that engages everyone affected by them which resonates with burning need to future proof employee experience, engagement and retention via digital roadmap which as per design thinking provides:

- Insight: learning from the lives of others go out into the world and observe the actual experiences [of people] as they improvise their way through their working lives.
- Observation: watching what people don't do, listening to what they don't say.
- Empathy: standing in the shoes of others.

The new generations of employees have huge opportunity to all become digital nomads leveraging wide range of remote working technologies already mentioned and hence Yohn (2016) in emphasising need for organizations to design their employee experiences as thoughtfully as they do their customers advances notion of using design thinking to map actual employee experience throughout employee journey fostering engagement and retention as follows:

- sourcing and recruiting.
- pre-boarding.
- onboarding (orientation and initial training).
- compensation and benefits.
- ongoing learning and development.
- ongoing engagement, communication, and community involvement.
- rewards and recognition.
- performance planning, feedback, and review.
- career advancement.
- retirement, termination, or resignation.

So each experience becomes a memorable moment of truth gaining insight and empathy as it relates to what employee thinks, feels, believes, expects and values as well as deeply intrinsically appreciates during each experience.

Arguably the second centrepiece of digital transformation roadmap which could have preceded the previous element of design thinking relates to what contemporary scholars Ulrich et al. (2017) as well as Boudreau and Ramstad (2007) and lastly Becker (1993) earlier referred to as need for HR practitioners to generate measurements, data and workplace analytics in order to provide robust evidence as to outcomes of their endeavours be it assessment, selection and or as in this case all that relates to the psychology of retention, engagement and the employee experience within a volatile digital landscape.

Barends et al. (2014) is of opinion that evidence-based practice relates specifically to making decisions through the conscientious, explicit and judicious use of the best available evidence from preferably secured via multiple credible sources by:

- Asking—translating a practical issue or problem into an answerable question.
- Acquiring—systematically searching for and retrieving evidence.
- Appraising—critically judging the trustworthiness and relevance of the evidence.
- Aggregating—weighing and pulling together the evidence.
- Applying—incorporating the evidence into a decision-making process.
- Assessing—evaluating the outcome of the decision taken so as to increase the likelihood of a favourable outcome.

As increasingly the case when everything nowadays is digital, and accordingly tracked, prioritized, systemised and managed with real time, just in time data practitioners have the opportunity, to demonstrate where and how much they directly impact strategic business goals via robust workplace analytics. Determining and calculating tangible benefits from improving time to market, continuous learning, responsiveness, and collaboration resulting from initiatives could be considered.

Data and insights arising from these analytics may be considered a source of evidence that is used in making more effective decisions especially those impacting financial business metrics relating to cost and value of savings generated from engagement and or retention initiatives. Here total revenue lost due to vacancy position days or improvement in revenue per employee following improved engagement or retention of key talent instantly comes to mind versus psychobabble relating to value of mindfulness exercise or possible improvements in effectiveness and productivity from neuroscience.

Often various surveys, events, initiatives or interventions lack business case and/or tangible evidence in monetary sense of benefits gained and the so-called return on investment lags intervention by months if not years e.g. between annual surveys void of any cost and or revenue returned per employee. Here various contemporary new generation platform based and wearable digital solutions will embarrass many a HR practitioner for example TrustSphere which provides online network employee relationship analytics in real time.

The final recommended centrepiece to enable digital transformation centres on need for HR practitioners to adopt a digital mindset as well as set of practices which doesn't require them to be technology experts but rather about curiosity, creativity, problem solving, empathy, flexibility, data informed decision making and team-based collaboration, cooperation and judgment to overall improve organization's nimbleness and overall responsiveness. It requires embracing and leveraging technology based solutions to effectively execute on business imperatives however equally critical is need to extend collaboration with other departments, incorporating mobile, analytics, social media and the cloud to ease their transition to be strategically more digitally transformative.

Gothelf (2017) shares story of large financial services concern who made every employee at its headquarters (nearly 3,500 people) re-interview for their job to bring about customer centricity and digital responsiveness. Staggeringly, 40% of people ended up in new positions or parted ways with the company. It wasn't about their skill sets. In fact, in many cases the employees' skill sets were still highly relevant. Rather, it was a specific mind-set that was lacking—one that could embrace the uncertainty, volatility, ambiguity and new the learning agility required for exponential organization.

It is increasingly becoming apparent that many organization's which are serious about its future sustainability and who are adopting agile mindset are amending their HR practitioner hiring approach as popularized by Bock (2015) former senior vice-president of people operations at Google to what is known as three thirds' hiring model. That means an HR department that breaks down as one third from HR backgrounds, one third from consultancy and business backgrounds and, crucially, one third from academic fields such as science and mathematics (people who are inculcated with the need for analytical proof). Keep in mind that organizations which fail to be more digitally agile and innovative as further mentioned by Bock (2015) half or 50% of the names of companies on the Fortune 500 have disappeared since the year 2000. Strangely Drucker (1978) shared this wisdom by stating that greatest danger in times of turbulence isn't the turbulence but to act with what he termed yesterday's logic.

Summary

This chapter explored how specifically digital disruption is impacting future of work and what work in the future is likely to look like. Given as HR practitioners we daily help organizations decode culture and grapple to understand the behaviours that drive innovation and performance, it remains pertinent to consider how everything is continually being disrupted digitally and is dramatically impacting future the of work and work of the future. It is more than obvious and ever increasingly pervasive that the current era of disengaged, transient talent impacts every aspect of the business, and the need to reignite purpose at work has never been more urgent. This might be via organizational network analysis or next generation engagement platform which aims to improve team effectiveness through measuring digital engagement and identifying areas of communication bias all aimed at futureproofing employee retention and sculpting a more meaningful employee experience. It remains ironic though that despite the more technologies, devices, sites, apps, and other digital touchpoints we have, the less connected we are as human beings. HR practitioners remain profoundly challenged to; via design thinking, workplace analytics and new digital mind-sets enable a work context which provides for both individual wellbeing as well as all-inclusive societal prosperity. This will, as decades pass, only be achieved through ensuring transparency and clarity of the organization's mission and core values, communicating why employees matter and the specific behaviours that exemplify those values throughout the organization irrespective of scale and/or maturity of the so called digital transformation.

References

Adams, L. (2017). *HR disrupted: It's time for something different*. London: Practical Inspiration Publishing.

Barends, E., Rosseau, D., & Briner, R. (2014). *Evidence-based management: The basic principles*. Amsterdam: Centre for Evidence Based Management.

Becker, G. S. (1993). *Human capital: A theoretical and empirical analysis with special reference to education*. Chicago: University of Chicago Press.

Bhaduri, A. (2016) *The digital tsunami: Succeeding in a world turned upside-down*. New.

Bock, L. (2015). *Work rules! Insights from inside Google that will transform how you live and lead*. New York: Hachette Book Group.

Boudreau, J., & Ramstad, P. M. (2007). *Beyond HR: The new science of human capital*. Boston: Harvard Business School Press.

Brown, T. (2009). *Change by design: How design thinking transforms organizations and inspires innovation*. New York: Harper Collins.

Brynjolfsson, E., & MacAfee, A. (2014). *The second machine age work, progress, and prosperity in a time of brilliant technologies*. New York: W.W. Norton & Company.

Davenport, T. H., & Kirby, J. (2016). *Only humans need apply winners and losers in the age of smart machines*. New York: Harper Collins.

Drucker, P. (1978). *The age of discontinuity*. New York: Harper & Row.

Gothelf, J. (2017). How HR can become agile (and why it needs to). *Harvard Business Review*. https://hbr.org/2017/06/how-hr-can-become-agile-and-why-it-needs-to.

Ingham, J. (2017). *The social organization: Developing employee connections and relationships for improved business performance*. London: Kogan Page.

Ismail, S., Malone, M. S., & Van Geest, Y. (2014). *Exponential organizations why new organizations are ten times better, faster, and cheaper than yours (and what to do about it)*. New York: Diversion Books.

Kolko, J. (2015). Design thinking comes of age. *Harvard Business Review*, September. https://hbr.org/2015/09/design-thinking-comes-of-age.

Kurzweil, R. (2005). *The singularity is near: When humans transcend biology*. New York: Penguin Group.
Mancini, J. (2015). *Collaborative workspaces: Making information work simpler, smarter, safer and faster*. New York: AIIM.
Mcgovern, M. (2017). *Thriving in the gig economy: How to capitalize and compete in the new world of work paperback*. New Jersey: The Career Press Inc.
McKinsey (2017). *Future of organizations and work*. https://www.mckinsey.com/global-themes/future-of-organizations-and-work/what-the-future-of-work-will-mean-for-jobs-skills-and-wage.
Meister, J. C., & Willyerd, K. (2010). *The 2020 workplace: How innovative companies attract, develop, and keep tomorrow's employees today*. New York: Harper Collins.
Miller, P., & Marsh, E. (2014). *The digital renaissance of work: Delivering digital workplaces fit for the future*. London: Routledge.
Morgan, J. (2017). *The employee experience advantage: How to win the war for talent by giving employees the workspaces they want, the tools they need, and a culture they can celebrate*. New Jersey: Wiley.
Parker, G. G., van Alstyne, M. W., & Choudary, S. P. (2017). *Platform revolution: How networked markets are transforming the economy—and How to make them work for you*. New York: W. W Norton.
Patterson, K., Wride, M., & Maylett, T. (2017). *The employee experience: How to attract talent, retain top performers, and drive results*. New Jersey: Wiley.
Pine, B. J., & Gilmore, J. H. (2011). *The experience economy: Work is theatre & every business a stage*. Cambridge, MA: Harvard Business Press.
Prensky, M. (2012). *From digital natives to digital wisdom*. London: Corwin.
Raskino, M., & Waller, M. (2015). Digital to the core. Remastering leadership for your industry, you're enterprise, and yourself. New York: Bibliomotion.
Surdak, C. (2014). *Data crush: How the information tidal wave is driving new business opportunities*. New York: American Management Association.
Ulrich, D. L., Kryscynski, D., Brockbank, W., & Ulrich, M. (2017). *Victory through organization: Why the war for talent is failing your company and what you can do about it*. New York: McGraw-Hill Education.
Yohn, D. L. (2016). *Design your employee experience as thoughtfully as you design your customer experience*. *Harvard Business Review*, December. https://hbr.org/2016/12/design-your-employee-experience-as-thoughtfully-as-you-design-your-customer-experience.

John Ludike is an executive human resource practitioner and has gained majority of his experience within the Financial Services, (FNB, RBS, Mashreq Bank, Barclays) Retail, (Sainsbury's) Telecoms (MTN, Etisalat) and more recently Hospitality (Yum Brands!) industries. His pioneering HR talent management achievements within MTN has been recognized by the Human Capital Management Institute and recently been published in book titled Human Capital Trends edited by Italia Boninelli & Terry Meyer (2011) as well as Managing Human Resource Development: an outcomes based approach edited by Marius Meyer. He has in addition also contributed chapters to publications titled The role of the Chief Human Resources Officer and Shaping Africa's Talent both published by Knowledge Resources. He specializes in automated digital design, development and facilitation of implementation of human capital systems and accordingly recalibration of leadership talent and organizational development change programs and solutions. John principally undertakes international consulting assignments in London, Middle East & Asia and aims to seldom experience a winter as he migrates from one assignment to the next.

Chapter 4
The Relevance of the Employee Value Proposition for Retention in the VUCA World of Work

Dieter Veldsman and Desiré Pauw

The war for talent is over ... and everybody lost.
(Chamorro-Premuzic & Yearsley 2017)

Abstract The organisational landscape is characterised by volatility, uncertainty, complexity, and ambiguity (VUCA). Organisations are ever-changing, and they are adapting and reinventing the world of work to become leaner, more agile, and sustainable. Talent has become a key ingredient of success, yet organisations are battling to attract, engage, and retain talent in an organisational landscape where those with critical talent are able to determine how, when, and where they want to work. Traditional retention mechanisms have become obsolete, and the focus has shifted towards crafting a holistic employee experience through an attractive, realistic, and coherent employee value proposition (EVP). This chapter explores the EVP as a method of retaining talent in the VUCA environment. The chapter focuses on defining the concept, different approaches associated with crafting a compelling EVP, and the challenges faced during EVP implementation. The chapter concludes with the discussion of an EVP implementation case study in the South African environment.

Keywords EVP · VUCA · EVP articulation and sense-checking
Implementation of an EVP

D. Veldsman (✉)
Mindset Management, Pretoria, South Africa
e-mail: dieter.veldsman@mmiholdings.co.za

D. Pauw
MMI Holdings Limited, Centurion, South Africa
e-mail: desire.pauw@mmiholdings.co.za

M. Coetzee et al. (eds.), *Psychology of Retention*,
https://doi.org/10.1007/978-3-319-98920-4_4

Introduction

Chaos has become the new order. The world based on predictability, control, and structure has become an ever-changing environment where adaptability, evolution, and constant reinvention are the norm. This has resulted in speed at the cost of quality, scale at the cost of personal relationships, and a virtual presence at the cost of a physical location (Korunka and Kubicek 2017). This business landscape, often referred to as 'the VUCA (volatility, uncertainty, complexity, and ambiguity) world of work,' has challenged organisations to reinvent and adapt if they are to survive. The acronym *VUCA* originated in the US military, where it was used to describe combat conditions during the cold war in the early 90s. It entered the business context after the global financial crisis, describing the multi-lateral world of work (Kinsinger and Walch 2012). Figure 4.1 provides a depiction of this VUCA landscape, including the trends that are informing the modern landscape and dictating the order of new world of work.

The VUCA environment has resulted in a change in the way in which work is organised. Organisations are becoming more distributed, not only in terms of physical location, but also by working across time zones and utilising different employee agreements. Social collaboration technologies have become the cornerstone of productive teams, with organisations such as Dropbox, Asana, and Cisco gaining traction for their products globally. A critical shortage of knowledge workers has created a global and mobile workforce that can adapt to various environments, is not tied to working in one location, and is open to new opportunities. However, this global pool is now being accessed by organisations across the globe, which has intensified competition between organisations to attract and

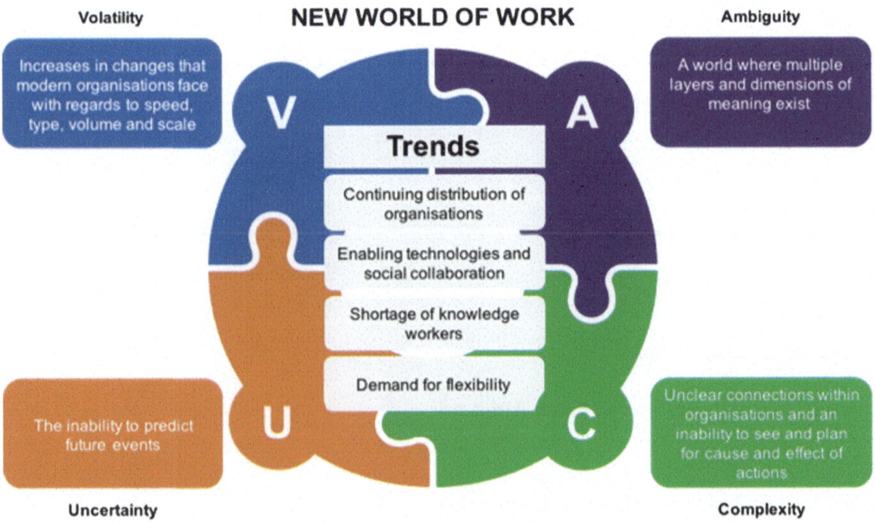

Fig. 4.1 The new world of work

retain talent. Talent is also demanding more flexibility, with these workers wanting to work where, how, and when they want to.

How and where work takes place and what constitutes work have also metamorphosed. A multi-generational workforce, co-located workspaces, and nomadic employees who work for more than one employer have become the norm. Human capital has become a critical asset of competitive advantage, and most organisations admit that they are struggling to attract and retain the required talent to build a sustainable organisation. Veldsman (2017) stated that human capital has become the wealth creators for organisations in the knowledge economy and, as such, should not be treated as an asset on the balance sheet, but rather as a partner in a relationship that should be harnessed over time to achieve the organisational mandate.

The real challenge for organisations is that talented workers can choose where and how they want to work. Organisational loyalty has become something of the past. Table 4.1 provides an overview of the average tenure of employees, highlighting the difficulty of retaining talent over the longer term.

Traditional approaches to attracting, developing, and retaining human capital have become largely irrelevant in the modern world of work. Concepts such as employee engagement, high-performance cultures, and organisational effectiveness have entered both practice and literature, and questions are being raised regarding the applicability of the rigid and process-driven traditional human resource practices. This shift has manifested in leading organisations such as Deloitte, Accenture, and Google abandoning formal performance management processes, a South African fast-food chain abandoning traditional leave practices, and organisations such as Zappos adopting a holacracy with no formal hierarchy and constantly shifting work teams. In the South African context, with the rise of an entrepreneurial culture, similar trends are observed as companies battle to create an environment where employees want to work:

- RetroRabbit, a fast-growing software development business, appointed a culture officer as its first non-core employee function, with a key focus on employee retention and establishing a defined culture aligned with their identity.
- Etiket, a creative agency, completely moved away from formal job titles, and adopted a flat hierarchy based on project teams, to retain their younger employees and provide new development opportunities.
- A small boutique consulting organisation employs only 22 full-time employees, yet has a global workforce of almost 150 employees who work according to flexible work arrangements, so that the organisation has uninterrupted access to topic experts across the globe.

Table 4.1 Average tenure at leading knowledge economy organisations. *Source* Business Insider UK (2018)

Organisation	Average employee tenure (years)
Google	1.9
Facebook	2.02
Apple	1.85
Amazon	1.84
Microsoft	1.81

Given this background, if organisations want to remain relevant in this new world of work, they need to answer the following questions:

- Why would top talent want to work here?
- What can our organisation offer to make us attractive to talent?
- How do we keep top talent engaged and retain them over the longer term?
- How do we create a value proposition that is coherent with the organisational identity and external brand perception?

This chapter will explore the concept of the employee value proposition (EVP) as a mechanism to answer the above questions and provide a framework for organisations to implement an authentic and relevant EVP that supports their current talent strategies in the VUCA world of work.

Defining the EVP

The EVP has been given new importance as organisations find it difficult to effectively compete in the talent war. The changing world of work places more pressure on organisations to ensure that their EVP is appealing to employees, to provide the organisation with a competitive advantage. The literature hails the EVP as a differentiator of sorts, yet, in practice, the EVP has largely been diluted to either an unarticulated concept that occurs 'by accident,' or as yet another people practice for which the box is ticked because it is 'the right thing to do.' Various definitions exist to conceptualise an EVP. The literature positions an EVP in terms of the following dimensions:

- the characteristics and appeal of working for an organisation, based upon a set of offerings and experiences that employers provide in exchange for the skills, capabilities, and experience that employees bring to the organisation;
- the employee's perception of whether what he or she receives equals or exceeds what he or she gives, based on the principles of equity theory (Munsamy and Venter 2009);
- the unique set of attributes and benefits that will motivate targeted candidates to join a company and current employees to stay (Meijerink et al. 2016); and
- the benefit or value that an employee perceives to gain from working for a certain employer (Heger 2007).

Across all these definitions, the following conclusions can be made in terms of defining an EVP. An EVP is based upon a reciprocal give-and-receive relationship between the organisation and current/potential employees, and will motivate them to stay/join. An EVP is based upon a psychological contract, equity theory, and social exchange, and creates an individual's perception of what he or she is entitled to in exchange for the services, time, and skills provided to the organisation. From these definitions, it also seems as if the EVP consists of both an internal and an external component, i.e. what employees experience internally, as well as how potential employees who are in the external market perceive the organisation. As such, the EVP seems to be closely aligned with the concept of an employer brand (Barrow and Mosley 2005). Mandhanya and Shah (2010) supported this view when they described an employer brand as a snapshot of the organisation that promotes and positions the perceived value of membership with potential employees. A unique EVP provides a clear picture of what sets a company apart as an employer, and refers to the distinctive set of attributes and benefits that will motivate targeted candidates to join a company and current employees to remain with the organisation (Brand Learning 2009). This implies that the EVP is crucial to retaining current talent, as it acts as the guiding framework for how the employee experiences the organisation.

According to the Corporate Leadership Council (2002), the perceived value of membership of an organisation is determined by five components:

- work environment (physical environment, safety, tools, and equipment);
- affiliation (this includes values, culture, and quality of colleagues, managers, and leaders);
- work content (this includes challenging work and a work–life balance);
- benefits, including development and career growth (indirect financial reward); and
- remuneration (direct financial reward).

These five pillars need to be utilised as a guiding framework for the development of an EVP that is authentic, attractive, and practically relevant to the organisation's needs.

The EVP should be viewed as a holistic concept that encapsulates all the factors mentioned above, to ensure a robust approach to defining, articulating, and implementing an EVP that drives retention and value for the organisation. Figure 4.2 provides an overview of the EVP landscape as painted by the literature. Central to the EVP is the psychological contract that determines the perceived fairness of the value exchange between what the organisation gives/receives and what the individual gives/receives. This social exchange between the individual and the organisation is a continuous process that is weighed during each interaction between employee and employer. The perceived fairness and experience of this exchange will determine whether employees are engaged, whether they stay, and whether they are motivated within the context of their internal perception of fairness. This experience will be rooted in the five pillars related to physical environment, affiliation, work content, benefits, and remuneration, which inform the experience of fairness from both the employee's and the employer's perspective.

From an external perspective, the EVP shapes perceived value that potential employees could derive from a relationship or association with the organisation. This could inform their decision whether to pursue a relationship with the organisation in question, as well as what the key differentiators are from an EVP perspective that makes the organisation attractive to potential talent. This perception is important, as current employees will continuously weigh the perceived value of their relationship with the employer against the perceived value of other employers

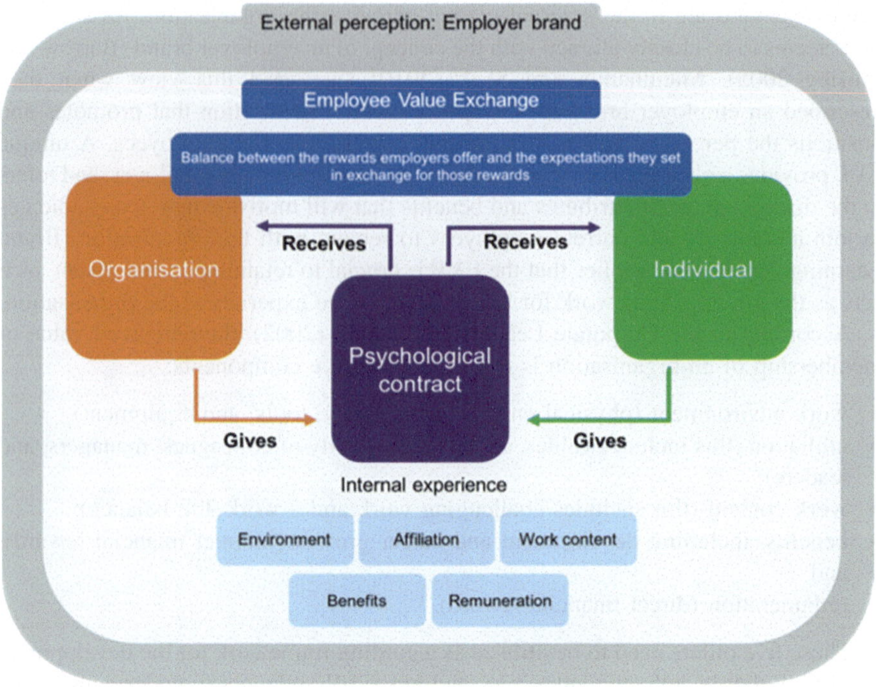

Fig. 4.2 The EVP landscape

in the market. The perception that 'the grass is greener on the other side' could then inform their decision to stay or leave.

From a business performance point of view, studies have shown that organisations with a well-articulated EVP that is authentic and attractive report higher performance. Towers-Watson (2010) reported that organisations with a well-articulated EVP perform better than their peers, and that 42% of high-performing organisations consciously craft and articulate their EVP. This is in contrast with organisations performing lower than their peers, of which only 28% spend time crafting a compelling EVP. Further benefits from an organisational perspective include the ability to improve the organisation's attractiveness and become an employer of choice, as well as greater employee commitment, engagement, and compensation savings (CEB 2006).

Challenges in the EVP Landscape

From the literature, it seems as if the business rationale and benefits of having a well-articulated EVP can be justified, but that several challenges exist in practice (Pandita 2011):

- Credibility: Lack of insight into what should constitute the EVP often leads to an EVP that does not seem credible or relevant to the organisation. Firstly, the EVP should align with the identity and culture of the business, while also being aspirational. Secondly, organisations often promise benefits they cannot deliver, often highlighted through other organisational practices. An example of this is the organisation stating, "We train our people to be at the top of their fields!" while no budget is visibly spent on training.
- Mismatched experience: A mismatch between the stated EVP and the actual employee experience can create the perception of inauthenticity, with employees losing trust and faith in the organisation, which is detrimental to the organisation's culture. This will influence the perception of fairness and the social exchange, leading to employee disengagement.
- Positioning: The positioning of the EVP seems to also fall largely within the HR domain, as opposed to being a mechanism that can be utilised by line managers to create an integrated employee experience. This approach leads to an inauthentic EVP experience and a perception by employees that the organisation is not keeping its promises in terms of the psycho-social contract. This could result in feelings of unfairness, culminating in talent seeking other opportunities outside of the organisation that they perceive to be better.
- Internally focused: Organisations also seem to craft EVP statements that are too internal and not comparable to those of other organisations in a similar field. Often, this leads to employees not understanding 'how good they have it here,' and leads them to view the benefits they have as the norm in the industry, as opposed to these being a key differentiator.
- Prioritisation: Organisations promise more than what they can currently deliver due to commercial restraints. This lack of prioritisation leads to the EVP being seen as disconnected and inauthentic, and as a concept that is never really implemented fully in practice.

The stated challenges can all be overcome through a structured and planned EVP implementation approach. The following section will discuss a framework for EVP implementation to ensure that organisations can leverage the envisaged benefits from the process while being cognisant of the potential pitfalls stated above.

Implementing the EVP in Practice

Various variations of and approaches to implementing a holistic EVP exist. The approach discussed below provides a generic framework that can be adapted to accommodate big and small organisations (Fig. 4.3).

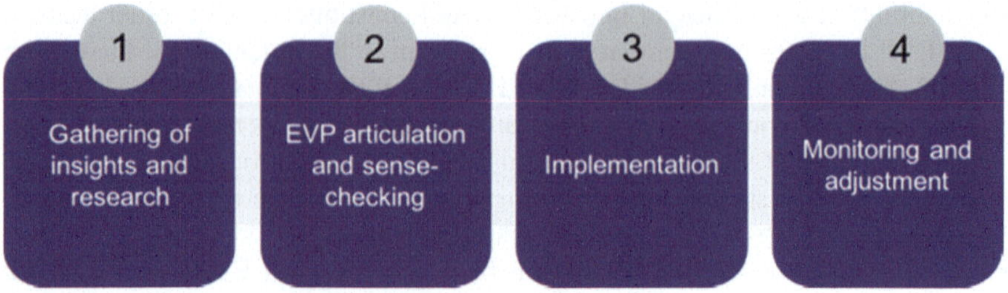

Fig. 4.3 Implementing the EVP in practice

Phase 1: Research and Gathering Insights

This phase focuses on researching current organisational practices to understand the current attributes of the EVP. A critical factor for the successful implementation of any EVP is authenticity of the EVP. As such, this phase aims to understand which artifacts should be included in the EVP. This phase also balances current reality with future aspirations, and organisations should, as far as possible, realistically balance factors that are already true and potential aspirational artifacts that need to be realised over time. This phase employs both quantitative and qualitative methods to build a coherent narrative around the strategic ambition of the organisation, its processes, and, above all, to align the EVP with the organisational identity and culture.

From an external perspective, this phase also includes evaluating current industry trends to understand what will differentiate the organisation's EVP from those of its competitors. This step gives the EVP comparability and plays a critical part in the attraction and retention of talent.

Key deliverables of this phase:

- opinion data from employees, gathered via surveys, focus groups, or semi-structured interviews;
- desktop research on the strategic ambition of the organisation, as well as the culture and value systems present within the organisation; and
- industry competitor analyses to understand competing EVP frameworks.

Phase 2: EVP Articulation and Sense-Checking

This phase focuses on articulating the EVP through a coherent narrative that can be sense-checked in collaboration with a representative group of stakeholders at all levels of the organisation, to ensure that the narrative is authentic, coherent, and believable. As a second step, the impact of the articulated EVP on organisational processes, with specific reference to human capital processes across the value chain, is evaluated, to understand the cost, time, and effort that will be required to implement the EVP. This step is crucial to allow for the prioritisation of key initiatives, as a holistic EVP can require multi-year implementation, and needs to be approached per manageable focus area. The output of this step will be a detailed implementation approach and plan to guide the next phase.

Key deliverables of this phase are:

- an articulated EVP;
- a sense-checking recommendations report; and
- an EVP impact report and implementation plan.

Phase 3: Implementation

This phase focuses on the execution of the crafted implementation plan, and involves the following activities:

- creation of visible EVP artifacts that are made part of an internal communication campaign to drive awareness of and attachment to the crafted EVP;
- integration of desired EVP outputs into key people processes, for example, on-boarding, performance, remuneration, and other practices;
- assigning senior leaders to drive EVP implementation;
- creation of an EVP task team to focus on implementing the EVP as a designated project—this task team should consist of members from both HR and business fields;
- creation of an EVP monitoring committee and change champion structure to drive EVP implementation as part of the EVP governance structure; and
- a transition and cut-over plan to conclude the EVP project and make it 'business as usual,' which concludes this phase.

Phase 4: Monitoring and Adjustment

The final phase is the continuous monitoring and evaluation of the relevance of the EVP artefacts to the changing business environment and industry focus. This function is usually performed by an organisational development or effectiveness function as part of an integrated report regarding human capital effectiveness in the organisation. From a leading practice perspective, if possible, the EVP committee should become a formal structure that forms part of the formal organisational governance structure, to ensure the relevance and sustainability of the EVP over the longer term.

The case study below is explored to illustrate the applicability of the framework in practice.

The Implementation of an EVP at MMI Holdings Limited

Context and Background

MMI Holdings Limited (MMI) is a financial services group that is based in South Africa and listed on the South African Stock Exchange. The group operates in the market through multiple client-facing brands, including insurance and investment brands Metropolitan and Momentum, South Africa's number one cell captive insurer Guardrisk, and wellness and rewards programme Multiply. MMI operates in several countries on the African continent, in the United Kingdom, and in India, through a direct presence, strategic partnerships, and joint ventures.

MMI's purpose is to enhance the lifetime financial wellness of people, their communities, and their businesses. Financial wellness is a continuous process of planning and management for individuals, households, and businesses, with the aim of affording expenses and achieving goals over one's lifetime. Our promise to our clients is to be their financial wellness partner over this life-long journey, using our expertise and solutions to help them develop and reach their goals.

The Brief from the MMI Leadership Team

The brief from the MMI leadership team was clear: Design, develop and implement an MMI EVP offering that would attract, retain, and engage employees. Also, this solution must proactively focus on enabling MMI employees to be well, specifically financially well, and to create an emotional connection between employees and MMI, in alignment with the identity and culture of the organisation.

Based upon this brief, MMI Holdings Limited, in 2015, embarked on a journey to develop a holistic MMI EVP. There were some complexities that needed to be taken into account, such as the following:

- MMI Holdings consists of four client-facing brands—Momentum, Metropolitan, Multiply, and Guardrisk.
- Like the segments these brands serve (upper, middle, and lower income), MMI employees are from various segments.
- MMI Holdings has approximately 17,500 employees across the globe, who have different contexts and needs.

To tackle these challenges, a core EVP team was mobilised to craft an approach and process that would be suited to MMI's environment. Originally, the core team consisted of human capital professionals, but, during the journey, the team evolved into one that consisted of various different role players across the organisation who could contribute to the development of an EVP solution that was credible, relevant, and authentic.

Phase I—Research and Gaining Insights

The journey started with an extensive research phase where data were gathered locally and internationally through a multi-method approach. The following information was included in the analysis:

- academic and theoretical research—best practice across industries, not just within financial services, to create a compelling benchmark to guide the MMI approach;
- internal MMI data (exit interviews, follow-up or stay interviews, and platforms that could give insight into an EVP, such as the Innovations Platform);
- competitor analysis;
- the various offerings across the Group within each of the brands and across various business units; and
- different EVP frameworks used in leading practice.

It was particularly important to understand the insights from the research to build an EVP solution for MMI that would address their specific needs and requirements. The research and analysis took the team approximately six months.

Phase II—Designing the MMI EVP Framework

The research provided clarity on what was happening within the EVP domain and the landscapes across various businesses and industries. The next step was to build a framework in line with the brief received from the leadership team.

The following were taken into account when building the framework:

- alignment with the MMI Strategy Map, Vision, and Purpose;
- enabling the organisation's culture—*The MMI Way*;
- attracting the right calibre employees from across the world;
- retaining talent in the MMI Group globally;
- enabling employees to contribute to MMI's success; and
- enabling employees to be well, specifically financially.

The team considered the following:

- different employee needs;
- reviewing the EVP framework and its relevance to MMI's requirements;
- understanding how this framework could show the importance of MMI's culture and enable it by creating an authentic EVP experience; and
- how employees could be held accountable in the give-and-get relationship within the EVP, based on social exchange theory and the psychological contract.

The decision was made to build the EVP around the MMI values of *Diversity, Excellence, Teamwork, Innovation, Accountability, and Integrity*, as well as the culture that was present within the organisation (*The MMI Way*). A further principle was to prioritise and focus the EVP on the needs of employees who fit into the organisational identity and culture of MMI, i.e. needs related to *Family and Community, Physical, Financial, Career, Growth, Emotional, Purpose, and Meaning*. Financial wellness was also included as a dimension, as this is core to the MMI offerings of *Financial Wellness, Opportunity, People, Organisation, Work, and Rewards*.

The team also aimed to articulate the reciprocal relationship between the employer and the employee as part of the EVP—emphasising that the employee also has a role to play in operationalising the EVP, and that the EVP represents a give-and-receive relationship. This was done to frame the context of the psychological contract as part of the core EVP offering. The following promise statements were created to articulate this relationship:

- **Financial wellness**: *Our employees are continuously encouraged and assisted to plan and manage their money, so that they may have control of their current and future financial wellness. They are also enthusiastic about improving the financial wellbeing of our clients.* This is also the definition used by MMI for financial wellness across the segments of the client base (upper, middle, and lower income).
- **Organisation**: *MMI employees are proud ambassadors who are passionate about our brands.*
- **Work**: *The MMI culture enables each individual to live his or her purpose and to enjoy meaningful work while contributing to the goals of MMI.*
- **People**: *Our people are the greatest contributors to our success. We embrace diversity and value different perspectives.*
- **Rewards**: *Our employees are innovative, collaborative, and solutions-driven. We recognise excellence and reward out-performance.*
- **Opportunity**: *MMI is a global organisation with vast career advancement opportunities.*

Therefore, both the employer and the employee have responsibilities. An employee gives something, and, in return, the employer gives something back. Figure 4.4 shows the EVP framework adopted by MMI.

- Central to the EVP is the individual in MMI, the "Me," highlighting the personal relationship and meaning given to the EVP within the context of the employee.
- On the left-hand side, the needs of the employee are articulated as part of the EVP focus.
- The right-hand side depicts the MMI values upon which the EVP is based and that govern *what and how we do things*.
- The circle in the middle shows the key focus areas of the EVP and the promises made as part of the exchange between employee and employer.

This framework was utilised to guide all decisions regarding focus and priority, while also creating a narrative in the organisation—*this is about us, together, going forward*.

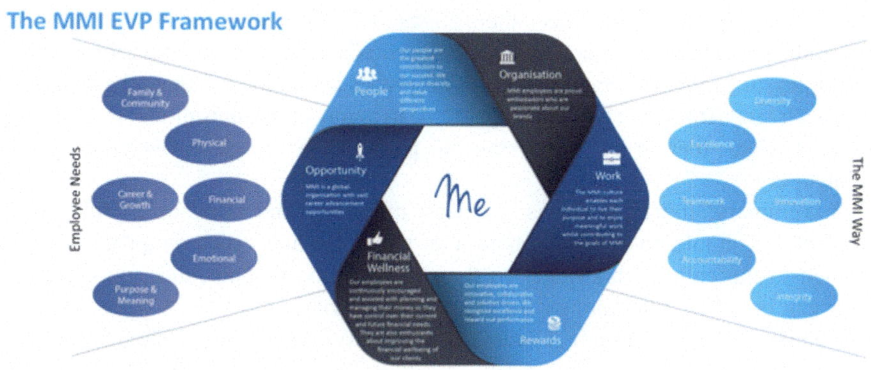

Fig. 4.4 The MMI EVP framework

Phase III—Implementation

Given the extensive nature of fully implementing the end-to-end EVP, the decision was made to prioritise steps in implementation according to areas of importance and impact. As financial wellness is what MMI stands for, the decision was taken to focus the first rollout of the MMI EVP on financial wellness. This was only one element in both the *Employee needs* and *Organisational offering* components, but it was agreed that it was an element that would have a significant impact. Being well in general will also allow an employee to make better financial decisions, and the key element for implementation in Phase I was an employee assistance programme that was branded *Wise and Well*, aimed at helping employees to be financially well by supporting them in gaining an understanding of their own financial options. Practically, this implied giving employees access to some of MMI's financial advisors to support them, not only by them experiencing the organisation's products, but also in making sound financial decisions.

MMI is currently entering the next phase of implementation, which will focus on integrating the other offerings into the EVP, as well as the creation of an EVP handbook for managers as part of the MMI leadership philosophy.

Conclusions and Implications for Retention

The focus of this chapter was on conceptualising the EVP as a construct applicable to the modern knowledge-economy organisation and the VUCA world of work. The findings from the literature indicate that the EVP is important to attract and retain top talent, as well as to be able to differentiate the organisation from its competitors. Talent retention is a critical challenge for organisational success, and it seems that a well-articulated EVP can support organisations to, not only attract top talent, but more importantly, keep them engaged over the longer term. The literature also indicates that organisations with a well-articulated EVP seem to perform better. A number of challenges regarding the EVP process were identified, and a proposed approach and framework were suggested to support organisations in realising benefits from their EVP processes in practice, while also overcoming the challenges.

In summary, the EVP seems to be an important and relevant organisational concept, but should be utilised as part of an integrated and structured process that is aligned to the culture and values of the organisation. Through this approach, the EVP can be a key differentiator for organisations within the VUCA landscape as a mechanism to attract and retain talent, as well as to achieve their desired ambitions.

Summary

This chapter explored the relevance of the EVP within the VUCA landscape as a mechanism for talent retention. The chapter conceptualised the theoretical rationale for the EVP and its relevance to practice. The chapter positioned an EVP implementation framework and process to address current challenges experienced in terms of the realisation of benefits associated with the EVP in practice. The chapter concluded by discussing MMI as a case study to reflect on the benefits of implementing an EVP in a South African services organisation.

Acknowledgements The authors would like to express their gratitude to MMI Holdings for giving permission to use the EVP process as a case study applicable to the new world of work.

References

Barrow, S., & Mosley, R. (2005). *The employer brand, bringing the best of brand management to people at work.* Chichester: Wiley.

Brand Learning. (2009). *Employee value propositions: A key marketing tool for talent management.* http://www.brandlearning.com/UploadedDocuments/Employee-Value-Propositions.pdf. Accessed 05 Oct 2010.

Corporate Leadership Council. (2002). Customizing the employment offer: Understanding employee job offer preferences across the workforce. Washington, DC: Corporate Executive Board.

Heger, B. K. (2007). Linking the employment value proposition (EVP) to employee engagement and business outcomes: Preliminary findings from a linkage research pilot study. *Organization Development Journal, 25*(2), 121.

http://www.oxfordleadership.com/leadership-challenges-v-u-c-world/.

https://www.fastcompany.com/3069078/the-war-for-talent-is-over-and-everyone-lost.

Kinsinger, P., & Walch, K. (2012). *Living and leading in a VUCA world.* Thunderbird University.

Korunka, C., & Kubicek, B. (2017). Job demands in a changing world of work. In *Job demands in a changing world of work* (pp. 1–5). Springer.

Mandhanya, Y., & Shah, M. (2010). Employer branding—a tool for talent management. *Global Management Review, 4*(2).
Meijerink, J. G., Bondarouk, T., & Lepak, D. P. (2016). Employees as active consumers of HRM: Linking employees' HRM competences with their perceptions of HRM service value. *Human Resource Management, 55*(2), 219–240.
Munsamy, M., & Venter, A. B. (2009). Retention factors of management staff in the maintenance phase of their careers in local government. *SA Journal of Human Resource Management, 7*(1), 1–9.
Pandita, D. (2011). HR redefined. *SAMVAD, 2,* 37–39.
Veldsman, T. H. (2017). *Talent in the new world.* Pretoria: SIOPSA Conference.
Watson, T. (2010). Creating a sustainable rewards and talent management model: Results of the 2010 global talent management and rewards study. Accessed 13 Dec 2017.

Dieter Veldsman (DCom) is a registered Psychologist (cat. Industrial) with the HPCSA with a key focus on organisational development, people analytics, people effectiveness and organisational design. He is currently the Head of Research and Development at Mindset Management, a people analytics software business that specialises in the development of human capital measurement models and supporting software. He has consulted across various industries and has completed numerous global consulting assignments across Africa, Europe and Asia. He is a regular speaker at international conferences on the topics of employee engagement, human capital metrics and organisational development. He lectures part-time at the University of Johannesburg and is involved in a variety of other academic institutions as lecturer and moderator.

Desiré Pauw is a registered Psychologist (cat. Industrial) with the Health Professions Council of South Africa (HPCSA). She is currently the Head of Human Capital for Client Engagement Solutions within MMI Holdings Limited, South Africa. She is part of the Client Engagement Solutions Exco team. She runs a Human Resources and Organisational Development capability in her team that enables employee engagement. She is also part of the team of thirteen Human Capital Heads that inform the business decisions from a people perspective within MMI. In addition to her role as Head of Human Capital, she runs the MMI Employee Value proposition with a team of employees. She also recently got involved with the Spatial Strategy of the MMI Group and is working closely with the Human Capital Group Executive to deliver this for MMI.

Part III
Internal Organisational Context

Overview and Insights

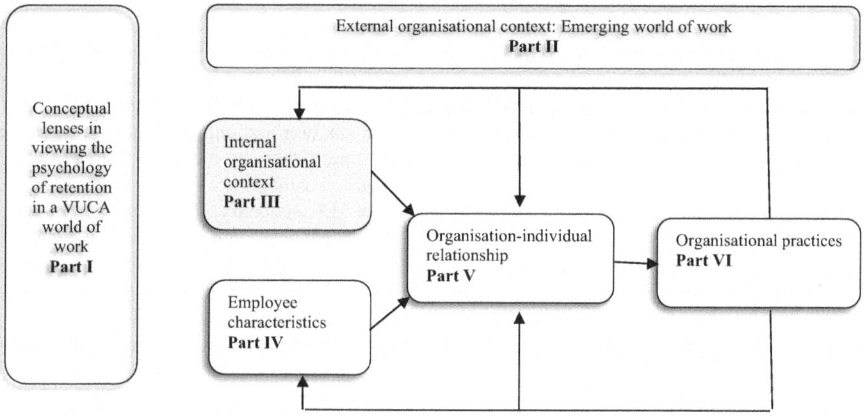

Towards an integrated conceptual framework for the psychology of retention

Part III, *Internal Organisational Context*, comprises four chapters that illustrate the dynamics of the psychology of retention within the internal organisational context. The dynamics of personal and organisational resources, factors influencing person–job fit and embeddedness, and the creation of need-supportive environments and practices are highlighted.

Part III: Overview

Chapter 5 by Brooks C. Holtom and Tiffany Darabi, *Job Embeddedness Theory as a Tool for Improving Employee Retention*, enriches the retention literature by unravelling the role of job embeddedness in the employee retention space. The authors elaborate on the antecedents, moderators and consequences of embeddedness and discuss practical implications for retention. The authors make a novel contribution to the embeddedness literature by arguing for the role of social networks as an aspect of embeddedness as seen through the lens of the well-known conservation of resources (COR) theory. This theory builds on the conceptual premises of the JD-R theory outlined in Chap. 1 (Part I of this book). The authors make a compelling argument for the principle of COR theory that employees strive to maximise their stock of resources at each level of embeddedness, while also viewing decisions to stay or leave from the calculus of potential resource sacrifices. They further argue that retention strategies should take cognisance of the underlying principles of COR theory to embed employees. Principles of job embeddedness as seen through the lens of COR may help organisations increase positive work behaviours such as organisational citizenship behaviours (OCBs) and task performance, while helping to curb counterproductive work behaviours (CWBs).

In Chap. 6, *Job Demands-Resources, Person-Job Fit and the Impact on Turnover Intention: Similar across Professional and Administrative Job-Types?*, Leon T. de Beer, Salomé Elizabeth Scholtz and Johanna Christina (Ina) Rothmann investigate the differences between professional and administrative occupation groups regarding the role workplace psychological factors play in retention (i.e. job demands, job resources and person–job fit perception). The authors draw from a data analysis based on a cross-sectional study of N = 745 participants (358 from professional occupations and 387 from administrative professions) in the South African work context. Building on the premises of the well-known job demands-resources (JD-R) model (see Chap. 1 in Part I), the authors show that job resources and person–job fit negatively relate with turnover intention in both professional and administrative occupations. Job overload and emotional load as well as person–job fit and career opportunities were stronger in relation to retention for the administrative group than in the professional group. The chapter makes a valuable contribution to the retention literature by highlighting that retention practices should consider the differences in importance of job demands, job resources and person–job fit for different occupational groups.

Sebastiaan Rothmann and Elmari Fouché critically review in Chap. 7, *School Principal Support, and Teachers' Work Engagement and Intention to Leave: The Role of Psychological Need Satisfaction*, the effects of manager behaviour (as perceived by employees) and flourishing of employees (as indicated by their psychological need satisfaction and engagement), on employee retention. The authors elucidate the associations between the factors by means of the well-known self-determination theory (SDT) of psychological needs satisfaction. Drawing from empirical findings of a cross-sectional study conducted among N = 513 secondary school teachers in public schools in South Africa, the authors made the premise that manager support for the satisfaction of employees' psychological needs for autonomy, competence and relatedness affects employees' autonomous motivation (and work engagement), which affect their intentions to leave. In the retention space, the authors conclude that autonomy satisfaction plays a significant role in the motivation and retention of employees because of its positive effect on work engagement and negative effect on intentions to leave.

Chapter 8 by Melinde Coetzee and Jeannette van Dyk, *Capitalising on Employee's Psychological Wellbeing Attributes in Managing Their Retention: The Adverse Influence of Workplace Bullying and Turnover Intention*, draws from the empirical findings of a cross-sectional study among a sample of N = 373 employees in the South African work context to evaluate the effect of the relationship dynamics among a number of psychological factors for employee retention. Building on the basic premises of broaden-and-build theory, the authors argue that employees' turnover intention and perceptions of workplace bullying are important to consider in retention strategies because of their link with employees' psychological wellbeing, engagement and commitment levels in the workplace. The new insights derived from the study findings indicate that for organisations to capitalise on employees' wellbeing attributes for retention purposes, leadership and human resource practices should counteract perceptions of workplace bullying and turnover intention in retention practices.

Part III: Key Insights

Part III of the book illustrates how the organisational context influences the psychology of retention. The basic premise is that employee behaviour is a function of personal and environmental factors that manifest within a specific organisational context. The interplay between these factors should be considered in understanding the reasons why employees decide to stay in or leave an organisation. The authors highlight key insights that inform retention practices.

Practice Guidelines

Chapter 5 focuses on the construct of job embeddedness operating across three key dimensions of fit, links and sacrifice (the totality of forces which cause employees to stay within an organisation) at the job, organisational and occupational levels. The authors of Chap. 5 illustrate the importance of measuring employees' job embeddedness as a retention practice. The chapter provides concrete research findings and examples from companies that have crafted retention strategies based on the measures of job embeddedness. The authors provide guidelines for practice including inter alia ways to enhance perceptions of fit, links and sacrifice. Such practice include, for example, newcomer socialisation tactics to proactively embed new employees in the social fabric of the firm by providing access to social capital resources; high-performance work practices (HPWPs) such as training, rotational programs, or performance incentives and awards, which can serve to increase the resources which employees accumulate at a particular organisation; creating occupational *links* through offering bonuses for referring employees who get hired; off-the-job retention resources and perks such as on-site daycare and preschools or extending access to fitness centres to family members, and work–family HRM bundles.

Chapter 6 demonstrates that retention strategies should address the differing needs and perceptions of person–job fit of various occupational groups in the organisation. The authors suggest organisational diagnostic surveys to proactively identify the job demands and job resources that influence perceptions of person–job fit for different occupational groups in departments. Chapter 7 focuses on retention practices in the school environment. The authors demonstrate the importance of principal support in improving engagement and lowering intentions to leave of teachers by focusing on psychological need satisfaction as an aspect of teachers' intrinsic motivation. Creating need-supportive environments initiated by principals contributes to teachers' engagement via the satisfaction of their autonomy needs, the relatedness satisfaction of teachers, characterised by experiences of a sense of communion and developing close and intimate relationships with others. Chapter 8 demonstrates the importance for organisations that act consistently against workplace bullying to create a climate where employees feel safe. Positive workplace conditions, policies and interventions for victims of bullying help increase employees' psychological wellbeing and decrease turnover intentions.

Research Gaps

The research represented in the various chapters was cross-sectional in nature and conducted within a specific organisational context. The authors in general recommend longitudinal research to be able to establish cause-effect links between the various factors that influence the psychology of retention in the internal organisational context. In addition, the authors recommend replication studies in various organisational contexts to be able to generalise the findings across various occupational and socio-demographic groups.

The authors of Chap. 5 emphasise the need for longitudinal studies that examine job embeddedness over the long term. The authors of Chap. 6 recommend further investigation into the differences in other occupational groups to assess the different dynamics that may emerge in these groups in different organisational contexts. In Chap. 7, the authors recommend future research that examines the antecedents and outcomes of psychological need satisfaction using a longitudinal design. The authors further suggest research regarding how social contextual factors influence the effects of principal support on psychological need satisfaction. They emphasise that future studies should also focus on the consequences of need thwarting and need satisfaction for outcomes such as teachers' engagement and intentions to leave. The authors of Chap. 8 recommend future longitudinal research that replicates the study with additional measures of wellbeing and retention-related attitudes in various occupational and socio-demographic contexts.

Chapter 5
Job Embeddedness Theory as a Tool for Improving Employee Retention

Brooks C. Holtom and Tiffany Darabi

Abstract In 2001, job embeddedness theory was introduced as a theory explaining why employees stay in organizations. The accumulated empirical results summarized in a compelling meta-analysis point to the predictive value of the theory. Across many contexts (e.g., for profit as well as not for profit, US and international), researchers have found that job embeddedness predicts staying as well as other positive work outcomes such as in-role and extra-role performance. Further, they have found that those who are more embedded are less likely to be absent or engage in counterproductive work behaviors. Recent theoretical elaborations identifying additional antecedents, moderators and consequences of embeddedness, have enriched both researcher and practitioner perspectives on staying. Based on theory and investigation, many practical implications for organizations seeking to enhance job embeddedness and its associated outcomes are advanced.

Keywords Job embeddedness · Turnover · Retention · Performance Organizational citizenship behaviors · Counterproductive work behaviors

Introduction

Given the extensive costs and disruptions that occur in organizations when valuable employees leave (Holtom et al. 2006), researchers have dedicated extensive efforts to better understanding why these employees leave. Decades of accumulated research have produced useful ideas and a clear understanding of many antecedents or predictors of leaving (e.g., Griffeth et al. 2000). However, relatively few attempts

B. C. Holtom (✉)
McDonough School of Business at Georgetown University, Washington, DC, USA
e-mail: Brooks.Holtom@Georgetown.edu

T. Darabi
ILR School, Cornell University, Ithaca, NY, USA
e-mail: tnd9@cornell.edu

M. Coetzee et al. (eds.), *Psychology of Retention*,
https://doi.org/10.1007/978-3-319-98920-4_5

had been made at understanding a related, but different, question: Why do people stay?

In 2001, Mitchell et al. articulated a theory of staying that they called job embeddedness (JE). Over time, researchers have found that job embeddedness not only predicts staying, but also other significant work outcomes such as absenteeism and counterproductive work behaviors as well as in-role and extra-role performance (Lee et al. 2004, 2014; Ng and Feldman 2009).

As a construct, job embeddedness has also been extended to explain other forms of staying such as embeddedness at the occupational (Ng and Feldman 2009) and organizational levels (Ng and Feldman 2007). Scholars have amassed enough detail over the past decade of focused study to yield a comprehensive meta-analysis of job embeddedness and its associated behavioral outcomes (Jiang et al. 2012). The strength and predictive value of JE makes it ripe for further theoretical expansion and study.

The purpose of this chapter is as follows: (1) to expand upon the fundamental components of the JE construct to articulate existing knowledge; (2) to propose new insights and suggestions for the future of job embeddedness research; and (3) to highlight practical implications of JE research for practitioners eager to apply such learnings to increase the probability of valued employees staying with their organizations.

Discussion

Research findings to date have established that individuals who are more embedded in their organizations and communities are more likely to stay in their jobs (Mitchell et al. 2001). Research has also shown that individuals are also influenced—through a process called 'social contagion'—by the attitudes and actions of co-workers and friends in the workplace, especially with regard to turnover decisions (Felps et al. 2009).

In this chapter, we also focus on recent research integrating social network theories with embeddedness. Work environments are inherently social and, therefore, how workers broker relationships with others and their perceived value and reputation within their social networks all have important impacts on turnover decisions (Feeley and Barnett 1997; Feeley et al. 2008; Mossholder et al. 2005; Ballinger et al. 2016). We also recast decisions to stay or leave as tradeoffs between resource gains and resource losses in discussing new aspects of the embeddedness construct (e.g. occupational embeddedness, family embeddedness in the community) that provide a richer understanding of job embeddedness through examining its deeper layers (Kaizad et al. 2015).

It is our hope that for practitioners looking to deepen their knowledge of how to structure effective HR practices or how to retain high performers this chapter provides the following: (1) job embeddedness as a theory to guide the development of an effective retention strategy; and (2) the importance of social networks in cultivating employee connections to reduce turnover and increase organizational commitment. In this chapter, we provide both empirical findings and established theories from decades of academic research on turnover and job embeddedness, as well as tangible examples from employers which can serve as examples of the types of practices that can be applied in the workplace in the service of a vibrant organizational community.

Theoretical Background

Job embeddedness was first conceived of by Mitchell et al. (2001) as a "higher-order aggregate of forces for retention." In other words, it represents the forces that influence an individual to become "stuck" within an organization (Mitchell et al. 2001). The notion of embeddedness is drawn conceptually from the sociological literature on the role of social relationships—specifically network ties—in constraining economic actions and social movement (Granovetter 1985; Uzzi 1996, 1997). In contrast to its sociological roots, the job embeddedness construct focuses on the individual as the unit of analysis (Mitchell et al. 2001).

Job embeddedness operates across three key dimensions—links, fit and sacrifice—at both the organizational and community levels (Mitchell et al. 2001). *Links* speak to the social ties individuals build and maintain with individuals, groups, and teams both on and off-the-job (Mitchell et al. 2001). *Fit* speaks to the association, affinity, or compatibility individuals feel for the job or community in which they are located (Mitchell et al. 2001). And lastly, *sacrifice*, refers to what an individual might lose or have to give up—materially or emotionally at both the organizational and community levels—by choosing to leave their job (Mitchell et al. 2001).

Although these three dimensions are intertwined and work in concert with one another through the job embeddedness construct, they each have distinct theoretical mechanisms which account for their effects. For example, *links* with friends, family or community organizations such as churches, influence staying (Hom et al. 2012; Maertz and Griffeth 2004) just as building social capital within the workplace may as well (Holtom et al. 2006). Both examples are evidence of the power of links to promote staying (Allen 2006; Mitchell and Lee 2001) by inducing normative pressures (Maertz et al. 2003) both on and off the job. Research regarding the relationship between social networks and turnover extends the impact of the links dimension even further. One of the assets which strong social capital in the workplace can provide is an enhanced reputation (Adler and Kwon 2002) through access to well-connected people within one's network (Ballinger et al. 2016). Employees with more prestigious network reputations are more likely to remain embedded within their organizations (Ballinger et al. 2016) with social capital—specifically the ability to broker relationships—becoming a more crucial component to success as employees advance up the hierarchy (Burt and Merluzzi 2014; Moran 2005; Rodan 2010). It follows then that strong social capital has a negative relationship with turnover for high-level employees (Ballinger et al. 2016). There is another social element that needs to be considered. Specifically, the notion of 'turnover contagion' characterizes turnover as having a contagious element much like a sickness spreading between co-workers (Felps et al. 2009). It appropriately describes the powerful influence that co-worker turnover can have on the turnover decisions of others within their network, potentially creating a ripple-effect within the organization (Felps et al. 2009).

The *fit* dimension of the job embeddedness construct at the community level can be described simply as an individual's affinity towards where they live as expressed through one or a number of items such as culture, locale or climate (Mitchell et al. 2001). As long as this affinity exists it is reasonable to assume that an individual might be less likely to engage in turnover intentions in many cases. The fit experienced on the job is best illustrated by the attraction-selection-attraction paradigm (ASA) (Schneider 1987). As the ASA wording implies, individuals and organizations select one another through a process of mutual attraction (Wheeler et al. 2007) with turnover occurring when one or both parties no longer experience such an attraction or fit (Wheeler et al. 2007). The importance of *fit* to employee retention should not be underestimated, especially amongst the Millennial population. Studies have found that Millennials do not feel swayed by paychecks and perks alone, but that they also need to feel connected to the mission, vision, and values of an organization to feel that their work is contributing to something larger (Slavin 2015). The mutual person-organization *fit* attraction also pays dividends overtime—as employee tenure increases so does the likelihood that they will stay (Holtom et al. 2013). As such, embeddedness can be characterized as having cumulative effects on employee turnover intentions (Holtom et al. 2013).

Decisions to leave require individuals to weigh the *sacrifices* they might have to make. Depending on the nature of the benefits and resources they have accumulated over time such a process can be quite complex (Kiazad et al. 2015). A number of turnover theories have naturally found that higher perceived costs of leaving serve to discourage individuals from leaving (Mobley 1977; Rusbult and Farrell 1983; Shaw et al. 1998). In an effort to conserve the resources they have accumulated (Kiazad et al. 2015), individuals will weigh the opportunities that leaving might provide against the sacrifices they will have to make in non-transferrable benefits such as training (Mitchell and Lee 2001) and the ability to navigate a familiar organizational culture and its associated politics. Fast food chain Pal's Sudden Service provides great evidence for the efficacy of the *sacrifices* domain with the 120 h of training they provide new hires even before they begin their jobs, which is supplemented by retraining, certifications, and pop-quizzes when employees switch jobs (Taylor 2016). The embedding effects of such investments are clear—Pal's boasts a 1.4% turnover rate amongst their assistant managers with only 7 general managers leaving voluntarily in the 33 years they have been in business (Taylor 2016). The *sacrifices* dimension also operates at the community embeddedness level, as individuals often choose to stay in certain locations due to the fact that they simply enjoy living there or that their children might be in good schools (Mitchell et al. 2001).

It is worth mentioning that job embeddedness itself is not an affective state—in contrast to organizational commitment (Allen and Meyer 1990), for example—but rather a construct caused by the accumulation of a number of different factors (Mitchell et al. 2001). As such, the links dimension is primarily about sheer numbers of connections via teams and colleagues, while fit is conceived of as a 'cognitive belief rather than an emotional response' (Cable and Parsons 1999: 24). Therefore, job embeddedness does not reflect one's affective affinity for particular organization or job, but simply the totality of elements both on-the-job and off-the-job—across the dimensions of links, fit, and sacrifice—that serve to bind an individual to a particular organization or job. The "binding" force of job embeddedness can serve useful for organizations at times when employees experience negative events in the workplace (Burton et al. 2010). Such events, known as "shocks" can often result in uprooting employees and have been proven to be the cause of turnover (Lee and Mitchell 1994). However, in cases where individuals are embedded on the job, embeddedness serves to soften the blow of negative events such that embedded individuals invest further in organizational citizenship behaviors and even improve their performance in efforts to help the organization weather its difficulties (Burton et al. 2010).

While much of the early literature on job embeddedness was primarily concerned with its on-the-job component, in recent years more studies have begun to delve into the multiple foci of the off-the-job component to better understand its impact on turnover and other workplace behaviors as well as to develop a richer understanding of how it relates to its on-the-job embeddedness counterpart. Perhaps not surprisingly, research has shown that off-the-job embeddedness (as opposed to on-the-job embeddedness) predicts voluntary turnover and absences, whereas on-the-job embeddedness (as opposed to off-the-job embeddedness) predicts both organizational citizenship and job performance (Lee et al. 2004). Ng and Feldman (2014) delve further into related questions, specifically examining the relationship between on-the-job and off-the-job embeddedness. They found that community and organizational embeddedness are directionally alike with organizational embeddedness serving as a proxy or mediator between community embeddedness and social networking behaviors, job motivation, and organizational identification (Ng and Feldman 2014).

The broad range of theories and cumulative findings overtime provide a solid foundation for the job embeddedness construct, thus making it especially noteworthy for firms seeking to enhance employee commitments and reduce turnover. Furthermore, the complex array of factors integrated within the job embeddedness construct is partly what makes it so effective in predicting turnover. Mitchell et al. (2001) found job embeddedness to be a stronger predictor of turnover than both job satisfaction and organizational commitment—factors encompassing one's desire to leave—as well as perceived job alternatives and job search engagement—factors related to how easily one might be able to leave. A longitudinal study confirmed these findings by developing and testing a global measure of job embeddedness which also found that job embeddedness predicted voluntary turnover beyond the traditionally used variables present in previous turnover studies (Crossley et al. 2007).

Key Predictive Relationships

Based on more than a decade of job embeddedness research, Jiang et al. (2012) published the first meta-analysis on the topic, evaluating its relationship to related constructs (e.g. job alternatives), demographics such as gender and national culture, and organizational types (e.g. public, private). The study draws from 52 published studies on job embeddedness with 65 independent samples (*N* 42,907), providing a comprehensive analysis (Jiang et al. 2012).

The findings provide clear evidence of the negative relationship that both on-the-job and off-the-job embeddedness have with turnover intentions and actual turnover, even after controlling for job attitudes and job alternatives.

Jiang et al. (2012) also examine the national cultural context to which organizations belong and how this might impact the embeddedness construct. Specifically, differences between individualistic and collectivist countries are explored, with the former defined as having a greater focus on self-concern as opposed to relationships with others and the latter characterized as valuing tight-knit relationships with important groups (Oyserman et al. 2002). In this context, it was hypothesized that those in collectivist countries who were embedded on and off-the job would be less likely to both intend to leave their organizations as well as less likely to actually leave (Jiang et al. 2012). Interestingly, the only finding of significance was that the negative relationship between off-the-job embeddedness and turnover intentions was significantly stronger in collectivist countries in comparison with individualistic countries.

The authors further postulated that women might be more susceptible to the influences of embeddedness both on and off-the-job due to the value they place on social and community-oriented ties and concerns for others as opposed to men who are more individualistic in their approach to work (Eagly and Wood 1991; Marsden et al. 1993). Findings indicate that gender does moderate or strengthen the link between on-the-job embeddedness and both turnover intentions and also actual turnover.

An analysis of organizational types, specifically public organizations as compared to private organizations, also provides an interesting lens by which to view embeddedness. Public organizations have been viewed synonymously with job security for quite some time—an attractive employment option for those who are risk averse (Bellante and Link 1981; Buelens and Van den Broeck 2007; Schneider 1987). The authors found that members of public organizations, as opposed to private organizations, were more embedded on-the-job (Jiang et al. 2012). While this was true for off-the-job embeddedness, such findings nevertheless provide another valuable variable to further contextualize the job embeddedness literature.

Future Research

Recent research examining job embeddedness from a conservation of resources (COR) perspective has created fresh new avenues for research (Kaizad et al. 2015). Below we discuss the following major developments: extensions of the original embeddedness construct into new embeddedness foci; variables that serve as antecedents to embeddedness; relationships between embeddedness foci and particular work outcomes such as performance; and interactions between embeddedness and social network theory. Lastly, we explore time dynamics in job embeddedness research to encourage researchers to collaborate with practitioners to test embeddedness in a dynamic fashion over the course of time.

The academic literature has recently expanded the foci within which individuals embed themselves (Feldman and Ng 2007; Feldman et al. 2012; Ramesh and Gelfand 2010). The various embeddedness foci go beyond just retention to also predict factors such as job performance and work-family conflict (Lee et al. 2004; Ng and Feldman 2009, 2012; Ramesh and Gelfand 2010). We provide an overview of the emerging research on multi-foci job embeddedness as a way to highlight key up-and-coming themes.

On-the-Job and Organizational Embeddedness

On-the-job and organizational embeddedness were long treated as one in the same. Only recently (Ng and Feldman 2007) have researchers begun to tease out their subtle, but significant differences and push past the original assumption that embeddedness in a job also signaled embeddedness in an organization (Mitchell et al. 2001). In many cases employees might very well enjoy their jobs and feel a fit between its tasks and their skills, but not necessarily feel in alignment with the values of an overall organization (Ng and Feldman 2007). Such individuals might even have strong network connections with co-workers in their work-unit, but at the same time might lack connections with colleagues across an organization. Further, firms such as Campbell Soup Company attempt to create organizational-level sacrifices with perks such as an on-site Kindergarten and after-school programs (Business Insider 2013). While it stands to reason that on-the-job embeddedness might very well yield higher workplace retention given that jobs are situated within firms, studies have shown that individuals embedded at the job level do chose to leave if they are forced to move to another job within the firm that they derive less enjoyment from or do not feel they excel at (Ng and Feldman 2007).

Occupational Embeddedness

Occupational embeddedness—also conceived of by Ng and Feldman (2007)—explains why individuals might chose to leave particular organizations but remain within a certain industry. Staying in this context is perceived in a broader sense with individuals gaining skills and making network connections not just within the firm but across firms within a particular occupation. At the same time, a healthy network of occupational links can be leveraged by organizations for their benefit as well. Hubspot offers employees $30,000 bonuses for recommending full-time employees who get hired (Van der Hoop 2016). Recruitment by referral can lead to greater retention rates given that employees already understand the firm's culture and will be better positioned to recommend individuals who might also be good fits (Van der Hoop 2016).

Initial empirical studies have found that after controlling for organizational embeddedness, occupational embeddedness explains unique variance across a number of valued outcomes such as task performance and creativity (Ng and Feldman 2009). Given the trend amongst millennials to change jobs and move from organization to organization quickly, understanding occupational embeddedness is crucial for firms to craft effective organization-level retention strategies.

Family Embeddedness in the Community

Mitchell et al. (2001) originally conceived of embeddedness through the lens of two primary foci—on and off-the-job embeddedness. Examples of external forces include recreational hobbies or activities that might embed an individual at the community level as well as embedding factors at the family level such as a spouse's employment in the area or children attending particular schools in the city, which might bind an individual to a location by proxy (Feldman et al. 2012). Also referred to as "family embeddedness in the community", this focal point examines external factors derived from the family that constrain an individual's mobility (Hom et al. 2012). Another potential dimension of off-the-job embeddedness—termed "family embeddedness" is when family members themselves become attached to an individual's workplace through means such as being beneficiaries of spousal health insurance benefits or befriending employees (Ramesh and Gelfand 2010). Hershey not only boasts its own fitness centers, but also opens them for use to employee spouses and dependents over the age of 18 (Business Insider 2013). Other potential examples of family embeddedness are a program at Mattel which defrays the costs of adoption or Microsoft's offering of Applied Behavioral Analysis therapy as an autism treatment (Business Insider 2013).

An individual may in many cases be giving way to the needs of family above their own to remain within a certain location (as with "family embeddedness in the community") or even to remain within a particular organization or position (as with "family embeddedness"). These embeddedness foci might lead to an individual reluctantly staying within a particular setting or other states of withdrawal (Hom et al. 2012) and perhaps even CWBs. The strength of these extrinsic forces has led scholars to propose that family embeddedness itself might explain additional turnover variance apart from on-the-job and community embeddedness (Ramesh and Gelfand 2010).

Antecedents to Embeddedness Foci

Now that we have explored the range of embeddedness foci in both workplace and community settings, we turn our attention to the antecedents of the embeddedness process itself. In other words, what valued resources are individuals receiving in each of the various contexts that induce them to become embedded in the first place? We draw on the conservation of resources perspective of embeddedness advanced by Kaizad and colleagues (Kiazad et al. 2015) to highlight *contextual variables* that create embedding resources—both within the workplace context and one outside of the workplace context. Our discussion of antecedents is not comprehensive nor is it inclusive of all elements or individual-level differences such as personality (Giosan et al. 2005).

Organizational Practices

High-performance work practices (HPWPs) have long been used by human resource management (HRM) scholars to describe groups of strategic practices undertaken by organizations to enhance firm performance outcomes (Becker and Huselid 1998). HPWPs such as training, rotational programs, or performance incentives and awards, can serve as embedding mechanisms. Pal's Sudden Service is certainly a model for utilizing HPWP to great ends—Pal's makes a mistake only once in 3,600 orders, which is ten times better than the average fast food chain (Taylor 2016). HPWPs are often deployed as bundles with the ability-motivation-opportunity (A-M-O) framework (Lepak and 2006; Combs et al. 2006) used as both a development aid as well as a descriptor for various HPWP configurations (*skill-enhancing*, *opportunity-enhancing*, and *motivation-enhancing*). These three descriptors offered by the A-M-O framework have been successful in capturing the range of HRM practices yielding embeddedness results (Allen 2006; Hom et al. 2009; Trevor and Nyberg 2008). The success at Pal's can be summarized in a similar manner—hiring for attitude and training for skill, providing constant opportunities for improvement, and molding leaders who are serious about teaching and training their staff (Taylor 2016). The skill-enhancing, opportunity-enhancing, and motivation-enhancing HPWP combinations provide different sets of resources to employees. As a result, individuals embed more strongly at either the job, organizational or occupational levels in correspondence to the various resources gained from the HPWP configuration.

Off-the-Job Characteristics

In our analysis of off-the-job embeddedness resources encouraging employees and their families to remain in the communities in which they reside, three key groupings emerge as being the most salient for providing resources to employees and their families: nearby extended family, community characteristics, and professional communities (Kaizad et al. 2015). Nearby extended family—especially in cases where familial ties are strong (Granovetter 1973; Lin 2001)—can provide support for family members to better manager conflict surrounding work and family demands through help with babysitting and a built-in network for birthdays, holiday celebrations, and the like (Kaizad et al. 2015). Communities that offer a wide range of resources to individuals that are in-line with their values and interests such as good schools or connections with like-minded individuals are embedding in the way that sacrificing such resources means sacrificing overall quality of life—a price some might find too high to pay (Kaizad et al. 2015). Professional communities—even those cultivated online—allow for development of occupational networks behind one's workplace and correlate highly with occupational embeddedness (Kaizad et al. 2015).

Embeddedness Foci and Work-Related Outcomes

As viewed from a COR perspective, the influence of job embeddedness goes well beyond reducing turnover intentions to impact organizational contributions in other areas as well (Jiang et al. 2012). Counter-productive work behaviors (CWBs), organizational citizenship behaviors (OCBs), and core task performance are three key categories of behavioral outcomes commonly associated with job embeddedness (Feldman et al. 2012; Lee et al. 2004; Ng and Feldman 2009). *CWBs* include negative behaviors ranging from wasting time at work to serious actions such as fraud or theft. Broadly, CWBs may contribute to a "dark side" of embeddedness—when employees stay but do so with reluctance or malicious intent (Spector et al. 2006). *OCBs* are directionally opposite of CWBs in that they capture an employees' positive actions towards or on behalf of an organization (Lee and Allen 2002). OCBs are not required by employee contract, and therefore demonstrate a level of commitment and affinity on the part of an employee towards their employer which can assist with various aspects of organizational functioning (e.g., attend voluntary functions, defending the company against criticism; Lee and Allen 2002). Lastly, *core task performance*—the tasks that are required by one's job to contribute directly to organizational outputs (Motowidlo et al. 1997)—has been demonstrated to be positively correlated with JE (Lee et al. 2004).

Below we discuss each of these three key organizational contributions in greater depth by employing a COR perspective of job embeddedness. Overall, we argue that based on COR theory embedded employees will likely have higher work performance due to the resources they hold (fit and links) and the advantages this provides for them to acquire yet more resources (i.e. pay increases, stock options) through excellent performance.

Direct Effects of Embeddedness Foci

On-the-job embeddedness has a stronger impact on workplace behaviors (i.e. performance) and attitudes (affective commitment, turnover intentions) as compared with off-the-job embeddedness (Allen 2006; Jiang et al. 2012; Ng and Feldman 2014; Wheeler et al. 2012). Additional research has shown, however, that both embeddedness foci increase OCBs and performance, while also decreasing turnover and absenteeism (Lee et al. 2004). The sections below will distinguish in greater detail between the various embeddedness foci across on and off-the-job embeddedness as they shape and impact the three aspects of organizational contributions highlighted above—CWBs, OCBs, and task performance.

CWBs. While the causes of CWBs can vary from person to person, the consequences of such behaviors (e.g. excessive internet surfing, abusing colleagues, etc.) do not. CWBs can damage employee reputations, promotional opportunities and—in their worst instances—even lead to termination (Feldman et al. 2012; Lee et al. 2004; Rotundo and Sackett 2002). From a COR perspective, CWBs result in a loss of resources at the job, organizational, and occupational levels.

The greatest implication for resource losses related to CWBs is at the occupational level (Ng and Feldman 2009). For example, those engaged in professional occupations such as doctors are more occupationally embedded than they are in any one organization or job. Furthermore, the implications of a malpractice suit or even absenteeism would impact a doctor at the occupational level—negative reputations spread amongst occupational communities and changing occupations can be difficult and sometimes impossible (Ng and Feldman 2009). As such, the threat of such resource losses amongst those highly embedded in occupations should curb CWBs (Blau 2000), making it more likely for such individuals to tweak the boundaries and alter the tasks of their jobs as a positive, "job-crafting" (Wrzesniewski and Dutton 2001) response to potential dissatisfaction which might otherwise lead to CWBs. Some employers have unknowingly adopted the philosophy behind "job-crafting" in their novel approaches to get the best out of their employees. Arrow Group of Companies, for example, gives their employees the flexibility and time—a few hours a week—to work from any location, on any project related to the organization (Van der Hoop 2016). According to CEO Sam Ibrahim, this practice has led to some of the firm's best innovations (Van der Hoop 2016).

OCBs. As previously stated, individuals embedded on-the-job at the job, organizational or occupational levels are more likely to exhibit OCBs. OCBs establish goodwill relationships between employees and their organizations, allowing employees to reap their associated rewards (Rioux and Penner 2001). Embeddedness—from a COR theory perspective—presupposes that individuals are prone to become embedded due to possibilities for resource gains or to avoid resource losses (Kaizad et al. 2015). Embedded individuals are driven to continually invest the instrumental resources (e.g. fit and links) they already have by virtue of their embedded status, in order to build additional resources in the future (Hobfoll 2001).

In the context of OCBs, employees with strong fit at the company-level and links across an organization, are most likely to gain from—and therefore invest in—OCBs. Such employees are likely to be viewed as congenial, more trustworthy, and as willing to work extra to help the firm (Bolino et al. 2006). The links such employees maintain within and outside the firm also allow them to offer important information such as the latest industry developments for the aid of the organization (Lee and Allen 2002). Other examples of OCBs include investing time and effort (Halbesleben et al. 2014) into socializing with co-workers or helping colleagues in order to gain resources such as recognition, peer support, or rewards (Halbesleben and Wheeler 2015; Ng and Feldman 2012; Podsakoff et al. 2009). An excellent example of this helping-to-gain principle is Google's practice of allowing employees to "own" their unused vacation time, providing flexibility for employees to donate vacation time to co-workers at their discretion and, in turn, offering another avenue for employees to exercise OCBs (Van der Hoop 2016).

Given that resources are best deployed with a clear sense for their utility and purpose (Hobfoll 2001), OCBs are most likely to be performed by employees who are organizationally embedded (Ng and Feldman 2009). For employees who are more embedded in the job than the organization, they may need to reduce task performance to allocate effort to OCBs. Thus, for those more highly embedded at the job and occupational levels, the return on investment from OCBs might not prove relevant enough to warrant equivalent efforts to those embedded at the organizational level.

Task performance. There exists a mutually reinforcing relationship between high performance and embeddedness as performance generally leads to extrinsic rewards (e.g., promotions, salary increases) and intrinsic benefits (e.g., praise) (Lanaj et al. 2012; Rotondo and Sackett 2002; Salamin and Hom 2005). For example, participation in professional associations or internal organizational committees allow employees to gain resources at the occupational and organizational levels and reveal a selectiveness about time allocation in order to build resources for the future (Halbesleben & Bowler, 2007). Such employees may be less likely to focus in the day-to-day task domain (Feldman and Ng 2007), consistently watching for future opportunities that might develop at the organizational or occupational levels. On the other hand, embeddedness at the job level tends toward greater performance motivation (Hom et al. 2012; Halbesleben et al. 2014), stronger demands-abilities fit (Kristof 1996), highly concentrated social capital networks

(Sparrowe et al. 2001) and lasting task-affinity (Hom et al. 2012). Such resources can then be used and reinvested by job embedded employees to reach even higher levels of task performance and increase team-level efficiency and effectiveness for enhanced individual and team-level rewards (Erdogan and Bauer 2005).

Network centrality. Another resource that can enhance embeddedness is the position one occupies in a social network. An employee receives valuable social capital assets through occupying a central position of prominence within their social network (Feeley and Barnett 1997; Feeley et al. 2008; Mossholder et al. 2005) through the links they foster between others (*betweenness centrality;* Mehra et al. 2001), the links they have to others (*out-degree centrality*), and how others are linked to them (*in-degree centrality*). By fostering links or creating bridges between others who are not connected with each other, employees control the flow of information across an organization (Feeley 2000; Mehra et al. 2001), increasing their social capital, influence and embeddedness. *Out-degree centrality* focuses on the number of links an employee thinks they have with others, while *in-degree* centrality focuses on the number of times network members claim to have a particular individual as a contact. While *out-degree centrality* has been the more long-standing measure associated with JE research, *in-degree centrality* has been the measure shown to be effective in decreasing turnover (Mossholder et al. 2005).

Network closure. Beyond simply network position, the structure of an individual's network also has implications for job embeddedness. Closed networks and open networks each have their advantages for enhancing social capital—closed networks operate on trust with mutually affiliated individuals sharing information (Burt 2001) and open networks rely on access to a greater variety of network connections and information sources. Being enmeshed in a closed network has the advantage of offering trusted relationships with network members being able to freely and amply exchange resources (e.g., Halbesleben and Wheeler 2015) and readily offer comfort (Balkundi and Harrison 2006) and other types of emotional support in greater quantity and in a timelier manner to assist with work stress (Lazarova et al. 2010). As such, network closure (Hom and Xiao 2011) bolsters embeddedness with individuals likely being reluctant to give up such coveted personal support resources by switching jobs, organizations or relocating in the case of off-the-job network closure.

Social capital losses. Decisions individuals make to stay or leave often cause them to experience losses in social capital. Deciding to stay in an organization when friends, co-workers, or bosses leave depletes valuable resources from a COR theory perspective, just as much as deciding to leave may cause a loss in accumulated social capital in the forms of organizational links one has already cultivated. While turnover can be contagious, "infecting" those already engaging in job search or others with low organizational embeddedness (Felps et al. 2009), it be an even greater risk in the event that a key network contact chooses to depart (Krackhardt and Porter 1986). Other research shows that subordinates of leaders with whom they have a positive LMX relationship, are more likely to follow their bosses when they depart the organization as opposed to having to rebuild ensuing LMX social capital losses (Ballinger et al. 2010). On an emotional level, just as there can be great benefits obtained from membership in a closed social network, employees often chose to depart organizations if such friends and emotional supporters are themselves leaving (Shah 2000). COR theory provides a rich lens through which the staying-leaving equation can be examined with network theory and social capital gains and losses being promising avenues for additional research.

Time Dynamics

The majority of studies examine job embeddedness at a static point in time as opposed to how it might evolve over the course of time. Recently there has been a call for more research utilizing longitudinal methods to capture such time sensitive nuances and changes (Ng and Feldman 2013). The relationship between resources and embeddedness as articulated by Kaizad et al. (2015) is a key component when examining embeddedness over the arc of an individual's career. Findings have indicated that different resources are more powerful embedding forces at different stages in an employee's career (Ng and Feldman 2007). As such, for younger employees an urban location might be more embedding, while for more established employees with families, suburban locations with good schools might be more powerful factors. The same can be said with on-the-job embedding factors—certain factors might be more salient at the start of an employees' career versus those that might matter more as one advances and becomes more established. As such, resource utility is very much dependent on context. If resources continue to satisfy needs and goals, individuals will embed further (Halbesleben et al. 2014) with more tenured employees being more likely to stay in the future (Holtom et al. 2013). Such findings are particularly useful for crafting retention strategies in a more targeted fashion. They also illustrate the need for expanding beyond the current body of research (Ng and Feldman 2007, 2013) addressing the time dynamics of embeddedness.

Implications for Retention Theory and Practice

The model presented in this chapter provides a holistic examination of the many dimensions involved in the retention equation. Employee decisions to stay or leave are in themselves complex and influenced by a confluence of factors. Job embeddedness theory offers a number of insights that go beyond traditional paradigms (e.g., organizational commitment or job satisfaction) to support organizations in crafting mindful retention strategies. The following topics serve to highlight key concepts from job embeddedness theory.

Beyond an Organization-Focused Approach

Often organizations focus on internal factors such as the rewards and incentives it provides. Job embeddedness theory pushes organizations to think more broadly about engaging employees in the full range of their experience—at work and outside of work. Many organizations such as Fifth Third Bancorp, Johnson & Johnson, Gusto, and KKR & Co. are putting in place practices (such as bringing nannies on work trips) that seek to increase embeddedness amongst working mothers (Feintzeig 2017). Fifth Third Bancorp in particular has employed a concierge service to tend to the needs of expectant mothers and parents with infants, providing services ranging from scheduling gender reveal parties to shopping for strollers (Feintzeig 2017). Examples of other tactics addressing full-spectrum work and community embeddedness include locating offices near to where employees live to ease commutes and maximize time spent at work and at home. In this way organizations engage employees in the communities where they already feel they *fit*. Offering paid time off for volunteer work like CRM Salesforce does by offering up to seven days for volunteering (Van der Hoop 2016), allows employees to build *links* in their community and strengthen existing network connections (Holtom et al. 2006). As another example, organizations can offer relocation or home-buying assistance to entice talent and ease the "*sacrifices*" and burdens associated with moving. Utilizing job embeddedness theory to think of retention in practical terms across its three dimensions as well as its two contexts—on and off-the-job—is essential for organizations seeking to attract and retain talent.

Supplementing Skill-Development with Opportunity-Enhancement

One of the most common approaches to retention is to provide training opportunities for employees. However, such skill-development HPWPs have a down side. In some cases, such training may serve to embed employees more at the occupational level as opposed to the organizational level. Occupational embeddedness does reduce CWBs, but it is less likely to foster long-term employment and motivate OCBs (Feldman and Ng 2007; Ng and Feldman 2009). Organizations must be careful to supplement skill-development offerings with opportunity-enhancing practices (e.g., cross-departmental collaboration, participative decision making) that can serve to bind employees at the job or organizational levels.

Supplementing Motivation-Enhancement with Opportunity-Enhancement

Providing incentives for employees switch to jobs within the firm entails some risk. In the event the new job is not as good of a fit as the old job, task performance levels may be diminished (Hom et al. 2012). Also, the use of incentives should be wisely applied, as OCBs that add value for the firm may typically reflect the commitment of intrinsically motivated employees to the organization. Similar to skill-development, motivation-enhancment practices should be supplemented with opportunity-enhancing practices in order to maximize worker performance and reduce turnover rates (Gardner et al. 2011).

The Possible Downside of Off-the-Job Embeddedness

As previously stated, off-the-job retention factors have traditionally been overlooked. Yet, the theoretical arguments and empirical evidence suggest that increasing off-the-job embeddedness benefits organizations. This is important for human resource professionals to be aware of when crafting employee wellness and support programs. Off-the-job embeddedness can serve to strengthen the person-organization bond in individuals who are already embedded on the job, reducing the likelihood of turnover and CWBs. However, it is often the case that off-the-job demands for parents can impact performance (Bakker et al. 2008). Implementing work-family HRM bundles such as flextime or on-site day care (Perry-Smith and Blum 2000) can provide much needed assistance and support to employees off-the-job, which also has the effect of freeing time and energy to contribute more effectively towards job demands (Trevor and Nyberg 2008).

Conclusion and Implications for Retention

In this chapter, we have conveyed foundational research and findings on job embeddedness summarized by the following points: (1) individuals who are more embedded in organizations and communities are more likely to stay in their jobs; (2) embeddedness as a construct provides valuable information on retention, OCBs, and performance beyond what job satisfaction and organizational commitment can predict; and (3) individual turnover decisions are greatly influenced by the attitudes and actions of co-workers, family members and others around them through the effects of social contagion.

The insights we have shared provide a summary of past research as well as the potential future agenda of job embeddedness research. Some of the recent work on job embeddedness has identified new embeddedness foci impacting the staying-leaving equation such as occupational embeddedness and family embeddedness in the community. COR theory adds theoretical depth to the complexity of the embeddedness construct. Recasting decisions to stay or leave as potential resource gains or losses has advanced understanding of the theoretical underpinnings of embeddedness. Lastly, recent research on the role social networks play in turnover decisions has deepened understanding of how network centrality, reputation amongst co-workers, and network brokerage play a role in turnover decisions.

Our goal with this chapter was also to assist practitioners seeking to craft meaningful retention strategies by not only unpacking the job embeddedness construct, but also through providing concrete examples from firms that have crafted retention strategies which exemplify the research findings around job embeddedness. Combining insights from social network analysis and job embeddedness can be a unique way to craft a retention strategy that goes beyond simply incentives to also look at the webs of interconnectedness employees form. The following are key strategies for organizations to take into account when crafting effective retention strategies.

- Crafting retention strategies with the three dimensions of job embeddedness (links, fit, and sacrifices) in mind is essential. For example, the *links* domain of job embeddedness theory (Mitchell et al. 2001) can be addressed by employing newcomer socialization tactics to proactively embed new employees in the social fabric of the firm by providing access to social capital resources. With the influx of Millennials in the work place *fit* becomes an even more essential component for any retention strategy aimed at this particular employee demographic given their need for identification with organizational mission.
- Employing high-performance work practices (HPWPs) such as training, rotational programs, or performance incentives and awards, can serve to assist to increase the resources which employees accumulate at a particular organization, thereby having an embedding effect.
- Acknowledging that embeddedness can take root in a multitude of foci—on-the-job, organizational, or occupational (Ng and Feldman 2007)—is an asset to organizations for crafting broad, creative retention strategies. For example, occupational embeddedness can be wielded effectively to an organization's advantage by taking advantage of employee's occupational *links* through offering bonuses for referring employees who get hired.
- Organizations should also ensure that retention strategies are holistic and not only reflective of on-the-job components. Providing perks such as on-site daycare and preschools or extending access to fitness centers to family members, are examples of attempts to embed employees beyond the work dimension. Such perks also become examples of *sacrifices*—benefits employees would have to give up if they were to leave.

Being mindful of these essential components of job embeddedness and their associated retention strategies, can assist organizations in increasing positive work behaviors such as OCBs and task performance, while helping to curb CWBs. It is also important to recognize that while strong retention strategies and low turnover rates are the marks of healthy organizations, not all staying is good and with turnover comes an influx of potentially new and creative perspectives to fuel an organization forward.

It is our hope that this chapter provides organizations with meaningful information to embed employees making meaningful contributions to their jobs, organizations, and occupations. As Pal's CEO Thomas Crosby has said, "People ask me, 'What if you spend all this time and money on training and someone leaves?' I ask them, 'What if we don't spend the time and money, and they stay?'" (Taylor 2016).

Summary

This chapter focuses on the construct of job embeddedness—operating across three key dimensions of fit, links and sacrifice—as the totality of forces which cause employees to stay within an organization (Mitchell et al. 2001). The original job embeddedness construct has been expanded to examine embeddedness at the job, organizational, and occupational levels (Ng and Feldman 2007, 2009) as well as to embrace off-the-job embeddedness factors such as family embeddedness in the community (Hom et al. 2012). More recent research has uncovered the pivotal role of social networks in the embeddedness equation through using COR theory as an essential lens from which to view embeddedness. COR theory states that employees strive to maximize their stock of resources at each level of embeddedness, while also viewing decisions to stay or leave from the calculus of potential resource sacrifices (Kaizad et al. 2015). Effectively designed retention strategies sensitive to the underlying forces of COR theory and drawing from organizational practices such as HPWPs can serve to embed employees, potentially increasing task performance and OCBs, while helping to curb CWBs.

References

Adler, P. S., & Kwon, S. W. (2002). Social capital: Prospects for a new concept. *Academy of Management Review, 27*(1), 17–40.

Allen, D. G. (2006). Do organizational socialization tactics influence newcomer embeddedness and turnover? *Journal of Management, 32,* 237–256.

Allen, N., & Meyer, J. (1990). The measurement and antecedents of affective, continuance, and normative commitment to the organization. *Journal of Occupational Psychology, 63,* 1–18.

Bakker, A. B., Demerouti, E., & Dollard, M. (2008). How job demands influence partners' experience of exhaustion: Integrating work-family conflict and crossover theory. *Journal of Applied Psychology, 93,* 901–911.

Balkundi, P., & Harrison, D. A. (2006). Ties, leaders, and time in teams: Strong inference about the effects of network structure on team viability and performance. *Academy of Management Journal, 49,* 49–68.

Ballinger, G. A., Cross, R., & Holtom, B. C. (2016). The right friends in the right places: Understanding network structure as a predictor of voluntary turnover. *Journal of Applied Psychology, 101*(4), 535.

Ballinger, G. A., Lehman, D. W., & Schoorman, F. D. (2010). Leader-member exchange and turnover before and after succession events. *Organizational Behavior and Human Decision Processes, 113,* 25–36.

Becker, B., & Huselid, M. (1998). High performance work systems and firm performance: A synthesis of research and managerial implications. *Research in Personnel and Human Resources, 16,* 53–101.

Bellante, D., & Link, A. N. (1981). Are public sector workers more risk averse than private sector workers? *Industrial and Labor Relations Review, 34,* 408–412.

Blau, G. (2000). Job, organisational, professional context antecedents as predictors of intent for inter-role work transitions. *Journal of Vocational Behavior, 56,* 330–445.

Bolino, M. C., Varela, J. A., Bande, B., & Turnley, W. H. (2006). The impact of impression-management tactics on supervisor ratings of organizational citizenship behavior. *Journal of Organizational Behavior, 27,* 281–297.

Buelens, M., & Van den Broeck, H. (2007). An analysis of differences in work motivation between public and private sector organizations. *Public Administration Review, 67,* 65–74.

Burt, R. S. (2001). Attachment, decay, and social network. *Journal of Organizational Behavior, 22*, 619–643.

Burt, R. S., & Merluzzi, J. (2014). Embedded brokerage: Hubs versus locals. In *Contemporary perspectives on organizational social networks* (pp. 161–177). Emerald Group Publishing Limited.

Burton, J., Holtom, B., Sablynski, C., Mitchell, T., & Lee, T. (2010). The buffering effects of job embeddedness on negative shocks. *Journal of Vocational Behavior, 76,* 42–51.

Business Insider, 18 of the Best Perks at Top Employers (2013).

Cable, D., & Parsons, C. (1999). Establishing person-organization fit during organizational entry. Paper presented at the Annual Meetings of the Academy of Management, Chicago, USA.

Combs, J., Liu, Y., Hall, A., & Ketchen, D. (2006). How much do high-performance work practices matter? A meta-analysis of their effects on organizational performance. *Personnel Psychology, 59,* 501–528.

Crossley, C. D., Bennett, R. J., Jex, S. M., & Burnfield, J. L. (2007). Development of a global measure of job embeddedness and integration into a traditional model of voluntary turnover. *Journal of Applied Psychology, 92*(4), 1031.

Eagly, A. H., & Wood, W. (1991). Explaining sex differences in social behavior: A meta-analytic perspective. *Personality and Social Psychology Bulletin, 17,* 306–315.

Erdogan, B., & Bauer, T. N. (2005). When do proactive individuals feel successful in their careers? The role of person-job and person-organization fit. *Personnel Psychology, 58,* 859–891.

Feeley, T. H. (2000). Testing a communication network model of employee turnover based on centrality. *Journal of Applied Communication Research, 28,* 262–277.

Feeley, T. H., & Barnett, G. A. (1997). Predicting employee turnover from communication networks. *Human Communication Research, 23,* 370–387.

Feeley, T. H., Hwang, J., & Barnett, G. A. (2008). Predicting employee turnover from friendship networks. *Journal of Applied Communication Research, 36,* 56–73.

Feldman, D., & Ng, T. (2007). Careers: Mobility, embeddedness, and success. *Journal of Management, 33,* 350–377.

Feldman, D., Ng, T., & Vogel, R. (2012). Off-the-job embeddedness: A reconceptualization and agenda for future research. *Research in Personnel and Human Resources Management, 31,* 209–251.

Felps, W., Mitchell, T., Hekman, D., Lee, T., Harman, W., & Holtom, B. (2009). Turnover contagion: How coworkers job embeddedness and coworkers job search behaviors influence quitting. *Academy of Management Journal, 52,* 545–561.

Feintzeig, R. (2017). When your employer plans your baby shower. *Wall Street Journal.*

Gardner, T. M., Wright, P. M., & Moynihan, L. M. (2011). The impact of motivation, empowerment, and skill enhancing practices on aggregate voluntary turnover: The mediating effect of collective affective commitment. *Personnel Psychology, 64,* 315–350.

Giosan, C., Holtom, B., & Watson, M. (2005). Antecedents of job embeddedness: The role of individual, organizational and market factors. *Revista De Psihologie Organizationala, 5,* 31–44.

Granovetter, M. (1973). The strength of weak ties. *American Journal of Sociology, 78,* 1360–1380.

Granovetter, M. (1985). Economic action and social structure: The problems of embeddedness. *American Journal of Sociology, 91,* 481–510.

Griffeth, R. W., Hom, P. W., & Gaertner, S. (2000). A meta-analysis of antecedents and correlates of employee turnover: Update, moderator tests, and research implications for the next millennium. *Journal of Management, 26,* 463–488.

Halbesleben, J. R. B., & Bowler, W. M. (2007). Emotional exhaustion and job performance: The mediating role of motivation. *Journal of Applied Psychology, 91,* 93–106.

Halbesleben, J. R. B., Neveu, J. P., Paustian-Underdahl, S. C., & Westman, M. (2014). Getting to the "COR": Understanding the role of resources in conservation of resources theory. *Journal of Management, 40,* 1334–1364.

Halbesleben, J. R., & Wheeler, A. R. (2015). To invest or not? The role of coworker support and trust in daily reciprocal gain spirals of helping behavior. *Journal of Management, 41*(6), 1628–1650.

Hobfoll, S. E. (2001). The influence of culture, community, and the nested self in the stress process: Advancing conservation of resources theory. *Applied Psychology: An International Review, 50,* 337–370.

Hobfoll, S. E. (2002). Social and psychological resources and adaptation. *Review of General Psychology, 6,* 307–324.

Holtom, B. C., Mitchell, T. R., & Lee, T. W. (2006). Increasing human and social capital by applying job embeddedness theory. *Organizational Dynamics, 35,* 316–331.

Holtom, B., Tidd, S., Mitchell, T., & Lee, T. (2013). Temporal dependency in the prediction of newcomer turnover. *Human Relations, 66,* 1337–1352.

Hom, P. W., Mitchell, T. R., Lee, T. W., & Griffeth, R. W. (2012). Reviewing employee turnover: Focusing on proximal withdrawal states and an expanded criterion. *Psychological Bulletin, 138,* 831–858.

Hom, P. W., Tsui, A., S., Wu, J. B., Lee, T., Zhang, Y., Fu, P. P., Li., L. (2009). Explaining employment relationship with social exchange and job embeddedness. *Journal of Applied Psychology, 94,* 277–297.

Hom, P. W., & Xiao, Z. (2011). Embedding social capital: How guanxi ties reinforce Chinese employees' retention. *Organizational Behavior and Human Decision Processes, 116,* 188–202.

Jiang, K., Liu, D., McKay, P., Lee, T., & Mitchell, T. (2012). When and how is job embeddedness predictive of turnover? A meta-analytic investigation. *Journal of Applied Psychology, 97,* 1077–1096.

Kiazad, K., Holtom, B., Newman, A., & Hom, P. (2015). Job embeddedness: An integrative review and research agenda. *Journal of Applied Psychology, 100,* 641–659.

Krackhardt, D., & Porter, L. (1986). The snowball effect: Turnover embedded in communication networks. *Journal of Applied Psychology, 71,* 50–55.

Kristof, A. (1996). Person-organization fit: An integrative review of its conceptualizations, measurement, and implications. *Personnel Psychology, 49,* 1–49.

Lanaj, K., Chang, C. H., & Johnson, R. E. (2012). Regulatory focus and work-related outcomes: A meta-analysis. *Psychological Bulletin, 138,* 998–1034.

Lazarova, M., Westman, M., & Shaffer, M. A. (2010). Elucidating the positive side of the work-family interface on international assignments: A model of expatriate work and family performance. *Academy of Management Review, 35,* 93–117.

Lee, K., & Allen, N. J. (2002). Organizational citizenship behaviour and workplace deviance: The role of affect and cognitions. *Journal of Applied Psychology, 87,* 131–142.

Lee, T., Burch, T., & Mitchell, T. (2014). The story of why we stay: A review of job embeddedness. *Annual Review of Organizational Psychology and Organizational Behavior, 1,* 199–216.

Lee, T. W., & Mitchell, T. R. (1994). An alternative approach: The unfolding model of voluntary employee turnover. *Academy of Management Review, 19*(1), 51–89.

Lee, T., Mitchell, T., Sablynski, C., Burton, J., & Holtom, B. (2004). The effects of job embeddedness on organizational citizenship, job performance, volitional absences, and voluntary turnover. *Academy of Management Journal, 47,* 711–722.

Lepak, D. P., Liao, H., Chung, Y., & Harden, E. E. (2006). A conceptual review of human resource management systems in strategic human resource management research. In J. J. Martocchio (Ed.), *Research in personnel and human resources management* (Vol. 25, pp. 217–271).

Lin, N. (2001). *Social capital: A theory of structure and action.* London and New York: Cambridge University Press.

Maertz, C. P., & Griffeth, R. W. (2004). Eight motivational forces and voluntary turnover: A theoretical synthesis with implications for research. *Journal of Management, 30,* 667–683.

Maertz, C. P., Stevens, M. J., & Campion, M. A. (2003). A turnover model for the Mexican maquiladoras. *Journal of Vocational Behavior, 63,* 111–135.

Marsden, P. V., Kalleberg, A. L., & Cook, C. R. (1993). Gender differences in organizational commitment. *Work and Occupations, 20,* 368–390.

Mehra, A., Kilduff, M., & Brass, D. (2001). The social networks of high and low self-monitors: Implications for workplace performance. *Administrative Science Quarterly, 46,* 121–146.

Mitchell, T., Holtom, B., Lee, T., Sablynski, C., & Erez, M. (2001). Why people stay: Using job embeddedness to predict voluntary turnover. *Academy of Management Journal, 44,* 1102–1121.

Mitchell, T. R., & Lee, T. W. (2001). The unfolding model of voluntary turnover and job embeddedness: Foundations for a comprehensive theory of attachment. *Research in Organizational Behavior, 23,* 189–246.

Mobley, W. (1977). Intermediate linkages in the relationship between job satisfaction and employee turnover. *Journal of Applied Psychology, 62,* 237–240.

Moran, P. (2005). Structural versus relational embeddedness: Social capital and managerial performance. *Strategic Management Journal, 26*(12), 1129–1151.

Mossholder, K. W., Settoon, R. P., & Henagan, S. C. (2005). A relational perspective on turnover: Examining structural, attitudinal, and behavioral predictors. *Academy of Management Journal, 48,* 607–618.

Motowidlo, S. J., Borman, W. C., & Schmit, M. J. (1997). A theory of individual differences in task and contextual performance. *Human Performance, 10,* 71–83.

Ng, T., & Feldman, D. (2007). Organizational embeddedness and occupational embeddedness across career stages. *Journal of Vocational Behavior, 65,* 336–351.

Ng, T., & Feldman, D. (2009). Occupational embeddedness and job performance. *Journal of Organizational Behavior, 30,* 863–891.

Ng, T., & Feldman, D. (2012). Employee voice behavior: A meta-analytic test of the conservation of resources framework. *Journal of Organizational Behavior, 33,* 216–234.

Ng, T., & Feldman, D. (2013). Changes in perceived supervisor embeddedness: Effects on employees' embeddedness, organizational trust, and voice behavior. *Personnel Psychology, 66,* 645–685.

Ng, T., & Feldman, D. (2014). Community embeddedness and work outcomes: The mediating role of organizational embeddedness. *Human Relations, 67,* 71–103.

Oyserman, D., Coon, H. M., & Kemmelmeier, M. (2002). Rethinking individualism and collectivism: Evaluation of theoretical assumptions and meta-analyses.

Perry-Smith, J. E., & Blum, T. C. (2000). Work-family human resource bundles and perceived organizational performance. *Academy of Management Journal, 43,* 1107–1117.

Podsakoff, N. P., Whiting, S. W., Podsakoff, P. M., & Blume, B. D. (2009). Individual- and organizational-level consequences of organizational citizenship behaviors: A meta-analysis. *Journal of Applied Psychology, 94,* 122–141.

Ramesh, A., & Gelfand, M. (2010). Will they stay or will they go? The role of job embeddedness in predicting turnover in individualistic and collectivistic cultures. *Journal of Applied Psychology, 95,* 807–823.

Rioux, S. M., & Penner, L. A. (2001). The causes of organizational citizenship behavior: A motivational analysis. *Journal of Applied Psychology, 86,* 1306–1314.

Rodan, S. (2010). Structural holes and managerial performance: Identifying the underlying mechanisms. *Social Networks, 32*(3), 168–179.

Rotundo, M., & Sackett, P. (2002). The relative importance of task, citizenship, and counterproductive performance to global ratings of job performance: A policy capturing approach. *Journal of Applied Psychology, 87,* 66–80.

Rusbult, C., & Farrell, D. (1983). A longitudinal test of the investment model: The impact on job satisfaction, job commitment, and turnover of variations in rewards, costs, alternatives, and investments. *Journal of Applied Psychology, 68,* 429–438.

Salamin, A., & Hom, P. W. (2005). In search of the elusive u-shaped performance–turnover relationship: Are high performing Swiss bankers more liable to quit? *Journal of Applied Psychology, 90,* 1204–1216.

Schneider, B. (1987). The people make the place. *Personnel Psychology, 40,* 437–454.

Shah, P. P. (2000). Network destruction: The structural implications of downsizing. *Academy of Management Journal, 43,* 101–112.

Shaw, J. D., Delery, J. E., Jenkins, G. D., & Gupta, N. (1998). An organization-level analysis of voluntary and involuntary turnover. *Academy of Management Journal, 41,* 511–525.

Slavin, A. (2015). 4 Ways to increase retention rates among millennial employees, Inc.

Sparrowe, R., Liden, R., Wayne, S., & Kraimer, M. (2001). Social networks and the performance of individuals and groups. *Academy of Management Journal, 44,* 316–325.

Spector, P. E., Fox, S., Penney, L. M., Bruursema, K., Goh, A., & Kessler, S. (2006). The dimensionality of counter productivity: Are all counterproductive behaviors created equal? *Journal of Vocational Behavior, 68,* 446–460.

Taylor, B. (2016). How one fast-food chain keeps its turnover rates absurdly low. *Harvard Business Review.*

Trevor, C. O., & Nyberg, A. J. (2008). Keeping your headcount when all about you are losing theirs: Downsizing, voluntary turnover rates, and the moderating role of HR practices. *Academy of Management Journal, 51,* 259–276.

Uzzi, B. (1996). The sources and consequences of embeddedness for the economic performance of organizations: The network effect. *American Sociological Review*, 674–698.

Uzzi, B. (1997). Social structure and competition in interfirm networks: The paradox of embeddedness. *Administrative Science Quarterly, 42,* 33–67.

Van der Hoop, J. (2016). 10 examples of innovative HR practices and policies that amplify success, *TalentSorter.*

Wheeler, A. R., Gallagher, V. C., Brouer, R. L., & Sablynski, C. J. (2007). When person-organization (mis) fit and (dis) satisfaction lead to turnover: The moderating role of perceived job mobility. *Journal of Managerial Psychology, 22,* 203–219.

Wheeler, A. R., Harris, K. J., & Sablynski, C. J. (2012). How do employees invest abundant resources? The mediating role of work effort in the job-embeddedness/job-performance relationship. *Journal of Applied Social Psychology, 42,* 244–266.
Wrzesniewski, A., & Dutton, J. E. (2001). Crafting a job: Re-envisioning employees as active crafters of their work. *Academy of Management Review, 26,* 179–201.

Brooks C. Holtom (PhD) is a Professor of Management at the McDonough School of Business at Georgetown University (Washington, DC, USA). His research focuses on how organizations acquire, develop and retain human and social capital. This research appears in the top journals in management (Academy of Management Journal, Journal of Applied Psychology, International Journal of Human Resource Management and others) and has high impact (e.g., h-index = 26, i-10 index = 33). He received the Human Resource Management Scholarly Achievement Award in 2013 from the Academy of Management and has twice received the Professor of the Year award for the Georgetown University Executive Masters of Leadership Program. He has performed research in or served as a consultant to many organizations including Bayer, Booz Allen Hamilton, Capital One, Citibank, International Monetary Fund, KPMG, Microsoft, Nordstrom, Rio Tinto, Rolls Royce, Sprint, United States Air Force, U.S. Chamber of Commerce, and the World Bank.

Tiffany Darabi is a PhD candidate in Organizational Behavior at Cornell University, USA. She previously worked as a research assistant at the McDonough School of Business at Georgetown University and the Ross School of Business at the University of Michigan. Her research focuses on how individuals engage in meaningful work, how social impact organizations sustain their missions, and how corporations engage in social action. Prior to her academic career, she spent nearly a decade and a half working for and consulting with mission-driven organizations in the international development sector on developing management systems and effective organizational practices. She holds a BA in International Relations from Johns Hopkins University.

Chapter 6
Job Demands-Resources, Person-Job Fit and the Impact on Turnover Intention: Similar Across Professional and Administrative Job-Types?

Leon T. de Beer, Salomé Elizabeth Scholtz and Johanna Christina Rothmann

Abstract The chapter investigated the differences between professional and administrative occupation groups regarding the role workplace psychological factors play in retention. The sample comprised 745 participants (358 from professional occupations and 387 administrative professions). Multi-group structural equation modelling methods were applied. The results showed that all of the correlational relationships were in the expected directions. With regards to the administrative group, overload and emotional load as well as person-job fit and career opportunities were stronger in relation to retention than in the professional group. Whereas communication was also significantly related to retention in the professional group but not in the administrative group. Lastly, similarities between the two groups were found with regards to remuneration as indicator of lower turnover intention, although of less importance compared to other motivational variables. This study indicates the importance of considering the qualitative differences in occupational groups when planning aspects such as retention strategies.

Keywords Retention · Turnover intention · Turnover · Administrative job
Professional job · Job demands-resources

Introduction

This chapter investigates differences between professional and administrative occupational groups regarding the role of psychological factors in employee retention (i.e. job demands, job resources and person-job fit perception). A brief overview of retention, the defining characteristics of professional and administrative jobs as well as data analysis and discussion are presented. This topic is important as the ability

L. T. de Beer (✉) · S. E. Scholtz · J. C. Rothmann
WorkWell Research Unit, North-West University, Potchefstroom, South Africa
e-mail: DeBeer.Leon@nwu.ac.za

M. Coetzee et al. (eds.), *Psychology of Retention*,
https://doi.org/10.1007/978-3-319-98920-4_6

Professional and Administrative Occupations

Muir and Li (2014) highlight the importance of considering job level when discussing retention, as psychological contracts differ across job levels and each level values different company features. Psychological contracts are seen as fair play, obligations, and rights employees believe should be provided to them by the employer in return for work (Grobler 2014). Tung (2016) as well as Zheng and Lamond (2010) supports the importance of job level consideration by also linking psychological contracts with employee turnover intention. Possible differences between professional and administrative job levels were therefore investigated as personnel in upper levels of an organization experience work that is "qualitatively different from work on other organizational levels" (Hambrick et al. 2005, p. 474). A comparison between professional occupations and administrative occupations, as defined by the Office of National Statistics (2010), highlights this difference. A professional occupation is a person, with a degree or equivalent qualification (frequently postgraduate degrees) who has experience and extensive knowledge in engineering, natural sciences, humanities as well as social and human sciences (Office of National Statistics 2010). The Office of National Statistics (2010) refers to persons in professional occupations as those that are concerned with applying their theoretical knowledge, developing or advancing this knowledge through research as well as teaching their knowledge to others. This professional occupation group is classified as a major group under the Standard Occupational Classification and includes the following sub-major groups each with its own minor group and unit groups (i.e. specific job indication) namely; Health Profession (e.g. therapy, nursing and health professionals with jobs such as psychologist, dietician etc.), science, research, engineering and technology profession (e.g. natural, chemical and humanities/social sciences with jobs such as chemist, geologist, historian, scientist, structural and power engineer etc.), teaching and educational profession (e.g. higher, secondary or special needs teaching professionals, includes jobs such as lecturer, teacher etc.), business media and public service professionals (e.g. legal, business, welfare, librarians, quality regulators, media and architect professionals with jobs such as advocate, coroner, accountants etc.) (Office of National Statistics 2010). The administrative and secretarial occupations are referred to as occupations wherein the person with standard, general or vocational training conducts client-oriented administrative duties, clerical secretarial work and general administrative work (Office of National Statistics 2010). Administrative occupations consist of two sub-major groups; administrative occupations and secretarial and related occupations (Office of National Statistics 2010). According to Office of National Statistics (2010) administrative occupations include the following minor groups with related unit groups: Other administrative occupations (e.g. sales administrators, other administrative occupations n.e.c.), administrative occupations: Records (e.g. library clerks and assistants, stock control clerks and assistants, transport and distribution clerks and assistants etc.), office managers and supervisors (e.g. office managers and supervisors), administrative occupations:

Finance (Credit controllers, Finance officers, Bank and post office clerks etc.), administrative occupations: Government and related organizations (e.g. national or local government and Officers of non-governmental organizations) (Office of National Statistics 2010). Secretarial and related occupations consist of the following minor groups with related unit groups; Secretarial and related occupations (e.g. personal assistants and other secretaries, school secretaries, receptionists, typists and related keyboard occupations etc.). Typical work-related tasks for persons in this occupation include;

> retrieving, updating, classifying and distributing documents, correspondence and other records held electronically and in storage files; typing, word-processing and otherwise preparing documents; operating other office and business machinery; receiving and directing telephone calls to an organisation; and routing information through organisations (Office of National Statistics 2010, p. 137).

The Job Demands-Resources Model

Due to the burden of employee turnover on organizations (Holtom et al. 2008; Ton and Huckman 2008), scholars have attempted to determine work characteristics in organizations that may influence an employee's intention to stay in their job (Cho and Song 2017). Concurrently a study by Knudsen et al. (2009) found evidence of turnover intention being influenced by job demands and job resources in upper-level employees in organizations. According to Schaufeli and Bakker (2004), turnover intention results from a job that is characterized by high job demands and low job resources, two aspects that form the base of the Job demands resource model. The JD-R model (Job demands-resources model) or JD-R theory as referred to in more recent studies (Bakker and Demerouti 2008, 2013), is one of the most influential occupational stress models (Schaufeli and Taris 2014), and posits that employee motivation and well-being is affected as the result of the interaction between two categories of workplace characteristics; overt job demands (negative) and job resources (positive) (Bakker and Demerouti 2007; Bickerton et al. 2015; Schaufeli and Taris 2014). Job demands refer to physical and psychological demands that are placed on the individual by their job, for example workplace experiences such as ambiguity and time pressure which can cause health impairment and further lead to negative job and health outcomes (Bakker and Demerouti 2007; Bickerton et al. 2015). Contrastingly, job resources are can be used to minimize job demands, examples being: peer support, autonomy and career opportunities which are aspects that promote positive job and personal outcomes via a motivational process (Bakker and Demerouti 2007; Bickerton et al. 2015; Urien et al. 2017). Dysvik and Kuvaas (2013) found that turnover is influenced by perceived autonomy whereas Jung (2014), found that turnover is negatively associated with goal setting. Additionally, Ertas (2015) found that turnover intention decreased in jobs that consisted of professional development, job satisfaction, creativity, promotion, pay satisfaction and having a good work group.

The JD-R model postulates that high levels of job resources can increase good outcomes through a motivational process whilst low levels of job resources in combination with high job demands can result in draining the employee's energy through stress (Hu et al. 2011; Urien et al. 2017). However, it is important to note that the JD-R model does not link specific job demands with specific job resources instead the model assumes an overall synthesis of job demands with a similar indicator of job resources (Bakker et al. 2003; Hu et al. 2011). Thus, employee wellbeing and health may be influenced by any job demand and any job resource (Schaufeli and Taris 2014). The JD-R model also assumes two moderating effects; *firstly*, the model assumes that challenging job demands in combination with optimal job resources leads to increased employee work engagement (Bakker et al. 2014). Work engagement refers to employee behaviour that includes absorption, vigour and dedication due to a fulfilling and positive work-related state of mind (Schaufeli et al. 2002) and is strongly related to work commitment and retention (Bakker and Demerouti 2007; De Beer et al. 2012). The *second* assumption places emphasis on the role that job resources play in minimizing the debilitating effects of high job demands on employee well-being (Bakker and Demerouti 2007). According to Jang et al. (2015) employee well-being has been explained by the JD-R model in various organizational contexts such as health, education, manufacturing and human services (Bakker et al. 2003; Delp et al. 2010; Hakanen et al. 2005; Knudsen et al. 2009; Korunka et al. 2009).

The inclusiveness and flexibility of the JD-R model makes it the model of choice when conducting research across various work settings (Schaufeli and Taris 2014). Additionally, the overall synthesis of job demands and job resources also supports the use of this model for investigating employee retention for the aim of this chapter.

Research Method

Approach

A quantitative research method, i.e. a survey within a cross-sectional research design, was used. Data were collected with a non-probability convenience sampling method. Convenience sampling is used when the sample is easily accessible to the researcher for data collection (Muijs 2011). This approach allows for the investigation of correlational data at one-point in time, by means of the most popular form of data collection in quantitative studies; a standardized questionnaire (Muijs 2011).

Participants

A database of 745 participants was extracted for the purposes of this study. The professional group consisted of 358 employees [Male = 190; Female = 168; Black African = 48; White = 168; Coloured = 10; Indian = 12; Other = 1] and the administrative group consisted of 387 employees [Male = 91; Female = 296; Black African = 64; White = 139; Coloured = 30; Indian = 30; Other = 1]. Table 6.2 presents a breakdown of the number of participants from the occupational groups' sub-categories.

Table 6.2 Participant groups

Occupational group and sub-categories	Number
Professional occupations	*358*
Architects, town planners and surveyors	12
Business, research and administrative professionals	72
Conservation and environment professionals	3
Engineering professionals	24
Health professionals	12
Information technology and telecommunications professionals	79
Legal professionals	11
Librarians and related professionals	2
Media professionals	11
Natural and social science professionals	21
Nursing and midwifery professionals	63
Quality and regulatory professionals	24
Research and development managers	3
Teaching and educational professionals	16
Therapy professionals	1
Welfare professionals	4
Administrative and secretarial occupations	*387*
Administrative occupations: Finance	117
Administrative occupations: Government and related organizations	10
Administrative occupations: Office managers and supervisors	29
Administrative occupations: Records	86
Other administrative occupations	102
Secretarial and related occupations	43

Measures

Scales from the South African Employee Health and Wellness Survey (SAEHWS; Rothmann and Rothmann 2007) were used. *Emotional load* ($\alpha = 0.71$) by four items, e.g. 'Do you have to deal with difficult people at work?'; *Overload*: ($\alpha = 0.79$) by four items, e.g. 'Do you have too much work to do?'; *Supervisor support*: ($\alpha = 0.84$) by three items e.g. 'Can you count on your direct supervisor when you come across difficulties in your work?'; *Colleague support*: ($\alpha = 0.74$) by three items, e.g. 'Can you count on your colleagues when you come across difficulties in your work?'; *Role clarity*: ($\alpha = 0.70$) by three items, e.g. 'Do you know exactly what your responsibilities are?'; *Communication*: ($\alpha = 0.81$) by three items, e.g. 'Is it clear to you whom you should address within the department/organization for specific problems?'; *Remuneration*: ($\alpha = 0.75$) by three items, e.g. 'Do you think you are paid enough for the work that you do?'; All of the above job demands and job resources were measured on four-point Likert scales ranging from Never (1) to Always (4). *Person-job fit*: ($\alpha = 0.89$) by four items was measured with a six-point Likert scale ranging from Strongly disagree (1) to Strongly agree (6), e.g. 'The requirements of my job match my specific talents and skills.'; Similarly, *Turnover intention*: ($\alpha = 0.91$) by three items, e.g. 'I am actively seeking a job elsewhere.' Employees were asked to indicate their profession as part of the biographical section.

Analysis

In terms of reliability the Cronbach's alpha coefficient was considered for each of the scales. Then, multi-group latent variable modelling methods were used to create a research model. Estimation was conducted with the Robust Maximum Likelihood estimator to guard against parameter bias due to potential non-normality of the data. To consider the fit of the model, the traditional Comparative Fit Index (CFI), Tucker-Lewis index (TLI) and Root mean squared error of approximation (RMSEA) were used. Given sufficient model fit the correlations between the variables and also the regressions were considered to answer the research questions. Specifically, the significance, direction and size of the standardised beta coefficients in the groups would be used to investigate similarity.

Results

Model Fit

The multi-group structural equation model executed successfully and presented the following fit statistics for the measurement model: $\chi^2 = 1116.59$ [Contribution from each group: Professional = 536.481 and Administrative = 580.113], df = 513, CFI = 0.92, TLI = 0.90 and RMSEA = 0.05. The CFI, TLI and RMSEA were all acceptable (Van de Schoot et al. 2012).

Correlations

Table 6.3 presents the correlation tables for the variables in each other groups from the structural equation modelling. The correlation table of both groups show that all of the relationships are in the expected directions as the job resources and person-job fit were negatively correlated with turnover intention. Therefore, there were no counter-intuitive signs in any of the significant relationships. Noteworthy, is that the correlation between overload and emotional load is higher in the Administrative occupation group ($r = 0.73$; large effect) compared to the Professional group ($r = 0.58$; large effect). Furthermore, the relationship between turnover intention with person-job fit and career opportunities was also higher in the administrative group (large effects) compared to the professional group (medium effects).

Path Analysis

The structural path model showed the following adequate fit indices: $\chi^2 = 1422.13$ [Contribution from each group: Professional = 681.22 and Administrative = 740.91], df = 705, CFI = 0.92, TLI = 0.90 and RMSEA = 0.05. The structural model revealed interesting results (see Table 6.4). Specifically, emotional load was shown to not significantly contribute to explained variance of turnover intention in the professional occupations, but had a significant positive relationship in the administrative group ($\beta = 0.66$, SE = 0.26; $p = 0.012$). Interestingly, overload did not have a significant regression to turnover intention in either of the groups ($ps > 0.05$), even though approaching significance in the administrative group ($p = 0.065$). In terms of the job resources, communication had a significant negative relationship to turnover intention in the professional group, even though being a borderline case ($\beta = -0.52$, SE = 0.26; $p = 0.048$)—but was not significant in the administrative group ($p = 0.637$). Remuneration was significantly negative related to turnover in both groups. Furthermore, person-job fit was also significantly negatively related to turnover intention in both groups, with a higher value in the professional group ($\beta = -0.39$, SE = 0.09; $p < 0.001$) compared to the administrative group ($\beta = -0.25$, SE = 0.09; $p = 0.005$).

Table 6.3 Correlations

Variables	1	2	3	4	5	6	7	8.	9	10
Group 1: Professional occupations (n = 358)										
1. Emotional load	1.00									
2. Overload	0.58	1.00								
3. Colleague support	−0.26	−0.07	1.00							
4. Supervisor support	−0.38	−0.10	0.47	1.00						
5. Role clarity	−0.40	−0.09	0.59	0.69	1.00					
6. Communication	−0.29	0.00	0.51	0.59	0.84	1.00				
7. Remuneration	−0.38	−0.23	0.18	0.26	0.21	0.22	1.00			
8. Career opportunities	−0.29	−0.04	0.36	0.39	0.42	0.54	0.31	1.00		
9. Person-job fit	−0.31	−0.03	0.24	0.29	0.45	0.33	0.16	0.36	1.00	
10. Turnover intention	0.41	0.14	−0.29	−0.39	−0.33	−0.41	−0.41	−0.38	−0.47	1.00
Group 2: Administrative occupations (n = 387)										
1. Emotional load	1.00									
2. Overload	0.73	1.00								
3. Colleague support	−0.43	−0.24	1.00							
4. Supervisor support	−0.52	−0.27	0.36	1.00						
5. Role clarity	−0.50	−0.07	0.35	0.73	1.00					
6. Communication	−0.48	−0.16	0.40	0.68	0.72	1.00				
7. Remuneration	−0.29	−0.11	0.17	0.30	0.25	0.36	1.00			
8. Career opportunities	−0.40	−0.12	0.22	0.38	0.36	0.48	0.53	1.00		
9. Person − job fit	−0.24	−0.02	0.23	0.31	0.43	0.39	0.32	0.50	1.00	
10. Turnover intention	0.46	0.10	−0.23	−0.37	−0.42	−0.38	−0.41	−0.51	−0.47	1.00

Discussion

This chapter explored the differences between professional and administrative occupations based on certain workplace psychological factors in employee retention in the context of the JD-R model. Job resources and person-job fit were found to negatively relate with turnover intention in both professional and administrative occupations, in line with expectations (see Schaufeli and Taris 2014). Additionally, four noteworthy differences between the two occupations were noted.

Firstly, the correlational relationships of overload and emotional load with turnover intention were higher in the administrative group than in the professional group. Role overload is often due to the scarcity of certain resources and can lead to burnout (Yip et al. 2008), whereas emotional load occurs when a person feels overwhelmed by work demands (Khan 2011) and is also implicit in the formation of burnout (Grandey 2003). Furthermore, in line with the general trend of our results, Khan (2011) found that secretarial jobs (administrative occupation) experience their work as more demanding than that of superiors and can only be conducted effectively by possessing the necessary abilities, skills and knowledge regarding their job. Thereby also emphasising the importance of person-job fit. In terms of the regression model, emotional load explained a significant amount of variance in turnover intention. The interaction between emotional exhaustion and

Table 6.4 Regression results for the multi-group research model

Structural path	Professional			Administrative		
	β	SE	p	β	SE	p
Emotional load → Turnover intention	0.19	0.12	0.123	0.66*	0.26	0.012
Overload → Turnover intention	0.02	0.11	0.817	0.42	0.23	0.065
Colleague support → Turnover intention	−0.11	0.08	0.151	0.03	0.07	0.654
Supervisor support → Turnover intention	−0.22	0.14	0.124	−0.08	0.15	0.588
Role clarity → Turnover intention	0.61	0.35	0.083	0.07	0.26	0.782
Communication → Turnover intention	−0.52*	0.26	0.048	0.07	0.14	0.637
Remuneration → Turnover intention	−0.22*	0.08	0.004	−0.14*	0.07	0.044
Career opportunities → Turnover intention	0.04	0.09	0.687	−0.13	0.10	0.213
Person-job fit → Turnover intention	−0.39*	0.09	0.001	−0.25*	0.09	0.005

Notes β = Standardised beta coefficient; SE = Standard error; *p* = Two-tailed statistical significance; * = significant

work environment characteristics are key role players in the JD-R model (Alarcon 2011; Bakker and Demerouti 2007) and may account for differences between these occupational groups. It is not hard to imagine that administrative occupations may face difficult clients, colleagues and superiors in the everyday workings of the organization—as they form an integral support function often being the first point of contact with clients and internal managers/supervisors—increasing their emotional load.

Secondly, even though not significant in the structural model, the correlations between career opportunities and person-job fit in relation to turnover intention were found to be higher in the administrative occupation group. Career opportunities provided by organizations are seen as a highly valued career resource (Lu et al. 2016) and can greatly impact an employee's career decisions (Kraimer et al. 2011; Weng and McElroy 2012; Weng et al. 2010). Similarly, Salamin and Hom (2005) found promotions and increased salary to be negatively associated with turnover. Lu et al. (2016) state that employees who are highly employable may experience lower turnover intention as they believe that the career opportunities made available to them is in line with their future career goals, whereas their turnover will result in loss of these career goals. In terms of person-job fit, persons in administrative occupations have shown lower job fit. For example, Truss et al. (2013) found that secretaries' role content was experienced by the majority as negative and that less than 30% experienced their job as utilizing their full set of skills. This is in line with person-job fit; the extent to which a job's requirements match the individual's abilities. Additionally, Truss et al. (2013) also state that those working in the secretarial occupation have a strong desire for a change of status and their contribution to the organization goals, an aspect that has not changed sufficiently in the last decade, which can be seen as the second component of person job fit namely; needs-supply (for example psychological desires and the need for recognition or decision-making latitude [Cable and DeRue 2002; Muchinsky and Monahan 1987]).

Thirdly, the regression model showed that communication explained a significant amount of variance in turnover intention in the professional group, but was not in the administrative group. Bakker et al. (2005) explained that job resources such as social interaction, supervisor relationship and feedback combats burnout as well as increases employee retention (Kim and Stoner 2008). Positive communication can also reduce job and role stress in professional occupations (Kim and Lee 2009). Similar findings have also been shown for administrative occupations (Nichols et al. 2016).

Lastly, the finding in the regression model that remuneration is important in retaining employees for both occupational groups is well established in literature (Akeyo and Wezel 2017; Brien et al. 2017; Larkin et al. 2016; Nawaz and Pangil 2016; Yang 2014). However, it is important to note that despite the role remuneration plays in retention, literature is also clear that it is not the sole motivator for turnover intention, e.g. Singh and Loncar (2010) found that job satisfaction for example was more crucial in retaining nurses. This is in line with the motivational theory of Herzberg (1966), indicating remuneration as a hygiene factor which becomes more important as a consideration for employees when it becomes problematic or absent as opposed to motivational factors when remuneration is present. In the current findings, it also had the lowest importance in the structural model of all the significant results.

Conclusion and Implications for Retention

This study has highlighted differences between work environment characteristics in different occupational groups with regards to turnover intention. Therefore, it is important to consider that different occupations have different needs with regard to support with job demands and job resources that impact their perceptions regarding turnover intention and thus their ultimate retention. Organizations should proactively investigate the job demands and job resources that are problematic and optimal in departments in order to address them and thereby increasing the likelihood of retaining talent. This can be done by implementing organizational diagnostic surveys which are valid and reliable—preferably with norm groups for the context. Person-job fit was also shown to be important in both occupational groups, not only should recruitment and selection be considered important but recent research has indicated that work engagement precedes person-job fit—and work engagement is most strongly predicted by job resources (De Beer et al. 2016), emphasising their importance. In terms of future studies, it is recommended that further investigation into the differences in other occupational groups be undertaken as it is highly likely that different dynamics could be evident given more complexity and the addition of additional occupational groups.

Summary

In this chapter, the authors provided insight into the dynamics of job demands-resources, person-job fit and turnover intention in administrative and professional occupations. Findings from this study highlight the importance of differences in occupational groups when considering aspects of turnover intention —by addressing the differences in importance of job demands, job resources and person-job fit.

References

Akeyo, M., & Wezel, F. (2017). Influence of remuneration factors on staff turnover in humanitarian sector. *Human Resource and Leadership Journal, 2*(1), 47–63.

Alarcon, G. M. (2011). A meta-analysis of burnout with job demands, resources, and attitudes. *Journal of Vocational Behavior, 79,* 549–562. https://doi.org/10.1016/j.jvb.2011.03.007.

Allen, D. G., & Shanock, L. R. (2013). Perceived organizational support and embeddedness as key mechanisms connecting socialization tactics to commitment and turnover among new employees. *Journal of Organizational Behaviour, 34,* 350–369. https://doi.org/10.1002/job.1805.

Bakker, A. B., & Demerouti, E. (2007). The job demands-resources model: State of the art. *Journal of Managerial Psychology, 22,* 309–328.

Bakker, A. B., & Demerouti, E. (2008). Towards a model of work engagement. *Career Development International, 13*(3), 209–223. https://doi.org/10.1108/13620430810870476.

Bakker, A. B., & Demerouti, E. (2013). La teoría de las demandasy los recursos laborales. *Revista de Psicología del Trabajo y de las Organizaciones, 29*(3), 107–115. https://doi.org/10.5093/tr2013a16.

Bakker, A. B., Demerouti, E., Taris, T. W., Schaufeli, W. B., & Schreurs, P. J. (2003). A multigroup analysis of the job demands-resources model in four home care organizations. *International Journal of Stress Management, 10,* 16–38.

Bakker, A. B., Demerouti, E., & Euwema, M. C. (2005). Job resources buffer the impact of job demands on burnout. *Journal of Occupational Health Psychology, 10*(2), 170–180.

Bakker, A. B., Demerouti, E., & Sanz-Vergel, A. I. (2014). Burnout and work engagement: The JD-R approach. *Annual Review of Organizational Psychology and Organizational Behaviour, 1,* 389–411.

Batt, R., & Valcour, R. M. (2003). Human resources practices as predictors of work-family outcomes and employee turnover. *Industrial Relations, 42,* 189–221.

Bickerton, G. R., Miner, M. H., Dowson, M., & Griffin, B. (2015). Incremental validity of spiritual resources in the job demands-resources model. *Psychology of Religion and Spirituality, 7*(2), 162.

Bidisha, L. D., & Mukulesh, B. (2013). Employee retention: A review of literature. *Journal of Business and Management, 14,* 8–16.

Boswell, W. R., Boudreau, J. W., & Tichy, J. (2005). The relationship between employee job change and job satisfaction: The honeymoon-hangover effect. *Journal of Applied Psychology, 90,* 882–892.

Branch, S. (1998). You hired 'em, but can you keep 'em. *Fortune, 138,* 247–249.

Brien, A., Thomas, N. J., & Brown, E. A. (2017). How hotel employee job-identity impacts the hotel industry: The uncomfortable truth. *Journal of Hospitality and Tourism Management, 31,* 235–243.

Cable, D. M., & DeRue, D. S. (2002). The convergent and discriminant validity of subjective fit perceptions. *Journal of Applied Psychology, 87*(5), 875–884.

Cho, Y. J., & Lewis, G. B. (2012). Turnover intention and turnover behavior implications for retaining federal employees. *Rev Public Person Adm., 32,* 4–23.

Cho, Y. J., & Song, H. J. (2017). Determinants of turnover intention of social workers: Effects of emotional labor and organizational trust. *Public Personnel Management, 46,* 41–65.

Christeen, G. (2015). Retaining professional workers: What makes them stay? *Employee Relations, 37,* 102–121. https://doi.org/10.1108/ER-10-2013-0151.

Das, B. L., & Baruah, M. (2013). Employee retention: A review of literature. *Journal of Business and Management, 14*(2), 8–16.

De Beer, L. T., Rothmann, S., Jr., & Pienaar, J. (2012). A confirmatory investigation of a job demands-resources model using a categorical estimator. *Psychological Reports, 111,* 528–544.

De Beer, L. T., Rothmann, S., Jr., & Mostert, K. (2016). Investigating the bidirectional relationship between person-job fit and work engagement: A three-wave study. *Journal of Personnel Psychology, 15,* 4–14.

Delp, L., Wallace, S., Geiger-Brown, J., & Muntaner, C. (2010). Job stress and job satisfaction: Home care workers in a consumer-directed model of care. *Health Services Research, 45,* 922–940.

Dess, G. G., & Shaw, J. D. (2001). Voluntary turnover, social capital, and organizational performance. *Academy of Management Review, 26*(3), 446–456.

Dupré, K. E., & Day, A. L. (2007). The effects of supportive management and job quality on the turnover intentions and health of military personnel. *Human Resource Management, 46*(2), 185–201.

Dysvik, A., & Kuvaas, B. (2013). Perceived job autonomy and turnover intention: The moderating role of perceived supervisor support. *European Journal of Work & Organizational Psychology, 22,* 563–573.

Edwards, J. R. (1991). Person-job fit: A conceptual integration, literature review, and methodological critique. In C. L. Cooper & I. T. Robertson (Eds.), *International review of industrial and organizational psychology* (Vol. 6, pp. 283–357). New York: Wiley.

Erasmus, B. J., Grobler, A., & Van Niekerk, M. (2015). Employee retention in a higher education institution from an organisational development perspective. *Progressio—South African Journal for Open and Distance Learning Practice, 37*(1), 33–63.

Ertas, N. (2015). Turnover intentions and work motivations of millennial employees in federal service. *Public Personnel Management, 44,* 401–423.

Fitz-enz, J. (1990). Getting and keeping good employees. *In personnel, 67*(8), 25–29.

Ghapanchi, A. H., & Aurum, A. (2011). Antecedents to IT personnel's intentions to leave: A systematic literature review. *Journal of Systems and Software, 84,* 238–249. https://doi.org/10.1016/j.jss.2010.09.022.

Glissmeyer, M., Bishop, J. W., & Fass, R. D. (2008). Role conflict, role ambiguity and intention to quit the organization: The case of law enforcement. *Academy of Management Journal, 40,* 82–111.

Grandey, A. A. (2003). When "The Show Must Go on": Surface acting and deep acting as determinants of emotional exhaustion and peer-rated service delivery. *The Academy of Management Journal, 46,* 86–96.

Grobler, A. (2014). Workplace alternatives—confront, conform, capitulate. *African Journal of Hospitality, Tourism and Leisure, 3*(2), 1–27.

Grobler, A., & Grobler, S. (2016). Intention to quit as precursor of voluntary turnover: Person—organisation fit and the psychological contract—a talent management quandary. *South African Journal of Labour Relations, 40*(2), 55–76.

Gurpreet, R. (2007). Relationship between job satisfaction and turnover intentions: An empirical analysis. *Indian Management Studies Journal, 4*(3), 1521–1531.

Hakanen, J. J., Bakker, A. B., & Demerouti, E. (2005). How dentists cope with their job demands and stay engaged: The moderating role of job resources. *European Journal of Oral Sciences, 113,* 479–487.

Hambrick, D. C., Finkelstein, S., & Mooney, A. C. (2005). Executive job demands: New insights for explaining strategic decisions and leader behaviors. *Academy of Management Review, 30,* 472–491.

Harrington, D., Bean, N., Pintello, D., & Mathews, D. (2001). Job satisfaction and burnout: Predictors of intentions to leave a job in a military setting. *Administration in Social Work, 25*(3), 1–16.

Herrbach, O., Mignonac, K., & Gatignon, A. (2004). Exploring the role of perceived external prestige in manager's turnover intentions. *International Journal of Human Resource Management, 15,* 1390–1408.

Herzberg, F. (1966). *Work and the nature of man.* Cleveland: World Publishing Company.

Holtom, B. C., Mitchell, T. R., Lee, T. W., & Inderrieden, E. J. (2005). Shocks as causes of turnover: What they are and how organizations can manage them. *Human Resource Management, 44,* 337–352.

Holtom, B. C., Mitchell, T. R., Lee, T. W., & Eberly, M. B. (2008). Turnover and retention research: A glance at the past, a closer review of the present, and a venture into the future. *Academy of Management Annals, 2,* 231–274.

Hom, P. W., Mitchell, T. R., Lee, T. W., & Griffeth, R. W. (2012). Reviewing employee turnover: Focusing on proximal withdrawal states and an expanded criterion. *Psychological Bulletin, 138,* 831–858. https://doi.org/10.1037/a0027983.

Hu, Q., Schaufeli, W. B., & Taris, T. W. (2011). The Job Demands-Resources model: An analysis of additive and joint effects of demands and resources. *Journal of Vocational Behavior, 79,* 181–190.

Jang, Y., Lee, A. A., Zadrozny, M., Bae, S. H., Kim, M. T., & Marti, N. C. (2015). Determinants of job satisfaction and turnover intent in home health workers: The role of job demands and resources. *Journal of Applied Gerontology, 36*(1), 56–70.

Jung, C. S. (2014). Why are goals important in the public sector? Exploring the benefits of goal clarity for reducing turnover intention. *Journal of Public Administration Research and Theory, 24,* 209–234.

Kaliprasad, M. (2006). The human factor I: Attracting, retaining, and motivating capable people. *Cost Engineering, 48*(6), 20–26.

Keaveney, S. M., & Nelson, J. E. (1993). Coping with organizational role stress: Intrinsic motivational orientation, perceived role benefits, and psychological withdrawal. *Journal of the Academy of Marketing Science, 21,* 113–124.

Khan, S. (2011). Relationship of job burnout and type A behaviour on psychological health among secretaries. *International Journal of Business and Management, 6,* 31.

Kim, H., & Lee, S. Y. (2009). Supervisory communication, burnout, and turnover intention among social workers in health care settings. *Social Work in Health Care, 48*(4), 364–385.

Kim, H., & Stoner, M. (2008). Burnout and turnover intention among social workers: Effects of role stress, job autonomy and social support. *Administration in Social Work, 32*(3), 5–25.

Knudsen, H. K., Ducharme, L. J., & Roman, P. M. (2009). Turnover intention and emotional exhaustion "at the top": Adapting the job demands-resources model to leaders of addiction treatment organizations. *Journal of Occupational Health Psychology, 14,* 84.

Korunka, C., Kubicek, B., Schaufeli, W. B., & Hoonakker, P. (2009). Work engagement and burnout: Testing the robustness of the job demands-resources model. *The Journal of Positive Psychology, 4,* 243–255.

Kossivi, B., Xu, M., & Kalgora, B. (2016). Study on determining factors of employee retention. *Open Journal of Social Sciences, 4,* 261–268. https://doi.org/10.4236/jss.2016.45029.

Kraimer, M. L., Seibert, S. E., Wayne, S. J., & Liden, R. C. (2011). Antecedents and outcomes of organizational support for development: The critical role of career opportunities. *Journal of Applied Psychology, 96,* 485–500. https://doi.org/10.1037/a0021452.

Kristof-Brown, A. L. (1996). Person-organization fit: An integrative review of its conceptualisations, measurement and implications. *Personnel Psychology, 49,* 1–9. https://doi.org/10.1111/j.1744-6570.1996.tb01790.x.

Larkin, I. M., Brantley-Dias, L., & Lokey-Vega, A. (2016). Job satisfaction, organizational commitment, and turnover intention of online teachers in the K-12 setting. *Online Learning, 20* (3), 26–51.

Loan-Clarke, J., Arnold, J., Coombs, C., Hartley, R., & Bosley, S. (2010). Retention, turnover and return—a longitudinal study of allied health professionals in Britain. *Human Resource Management Journal, 20,* 391–406. https://doi.org/10.1111/j.1748-8583.2010.00140.x.

Lu, C. Q., Sun, J. W., & Du, D. Y. (2016). The relationships between employability, emotional exhaustion, and turnover intention: The moderation of perceived career opportunity. *Journal of Career Development, 43,* 37–51.

Masoga, L. (2013). *The role of personality and organisational climate in employee turnover.* Unpublished Doctoral thesis, University of South Africa, Pretoria.

Mita, M., Aarti, K., & Ravneeta, D. (2014). Study on employee retention and commitment. *International Journal of Advance Research in Computer Science and Management Studies, 2,* 154–164.

Mitiku, M. (2010). *An investigation of the nature of academic staff turnover: The case of Addis Ababa University.* Unpublished MBA thesis, Addis Ababa University, Ethiopia.

Moynihan, D. P., & Landuyt, N. (2008). Explaining turnover intention in state government: Examining the roles of gender, life cycle, and loyalty. *Review of Public Personnel Administration, 28,* 120–143.

Muchinsky, P. M., & Monahan, C. J. (1987). What is person-environment congruence? Supplementary versus complementary models of fit. *Journal of Vocational Behavior, 31*(3), 268–277.

Muijs, D. (2011). *Doing quantitative research in education with SPSS* (2nd ed.). Thousand Oaks, CA: Sage.

Muir, M. R., & Li, L. (2014). *What are the top factors that drive employee retention and are there demographic (gender, generation, ethnicity, geography, etc.) differences in these factors?* Retrieved from http://digitalcommons.ilr.cornell.edu/student/59.

Nawaz, M., & Pangil, F. (2016). The relationship between human resource development factors, career growth and turnover intention: The mediating role of organizational commitment. *Management Science Letters, 6*(2), 157–176.

Newman, S. J., Ye, J., & Leep, C. J. (2014). Workforce turnover at local health departments: nature, characteristics, and implications. *American Journal of Preventive Medicine, 47*(5 suppl 3), S337–S343.

Nichols, H. M., Swanberg, J. E., & Bright, C. L. (2016). How does supervisor support influence turnover intent among frontline hospital workers? The mediating role of affective commitment. *The Health Care Manager, 35*(3), 266–279.

Office for National Statistics. (2010). *Standard occupational classification 2010; Volume 1 Structure and descriptions of unit groups.* Palgrave, Macmillain, Newport.

Pfeffer, J. (2005). Changing mental models: HR's most important task. *Human Resource Management, 44,* 123–128.

Pourshaban, D., Basurto-Davila, R., & Shih, M. (2015). Building and sustaining strong public health agencies: determinants of workforce turnover. *The Journal of Public Health Management and Practice, 21*(6), S80–S90.

Rothmann, J. C. (2017). The cost of not knowing: The importance of employee and workplace risk management. In *Keynote at SIOPSA conference*, Pretoria, South Africa.

Rothmann, J. C., & Rothmann, S. (2007). *The South African employee health and wellness survey: User manual.* Potchefstroom: Afriforte (Pty) Ltd.

Salamin, A., & Hom, P. W. (2005). In search of the elusive U shaped performance-turnover relationship: are high performing Swiss bankers more liable to quit? *Journal of Applied Psychology, 90*(6), 1204–1216.

Schaufeli, W. B., & Bakker, A. B. (2004). Job demands, job resources, and their relation with burnout and engagement: A multi-sample study. *Journal of Organizational Behavior, 25,* 293–315.

Schaufeli, W. B., & Taris, T. W. (2014). A critical review of the Job Demands-Resources Model: Implications for improving work and health. In G. F. Bauer & O. Hämmig (Eds.), *Bridging occupational, organizational and public health* (pp. 43–68). Dordrecht, Netherlands: Springer.

Schaufeli, W. B., Salanova, M., Gonzalez-Roma, V., & Bakker, A. B. (2002). The measurement of engagement and burnout: A two sample confirmatory factor analytic approach. *Journal of Happiness Studies, 3,* 71–92. https://doi.org/10.1023/A:1015630930326.

Scott, D., McMullen, T., & Royal, M. (2012). *Retention of key talent and the role of rewards*. Retrieved from https://www.worldatwork.org/waw/adimLink?id=62016.

Shimp, K. M. (2017). Systematic review of turnover/retention and staff perception of staffing and resource adequacy related to staffing. *Nursing Economics, 35*(5), 239–266.

Singh, P., & Loncar, N. (2010). Pay satisfaction, job satisfaction and turnover intent. *Relations industrielles/industrial relations, 65*, 470–490.

Ton, Z., & Huckman, R. S. (2008). Managing the impact of employee turnover on performance: the role of process conformance. *Organization Science, 19,* 56–68.

Truss, C., Alfes, K., Shantz, A., & Rosewarne, A. (2013). Still in the ghetto? Experiences of secretarial work in the 21st century. *Gender, Work and Organization, 20*(4), 349–363.

Tung, R. L. (2016). New perspectives on human resource management in a global context. *Journal of World Business, 51,* 142–152.

Urien, B., Osca, A., & García-Salmones, L. (2017). Role ambiguity, group cohesion and job satisfaction: A Demands-Resources Model (JD-R) study from Mexico and Spain. *Revista Latinoamericana de Psicología, 49*(2), 137–145.

Van de Schoot, R., Lugtig, P., & Hox, J. (2012). A checklist for testing measurement invariance. *European Journal of Developmental Psychology, 9*, 486–492.

Weng, Q. X., & McElroy, J. C. (2012). Organizational career growth, affective occupational commitment and turnover intentions. *Journal of Vocational Behavior, 80,* 256–265. https://doi.org/10.1016/j.jvb.2012.01.014.

Weng, Q., McElroy, J. C., Morrow, P. C., & Liu, R. (2010). The relationship between career growth and organizational commitment. *Journal of Vocational Behavior, 77,* 391–400. https://doi.org/10.1016/j.jvb.2010.05.003.

Workforce Planning for Wisconsin State Government. (2005). *Employee Retention*. Retrieved from http://workforceplanning.wi.gov/category.asp?linkcatid=15&linkid=18.

Yang, Y. (2014). Effect of gender, compensation on employee turnover in the Chinese hotel industry. *Tourism Tribune, 29*(4), 38–47.

Yip, B., Rowlinson, S., & Siu, O. L. (2008). Coping strategies as moderators in the relationship between role overload and burnout. *Construction Management and Economics, 26*(8), 871–882.

Zheng, C., & Lamond, D. (2010). Organisational determinants of employee turnover for multinational companies in Asia. *Asia Pacific Journal of Management, 27,* 423–443.

Zineldin, M. (2000). Total relationship management (TRM) and total quality management (TQM). *Managerial Auditing Journal, 15*(1/2), 20–28. https://doi.org/10.1108/02686900010304399.

Leon T. de Beer (Ph.D.) is an Associate Professor at the North-West University's WorkWell Research Unit, South Africa. He holds professional registrations as an Industrial Psychologist and also Research Psychologist with the Health Professions Council of South Africa (HPCSA). He has published numerous academic articles—mostly focused on employee work-related well-being and its link to organisational outcomes.

Salomé Elizabeth Scholtz is a Research Assistant at the North-West University's WorkWell Research Unit, South Africa. She holds a Masters degree in Research Psychology and is currently completing her PhD in Psychology at the North-West University.

Johanna Christina (Ina) Rothmann (Ph.D.) is an extra-ordinary Associate Professor at the North-West University's WorkWell Research Unit, South Africa. She is also the Managing Director of Afriforte (Pty) Ltd., the commercial arm of the WorkWell Research Unit, directing, assisting and managing action-research projects within organisations both locally and internationally.

Chapter 7
School Principal Support, and Teachers' Work Engagement and Intention to Leave: The Role of Psychological Need Satisfaction

Sebastiaan Rothmann and Elmari Fouché

Abstract The study reported in this chapter contributes to understanding the retention of teachers by analysing the relationships between perceived school principal support, and teachers' psychological need satisfaction, engagement and intention to leave. A total of 513 secondary school teachers in public schools in South Africa participated in a cross-sectional survey. The School Principal Behaviour Scale, Work-related Basic Need Satisfaction Scale, Work Engagement Scale and Intention to Leave Scale were administered. Principal support was positively related to teachers' psychological need satisfaction and work engagement, and negatively related to intention to leave. Principal support affected work engagement positively and intention to leave negatively via teachers' autonomy satisfaction.

Keywords Engagement · Retention · Intention to leave · Principal Psychological need satisfaction · Self-determination · Manager support

Introduction

The relationships between individuals and their managers are vital drivers for individuals' work engagement (Harter and Adkins 2015) and retention (Gu and Day 2013). This is also true for school principals (in their role as managers) and teachers (Lee and Nie 2014). Studies use intention to leave as an indicator of actual turnover or retention. The reason is that evidence suggests that before actually leaving the job, workers typically make a conscious decision to do so (Coward et al. 1995). Intention to quit is a strong predictor of turnover (Mor Barak et al. 2001), and it is, therefore, legitimate to use it as an outcome variable in retention studies.

S. Rothmann (✉) · E. Fouché
North-West University, Vanderbijlpark, South Africa
e-mail: ian@ianrothmann.com

M. Coetzee et al. (eds.), *Psychology of Retention*,
https://doi.org/10.1007/978-3-319-98920-4_7

Organisational scholars have emphasised the importance of self-determination for engagement of individuals as well as organisational outcomes (Graves and Luciano 2013; Van den Broeck et al. 2008). Self-determination theory (SDT; Deci and Ryan 2008a) can explain how principals' behaviours affect work engagement and retention via autonomous regulation of behaviour. Such effects might occur through identification (attaining a valued personal goal) and integration (expressing one's sense of self). All individuals inherently strive towards developing and actualising their potential. According to the SDT, this is subservient to individuals' ability to satisfy their three basic psychological needs for autonomy, competence, and relatedness (Deci and Ryan 2008a). The self-determination literature acknowledges the role of the manager in affecting psychological need satisfaction and autonomous motivation of individuals (Gagné and Deci 2005). A study by Graves and Luciano (2013) showed how leader-member exchange evokes psychological need satisfaction. Research (Hetland et al. 2011; Kovjanic et al. 2013) showed that transformational leadership has positive effects on psychological need satisfaction and work engagement. Teachers' work engagement are negatively related to their organisational commitment and retention (Jackson et al. 2006). Rothmann et al. (2013) found associations among manager behaviour, psychological need satisfaction and intention to leave.

The psychological functioning of teachers in terms of school leaders' empowering behaviour is largely unexplored, particularly in emerging economies (Lee and Nie 2014). A study by Liebenberg and Hattingh (2017) showed that 29740 educators in South Africa left the profession from 2011 to 2015. For the period 2008 to 2013, a total of 43.9% of educators was lost because they resigned from their work. Therefore, the turnover behaviour of educators should be regarded as a concern. Moreover, resignations of educators have been linked to low morale, and relationships between principals and teachers (Liebenberg and Hattingh 2017).

Scientific information is lacking regarding specific principal behaviours that affect work engagement and turnover intention of teachers via psychological need satisfaction. The current study aims to fill this void in the literature by making two important contributions. Firstly, it identifies the specific behaviours of school principals that might elicit autonomy, competence and relatedness support. Previous studies (e.g. Janik and Rothmann 2015; May et al. 2004; Rothmann et al. 2013) focused on leader relations without linking these relations to a motivation theory (e.g. SDT). Secondly, it investigates the effects of both leader behaviour and psychological need satisfaction on work engagement and retention of teachers. The focus is on teachers' perceptions and interpretations of principals' behaviours. Individuals' interpretations of their relationships with managers are conceptually distinct from managers' interpretations and may be differentially related to individual and organisational outcomes (Graves and Luciano 2013). Individuals' interpretations are most likely to influence their internal motivational mechanisms (e.g. psychological need satisfaction) and outcomes such as work engagement and intentions to leave. In developing the theoretical model of the processes by which the teachers' perception of the supervisor-employee relationship influences outcomes such as work engagement and intention to leave, this study drew on SDT.

Principal Support and Psychological Need Satisfaction

The satisfaction of psychological needs (i.e. autonomy, competence, and relatedness) results in people aligning their behaviour, values, beliefs and interests (Deci and Ryan 2011; Greguras and Diefendorff 2010). Psychological needs provide the energy and direction for people to engage in activities that influence need satisfaction (Deci and Ryan 2011). The need for *autonomy* is the desire to experience freedom and choice to engage in behaviour that is compatible with individuals' values. The need for *competence* refers to individuals' inherent desire to feel effective in interacting with the environment. The need for *relatedness* concerns the innate need of individuals to feel connected to others, to love and be loved, and to care for others and be cared for (Deci and Ryan 2011).

If a work environment provides adequate support for the satisfaction of the three needs, it should generate more participation from individuals, as it would be associated with more autonomous motivation (Milyavskaya and Koestner 2011). Employees setting themselves autonomous goals attain more goals, which then motivate them to set and attain more autonomous goals in the future and in so doing enhance their well-being (Sheldon and Houser-Marko 2001). The extent to which goals are autonomous will determine individuals' energy in achieving their goals. Goals that are achieved relate to psychological need satisfaction for autonomy, competence, and relatedness.

In the workplace, leadership is one of the most critical factors affecting the motivation of others (Gagné and Deci 2005). The control that leaders wield over policies, job characteristics, goals, and rewards give them considerable influence over individuals' perceptions of the work environment as controlling versus autonomous. Such control affects individuals' sense of self-determination (Gilbert and Kelloway 2014).

Various leadership theories, including transformational leadership (Hetland et al. 2011; Kovjanic et al. 2012; Kovjanic et al. 2013), leader-member exchange (Graves and Luciano 2013), and authentic leadership, have linked follower needs to leadership. In fact, Burns' (1978) and Bass' (1985) definitions of transformational leadership state that the leader attempts to find and satisfy followers' higher-order needs. Therefore, manager behaviours that promote the satisfaction of three basic psychological needs of individuals (Hetland et al. 2011) produce positive outcomes (e.g. engagement). Behaviours that prevent need satisfaction will likely lead to negative outcomes (e.g. intention to leave) (Gilbert and Kelloway 2014).

Principal behaviour can be autonomy supportive or controlling (Ryan and Deci 2000; Fernet et al. 2012). Autonomy-supportive principals allow individuals to make choices about their work, give them influence over their workplace, provide feedback in a non-controlling way, eliminate excessive rules, and acknowledge individuals' talents (Fernet et al. 2012; Gilbert and Kelloway 2014). Autonomy support relies on managers' understanding and acknowledgement of individuals' perceptions, supplying information, providing opportunities and encouraging self-initiation. People feel autonomous when they understand the value and relevance of the task in which they are engaged, and can identify with it. According to Katz and Assor (2007), autonomy satisfaction is especially strong when the task is viewed as being closely connected to the individual's values, interests and goals. Individuals' sense of autonomy increases when managers minimise coercion and interference, show understanding for individuals' perspectives and feelings, provide a meaningful rationale for doing a task, and offer choice by allowing individuals to participate in the choice of tasks and goals in their jobs (Deci and Ryan 2011).

Competence-support of the principal is evident from behaviours such as providing challenges, supporting individuals to acquire skills, showing confidence in them, giving helpful feedback and coaching on performance, making sure that they get the credit for accomplishments, praising good work, and allowing them to learn from their mistakes (Darling-Hammond 2003; May et al. 2004; Reeve 2009). Clarifying expectations is vital to competence building; principals should frequently talk with teachers about their responsibilities, performance and progress (Harter and Adkins 2015).

Principal behaviours that are conducive to the satisfaction of relatedness needs of individuals include regular communication and building genuine, supportive relationships with them (Harter and Adkins 2015). The manager should show support, be dependable, and strengthen team spirit and co-worker relations (Deci and Ryan 1985; Kovjanic et al. 2013; May et al. 2004). Trusting relationships with managers, characterised by a focus on individuals' individuality and what they need to fulfil their roles, result in individuals feeling connected to them and the missions they embody (Kahn and Heaphy 2014). Relatedness satisfaction is supported when managers are accessible, treat employees fairly, show commitment to protect their interests, keep promises, and demonstrate that they can be trusted (May et al. 2004).

Principal Support, Basic Needs Satisfaction, and Work Engagement

Two outcomes strongly related to self-determination, given and Intention to Leave their relationships with motivation and leadership, are work engagement and intention to leave (Kahn and Heaphy 2014). Studies (Janik and Rothmann 2015; May et al. 2004; Rothmann et al. 2013; Schaufeli and Bakker 2004) confirm the importance of manager support for the engagement and retention of employees.

If a manager provides adequate support for satisfying the three needs, it should generate higher work engagement and lead to lower turnover intention because of greater autonomous motivation (Deci and Ryan 2008a). Studies by Baard et al. (2004), Thomas (2000) and Rothmann et al. (2013) showed that autonomy-supportive behaviour by managers affects work engagement positively, and intention to leave negatively. However, these studies had three limitations. First, psychological need satisfaction was not linked to specific manager behaviours (derived from SDT) that support the satisfaction of the three psychological needs (i.e. autonomy, competence and relatedness) of people. Second, at least two of the three studies were not done in the South African context. Third, none of the studies were conducted in educational contexts.

Work engagement is defined as the mobilisation of individuals' selves in their work roles so that they express themselves physically, cognitively, and emotionally during role performance (Kahn 1990). Work engagement is regarded as an experience, i.e. a psychological state in which individuals are intrinsically motivated (Schaufeli 2014). Supervisors play a pivotal role in creating an environment conducive to work engagement (Soane 2014). Manager-follower relationships can offer a sense of connectedness and opportunities to attach to a purpose (Kahn and Heaphy 2014), as well as individualised consideration (Soane 2014).

Intention to leave entails a subjective evaluation of the probability that an individual will quit an organisation shortly (Vandenberg and Nelson 1999). It represents a behavioural intention that precedes actual turnover of staff. A low turnover of staff is desirable because it reduces expensive replacement costs and keeps competent staff in organisations. The satisfaction of the psychological needs for autonomy, competence and relatedness should be negatively associated with intentions to leave a job (Otis and Pelletier 2005).

Aim and Hypotheses

This study aimed to determine the relationships between perceived school principal support, and teachers' psychological need satisfaction, engagement and intention to leave. The following hypotheses were set for this study:

Hypothesis 1 Principal support relates positively to need satisfaction.

Hypothesis 2 Psychological need satisfaction relates positively to teachers' engagement.

Hypothesis 3 Psychological need satisfaction relates negatively to teachers' intentions to leave.

Hypothesis 4 Principal support relates positively to teachers' engagement.

Hypothesis 5 Principal support relates negatively to teachers' intentions to leave.

Hypothesis 6 Principal support indirectly affects teachers' engagement via psychological need satisfaction.

Hypothesis 7 Lack of principal support indirectly affects teachers' intentions to leave via psychological need satisfaction.

Method

Setting and Participants

The setting for this study was 40 public secondary schools within the Kenneth Kaunda District in the North West Province. The number of participants in this study varied from 8 to 20 educators per school. There are 334 secondary schools located in 109 cities and towns in the province (http://www.schools4sa.co.za). A total of 800 respondents representing 40 secondary schools were approached to take part in this study. A final sample of 513 completed the survey, and a usable survey was obtained for a response rate of 64.13%. (See Table 7.1 for a description of the participants.) Males comprised 38.99% of the sample and females 61.01%. The ages of the participants varied from 19 to 65 (Mean = 42). The length of service in the various schools varied between one year and 38 years. The distribution of participants' job position was: student teacher (3.91%), junior teacher (13.79%), senior teacher (67.90%) and head of the department (14.40%).

Table 7.1 Characteristics of participants (N = 513)

Item	Category	Frequency	Percentage
Gender	Male	200	38.99
	Female	313	61.01
Age	Below 23	9	1.96
	23–30	97	21.23
	31–39	70	15.32
	40–45	113	24.73
	46–55	118	25.82
	Over 55	50	10.94
Job level	Student teacher	19	3.91
	Junior teacher	67	13.79
	Senior teacher	330	67.90
	Head of department	70	14.40
Years in teaching	1–2	36	9.16
	3–5	44	11.20
	6–10	77	19.59
	11–20	121	30.79
	21–30	84	21.37
	More than 30 years	31	7.89
Home language	Afrikaans	222	57.66
	English	31	8.05
	Setswana	132	34.29

Measuring Instruments

The School Principal Behaviour Scale (SPBS) was developed to measure participants' perceptions of the behaviours of their school principals. A total of 29 items which refer to autonomy, competence, and relatedness support by manager were identified from the literature on work engagement (Truss et al. 2014), manager behaviour (Kahn and Heaphy 2014; May et al. 2004; Rothmann et al. 2013), and self-determination (Deci and Ryan 2000, 2002, 2008a, b, 2011). We asked five experts to classify the 29 items regarding three dimensions, namely autonomy, competence, and relatedness support. Twelve items were not consistently correctly classified and were thus removed from the initial questionnaire. The SBS consists of 17 items that measure three factors applicable to principals, namely autonomy, competence, and relatedness support (see Table 7.2). Autonomy support was measured by using five items (e.g. "My principal encourages people to speak up when they disagree with a decision"). Competence support was measured by using six items (e.g. "My principal gives me helpful feedback about my performance"). Relatedness support was measured by six items (e.g. "My principal is accessible"). All items were rated on an agreement-disagreement Likert format varying from 1 (*strongly disagree*) to 5 (*strongly agree*).

The *Work-related Basic Need Satisfaction Scale* (WBNSS; Van den Broeck et al. 2010) was used to measure psychological need satisfaction. The WBNSS

Table 7.2 Items of the SPBS

Autonomy support
• encourages me to participate in important decisions • encourages me to speak up when I disagree with a decision • encourages everyone to speak about what they feel • listens carefully to different points of view before making conclusions • seeks feedback to improve interactions with others
Competence support
• takes the time to learn about my career goals and aspirations • cares about whether or not I achieve my goals • makes sure I get the credit when I accomplish something substantial on the job • gives me helpful feedback about my performance • gives me helpful advice about improving my performance when I need it • supports my attempts to acquire additional training or education to further my career
Relatedness support
• treats people fairly • is committed to protecting my interests • does what he/she says he/she will do • can be trusted • is accessible • has confidence in my abilities

Note Each statement starts with "My principal"

measures the satisfaction of three psychological needs: autonomy (five items, e.g. "I feel like I can pretty much be myself at work"); competence (four items, e.g. "I feel competent at work"), and relatedness (six items, e.g. "People at work care about me"). The items were evaluated on a five-point scale ranging from 1 (*totally disagree*) to 5 (*totally agree*). Research by Diedericks (2012) supported the three-factor structure of the WBNSS. Alpha coefficients of 0.81, 0.79 and 0.79 confirm the reliability for autonomy, competence, and relatedness satisfaction respectively.

The *Work Engagement Scale* (WES; Rothmann et al. 2013) was applied to measure work engagement. The WES has 13 items. A seven-point frequency scale ranging from 1 (*almost never or never*) to 7 (*always or almost always*) was used for all items. The three components of Khan's (1990) conceptualisation of engagement are reflected in the items, namely cognitive, emotional and physical engagement. Rothmann et al. (2013) found evidence for the construct validity of the WES. They reported an alpha coefficient of 0.72 for the WES.

The *Turnover Intention Scale* (TIS) (Diedericks 2012) was used to measure intentions to leave. The TIS consists of two items (e.g. "If I were completely free to choose, I would leave this job"). The items are rated on a scale varying from 1 (*strongly disagree*) to 5 (*strongly agree*). An alpha coefficient of 0.83 was reported for the TIS. Diedericks (2012) found an alpha coefficient of 0.79 for the TIS in a study in South Africa.

Data Analysis

We performed latent variable modelling using Mplus version 7.31 (Muthén and Muthén 1998–2014). A weighted least squares with mean and variance adjustment (WLSMV) estimator was used to test the measurement and structural models. Given that we wanted to test a theoretical model, we decided to employ a confirmatory factor analysis strategy.

The following Mplus fit indices were used in this study: absolute fit indices, which included the Chi-square statistic, the weighted root mean square residual (WRMR), and the root mean square error of approximation (RMSEA); incremental fit indices, which included the Tucker–Lewis Index (TLI); and the Comparative Fit Index (CFI) (West et al. 2012). According to Wang and Wang (2012), CFI and TLI values higher than 0.90 are acceptable. Hu and Bentler (1999) suggested a cut-off value of 0.95. The RMSEA should be 0.05 or less and should not exceed 0.08. West et al. (2012) pointed out that cut-off values recommended by Hu and Bentler (1999) were based on simulation studies. Therefore, these cut-off values should be used as rough indicators only, especially when models and data further away from confirmatory factor analysis models with complete data are studied. Raykov's (2009) confirmatory factor analysis-based estimate of scale reliability (ρ) was computed for each scale.

Research Procedure

The ethics committee at the university where the study was undertaken provided ethical approval for the study. The director of the district where participants were employed permitted the study. The researchers contacted the secondary schools' principals in the North West Province and obtained permission to conduct the research. A cover letter explained the purpose of the study, and emphasising the confidentiality of the research project, accompanied the questionnaire. Participants completed a consent form. Participation in the project was voluntary, and respondents had the option to withdraw at any time. Participants completed the questionnaires in hard-copy format and responses to items were captured in an Excel spreadsheet and subsequently analysed using the Mplus 7.31 software program.

Results

Testing the Measurement Model

Using confirmatory factor analysis (CFA), a five-factor measurement model and four alternative models were tested. Survey items were used as indicators of first-level latent variables. Model 1 consisted of five latent variables: (a) principal support, a second-order latent variable which consisted of three first-order latent variables: autonomy support (measured using five items), competence support (measured using six items), and relatedness support (measured using six items); (b) psychological need satisfaction, which consisted of three related first-order latent variables: autonomy satisfaction (measured using five items), competence satisfaction (measured using four items), relatedness satisfaction (measured using six items); (c) work engagement, a second-order latent variable which consisted of three first-order latent variables: cognitive, emotional and physical engagement (each measured using three items), and (d) intention to leave (which consisted of two items). Correlations were allowed among all latent variables in model 1.

Model 2 was specified with 17 observed variables measuring principal support (without the three first-order latent variables, namely autonomy support, competence support, and relatedness support); model 3 was specified with 17 observed variables measuring principal support (without the three first-order latent variables, namely autonomy support, competence support, and relatedness support) and 15 observed variables measuring psychological need satisfaction (without the three first-order latent variables, namely autonomy, competence and relatedness satisfaction); model 4 was specified with 15 observed variables measuring psychological need satisfaction (without the three first-order latent variables, namely autonomy, competence, and relatedness satisfaction); model 5 was specified with 43 observed variables measuring one latent factor.

Table 7.3 presents the fit statistics for the different models.

Table 7.3 Fit statistics of competing measurement models

Model	χ^2	*df*	TLI	CFI	RMSEA	WRMR
1	1934.54*	798	0.97	0.97	0.05* [0.049, 0.055]	1.39
2	2513.27*	807	0.96	0.95	0.06* [0.061, 0.067]	1.71
3	2322.81*	801	0.93	0.93	0.06* [0.058, 0.063]	1.59
4	2743.58*	801	0.95	0.95	0.07* [0.066, 0.071]	1.75
5	9774.02	819	0.77	0.76	0.15* [0.143, 0.148]	4.11

*$p < 0.01$ χ^2: chi-square statistic; *df*: degrees of freedom; TLI: Tucker–Lewis Index; CFI: Comparative Fit Index; RMSEA: root mean square error of approximation; WRMR: weighted root mean square residual

The results in Table 7.3 show a χ^2 value of 1934.54 ($df = 798$) for the hypothesised measurement model. The fit statistics on four fit indices were acceptable: TLI = 0.97, CFI = 0.97, RMSEA = 0.05 and WRMR = 1.39. The hypothesised model showed acceptable fit with the data on four of the five fit indices. The standardised regression coefficients were all statistically significant and varied from 0.22 to 0.78.

Testing the Structural Model

Table 7.4 shows the reliabilities and correlations of the latent variables.

Table 7.4 shows scale reliabilities ranging from 0.72 to 0.93, which indicate acceptable internal consistency of all the scales. The measurement model was used as the basis for the test of three competing structural models. Model 1 included paths from principal support to psychological need satisfaction, from principal support to engagement and intention to leave, and from psychological need satisfaction to engagement and intention to leave. Table 7.5 shows the fit statistics and standardised regression coefficients for the three competing structural models.

This model yielded the following fit statistics: $\chi^2 = 1934.54$, $df = 798$; $p < 0.001$; CFI = 0.97; TLI = 0.97; RMSEA = 0.05 [90% CI 0.049, 0.055]; WRMR = 1.39. These statistics show a good fit for the hypothesised model. Because a cross-sectional survey was used in this study, two additional competing structural models were tested (see Table 7.5). Model 2 (the direct effects model) included paths from principal support and psychological need satisfaction to engagement and intention to leave. However, the paths from principal support to psychological need satisfaction were constrained to zero. Model 3 (the indirect effects model) included paths from principal support to psychological need satisfaction, and from psychological need satisfaction to engagement and intention to leave. However, the paths from principal support to engagement and intention to leave were constrained to zero. The following changes in chi-square ($\Delta\chi^2$) were recorded: Models 1 and 2 ($\Delta\chi^2 = 287.34$, $\Delta df = 3$, $p < 0.001$), and models 1 and 3 ($\Delta\chi^2 = 1.02$, $\Delta df = 2$, $p = 0.60$).

Table 7.4 Reliability coefficients and correlations of the scales (N = 513)

Variable	ρ	1	2	3	4	5	6	7	8
1. Autonomy support	0.72	–	–	–	–	–	–	–	–
2. Competence support	0.72	0.78	–	–	–	–	–	–	–
3. Relatedness support	0.73	0.86	0.81	–	–	–	–	–	–
4. Principal behaviour	0.81	0.91	0.86	0.95	–	–	–	–	–
5. Autonomy satisfaction	0.93	0.58	0.55	0.61	0.64	–	–	–	–
6. Competence satisfaction	0.89	0.24	0.23	0.25	0.26	0.66	–	–	–
7. Relatedness satisfaction	0.93	0.41	0.39	0.43	0.45	0.79	0.65	–	–
8. Engagement	0.90	0.44	0.41	0.45	0.48	0.77	0.57	0.57	–
9. Turnover intention	0.84	−0.33	−0.32	−0.35	−0.37	−0.56	−0.32	−0.49	−0.53

Note The correlations among all variables are statistically significant ($p < 0.001$)

These results show that model 3 was the best-fitting model. Figure 7.1 and Table 7.5 show the standardised path coefficients estimated by Mplus for the hypothesised model. Correlations were allowed between engagement and intention to leave. Next, the obtained relations of the best fitting and most parsimonious structural model (model 3) are discussed regarding the hypotheses of this study.

Regarding *psychological need satisfaction*, Table 7.5 shows that the path coefficients of principal support were statistically significant for autonomy ($\beta = 0.84$, $p < 0.01$), competence ($\beta = 0.27$, $p < 0.01$), and relatedness satisfaction ($\beta = 0.51$, $p < 0.01$), and had the expected signs. Hypotheses 1 and 2 are accepted.

Relating to the portion of the model predicting *engagement,* the path coefficients of autonomy ($\beta = 0.80$, $p < 0.01$) and competence ($\beta = 0.14$, $p < 0.05$) were statistically significant and had the expected signs. However, the path coefficient of autonomy satisfaction was almost four times stronger than that of competence. Hypothesis 3 is accepted.

Relating to the portion of the model predicting *intention to leave*, the path coefficient of autonomy ($\beta = -0.50$, $p < 0.01$) was statistically significant and had the expected sign. Autonomy had a negative relation with intention to leave. Hypothesis 4 is accepted.

Table 7.5 Fit indices and standardised path coefficients of the structural models

Measures		Indirect effects (Model 3)	Direct effects (Model 2)	Direct and indirect effects (Model 1)
Fit Indices	χ^2	1929.27*	4712.96*	1934.54*
	Df	800	801	798
	TLI	0.97	0.89	0.97
	CFI	0.97	0.90	0.97
	RMSEA	0.05	0.10	0.05
	RMSEA 90% CI	[0.049, 0.055]	[0.09, 0.10]	[0.049, 0.055]
	WRMR	1.39	3.03	1.39
Direct effects on autonomy	Principal behaviour	0.84**	–	0.81**
Direct effects on competence		0.27**	–	0.27**
Direct effects on relatedness		0.51**	–	0.51**
Direct effects on engagement	Principal behaviour	–	0.48**	0.08
	Autonomy	0.80**	0.72**	0.83**
	Competence	0.14**	0.17**	0.28**
	Relatedness	−0.16	−0.10	−0.15
Direct effects on intention to leave	Principal behaviour	–	−0.37*	−0.04
	Autonomy	−0.50**	−0.45**	−0.40**
	Competence	0.12	0.10	0.11
	Relatedness	−0.17	−0.21**	−0.22**

*$p < 0.05$; **$p < 0.01$

df = degrees of freedom; CFI: Comparative Fit Index; TLI: Tucker–Lewis Index; RMSEA: root mean square error of approximation; WRMR: weighted root mean square residual

Indirect Effects

To evaluate indirect effects of principal support on the outcome variables, bootstrapping (with 10 000 samples; Hayes 2013) was used. Table 7.6 shows the indirect effects, as well as the lower and upper CIs.

The total direct effect of principal support on engagement was 0.48 [0.40, 0.56], while the total indirect effect was 0.43 [0.30, 0.56]. Table 7.6 shows that principal support had a significant effect on engagement via autonomy satisfaction: $\beta = 0.43$, $p < 0.01$, 95% BC CI [0.24, 0.62]. Principal support also had a significant effect on engagement via competence satisfaction: $\beta = 0.05$, $p < 0.01$, 95% BC CI [0.01, 0.09]. Hypothesis 5 is partially supported. The total direct effect of principal support on intention to leave was −0.37 [−0.46, −0.27], while the total indirect effect was

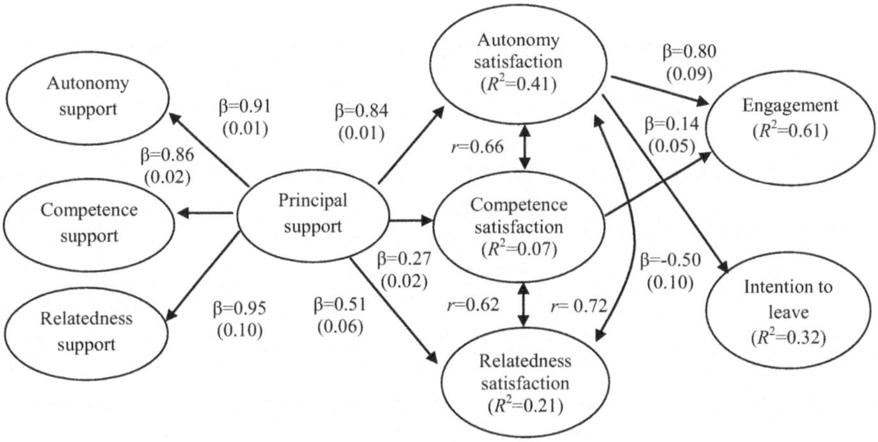

Fig. 7.1 The structural model (standardised solution with standard errors in parentheses)

Table 7.6 Indirect effects of principal behaviour on engagement and intention to leave

	Engagement			Intention to leave		
Variable	Estimate	SE	95% BC CI	Estimate	SE	95% BC CI
Autonomy	0.43	0.10	[0.24, 0.62]	−0.27	0.10	[−0.47, −0.06]
Competency	0.05	0.02	[0.01, 0.09]	0.02	0.03	[−0.03, 0.08]
Relatedness	−0.05	0.05	[−0.14, 0.05]	−0.09	0.06	[−0.21, 0.02]

SE: standard error, BC CI: bias-corrected confidence interval

−0.34 [−0.46, −0.21]. Principal support had a significant indirect effect on intention to leave via autonomy satisfaction: β = −0.27, $p < 0.01$, 95% BC CI [−0.47, −0.07]. Hypothesis 6 is partially supported.

The indirect effects model accounts for the following percentages of the variance (Cohen 1988): autonomy satisfaction = 41% (large effect), competence satisfaction = 7% (small effect), relatedness satisfaction = 21% (moderate effect), engagement = 61% (large effect), and intention to leave = 32% (large effect). These results lend empirical support for the model's fit.

Discussion

This study investigated the role of school principal support in facilitating psychological need satisfaction, work engagement, and intention to leave of teachers. School principal support for psychological need satisfaction had a substantial effect on autonomy satisfaction, a moderate effect on relatedness satisfaction, and a small effect on competence satisfaction. Psychological need satisfaction, and specifically autonomy satisfaction, had a significant positive effect on work engagement and a moderately adverse effect on teachers' intentions to leave. Competence satisfaction had a small effect on work engagement, while relatedness satisfaction had a small negative effect on intention to leave. Autonomy satisfaction played a pivotal role, not only because of its direct effects on teachers' work engagement and intentions to leave but also because it mediated the relation between support for psychological need satisfaction and these outcomes. Work engagement was strongly and negatively associated with intention to leave, indicating that teachers who could not express themselves in their roles also thought of leaving the profession.

School principals that create a climate for psychological need satisfaction of teachers support their autonomy (by encouraging them to participate in meaningful decisions, strengthening them to speak about what they feel, listening to different points of view before making conclusions, and by encouraging them to speak up when they disagree with a decision). Furthermore, they support individuals' competence by supporting teachers' attempts to acquire additional training or education to further their careers. Lastly, principals support teachers' relatedness satisfaction by treating them fairly, showing commitment to protect teachers' interests, doing what they say they will do, demonstrating that they can be trusted, being accessible, and by having confidence in teachers' abilities.

Our findings suggest that teachers' perceptions of supportive principal support fulfil their needs for autonomy, competence, and relatedness satisfaction. Increases in psychological need satisfaction may result in increases in work engagement of teachers and decreases in their intentions to leave. Our findings suggest that satisfaction of autonomy needs is crucial. Autonomy satisfaction was paramount for being engaged at work and not intending to leave the school. Competence satisfaction did play a role in work engagement, but its effect was small. The results of this study supported a model in which poor autonomy support from principals indirectly and negatively affected teachers' work engagement, primarily via a lack of autonomy satisfaction. Autonomy support strengthens teachers' social identity and generates greater meaningfulness within the workplace, which results in work engagement (May et al. 2004).

Relatedness satisfaction implies that individuals experience a sense of communion and develop close and intimate relationships with others (Deci and Ryan 2011). Therefore, support by the principal plays a significant role in psychological need satisfaction in the work context (Deci and Ryan 2000). Supportive behaviours of principals contributed statistically significantly to competence satisfaction of teachers in this study. Competence satisfaction occurs when teachers feel that they are mastering their tasks (Deci and Ryan 2011). Principals might not be sufficiently skilled and motivated to demonstrate behaviour that elicits competence satisfaction of teachers (Bandura 2000).

Satisfaction of the psychological need for autonomy and competence explained a large percentage of the variance in engagement. In line with SDT, adequate experiences of freedom and choice at work result in engagement because these experiences lead to self-regulation of behaviour. Engagement is strengthened when teachers master tasks and feel efficious at work (Deci and Ryan 2011). However, principal behaviours affected work engagement via fulfilment of the psychological need for autonomy (Gagné and Deci 2005). If teachers experience that principals are supportive and that they can be trusted, they will experience more autonomy satisfaction, which leads to engagement. Autonomy satisfaction is thus a crucial psychological condition that mediates between principal support and teachers' engagement (Deci and Ryan 2008a, b). Although need-supportive principal behaviours did not affect work engagement indirectly via relatedness, this does not mean that such effects do not exist in practice. Competence and relatedness satisfaction might affect motivational outcomes (such as work engagement) via autonomy satisfaction (Deci and Ryan 2000).

It is crucial to study and promote the psychological functioning of teachers, especially in emerging economies where teachers work is becoming increasingly complex and demanding (Lee and Nie 2014). Our findings confirm the value of psychological need satisfaction in understanding the association between principal support on the one hand and work engagement and intention to leave on the other hand. Need-supportive environments initiated by principals contributed to teachers' engagement via the satisfaction of their autonomy needs. Furthermore, need-supportive principal behaviours contribute to relatedness satisfaction of teachers, characterised by experiences of a sense of communion and developing close and intimate relationships with others.

Principals contributed to the well-being of teachers because they encouraged them to participate in meaningful decisions and to develop new skills, gave them helpful feedback on their performance, and helped them to solve work-related problems. Supportive principals showed the following types of behaviour towards teachers: confidence in their abilities, support for the development of their potential, provide direction when needed, understand what motivates them, and communicate in a way that workers understand. Principal behaviour affected psychological need satisfaction and engagement of employees, positively, and intention to leave, negatively.

This study had various limitations. Firstly, self-reports were used to gather data. Common method variance could have resulted in correlations between constructs. Secondly, the cross-sectional design used in this study makes it impossible to establish causality. The findings of this study suggest that managerial support and psychological need satisfaction are valuable concepts in understanding the engagement and intentions to leave of teachers. The sampling in this study might limit the generalisability of the findings. Participants were secondary school teachers in one province in South Africa.

Conclusions and Implications for Retention Practice and Research

Addressing the needs of teachers and supporting them can assist in their engagement and retention. Educational organisations should invest in training in self-determination theory for school principals so that they can understand the importance of psychological need satisfaction in the intrinsic motivation of teachers. Principals need to articulate their visions and expectations to teachers and should be available to assist, support and encourage them. Principals should be prepared to improve engagement and intentions to leave of teachers by focusing on psychological need satisfaction.

Future research should examine the antecedents and outcomes of psychological need satisfaction using a longitudinal design. More research is needed regarding how social-contextual factors influence the effects of principal support on psychological need satisfaction. Future studies should also focus on the consequences of need thwarting and need satisfaction for outcomes such as teachers' engagement and intentions to leave.

Summary

This chapter focused on the effects of manager behaviour (as perceived by employees) and flourishing of employees (as indicated by their psychological need satisfaction and engagement), on employee retention. An individual's intention to leave is a good indicator of his or her actual turnover (which results in poor retention).

Using SDT as a theoretical framework, it was argued that manager support for the satisfaction of employees' psychological needs for autonomy, competence and relatedness affect employees' autonomous motivation (and work engagement), which affect their intentions to leave. We stressed that individuals' interpretations are likely to influence internal motivational mechanisms (e.g. their psychological need satisfaction) which affect employees' engagement and intentions to leave. Through psychological need satisfaction, individuals align their behaviour, values, beliefs and interests. Therefore, psychological need satisfaction provides the energy and direction for people to engage or disengage in specific roles and to remain in an organisation.

A work environment (and leader behaviour) that provide support for psychological need satisfaction of employees lead to autonomous goal-setting and motivation. The extent to which leaders affect perceptions of the work environment as autonomous versus controlling will affect the satisfaction of employees' psychological needs for autonomy, competence and relatedness. Autonomy-supportive leaders allow individuals to make choices at work, give them influence over the workplace, eliminate excessive rules and acknowledge individual talents.

Competence-supportive leaders provide challenges to individuals, support them to acquire skills, provide helpful feedback and coaching. Relatedness-supportive leaders communicate genuinely and facilitate relationship building.

Applied to a secondary school setting in South Africa, our empirical study showed that managerial support affected teachers' psychological need satisfaction. Psychological need satisfaction, and particularly autonomy satisfaction, had a strong effect on work engagement and a moderately negative effect on intentions to leave. Satisfaction of the need for competence contributed to work engagement. Satisfaction of relatedness needs impacted teachers' intention to leave.

Most importantly, the findings in this chapter suggest that autonomy satisfaction plays a significant role in the motivation and retention of employees. Autonomy satisfaction impacts work engagement positively and intentions to leave negatively. It also transfers the effects of leader behaviour to work engagement and turnover intentions. Finally, individuals who cannot express themselves in their roles also thought of leaving the organisation.

References

Baard, P. P., Deci, E. L., & Ryan, R. M. (2004). Intrinsic need satisfaction: A motivational basis of performance and well-being in two work settings. *Journal of Applied Social Psychology, 34,* 2045–2068.

Bandura, A. (2000). Cultivate self-efficacy for personal and organizational effectiveness. In E. A. Locke (Ed.), *Handbook of principles of organization behaviour* (pp. 120–136). Oxford, UK: Blackwell.

Bass, B. M. (1985). *Leadership and performance beyond expectations.* New York, NY: Free Press.

Burns, J. M. (1978). *Leadership.* New York, NY: Harper & Row.

Cohen, J. (1988). *Statistical power analysis for the behavioral sciences* (2nd ed.). Hillsdale, NJ: Lawrence Erlbaum Associates.

Coward, R. T., Hogan, T. L., Duncan, R. P., Horne, C. H., Hilker, M. A., & Felsen, L. M. (1995). Job satisfaction of nurses employed in rural and urban long-term care facilities. *Research in Nursing & Health, 18,* 271–284.

Darling-Hammond, L. (2003). Keeping good teachers: Why it matters, what leaders can do. *Educational Leadership, 60*(8), 6–13.

Deci, E. L., & Ryan, R. M. (1985). *Intrinsic motivation and self-determination in human behavior.* New York, NY: Plenum.

Deci, E. L., & Ryan, R. M. (2000). The "what" and "why" of goal pursuits: Human needs and the self-determination of behaviour. *Psychological Inquiry, 11,* 227–268.

Deci, E. L., & Ryan, R. M. (2002). *Handbook of self-determination research.* New York, NY: University of Rochester Press.

Deci, E. L., & Ryan, R. M. (2008a). Self-determination theory: A macrotheory of human motivation, development, and health. *Canadian Psychology, 49*(3), 182–185.

Deci, E. L., & Ryan, R. M. (2008b). Facilitating optimal motivation and psychological well-being across life's domains. *Canadian Psychology, 49,* 14–23.

Deci, E. L., & Ryan, R. M. (2011). Levels of analysis: Regnant causes of behavior and well-being: The role of psychological needs. *Psychological Inquiry, 22,* 17–22.

Diedericks, E. (2012). *Flourishing of employees in the information technology industry in South Africa.* Unpublished doctoral thesis. Vanderbijlpark, South Africa: North-West University.

Fernet, C., Guay., F., Senécal, C., & Austin, S. (2012). Predicting intra-individual changes in teacher burnout: The role of perceived school environment and motivational factors. *Teaching and Teacher Education, 28*, 514–525.

Gagné, M., & Deci, E. L. (2005). Self-determination theory and work motivation. *Journal of Organizational Behaviour, 26*, 331–362.

Gilbert, S. L., & Kelloway, E. K. (2014). Leadership. In M. Gagné (Ed.), *The Oxford handbook of work engagement, motivation, and self-determination theory* (pp. 181–198). Oxford, UK: Oxford University Press.

Graves, L. M., & Luciano, M. M. (2013). Self-determination at work: Understanding the role of leader-member exchange. *Motivation and Emotion, 37*, 518–536.

Greguras, G. J., & Diefendorff, J. M. (2010). Why does proactive personality predict employee life satisfaction and work behaviors? A field investigation in the mediating role of the self-concordance model. *Personnel Psychology, 63*, 539–560.

Gu, Q., & Day, C. (2013). Challenges to teacher resilience: Conditions count. *British Educational Journal, 39*(1), 22–44.

Harter, J., & Adkins, A. (2015, April). What great managers do to engage employees. *Harvard Business Review*. Retrieved October 9, 2016 from https://hbr.org/2015/04/what-great-managers-do-to-engage-employees.

Hayes, A. F. (2013). *Introduction to mediation, moderation, and conditional process analysis: A regression-based approach*. New York, NY: The Guilford Press.

Hetland, H., Hetland, C., Andreassen, C. S., Pallesen, S., & Notelaers, G. (2011). Leadership and fulfillment of the three basic psychological needs at work. *Career Development International, 16*, 507–523.

Hu, L. T., & Bentler, P. M. (1999). Cut-off criteria for fit indexes in covariance structure analysis: Conventional criteria versus new alternatives. *Structural Equation Modeling: A Multidisciplinary Journal, 6*, 1–55.

Jackson, L. T. B., Rothmann, S., & Van De Vijver, A. J. R. (2006). A model of work-related well-being for educators in South Africa. *Stress and Health, 22*, 263–274.

Janik, M., & Rothmann, S. (2015). Meaningful work and secondary school teachers' intention to leave. *SA Journal of Education, 35*(2), 13. https://doi.org/10.15700/saje.v35n2a1008. Art. 1008

Kahn, W. A., & Heaphy, E. D. (2014). Relational context of personal engagement at work. In C. Truss, R. Delbridge, E. Soane, K. Alfes & A. Shantz (Eds.), *Employee engagement in theory and practice* (pp. 163–179). Abingdon, UK: Routledge.

Kahn, W. A. (1990). Psychological conditions of personal engagement and disengagement at work. *Academy of Management Journal, 33*, 692–724.

Katz, I., & Assor, A. A. (2007). When choice motivates and when it does not. *Educational Psychology Review, 19*, 429–442.

Kovjanic, S., Schuh, S. C., Jonas, K., Van Quaquebeke, N., & Van Dick, R. (2012). How do transformational leaders foster positive employee outcomes? A self-determination-based analysis of employees' needs as mediating links. *Journal of Organizational Behavior, 33*(8), 1031–1052.

Kovjanic, S., Schuh, S. C., & Jonas, K. (2013). Transformational leadership and performance: An experimental investigation into the mediating effects of basic needs and work engagement. *Journal of Occupational and Organizational Psychology, 86*, 543–555.

Lee, A. N., & Nie, Y. (2014). Understanding teacher empowerment: Teachers' perceptions of principal's and immediate supervisor's empowering behaviours, psychological empowerment and work-related outcomes. *Teaching and Teacher Education, 41*, 67–79.

Liebenberg, K., & Hattingh, C. (2017). 'n Evaluering van opvoedermoreel in skole in Wellington. *LitNet Akademies, 14*(3), 661–717.

May, D. R., Gilson, R. L., & Harter, L. M. (2004). The psychological conditions of meaningfulness, safety and availability and the engagement of the human spirit at work. *Journal of Occupational and Organizational Psychology, 77*, 11–37.

Milyavskay, M., & Koestner, R. (2011). Psychological needs, motivation, and well-being: A test of self-determination theory across multiple domains. *Personality and Individual Differences, 50,* 387–391.
Mor Barak, M. E., Nissly, J. A., & Levin, A. (2001). Antecedents to retention and turnover among child welfare, social work, and other human service employees: What can we learn from past research? A review and metanalysis. *Social Service Review, 75,* 625–661.
Muthén, L. K., & Muthén, B. O. (1998–2014). *Mplus users' guide* (6th ed.). Los Angeles, CA: Muthén & Muthén.
Otis, N., & Pelletier, L. G. (2005). A motivational model of daily hassles, physical symptoms, and future work intentions among police officers. *Journal of Applied Social Psychology, 35,* 2193–2214.
Raykov, T. (2009). Evaluation of scale reliability for unidimensional measures using latent variable modeling. *Measurement and Evaluation in Counseling and Development, 42,* 223–232.
Reeve, J. (2009). Why teachers adopt a controlling motivating style toward students and how they can become more autonomy supportive. *Educational Psychologist, 44,* 159–175.
Rothmann, S., Diedericks, E., & Swart, J. P. (2013). Manager relations, psychological need satisfaction and intention to leave in the agricultural sector. *SA Journal of Industrial Psychology, 39*(2), 11. https://doi.org/10.4102/sajip.v39i2.1129.
Ryan, R. M., & Deci, E. L. (2000). Self-determination theory and the facilitation of intrinsic motivation, social development and well-being. *American Psychologist, 55,* 68–78.
Schaufeli, W. B. (2014). What is engagement? In C. Truss, R. Delbridge, E. Soane, K. Alfes, & A. Shantz (Eds.), *Employee engagement in theory and practice* (pp. 15–35). Abingdon, UK: Routledge.
Schaufeli, W. B., & Bakker, A. B. (2004). Job demands, job resources, and their relationship with burnout and engagement: A multi-sample study. *Journal of Organizational Behavior, 25,* 293–315.
Sheldon, K. M., & Houser-Marko, L. (2001). Self-concordance, goal attainment, and the pursuit of happiness: Can there be an upward spiral? *Journal of Personality and Social Psychology, 80,* 152–165.
Soane, M. (2014). Leadership and employee engagement. In C. Truss, R. Delbridge, E. Soane, K. Alfes, & A. Shantz (Eds.), *Employee engagement in theory and practice* (pp. 149–162). London, UK: Routledge.
Thomas, K. W. (2000). *Intrinsic motivation at work: Building energy and commitment.* San Francisco, CA: Berrett-Koehler.
Truss, C., Delbridge, R., Soane, E., Alfes, K., & Shantz, A. (2014). *Employee engagement in theory and practice.* Abingdon, UK: Routledge.
Van den Broeck, A., Vansteenkiste, M., De Witte, H., & Lens, W. (2008). Explaining the relationships between job characteristics, burnout, and engagement: The role of basic psychological need satisfaction. *Work and Stress, 22,* 277–294.
Van den Broeck, A., Vansteenkiste, M., De Witte, H., Soenens, B., & Lens, W. (2010). Capturing autonomy, competence, and relatedness at work: Construction and initial validation of the work-related basic need satisfaction scale. *Journal of Occupational and Organizational Psychology, 83,* 981–1002.
Vandenberg, R. J., & Nelson, J. B. (1999). Disaggregating the motives underlying turnover intentions: When do intentions predict turnover behavior? *Human Relations, 52,* 1313–1336.
Wang, J., & Wang, X. (2012). *Structural equation modeling: Applications using Mplus.* Chichester, United Kingdom: Wiley.
West, S. G., Taylor, A. B., & Wu, W. (2012). Model fit and model selection in structural equation modeling. In R. H. Hoyle (Ed.), *Handbook of structural equation modeling* (pp. 209–231). New York, NY: Guilford Press.

Sebastiaan (Ian) Rothmann (PhD) is a professor in Industrial Psychology and Director of the Optentia Research Focus Area at the North-West University in South Africa. Ian's research interest is the assessment and development of human potential and flourishing in institutions within multicultural contexts. He is author/co-author of 200 peer-reviewed journal articles and chapters in handbooks. Ian is an honorary fellow of the Society of Industrial and Organizational Psychology in South Africa (SIOPSA) and an international affiliate of the American Psychological Association, a member of the Society of Industrial/Organizational Psychology (SIOP–USA), and the Academy of Management (USA).

Elmari Fouché (PhD) is a registered industrial psychologist with six years of experience in private practice, two years of experience as manager of the School-Based Educator Training (SBET) program as well as 10 years of experience as a lecturer in Educational psychology, Life Orientation, Learner Support and Religion Studies at the North-West University, Potchefstroom Campus, South Africa.

Chapter 8
Capitalising on Employee's Psychological Wellbeing Attributes in Managing Their Retention: The Adverse Influence of Workplace Bullying and Turnover Intention

Melinde Coetzee and Jeannette van Dyk

Abstract This chapter explores the role of a broad array of wellbeing dispositional attributes (i.e. self-esteem, emotional intelligence, hardiness, work engagement and flourishing) in the retention context and evaluates the relationship dynamics between these attributes and employees' perceptions of workplace bullying and turnover intention. Although workplace bullying and turnover intention are well-researched in the retention context, the role of employees' psychological wellbeing attributes in explaining turnover intention and workplace bullying and vice versa is not clear. Building on the theoretical premises of broaden-and build theory, we propose that employees' perceptions of workplace bullying and turnover intention reflect negative retention-related attitudes that adversely influence their psychological wellbeing resources. Canonical results of a study conducted on a convenience sample of (N = 373) employees in the South African work context suggested that negative feelings (i.e. low levels of work engagement and hardiness commitment) generally create the urge to escape (i.e. high turnover intentions). Perceptions of workplace bullying and turnover intention further seem to lower the propensity to create personal resources to cope with difficult work circumstances (i.e. resulting in stronger perceptions of falling victim to workplace bullying and person-related bullying). The results substantiate that employees' turnover intention and perceptions of workplace bullying are important to consider in retention strategies because of their link with employees' psychological wellbeing, engagement and commitment levels in the workplace. The new insights derived from the study findings indicate that for organisations to capitalise on employees' wellbeing attributes for retention purposes, leadership and human resource practices should counteract perceptions of workplace bullying and turnover intention.

M. Coetzee (✉) · J. van Dyk
Department of Industrial and Organisational Psychology, University of South Africa, Pretoria, South Africa
e-mail: coetzm1@unisa.ac.za

M. Coetzee et al. (eds.), *Psychology of Retention*,
https://doi.org/10.1007/978-3-319-98920-4_8

Keywords Psychological wellbeing · Self-esteem · Emotional intelligence Hardiness · Work engagement · Flourishing · Turnover intention Workplace bullying

Introduction

Turnover intention continues to be an important area of inquiry in retention research and practice. Globalised business competitiveness, technological advances, and the competition for critical and scarce skilled knowledge workers all contribute to the need to better understand employees' turnover intention as part of the organisation's retention strategy (Holtom et al. 2008; Kalliath and Kalliath 2012; Kim 2017). Employees turnover intention reflects their attitudinal (i.e. thoughts of leaving), decisions (i.e. plans to exit) and behaviours (i.e. searching for alternative employment opportunities) that occur before actual turnover (Van Dyk 2016). In the retention context, the high turnover intention of high performing valuable human capital may become dysfunctional voluntary turnover behaviour that is costly for the organisation (Ozolina-Ozola 2014). Turnover intention is generally the final stage before employees display actions to exit the organisation. Proactive actions to address employees' turnover intention may help to shift their minds toward staying at the organisation (Dysvik and Kuvaas 2010). For this reason, managers, practitioners and scholars remain interested in the psychosocial factors that contribute to employees' turnover intention (Kim 2017; Van Dyk 2016).

Workplace bullying, a form of recurrent negative interpersonal behaviour (for example, victimization, personal attacks, unrealistic work overload, isolation, excessive humiliation and criticism, and unspoken threats) is a psychological factor related to high turnover intention (Nami and Nami 2011; Renn et al. 2013; Van Dyk 2016). While turnover intention signals an affective-cognitive state of psychological distress, acts of workplace bullying cause physical, mental and affective distress and are therefore seen as antecedents of turnover intention (Greenbaum et al. 2015; Rodwell et al. 2014). In the context of this chapter, employees' turnover intention and their perceptions of workplace bullying are therefore associated with lower levels of wellbeing at work (Zhang and Lee 2010; Van Dyk 2016). Negative health and psychological consequences such as anxiety and depression have been reported for targets of bullying (Hauge et al. 2010; Hogh et al. 2011). Victims generally report negative feelings of isolation, lowered self-esteem, anger, fear, mood swings, and lower motivation and engagement levels (Oade 2009). Research shows that negative affective states impact how employees perceive their jobs and work and life experiences and are reported to be associated with stressors and strains (Allen et al. 2012; Spector and Bruk-Lee 2008).

In this chapter, we propose that employees' perceptions of workplace bullying and turnover intention reflect negative retention-related attitudes that adversely influence their psychological wellbeing. The purpose of the current chapter is to extend what is known about the link between wellbeing-related dispositional attributes and the retention-related attitudes of workplace bullying and turnover intention. Employees' wellbeing is associated with dispositional attributes that predispose them to positive behaviours and responses that serve as important personal resources in performing better on the job and achieving career success (Allen et al. 2012; Van Dyk 2016). The intent was to study the role of a broad array of wellbeing dispositional attributes (i.e. self-esteem, emotional intelligence, hardiness, work engagement and flourishing) in the retention context and explore the relationship dynamics between these attributes and employees' perceptions of workplace bullying and turnover intention. To date, retention research has neglected studying these wellbeing attributes jointly and in relation to the two constructs of workplace bullying and turnover intention in a single study. Research tends to overemphasise work engagement as an important predictor of turnover intention and neglects evaluating the role of other positive dispositional attributes along with work engagement in the retention context (Kim 2017; Schaufeli and Bakker 2004). This chapter addresses this gap in research and extends retention theory. An investigation of wellbeing dispositional attributes in relation to retention-related attitudes may offer new insights that can be used to empower employees with the necessary personal and organisational support they need to experience wellbeing in demanding environments. Wellbeing is seen as an important precursor of employees' intention to remain at an organisation (DeTienne et al. 2012; Paillé 2011).

Theoretical Support for Linking Workplace Bullying, Turnover Intention and Wellbeing Dispositional Attributes

The broaden-and build theory of Fredrickson (1998, 2001, 2004) seems to offer an explanation for the link between employees' perceptions of workplace bullying, turnover intention, and wellbeing dispositional attributes. The theory explains that prolonged negative feelings result in narrow-mindedness (i.e. psychological distress and lack of creative responsiveness) with individuals feeling trapped and isolated in an adverse situation which may create the urge to attack or escape (i.e. withdraw from the situation). Workplace bullying refers to a situation in which employees are subjected to prolonged deliberate negative acts at work. Negative acts may be work-related (for example, withholding information, job characteristics such as unrealistic workloads, allocation of insignificant tasks), person-related (for example, humiliation and excessive criticism, incessant disapproval, and psychological threats) and physical intimidation and abuse (Einarsen et al. 2003, 2009). Workplace bullying is seen as a major predictor of psychological distress, negative health (i.e. depression and anxiety), and negative affective-cognitive states (Hogh et al. 2011; Oade 2009). Research indicates links between bullying and reports of cognitive and emotional demands, job insecurity, role problems and negative links with job autonomy, skill utilisation and social support, all of which are also associated with antecedents of turnover intention (Greenbaum et al. 2015; Kim 2017; Van den Broeck et al. 2011).

Broaden-and build theory (Fredrickson 1998, 2001, 2004) further posits that positive feelings such as happiness and satisfaction have the predisposition to broaden individuals' mindsets and thought-behavioural repertoire in a manner that supports their wellbeing. Constructive actions may further enhance existing positive feelings, cause creativity and build interpersonal connections through which people's personal resources are enhanced. Personal resources help individuals enhance their chances to effectively manage and creatively cope with difficult circumstances in the long run (Fredrickson 2004). In the context of this chapter, the wellbeing attributes of self-esteem, emotional intelligence, hardiness, work engagement and flourishing are seen as important personal resources that enrich individuals' affective-cognitive mindsets and thought-behavioural repertoire, including their intention to remain at the organisation. Research shows that positive dispositional attributes (for example, positive affect, self-efficacy, optimism, resilience, engagement, hardiness, self-esteem, flourishing) promote wellbeing and may protect individuals from adverse demands and lower their perceptions of stressors and strains (Allen et al. 2012; Ciarrochi et al. 2002; Hansen et al. 2014; Kardum et al. 2012; Vazi et al. 2013; Wu et al. 2011). It therefore stands to reason that higher levels of wellbeing dispositional attributes may be associated with lower perceptions of workplace bullying and turnover intention. However, on the side of the retention spectrum, due to the adverse effects of workplace bullying, strong perceptions of workplace bullying and high turnover intention may be linked to low levels of wellbeing attributes. The following research hypothesis was formulated:

Research hypothesis: Low levels of wellbeing dispositional attributes will explain high levels of turnover intention and strong perceptions of workplace bullying and vice versa.

Figure 8.1 gives an overview of the elements of the various wellbeing dispositional attributes as relevant to the retention context:

- Self-esteem (i.e. feelings, perceptions and aspirations regarding one's worth as a person) functions as a significant personal resource during strenuous events. High self-esteem seems to lower the effects of stressors and improves mental health (Battle 1992; Sowislo and Orth 2013; Wu et al. 2011).
- Emotional intelligence (i.e. the ability to observe and manage one's own and others' feelings and emotions and utilising them to direct one's actions). The capability to regulate emotions enables people to maintain positive interpersonal relations and cope more effectively with stressors (O'Boyle et al. 2011; Schutte et al. 2009).
- Hardiness (i.e. mental toughness or the ability to view stressful life situations as challenges and treating them as opportunities for personal development). The hardiness aspects of commitment (i.e. personal engagement with environment, viewing tasks as meaningful), challenge (i.e. ability to put stressful situation into perspective and looking at alternatives to solving a problem) and control (i.e. predisposition to trust in one's capability to deal successfully with situations;

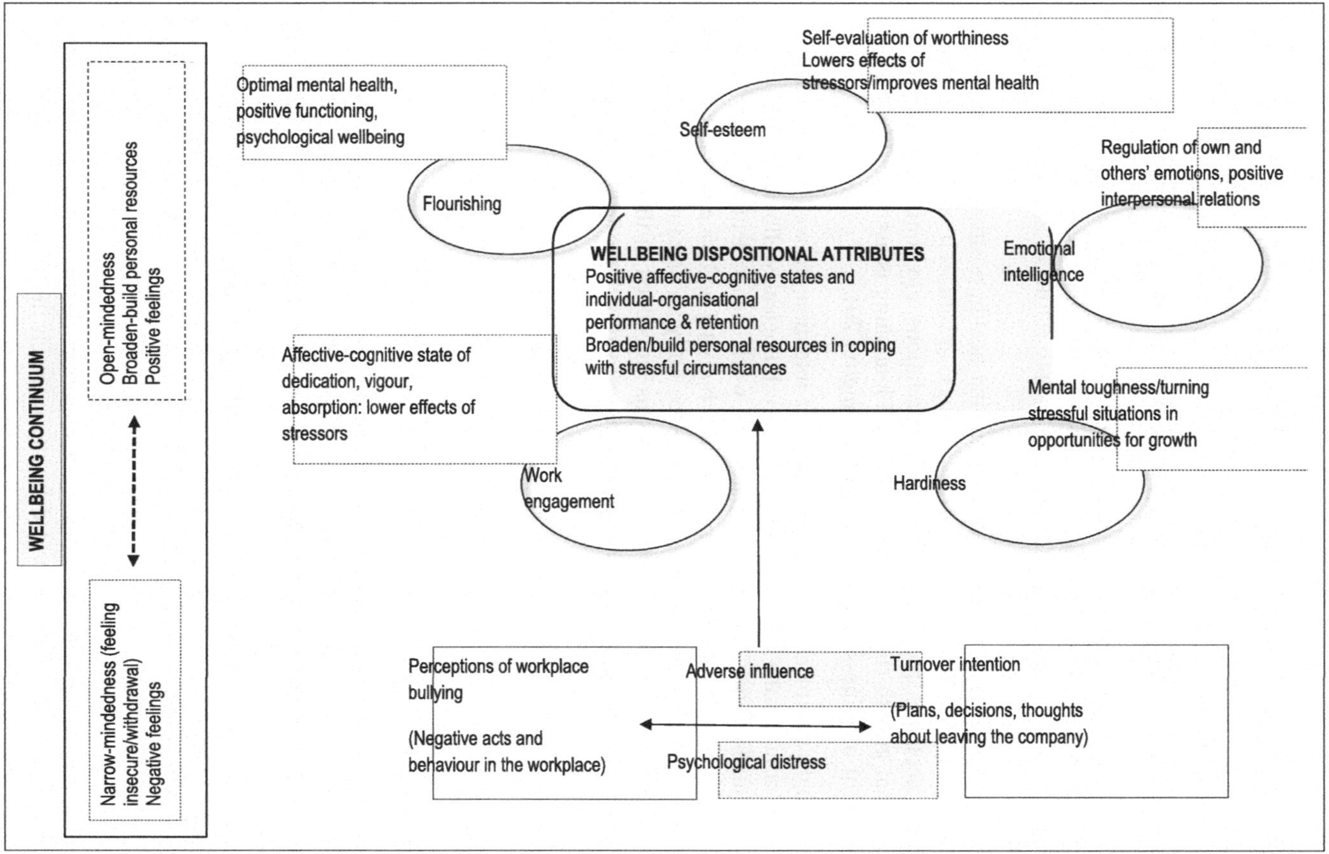

Fig. 8.1 The role of wellbeing dispositional attributes, perceptions of workplace bullying and turnover intention in the retention context (Authors'own compilation)

feeling in control) function as resources of resilience and health-protectors during stressful life occurrences in the workplace (Kardum et al. 2012; Kobasa et al. 1982).

- Work engagement is the positive affective-cognitive motivational state of dedication (commitment), vigour (drive) and absorption (focused attention) through which individuals exhibit physical exertion, mental vitality and an emotional bond with their work (Rich et al. 2010; Schaufeli et al. 2002). Work engagement lowers the effect of stressors and protect individuals' physical and mental health. Highly engaged people are able to apply effective coping strategies when exposed to stressors (Hansen et al. 2014). Work engagement is associated with higher work performance and intention to stay (Gruman and Saks 2011; Kim 2017).
- Flourishing is a condition of optimal mental health, positive functioning, psychological wellbeing and positive feelings toward self and life, including self-acceptance, purpose in life, positive relations, environmental mastery and personal growth (Ryff and Keyes 1995). Flourishing is associated with greater levels of happiness and satisfaction (Harrington 2013).

Although workplace bullying and turnover intention are well-researched in the retention context, the role of employees' psychological wellbeing attributes (i.e. self-esteem, emotional intelligence, hardiness, work engagement and flourishing) in explaining turnover intention and workplace bullying and vice versa is not clear. Understanding also the influence of workplace bullying and turnover intention on employees' repertoire of personal resources as embedded in their wellbeing attributes, may help inform retention practices concerned with the wellbeing support of employees.

Method

Participants and Procedure

A convenience sample of staff level employees (N = 373) employed in various South African organisations was involved in the study. Data were collected through a combination of an online (a copy of the questionnaire emailed to participants) and paper-based survey (participants completing the questionnaires in group sessions). The sample was represented by white (68%) and African (32%) employees and females (63%) and males (37%). The mean age of the participants was 44 years (SD: 8.47). The participants were represented by employees who had more than five years of tenure in the company (53%) and those with less than five years (47%). Permission to conduct the survey was obtained from the participating organisations and ethical clearance was provided by the research institution. Participation was voluntary and anonymous.

Measures

Self-esteem. The culture free self-esteem inventory for adults (CFSEI-AD) developed by Battle (1992) was utilised to measure participants' self-esteem in terms of their general self-esteem (16 items; e.g. "I am as important as most people"), social self-esteem (8 items; e.g. "Most people I know like me"), and personal self-esteem (8 items; e.g. "I am as nice looking as most people"). A seven-point likert-type scale was used to capture responses (1 = strongly disagree; 7 = strongly agree). Battle (1992) reports evidence of construct validity and test-retest reliability of the scale. Acceptable internal consistency reliabilities were obtained for the present study with composite reliabilities ranging between 0.66 and 0.86.

Emotional intelligence. The assessing emotions scale (AES) developed by Schutte et al. 2009) was utilised to measure participants' emotional intelligence in terms of their perceptions of emotions (10 items; e.g. "By looking at their facial expressions, I recognise the emotions people are experiencing"), managing own emotions (9 items, e.g. "When I experience a positive emotion, I know how to make it last"), managing others' emotions (8 items, e.g. "I help other people feel better when they are down"), and utilisation of emotions (6 items; e.g. "When I feel a change in emotions, I tend to come up with new ideas"). A five-point likert type scale was used to capture responses (1 = strongly disagree; 5 = strongly agree). Schutte et al. (2009) report evidence of construct validity and test-retest reliability. Acceptable internal consistency reliabilities were obtained for the present study with composite reliabilities ranging between 0.76 and 0.84.

Hardiness. The personal views survey II (PVS-II) developed by Kobasa (1982) was utilised to measure participants' hardiness in terms of their hardiness commitment (15 items; e.g. "I find it difficult to imagine getting excited about working"), hardiness control (17 items; e.g." I usually feel that I can change what might happen tomorrow, by what I do today"), and hardiness challenge (18 items, e.g. "A person whose mind seldom changes can usually be depended on to have reliable judgements"). Responses were captured on a four-point likert type scale (0 = not at all true; 3 = completely true). Maddi (1987; 2008) reports evidence of the construct validity and test-retest reliability of the scale. Acceptable internal consistency reliabilities were obtained for the present study with composite reliabilities ranging between 0.73 and 0.89.

Work engagement. The Utrecht work engagement scale developed by Schaufeli et al. (2002) was utilised to measure participants work engagement in terms of their sense of vigour (8 items; e.g. "I feel strong and vigorous in my job"), dedication (5 items; e.g. "To me, my work is challenging") and absorption (8 items; e.g. "I am immersed in my work"). Responses were captured on seven-point likert type scale (0 = never; 6 = every day). Schaufeli et al. (2002) reports evidence of the construct validity of the scale and internal consistency reliability. Acceptable internal consistency reliabilities were obtained for the present study with composite reliabilities ranging between 0.89 and 0.92.

Flourishing. The eight-item flourishing scale (FS) developed by Diener et al. (2010) was utilised to measure participants overall sense of flourishing (e.g. "I lead a purposeful and meaningful life"). Responses were captured on a seven point likert type scale (1 = strongly disagree; 7 = strongly agree). Diener et al. (2010) report evidence of construct validity and internal consistency reliability of the scale. A high internal consistency (composite) reliability coefficient of 0.92 was obtained for the present study.

Workplace bullying. The negative acts questionnaire- revised (NAQ-R) developed by Einarsen et al. (2009) was utilised to measure participants' perceptions of workplace bullying in terms of work-related bullying (7 items, e.g. "Pressure not to claim something to which by right you are entitled e.g. sick leave, holiday entitlement, travel expenses"), person-related bullying, (12 items; e.g. "Being the subject of excessive teasing and sarcasm") and physical intimidation (3 items; e.g. "Threats of violence or physical abuse or actual abuse"). A five-point likert type scale was used to capture responses (0 = never; 4 = daily). Einarsen et al. (2009) report evidence of the construct validity and reliability of the scale. Acceptable internal consistency reliabilities were obtained for the present study with composite reliabilities ranging between 0.75 and 0.93.

Turnover intention. The five-item turnover intention scale (TIS) developed by Dysvik and Kuvaas (2010) was utilised to measure participants' overall turnover intention (e.g. "I often think about quitting my present job"). A five-point likert type scale wad used to capture responses (1 = strongly disagree; 5 = strongly agree). Dysvik and Kuvaas (2010) report evidence of the construct validity and internal consistency reliability of the scale. A high internal consistency (composite) reliability coefficient of 0.90 was obtained for the present study.

Statistical Analysis

Canonical correlation analysis (CCA) was used to assess the link between the wellbeing-related dispositions (self-esteem, emotional intelligence, hardiness, work engagement and flourishing) as a composite variable set and the retention-related constructs of workplace bullying and turnover intention as a composite variable set. CCA allows for the calculation of a multivariate statistical model for assessing links between multiple variable sets and identifying the variables that contribute the most in explaining the links between the two sets of variables (De Guzman and Choi 2013; Sherry and Henson 2005). The SAS (2013) MANOVA procedure was utilised for the CCA. The Wilk's multivariate criterion lambda (λ) was used to assess the significance of the overall canonical correlation between the two composite sets of latent variables because it allows researchers to assess the practical significance ($1 - \lambda = r^2$-type metric of effect size) of the full canonical model (Sherry and Henson 2005). CCA also limits the chances of committing type I errors. The cut-off criterion for interpreting canonical loadings was set at $Rc \geq 0.40$ (moderate to large practical effect). The redundancy index was also considered in determining the magnitude of the overall relationships (correlational) between the two variates of a canonical function. The interpretation of the squared canonical correlation (Rc^2) values were based on the following effect sizes in line with guidelines set by Cohen (1992): a large practical effect: $Rc^2 \geq 0.26$; medium practical effect: $Rc^2 \geq 0.13 \leq 0.25$; small practical effect: $Rc^2 \leq 0.12$. Only the singular canonical structure correlations (loadings) and the squared canonical structure correlations (loadings) were deliberated upon in the interpretation of the practical significance and importance of the derivation of the two canonical variate constructs. This approach was based on the variability of the canonical weights and multi-collinearity apprehensions (Hair et al. 2010).

Results

Descriptive Statistics and Zero-Order Correlations

Table 8.1 reports the means, standard deviations, composite reliability coefficients and zero-order correlations for the subscales. The correlations between the subscales were in the expected direction (i.e. the psychological wellbeing attributes variables correlated negatively with the retention-related constructs of workplace bullying and turnover intention; workplace bullying correlated positively with turnover intention). The correlations were below the threshold value of $r \geq 0.80$ for multicollinearity concerns (Hair et al. 2010).

Correlation Analysis

Table 8.2 reports the overall model fit statistics while Table 8.3 summarises the results of the first canonical function. As shown in Table 8.2, the full model r^2 type's effect size (yielded by $1 - 0.\lambda$: $1 - 0.425$) was $r^2 = 0.58$ (large practical effect; $Fp = 0.001$), indicating that the full model explained a substantial proportion (approximately 58%) of the variance shared between the two canonical variate sets. The variables of the two canonical variates of the first function accounted for 42% (overall $Rc^2 = 0.42$; large practical effect) of the data variability. Only the results of the first canonical were therefore considered for testing the research hypothesis. The second function explained only an additional 18% of the variance shared between the two canonical variate sets, and the data variability and the third function only 8%.

Table 8.1 Descriptive statistics, reliabilities and zero-order correlations

	Variable	Mean (SD)	α	1	2	3	4	5	6	7	8	9	10	11	12	13	14	15	16	17	18
1	General self esteem	5.36(.96)	.86	-																	
2	Social self esteem	4.88(.68)	.66	.52**	-																
3	Personal self esteem	4.72 (1.31)	.83	.75**	.41**	-															
4	Perception of emotion	3.86(.68)	.84	.45**	.33**	.36**	-														
5	Managing own emotions	4.19(.62)	.84	.67**	.46**	.59**	.57**	-													
6	Managing others' emotions	4.05(.58)	.76	.41**	.38**	.29**	.68**	.65**	-												
7	Utilisatioof emotions	4.07(.61)	.76	.36**	.28**	.24**	.54**	.65**	.64**	-											
8	Hardiness commitment	2.20(.51)	.86	.54**	.35**	.44**	.39**	.44**	.26**	.26**	-										
9	Hardiness control	2.24(.40)	.79	.55**	.35**	.50**	.43**	.48**	.33**	.24**	.78**	-									
10	Hardiness challenge	1.63(.42)	.73	.32**	.20**	.29**	.23**	.14**	.08	.07	.56**	.55**	-								
11	Vigour	4.46(1.18	.89	.38**	.27**	.33**	.30**	.39**	.26**	.26**	.53**	.38**	.21**	-							
12	Dedication	4.50(1.45	.92	.29**	.19**	.23**	.19**	.29**	.17**	.18**	.50**	.31**	.18**	.87**	-						
13	Absorption	4.32(1.25	.89	.25**	.17**	.18**	.21**	.24**	.17**	.20**	.43**	.24**	.15**	.85**	.83**	-					
14	Psychosocial flourishing	6.04(.89)	.90	.60**	.46**	.50**	.46**	.66**	.49**	.45**	.51**	.45**	.19**	.51**	.43**	.37**	-				
15	Workrelated bullying	.92(.76)	.82	-.21**	-.13*	-.25**	-.14**	-.18**	-.16**	-.02	-.39**	-.37**	-.08	-.31**	-.35**	-.27**	-.22**	-			
16	Persorrelated bullying	.54(.64)	.93	-.23**	-.12*	-.26**	-.18**	-.17**	-.10	.02	-.40**	-.41**	-.15**	-.28**	-.30**	-.25**	-.20**	.74**	-		
17	Physical intimidation bullying	.36(.60)	.75	-.14**	.00	-.18**	-.16**	-.14**	.08	-.02	-.36**	-.38**	-.13*	-.21**	-.22**	-.17**	-.18**	.60**	.79**	-	
18	Turnover intention	2.67(1.32	.90	-.18**	-.03	-.17**	-.04	-.17**	-.05	-.05	-.34**	-.14**	.03	-.43**	-.53**	-.40**	-.21**	.45**	.34**	.24**	-

Table 8.2 Canonical correlation results: Overall model fit statistics

	Measures of overall model fit for canonical correlation analysis				
Canonical function	Overall canonical correlation (*Rc*)	Overall squared canonical correlation (Rc^2)	Eigenvalue	*F* statistics	Probability (*p*)
1	0.65	0.42	0.7184	5.29	<0.0001***
2	0.42	0.18	0.2145	2.61	<0.0001***
3	0.28	0.08	0.0861	1.57	0.03*
Multivariate tests of significance					
Statistics		Value	Approximate F statistic		Probability (*p*)
Wilks's lambda		0.425	5.29		<0.0001***
Pillai's trace		0.711	4.81		<0.0001***
Hotelling-Lawley trace		1.057	5.81		<0.0001***
Roy's greatest root		0.718	15.98		<0.0001***

Notes N = 373

Variables Explaining the Wellbeing Dispositional Attributes Canonical Variate

Based on the cut-off criterion of $Rc \geq 0.40$, Table 8.3 shows that the variables that contributed the most in explaining the overall canonical psychological wellbeing attributes construct variate were the three engagement variables (dedication: $Rc = -0.84$; vigour: $Rc = -0.70$; absorption: $Rc = -0.64$) and two of the hardiness variables (commitment: $Rc = -0.68$; control: $Rc = -0.44$). Although canonical correlation does not imply causality, the negative direction of the values suggests that the lower the participants' sense of wellbeing as explained by their work engagement, hardiness, managing own emotions, self-esteem and flourishing, the greater the likelihood that their overall sense of psychological wellbeing will be lower.

Variables Explaining the Retention-Related Attitudes Canonical Variate

Table 8.3 shows that all the variables contributed in explaining the overall canonical retention-related attributes construct variate. Turnover intention ($Rc = 0.92$) accounted the most in explaining the retention-related canonical construct variate, followed by work-related bullying ($Rc = 0.71$), person-related bullying ($Rc = 0.63$) and physical intimidation ($Rc = 0.54$).

Table 8.3 Results of the standardised canonical correlation analysis for the first canonical function

Variate/variables	Canonical coefficient (Weight)	Structure coefficient (Canonical Loading) (Rc)	Canonical cross-loadings (Rc)	Squared multiple correlation (Rc^2)
Psychological wellbeing attributes canonical variate (composite set of latent independent variables)				
General self-esteem	−93.84	−0.35	−0.23	0.05
Social self-esteem	−32.78	−0.09	−0.06	0.004
Personal self-esteem	−64.30	−0.37	−0.24	0.06
Perception of emotion	0.06	−0.16	−0.10	0.01
Managing own emotions	−0.01	−0.31	−0.20	0.04
Managing others' emotions	−0.10	−0.15	−0.10	0.01
Utilisation of emotion	−0.13	−0.08	−0.05	0.003
Hardiness commitment	−0.66	−0.68	−0.44	0.19
Hardiness control	−0.03	−0.44	−0.29	0.08
Hardiness challenge	0.43	−0.05	−0.03	0.001
Vigour	0.19	−0.70	−0.45	0.20
Dedication	−0.87	−0.84	−0.54	0.29
Absorption	0.10	−0.64	−0.41	0.17
Psychosocial flourishing	0.09	−0.39	−0.25	0.06
Percentage of overall variance of variables explained by their own canonical variables: 0.19				
Retention-related attitudes canonical variate (composite set of latent dependent variables)				
Work-related bullying	0.59	0.71	0.46	0.21
Person-related bullying	−0.24	0.63	0.41	0.17
Physical-intimidation bullying	0.07	0.54	0.35	0.12
Turnover intention	0.75	0.92	0.60	0.36
Percentage of overall variance of variables explained by their own canonical variables: 0.51				
Overall model fit measure (function1)				
Redundancy index: $Rc^2 = 0.21$ (percentage of overall variance in workplace bullying and turnover intention (dependent) canonical construct variables accounted for by the psychological wellbeing-related (independent) canonical construct variables): moderate effect				

Note N = 373

Wellbeing Dispositional Attributes Accounting for the Variance in the Retention-Related Canonical Construct Variate Variables

As shown in Table 8.3, the wellbeing attributes contributed significantly ($Rc^2 = 0.21$; moderate practical effect) in explaining the variance in the retention-related variables of workplace bullying and turnover intention. Using the cut-off guideline of $Rc \geq 0.40$, dedication ($Rc^2 = -0.54$; 29%; large practical effect), followed by vigour ($Rc^2 = -0.45$; 20%; large practical effect), hardiness commitment ($Rc^2 = -0.44$; 19%; large practical effect), and absorption $Rc^2 = -0.41$; 17%; large practical effect), accounted the most for the variance in the workplace bullying and turnover intention canonical variate variables. The negative direction of the loadings suggests that the lower participants' sense of engagement (vigour, dedication and absorption) and hardiness commitment (i.e. higher sense of alienation), the greater the likelihood that their perceptions of work-related and person-related bullying and turnover intention will be higher.

Retention-Related Attitudes Accounting for the Variance in the Wellbeing Dispositional Attributes Canonical Construct Variate Variables

High turnover intention ($Rc^2 = 0.60$; 36%; large practical effect), contributed the most in explaining the variance in the wellbeing dispositional attributes followed by the other three workplace bullying variables (small to moderate practical effect). High retention-related attitudes are associated with lower wellbeing, with turnover intention having the largest explanatory power.

The results provided evidence in support of the research hypothesis: Low levels of wellbeing dispositional attributes will explain high levels of turnover intention and strong perceptions of workplace bullying and vice versa.

Discussion

The research presented in this chapter explored the relationship dynamics between a composite set of wellbeing attributes (self-esteem, emotional intelligence, hardiness, work engagement and flourishing) and the retention-related attitudes of workplace bullying and turnover intention as a composite set of variables. The results highlighted work engagement (i.e. the positive fulfilling state of mind characterised by dedication, vigour and absorption) and hardiness commitment as key wellbeing attributes in explaining participants' perceptions of work-related and person-related bullying and their turnover intention. The findings corroborate previous research showing that work engagement related negatively to employees' turnover intention (Kim 2017; Shuck et al. 2011). Previous research also indicates work engagement as a buffering mechanism in the workplace bullying-turnover intention link (Coetzee and Van Dyk 2018). Research further shows negative links between high levels of hardiness commitment and low turnover intention and less strong perceptions of workplace bullying (Van Dyk 2016). Generally, hardiness broadens individuals' mindsets which allow them to appraise stressors in a way that minimises the level of threat perceived and limits the amount of negative arousal experienced (Kobasa 1982). However, the results showed that strong perceptions of workplace bullying and turnover intention were likely to adversely influence the hardiness commitment attributes of feeling excited and a strong sense of community and motivation to remain engaged during difficult times, which could also explain the lower levels of work engagement.

The four wellbeing attributes allude to intrinsic affective-cognitive states of motivation, persistence, excitement, meaningfulness and challenge (Ferreira 2012; Rich et al. 2010; Reijseger et al. 2017; Schaufeli and Bakker 2004; Van Dyk 2016). Extending on the reasoning of Frederickson's (2004) broaden-and-build theory, low levels of engagement and hardiness commitment reflect a negative emotional-cognitive state alluding to low levels of wellbeing at work which may result in narrow-mindedness and the inability to build the personal resources needed to cope with stressful work experiences. The findings suggest that negative feelings (i.e. low levels of work engagement and hardiness commitment) generally create the urge to escape (i.e. high turnover intentions) and lower the propensity to create personal resources to cope with difficult work circumstances (i.e. resulting in stronger perceptions of falling victim to workplace bullying and person-related bullying). On the other hand, building on the premises of broaden-and-build theory (Frederickson 2004), the presence of positive levels of engagement and hardiness commitment may help to broaden employees' mindsets about their experiences in the workplace which may help them to build the interpersonal connections that enhance their personal resources, which in turn, may help them to cope constructively with difficult circumstances (i.e. resulting in lower turnover intention and less strong perceptions of bullying).

Dedication (i.e. feeling inspired by and taking pride in one's work, seeing work as meaningful and challenging) was highlighted as the strongest attribute in explaining participants' turnover intention and perceptions of bullying. The results suggest that work that fails to engender these feelings may result in higher turnover intention. Research by Karlowicz and Ternus (2007) supports the link between dedication and turnover intention. The significant link between low levels of dedication and strong perceptions of workplace bullying could be attributed to research showing that acts of workplace bullying engender feelings of helplessness, anxiety and emotional exhaustion caused by perceiving impending threatening working conditions which lower employees' levels of wellbeing (Nielsen and Einarsen 2012; Razzaghian and Shah 2011). Meaningful work and positive workplace experiences have been found to increase employees' sense of dedication and overall work engagement (Hirschi 2012; Mendes and Stander 2011).

On the retention-related attitudes spectrum, high turnover intention followed by work-related bullying (i.e. lack of information, performing tasks below one's level of competence, unmanageable workloads: Einarsen et al. 2009) had a large practical effect in explaining low work engagement and hardiness alienation (i.e. low commitment). Moderate practical effects were observed in terms of the explanatory power of perceptions of person-related bullying (i.e. hostile behaviour, excessive humiliation and criticism, being ignored: Einarsen et al. 2009). The correlation results further showed positive associations between workplace bullying and turnover intention. The findings highlight the negative effect of turnover intentions and perceived acts of bullying on employees' sense of wellbeing as reflected in their low levels of work engagement and hardiness commitment. Turnover intention is regarded as a signal of psychological distress resulting from negative workplace and job experiences such as for example workplace bullying, leadership practices and job characteristics (Alhamwan and Matt 2015; Renn et al. 2013). Research provides evidence that exposure to bullying behaviour in the workplace results in experiences of psychological distress and health problems (Hogh et al. 2011; Nami and Nami 2011). Vague job descriptions, lack of clear work expectations and resources for work task performance have been found to be meaningful indicators of workplace bullying, which could result in lower levels of job performance, engagement, and commitment, and higher turnover intention (Balducci et al. 2012; Van Dyk 2016).

Implications for Retention Practice

The findings suggest that organisations need to be more aware of the negative consequences of work-related and person-related bullying behaviour in the workplace for the retention of valuable employees. Employees' turnover intentions are often signals of psychological distress as a consequence of perceptions of workplace bullying behaviour. Turnover intention (i.e. thoughts of leaving, plans and actions taken to leave the organisation) may lead to actual turnover behaviour and be costly for organisations and should not be ignored by organisations challenged by staff retention (Ozolina-Ozola 2014).

Organisations that tolerate bullying behaviour can enforce misbehaviour and be seen to endorse a culture that permits bullying behaviour. Interpersonal conflict, aggressive personality types, work stress, restrictive job characteristics, person-job/workplace misfit and poor leadership practices often act as antecedents of bullying behaviour and should be formally addressed by management policies and procedures (Einarsen et al. 2009; Glasø et al. 2011; Van Dyk 2016). On the other hand, organisations that act consistently against workplace bullying will create a climate where employees feel safe, and consequently increase their psychological wellbeing and decrease turnover intentions (Van Dyk 2016). Offering efficient support and rehabilitation systems for victims of bullying behaviour and establishing organisational policies and structures that aim to prevent and manage acts of workplace bullying may help to mitigate the occurrence of bullying and reduce turnover intentions (Einarsen et al. 2003).

The findings of the present research showed that turnover intention and perceptions of work-related and person-related bullying had potentially adverse effects on employees' sense of wellbeing at work, and especially their work engagement and hardiness commitment. Fostering employees' work engagement has been acknowledged by scholars, managers and practitioners as the key to an organisation's success and competitiveness because of its link with organisational performance, productivity, retention, financial performance and shareholder return (Gruman and Saks 2011; Schaufeli and Salanova 2007). May et al (2004) further regard engagement as key to address employees' lack disengagement or alienation (i.e. low hardiness commitment) and motivation. Organisations can foster psychological conditions that broaden and build employees' beliefs regarding how meaningful it is to bring themselves to a role performance (i.e. providing incentives to engage; feedback on their value to the company). Conditions that foster psychological safety (i.e. perceptions of feeling safe to bring oneself to a role performance without fear or damage to self-image, status or career) is also essential for enhancing employees' engagement. Fostering psychological availability (i.e. the perception of how available one is to bring oneself into a role, including having the physical, emotional and psychological resources one can bring into the role) is another condition in enhancing employees' engagement (Gruman and Saks 2011). Acts of bullying may be distractions of engagement that adversely affect the psychological conditions of work engagement because they result in the depletion of physical, mental and emotional energy, and enhance feelings of insecurity, all of which allude to psychological distress and narrowmindedness in coping (Gruman and Saks 2011).

Apart from designing jobs and performance management systems that facilitate employees' sense of dedication, vigour, absorption and hardiness commitment, organisations must also foster a work climate, policies and practices that support and reward worker commitment and dedication toward their jobs. Such an approach generally culminates in high job performance and low turnover intention which benefit both the individual and the organisation. Meaningful work that fits the occupational identity of the employee and work that fulfils employees' psychological needs for autonomy, competence and relatedness may enhance their work engagement and commitment, and by implication reduce their turnover intention (Hirschi 2012; McAllister et al. 2017). Employees' work engagement and hardiness commitment could be managed and enhanced through human resource and leadership practices that mitigate and prevent workplace bullying behaviour and provide organisational support in the form of job resources (i.e. benefits, autonomy, performance feedback, social support, manageable and flexible work schedules, learning and career development opportunities) and personal support in the form of mentoring, counselling and wellness practices (Kim 2017; Takawira 2017; Skogstad et al. 2011).

Limitations and Directions for Future Research

The findings of the study should be interpreted with caution due to the exploratory correlational design. No cause-effect relations could be established but merely the magnitude and direction of associations between the variables. Longitudinal research designs are recommended for future studies. The cross-sectional research design limits the generalisability of the findings to the study population. Future research should consider replicating the study with additional measures of well-being and retention-related attitudes in various occupational and socio-demographic contexts. Although common method bias as a result of the self-report measures was limited by treating the respondents' responses as anonymous and confidential, future research designs should consider the possibility of common method variance.

Summary

The study extended retention theory by providing new insights on the relationship dynamics between wellbeing attributes and retention-related attitudes as seen through the theoretical lens of the broaden-and-build theory. The results substantiated that employees' turnover intention and perceptions of workplace bullying are important to consider in retention strategies because of their negative link with employees' psychological wellbeing, engagement and commitment levels in the workplace. The new insights derived from the study findings indicate that for organisations to capitalize on employees' wellbeing attributes for retention purposes, leadership and human resource practices should counteract perceptions of workplace bullying and turnover intention.

References

Alhamwan, M., & Mat, N. (2015). Antecedents of turnover intention behavior among nurses: A theoretical review. *Journal of Management and Sustainability, 5*(1), 84–89.

Allen, T. D., Johnson, R. C., Saboe, K. N., Cho, E., Dumani, S., & Evans, S. (2012). Dispositional variables and work-family conflict: a meta-analysis. *Journal of Vocational Behavior, 80,* 17–26.

Balducci, C., Cecchin, M., & Fraccaroli, F. (2012). The impact of role stressors on workplace bullying in both victims and perpetrators, controlling for personal vulnerability factors: A longitudinal analysis. *Work & Stress, 23*(3), 195–212.

Battle, J. (1992). *Culture-free self-esteem inventories for children and adults*. Texas: Pro-Ed.

Ciarrochi, J. V., Deane, F. P., & Anderson, S. (2002). Emotional intelligence moderates the relationship between stress and mental health. *Personality and Individual Differences, 32*(2), 197–209.

Coetzee, M. & Van Dyk, J. (2018). Workplace bullying and turnover intention: Exploring work engagement as a potential mediator. *Psychological Reports*, in press.

Cohen, J. (1992). Quantitative methods in psychology: A power primer. *Psychological Bulletin, 112*(1), 153–159.

De Guzman, A. B., & Choi, K. O. (2013). The relations of employability skills to career adaptability among technical school students. *Journal of Vocational Behavior, 82*, 199–207.

DeTienne, K. B., Agle, B. R., Phillips, J. C., & Ingerson, M. (2012). The impact of moral stress compared to other stressors on employee fatigue, job satisfaction, and turnover: An empirical investigation. *Journal of Business Ethics, 110*(3), 377–391.

Diener, E., Wirtz, D., Tov, W., Kim-Prieto, C., Choi, D., Oishi, S., et al. (2010). New wellbeing measures: Short scales to assess flourishing and positive and negative feelings. *Social Indicators Research, 97*(2), 143–156.

Dysvik, A., & Kuvaas, B. (2010). Exploring the relative and combined influence of mastery-approach goals and work intrinsic motivation on employee turnover intention. *Personnel Review, 39*(5), 622–638.

Einarsen, S., Hoel, H., Zapf, D., & Cooper, C. L. (2003). The concept of bullying at work: The European tradition. In S. Einarsen, H. Hoel, D. Zapf, & C. L. Cooper (Eds.), *Bullying and emotional abuse in the workplace: International perspectives in research and practice* (pp. 3–30). London, UK: Taylor & Francis.

Einarsen, S., Hoel, H., & Notelaers, G. (2009). Measuring exposure to bullying and harassment at work: Validity, factor structure and psychometric properties of the Negative Acts Questionnaire-Revised. *Work & Stress, 23*(1), 24–44.

Ferreira, N. (2012). Hardiness in relation to organisational commitment in the human resource management field. *Journal of Human Resource Management, 10*(2), 1–10.

Fredrickson, B. L. (1998). What good are positive emotions? *Review of General Psychology, 2*(3), 300–319.

Fredrickson, B. L. (2001). The role of positive emotions in positive psychology: The broaden-and-build theory of positive emotions. *American Psychologist, 56*(3), 218–226.

Fredrickson, B. L. (2004). The broaden-and-build theory of positive emotions. *Philosophical Transactions: Biological Sciences, 359*(1449), 1367–1377.

Glasø, L., Vie, T. L., Holmdal, G. R., & Einarsen, S. (2011). An application of affective events theory to workplace bullying: The role of emotions, trait anxiety, and trait anger. *European Psychologist, 16*(3), 198–208.

Greenbaum, R. L., Mawritz, M. D., & Piccolo, R. F. (2015). When leaders fail to 'walk the talk': Supervisor undermining and perceptions of leader hypocrisy. *Journal of Management, 41*(3), 929–956.

Gruman, J. A., & Saks, A. M. (2011). Performance management and employee engagement. *Human Resource Management Review, 21*, 123–136.

Hair, J., Black, W., Babin, B., & Anderson, R. (2010). *Multivariate data analysis*. Englewood Cliffs, NJ: Pearson Education.

Hansen, A., Byrne, Z., & Kiersch, C. (2014). How interpersonal leadership relates to employee engagement. *Journal of Managerial Psychology, 29*(8), 953–972.

Harrington, R. (2013). *Stress, health, and wellbeing: Thriving in the 21st century*. Belmont, CA: Wadsworth Cengage Learning.

Hauge, L. J., Skogstad, A., & Einarsen, S. (2010). Personality and social sciences: The relative impact of workplace bullying as a social stressor at work. *Scandinavian Journal of Psychology, 51*(5), 426–433.

Hirschi, A. (2012). Callings and work engagement: Moderated mediation model of work meaningfulness, occupational identity, and occupational self-efficacy. *Journal of Counseling Psychology, 15*(3), 479–485.

Hogh, A., Mikkelsen, E. G., & Hansen, A. M. (2011). Individual consequences of workplace bullying/ mobbing. In S. Einarsen, H. Hoel, D. Zapf, & C. L. Cooper (Eds.), *Bullying and harassment in the workplace. Developments in theory, research, and practice* (pp. 107–128). Boca Raton, FL: CRC Press.

Holtom, B. C., Mitchell, T. R., Lee, T. W., & Eberly, M. B. (2008). Turnover and retention research: A glance at the past, a closer view of the present, and a venture into the future. *The Academy of Management Annals, 2*(1), 231–274.

Kalliath, T., & Kalliath, P. (2012). Changing work environments and employee wellbeing: An introduction. *International Journal of Manpower, 33*(7), 729–737.
Kardum, I., Hudek-Knežević, J., & Krapić, N. (2012). The structure of hardiness, its measurement invariance across gender and relationships with personality traits and mental health outcomes. *Psychological Topics, 21*(3), 487–507.
Karlowicz, K. A., & Ternus, M. P. (2007). Issues influencing psychiatric nurse retention during the first year of employment: a case analysis. *Journal of Nursing Management, 17*(1), 49–58.
Kim, W. (2017). Examining mediating effects of work engagement among job resources, job performance and turnover intention. *Performance Improvement Quarterly, 29*(4), 407–425.
Kobasa, S. C. (1982). The hardy personality: Toward a social psychology of stress and health. In G. S. Sanders & J. Suls (Eds.), *Social psychology of health and illness* (pp. 3–32). Hillsdale, NJ: Lawrence Erlbaum.
Kobasa, S. C., Maddi, S. R., & Kahn, S. (1982). Hardiness and health: A prospective study. *Journal of Personality and Social Psychology, 42*(1), 168–177.
Maddi, S. R. (1987). Hardiness training at Illinois Bell Telephone. In J. P. Opatz (Ed.), *Health promotion evaluation: Measuring the organizational impact* (pp. 101–115). Stevens Point, WI: National Wellness institute.
Maddi, S. R. (2008). The courage and strategies of hardiness as helpful in growing despite major, disruptive stresses. *American Psychologist, 63*(6), 563–564.
May, D. R., Gilson, R. L., & Harter, L. M. (2004). The psychological conditions of meaningfulness, safety and availability and the engagement of the human spirit at work. *Journal of Occupational and Organizational Psychology, 77,* 11–37.
McAllister, C. P., Harris, J. N., Hochwarter, W. A., Perrewé, P. L., & Ferris, G. R. (2017). Got resources? A multi-sample constructive replication of perceived resource availability's role in work passion-job outcomes relationships. *Journal of Business and Psychology, 32,* 147–164.
Mendes, F., & Stander, M. W. (2011). Positive organisation: The role of leader behaviour in work engagement and retention. *South African Journal of Industrial Psychology, 37*(1), 1–13.
Nami, G., & Nami, R. F. (2011). *The bully-free workplace: Stop jerks, weasels, and snakes from killing your organization.* Hoboken, NJ: Wiley.
Nielsen, M. B., & Einarsen, S. (2012). Outcomes of exposure to workplace bullying: A meta-analytic review. *Work & Stress, 26*(4), 309–332.
Oade, A. (2009). *Managing workplace bullying: How to identify, responds to and manage bullying behaviour in the workplace.* Basingstoke, UK: Palgrave Macmillan.
O'Boyle, E. H., Jr., Humphrey, R. H., Pollack, J. M., Hawver, T. H., & Story, P. A. (2011). The relation between emotional intelligence and job performance: A meta-analysis. *Journal of Organizational Behavior, 32*(5), 788–818.
Ozolina-Ozola, I. (2014). The impact of human resource management practices on employee turnover. *Social and Behavioral Sciences, 156,* 223–226.
Paillé, P. (2011). Perceived stressful work, citizenship behaviour and intention to leave the organization in a high turnover environment: Examining the mediating role of job satisfaction. *Journal of Management Research, 3*(1), 1–16.
Razzaghian, M., & Shah, A. (2011). Prevalence, antecedents, and effects of workplace bullying: A review. *African Journal of Business Management, 5*(35), 13419–13427.
Renn, R., Allen, D., & Huning, T. (2013). The relationship of social exclusion at work with self-defeating behavior and turnover. *The Journal of Social Psychology, 153*(2), 229–249.
Reijseger, G., Peeters, M. C. W., Taris, T. W., & Schaufeli, W. B. (2017). From motivation to activation: Why engaged workers are better performers. *Journal of Business and Psychology, 32,* 117–130.
Rich, B. L., Lepine, J. A., & Crawford, E. R. (2010). Job engagement: Antecedents and effects on job performance. *Academy of Management Journal, 53*(3), 617–635.
Rodwell, J., Brunetto, Y., Demir, D., Shacklock, K., & Farr-Wharton, R. (2014). Supervision and links to nurse intentions to quit. *Journal of Nursing Scholarship, 46*(5), 357–365.
Ryff, C. D., & Keyes, C. L. M. (1995). The structure of psychological wellbeing revisited. *Journal of Personality and Social Psychology, 69*(4), 719–727.

SAS. (2013). *Statistical Analysis System, Version 6.1.* Cary, NC: SAS Institute Inc.
Schaufeli, W. B., & Bakker, A. B. (2004). Job demands, job resources and their relationship with burnout and engagement: A multi-sample study. *Journal of Organisational Behaviour, 25*(3), 293–315.
Schaufeli, W. B., & Salanova, M. (2007). Work engagement: An emerging psychological concept and its implications for organizations. In S. W. Gilliland, D. D. Steiner, & D. P. Skarlicki (Eds.), *Managing social and ethical issues in organizations* (pp. 135–177). Greenwich, CT: Information Age Publishing.
Schaufeli, W. B., Salanova, M., González-Romá, V., & Bakker, A. B. (2002). The measurement of engagement and burnout: A confirmatory factor analytic approach. *Journal of Happiness Studies, 3*(1), 71–92.
Schutte, N. S., Malouff, J. M., & Bhullar, N. (2009). The Assessing Emotions Scale. In C. Stough, D. Saklofske, & J. Parker (Eds.), *The assessment of emotional intelligence* (pp. 119–135). New York: Springer.
Sherry, A., & Henson, R. K. (2005). Conducting and interpreting canonical correlation analysis in personality research: a user-friendly primer. *Journal of Personality Assessment, 84,* 37–48.
Shuck., B., Reio, T. G., Jr., & Rocco, T. S. (2011). Employee engagement: An examination of antecedent and outcome variables. *Human Resource Development International, 14*(4), 427–445.
Skogstad, A., Torsheim, T., & Einarsen, S. (2011). Testing the work environment hypothesis of bullying on a group level of analysis: Psychosocial factors as precursors of observed workplace bullying. *Applied Psychology: An International Review, 60,* 475–495.
Sowislo, J. F., & Orth, U. (2013). Does low self-esteem predict depression and anxiety? A meta-analysis of longitudinal studies. *Psychological Bulletin, 139*(1), 213–240.
Spector, P. E., & Bruk-Lee, V. (2008). Conflict, health, and well-being. In C. K. W. de Dreu & M. J. Gelfand (Eds.), *The psychology of conflict and conflict management in organizations* (pp. 267–288). San Francisco: Jossey-Bass.
Takawira, N. (2017). *Constructing a psychosocial profile for enhancing the career success of South African professional women.* (Unpublished doctoral thesis), University of South Africa, Pretoria, South Africa.
Van den Broeck, A., Baillien, E., & De Witte, H. (2011). Workplace bullying: A perspective from the Job Demands-Resources model. *South African Journal of Industrial Psychology, 37*(2), Art. #879, 12 pages. https://doi.org/10.4102/sajip.v37i2.879.
Van Dyk, J. (2016). *The mediating effect of a psychological wellbeing profile in the bullying and turnover intention relation.* (Unpublished doctoral dissertation), University of South Africa, Pretoria, South Africa.
Vazi, M. L. M., Ruiter, R. A. C., van den Borne, B., Martin, G., Dumont, K., & Reddy, P. S. (2013). The relationship between wellbeing indicators and teacher psychological stress in Eastern Cape public schools in South Africa. *SA Journal of Industrial Psychology, 39*(1), 1–10.
Wu, K., Li, C., & Johnson, D. E. (2011). Role of self-esteem in the relationship between stress and ingratiation. *Psychological Reports, 108*(1), 239–251.
Zhang, G., & Lee, G. (2010). The moderation effects of perceptions of organizational politics on the relationship between work stress and turnover intention: An empirical study about civilian in skeleton government of China. *iBusiness, 2,* 268–273.

Melinde Coetzee (DLitt et Phil) is a Professor in the Department of Industrial and Organisational Psychology at the University of South Africa, Pretoria, South Africa. She has extensive experience in the corporate environment on psychological interventions pertaining to organisational development, human capacity and career development and talent retention. Her research interests include issues of employability and career and retention psychology in multi-cultural work contexts. She is Chief Editor of the *South African Journal of Industrial Psychology* and also the author, co-author and editor of a number of academic books. She has published in numerous accredited academic journals. She has also co-authored and contributed chapters to books nationally and internationally. She has presented numerous academic papers and posters at national and international conferences. She is a professionally registered Psychologist (cat. Industrial) with the Health Professions Council of South Africa (HPCSA) and a master human resource practitioner with the South African Board for People Practice (SABPP). She is a member of SIOPSA and IAAP.

Jeannette van Dyk (DCom) is an industrial psychologist, independent practice affiliated with the Department of Industrial and Organisational Psychology, University of South Africa, South Africa. Her research interests are retention and turnover intention. She has published various scientific articles on the theme and has presented papers at conferences.

Part IV
Employee Characteristics

Overview and Insights

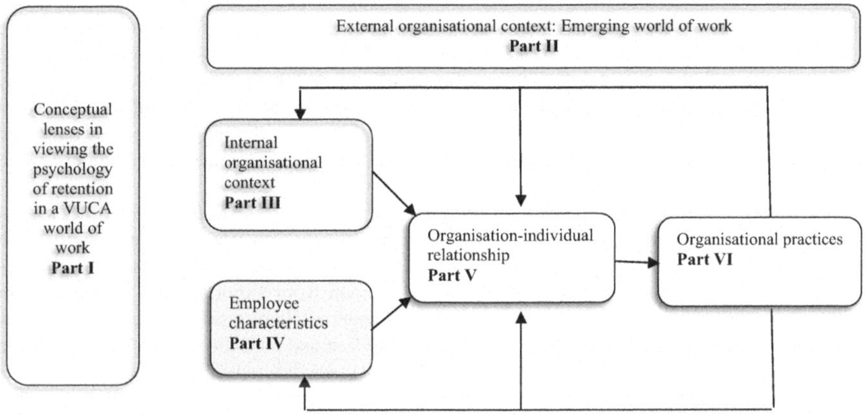

Towards an integrated conceptual framework for the psychology of retention

Part IV, *Employee Characteristics*, comprises five chapters that explore the role of employee characteristics in the psychology of retention. The various chapters extend on the basic premise of Part III that behaviour is a function of personal and environmental factors within a specific organisational context which should be considered in understanding the reasons why employees decide to stay in or leave an organisation. Part IV emphasises the unique characteristics of the individual and highlights issues of multi-generational theory and diversity that should be considered in the psychology of retention. The chapters in Part IV demonstrate how socio-demographic diversity impacts on retention by examining how person–organisational factors interact with individuals' socio-demographic characteristics.

Part IV: Overview

In Chap. 9, *Personal Attributes Framework for Talent Retention*, Ingrid Potgieter makes a compelling case for the role of personal attributes such as self-esteem, employability attributes, organisational commitment and career adaptability in the retention of valuable employees.

Anchored in a review of the retention research literature, the author describes these personal attributes as important psychological career resources essential for the retention of employees. The author recommends that human resource practitioners and industrial psychologists should utilise interventions that assist individuals in developing these personal attributes in order to enhance their intention to stay. The chapter makes a valuable contribution to the retention literature by presenting a personal attributes framework for retention which includes practical intervention suggestions relating to the personal attributes discussed in the chapter.

In Chap. 10, *Multi-generational Workforce and its Implication for Talent Retention Strategies*, Edyta Kostanek and Violetta Khoreva provide a discussion on the current multi-generational workforce's (i.e. Silent Generation, Baby Boomers, Generation X and the Millennials) values and expectations. The authors argue that for organisations to keep up with the different generation's values, attitudes, behaviours and expectations, managers must be able to diversify, customise and adjust their approaches to talent management and retention practices. The chapter makes a valuable contribution by translating the unique needs and expectations of the various generational cohorts into specific retention practices proposed for each generational cohort. The authors also argue that talent management practices will look differently in organisations that are undergoing rapid organisational transformations than in more stable multi-national companies (MNCs) and that the former should approach their talent retention from a strategic perspective.

Chapter 11 by Nadia Ferreira, *Talent Retention Strategies: The Role of Self-regulatory Career Behaviour among Working Adults*, makes a convincing case for the role of self-regulatory career behaviours (i.e. career adaptability, employability attributes and organisational commitment) in designing career development interventions for employee retention. Based on a review of the research literature, the author explains the relationship dynamics among self-regulatory behaviour and outlines how various retention factors can be considered in designing career development interventions that support employee retention. A novel contribution is the self-regulatory career behaviour profile that is positioned in the context of retention practices.

In Chap. 12, *Career Development of Professional Women: The Role of Person−Centered Characteristics on Career Satisfaction*, Ndayiziveyi Takawira focuses on the unique career development needs of professional women that need to be considered in talent retention strategies. Drawing from a sample of professionally qualified women from various South African organisations (N = 606), the author shows that core person-centered characteristics (race, job level and total monthly income, age, marital status, number of children and education level) were significant predictors of their career satisfaction. The author also discusses differences among the biographical groups regarding career satisfaction, indicating differing needs. The chapter extends retention research and practice by providing new insights that could inform the design of career development interventions to address the unique career needs of women.

Chapter 13 by Rodrigo Serrat, Feliciano Villar and Montserrat Celdrán, *Encouraging Older People to Continue Participating in Civil Society Organizations: A Systematic Review and Conceptual Framework*, makes an important case for older people's participation in civil society organisations. The chapter identifies and classifies factors associated with the retention of older participants in civil society organisations and explores empirically based measures for promoting retention of older participants in civil society organisations. A novel contribution to the retention literature is the proposed conceptual framework that deepens insight into these factors (classified as means-related, motives-related, or organisational and opportunity context-related). The authors discuss the implications of the factors for retention theory and practice. The authors convincingly argue that strategies to promote continued participation among older people are important for the sustainability of organisations in the future.

Part IV: Key Insights

Part IV of the book illustrates the dynamics of employee characteristics in the psychology of retention and how these characteristics inform retention practices.

Practice Guidelines

The author of Chap. 9 suggests a range of interventions to address the psychological needs, intrinsic motivational functioning and personal attributes of employees. The author also recommends career supportive interventions that enhance the self-esteem, employability, career adaptability and organisational commitment of the employee. In Chap. 10, the authors emphasise formal assessments of workplace values and attitudes of the generations represented in the company's workforce. The needs of the young talent groups (e.g. Millennials) in contemporary organisational transformation contexts are highlighted. The authors suggest flexible talent management and retention practices that offer a more personalised approach that would be more suitable to the workforce that is increasingly made of independent and flexibility-seeking Millennials. They also suggest developmental opportunities, meaningful job tasks across all generational cohorts, providing Silent Generation with benefits and retirement plans and Millennials with increased job flexibility and self-reliance at workplace.

The author of Chap. 11 highlights the importance of understanding and measuring how employees' self-regulatory career behaviour influences their perception of retention practices. The author recommends a partnership between managers, career counsellors and HR practitioners in developing employees' career adaptability, employability attributes and organisational commitment by implementing training and development programmes, career development opportunities and continuous learning programmes, as well as interventions to assist them in gaining career self-management skills. In Chap. 12, the author illustrates the importance of understanding the unique career development needs of professional women and the influence of person-centered characteristics on the career satisfaction of professional women across different career stages. Career development support is seen as an important retention practice including flexible career paths for individual development to increase satisfaction with careers, training interventions to increase a sense of control over career decisions and mentoring networks and coaching practices. In Chap. 13, the authors illustrate the importance of interventions to keep older people as a valuable resource for the sustainability of the organisation optimally engaged. Some retention practices include inter alia adapting tasks and allowing less time-intensive forms of participation for older participants with disabilities or in poor health, or those with care commitments or those engaged in other productive activities; ride-share opportunities for those experiencing transport problems or who live in rural areas and virtual- or home-based participation opportunities.

Research Gaps

The research presented in the various chapters mostly represented a Western view of the manifestation of employee characteristics in specific organisational and cultural settings. In general, the authors recommend additional measures of diversity to assess the influence of diverse socio-demographic and cultural factors on the psychology of retention. More theoretical and empirical research is encouraged to investigate the role of various employee characteristics and diversity measures in relation to talent retention strategies.

The author of Chap. 9 based her theoretical personal attributes framework on research conducted in various organisational settings among various occupational groups. Future research should explore the application of the framework in global contexts and its relevance to the digital and VUCA world of work context. The authors of Chap. 10 recommend inter alia research that helps uncover whether generational values and attitudes towards workplace depend on a societal, cultural and contextual issues. Research should further investigate generational, national and cultural differences in relation to talent retention and should focus on other than Western perspectives and organisations. In Chap. 11, the author recommends continued research on the manifestation of employee self-regulatory behaviour in relation to their career adaptability, employability attributes and organisational commitment for diverse groups in diverse settings. The author of Chap. 12 recommends longitudinal studies among diverse occupational, gender, race and age groups in various occupational contexts to assess differences regarding the factors influencing their career satisfaction. In Chap. 13, the authors recommend the development of a standardised instrument measuring the retention of older participants that takes into account the results from previous research and the conceptual framework they propose in this chapter.

Chapter 9
Personal Attributes Framework for Talent Retention

Ingrid L. Potgieter

Abstract The 21st century world of work is characterised by exceptional levels of talent mobility as employees try to satisfy their own requirements, with a resultant growing concern among organisations about the retention of talented employees. Organisations in the 21st-century workplace are increasingly realising that employees are their most valuable asset, and as a result they are constantly trying to create an employment brand that is attractive to both existing employees and potential talent, while competing in a "war for talent". Recent research emphasised that it is not only monetary awards or stability that influences an individuals' decision to remain with an organisation, but that several personal attributes also play a role in the retention of valuable employees. These personal attributes include self-esteem, employability attributes, organisational commitment and career adaptability. Based on the relationship found between these personal attributes and retention, human resource practitioners and industrial psychologists should utilise interventions to assist individuals to enhance their personal attributes in order to enhance their intention to stay.

Keywords Talent retention · Personal attributes · Self-esteem · Employability attributes · Organisational commitment · Career adaptability

Introduction

Numerous changes took place in the 21st century workplace. Individuals are now faced with lower job security, limited employment opportunities, rapid changing technology, international pressures and competition, as well as increasing pressures to perform, to be adaptable and to become and remain employable (Ineson et al. 2013; Marock 2008). These fast-paced changes have created the question of

I. L. Potgieter (✉)
Department of Human Resource Management, University of South Africa, Pretoria, South Africa
e-mail: visseil@unisa.ac.za

M. Coetzee et al. (eds.), *Psychology of Retention*,
https://doi.org/10.1007/978-3-319-98920-4_9

whether individuals will be able to cope with these changes, be more adaptable and whether they will stay loyal to one organisation (Mclaggan et al. 2013). It is evident that in recent days, it is expected from employees to take control of their own career development and career management and constantly improve their knowledge, skills and competencies to remain employable (De Guzman and Choi 2013; Froehlich et al. 2014; Lent 2013; Savickas 2012). Strategies in order to increase employees' employability and personal attributes may contribute towards higher retention within organisations.

This chapter therefore focuses on the personal attributes important for the successful retention of valuable employees. The concept of personal attributes refers to a set of psychological career resources essential for the retention of employees. Although several definitions for this term can be found, for the purpose of this study, psychological career resources refer to personal attributes and abilities, such as career orientation awareness, sense of purpose, self-esteem, emotional intelligence, behavioural adaptability and self-knowledge. These attributes and abilities enables individuals to manage their own careers and to be self-sufficient learners (Briscoe and Hall 1999; Coetzee 2008; Coetzee and Roythorne-Jacobs 2012; Hall and Chandler 2005; Herr et al. 2004). Several research found that individuals with a high number of psychological career resources are able to adapt to changing career circumstances relatively easy and also demonstrates high levels of employability (Fugate et al. 2004; Griffen and Hesketh 2005). Given the evidence that personal attributes can be taught and learned (Baumeister and Leary 1995; Pool and Sewell 2007; Salovey and Meyer 1990) and that more emphasis are recently placed on developing an enhancing an individual's employability skills (Coetzee and Beukes 2010; Pool and Sewell 2007), a framework linking personal attributes variables together may be a useful tool in retention practices. This chapter discusses a psychological profile constituting the personal attributes required for effective retention of valuable employees.

Theoretical Support for Linking Self-esteem, Organisational Commitment, Career Adaptability and Employability to Retention

Self-esteem refers to an individual's general feeling of self-worth (Battle 1992; Coetzee 2005; Hewitt 2002; Maslow 1970; Potgieter 2012; Quick and Nelson 2013). It is defined by several components, namely, general, social or peer and personal self-esteem. Kim (2015) found that individuals with a high self-esteem are more likely to remain loyal to a company. Potgieter (2012) also pointed out that self-esteem is an important psychological factor to consider in retention strategies. It is thus evident that by enhancing self-esteem, employees will more likely remain with a company, thereby increasing retention of employees (De Cuyper et al. 2012).

Organisational commitment is a psychological situation that binds an employee to an organisation which will positively influence an employee to remain with an organisation (Allen and Meyer 1996; Meyer and Allen 1997). Tsai and Cheng (2011) included general interests, principles, values, objectives and goals (all related to emotional components) in their definition of organisational commitment. In this study, organisational commitment specifically includes the psychological state that exposes the level of an individual's commitment and emotional attachment towards the organisation (affective commitment), the pre-existing behaviours that are expected to result from this commitment (normative commitment) and the necessity to remain with an organisation as the cost of leaving will be too high (continuance commitment).

According to Ahmad and Oranye (2010), employees with a high level of organisational commitment identify with the organisational morals, goals and objectives, devote their energies to achieving organisational objectives and choose to remain with the organisation (Fisk and Friesen 2012). Nawab and Bhatti's (2011) research findings suggest that organisational commitment increases employee commitment, which in turn influences employees' intention to stay in a positive way. Several research found a positive and significant link between organisation commitment and retention (Chang et al. 2013; Dhar 2015; Döckel 2003, 2006; Guchait and Choi 2012; Khasawneh et al. 2012; Krüger and Rootman 2010; Srivastava 2013). It is therefore evident that if contemporary organisations keep their employees loyal and committed, they will be more likely to retain valuable skills and competencies (Ferreira et al. 2010; Lumley et al. 2011; Neininger et al. 2010; Stoltz 2014).

Career adaptability as defined as the psychological ability to adapt to and cope with changing career circumstances (Savickas 1997; Savickas and Porfelli 2012). Tolentino et al. (2013) states that career adaptability include a range of attitudes, behaviours and competencies that employees need to have in order to successfully adapt to career transitions and change within the work context. Relevant to this study, career adaptability includes the elements of career concern, career control, career cusiosity and career confidence. Several authors noted that career adaptability has become essential for employees in todays' fast changing workplace (Coetzee and Harry 2014; Savickas and Porfeli 2012). This has led to career adaptability becoming a core construct in the field of vocational psychology and in career management (Brown and Lent 2016).

Employees with high levels of career adaptability has been found to cope better (both cognitively and emotionally) with unpredictable changes in tasks (Savickas and Porfelli 2012).

Lent (2013) also found that, in general, employees with high levels of career adaptability, proactively manage their personal lives and development and put an effort in promoting their own careers. Savickas (2013) further found that employees with high levels of career adaptability has more psychosocial career resources that assist them to adapt and manage career and work-related changes and demands. Several studies have now shown that career adaptability is positively related to subjective career success, career satisfaction and minimal work stress (Johnston et al. 2013; Spurk and Volmer 2013; Zacher 2014; Zacher and Griffin 2015). Career success and satisfaction again has been positively linked to retention (Chan and Mai 2015). Ferreira et al. (2013) as well as Savickas et al. (2009) further supports these finding by providing empirical evidence of the link between career adaptability and retention. It is therefore seems evident that organisations should assist employees to continuously develop lifelong career strategies for individual career development, as well as to set and pursue their career goals (Chan and Mai 2015; Klehe et al. 2011).

Employability attributes refers to the set of skills, knowledge and attributes that all employees (and potential employees) should have in order to be effective in the workplace as well as to obtain, maintain and retain employment (Beukes 2010; McGrath 2009; Yorke and Knight 2007). Bezuidenhout and Coetzee (2011) view employability as a pscyhosocial construct consisting of various attributes. These attributes are values, dispositions and skills which promote proactive adaptability in changing environments. They enhance an individual's suitability for employment and the likelihood of career success. In this research, employability is viewed as a career meta-competency construct or a balance between the individual's competencies and skills and the labour market requirements (Nielsen 1999; Potgieter 2012).

According to Moore (2010), an employable worker demonstrates the following characteristics; flexible personality, willingness to learn, sufficient communicator, entrepreneur, employable, continuous learner, self-managed, innovator and independent thinker. Potgieter and Coetzee (2013) also found that employability is a personal attribute essential for employability. In the present study, employability is a psychosocial construct consisting of career related attributes which include career self-management; cultural competence; self-efficacy; career resilience; sociability; entrepreneurial orientation; proactivity and emotional literacy.

According to Sinha and Sinha (2012) employees need to enhance their employability on a continuous basis by focusing on their own professional development. According to Blackford (2013), career development, providing training opportunities for staff and continuous professional development can help an organisation to attract and retain highly talented employees. Training new employees and providing them with developmental opportunities diminishes their intention to leave the organisation (Khan et al. 2011; Singh 2013). Erasmus et al. (2015) also found a significant and positive relationship between employability and retention.

It is evident from the literature that several personal factors are essential for the effective and successful retention of valuable employees. Figure 9.1 gives an overview of the variables (and sub-variables) of the various personal attributes relevant to the retention context.

Previous research provided support on the link between the variables. However, no integrated study could be found linking these variables as a set of personal attributes to retention. Pool and Sewell (2007) found that self-esteem relates positively and significantly to employability. Individuals who feel and think that they can achieve anything (therefore displaying a high self-esteem) are more likely to

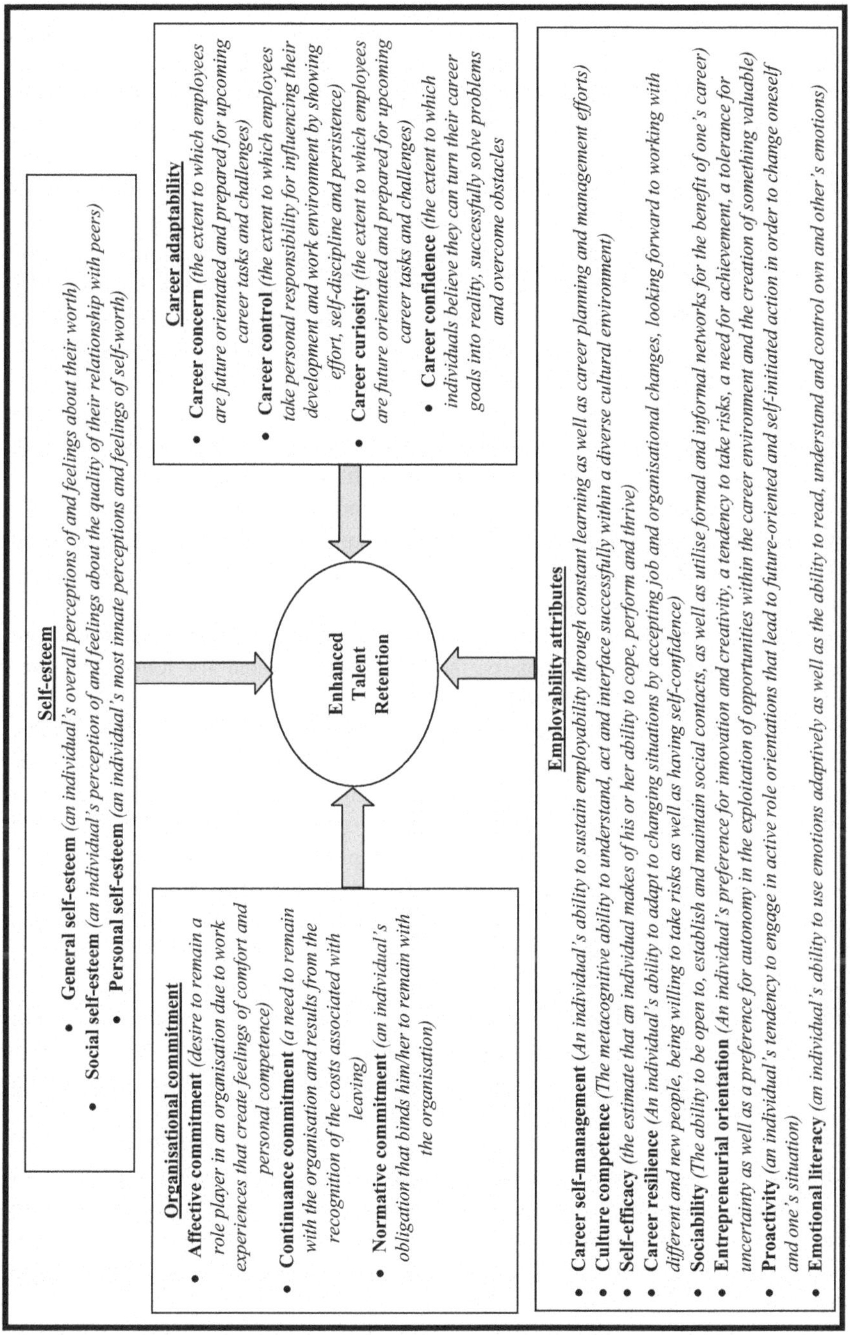

Fig. 9.1 Personal attributes relevant to retention

succeed in any occupation they choose as oppose to individuals with a lower self-esteem (Yorke and Knight 2004). The development of a healthy, high self-esteem therefore relates positively to employability (Coetzee 2008). These findings are in line with the findings of van Dyk (2011), Lane et al. (2004) and Potgieter (2012), who also found that individuals with higher self-esteem are more able to demonstrate employability attributes as opposed to individuals with low self-esteem.

Heimpel, Elliot and Wood (2006) found that people with high self-esteem are more likely than those with a low self-esteem to engage in adaptive coping efforts. Literature provides a theoretical connection between career adaptability and utilising one's strength (Heimpel et al. 2006). Similarly, a study done by Ismail (2015) found a positive relationship between self-esteem and career adaptability. Having high levels of self-esteem results in individuals who is able to effectively adapt to changing contexts and situations. Individuals with a low level of self-esteem were found to be less likely to engage in adaptive behaviours. Employers require their employees to be able to adapt to changing situations, as well as to have a good self-concept, greater self-confidence and thus high self-esteem.

A positive and healthy self-esteem is an important work participation resource in that it enhances the individual's motivation to remain loyal to the company (Kim 2015). Focusing on individuals' positive self-esteem makes them content and remain loyal to the organisation (Kim 2015), resultantly influencing their organisational commitment (Stoltz 2014). This is in line with the findings of Shahid and Azhar (2013) who found that positive self-esteem is critical for long term commitment to the organisation by employees.

Several studies found a positive link between career adaptability and organisational commitment (Coetzee and Schreuder 2014; Ellison and Schreuder 2000; Ndzube 2013). According to these authors, employees who are not adaptable tend to seek for alternative careers outside of their current organisations (Kim 2015). It seems evident from the literature that when employees are provided with many opportunities for career development within their organisations, they are less likely to leave (Abdulkareem et al. 2015; A'yuninnisa and Saptoto 2015; Chew and Chan 2008; Dardar et al. 2012; Juhdi et al. 2013; Samuel and Chipunza 2009; Yean and Yahya 2013).

Benson (2006) as well as De Cuyper et al. (2011) found a positive relationship between organisational commitment and employability. According to De Cuyper et al. (2011), employability may provide opportunities to enhance commitment among workers, and concern only rises when workers perceive better alternative employment opportunities outside of their current organisation. Potgieter et al. (2016) confirms this significant relationship as their study revealed that employability attributes provide security to employees. Employees with high employability attributes is likely to find a new job easily if required, and this allows them to develop a sense of commitment to their careers and occupations rather than to the organisation.

Career adaptability improves employability both within and separate from an organisation (Ito and Brotheridge 2005). De Guzman and Choi (2013) found that adolescents who show high career adaptability levels showed high confidence in their employability attributes. This in turn emphasises that people with higher levels of adaptability have a greater possibility of finding a suitable job. Porfeli and Savickas (2012) found that career adaptability was strongly associated with career identity (specifically with identification with career commitments as well as vocational exploration and) which emphasises that identity and career adaptability are fundamental in career construction (Savickas 2011). McArdle et al. (2007) supported these findings when they discovered that career adaptability predicted employability.

A Personal Attributes Framework for Talent Retention

Personal attributes (that is, self-esteem, organisational commitment, career adaptability and employability attributes) should theoretically be considered for a psychological framework to be used talent retention interventions and strategies.

It is important to explore the relationship between the sub elements of each of the four relevant constructs as this might guide organisations and human resource practitioners to develop and implement effective retention strategies. Such guidance can assist organisations to help individuals to increase and enhance their less developed personal attributes, which will positively influence retention. As a further aid to organisations and human resource practitioners, this research has attempted to develop a psychological framework consisting of personal attributes (self-esteem, organisational commitment, career adaptability and employability) in order to increase retention in the 21st century world of work.

Table 9.1 illustrates the psychological profile made up of an individual's personal attributes (self-esteem, organisational commitment, career adaptability and employability attributes). Because the psychological profile constitutes psychological career-related attributes, they are described in terms of personal and interpersonal behavioural attributes. This classification will also assist organisations and human resource practitioners to develop the personal attributes on the correct level.

Potgieter (2012), Jabaar (2017), Gani (2017) and Potgieter and Mawande (2017) recently conducted empirical investigations into the statistical interrelationship between the personal attributes construct variables (self-esteem, organisational commitment, career adaptability and employability attributes) and their implication on retention.

According to Potgieter and Mawande (2017), employees displaying high levels of self-esteem has sufficient confidence in their employabiltiy attributes. It is thus likely that individuals with high general, social and personal self-esteem are also likely to display high confidence in their career self-management, cultural competence, self-efficacy, career resilience, sociability, entrepreneurial orientation, proactivity, emotional literacy and overall employability attributes. This study also revealed that all sub elements of self-esteem and employability attributes are essential in the retention of valuable employees.

Table 9.1 Psychological profile reflecting personal attributes

Personal attributes	Personal level	Interpersonal level
Self-esteem	General self-esteem Social/peer self-esteem	Personal self-esteem
Organisational commitment	Normative commitment Continuance commitment	Affective commitment
Career adaptability	Concern Control Curiosity	Confidence
Employability	Career self-management Self-efficacy Career resilience Entrepreneurial orientation Proactivity	Emotional literacy Cultural competence Sociability

Jabaar (2017) found that employees who displayed high normative, affective as well as continuance commitment were highly adaptable and that all of these sub-variables were important for the retention of employees. Organisational commitment has shown significant positive correlations with all the career adaptability sub-variables as well (Jabaar 2017). Savickas (2013) notes that if employees are to feel concerned about their future career, they need to have a level of self-awareness, involvement and preparation. It is imperative for employees to be concerned, to demonstrate future orientated attitudes, to feel optimistic and to be future orientated about their careers (Hartung 2013). It is therefore important for retention interventions to focus on supporting employees with career-related decisions because most employees require guidance and support in planning and managing future careers (Maree 2015). In addition, employees need to be equipped with coping skills and assisted to find means to deal with career anxiety and career uncertainty as well as changes within the careers (Maree 2015). This may increase employees' ability to cope with and adapt to changing circumstances (such as changes in work tasks and work roles).In addition, it may assist employees to accept and embrace multi-tasking and job rotation (Spurk et al. 2016).

Employees who possess of high levels of organisational commitment react to the organisation with positive feelings (Ng 2015). According to Nayak and Sahoo (2015), highly committed employees have higher levels of career adaptability, have a high sense of responsibility and are likely less of a financial risk to the organisation. It is thus evident that employees with high career adaptability are more committed to the organisation (and thus have stronger feelings for, connection to and association with the organisation. Such employees are more likely to stay at the organisation for a longer period of time (Ferreira 2012). The results of this research therefore seem to be in line with several other studies that also found positive correlations between organisational commitment and career adaptability.

In the study done by Potgieter and Mawande (2017), all self-esteem variables positvley correlated with all sub elements of employability. It seems evident that employees with a high self-efficacy and emotional awareness may be more confident in displaying employabiltiy attributes. These employees may be more effective and succesful in managing their own careers, have a high sense of self-efficacy, be culturally competent, display career resilience, be sociable and proactive, display an orientation towards enterpreneurship and have a high emotional literacy. Several authors also reported a significant relationship between self-esteem and employability (Briscoe and Hall 1999; Coetzee and Roythorne-Jacobs 2012; Hall and Chandler 2005; Herr et al. 2004; Van der Velde and Van den Berg 2003; Weng and McElroy 2010).

It is interesting to note that personal and interpersonal psychological dimensions are found to be significant and important in a psychological profile for retention strategies. It thus seems that organisations should assist individuals to develop their personal attributes on a personal and interpersonal level in order to positively influence retention.

On a **personal level**, individuals' general self-esteem (Bandura 1999; Coetzee 2008; Pool and Sewell 2007; Potgieter and Mawande 2017; Yorke and Knight 2004), normative commitment (Jabaar 2017; Kuo 2013; Ojakaa et al. 2014), continuance commitment (Jabaar 2017; Mehta et al. 2014), career concern (Jabaar 2017; Šverko and Babarović 2016), career control (Jabaar 2017), career curiosity (Bezuidenhout and Coetzee 2011), career self-management (Bezuidenhout and Coetzee 2011; Coetzee and Beukes 2010), self-efficacy (Bezuidenhout and Coetzee 2011), career resilience, entrepreneurial orientation and proactivity (Bezuidenhout and Coetzee 2011; Coetzee 2012) may positively influence individuals intention to stay with an organisation (and therefore influence retention). Retention strategies should thus focus on creating self-awareness to make it possible to recognize (and improve) on underdeveloped personal attributes. By focusing on employability on a personal level may assist individuals to obtain employment and thereby enhance their employability as well as increase retention within an organisation. By increasing career concern, retention may also increase (Jabaar 2017). Furthermore, individuals should be assisted to enhance their general self-esteem and engage in managing their own careers. Such interventions could possibly increase the retention of valuable employees within an organisation. Retention strategies consisting of interventions to improve employees' confidence to become more willing to take risks and try creative solutions to problems when confronted with changing situations within the new world of work as well as to encourage employees to be inquisitive, may also increase retention within an organisation.

On an **interpersonal**, individuals' personal self-esteem (Coetzee 2008; Pool and Sewell 2007; Yorke and Knight 2004), social/peer-related self-esteem (Bandura 1999; Coetzee 2008; Pool and Sewell 2007; Yorke and Knight 2004), affective commitment (Gani 2017; Jabaar 2017), career confidence (Jabaar 2017), cultural competence and sociability (Bezuidenhout and Coetzee 2011; Coetzee 2012) and emotional literacy (Ashkanasy and Daus 2002; Brown et al. 2003; Bezuidenhout and Coetzee 2011; Coetzee and Beukes 2010; Jeager 2003; Yorke and Knight 2007) may influence the retention of valuable employees. Interventions on an interpersonal level may influence their ability to interact and network with others.

Effective interaction and networking may create employment opportunities for individuals and thereby enhance their employability and influencing an individual's willingness to stay within an organisation.

Retention strategies should help individuals to gain personal insight. This could enable individuals to improve on their personal self-esteem, display higher affective commitment and thus create a desire with employees to remain with an organisation. It could further enhance employees' career confidence and assist them to be able to manage and utilise emotions effectively. Furthermore, retention strategies on an interpersonal level could assist individuals to communicate and connect with people from other cultures or backgrounds. Positive and healthy relationships within the workplace positively influences retention. Such interventions could possibly influence the career success and satisfaction of employees and therefore increase the retention of valuable employees within an organisation.

Based on the literature review it seems as if all sub elements of the personal attributes (general self-esteem, social self-esteem, personal self-esteem, affective commitment, normative commitment, continuance commitment, career control, career concern, career curiosity, career self-management, self-efficacy, cultural competence, career resilience, sociability, entrepreneurial orientation, proactivity and emotional literacy) should be developed in order to increase the retention of valuable employees.

The following psychological profile for retention strategies (as shown in Table 9.2) are therefore included in the proposed personal attributes framework for retention.

Implications for Retention Theory and Practice

Jabaar (2017), Gani (2017), Harmsey (2017) and Potgieter and Mawande (2017) suggest that research on personal attributes (self-esteem, organisational commitment, career adaptability and employability) within the South African organisational context will provide valuable new insights to the body of knowledge relating to employee retention. Several research supports this notion by stating that employees are now more committed to their organisation if their psychological needs have been addressed (Ferreira and Coetzee 2013; Kim 2015).

Mercurio (2015) suggests that as human resource managers and practitioners seek to build organisational commitment and career adaptability, is it important to focus on what current practices are in place to address the psychological needs and personal attributes of employees.

Many organisations and research only focus on retention factors (for example salaries, benefits, positions, and career advancement structures) as a manner of increasing organisational commitment and career adaptability, thus they may be overlooking more personal factors which may influence an employees' intention to remain with a company (Mercurio 2015). Mercurio (2015) further found that the positive emotional connection employees have with their organisation improves

Table 9.2 Personal attributes framework for retention

Psychological dimension	Personal Attributes			
	Self-esteem	Organisational Commitment	Career adaptability	Employability attributes
Personal level	• Increase an individuals overall perceptions and feelings about themselves	• Increase an employees sense of obligation to remain with the organisation. • Provide good benefits which will increase the perceived cost of leaving the organisation	• Assist employees to be future orientated and help them to prepare for upcoming events and challenges • Assist employees to take personal responsibility for their own development. • Assist employees to be future orientated and help them to prepare for upcoming events and challenges	• Assist employees to engage in constant learning. Boost employees' confidence and thus increasing their perception of their ability to perform and cope • Create a safe working environment so that employees feel safe to take risks; assist employees to adapt to changing work situations. • Create a space for employees to be creative • Create opportunities for employees to engage in active role orientations
Interpersonal level	• Increase an employees feelings and perception about him/ herself • Assist in increasing interpersonal relationship amongst colleagues	• Create a healthy and fun environment which will increase the employee's desire to stay with the organisation	• Create a safe working environment to enable employees to turn their goals into reality, thereby boosting their confidence	• Assist employees read, understand and control their own emotions • Create cultural awareness and make an effort to engage employees from different cultures to one another • Create opportunities for social interaction between colleagues

organisational commitment and career adaptability. A higher self-esteem and confidence in displaying employability attributes contributes towards affective commitment within an organisation. It is therefore recommended that HR practices should consider more personal attributes when developing possible retention strategies and practices, as it is critical component of the retention of skilled, talented and valuable employees.

Spurk et al. (2016) recommend that organisations should implement training and coaching interventions that directly focus on developing employees' career adaptability. These practical recommendations will also be beneficial for employees who want to improve their loyalty and commitment to the organisation and their future careers (Spurk et al. 2016). In addition, it will support employees to adjust or increase job responsibilities for the future (Chong and Leong 2015) and in turn enhance their skills and commitment. Maggiori et al. (2013) also suggest that career adaptability leads to positive effects in the organisation. Employees who are thus more satisfied with their job environments, has a higher feeling of empowerment, are able to cope better with their working environmental challenges and therefore positively influences employees' self-esteem (Fiori et al. 2015).

According to Beeftink et al. (2012), emphasis should be placed on the development of self-esteem amongst individuals as a high self-esteem may foster faster and more effective task completion in order to meet organisational goals. Davis (2015) confirmed that it is essential to develop a supportive working environment that increases employee morale in order to retain talented employees.

Furthermore, Clarke (2008) emphasises that employability is partly dependent on the agency of the individual and the organisation. Therefore, organisations have a responsibility for supporting employees to manage their careers and employability. This benefits the organisation by creating a more employable workforce and succeeding in retaining them (Clarke 2008).

In conclusion, managers and human resource practitioners have the responsibility to provide employees with career development support, especially for talent retention and organisational success (Ferreira and Coetzee 2013). Other researchers agree that self-esteem, organisational commitment, employability and career adaptability have become essential ingredients for career success (Savickas and Porfeli 2012; Tolentino et al. 2014). It is therefore imperative that individuals develop a healthy self-esteem that will enhance their employability, career adaptability and organisational commitment (Coetzee and Potgieter 2014), which potentially could optimise individuals' intention to stay within an organisation (Coetzee et al. 2014).

In conclusion, it is evident that several personal attributes (which is self-esteem, organisational commitment, career adaptability and employability) should be considered during the design and implementation of retention strategies.

Summary

This chapter discussed self-esteem, organisational commitment, career adaptability and employability (as a set of composite personal attributes) and proposed a personal attributes framework that can be used for retention strategies focused on addressing the psychological needs of employees. It is concluded that these competencies and attributes need to be developed to help the individuals to stay committed to an organisation and therefore increase retention of valuable and knowledgeable employees in the contemporary world of work.

References

Abdulkareem, R., Chauhan, A., & Maitama, K. (2015). The relationship between human resource management practices and employee's turnover intention among registered nurses in Nigerian public hospitals: The mediating role of organisational trust. *UTM Press, 2,* 95–98.

Ahmad, N., & Oranye, O. (2010). Empowerment, job satisfaction and organisational commitment: A comparative analysis of nurses working in Malaysia and England. *Journal of Nursing Management, 18,* 582–591.

Allen, N. J., & Meyer, J. P. (1996). Affective, continuance and normative commitment to the organisation: An examination of the construct validity. *Journal of Vocational Behaviour, 49* (3), 252–276. http://dx.do.org/10.1006/jvbe.1996.0043.

Ashkanasy, N., & Daus, C. (2002). Emotion in the workplace: The new challenge for managers. *Academy of Management Executive, 16*(1), 76–86.

A'yuninnisa, R. N. A., & Saptoto, R. (2015). The effects of pay satisfaction and affective commitment on turnover intention. *International Journal of Research Studies in Psychology, 4* (2).

Bandura, A. (1999). *Self efficacy: The exercise of control.* New York: Freeman.

Battle, J. (1992). *Culture-free self-esteem inventoriess for children and adults.* Texas: Pro-Ed.

Beeftink, F., Van Eerde, W., Rutte, C. G., & Bertrand, J. W. M. (2012). Being successful in a creative profession: The role of innovative cognitive style, self-regulation, and self-efficacy. *Journal of business and psychology, 27*(1), 71–81.

Beukes, C.J. (2010). *Employability and emotional intelligence of the individual within the school-to-work transition phase.* Unpublished masters' dissertation. University of South Africa, Pretoria, South Africa.

Baumeister, R., & Leary, M. (1995). The need to belong: Desire for interpersonal attachments as a fundamental human motivation. *Psychological Bulletin, 117,* 497–529.

Benson, G. S. (2006), Employee development, commitment and intention to turnover: a test of 'employability' policies in action. *Human Resource Management Journal, 16,* 173–192.

Bezuidenhout, M., & Coetzee, M. (2011). Preliminary Exploratory Factor Analysis: Student Employability Scale. Unpublished research report, Department of Industrial and Organisational Psychology, University of South Africa, Pretoria.

Blackford, S. (2013). *Career planning for research Bioscientists.* UK: John Wiley and Sons Ltd.

Briscoe, J., & Hall, D. (1999). Grooming and picking leaders using competency frameworks: Do they work? An alternative approach and new guideline for practice. *Organisational Dynamics, 28*(2), 37–52.

Brown, P., Hesketh, A., & Williams, S. (2003). Employability in a knowledge-driven economy. *Journal of Education and Work, 16*(2), 107–126.

Brown, S. D., & Lent, R. (2016). Vocational psychology: Agency, equity and well-being. *Annual Review of Psychology, 67*, 27.21–27.25. https://doi.org/10.1146/annurev-psych-122414-003237.

Chew, J., & Chan, C. C. (2008). Human resource practices, organisational commitment and intention to stay. *International Journal of Manpower, 29*(6), 503–522.

Chan, S. H. J., & Mai, X. (2015). The relation of career adaptability to satisfaction and turnover intentions. *Journal of Vocational Behaviour, 89*, 130–139.

Chang, W., Wang, Y., & Huang, T. (2013). Work-design-related antecedents of turnover intention: A multi-level approach. *Human Resources Management, 52*(1), 1–26.

Chong, S., & Leong, F. T. L. (2015). Antecedents of career adaptability in strategic career management. *Journal of Career Assessment*, 1–13. https://doi.org/10.1177/1069072715621522.

Clarke, M. (2008). Understanding and managing employability in changing career contexts. *Journal of European Industrial Training, 32*(4), 258–284.

Coetzee, M. (2005). The relationship between personality preferences, self-esteem and emotional competence. Unpublished doctoral degree. Department of Organisational Psychology, University of South-Africa.

Coetzee, M. (2008). Psychological career resources of working adults: A South African survey. *SA Journal of Industrial Psychology, 34*(2), 32–41.

Coetzee, M. (2012). Distance learning students' graduateness as predictors of their job satisfaction and optimism about future career prospects. *Journal of Social Sciences, 33*(3), 305–313.

Coetzee, M., & Beukes, C. (2010). Employability, emotional intelligence and career preparation support satisfaction among adolescents in the school-to-work transition phase. *Journal of Psychology in Africa, 20*(3), 439–446.

Coetzee, M., & Harry, N. (2014). Emotional intelligence as predictor of employees' career adaptability. *Journal of Vocational Behaviour, 84*, 90–97. https://doi.org/10.1016/j.jvb.2013.09.001.

Coetzee, M., & Potgieter, I. L. (2014). Mediating effect of self-esteem on the career self-management and career resilience of early-career staff in the business management field. *Southern African Business Review, 18*(2), 65–82.

Coetzee, M., & Roythorne-Jacobs, H. (2012). *Career counselling and guidance in the workplace: A manual for career practitioners* (2nd ed.). Cape Town: Juta.

Coetzee, M., & Schreuder, D. A. (2014). *Career anchors as a meta-capacity in organisational career development.* In M. Coetzee (Ed.), Psycho-social career meta-capacities: Dynamics of contemporary career development (pp. 139–154). Dordrecht: Springer International Publishing. http://doi.dx.org/10.1007/978-3-319-00645-1.

Coetzee, M., Schreuder, D., & Tladinyane, R. (2014). Employees' work engagement and job commitment: The moderating role of career anchors: Original research. *SA Journal of Human Resource Management, 12*(1), 1–12.

Dardar, A. H. A., Jusoh, A., & Rasli, A. (2012). The impact of job training, job satisfaction and alternative job opportunities on job turnover in Libyan oil companies. *Procedia-Social and Behavioural Sciences, 40*, 389–394.

Davis, P. J. (2015). Implementing an employee career-development strategy: How to build commitment and retain employees. *Human Resource Management International Digest, 23*(4), 28–32.

De Cuyper, N., Mauno, S., Kinnunen, U., & Mäkikangas, A. (2011). The role of job resources in the relation between perceived employability and turnover intention: A prospective two-sample study. *Journal of Vocational Behaviour, 78*(2), 253–263.

De Cuyper, N., Raeder, S., Van der Heijden, B.I.J.M., & Wittekind, A.)2012). The association between workers' employability and burnout in a reorganization context: Longitudinal evidence building upon the conservation of resources theory. *Journal of Occupational Health Psychology, 17*(2), 162–174.

De Guzman, A. B., & Choi, K. O. (2013). The relations of employability skills to career adaptability among technical school students. *Journal of Vocational Behaviour, 82*(3), 199–207.

Dhar, R. L. (2015). Service quality and the training of employees: The mediating role of organisational commitment. *Journal of Tourism Management, 46*, 419–430. http://doi.org/10.1016/j.tourman.2014.08.001.

Döckel, A. (2003). The effect of retention factors on organisational commitment: An investigation of high technology employees (Unpublished master's thesis). University of Pretoria, Pretoria, South Africa.

Döckel, A., Basson, J. S., & Coetzee, M. (2006). The effect of retention factors on organisational commitment: An investigation of high technology employees. *SA Journal of Human Resource Management, 4*(2), 20–28.

Erasmus, B. J., Grobler, A., & Van Niekerk, M. (2015). Employee retention in a higher education institution: An organisational development perspective. *Progressio, 37*(2), 33–63.

Ellison, J. A., & Schreuder, A. M. G. (2000). The relation between career anchors, occupational types and job satisfaction of mid-career employees. *SA Journal of Industrial Psychology, 26* (2), 1–6.

Ferreira, N. (2012). *Constructing a psychological career profile for staff retention (Unpublished doctoral thesis)*. Pretoria, South Africa: University of South Africa.

Ferreira, N., Basson, J., & Coetzee, M. (2010). Psychological career resources in relation to organisational commitment: An exploratory study. *SA Journal of Human Resource Management/SA Tydskrif vir Menslikhulpbronbestuur, 8*(1). https://doi.org/10.4102/sajhrm.v8i1.284.

Ferreira, N., & Coetzee, M. (2013). The influence of job embeddedness on black employees' organisational commitment. *Southern African Business Review, 17*(3), 239–255.

Ferreira, N., Coetzee, M., & Masenge, A. (2013). Psychological career resources, career adaptability and hardiness in relation to job embeddedness and organisational commitment. *Journal of Psychology in Africa, 23*(1), 31–40.

Fiori, M., Bollmann, G., & Rossier, J. (2015). Exploring the path through which career adaptability increases job satisfaction and lower stress: The role of affect. *Journal of Vocational Behaviour, 91*, 113–121.

Fisk, G. M., & Friesen, J. P. (2012). Perceptions of leader emotion regulation and LMX as predictors of followers' job satisfaction and organisational citizenship behaviours. *Leadership Quarterly, 23*, 1–12.

Froehlich, D. E., Beausaert, S., Segers, M., & Gerken, M. (2014). Learning to stay employable. *Career Development International, 19*(5), 508–525. http://dx.doi.org/10.1018/CDI-11-2013-0139.

Fugate, M., Kinicki, A., & Ashforth, B. (2004). Employability: A psycho-social construct, its dimensions and applications. *Journal of Vocational Behaviour, 65*, 14–38.

Gani, K. (2017). *Employability attributes, organisational commitment and retention factors in the 21st century world of work* (Unpublished masters thesis). University of South Africa, Pretoria, South Africa.

Griffen, B., & Hesketh, B. (2005). Adaptable behaviours for successful work and career adjustment. *Australian Journal of Psychology, 55*(2), 65–73.

Guchait, P., & Choi, S. (2012). The impact of human resource management practices on intention to leave of employees in the service industry in India: The mediating role of organisational commitment. *International Journal of Human Resource Management, 21*(8), 1228–1247.

Hall, D., & Chandler, D. (2005). Psychological succes: When the career is a calling. *Journal of Organizational Behaviour, 26*(2), 155–176.

Harmsey, S. K. (2017). Development of a retention framework for the banking industry (Unpublished masters dissertation). South Africa: University of South Africa.

Hartung, P. J. (2013). The life-span, life-space theory of careers. In S. D. Brown & R. W. Lent (Eds.), *Career development and counselling: Putting theory and research to work* (2nd ed., pp. 187–214). Hoboken: Wiley.

Heimpel, S. A., Elliot, A. J., & Wood, J. V. (2006). Basic personality dispositions, self-esteem, and personal goals: An approach-avoidance analysis. *Journal of Personality, 74,* 1293–1320. https://doi.org/10.1111/j.1467-6494.2006.00410.x.

Herr, E., Cramer, S., & Niles, S. (2004). *Career guidance and counselling through the lfespan.* London: Prentice Hall.

Hewitt, J. (2002). The social construction of self-esteem. In C.R. *Snyder* (2002). *Handbook of positive psychology,* 135–147.

Ineson, E. M., Benke, E., & Laszlo, J. (2013). Employee loyalty in Hungarian hotels. *International Journal of Hospitality Management, 32,* 31–39.

Ismail, I. (2005). Self-esteem, graduateness skills and attributes and career adaptability of the young adult in the school-to-work transition phase (Unpublished masters dissertation). South Africa: University of South Africa.

Ito, J. K., & Brotheridge, C. M. (2005). Does supporting employees' career adaptability lead to commitment, turnover, or both? *Human Resource Management, 44*(1), 5–19.

Jabaar, R (2017). The relationship between organisational commitment, career adaptability and retention factors within the retail sector in the Western Cape (Unpublished masters thesis). University of South Africa, Pretoria, South Africa.

Jeager, A. (2003). Job competencies in the curriculum: An inquiry into emotional intelligence in graduate professional education. *Research in Higher Education, 44*(6), 615–639.

Johnston, C. S., Luciano, E. C., Maggiori, C., Ruch, W., & Rossier, J. (2013). Validation of the German version of the career adapt-abilities scale and its relation to orientations to happiness and work stress. *Journal of Vocational Behaviour, 83*(3), 295–304.

Juhdi, N., Pa'wan, F., & Hansaram, R. M. K. (2013). HR practices and turnover intention: The mediating roles of organisational commitment and organisational engagement in a selected region in Malaysia. *The International Journal of Human Resource Management, 24*(15), 3002–3019.

Khan, A. A., Mahmood, B., Ayoub, M. & Hussain, S. (2011). An empirical study of retention issues in hotel industry: A case study of Serena Hotel, Faisalabad, Pakistan. *European Journal of Economics, Finance and Administrative Sciences, 1*(29), 7–18.

Khasawneh, S., Omari, A., & Abu-Tineh, A. M. (2012). The relationship between transformational leadership and organisational commitment: The case of vocational teachers in Jordan. *Educational Management Administration and Leadership, 40*(4), 494–508.

Kim, J. (2015). What increases public employees' turnover intention? *Public Personne Management, 44*(4), 496–519.

Klehe, U. C., Zikic, J., Van Vianen, A. E. M., & De Pater, I. E. (2011). Career adaptability, turnover and loyalty during organisational downsizing. *Journal of Vocational Behaviour, 79* (1), 217–229.

Krüger, J., & Rootman, C. (2010). How do small business managers influence employee satisfaction and commitment? *Acta Commercii, 10*(2), 59–72.

Kuo, Y. (2013). Organisational commitment in an intense competition environment. *Industrial Management & Data Systems, 113*(1), 39–56.

Lane, J., Lane, A., & Kyprianou, A. (2004). Self-efficacy, self-esteem and their impact on academic performance. *Social behavior and personality, 32*(3), 247–256.

Lent, R. W. (2013). Career-life preparedness: Revisiting career planning and adjustment in the new workplace. *The Career Development Quarterly, 61*(1), 2–14.

Lumley, E. J., Coetzee, M., Tladinyane, R., & Ferreira, N. (2011). Exploring the job satisfaction and organisational commitment of employees in the information technology environment. *Southern African Business Review, 15*(1), 100–118. http://www.ajol.info/index.php/sabr/article/view/76394.

Maggiori, C., Johnston, C. S., Krings, F., Massoudi, K., & Rossier, J. (2013). The role of career adaptability and work conditions on general and professional well-being. *Journal of Vocational Behaviour, 83*(3), 437–449. https://doi.org/10.1016/j.jvb.2013.07.001.

Maree, J. G. (2015). *Career construction counseling: A thematic analysis of outcomes for four clients.* South Africa: University of Pretoria.

Marock, C. (2008). *Grappling with your employability in South Africa*. Pretoria: Human Sciences Research Council.

Maslow, A. (1970). *Motivation and personality*. New York: Harper & Row.

McArdle, S., Waters, L., Briscoe, J. P., & Hall, D. T. (2007). Employability during unemployment: Adaptability, career identity and human and social capital. *Journal of Vocational Behavior, 71*(2), 247–264. https://doi.org/10.1016/j.jvb.2007.06.003.

McGrath, S (2009). What is employability? UNESCO centre for comparative education research. University of Nottingham.

Mclaggan, E., Bezuidenhout, A., & Botha, C. T. (2013). Leadership style and organisational commitment in the mining industry in Mpumalanga. *SA Journal of Human Resource Management/SA Tydskrif vir Menslikehulpbronbestuur, 11*(1), Art. #483, 9 pages. https://doi.org/10.4102/sajhm.v11i1.483.

Mehta, M., Kurbetti, A., & Dhankhar, R. (2014). Review paper: Study of employee retention and commitment. *International Journal of Advance Research in Computer Science and Management Studies, 2*(2), 154–164.

Mercurio, A. (2015). Affective commitment as a core essence of organisational commitment: An integrative literature review. *Human Resource Development Review, 14*(4), 389–414.

Meyer, J. P., & Allen, N. J. (1997). *Commitment in the workplace*. Thousand Oaks: Sage Publications.

Moore, P. (2010). *The International political economy of work and employability*. London: Palgrave Macmillan.

Nawab, S., & Bhatti, K. K. (2011). Influence of employee compensation on organisational commitment and job satisfaction: A case study of educational sector of Pakistan. *International Journal of Business and Social Science, 2*(8), 25–32.

Nayak, T., & Sahoo, C. K. (2015). Quality of work life and organisational performance: The mediating role of employee commitment. *Journal of Health Management, 17*(3), 263–273. https://doi.org/10.1177/0972063415589236; https://urldefense.proofpoint.com/v2/url?u=http-3A__jhm.sagepub.com&d=DwIGaQ&c=vh6FgFnduejNhPPD0fl_yRaSfZy8CWbWnIf4XJhSqx8&r=Rd8o2pKscGmSdcWURPJ1G8FbYLBbujcShNE6HJFXXvEEwEmtrRmRg1nVBBcF5W8F&m=Y0i9kKhp8PCmTL4aZkIbSJA92Snwwy7p7cLmuFpm4X8&s=PhZY8izK9gHWN2uDec-eFm9c-NOiO6Ng3CODVB4pegY&e=.

Neininger, A., Lehmann-Willenbrock, N., Kauffeld, S., & Henschel, A. (2010). Effects of team and organisational commitment: A longitudinal study. *Journal of Vocational Behaviour, 76*, 567–579.

Ndzube, F. (2013). The relationship between career anchors and employability (Unpublished master's dissertation). Department of Industrial and Organisational Psychology, University of South Africa, Pretoria, South Africa.

Ng, T. W. H. (2015). The incremental validity of organisational commitment, organisational trust and organisational identification. *Journal of Vocational Behaviour, 88*, 154–163.

Nielsen, J. (1999). Employability and workability among Danish employees. *Experimental Aging Research, 25*(4), 393–397.

Ojakaa, D., Olango, S., & Jarvis, J. (2014). Factors affecting motivation and retention of primary health care workers in three disparate regions of Kenya. *Human Resources for Health, 12*(1), 1–13. https://doi.org/10.1186/1478-4491-12-33.

Pool, L., & Sewell, P. (2007). The key to employability: Developing a practical model of graduate employability. *Education and Training, 49*(4), 227–289.

Porfeli, E. J., & Savickas, M. L. (2012). Career adapt-abilities scale—USA form: Psychometric properties and relation to vocational identity. *Journal of Vocational Behaviour, 80*, 748–753.

Potgieter, I. L. (2012). The development of a career meta-competency model for sustained employability. Unpublished doctoral degree. Department of Organisational Psychology, University of South-Africa.

Potgieter, I. L., & Coetzee, M. (2013). Employability attributes and personality preferences of postgraduate business management students. *SA Journal of Industrial Psychology, 39*(1), 01–10.

Potgieter, I. L., Coetzee, M., & Ferreira, N. (2016). Employability capacities and organisational commitment foci of human resource professionals : An exploratory study. *Journal of Psychology in Africa, 26*(5), 436–442 https://doi.org/10.1080/14330237.2016.1219549.

Potgieter, I. L., & Mawande, L. (2017). Self-esteem, employability attributes and retention factors of employees within the financial sector. *Journal of Psychology in Africa, 27*(5), 393–399.

Quick, J. C., & Nelson, D. L. (2013). *Principles of organisational behaviour: Realities and challenges*. Australia: South-Western Cengage Learning.

Salovey, P., & Mayer, J. (1990). Emotional intelligence. *Imagination, Cognition, and Personality, 9,* 185–221.

Samuel, M., & Chipunza, C. (2009). Employee retention and turnover: Using motivational variables as a panacea. *African Journal of Business Management, 3*(8), 410–415.

Savickas, M. L. (1997). Career adaptability: An integrative construct for life-span, life-space theory. *Career Development Quarterly, 45*, 247–259. https://doi.org/10.1002/j.2161-0045.1997.tb00469.x.

Savickas, M. L. (2011). *Career counselling*. Washington, DC: American Psychological Association.

Savickas, M. L. (2012). Life design: A paradigm for career intervention in the 21st century. *Journal of Counselling & Development, 90,* 13–19.

Savickas, M. L. (2013). Career construction theory and practice. In R. W. Lent & S. D. Brown (Eds.), *Career development and counselling: Putting theory and research to work* (2nd ed., pp. 147–183). Hoboken, NJ: John Wiley.

Savickas, M. L., & Porfeli, E. J. (2012). Career adapt-abilities scale: Construction, reliability, and measurement equivalence across 13 countries. *Journal of Vocational Behavior, 80,* 661–673.

Savickas, M., Nota, L., Rossier, J., Dauwalder, J., Duarte, M., Guichard, J., et al. (2009). Life designing: A paradigm for career construction in the 21st century. *Journal of Vocational Behavior, 75,* 239–325.

Shahid, A., & Azhar, S. M. (2013). Gaining employee commitment: Linking to organizational effectiveness. *Journal of Management Research, 5*(1), 250–268.

Singh, A. (2013). An analysis of employee retention in its industry. *Asian Journal of Multidisciplinary Studies, 1*(5), 55–60.

Sinha, C., & Sinha, R. (2012). Factors affecting employee retention: A comparative analysis of two organisations from heavy engineering industry. *European Journal of Business and Management, 4*(3), 145–162.

Spurk, D., Kauffeld, S., Meinecke, A. L., & Ebner, K. (2016). Why do adaptable people feel less insecure? Indirect effects of career adaptability on job and career insecurity via two types of perceived marketability. *Journal of Career Assessment, 24*(2), 289–306. https://doi.org/10.1177/1069072715580415.

Spurk, D., & Volmer, J. (2013). Validierung einer deutschen version des career futures inventory (CFI): Berufliche Anpassungsfahigkeit, beruflicher Optimismus, Arbeitsmarktwissen und Berufserfolg [Validation of a German version of the career futures inventory (CFI): Career adaptability, career optimism, job market knowledge, and career success]. *Zeitschrift fur Arbeits-und Organisationspsychologie, 57,* 77–95. https://doi.org/10.1026/0932-4089/a000106.

Srivastava, S. (2013). Job satisfaction and organisational commitment relationship: Effect of personality variables. *Vision, 17*(2), 159–167. https://doi.org/10.1177/0972262912483529.

Stoltz, E. (2014). *Employability attributes and career adaptability as predictors of staff satisfaction with retention factors (Unpublished master's thesis)*. Pretoria, South Africa: University of South Africa.

Šverko, I., & Babarović, T. (2016). Integrating personality and career adaptability into vocational interest space. *Journal of Vocational Behaviour, 94,* 89–103.

Tsai, M. T., & Cheng, N. C. (2011). Understanding knowledge sharing between IT professionals: An integration of social cognitive and social exchange theory. *Behavioural Information & Technology, 31*(11), 1–12.

Tolentino, L., Garcia, P., Lu, V. N., Restubog, S., Bordia, P., & Plewa, C. (2014). Career adaptation: The relation of adaptability to goal orientation, proactive personality, and career optimism. *Journal of Vocational Behaviour, 84*, 39–84. http://dx.doi.org/10.1016j.jvb.2013.10.004.

Tolentino, L. R., Garcia, P. R., Restubog, S. L. D., Bordia, P., & Tang, R. L. (2013). Validation of the career-adapt-abilities scale and an examination of a model of career adaptation of the Philippine context. *Journal of Vocational Behaviour, 83*(3), 410–418.

Van der Velde, M., & Van den Berg, P. (2003). Managing functional flexibility in a passanger transport firm. *Human Resource Management Journal, 13*(4), 45–55.

Van Dyk, J. (2011). *The relationship between organisational commitment, retention factors and perceived job embeddedness (Unpublished master's dissertation).* South Africa: University of South Africa, Pretoria.

Weng, Q., & McElroy, J. C. (2010). Vocational self-concept crystallization as a mediator of the relationship between career self-management and job decision effectiveness. *Journal of Vocational Behavior, 76,* 234–243.

Yean, T. F., & Yahya, K. K. (2013). The influence of human resource management practices and career strategy on career satisfaction of insurance agents. *International Journal of Business and Society, 14*(2), 193–206.

Yorke, M., & Knight, P. (2004). *Embedding employability in the curriculum.* New York: Higher Education Academy.

Yorke, M., & Knight, P. (2007). Evidence-informed pedagogy and the enhancement of student employability. *Teaching in Higher Education, 12*(2), 117–157.

Zacher, H. (2014). Career adaptability predicts subjective career success above and beyond personality traits and core self-evaluations. *Journal of Vocational Behaviour, 84*(1), 21–30. http://dx.doi.org/10.1016/j.jvb.2013.10.0012.

Zacher, H., & Griffin, B. (2015). Older workers' age as a moderator of the relationship between career adaptability and job satisfaction. *Work, Aging and Retirement, 1*(2), 227–236. https://doi.org/10.1093/worker/wau009.

Ingrid L. Potgieter (DCom) is an Associate Professor in Human Resource Management at the Department of Human Resource Management at the University of South Africa (Unisa), South Africa. She is a registered Psychologist (cat. Industrial) at the Health Professions Council of South Africa (HPCSA) since 2009 and also a registered human resource practitioner and the South African board for people practices (SABPP). She is also an author and co-author of several published articles in local and international journals. In addition, she presented several papers at national and international conferences.

Chapter 10
Multi-generational Workforce and Its Implication for Talent Retention Strategies

Edyta Kostanek and Violetta Khoreva

Abstract Talent recruitment and retention research has traditionally looked at such characteristics as age, gender, ethnicity, tenure, and more. There is however an increasing demand to add multigenerational diversity to this list. The current multi-generational workforce of Silent Generation, Baby Boomers, Generation X, and the Millennials generates a need for organizations to manage a highly diverse set of employees whose work habits and expectations vary widely. A generic approach to attracting and managing this multi-generational type of workforce is unlikely to work, mostly due to markedly distinct needs and wants by each generation. To keep up with multi-generational workforce, organizations need to respond to these varying needs and develop innovative ways to attract, manage, and retain talents. This chapter will give insight into the most effective talent management and retention practices per each generation and contextualize them in relation to stability of work environments.

Keywords Talent retention · Generational cohorts · Silent generation Baby boomers · Generation X · Millennials

Introduction

In today's global economy, multinational corporations (MNCs) are increasingly reliant on the ability to manage their international operations effectively, realizing the need to recruit, develop and retain high-potential employees (Björkman et al. 2017;

E. Kostanek (✉)
Faculty of Business and Law, School of Strategy and Leadership, Coventry University, Coventry CV1 5FB, UK
e-mail: edyta.kostanek@coventry.ac.uk

V. Khoreva
Department of Management and Organization, Hanken School of Economics, Biblioteksgatan 16, PB 287, 65100 Vaasa, Finland
e-mail: violetta.khoreva@hanken.fi

M. Coetzee et al. (eds.), *Psychology of Retention*,
https://doi.org/10.1007/978-3-319-98920-4_10

Farndale et al. 2014). Scholars have also identified the link between MNCs' competitive advantage and talent management (TM) (Ashton and Morton 2005; Collings 2014; Collings and Mellahi 2009; Latukha 2018; Sidani and Ariss 2014), which focuses on a pool of employees who rank at the top in terms of performance and competencies, and are thus considered leaders or key professionals either at the moment or at some point in future (Björkman et al. 2013). Talent management likewise keeps on being one of the main concerns for organizations that understand that they need to attract, manage, and retain talent so as to prevail in the current competitive and progressively multifaceted global economy (Cascio and Boudreau 2010; Latukha 2018; Meyers and van Woerkom 2014).

The research field of talent management has received a significant interest from both academic and practitioner perspectives in the past two decades (Cascio and Boudreau 2015; Collings et al. 2015; Malik et al. 2017; Scullion et al. 2016; Thunnissen 2016; Meyers and van Woerkom, 2014; Khoreva et al. 2017). Drawing upon ideas from various areas such as human resource management, organizational behaviour, resource-based view, talent management is now slowly maturing (Cascio and Boudreau 2015; Gallardo-Gallardo and Thunnissen 2016; Sparrow and Makram 2015). Talent recruitment and retention research has traditionally looked at such characteristics as age, gender, ethnicity, tenure, and more. There is however an increasing demand to add multigenerational diversity to this list. The current multi-generational workforce of Silent Generation, Baby Boomers, Generation X, and the Millennials generates a need for organizations to manage a highly diverse set of employees whose work habits and expectations vary widely (DelCampo et al. 2011). Each generation has its own qualities, values, work attitudes, and expectations (Hu et al. 2004; Altimier 2006; de Waal et al. 2017; Glass 2007; Gursoy et al. 2008; Johnson 2017; Lyons and Kuron 2014; Marcus and Leiter 2017). Baby Boomers expect stability, job security, and organizational polices, while Generation Y members expect learning opportunities and career development. Generation Y requires from their employer to provide work-life balance, while Baby Boomers do not perceive it as equally important.

Research so far has treated talented individuals as subjects that need to be managed, while forgetting to study their preferences, needs, and expectations (Gallardo-Gallardo et al. 2017; Tansley 2011; Thunnissen et al. 2013). Consequently, managing these diverse cohorts of employees requires employers that can adjust themselves or the organizational context, or who can tackle the qualities of each generation to address the priorities of their particular organizational context. A generic approach to attracting and managing the multi-generational type of workforce is unlikely to work, mostly due to markedly distinct needs and wants by each generation. To keep up with multi-generational workforce, organizations need to respond to these varying needs and develop innovative ways to attract, manage, and retain talents. Understanding the generational differences and their impact on talent management practices has been acknowledged as one the major challenges of the TM field (Benson and Brown 2011; Jenkins 2008; Schuler et al. 2011; Tarique and Schuler 2010). However, the research that would thoroughly discuss such generational aspect in this particular context is sparse (Al Ariss et al. 2014; Tarique and Schuler 2010). This means, that organizations have little theoretical and empirical guidance on how to implement effective talent retention strategies for the multi-generational workforce, which we see as a significant omission in TM research. This chapter will therefore give insight into the most effective talent management and retention practices per each generation and contextualize them in relation to stability of work environments.

Talents

In a growing number of MNCs, strategic human resource (HR) decisions and processes are primarily focused on attracting high-potential employees, their continuous motivation and professional development through the creation of conditions enabling and supporting organizational learning, knowledge transfer between employees and teams within the MNC and implementation of innovative solutions. It is generally known that the most profitable business personal strategy is hiring the right people, creating the conditions for the development and maintenance of high-potential employees (Pfeffer and Veiga 1999).

As mentioned by Mellahi and Collings (2010, p. 148), "effective TM has been hailed as a valuable competitive advantage weapon". TM has been thus studied under various labels, namely as human resource development (Bartlett et al. 2002), organizational learning (Adler and Bartholomew 1992), and succession (Daily et al. 2000). There still is lack of consensus on the definition of talent, despite significant theoretical development in this context over the past two decades (Collings et al. 2015; Dries 2013; Nijs et al. 2013; Sonnenberg et al. 2014; Sparrow et al. 2014; Thunnissen 2016). Although the term 'talent' has been frequently used in the management literature, its understanding is still limited, and the topic of TM seems to be rather underdeveloped (Collings and Mellahi 2009). According to Collings and Mellahi (2009, p. 304), talent management refers to "activities and processes that involve the systematic identification of key positions which differentially contribute to the organization's sustainable competitive advantage, the development of a talent pool of high potential and high performing incumbents to fill these roles, and the development of a differentiated human resource architecture to facilitate filling these positions with competent incumbents and to ensure their continued commitment to the organization". Stahl et al. (2007) broadly describes TM as an organization's ability to attract, select, develop, manage, and retain key employees.

In the literature talent has generally been understood in two ways. First, talent has been defined as a set of features in terms of innate predispositions, acquired competencies, level of intelligence, "characteristics of a person that allow them to perform well or at their personal best" (Wood et al. 2011, p. 15). Second, it has been described as a group of specific employees with high competence and potential (CIPD 2006; Silzer and Church 2009). These two approaches take at least two mutually exclusive assumptions: either only a few have talent clearly being better than others in terms of selected features, or all employees have hidden talents and the role of managers is to discover the often latent and invisible strengths of each of the employees. On the one hand, the aim of TM programs is to recognize that all employees have talent. On the other hand, assuming that the talent is a highly skilled worker means that TM is directed only towards a specified pool of employees who rank at the top in terms of capability and performance (Stahl et al. 2007).

In this chapter, we use the term 'talents' and define them as "high performers who are pivotal for the organization" (Festing and Schäfer 2014, p. 263). Talents can be described through a set of attributes, for instance, their intelligence and knowledge, experience, capabilities, aptitudes, skills, passion, performance, the capacity to learn and develop, etc. (Ulrich 2008). These employees are valuable, rare and difficult to imitate (Vance and Vaiman 2008). They are key strategic resources (Collings and Mellahi 2009) because they have a considerable impact on company's overall organizational performance (Collings and Mellahi 2009; Tansley et al. 2007) and on creating sustainable competitive advantage for a corporation (Sparrow and Makram 2015; Tatoglu et al. 2016).

Generational Cohorts

Understanding generational differences is key to understanding employee engagement, motivational issues, career direction and the expectations employees hold towards the organization (Cheese et al. 2008). Generation is typically defined as the group of people of the similar age, born in the similar time of history (Palese et al. 2006) who share common life events during a formative period (e.g. during childhood and adolescence), which subsequently leads to similar values, views, and attitudes (Arsenault 2004; Ng et al. 2012; Smola and Sutton 2002; Twenge et al. 2010). Despite the fact that there is no absolute agreement about beginning or end to the generational distinctions, with boundaries of each generations somewhat arbitrary, they typically span across around 20 years (Weingarten 2009) and literature has identified several such generations that are present in current workforce. According to Lancaster and Stillman (2002) and Twenge et al (2010) there are currently four generations in the workplace: Silent Generation[1] (born 1925–1945), Baby Boomers (born 1946–1964), Generation X[2] (born 1965–1981) and Millennials[3] (born 1982–1999). While these generational cohorts are not rigid, they provide useful insights into talent motivations, expectations and work styles.

Each generation has its distinctive values, attitudes, behaviours and expectations (Crampton and Hodge 2007; Jenkins 2008). Because employment relationships and

---

[1]Also known as "Veterans" or "Traditionalists".

[2]Also known as "Gen Xers", "13th generation", "Latchkey generation".

[3]Also known as "Generation Y".

workplace contexts have changed over time, each of these generations also have developed differing values and expectations related to work life. These are key specifically when investigating the psychological contract of talents from each generational cohort. (Benson and Brown 2011; D'Amato and Herzfeldt 2008).

Academic research that investigates generational differences in relation to such work values and attitudes as job satisfaction, organizational commitment, company loyalty, lifetime employment, and work-life balance is still reasonability scarce (Arsenault 2004; Benson and Brown 2011; Bennett et al. 2017; Giancola 2006; Gibson et al. 2009; Marcus and Leiter 2017; Singh and Gupta 2015; Twenge et al. 2010). Yet, the existing studies show that differences in such work-related values and attitudes, are more likely to be influenced by the generational experiences than by the differences in career stages or maturity (Benson and Brown 2011; Crampton and Hodge 2007; Dries et al. 2008; Jenkins 2008; Twenge et al. 2010). Therefore, considering the context in which a member of a generation was born—can also provide helpful information to effectively attract, manage and retain talents (DelCampo et al. 2011; Dries et al. 2008).

In what follows, we discuss briefly each of the generations along with their specific characteristics and approaches to workplace, which we summarise also in Table 10.1.

Silent Generation

Silent Generation are individual born between 1925–1945 and compose approximately 5% of today's workforce (Schullery 2013, Wiedmer 2015). Even though most of this generation has already retired from the workforce, their impact is still felt within organizations which they created. Silent Generation was heavily impacted by the events of Ward Wars and the military leadership style of that time; hence they are very procedural, feel most comfortable within the top-down management structures. They are very cautious about their savings and protecting their wealth. Their typical aspiration was to join an organization and stay with it until retirement. Job loyalty, security and stability are very important aspects of their work life.

Baby Boomers

Baby Boomers were born between 1946–1964 and compose approximately 30% of today's workforce (Schullery 2013; Wiedmer 2015). Baby Boomers are the post-World War II generation and until recently they were the most dominant generation in the corporate context. They were raised in the era of optimism, opportunity and progress; therefore, their key values are optimism, personal growth and health (Duchscher and Cowan 2004; Weingarten 2009). However, due to sheer

Table 10.1 Generational cohorts, their values and work attitudes, and retention strategies

	Silent Generation (1925–1945)	Baby Boomers (1946–1964)	Generation X (1965–1981)	Millennials (1982–1999)
I see work as…	…an obligation	…an adventure	…a contract	…a means to an end
I want…	…benefits and retirement options	…money	…time	…meaningfulness
Views on changing jobs	Stay for life at the same workplace	Stay at the same workplace if you are moving up	Changing jobs is necessary	Changing jobs is expected
Job loyalty	Loyalty pays off	You need to pay your dues	I need to know my options	Will switch frequently and fast
Values	• Loyalty •Leadership • Team working • Legacy	•Recognition, Competition • Hard work • Loyalty	• Independence • Flexibility • Informal relationships • Resilience • Having fun	• Optimism • Morality • Flexibility • Informal relationships • Creating meaningful work and life • Achievement
Work style	• Team player • Top-down management • Communication on a "need to know basis" • All information must go through appropriate channels • Procedural	• Team player • Competitive • Hard-working • Information is power	• Entrepreneurial • Independent • Adaptable • Straightforward • Sceptical of authority	• Flexibility • Collaborative • Tech-savvy • Expect information immediately • Reject traditional top-down communication • Distrust bureaucracy
Work expectations	• Job security • Benefit and retirement plan	• Job security •Recognition • Democratic approach to work	•Advancement opportunities • Care benefits • Work-life balance • Incentive and compensation plans	•Advancement opportunities • Working remotely • Competitive salary • Friendly and convenient work environment

(continued)

Table 10.1 (continued)

	Silent Generation (1925–1945)	Baby Boomers (1946–1964)	Generation X (1965–1981)	Millennials (1982–1999)
Motivated by	• Organization's success	• Opportunities for advancement •Compensation, Recognition	• Opportunities for advancement • Casual work environment	• Challenging and meaningful work
Retaining strategies focus	•Benefits • Retirement plans	•Career development • Competitive wages and benefits • Flexible job arrangements	• Providing freedom and mobility	• Instant feedback on how to do better • Career advancements • Volunteering and philanthropic activities

size of this generation, they had to fight for everything and hence became very competitive, loyal, with strong work ethic. Studies have found that they are generally more satisfied with and less likely to change their jobs, compared to Generation X (Benson and Brown 2011; Crampton and Hodge 2007). Baby Boomers prefer to seek consensus and treat other employees equally. They prefer when organizations are democratic and caring. They also seek challenging and meaningful work and developmental opportunities (Dowd-Higgins 2013).

While Silent Generation and Baby Boomers are significantly different from each other when it comes to management and communication style, they do share similar approach to loyalty to their employers. This is quite different when it comes to two next generations: Generation X and Millennials.

Generation X

Generation X are individuals born between 1965–1981 and compose approximately 34% of today's workforce (Schullery 2013; Eastman and Liu 2012). Representatives of Generation X witnessed the development of personal computer and birth of the Internet, cable TV and mobile phones and hence are more technology-wise than previous generations (Benson and Brown 2011; Burke 2004; Smola and Sutton 2002; Twenge et al. 2010). They were exposed to and impacted greatly by the rise of two-career families, as well as massive layoffs, and a sharp increase in the divorce rates. All these experiences created a generation that is extremely independent, resilient, adaptable to changing circumstances, and thrives on change (Murphy 2007; Dowd-Higgins 2013).

Generation X has a completely different work ethic than their parent meaning that they would like to keep a good work-life balance and job that would offer them schedule flexibility, fun (Irvine 2010) and autonomy, rather than spend as much time away from family as the organization requires. They are sceptical towards authority and their expectation that workplace will be able to accommodate their flexibility toward how, when and where the work gets done. Their core values are having fun, travel, meet people, be independent, appreciate diversity (Weingarten 2009). They recognize that job security is a thing of the past, hence they place less value on loyalty toward their employers and would take on a job opportunity if it provides them with possibility to develop their skills further.

Millennials

Millennials were born between 1982–2000 and compose approximately 12% of today's workforce (Schullery 2013; Allison 2013). Millennials are substantially different from other generations (Festing and Schäfer 2014; Vaiman et al. 2012). They do share some of qualities with Generation X, but they often represent them in a more extreme way. As children, Millennials have been brought up in the notion of being special, they have been included in family decision making and their opinions mattered. Because of these experiences, they are comfortable in providing feedback, expressing themselves, and giving opinions to other employees and supervisors.

The key values that Millennials share are corporate social responsibility, work-life balance, development and learning, mobility (Cennamo and Gardner 2008; DelCampo et al. 2011; DelCampo 2007; Vaiman et al. 2012; Vaiman et al. 2015). Millennials expect convenient work environment with personalised community and thought-provoking work communication (Festing and Schäfer 2014). As they have grown up in a world with massive amount of information at one's fingertips, they are extremely technology savvy, value multitasking and collaborative work as much as possible. They are not interested in having the same job until retirement, in fact, they believe that changing jobs is expected. Finally, they are not solely looking for financial gratification and rapid promotion, instead they value career development and advancement opportunities, which means they are likely to select their new workplace in a very thoughtful and strategic manner.

All these generational cohorts appreciate meaningful work, learning opportunities, development, and want to be treated fairly. Organizations therefore should therefore focus on appreciating key differences and focus on similarities when developing their talent management practices. Those who will be proactive in addressing these generational differences will be likely to gain benefits, while others organizations that ignore the multigenerational aspect of current workforce will be likely to lose the war for talent.

Generational Cohorts and Talent Retention Strategies

Talent retention is one of the most important aspects of a successful human resource management and is key for maintaining institutional knowledge, high employee morale, competitive advantage and organizational performance. Losing key talents can impact productivity, damage morale and increase costs as organizations need to attract and train replacements. Understanding why people leave organizations is important but understanding what makes people stay within organizations is even more crucial (George 2015). While most of managers would assume that the financial aspect may be the most important issues in talent retention, the reality is that it is a set of other factors can contribute to talent retention (i.e. job satisfaction, development opportunities, effectiveness of management, favourable work environment, social support, compensation, work-life balance, etc. (George 2015).

The ascent of a multi-generational workforce has a major influence on talent management practices and creates unique challenges and opportunities for organizations who want to benefit from each generation's talents and strengths. With the increase in world population numbers, Millennials enter the workforce in high numbers and it is predicted that they will make up 50% of the worldwide workforce by 2020 (PricewaterhouseCoopers 2011). In the meantime, Baby Boomers either do not want to retire or are unfit to leave their work due to financial or personal reasons. While the landscape of workforce is changing with Millennials as a main source of talent pool, baby boomers still continue to be valuable organizational assets. The existence of all the different generations in the workplace, has the potential to create a very real challenge for any organization that want to retain their talent. A generic approach to managing and retaining this new type of workforce is unlikely to work, mostly due to markedly distinct needs and wants by each generation. As such, it is crucial to implement effective strategies that recognize and address issues of retention for all generational cohorts within an organization. Failure to account for these differences has the potential to undermine talent retention within organization which in consequence may put the organization at a competitive disadvantage.

The key understanding of generational cohorts in workplace is related to identification of how important is work for them (see also Table 10.1). For instance, Silent Generation and Baby Boomers "live to work", while Generation X and Millennials organized their job around their lives and as such "work to live". Research suggests that it is essential for organizations to comprehend the basic values and attitudes of each generation if they want develop and maintain a work environment that would promote leadership, motivation, and communication between generations and help retain the employees (Gursory et al. 2013).

Silent Generation is now the least represented among the current workforce and its representatives are approaching or thinking about retirement, they would prefer to work for an organization that offers them a good benefits and retirement plan. Many of the *Baby Boomers* are interested in continuing to work past retirement eligibility, but only in the roles that interest them or would allow them to move up. If organizations would like to retain Baby Boomer talent within their employees, then they would need to focus on developing practices that would allow these talents to develop competences and allow for career advancements, while at the same time offer good set of benefits and compensation for their experience and skills. Organizations should also offer them flexible work arrangements and phased retirement plans that would allow Baby Boomers to work longer and allow for knowledge transfers to younger generations.

The *Generation X* is independent, self-reliant, team-work oriented, and values workplace flexibility. Working on multiple assignments keeps them motivated and engaged. Their key expectation is to be offered consistent learning opportunities and experiences that would allow them to develop their skills and competencies and ultimately (Hernaus and Vokic 2014). Because they are independent and self-reliant, the best retention practice that an organization can offer for them is a flexible work environment that offers a lot of freedom and mobility.

Finally, *Millennials* are very focused on learning and development opportunities, career development, and work-life balance (D'Amato and Herzfeldt 2008; DelCampo et al. 2011; Twenge et al. 2010) and so this this may be a crucial element of talent retention strategy for that specific generational cohort. Moreover, Millennials have been described as less loyal and more individualistic, compared to other generations, and in their choice of employers, they value those organizations that care about their employees as individuals and about employee's personal development (Terjesen and Frey 2008). Therefore, we can assume that a good talent retention practice would retain elements that address the above-mentioned values and attitudes and create practices that will allow talents representing Millennials to feel that their developmental needs are being met. As delivering a meaningful work and leading a meaningful life seems to be a crucial value for Millennials, organizations could also provide them with developmental opportunities through volunteering or philanthropic types of assignments (Murphy 2007)

This multi-generational workforce with the Millennials slowly taking over the majority, urges organizations to customize and adjust their talent management approaches. In order to keep up with this changing landscape, it is crucial for organizations to develop and deliver continuous training, developmental opportunities, and meaningful job tasks to its talent, which involve a high degree of creativity, independence and meaningfulness (Cooke et al. 2014; Farndale et al. 2014). Organizations should also focus on providing Millennials with increased job flexibility, self-reliance and accelerated career advancements opportunities.

The key to efficient talent management lies in the ability to predict the need for key talent positions, and then setting up and implementing the plan to meet this need. Practice shows that organizations typically choose between two approaches: being reactive and being proactive. The first approach is typical for organizations that operate in fairly stable contexts, that have a stable organizational structure, or when organizations have a large pool of talents available. Research in talent management has so far been widely focused on studying relatively stable organization (Björkman et al. 2013; Cooke et al. 2014; Tatoglu et al. 2016; Valverde et al. 2013). These organizations typically will have a well-defined set of structured talent practices focused on talents as a one unified group of employees, and they would address the retention problems only when there is a suspicion that a specific talent may want to leave. The typical answer in this scenario is to offer the employee a better salary or benefits package. While this approach may cater for the needs of the Silent Generation or Baby-Boomers, this will not address the needs and wants of the two younger generations present in the workforce, neither can it be a long-term solution.

On the other hand, many organizations are currently facing the need to rearrange and strategically renew themselves due to global environment becoming increasingly volatile. Strategic renewal refers to "the process, content, and outcome of refreshment or replacement of attributes of a company that has the potential to substantially affect its long-term prospects" (Agarwal and Helfat 2009, p. 282). This renewal may cover goals and organizational identity (Tripsas 2009) or resources and capabilities (Capron and Mitchell 2009). Given the changing nature of organizational designs and work itself and given the increasing number of independent and self-reliant Millennials coming into workforce, organizations must take the second more proactive approach to their talent retention. This becomes a great challenge for organizations that are going through rapid organizational transformation or through strategic renewal, because they are facing the risk of losing a significant talent who may be looking for options for career advancement and development and may ultimately want to take up jobs elsewhere. Therefore, in order to retain the high-potential employees, it is imperative for those organizations to tackle the issues of retention from a strategic perspective and offer a flexible set of talent management and retention practices, with particular focus on those practices those that would offer flexible work patterns, career development and advancement options, as well as challenging and meaningful projects to engage in, and by that cater also specifically to the needs of Generation X and Millennials.

Conclusions and Implications for Retention Practice

With the current demographic situation and shortage of skilled labour in many countries (Ward 2011), it has become crucial to retain talent within the organizations. Considering that workforces are not homogenous, one way to embrace and address this diversity is to adopt a generational lens and try to understand what impact the different generations' values and work attitudes would have on talent management. By suggesting the diversified approach to talent retention practices for each of the generational cohorts, we contribute to a theoretical research on talent management. We argue that a generic approach attracting and managing this multi-generational type of workforce is unlikely to work organizations need to respond to their varying needs and develop innovative ways to attract, manage, and retain talents.

Organizations are making substantial investments in talent management development (Dries 2013), and the outcomes of talent retention practices are crucial for their future competitiveness Consequently, a better understanding of the multi-generational workforce may enable organizational decision makers to come up with more accurate choices when it comes to talent retention strategies. Managers, administrators, and other individuals who hold top decision-making positions could use the suggestions of this chapter to increase the retention rates of generational workers, and thereby improving both organizational and people relations. We however suppose that the suggested talent retention approaches would apply mainly to developed countries and larger organizations. This is because they would either have multiple generations represented in their current workforces or have required resources to invest in specific tailored talent retention practices.

To keep up with multi-generational workforce, organizations should diversify their approaches to talent management and retention practices. Following, Costanza et al. (2012), who noted that such practices could have counterproductive outcomes if implemented too early, we suggest that a more thoughtful and carefully planned approach to diversified set of talent retention practices should be used. This could include an initiation phase where organizations would conduct an assessments of workplace values and attitudes of generations represented in their workforce. Such an assessment would also be beneficial to those organizations that already have a talent retention program in place and would allow them to make adjustments and corrections to existing practices.

Efficient talent management can be built upon the ability to predict the need for key talent positions, and then setting up and implementing the plan to meet this need, and the ability to adjust to the more and more often changing business environment. HR managers should therefore understand that their talent management practices should look differently in organizations undergoing rapid organizational transformations (i.e. strategic renewals, restructuring) than in more stable ones. Organizations undergoing rapid organizational transformation should therefore focus on implementing flexible talent management and retention practices, and in fact offer a more personalised approach that would be more suitable to the workforce that is increasingly made of independent and flexibility-seeking Millennials.

Limitations and Suggestions for Further Research

Based on the purely theoretical nature of this chapter, there are several limitations. First of all, this chapter is focused on four generational cohorts and discusses their distinct values and attitudes. However, there is always a risk of over-generalizing the different generational cohorts. We understand that here is a fine line between unique characteristics of each generational cohort and stereotypes about these groups, and as such we aimed to present a discussion that would be based on the first.

Second, generational cohorts, though a very popular concept in consumer marketing studies, are approached by management researchers with a big dose of caution due to classification concerns and lack of mutual exclusiveness between various generations. As mentioned earlier, it is typically understood that a generational cohort spans a period of around 20 years. This means that some representatives of the same cohort are born at the beginning of the specific period while some are born only at the end of it. This means that the latter will most likely share experiences of the two generations: their own and the next one (Arsenault 2004). Arsenault (2004) labelled these individuals born at the generations' classification boundaries as 'tweeners'. Tweeners would most likely share the work values and attitudes of the two generations and hence would respond to even more varied set of talent retention practices. We therefore suggest that further theoretical studies should address the concept of tweeners in the context of talent management. Quantitative research should also be cautious when conceptualizing their research in order to address these kinds of generational subgroups when investigating employee work values and attitudes in organizational context.

Finally, while the focus of this paper is generational differences and their effect on the choice of talent retention strategies, we acknowledge that other diversity measures, such as gender or cultural background, could provide additional insights into talent retention. Research referred to in this chapter presents primarily a Western view of generational cohorts. It would be therefore particularly valuable to uncover whether generational values and attitudes towards workplace depend on a societal, cultural and contextual issues, and whether these aspects would lead to different approaches to talent retention. Future research should investigate the impact of contextual factors on talent retention explicitly and deliberately, as it may help clarify how to retain talent in an effective manner (Gallardo-Gallardo and Thunnissen, 2016). With increasingly diverse workforces and existing cultural differences, research should further investigate national and cultural differences in relation to talent retention and should focus on other than Western perspectives and organizations (Collings et al. 2011; Scullion and Collings 2011).

We also acknowledge that no two individuals are exactly the same, and even though members of the same generations are born around the same time they may have completely different life experiences that would shape their values, beliefs, expectations and work attitudes. More theoretical and empirical research is encouraged to investigate the role of various diversity measures in relation to talent retention strategies. To that end, we believe our review of generational cohort and their application to the context of talent retention will add to current research and we hope that an abundance of new research on generational-focused talent management research will follow.

Summary

Multigenerational workforce creates unique challenges and opportunities for organizations in regard to their talent management practices. To keep up with different generation's values, attitudes, behaviours, and expectations, organizations must be able to diversify, customize, and adjust their approaches to talent management and retention practices. This chapter provided a discussion on generational cohorts' values and expectations, which we translated into specific retention practices proposed for each generational cohort. We suggest that organizations should offer innovative ways to attract, manage, and retain talent, for instance by offering developmental opportunities, meaningful job tasks to its talent pool across all generational cohorts, providing Silent Generation with benefits and retirement plans and Millennials with increased job flexibility and self-reliance at workplace.

We also suggest that talent management practices look differently in organizations that are undergoing rapid organizational transformations than in more stable MNCs, and that the former should approach their talent retention from a strategic perspective. This could be done by providing a flexible, even set of diversified and even personalised practices that would cater talents representing various generational cohorts, such as flexible work patterns, career development and advancement options, offering meaningful projects for talent to engage in.

References

Adler, N. J., & Bartholomew, S. (1992). Managing globally competent people. *Academy of Management Executive, 6,* 52–65.

Agarwal, R., & Helfat, C. E. (2009). Strategic renewal of organizations. *Organization Science, 20,* 281–293.

Al Ariss, A., Cascio, W. F., & Paauwe, J. (2014). Talent management: Current theories and future research directions. *Journal of World Business, 49*(2), 173–179.

Allison, S. (2013). Employment and the millennials. *Youth Studies Australia, 32,* 81–84.

Altimier, L. (2006). Leading a new generation. *Newborn and Infant Nursing Reviews, 6*(1), 7–9.

Arsenault, P. M. (2004). Validating generational differences: A legitimate diversity and leadership issue. *Leadership and Organization Development Journal, 25*(2), 124–141.

Ashton, C., & Morton, L. (2005). Managing talent for competitive advantage: Taking a systemic approach to talent management. *Strategic HR Review, 4*(5), 28–31.

Bartlett, K. R., Lawler, J. J., Bae, J., Chen, S., & Wan, D. (2002). Differences in international human resource development among indigenous firms and multinational affiliates in East and Southeast Asia. *Human Resource Development Quarterly, 13,* 383–405.

Bennett, M. M., Beehr, T. A., & Ivanitskaya, L. V. (2017). Work-family conflict: Differences across generations and life cycles. *Journal of Managerial Psychology, 32*(4), 314–332.

Benson, J., & Brown, M. (2011). Generations at work: Are there differences and do they matter? *International Journal of Human Resource Management, 22*(9), 1843–1865.

Björkman, I., Ehrnrooth, M., Mäkelä, K., Smale, A., & Sumelius, J. (2013). Talent or not? Employee reactions to talent identification. *Human Resource Management, 52*(2), 195–214.

Björkman, I., Ehrnrooth, M., Mäkelä, K., Smale, A., & Sumelius, J. (2017). Talent management in multinational corporations. In D. G. Collings, K. Mellahi, & W. F. Cascio (Eds.), *The Oxford handbook of talent management*. Oxford: Oxford University Press.

Burke, M. E. (2004). *Generational differences. Survey report.* Alexandria: Society for Human Resource Management (SHRM). Retrieved from http://www.shrm.org/research/survey-findings/documents/generational%20differences%20survey%20report.pdf.

Capron, L., & Mitchell, W. (2009). Selection capability: How capability gaps and internal social frictions affect internal and external strategic renewal. *Organization Science, 20,* 294–312.

Cascio, W. F., & Boudreau, J. W. (2015). *Investing in people: Financial impact of human resource initiatives*. New Jersey: Pearson Education.

Cennamo, L., & Gardner, D. (2008). Generational differences in work values, outcomes and person-organisation values fit. *Journal of Managerial Psychology, 23*(8), 891–906.

Cheese, P., Thomas, R. J., & Craig, E. (2008). *The talent powered organization. Strategies for globalization, Talent Management and high performance*. London, UK: Kogan Page Limited.

CIPD. (2006). *Reflections on talent management: Change agenda.* London: Chartered Institute of Personnel and Development.

Collings, D. (2014). Integrating global mobility and global talent management: Exploring the challenges and strategic opportunities. *Journal of World Business, 49*(2), 253–261.

Collings, D. G., & Mellahi, K. (2009). Strategic talent management: A review and research agenda. *Human Resource Management Review, 19*(4), 304–313.

Collings, D. G., Scullion, H., & Vaiman, V. (2011). European perspectives on talent management. *European Journal of International Management, 5*(5), 453–462.

Collings, D. G., Scullion, H., & Vaiman., V. (2015). Talent management: Progress and prospects. *Human Resource Management Review, 25,* 233–235.

Costanza, D. P., Badger, J. M., Fraser, R. L. (2012). Generational differences in work-related attitudes: A meta-analysis. *Journal of Business and Psychology, 27,* 375–394.

Cooke, F. L., Saini, D. S., & Wang, J. (2014). Talent management in China and India: A comparison of management perceptions and human resource practices. *Journal of World Business, 49,* 225–235.

Crampton, S. M., & Hodge, J. W. (2007). Generations in the workplace: Understanding age diversity. *The Business Review, 9*(1), 16–22.

D'Amato, A., & Herzfeldt, R. (2008). Learning orientation, organizational commitment and talent retention across generations. A study of European managers. *Journal of Managerial Psychology, 23*(8), 929–953.

Daily, C. M., Certo, S. T., & Dalton, D. R. (2000). International experience in the executive suite: The path to prosperity. *Strategic Management Journal, 21,* 515–523.

de Waal, A., Peters, L., & Broekhuizen, M. (2017). Do different generations look differently at high performance organizations? *Journal of Strategy and Management, 10*(1), 86–101.

DelCampo, R. G. (2007). Understanding the psychological contract: A direction for the future. *Management Research News, 30*(6), 432–440.

DelCampo, R. G., Haggerty, L. A., Haney, M. J., & Knippel, L. A. (2011). *Managing the multi-generational workforce: From the GI Generation to the Millennials.* Surrey, UK , Burlington, VT: Gower. Routledge.

Dowd-Higgins, C. (2013). *How to play together in the multigenerational sandbox at work. Huffington Post.* Retrieved from http://www.huffingtonpost.com/caroline-dowdhiggins/how-to-play-together-in-t_b_2989568.html.

Dries, N. (2013). The psychology of talent management: A review and research agenda. *Human Resource Management Review, 23*(4), 272–285.

Dries, N., Pepermans, R., & de Kerpel, E. (2008). Exploring four generations' beliefs about career. Is "satisfied" the new "successful"? *Journal of Managerial Psychology, 23*(8), 907–928.

Duchscher, J. E., & Cowan, L. (2004). Multigenerational nurses in the workplace. *The Journal of Nursing Administration, 34*(11), 495–501.

Eastman, J., & Liu, J. (2012). The impact of generational cohorts on status consumption: An exploratory look at generational cohort and demographics on status consumption. *Journal of Consumer Marketing, 29,* 93–102.

Farndale, E., Pai, A., Sparrow, P., & Scullion, H. (2014). Balancing individual and organizational goals in global talent management: A mutual-benefits perspective. *Journal of World Business, 49,* 204–214.

Festing, M., & Schäfer, L. (2014). Generational challenges to talent management: A framework for talent retention based on the psychological-contract perspective. *Journal of World Business, 49,* 262–271.

Gallardo-Gallardo, E., & Thunnissen, M. (2016). Standing on the shoulders of giants? A critical review of empirical talent management research. *Employee Relations, 38,* 31–56.

Gallardo-Gallardo, E., Thunnissen, M., & Scullion, H. (2017). Special issue of International Journal of Human Resource Management. A contextualized approach to Talent Management: Advancing the field. *The International Journal of Human Resource Management.* https://doi.org/10.1080/09585192.2016.1275292.

George, C. (2015). Retaining professional workers: What makes them stay? *Employee Relations, 37,* 102–121.

Giancola, F. (2006). The generation gap: More myth than reality. *Human Resource Planning, 29* (4), 32–37.

Gibson, J. W., Greenwood, R. A., & Murphy, E. F., Jr. (2009). Generational differences in the workplace: Personal values, behaviors, and popular beliefs. *Journal of Diversity Management, 4*(3), 1.

Glass, A. (2007). Understanding generational differences for competitive success. *Industrial and Commercial Training, 39*(2), 98–103.

Gursoy, D., Maier, T. A., & Chi, C. G. (2008). Generational differences: an examination of work values and generational gaps in the hospitality workforce. *International Journal of Hospitality Management, 27*(3), 448–458.

Gursoy, D., Chi, C., & Karadag, E. (2013). Generational differences in work values and attitudes among frontline and service contact employees. *International Journal of Hospitality Management, 32,* 40–48.

Hernaus, T., & Vokic, N. P. (2014). Work design for different generational cohorts: Determining common and idiosyncratic job characteristics. *Journal of Organizational Change Management, 27*(4), 615–641.

Hu, J., Herrick, C., & Hodgin, K. A. (2004). Managing the multigenerational nursing team. *Health Care Management, 23*(4), 334–340.

Irvine, D. (2010). How to reward a multigenerational and culturally diverse workforce. *Workspan, 04*(10), 6268.

Jenkins, J. (2008). Strategies for managing talent in a multi-generational workforce. *Employment Relations Today, 34*(4), 19–26.

Johnson, M. H. (2017). *Multi-Generational workforce: Understanding generational differences*. Trevecca Nazarene University.

Khoreva, V., Vaiman, V., & van Zalk, M. (2017). Talent management practice effectiveness: investigating employee perspective. *Employee Relations, 39*(1), 19–33.

Lancaster, L. C. & Stillman, D. (2002). *When generations collide. Who they are. Why they clash. How to solve the generational puzzle at work*. New York: Collins Business.

Latukha, M. O. (2018). Can talent management practices be considered as a basis fr sustainable competitive advantages in emerging-market firms? evidence from Russia. *Thunderbird International Business Review, 60,* 69–87.

Lyons, S., & Kuron, L. (2014). Generational differences in the workplace: a review of the evidence and directions for future research. *Journal of Organizational Behavior, 35*(S1), S139–S157.

Malik, A. R., Singh, P., & Chan, C. (2017). High potential programs and employee outcomes: The roles of organizational trust and employee attributions. *Career Development International, 22*(7), 772–796.

Marcus, J., & Leiter, M. P. (2017). Generational differences: Effects of job and organizational context. *Age Diversity in the Workplace*. Published online: August 03, 2017; 65–94.

Mellahi, K., & Collings, D. G. (2010). The barriers to effective global talent management: The example of corporate elites in MNEs. *Journal of World Business, 45,* 143–149.

Meyers, M., & van Woerkom, M. (2014). The influence of underlying philosophies on talent management: Theory, implications for practice, and research agenda. *Journal of World Business, 49,* 192–203.

Murphy, S. (2007). *Leading a multigenerational workforce*. Washington, D.C.: AARP.

Ng, E. S., Lyons, S., & Schweitzer, L. (2012). *Managing the new workforce. International perspectives on the millennial generation*. Cheltenham, UK & Northhampton, MA: Edward Elgar.

Nijs, S., Gallardo-Gallardo, E., Dries, N., & Sels, L. (2013). A multidisciplinary review into the definition, operationalization, and measurement of talent. *Journal of World Business, 49,* 180–191.

Palese, A., Pantali, G., & Saiani, L. (2006). The management of a multigenerational nursing team with different qualifications: A qualitative study. *Health Care Management, 25,* 173–193.

Pfeffer, J., & Veiga, J. F. (1999). Putting people first for organizational studies. *The Academy of Management Executive, 13*(2), 37–48.

PricewaterhouseCoopers. (2011). *Millennials at work. Reshaping the workplace.* Retrieved from https://www.pwc.com/gx/en/managing-tomorrows-people/future-of-work/assets/reshaping-the-workplace.pdf.

Schullery, N. (2013). Workplace engagement and generational differences in values. *Business and Professional Communication Quarterly, 76,* 252–265.

Schuler, R. S., Jackson, S. E., & Tarique, I. (2011). Global talent management and global talent challenges: Strategic opportunities for IHRM. *Journal of World Business, 46*(4), 506–516.

Scullion, H., & Collings, D. G. (2011). *Global talent management*. London: Routledge.

Scullion, H., Vaiman, V., & Collings, D. G. (2016). Guest editorial: Strategic talent management. *Employee Relations: The International Journal, 38*(1), 1–7.

Sidani, Y., & Ariss, A. A. (2014). Institutional and corporate drivers of global talent management: Evidence from the Arab Gulf region. *Journal of World Business, 49,* 215–224.

Silzer, R., & Church, A. H. (2009). The pearls and perils of identifying potential. *Industrial and Organizational Psychology, 2,* 377–412.
Singh, A., & Gupta, B. (2015). Job involvement, organizational commitment, professional commitment, and team commitment: A study of generational diversity. *Benchmarking: An International Journal, 22*(6), 1192–1211.
Smola, K., & Sutton, C. (2002). Generational differences: Revisiting generational work values for the new millennium. *Journal of Organizational Behaviour, 23*(4), 363–382.
Sonnenberg, M., van Zijderveld, V., & Brinks, M. (2014). The role of talent-perception incongruence in effective talent management. *Journal of World Business, 49,* 272–280.
Sparrow, P. R., & Makram, H. (2015). What is the value of talent management? Building value-driven processes within a talent management architecture. *Human Resource Management Review, 25,* 249–263.
Sparrow, P., Scullion, H., & Tarique, I. (2014). Multiple lenses on talent management: Definitions and contours of the field. In P. Sparrow, H. Scullion, & I. Tarique (Eds.), *Strategic talent management*. Cambridge: Cambridge University Press.
Stahl, G. K., Björkman, I., Farndale, E., Morris, S. S., Paauwe, J., Stiles, P., (2007). Global talent management: How leading multinationals build and sustain their talent pipeline. In *INSEAD Working Papers Collection* (pp. 1–36).
Tansley, C. (2011). What do we mean by the term "talent" in talent management? *Industrial & Commercial Training, 43*(5), 266–274.
Tansley, C., Turner, P. A., Foster, C., Harris, L. M., Stewart, J., & Sempik, A. (2007). *Talent: Strategy, management measurement*. Plymouth, UK: Chartered Institute of Personal & Development.
Tarique, I., & Schuler, R. S. (2010). Global talent management: Literature review, integrative framework, and suggestions for further research. *Journal of World Business, 45*(2), 122–133.
Tatoglu, E., Glaister, A. J., & Demirbag, M. (2016). Talent management motives and practices in an emerging market: A comparison between MNEs and local firms. *Journal of World Business, 51,* 278–293.
Terjesen, S., & Frey, R.-V. (2008). Attracting and retaining Generation Y knowledge worker talent. In V. Vaiman & C. M. Vance (Eds.), *Smart talent management* (pp. 66–89). Cheltenham, UK & Northampton, MA: Edward Elgar.
Thunnissen, M. (2016). Talent management: For what, how, and how well? An empirical exploration of talent management in practice. *Employee Relations: The International Journal, 38*(1), 57–72.
Thunnissen, M., Boselie, P., & Fruytier, B. (2013). Talent management and the rele-vance of context: Towards a pluralistic approach. *Human Resource Management Review, 23*(4), 326–336.
Tripsas, M. (2009). Technology, identity, and inertia through the lens of "the digital photography company". *Organization Science, 20,* 441–460.
Twenge, J. M., Campbell, S. M., Hoffman, B. J., & Lance, C. E. (2010). Generational differences in work values: Leisure and extrinsic values increasing, social and intrinsic values decreasing. *Journal of Management, 36*(5), 1117–1142.
Ulrich, D. (2008). Call for talent: What is the best solutions. *Leadership Excellence, 25*(5), 17.
Vaiman, V., Haslberger, A., & Vance, C. M. (2015). Recognizing the important role of self-initiated expatriates in effective global talent management. *Human Resource Management Review, 25,* 280–286.
Vaiman, V., Scullion, H., & Collings, D. (2012). Talent management decision making. *Management Decision, 50*(5), 925–941.
Valverde, M., Scullion, H., & Ryan, G. (2013). Talent management in Spanish medium-sized organizations. *The International Journal of Human Resource Management, 24,* 1832–1852.
Vance, C. M., & Vaiman, V. (2008). Smart talent management: On the powerful amalgamation of talent management and knowledge management. In V. Vaiman & C. M. Vance (Eds.), *Smart talent management* (pp. 1–15). Cheltenham UK & Northampton, MA: Edward Elgar.
Ward, K. (2011). *The world in 2050: Quantifying the shift in the global economy*. London: HSBC.

Weingarten, R. M. (2009). Four generations, one workplace: a gen X-Y staff nurses view of team building in the emergency department. *Journal of Emergency Nursing, 35*(1), 27–30.
Wiedmer, T. (2015). Generations do differ: Best practices in leading traditionalists, boomers, and generations X, Y, and Z. *Delta Kappa Gamma Bulletin, 82,* 51–58.
Wood, A. M., Linley, P. A., Maltby, J., Kashdan, T. B., & Hurling, R. (2011). Using personal and psychological strengths leads to increases in well-being over time: A longitudinal study and the development of the strengths use questionnaire. *Personality and Individual Differences, 50*(1), 15–19.

Edyta Kostanek is a Senior Lecturer in Project Management at the School of Strategy and Leadership, Coventry University in United Kingdom. Her research interests include language issues in international management, international human resource management (specifically talent management in multinational companies), and international project management.

Violetta Khoreva is an Assistant Professor at Hanken School of Economics in Finland. Her research interests include issues of international human resource management, specifically talent management and leadership in multinational companies. She has appeared in several academic journals, including Corporate Governance: An International Review, Journal of Managerial Psychology, Personnel Review and Career Development International.

Chapter 11
Talent Retention Strategies: The Role of Self-regulatory Career Behaviour Among Working Adults

Nadia Ferreira

Abstract The increasing demand for proactive career self-management in working adults in a business environment that competes for scarce and critical skills necessitates self-regulatory career behaviour which relates to the retention of employees in uncertain employment markets. The unpredictable and rapidly changing world of work, requires employees to be more accountable and responsible for their own careers and to thus remain employable, adaptable, committed and retainable. Security lies in employability, rather than in employment. Hence the investigation of the relationship between self-regulatory career behaviours and retention factors has become vital in light of the dynamic nature of the current world of work, and the scarcity of talent. These self-regulatory career behaviours include career adaptability, employability attributes and organisational commitment. Based on the relationship found between these self-regulatory career behaviours and retention, human resource practitioners and industrial psychologists should utilise interventions and strategies to promote individual self-regulatory career behaviours in order to increase the retention of talented staff.

Keywords Self-regulatory career behaviour · Employability · Career adaptability Organizational commitment

Introduction

The workplace today utilizes flatter organisational structures, deal with rapid changes in terms of consumer strains and empowerment practices as predominant. It is expected from employees to be more focused on self-regulatory career behaviour in order to be more proactive in the workplace as well as their own careers. Self-regulatory career behaviours, include those that are self-initiated,

N. Ferreira (✉)
Department of Human Resource Management, University of South Africa, Pretoria, South Africa
e-mail: ferren@unisa.ac.za

M. Coetzee et al. (eds.), *Psychology of Retention*,
https://doi.org/10.1007/978-3-319-98920-4_11

future-orientated and change-inducing. The modern workplace perceived a reduction in stability and security in careers (Ferreira 2012; Harry and Coetzee 2013). Employees are required to take greater ownership of their own careers as well as their own career development (Lent 2013). In the current unpredictable and fast changing environment, it is particularly important for individuals to take full accountability and responsibility for their own careers in order to ensure that they remain employable (Thrift 2012). Within this fast-moving and volatile employment, setting the ability to remain employable is seen as an important and needed skill (Blackford 2013).

Working in a fast-paced world of work, creates more diversity and a less predictable environment for most employees (Lent 2013). The rise of protean and boundaryless careers suggests an erosion of a career with a single employer and has to effect more changes within an individual's career path (Lent 2013). In turn, proactive careers necessitate greater levels of self-regulatory career behaviour among individuals (Beukes 2009) as well as organisational commitment (Meyer and Allen 1997). The concept of protean career (Hall 2002, 2013) refers to the career attitude where employees or individuals are in charge of their own careers, instead of the organisation. Employees with high proactive career attitudes are more likely and capable of managing their own careers (Gulyani and Bhatnagar 2016; Jawahar and Liu 2016) by means of self-regulatory skills that support continued employability, adaptability and commitment toward the organisation. Proactive career behaviour can help contribute to the career success of individuals (Parker and Liao 2017).

The increasing demand for employable, adaptable and committed adult workers in a business environment that competes for scarce and critical skills necessitates a study on how self-regulatory career behaviour relates to working adults' commitment in uncertain employment markets. However, in the career self-management context, it is not clear from the research literature how individuals' self-regulatory employability, career adaptability skills and organisational commitment (these constructs relate to self-regulatory capacities considered important for contemporary career management (Ruvimbo and Hlanganipai 2016; Savickas 2013; Van der Heijde and Van Der Heijden 2006) relate to employee retention. To address this research gap, the objective of this chapter was to explore the associations between employees' self-regulatory career behaviour, which include: employability skills, career adaptability, organisational commitment and employee retention factors in the South African workplace context. This chapter further addresses this gap in the research and add value to retention theory. An exploration of self-regulatory career behaviour in relation to employee retention factors may offer new insights that can be used to empower employees as well as organisations with the needed personal and organisational support they need to ensure higher levels of organisational commitment and successful retention of valuable staff.

Theoretical Support for Linking Self-regulatory Career Behaviour (Employability Attributes, Career Adaptability and Organisational Commitment) and Retention Factors

The self-regulatory career behaviour included in this chapter have been identified as employability attributes, career adaptability and organisational commitment.

Self-regulatory Employability Skills

Self-regulatory employability represents the capacity to apply and continuously develop a range of helpful competencies and attributes by including a range of reiterative developmental stages that improves the employee's opportunities for accessing and sustaining employment opportunities (Beukes 2009; Coetzee and Beukes 2010). The application and development of competencies are self-directed and denote proactive career self-management (Van der Heijde and Van Der Heijden 2006). Beukes (2009) notion of employability parallels Pool and Sewell's (2007) understanding of employability. They described employability as possessing a set of skills, knowledge, understanding and personal attributes that make a person more likely to choose will assist the individual to choose a secure occupation in which they can be satisfied and successful, to benefit themselves, the workforce, the community and the economy. Through supportive career services, these skills, knowledge, understanding and personal attributes may be developed in such a manner that it can assist the employee to maintain suitable employment (Beukes 2009; Coetzee and Beukes 2010). Being employable has become an essential key factor of global working life. Employability has further become the first pillar in global employment and simplifying employee entree to the labour market, as well as ensuring attractiveness and marketability within today's changing and unpredictable work setting (Coetzee et al. 2016; Jackson and Wilton 2017; Potgieter et al. 2016). Employability is a set of competencies, skills and expertise that enables an individual to secure sustained employment, maintain employment and obtain new employment if the need arises even in the face of joblessness (Botha et al 2015; De Fruyt et al. 2015). Bezuidenhout (2011) differentiates between eight core employability attributes that are presented in Table 11.1 .

Self-regulatory employability has been associated with positive career behaviours (Coetzee and Beukes 2010) and learning and goal-directed behaviours that support individuals' employability and career success (Van der Heijde and Van Der Heijden 2006). According to Coetzee and Schreuder (2013) and Reid (2016) employable individuals are more self-directed, have an inner sense of stability and personal plan in keeping a job, based on the set of attributes and competencies in an uncertain and unpredictable employment context. Employees that are more employable tend to have more courage and strength to take control and realise the potential presented in the current and future career path (Babos et al. 2015; Taylor 2016).

Table 11.1 Employability attributes

Career self-management	The ability to remain employable through continuous learning and career planning and self-management
Cultural competence	The ability to interact, understand and function in a diverse cultural environment
Self-efficacy	The evaluation individuals create of their own capability to manage, achieve and succeed
Career resilience	The level of adaptability, flexibility, self-confidence and competence regardless of opposing career circumstances
Sociability	The ability of openness, establishment, and maintaining social contacts (formal and informal linkages) to the benefit of one's career
Entrepreneurial orientation	The ability to be innovative and creative, taking risks, desire for success, an open-mindedness for uncertainty and self-sufficiency in taking advantage of opportunities within one's career
Proactivity	The ability to actively engage in a direction that steers one to be more future-oriented and self-initiated in the actions taken in order to adapt to changing situations
Emotional literacy	The ability to adapt one's emotions, to read, apprehend and control one's and others' emotions

Career Adaptability

Career-adaptability can assist employees to be prepare for, and having the necessary resources, to cope with work distresses, career development tasks, and changes in their careers throughout their whole life span (Brown and Lent 2013; Coetzee and Harry 2015). Career adaptability integrates aspects such as, plan-fullness, exploration, decision making, information and realism (Super 1974), career planning and career exploration (Zikic and Klehe 2006), a boundaryless mind-set (McArdle et al. 2007) of career planning, career decidedness and career confidence (Skorikov 2007). Savickas (1997), Savickas and Porfeli (2012) theorize that career adaptability includes the concern as planning, expectancy and mindfulness for one's future. Control is taking full responsibility for constructing one's career through taking decisive, assertive and conscientious actions. Curiosity is taking initiative learning about the world of work that leads to information seeking behaviours. Curiosity is openness to new experiences, inquisitive exploration, and reflection about the fit between self and the world of work. Confidence is defined as serious engagement in designing one's occupational futures and executing plans in order to actualise their choices (Coetzee and Stoltz 2015; Oncel 2014; Rottinghaus et al. 2012; Savickas and Porfeli 2011; 2012; Savickas 1997).

Research has shown that the four psychosocial resources, which are also referred to as four major dimensions of career adaptability, namely concern, control curiosity and confidence are important in life in order to remain employable (Ferreira and Mujajati 2017). It can be argued that the four dimensions of career adaptability (career planning, decision making, exploration and confidence) refer to

Table 11.2 Dimensions of career adaptability

Concern	A propensity to reflect on life within a certain period of life secured in hope and confidence (becoming apprehensive about one's career and occupation)
Control	The belief that it is a benefit for individuals to be able not only to use self-regulatory career behaviour to adjust in diverse situations, but also to apply some sort of power and control over the context (to be more in control of one's vocational future)
Curiosity	Implicates that selves and social opportunities enhance individuals's dynamic exploration activities (demonstrating curiosity by exploring possible selves and prospect advances)
Confidence	The ability to stand by one's own goals and objectives, even when facing difficulties and obstacles (enhancing self-assurance to follow one's aspirations)

an individual's preparation and psychological willingness to use diverse job search strategies, which in turn can influence the individual's re-employment results (Koen et al. 2010). Understanding an individual's career adaptability profile may directly influence staff retention in an organisation.

Bearing in mind adaptability, the career construction theory (Savickas 2005) highlights a set of specific attitudes, beliefs and competencies, which shape the actual problem-solving strategies and self-regulatory career behaviour that individuals use to integrate their vocational self-concepts with their work roles. Table 11.2 represents the four dimensions of career adaptability.

These four dimensions (4 Cs) signifies over-all adaptability resources and approaches that individuals use to construct their careers as well as coping with developmental tasks, changes in work settings and work disturbances (Luke et al. 2016; Tak 2012).

Organisational Commitment

Generally, the research literature describes organisational commitment as a set of distinct mindsets such as emotional attachment to the organisation, having a sense of obligation to the organisation or concerns about the perceived cost of leaving the organisation (Meyer et al. 2012). Research on mindsets towards specific targets or commitment within the organisation is rare (Meyer et al. 2015; Roodt 1997), especially within the South African work context. According to O'Reilly 1989, organisational commitment is the psychological connection an individual has with the organisation, which includes a sense of job involvement, faithfulness and confidence in the organisation's values. Organisational commitment is further regarded as an employee's acknowledgement of organissational goals and his or her enthusiasm into making these goals their own (O'Reilly 1989).

Research suggests that individuals may experience conflict regarding their target of commitment whereas similarity of commitment to the various foci of commitment may be possible (Meyer et al. 2015). Regulatory focus theory (Higgins 1998) posits that employees' regulatory focus can influence the nature of the commitments they develop, they can commit to one or more or neither targets and can experience different mindsets towards each target. Similarly, research has revealed that individuals' inner work lives, career goals, motivations and desires act as self-regulated motivating forces that influence their attitudes toward their jobs, careers as well as their organisation (Coetzee 2015; Bothma and Roodt 2012; Ferreira and Coetzee 2010; Hirschi 2012). It therefore stands to reason that individuals' perceptions about their self-regulatory employability skills may potentially influence their organisational commitment. An individual's commitment to and involvement in their work, job and career revolve around an attitude of active engagement in their work, job and career areas because of the desire to achieve set goals within these areas (Coetzee 2015; Coetzee et al. 2014; Puah and Ananthram 2006; Tladinyane et al. 2013). Meyer and Allen (1997), describe organisational commitment as a psychological connection between the employee and his or her organisation that makes it less likely for the employee to voluntary leave the organisation

Organisational commitment leads to positive organisational outcomes, comprising improved performance on individual and organisational level, organisational efficiency and reduces employee turnover (Saif et al. 2012). Mujajati (2017) proclaims highly committed individuals opt to remain with their current organisation even if the circumstances are less than ideal. Committed employees are more satisfied with their jobs, due to be more likely to focus on the positive, rather than the negative elements of their working environment (Knapp et al. 2014).

In this chapter, the notion of organisational commitment is based on Meyer and Allen (1997) three-component model of organisational commitment as described in Table 11.3.

Retention Factors

The success, effectiveness and survival of organisations are determined by the retention of highly talented, dedicated and exceptional individuals (Olckers and Du Plessis 2015; Zhang et al. 2015). The competency, efficacy, profitability and sustainability of any organisation in the 21st century world of work depend on attracting and retaining key and valuable employees (Malcolm et al. 2015). Highly professional, talented and educated employees are the most vital and dynamic irreplaceable resources that deliver great products and services, provide their customers and colleagues with immense satisfaction, increase product sales, and make organisations great and effective (Graen and Grace 2015). It is important that organisations create good and healthy working environments and work/life policies that will attract and retain bright and productive individuals, this will assist organisations to be able to retain rare talents who are resilient, adaptive, intellectual, agile and versatile, (Deery and Jago 2015; Du Plessis and Sukumaran 2015).

Table 11.3 Dimensions of organisational commitment

Affective commitment	Refers to the affecting connection of an individual, recognition as part of and participation in the organisation. Employees with high levels of affective commitment towards the organisation will probably remain with the organisation because they want to (Meyer and Allen 1991). Recognition of the organisation and internalisation of organisational principles and standards, form part of the development of affective commitment (Beck and Wilson 2000)
Continuance commitment	Comprises the consciousness of the costs involved with leaving the organisation (Meyer and Allen 1997, p. 11). Kanter (1968) agrees with this definition affirming that it is the advantage associated with sustained involvement and the costs associated with leaving the organisation. Individuals, whose connection to the organisation is based on continuance commitment, stay because they need to (Allen and Meyer 1990)
Normative commitment	A sense of responsibility to remain with the currently employed organisation (Meyer and Allen 1997). Allen and Meyer (1990) indicate that the adopted normative idea of responsibility and commitment permits employees to appreciate sustained involvement of a specific organisation. The commitment individuals think about morally concerning their right to continue with their current organisation, in spite of how much status improvement or fulfilment the organisation provides them over the years is seen as the normative element of commitment (March and Mannari 1977)

Retention factors are aspects that facilitate the retention or departure of employees. These decisions to leave or stay with an organisation be contingent on the employee's priorities (Coetzee et al. 2016; Okech 2015; Ratna and Chawla 2012; Van Dyk and Coetzee 2012). Dockel (2003) identified the six retention factors identified by Dockel (2003) are presented in Table 11.4.

Table 11.4 Retention factors explained

Compensation	The attractiveness of salary package, value of benefits and organisational remuneration policies
Job characteristics	The facets of the job, which include varied work, problem-solving opportunities and to work with the best people, freedom, flexibility, and the ability to pursue interesting assignments
Training and development opportunities	Job-specific training, opportunity for personal growth and development, application of learning in the workplace
Supervisor support	The feedback from supervisors on personal performance, praise and appreciation, reward and acknowledgement outstanding performance
Career opportunities	Progression and individual career development opportunities within the organisation
Work-life balance	The ability to balance one's work and life (personal) domain

Retaining highly talented, adaptable and employable employees within the South African context have become important due to the uncertainty in the ever changing and unstable labour market. By assisting employees, they are to develop the necessary self-regulatory career behaviour. Employees will be able to take self-responsibility for developing the necessary skills and managing their own careers as successfully as possible. Individuals can engage in career counselling and career development activities. By engaging in career development activities individuals will be able to identify their own strengths and weaknesses and develop these self-regulatory career behaviour as a tool for enhancing their skills. Retention strategies within an organisation would therefore be a powerful tool for industrial psychologists, human resource practitioners, managers, career counsellors, individuals as career agents and all those involved in career counselling. These retention strategies could be used to deepen the understanding of how employees can influence and enhance their self-regulatory career behaviour. This knowledge could be useful in the design of retention practices on an individual and organisational level in order to retain talented staff.

Rothausen et al. (2015) indicated that retention challenges are now even more related to employee well-being. Working environment, training and development, career development opportunities as well as work-life balance are some other factors which have a direct influence on employee retention (Hassan et al. 2013). Employees must be able to vision a clear career path within the organisation in order to be more loyal and more committed and only then, will they remain with the organisation (Bagga 2013). Employees' must have clear career ambitions and must therefore be able to recognise the skills and competencies that are required to achieve those career goals (Bezuidenhout 2011). These findings by Bezuidenhout (2011) further indicate that employees must continuously be engaged, committed and focused on these skills development activities. The study results by Coetzee (2015), provide evidence that employees who take personal responsibility for their career development and goals, who manage their own action plans, experience greater satisfaction with training and development opportunities and career development opportunities. Well-managed organisations should develop their specific talent retention strategies and implement policies and practices from the date of hire of new employees. Such strategies and policies can include career development opportunities used as a tool for talent retention, new employees are briefed on this during their on-boarding, in order for them to prepare their mind-set for career development and aspirations (Bhattacharyya 2015). Dhar (2015) states that training also helps to develop employee networks, abilities and improve their performance. Training further assist employees to clarify their career objectives and provide them with the opportunity to pursue new career goals and paths.

The global skills shortages require managers, industrial psychologists and human resource practitioners to not only understand the reasons why people leave their organisations, but also the factors that influence turnover and the retention of employees (Coetzee et al. 2015). By looking at the current literature, it is clear that the work context has changed radically during the 21st century. Careers have also changed and moved away from what was known as the traditional career to the boundaryless career, as a result of the changes in the work context. The developments in the career context have highlighted the need for more self-regulatory career behaviour. The highest qualification or the best skills does not necessarily secure the best job anymore. Employability, career adaptability and organisational commitment as self-regulatory career behaviour influence the retention of valuable employees in an organisation (Coetzee et al. 2017; Ferreira and Mujajati 2017).

Proposed Strategies for Talent Retention

The findings of this chapter is based on recent studies conducted by Jabaar (2017) and Ferreira and Mujajati (2017). As shown in Table 11.5, the theoretical self-regulatory career behaviour framework is described in terms of the psychological behavioural dimensions: cognitive, affective, conative and interpersonal levels.

On a **cognitive level**, the retention of individuals may be influenced by their career self-management and self-efficacy (employability attributes), concern and control (career adaptability) and normative commitment (organisational commitment) (Ferreira 2012; Ferreira and Mujajati 2017; Jabaar 2017; Savickas 2002; Schreuder and Coetzee 2011). Career development support practices and career counselling should focus on creating a work environment that provide employees with the opportunity to be able to manage their own careers and develop the skills to cope, perform and thrive within the organisation. Furthermore, it is important for organisations to assist individuals with the preparation for upcoming career challenges as well as providing them with opportunity to be self-responsible and determined in terms of taking control of career and work situations. Organisations should also be assisted within these interventions to enhance the idea of responsibility and commitment of individuals in order to engage them in managing their

Table 11.5 Theoretical self-regulatory career behaviour profile

	Self-regulatory career behaviour		
	Employability	Career adaptability	Organisational Commitment
Cognitive	• Career self-management • Self-efficacy	• Concern • Control	• Normative commitment
Affective	• Emotional literacy	• Curiosity	• Affective commitment
Conative	• Career resilience • Entrepreneurial orientation • Proactivity	• Cooperation • Confidence	• Normative commitment • Continuance commitment
Interpersonal	• Cultural competence • Sociability	• Cooperation • Concern	• Affective commitment • Normative commitment • Continuance commitment

own careers by developing these self-regulatory career behaviours on a cognitive level. Such interventions could possibly assist organisation with the development of effective retention strategies within the company.

On an **affective level**, individuals' retention may be influenced by their emotional literacy (employability attributes), curiosity (career adaptability) and affective commitment (organisational commitment) (Allen and Meyer 1990; Brown et al. 2003; Coetzee and Bergh 2009; Ferreira et al. 2010; Ferreira and Mujajati 2017; Jabaar 2017). Career development support practices and career counselling should assist individuals by developing their ability to use their emotions effectively and manage and control their emotions in all situations. This may help individuals to improve their emotional intelligence, social connectivity, curiosity and commitment but also to utilise their emotions appropriately within the work context. Career development support practices will create a feeling of belonging among employees in their current organisation and demonstration and develop an emotional connection with the organisation. By creating employees with the ability to manage and utilise their emotions within their career context and having a sense of belonging, could possibly assist organisations with the retention of talented staff.

On a **conative level**, individuals' retention may be influenced by their career resilience, entrepreneurial orientation and proactivity (employability attributes), cooperation and confidence (career adaptability) and continuance- and normative commitment (organisational commitment) (Ferreira and Mujajati 2017; Jabaar 2017; Koen et al. 2010; Maddi 2002; Meyer and Allen 1991; Mitchell and Lee 2001; Savickas 1997). Career development support practices and career counselling could possibly assist individuals by encouraging their level of adaptability, flexibility and self-confidence as well as their ability to act proactively in order to adapt in changing situations. Furthermore, employees need encouragement to be more innovative, creative and taking and managing risks within their careers and organisations. Cooperation, confidence and commitment among employees towards the organisation might increase by supporting employees with the correct career support practices and career counselling. This in turn might assist organisations with the retention of talented staff.

On an **interpersonal level**, individuals' retention may be influenced by their cultural competence and sociability (employability attributes), cooperation and concern (career adaptability and affective-, continuance- and normative commitment (organisational commitment) (Ferreira et al. 2010; Ferreira and Mujajati 2017; Jabaar 2017; Koen et al. 2010; Maddi 2002; Meyer and Allen 1991; Mitchell and Lee 2001; Savickas 1997; 2001; 2002). Effective interaction and social connectivity with others in a diverse cultural environment may create a feeling of security within the individual, which might have a positive effect on the retention of talented staff. Career development support practices and career counselling could assist individuals to enhance their ability to interact, understand and function within a diverse cultural environment as well as to establish and maintain social connections, which might have a positive effect on their commitment towards the organisation. By developing these self-regulatory career behavioural skills on an interpersonal level might have a positive influence on the retention of staff within the organisation.

Keeping employees employable, adaptable and committed to the organisation is a top priority for many contemporary organisations in order to retain their assets (Coetzee et al. 2017; Fereira and Mujajati 2017; Neininger et al. 2010). Especially in times of uncertainty and retrenchments, committing top performers to the organisation becomes a concern. It is critical for organisation to determine retention strategies within the organisation on both an individual and organisational level in order to ensure successful retention of employees. Table 11.6 present possible retention stretegies on these two levels: individual level and organisational level.

Table 11.6 Possible retention strategies

Individual level
• Individuals should think, plan and prepare for the future and realise that the choices made today have an influence on their future • Plan on how to achieve personal goals and make better and independent decisions • Individuals should strive to be more persistent, patient and explore their surroundings • Individuals should observe different ways of doing things and consider all possible alternatives to a situation • Individuals should try to perform all tasks efficiently and learn from their mistakes • Individuals should strive to improve your self-confidence by learning new skills and challenging themselves • Individuals must have clear career aspirations and take into account others' opinions regarding their strengths and weaknesses in the workplace • Individuals should try to get along with other colleagues and people and form part or a team (specifically in a diverse cultural environment) • Individuals should develop their ability to be more emotionally literate, compromising as well as being a good listener • Individuals should be more adaptable to changing situations in their career • Individuals should contribute to the community as part of their career • Employees should be supported in terms of career development and career counselling. Such support can help individuals to enhance deeper understanding, improve their own personal self-esteem and to manage their own emotions as well as use their emotions appropriately within the new world of work
Organisational level
• Organisations should ensure that their remuneration policies and procedures are faire and consistent with both internal and external roles of similarity • Organisations should ensure that their pay structures are competitive • Organisations should create a work context that is challenging and provides employees with the level of skills and experience aligned with their personal and professional growth needs • Organisations should develop a career development-counselling framework that can be used to assist employees to develop their employability and adaptability skills. This would assist individuals in developing their self-regulatory career behaviour by identifying the relationship between their own employability, career adaptability, organisational commitment and their retention factors • Organisations should use the Employability Attributes Scale (EAS), Career Adaptability Inventory (CAI) and the Organisational Commitment Survey (OCS) in career counselling to help individuals identify their self-regulatory career behaviour that affect their retention factors within an organisation

Implications for Retention Practices

The fresh perceptions resulting from the findings may provide a deeper understanding on how individuals' self-regulatory career behaviour (employability, career adaptability and organisational commitment) explain their retention factors (Ferreira and Mujajati 2017; Jabaar 2017). Furthermore, the findings could be used to assist individuals developing stronger self-regulatory career behaviour. These findings may in turn improve the career decision making and retention of talented staff within an organisation. Based on the findings (Ferreira and Mujajati 2017; Jabaar 2017), organisations should gain a better understanding of the employability skills, career adaptability and organisational commitment levels that individuals have towards remaining in an organisation. Organisations should be able to adjust their retention strategies accordingly.

Managers and industrial psychologists should take into account the different theoretical models and concepts that impact on the variables included in self-regulatory career behaviour (employability, career adaptability and organisational commitment) when working in the field of career development, and should take cognisance of the strengths and weaknesses of the four measuring instruments used in the studies done by Ferreira and Mujajati (2017) and Jabaar (2017).

Prior to utilising the psychometric properties in organisational initiatives, managers, career counsellors and industrial psychologists should be mindful of the psychometric properties of the different measuring instruments (EAS, CAI, OCS and RMFS). The instruments should be supported by sufficient reliability and validity data for use in the South African context in particular. In order to ensure successful career decision making and retention strategies that are fair and unbiased, it is necessary to take into account the needed integrity in selecting, administering and interpreting instruments and providing individual feedback.

Individuals can apply a career decision-making strategy. Such career decision-making strategies will meet their different career and stage developmental needs and prevent as much career indecisiveness as possible, only when managers assist them with career advice, and remove as much uncertainty in them as possible about their career choice and environment. Furthermore, if organisations invest in positive psychological contracts with their employees, it could result in employees who are even more committed, motivated and trustworthy towards the organisation.

According to Ferreira and Mujajati (2017) and Jabaar (2017), based on the research findings and relationships that emerged, the following organisational interventions in terms of career decision making and retention strategies are recommended:

- Organisations should consider offering attractive salary packages, value of the benefit offered and clear organisational remuneration policies.
- Organisations should take into account the different aspects of a specific job such as varied work, provide employees with opportunities to solve problems and the opportunity to pursue interesting assignments.

- Organisations should assist employees with specific training needed to provide opportunity to grow and develop, as well as to be able to apply learning in the workplace.
- Supervisors should ensure that feedback is provided on personal performance praise and appreciation, reward as well as the necessary acknowledgement.
- Organisations should provide employees with the necessary progression and individual career development opportunities within the organisation.
- Organisations should support individuals with the ability to balance their work and personal life.

The following practical recommendations apply to industrial psychologists working in the field of career development and retention:

- Both the manager and industrial psychologist's role is that of a career counsellor. To successfully fulfil this role, it is needed to understand all the facets of an individual's self-regulatory career behavioural skills and understand what motivates him or her in the workplace. This will ensure that the manager and career counsellor guide employees successfully in their career choices in order to strengthen the commit towards the employer or organisation.
- Self-reflection can be engaged on by individuals when receiving feedback on their self-regulatory career behaviour (employability, career adaptability and organisational commitment) at a cognitive, affective, conative and interpersonal level.
- Individuals can participate in career development in order to improve their self-regulatory career behaviour (employability, career adaptability and organisational commitment) at a cognitive, affective, conative and interpersonal level.
- Interventions to facilitate the enhancement of employability skills, career adaptability and organisational commitment for the retention of highly talented employees, should be engaged in by Human resource practitioners, managers and career counsellors.
- HR practitioners and Career counsellors should partner with employers to appreciate the importance of and reach consensus on how to support employees in bettering their career adaptability, employability attributes and organisational commitment to strengthen their retention strategies.
- Managers, Career counsellors and HR practitioners can develop employees' career adaptability, employability attributes and organisational commitment in the world of work by implementing training and development programmes, career development opportunities and continuous learning programmes, as well as interventions to assist them in gaining these necessary skills.

On *a practical level*, if managers, human resource practitioners and industrial psychologists could better understand the self-regulatory career behaviours and the facets thereof in considering organisational retention strategies. A better understanding could have a positive impact on the retention of valuable talented employees. The positive outcomes of possible future research could include raising awareness of the fact that individuals in the workplace have different employability attributes, career adaptability and organisational commitment levels. Every individual needs to be treated in a manner that is appropriate to him or her in order to promote a successful career, filled with job and career satisfaction. This will culminate in the successful retention of employees. The realisation of the way in which employees' self-regulatory career behaviours influence their retention factors towards the employing organisation was another positive outcome. These studies also emphasises the significance of mentoring and succession planning in career development and retention practices (Ferreira and Mujajati 2017; Jabaar 2017). Furthermore, the research results contributed to the body of knowledge relating to the self-regulatory career behaviour that influence employee retention in the retail sector organisational context.

There is a need for future research on employability attributes, career adaptability, organisational commitment and retention factors, specifically in South Africa. Further studies would be valuable for career development and guidance purposes because it would assist managers to provide guidance to individuals when making career choices, based on their ability to translate their self-regulatory career behaviour into jobs what would fulfil their personal needs.

Conclusions

Based on the literature review and the study done by Ferreira and Mujajati (2017) and Jabaar (2017), it seems as if employees' employability attributes, career adaptability and organisational commitment levels should be developed in order to increase their retention factors within an organisation. Furthermore, employability attributes, career adaptability and organisational commitment seem to be the most important attributes to consider in career counselling and career development when focusing on individuals' self-regulatory career behaviour. These constructs therefore need to be developed to assist individuals to proactively manage their own career development and assist organisations in the retention of valuable staff. Insights into how the inter- and overall relationships between the constructs of relevance to the studies have contributed to explore the relationship between these constructs. Hopefully industrial and organisational psychologists and managers will be able to successfully utilise the new understandings in enhancing retention strategies within an organisation. Talent retention has become a prominent focus of many organisations because of the competitive nature of today's work environment.

Summary

This chapter identified the implications of the theoretical relationship between employability attributes, career adaptability and organisational commitment (Self-regulatory career behaviour) and retention factors proposed a self-regulatory career behaviour profile for staff retention that can be used during career counselling and career development interventions.

References

Allen, N. J., & Meyer, J. P. (1990). The measurement and antecedents of affective, continuance and normative commitment to the organisation. *Journal of Occupational Psychology, 63*, 1–18.

Babos, P., Lubyova, M., & Student, I. (2015). Policy brief: Proceedings of Light in Europe. *Research Project*, 1–27.

Bagga, G. (2013). How to keep the talent you have got. *Human Resource Management International Digest, 21*(1), 3–4. https://doi.org/10.1108/09670731311.

Beck, N., & Wilson, J. (2000). Development of affective organizational commitment: A cross-sequental examination of change with tenure. *Journal of Vocational Behaviour, 56*, 114–136.

Beukes, C. (2009). *The relationship between employability and emotional intelligence.* Unpublished research report, Department of Industrial and Organisational Psychology, University of South Africa, Pretoria.

Bezuidenhout, M. (2011). *The development and evaluation of a measure of graduate employability in the context of the new world of work* (Unpublished master's dissertation). Department of Human Resources, University of Pretoria, Pretoria, South Africa.

Bhattacharyya, D. K. (2015). Compensation and benefits program a mediating variable for talent retention: A study of two centuries old Indian organisations. *Compensation and Benefits Review, 30,* 1–16.

Botha, J., Coetzee, M., & Coetzee, M. (2015). Exploring adult learners' self-directedness in relation to their employability attributes in open distance learning. *Journal of Psychology in Africa, 25*(1), 65–72. https://doi.org/10.1080/14330237.2015.1007603.

Bothma, F. C. & Roodt, G. (2012). 'Work-based identity and work engagement as potential antecendents of task performance and turnover intention: Unravelling a complex relationship'. *South African Journal of Industrial Psychology,* 38(1), Art #893. https://doi.org/10.4102/sajip.v38i1.893.

Blackford, S. (2013). *Career planning for research Bioscientists*. UK: Wiley.

Brown, S. D., & Lent, R. W. (2013). *Career development and counselling: Putting theory and research to work* (2nd ed.). USA: Wiley.

Brown, C., George-Curran, R., & Smith, M. (2003). The role of emotional intelligence in the career commitment and decision making process. *Journal of Career Assessment, 11*(4), 379–392.

Coetzee, M. (2015). Employees' psychosocial career preoccupations in relation to their work-related commitment. *Southern African Business Review, 19*(3), 30–47.

Coetzee, M., & Bergh, Z. (2009). Psychological career resources and subjective work experiences of working adults: An exploratory study. *South African Business Review, 13*(2), 1–31.

Coetzee, M., & Beukes, C. J. (2010). Employability, emotional intelligence and career preparation support satisfaction among adolescents in the school-to-work transition phase. *Journal Psychology in Africa, 20*(3), 439–446.

Coetzee, M., & Stoltz, E. (2015). Employees' satisfaction with retention factors: Exploring the role of career adaptability. *Journal of Vocational Behaviour, 89,* 83–91.

Coetzee, M., & Harry, N. (2015). Gender and hardiness as predictors of career adaptability: An exploratory study among black call centre agents. *South African Journal of Psychology, 45*(1), 81–92.

Coetzee, M., Ferreira, N., & Pogieter, L. (2015). Assessing employability capacities and career adaptability in a sample of human resource professional. *SA Journal of Human Resource Management/ SA Tydskrif vir Menslikehulpbronbestuur, 13*(1), a682, 9 pages. http://dx.doi.org/10.4102/sajhrm.v13i1.682.

Coetzee, M., Ferreira, N., & Shunmugum, C. (2017). Psychological career resources, career adaptability and work engagement of generational cohorts in the media industry. *SA Journal of Human Resource Management/SA Tydskrif vir Menslikehulpbronbestuur, 15*(0), a868. https://doi.org/10.4102/sajhrm.v15i0.868.

Coetzee, M., Oosthuizen, R. M., & Stoltz, E. (2016). Psychosocial employability attributes as predictors of staff satisfaction with retention factors. *South African Journal of Psychology, 46* (2), 232–243. https://doi.org/10.1177/0081246315595971.

Coetzee, M., & Schreuder, D. (2013). Career anchors and emotional intelligence as predictors of human resource staff graduateness skills and employability attributes. *South African Journal of Labour Relations, 37*(2), 97–117.

Coetzee, M., Mitonga-Monga, J. & Swart, B. (2014). Human resource practices as predictors of engineering staff's organizational commitment. *South African Journal of Human Resource Management,* 12(1), 12. https://doi.org/10.4102/sajhrm.v12.i1.604.

Deery, M., & Jago, L. (2015). Revisiting talent management, work—life balance and retention strategies. *International Journal of Contemporary Hospital Management, 27*(3), 453–472.

De Fruyt, F., Willie, B., & John, O. P. (2015). Employability in the 21st century: Complex (interactive) problem solving and other essential skills. *Journal of International Studies, 8*(2), 276–281.

Dhar, R. L. (2015). Service quality and the training of employees: the mediating role of organisational commitment. *Tourism Management, 46*(2015), 419–430.

Dockel, A. (2003). *The effect of retention factors on organisational commitment: An investigation of high technology employees*. Unpublished Masters dissertation, University of South Africa, Pretoria.

Du Plessis, A., & Sukumaran, S. (2015). The role of HRM in leadership development, talent retention, knowledge management and employee engagement. *World Journal of Social Sciences, 5*(1), 93–110.

Ferreira, N. (2012). *Constructing a psychological career profile for staff retention.* Unpublished doctoral dissertation, University of South Africa, Pretoria: South Africa.

Ferreira, N., Basson, J., & Coetzee, M. (2010). Psychological career resources in relation to organisational commitment: An exploratory study. *South African Journal of Human Resource Management, 8*(1), 1–9.

Ferreira, N., & Coetzee, M. (2010). Psychological career resources and organisational commitment: Exploring socio-demographic differences. *South African Journal of Labour Relations, 34*(2), 25–41.

Ferreira, N., & Mujajati, E. (2017). Career meta-capacities and retention factors of recruitment advertising agencies: An exploratory study. *Journal of Psychology in Africa, 27*(5), 405–411. https://doi.org/10.1080/14330237.2017.1379659.

Graen, G., & Grace, R. (2015). New talent strategy: Attract, process, educate, empower, engage and retain the best. *Society for Human Resource Management*, 23–34.

Gulyani, G., & Bhatnagar, J. (2016). Mediator analysis of passion for work Indian millennials: Relationship between protean career attitude and proactive work behavior. *Career Development International,* 22(1), 50–69. https://doi.org/10.1108/CDI-04-2016-0057.

Hall, D. T. (2002). *Protean careers in and out of organisations*. Thousand Oaks, CA: Sage.

Hall, D. T. (2013). Protean careers in the 21st century. In K. Inkson & M. L. Savickas (Eds.), *Career studies* (Vol. I, pp. 245–254)., Foundations of career studies London: Sage.

Hassan, W., Razi, A., Qamar, R., Jaffir, R., & Suhail, S. (2013). The effect of training on employee retention. *Global Journal of Management and Business Research Administration and Management, 13*(6), 16–20.

Harry, N., & Coetzee, M. (2013). Sense of coherence, career adaptability and burnout of early-career Black staff in the call centre environment. *SA Journal of Industrial Psychology, 39* (2), 1138–1148. https://doi.org/10.4102/sajip.v39i2.1138.

Higgins, E. T. (1998). Promotion and prevention: regulatory focus as a motivational principle. *Advances in Experimental Social Psychology, 30,* 1–46.

Hirschi, A. (2012). The career resources model: an integrative framework for career counsellors. *British Journal of Guidance & Counselling,* 40(4), 369–383. https://doi.org/10.1080/03069885.2012.700506.

Jabaar, R. (2017). The relationship between organizational commitment, career adaptability and retention factors within the retail sector in the Western Cape. Unpublished doctoral dissertation, University of South Africa, Pretoria, South Africa.

Jackson, D., & Wilton, N. (2017). Perceived employability among undergraduates and the importance of career self-management, work experience and individual characteristics. *Higher Education Research and Development, 36*(4), 747–762. https://doi.org/10.1080/07294360.2016.1229270.

Jawahar, I. M. & Liu, Y. (2016). Why are proactive people more satisfied with their job, career, and life? An examination of the role of work engagement. *Journal of Career Development, 2016,* 1–15. https://doi.org/10.1177/0894845316656070.

Kanter, R. (1968). Commitment and social organisation: A study of commitment mechanisms in Utopian communities. *American Sociological Review, 33,* 499–517.

Knapp, R., Smith, B. R. & Sprinkle, T. A. (2014). Clarifying the retaional ties of organisational belonging: Understanding the roles of perceives insider status, psychological ownership and organisational identification. *Journal of Leadership & Organisational Studies, 2014.* https://doi.org/10.1177/1548051814529826.

Koen, J., Klehe, U. S., Van Vianen, A. E. M., Zikic, J., & Nauta, A. (2010). Job-search strategies and reemployment quality: The impact of career adaptability. *Journal of Vocational Behaviour, 77*(1), 126–139.

Lent, R. W. (2013). Career-life preparedness: revisiting career planning and adjustment in the new workplace. *The Career Development Quartely, 61*(1), 2–14. https://doi.org/10.1002/j2161-0045.201300031.x.

Luke, J., McIlveen, S., & Perera, H. N. (2016). A thematic analysis of career adaptability in retirees who return to work. *Frontiers in Psychology, 7,* 193–198.

Maddi, S. (2002). The story of hardiness: Twenty years of theorizing, research, and practice. *Consulting Psychology Journal: Practice and Research, 54*(3), 175–185.

Malcolm, J. B., Jones, P., Pickernell, D., & Packham, G. (2015). Investigating the impact of training influence on employee retention in small and medium enterprises: A regression-type classification and ranking believe simplex analysis on sparse data. *Expert Systems, 32*(1), 141–154.

March, R., & Mannari, H. (1977). Organisational commitment and turnover: A predictive study. *Administrative Science Quarterly, 22,* 57–75.

McArdle, S., Waters, L., Briscoe, J., & Hall, D. (2007). Employability during unemployment: Adaptability, career identity and human and social capital. *Journal of Vocational Behaviour, 71*(2007), 247–264.

Meyer, J., & Allen, N. (1991). A three-component conceptualisation of organisational commitment. *Human Resource Management Review, 1,* 61–89.

Meyer, J., & Allen, N. (1997). *Commitment in the workplace, theory, research and application.* Thousand Oaks, CA: Sage.

Meyer, J. P., Morin, A. J. S., & Vandenberghe, C. (2015). Dual commitment to organization and supervisor: a person-centred approach. *Journal of Vocational Behaviour, 88,* 56–72.

Meyer, J. P., Stanley, L. J., & Parfyonova, N. M. (2012). Employee commitment in context: The nature and implication of commitment profiles. *Journal of Vocational Behaviour, 80*(1), 1–16.

Mitchell, T., & Lee, T. (2001). The unfolding model of voluntary turnover and job embeddedness: Foundations for a comprehensive theory of attachment. *Research in Organizational Behaviour, 23,* 189–246.

Mujajati, N. (2017). Investigating the relationship between career adaptability, employability attributes and retention factors of employees in selected 21st century recruitment agancies. Unpublished doctoral dissertation, University of South Africa, Pretoria, South Africa.

Neininger, A., Lehmann-Willenbrock, N., Kauffeld, S., & Henschel, A. (2010). Effects of team and organizational commitment—A longtitudinal study. *Journal of Vocational Behaviour, 76,* 567–579.

Okech, V. A. (2015). Human resource management practices influencing staff retention in non-governmental organisations in Kenya: A case study of Kenya red—cross society Eastern and Central Kenya regions. *Strategic Journal of Business and Change Management, 2*(89), 1224–1242.

Olckers, C., & Du Plessis, Y. (2015). Psychological ownership as a requisite for talent retention: The voice of highly skilled employees. *European Journal of Internal Management, 9*(1), 52–72.

Oncel, L. (2014). Career adapt-abilities scale: Convergent validity of subscale scores. *Journal of Vocational Behaviour, 83,* 13–17.

O'Reilly, A. (1989). People and organizational culture: A profile comparison approach to assessing person-organisation fit. *The Academy of Management Journal, 34*(3), 487–516.

Parker, S. K. & Liao, J. (2017). Wise Proactivity: How to be proactive and wise in building your career. *Organizational Dymanics,* 1–15 (In Press).

Ratna, R., & Chawla, S. (2012). Key factors of retention and retention strategies in Telecom sector. *Sola Global Management Review, 6*(3), 35–46.

Reid, J. (2016). Redefining "employability" as something to be achieved: Utilising Toronto" conceptual framework of care to refocus the debate. *Higher Education, Skills and Work-Based Learning, 6*(1), 55–68.

Pool, L. D., & Sewell, P. (2007). The key to employability: Developing a practical model of graduate employability. *Education and Training, 49*(4), 277–289.

Potgieter, I. L., Coetzee, M., & Ferreira, N. (2016). Employability capacities and organisational commitment foci of human resource professionals: An exploratory study. *Journal of Psychology in Africa, 26*(5), 436–442. https://doi.org/10.1080/14330237.2016.1219549.

Puah, P., & Ananthram, S. (2006). Exploring the antecedents and outcomes of career development initiatives: Empirical evidence from Singaporean employees. *Research and Practice in Human Resource Management, 14*(1), 112–142.

Roodt, G. (1997). Theoretical and empirical linkages between work-related commitment foci. *Journal of Industrial Psychology, 23*(2), 6–13.

Rothausen, T. J., Henderson, K. E., Arnold, J. K. & Malshe, A. (2015). Should I stay or should I go? Identify and well-being in sensemaking about retention and turnover. *Journal of Management, 43*(7), 2357–2385. https://doi.org/10.1177/0149206315569312.

Rottinghaus, P. J., Buelow, K. L., Matyja, A., & Schneider, M. R. (2012). The career futures inventory-revised: Measuring dimensions of career adaptability. *Journal of Career Assessment, 20*(2), 123–139.

Ruvimbo, T. S., & Hlanganipai, N. (2016). Organisational commitment and job retention among nurses in a South African setting: An exploratory study. *Journal of Psychology in Africa, 26* (1), 74–77. https://doi.org/10.1080/14330237.2015.1101283.

Saif, S. K., Nawaz, A., Jan, E. A., & Khan, M. I. (2012). Synthesizing the theories of job satisfaction across the cultural/attitudinal dimensions. *Interdisciplinary journal of contemporary research in business, 3*(9), 1382–1396.

Savickas, M. L. (1997). Adaptability: An integrative construct for life-span, life-space theory. *Career Development Quarterly, 45,* 247–259.

Savickas, M. (2002). Career construction: A development theory of vocational behaviour. In D. Brown, Associates (Eds). *Career choice and development* (4th ed.). San Francisco: Jossey-Bass.

Savickas, M. L. (2005). The theory and practice of career construction. In S. D. Brown & R. W. Lent (Eds.), *Career development and counselling: Putting theory and research to work* (pp. 42–70).

Savickas, M. L. (2013). Career construction theory and practice. In R. W. Lent & S. D. Brown (Eds.), *Career development and counselling: putting theory and research to work* (2nd ed., pp. 147–183). Hoboken, NJ: Wiley.

Savickas, M. L., & Porfeli, E. J. (2011). Revision of the career maturity inventory: The adaptability form. *Journal of Career Assessment, 19*(4), 355–374.

Savickas, M. L., & Porfeli, E. J. (2012). Career adapt-abilities scale: Construction, reliability and measurement equivalence across 13 countries. *Journal of Vocational Behaviour, 80,* 661–673.

Schreuder, A., & Coetzee, M. (2011). *Careers: An organisational perspective* (4th ed.). Cape Town: Juta.

Skorikov, V. (2007). Continuity in adolescent career preparation and its effects on adjustment. *Journal of Vocational Behaviour, 70,* 8–24.

Super, D. E. (1974). Career counselling in a post-industrial society. *Canadian Counsellor, 8,* 21–29.

Tak, J. (2012). Career adapt-abilities scale Korea form: Psychometric properties and construct validity. *Journal of Vocational Behaviour, 80,* 712–715.

Taylor, L. (2016). *How to develop your healthcare career: A guide to employability and professional development.* UK: Wiley.

Thrift, J. (2012). *An examination of talent management strategies for a large investor-owned utility company: Facing the market pressures of the 21st century.* Doctoral thesis, Pepperdine University, California, United States.

Tladinyane, R. T., Coetzee, M., & Masenge, A. (2013). Psychological career meta-capacities in relations to employees' retention-related dispositions. *Southern African Business Review, 17* (2), 140–163.

Van Der Heijde, C. M., & Van Der Heijden, B. I. J. M. (2006). A competence-based and multidimensional operationalisation and measurement of employability. *Human Resource Management, 45*(3), 449–476.

Van Dyk, J., & Coetzee, M. (2012). Retention factors in relation to organisational commitment in medical and information technology services. *South African Journal of Human Resource Management, 10*(2), 1–11.

Zhang, J., Ahammad, M. F., Tarba, S., Cooper, C. L., Glaiser, K. W., & Wang, J. (2015). The effect of leadership style on talent retention during merger and acquisition integration: Evidence from China. *The International Journal of Human Resource Management, 26*(7), 1021–1050.

Zikic, J., & Klehe, U. C. (2006). Job loss as a blessing in disguise: The role of career exploration and career planning in predicting reemployment quality. *Journal of Vocational Behavior, 69,* 391–409.

Nadia Ferreira (DCom) is an Associate Professor in Human Resource Management at the Department of Human Resource Management at the University of South Africa (Unisa), South Africa. She is a registered human resource practitioner with the South African Board for People Practices (SABPP). She is also an author and co-author of several published articles in local and international journals. In addition, she presented several papers at national and international conferences.

Chapter 12
Career Development of Professional Women: The Role of Person—Centered Characteristics on Career Satisfaction

Ndayiziveyi Takawira

Abstract The female workforce represents talent with a different career mind-set and adaptive strategies reflecting their unique career needs are necessary for retention and organisational competitiveness. This chapter provides insight into the role of person−centered characteristics on the career development and satisfaction of professional women across different career stages. A sample of professional women from various South African organisations (N = 606; Age 25–44 years: 85%) participated in the study. The empirical study showed that core person −centered characteristics (race, job level and total monthly income) were significant predictors of career satisfaction, along with age, marital status, number of children and education level indicating significant difference on the career satisfaction of professional women. The chapter and results of the study provide valuable new knowledge and insights relevant to the career development theory that could potentially inform human resource practitioners with the aim of enhancing the career satisfaction and subsequent retention of professional women.

Keywords Career development · Career satisfaction · Employee retention Person–centered characteristic · Professional women

Introduction

Today's modern careers, with a high degree of uncertainty due to the changing nature of work, have had far—reaching implications in experiencing work and careers (Srikanth and Israel 2012). While effect of these shifts on careers undoubtedly varies between contexts and occupational groups, changes to the nature of work has led to a weakening relationship between employer and employee and a shift in responsibility for career development from the organisation to the

N. Takawira (✉)
Department of Human Resource Management, University of South Africa, Pretoria, South Africa
e-mail: takawn@unisa.ac.za

M. Coetzee et al. (eds.), *Psychology of Retention*,
https://doi.org/10.1007/978-3-319-98920-4_12

individual (Hall 2013; Jackson and Wilton 2016). Previously, organisations operated in a rigid hierarchical structure within a stable environment, and career success was evaluated by upward mobility, clear career paths, salary increases and social status (Baruch 2006; Gerli et al. 2015). In contrast, careers have become transitional, flexible and dynamic, forcing new perspectives of career success in terms of a sideway move in the organisation, physical career mobility, change of aspiration, life satisfaction or work–family balance (Baruch 2004; Chu et al. 2015).

Career development is viewed as a continuous stream of career-relevant events with a total collection of psychological, social, physical, economic and individual characteristics that combine to shape the career of the individual over a life span (Patton and McMahon 2014). Career, as traditionally portrayed, is commonly considered a notion that relates to a lifelong sequence of events of the individual's work-related experiences (Greenhaus et al. 2010). Generally, work-related experiences encompass objective occurrences such as job positions or work-related decisions whereas subjective perceptions of work-related events could reflect work aspirations and needs, values or feelings about a particular work experience (Greenhaus et al. 2010). Career success is portrayed as the positive perceptions of accomplishments or achievements individuals will have accumulated as a result of their work experiences (Judge et al. 1995; Koekemoer 2014). These work experiences or outcomes are viewed as having both objective and subjective successes (Callanan 2003; Dai and Song 2016). A key element that differentiate subjective career success from objective career success is the perception of career satisfaction as a measure of subjective career success rather than the actual visible external career achievements (Dai and Song 2016; Du Toit and Coetzee 2012).

This chapter explores whether professional women's person–centered characteristics influence their experiences of career satisfaction. The career satisfaction of women has significant consequences for their future work experiences, which include economic and social status, satisfaction with overall career goals for advancement and development of new skills–all of which are seen as important employee retention and career development outcomes (Coetzee 2017; Yap et al. 2010). Although career satisfaction has been widely researched, little is known about the influence of the person–centered characteristics on the career satisfaction of professional women. In this regard, the chapter potentially extends women's career development by exploring the role of person–centered characteristics on career satisfaction in the workplace.

Theoretical Background

Despite significant improvements over the past years, South African women remain underrepresented in professional career fields of sciences, technology, engineering and math (Shepherd 2017). A review of literature indicates that unique challenges of the career development of professional women include personal, interpersonal, organisational and societal factors (Linge 2015; Napasri and Yukongdi 2015;

Rowe and Crafford 2003; Shrestha 2016). These have implications not only for the career development and retention of female talent, but also for social inequality as women continue to have lower access to employment opportunities that offer higher salary income (Shepherd 2017). A number of socially constructed internal and external challenges relating to early gender role stereotypes, family responsibilities, and employment inequities were perceived to be key obstacles to the career choices, advancement and career development for women (Coogan and Chen 2007; Linge 2015; Napasri and Yukongdi 2015; Shrestha 2016). These challenges pose threats to women's vocational lives and hinder their career development processes when motivated to opt-out of the workforce for complex career reasons (Deemer et al. 2014; Sullivan and Mainiero 2008).

Research evidence suggests that gender-based impediments have a negative impact on women who aspire to experience the full realisation of career development in the workplace (Kelly and Breslin 2010; Napasri and Yukongdi 2015). Likewise, the presence of children, employment status of one's partner and household responsibilities influence the perception of work importance and experienced work—related outcomes for women (Mayrhofer et al. 2008). In that view, gender stereotypes concerning both life and occupational roles may cause women to place less emphasis on pursuing successful careers as compared to their male counterparts (Coogan and Chen 2007; Moore 2011).

Career scholars have identified that social values lower the career aspirations of women's career advancement, given the cultural beliefs which expect women to put their families first (Chou et al. 2005; Napasri and Yukongdi 2015). Although women have a clear ability to perform with the same skill and success in every endeavour engaged by men in the workplace, stereotypical attitudes remain a hindrance towards women's career advancement and success (Napasri and Yukongdi 2015; Shrestha 2016). This is not surprising as women tend to avoid stereotypically male occupations, which demand increased responsibility and pressurised obligations due to family responsibilities (Moore 2011). To overcome these challenges, women often choose to pursue female—type occupations that tend to be family—friendly and flexible (Coogan and Chen 2007). Ultimately, the potential breaks of employment for childbearing constrain women to choose occupations with lower interruption costs and career development opportunities (Moore 2011).

The incompatibility of role pressures as a result of a shortage of time to participate in the work and home domains results in situations where participation in one role makes it difficult to function successfully in another role (Greenhaus and Kossek 2014). Moreover, careers are frequently experienced differently by women and men, partly because women are more likely than men to view work and home as entangled strands (Greenhaus and Kossek 2014; Lee et al. 2011). Women's value for relationships may force choices that require evaluation of the needs of children, spouses or aging parents as part of the whole in making career decisions (Sullivan and Mainiero 2008). Hence, family responsibilities (home and childcare) can be a major factor in women experiencing career interruptions, decreased career advancement opportunities or opting-out of the workforce (Coogan and Chen 2007; Sullivan and Mainiero 2008).

Research findings indicate that couples still divide their family responsibilities according to traditional gender roles that expect women to interrupt their careers for family reasons (Evers and Sieverding 2013). For instance, the number of children was found to significantly and positively relate to career interruptions whereas for men the number of children was significantly but negatively related to career interruptions (Evers and Sieverding 2013). Likewise, a study by Miles (2013) indicated that women leave the workforce because they cannot balance home and work responsibilities. Consequently, women may adjust their career ambitions to obtain a more flexible schedule or put aside personal needs for authentic work or meaningful experience in favour of significant others (Sullivan and Mainiero 2008).

Although the South African Employment Equity Amendment Act (EEAA), No. 47 of 2013 represents a milestone to create an equitable, fair and balanced employment environment to ensure that women are equally represented across all occupational levels in the workforce (Republic of South Africa 2014). Yet, the representation of South African women in top management has declined from 3.9% in 2008 to 3.6% in 2012 (Business Women's Association [BWA] 2012; Doubell and Struwig 2014). Grala (2013) further indicates that by 2013, only 28% of South African senior management positions were occupied by women and this status has remained flat lining for at least five years (i.e. 2009–2013). Interestingly, Brown's (2016) latest survey shows that the number of female accountants in South Africa has increased from 16.3% to 34.5% over the period (2002–2016). However, the latest report by Business Report (2017) confirms that senior management roles in South Africa held by women has remained flat lined at 28%. Likewise, the Public Works Committee (2013) lamented that transformation was taking place too slowly and failing the women of South Africa as the male versus female ratio in the built and engineering profession was 86.3 to 13.7%.

There is a real disparity between the traditional career model, characterised by uninterrupted, full-time, long-term employment and extrinsic measures of success, such as salary income and promotions in relation to the needs of women employees (Cabrera 2009). New career theories like boundaryless and protean career approaches, the kaleidoscope career model (KCM) and the ecological model are emerging, which better reflect the needs of women to adapt to career transitions or dynamic work environments (Cabrera 2009; Cook et al. 2005; Briscoe and Hall 2006). On the one hand, the boundaryless career emphasises the seemingly positive experiences which allow individuals to broaden their mind-set and to recognise possibilities the career presents as well as taking advantage of opportunities that could lead to career satisfaction (Briscoe and Hall 2006; Fleisher et al. 2014). Individuals might perceive a boundaryless future as one of independence, driven by inner-directed choices and crossing organisational boundaries in employment mobility (Briscoe and Hall 2006; Chin and Rasdi 2014). On the other hand, a protean career is one that emphasises a self-directed approach (taking control of one's career) driven by one's own values (awareness of one's personal priorities) for professional success (Briscoe and Hall 2006; Waters et al. 2014). Hence, the protean individuals value individual freedom, self-growth and define career success in terms of subjective factors such as the degree of career satisfaction, a sense of self-fulfilment and personal accomplishment (Chin and Rasdi 2014; Hall and Chandler 2005).

Women's career and life responsibilities flow according to life/career stage concerns and career decisions are usually part of a larger and intricate web of interconnected issues and people, and these aspects come together to form a delicate balance (Mainiero and Sullivan 2005). The KCM evaluates women's career choices holistically in the context of relationships, constraints and opportunities to achieve a balance and find the pattern that best resembles women's life circumstances and needs (Mainiero and Sullivan 2006; O'Neil et al. 2008). The KCM provides three parameters or needs (authenticity, balance and challenge) which are always present and ever interacting but take on different levels of importance or intensity based on the woman's life occurrences at a specific point to influence her career decisions (Sullivan and Mainiero 2008). Issues of authenticity and being true to oneself are paramount in late career, balance between career and life responsibilities mostly manifest in mid-career and engaging challenging work are the primary focus of women in early career stages (O'Neil et al., 2008).

Developed in response to limits of the traditional career development theory, the ecological model (Bronfenbrenner's 1977) attempts to comprehend the dynamics of women's career behaviour (Patton 2013). Essentially, the ecological perspective suggests that human behaviour is a result of the continuing dynamic interaction between the person and the environment (Cook et al. 2002). For instance, from early childhood, women's perceptions about themselves and their possibilities are shaped by enduring interactions with others within their immediate environment (Cook et al. 2005). Hence, any perspective that is used to postulate the career development of women must accommodate multiple influences that shape women's experiences simultaneously and over time (Cook et al. 2005). In this regard, it appears that boundaryless and protean career approaches, the KCM and the ecological model are important career orientations that could assist women to develop their careers, achieve work-life balance and experience satisfaction with careers.

Person−centered characteristics entail biographical factors (i.e., age, race, marital status, job level or education level) which may influence objective and subjective career success outcomes (Judge et al. 1995; Pachulicz et al. 2008). These outcomes vary from objective success (i.e., high—income, promotion or high-skilled occupational status) to more subjective terms such as progression with career goals (Doubell and Struwig 2014; Yap et al. 2010). In a study of professional and business women in South Africa, Doubell and Struwig (2014) found significant relationships between groups of women on their biographical factors (different birth orders, marital status and respondents with children aged seven to twelve and older than eighteen) and their experiences of career success. Bakan and Buyukbese (2013) indicate that employees with high income levels reported significantly higher levels of satisfaction than did employees with low income levels. Research findings also indicate that current salary and length of marriage positively affect career satisfaction (Amdurer et al. 2014). Likewise, length of marriage suggests stability at home, which in turn, allows for energy and attention to be devoted at work and to one's career, whereas, having many children might put a strain on an individual's ability to engage in work (Amdurer et al. 2014).

Career scholars have addressed subjective career success as experienced directly by the individual who is engaged in her career, where success is measured according to her own standard (Gu and Su 2016; Hall and Chandler 2005; Heslin 2003). Du Toit and Coetzee (2012) describe subjective career success as the individual's perception or self-evaluation of her own success (e.g. personal satisfaction, a sense of accomplishment or self—worth) in the current organisation as well as in the career in general. Unlike the objective career success, subjective success as perceived by the self instead of the organisation is defined as psychological success emanating from a sense of pride and personal accomplishment regarding various goals in one's career (Hall and Chandler 2005; Gu and Su 2016). Career satisfaction is a subjective measure of career success that stems from individuals' perceptions of their satisfaction with their overall career goals, for instance, income, advancement or development of new skills (Karavardar 2014; Yap et al. 2010). Personal goal accomplishment is a major source of subjective wellbeing and satisfaction, and is enhanced by accessibility of resources such as person−centered characteristics, abilities or material resources in the form of status or income, and social factors (Sirgy 2012). Hence, career satisfaction is a measure of the extent to which individuals believe their career progress is consistent with their own goals, values, preference and reflects how individuals feel about their career-related roles, accomplishments and success (Karavardar 2014).

Research findings by Snyder (2011) showed that women were satisfied with four of the career satisfaction areas: career success, meeting overall career goals, professional development goals, and the development of new professional skills, but not with progress toward meeting goals for income. Career satisfaction may be attributed to the development of competencies associated with one's job and provide opportunities for career advancement (Srikanth and Israel 2012). Leigh et al. (2009) observed that more mature physicians experienced high levels of career satisfaction. Burke (2005) found that individuals at lower organisational levels were less satisfied with their careers than those at higher levels. Yap et al. (2010) found that black, South Asian and Chinese employees working in information and communications technology and financial services sectors were less satisfied with their careers than white employees, with black employees being the least satisfied. Research by Bakan and Buyukbese (2013) also indicated that participating employees with high income levels reported significantly higher levels of career satisfaction than did employees with low income levels. In this regard, research on the relationship between person−centered characteristics and career satisfaction could contribute to the career development and satisfaction among professional women in the diverse South African workforce.

Problem Statement and Objectives

Shepherd (2017) emphasise the continual under-representation of women in professional careers and the role of individual differences in accessing higher paying employment opportunities. Despite the extensive research that has identified factors that hinder the career development and satisfaction of women in organisations (Linge 2015; O'Neil et al. 2008; Patton and McMahon 2014), empirical studies considering the influence of person−centered characteristics on the career satisfaction of professional women seem to be scarce, especially in the diverse South African context. The present study aimed at addressing this gap in the research literature by exploring the influence of person−centered characteristics on the career satisfaction of professional women in the career development context.

Research Design

Participants and Procedure

The study formed part of a larger research project on the career success (satisfaction) of professionally qualified South African women who were employed full-time in the human resource, engineering and financial fields. The study followed a cross-sectional quantitative research approach. A purposive sample of N = 606 employed qualified professional women registered as members of the South African Board for People Practices (SABPP), Engineering Council of South Africa (ECSA) and the South African Institute for Chartered Accountants (SAICA) participated in the study by means of an online web survey. The participants were predominantly white (62%) and the majority was married (67%). In terms of age, the participants were predominantly in the early to middle adulthood life stages (25 to 44 years: 85%) and skewed towards women with children (58%). The majority of participants had a post-graduate degree (74%) with 66 percent employed at management level positions. The majority (76%) had more than 6 years of experience years in the respective career.

Ethical clearance for the research project was obtained from the university and permission to conduct the research among the respective members were obtained from the Professional Bodies. Participation in the project was voluntary and anonymous, and informed consent to use the data for research purposes was obtained from the participants.

Measures

Biographical questionnaire. Age, race, marital status, number of children, job level, total monthly income and education level were included in the biographical questionnaire and were only used as biographical variables to get a relative estimate in terms of sample profile. However, the perceptions regarding job level and total monthly income as career success outcomes are not measured. Such measurement can be done by means of qualitative studies and was not the focus of the present study.

Career satisfaction. The construct was measured by means of the career satisfaction scale (CSS) developed by Greenhaus et al. (1990). The CSS measures career satisfaction as a global factor through five-items and five-point Likert-type scale ranging from (1) strongly disagree to (5) strongly agree (e.g. "*I am satisfied with the progress l have made towards meeting my overall career goals*"). The Cronbach's coefficient obtained for the CSS was $\alpha = 0.92$.

Data Analysis

Descriptive, correlation, multiple regression analysis and test for significant mean differences were conducted to analyse the association between the variables. Age, race, marital status, number of children, job level, total monthly income and education level were used as variables in the multiple regression analysis based on previous research showing an association between age, race, marital status and education level (Amdurer et al. 2014; Kirkbesoglu and Ozder 2015; Payne et al. 2010; Leigh et al. 2009; Yap et al. 2010). Coding of the biographical variables was as follows: age = $\leq$ 44 years: 0, $\geq$ 45 years: 1; race = black: 0, white: 1; marital status = single/divorced or separated/widowed: 0, married: 1; number of children = 0:0, 1 + :1, job level = employee: 0, management: 1; total monthly income = $\leq$ 29 999 = 0, $\geq$ 30 000 + : 1, education level = certificate/diploma/degree: 0, postgraduate: 1.

Results

Correlations

Table 12.1 shows the descriptive statistics and correlations for all variables. The practical effect of the significant correlations between the biographical characteristics and the career satisfaction variable ranged between $r \geq 0.16 \leq 0.36$ (small to medium practical effect size; $p \leq 0.001$). However, the associations between (age, race, marital status, number of children, total monthly income and education level) and career satisfaction were small in practical effect ($r \geq 0.16 \leq 0.28$; $p \leq 0.001$) and overall, regarded as negligible.

Predictor Effects

The regression model in Table 12.2 showed that the predictor biographical variables (age, race, marital status, number of children, job level, total monthly income and education level) explained 13% ($R^2 = 0.13$; medium practical effect) of the variance in overall career satisfaction. Only the biographical variables race ($\beta = 0.21$; $t = 2.49$; p 0.05), job level ($\beta = 0.39$; $t = 4.08$; $p \leq 0.001$), and total monthly income ($\beta = 0.32$; $t = 3.05$; $p \leq 0.01$) contributed statistically significantly and positively in explaining the variance in overall career satisfaction, with job level accounting for most of the variance in career satisfaction. However, age, marital status, number of children and education level did not predict career satisfaction.

Significant Differences in Biographical Characteristics

As can be seen in Table 12.3, the ANOVA for biographical characteristics (age, race, marital status, number of children, job level, total monthly income and education level) showed significant differences in terms of career satisfaction. As shown in Table 1.3, the ANOVA for age shows significant differences in terms of career satisfaction ($F = 4.65$; $p \leq 0.01$). The Tukey's HSD pairwise comparison test showed that 64 (12%) participants aged between 45–60 years (management career stage) mostly reported satisfaction with their careers as compared to participants aged between 25–44 years (establishment careers stage) ($M = 4.08$ versus 3.70). The differences between the groups are small in magnitude ($d = 0.38$; $p \leq 0.05$).

Race showed significant differences in terms of career satisfaction for the race groups ($F = 11.40$; $p \leq 0.001$). White participants obtained significantly higher mean scores than Black participants in terms of career satisfaction ($M = 3.93$ versus 3.38 to 3.90; $d = \geq 0.34 \leq 0.50$; small to medium practical effect; $p \leq 0.05$).

The career satisfaction of the marital status groups (divorced/separated and single; married and single) differed significantly ($F = 8.70$; $p \leq 0.001$). Divorced/separated participants obtained significantly higher mean scores than the single and married participants in terms of career satisfaction ($M = 4.05$ versus 3.45 to 3.88; $d = \geq 0.39 \leq 0.55$; small to medium practical effect; $p \leq 0.05$).

Number of children groups showed significant differences in terms of career satisfaction for the number of children groups (2 and 1; 2 and 0) ($F = 4.35$; p 0.01). The participants with two children obtained significantly higher mean scores than the participants with one or no children on career satisfaction ($M = 4.04$ versus 3.61 to 3.64; $d = \geq 0.39 \leq 0.43$; small practical effect $p \leq 0.05$).

Job level groups showed significant differences in terms of career satisfaction ($F = 18.11$; $p \leq 0.001$). Executive participants obtained significantly higher mean scores than the employee and senior management participants in terms of career satisfaction ($M = 4.35$ versus 3.36 to 4.27; $d = \geq 0.32 \leq 0.95$; small to large practical effect; $p \leq 0.05$).

Total monthly income showed significant differences in terms of career satisfaction ($F = 11.02$; $p \leq 0.001$). Participants earning R50 000 and over obtained significantly higher mean scores than the participants earning less than R15 000 and between R15 000 and R49 999 in terms of career satisfaction ($M = 4.04$ versus 3.08 to 3.86; $d = \geq 0.41 \leq 0.92$; small to large practical effect; $p \leq 0.05$).

Education level showed significant differences in terms of career satisfaction ($F = 5.57$; $p \leq 0.01$). Master's participants obtained significantly higher mean scores than the degree/honours participants in terms of career satisfaction ($M = 3.97$ versus 3.40 to 3.82; $d = \geq 0.39 \leq 0.52$; small to medium practical effect; $p \leq 0.05$).

Discussion

This chapter approached person−centered (biographical) characteristics as significant predictors of career satisfaction for professional women. The results of the multiple regression analysis has provided new insight into how professional women's person−centered characteristics and their career satisfaction experiences are related. The findings advance the literature on career satisfaction in the contemporary career development context. Overall, the findings suggest that race, job level and total monthly income were instrumental in explaining the career satisfaction of professional women. The white race group experienced higher levels of career satisfaction than their black counterparts. On the basis of Bronfenbrenner's (1977) ecological model, individuals operate within a unique ecosystem (i.e., the continuing dynamic interaction between the person and the environment); thus, race groups play a significant role in the career development of women (Cook et al. 2002). Fouad and Byars-Winston (2005) indicated that race differences do not play a major role in career aspirations and career development, but they are differences among racial groups in perceptions of related career opportunities and barriers that influence career development. Fouad and Byars-Winston (2005) also suggest that, although the career aspirations of individuals are similar, perceptions of the opportunities for career development differ by race. In the present study, it might be that black women were more concerned about opportunities for career development as compared to their white counterparts.

Peterson et al. (2004) suggest that employees who experience racial prejudice are less likely to feel satisfied with their careers and often feel less welcomed by the organisation. Faupel-Badger et al. (2017) indicates that race groups other than the white group are associated with low satisfaction in terms of their career trajectory and career development opportunities for career growth. Organisations could inevitably encourage fair opportunities for career development, supportive environments and favourable work experiences for all race groups, which encourage employees to actively make use of opportunities for career development to enhance their career satisfaction (De Vos et al. 2011).

Women in senior management were found to have higher career satisfaction levels than their employee counterparts. Similarly, Burke (2005) found that individuals at lower organisational levels were less satisfied with their careers than their counterparts at managerial levels. The findings are useful, suggesting that organisations could improve the career satisfaction of all employees by implementing career development programmes and also create opportunities for career development, which address the unique needs of women in different life/career stages (Cabrera 2009). Women who earned R50 000 were found to have higher career satisfaction levels than the less than R15 000 income group. Likewise, Bakan and Buyukbese (2013) found that participating employees with high income levels reported significantly higher levels of career satisfaction than did employees with low income levels. The findings are in line with the career stage model (Super 1990), which acknowledges career progression, suggesting that as individuals progress through the career stages, income increases in relation to increase in work experience (Young et al. 2014). This finding could suggest that organisations should implement objective and clear career progression maps, which employees can use to track their achievement of career goals in relation to a positive income progression (Gu and Su 2016).

Implications for Career Development and Retention Practice

Despite the limitations of the research design, the study adds valuable insight to the research literature on career satisfaction by introducing the concept of person−centered characteristics in relation to the career satisfaction and retention of professional women in the workforce. Insight into the career satisfaction of professional women has become important in light of the unique career needs and changing patterns of women's careers. The findings of the study are valuable inputs that can inform the design of key career development and retention strategies, which support the career advancement of professional women to enhance their career satisfaction. Such interventions should promote protean career orientations and a boundaryless mind-set regarding career pathways, which require individualised career management approaches to enhance the career satisfaction and retention of professional women. Organisations might clearly communicate support for use of work-life balance benefits (i.e., telecommuting or flexible work schedules) to retain the valuable talent of professional women. Organisations willing to retain female talent provide flexibility across careers and support flexible career paths for individual development to increase satisfaction with careers.

Career development support in the form of training interventions to increase a sense of control over career decisions and career paths are important to encourage continuous learning, skills development and achievement of career goals. Retention programmes through mentoring networks and coaching practices empower professional women for promotion to leadership positions and higher income. Advice and information sharing on professional development opportunities and acquisition of tacit knowledge could contribute to career advancement aimed at enhancing career satisfaction. Understanding the dynamic interaction between person−centered characteristics and career satisfaction, could play an important role to the career development and retention of professional women.

Limitations and Recommendations

Several limitations need to be considered in interpreting the results of the present study. Firstly, the present results are based on a sample of predominantly women in the emerging to mid-career adulthood stage employed in the South African financial, engineering and human resource fields. The findings may not necessarily be generalised to professional women in other organisational fields, and future studies should maybe also consider men, given shifting roles of dual career couples. A second limitation is the use of self-report measures as data collection tools. A certain amount of social desirability and acquiescent responding in self-report measures might affect the internal consistency of measures. However, acceptable internal consistency reliabilities were reported for the career satisfaction measuring instrument. Lastly, the participants were predominantly represented by white women and future research should consider a more diverse group to assess whether the career satisfaction of women manifest in the same way or differently in varying individual biographical characteristics (i.e., age, race, marital status, number of children, job level, total monthly income and education level).

Despite the limitations, the findings of this study has contributed to the current understanding of the unique career development needs and the career satisfaction of professional women in career construction theory approaches to career counselling and career development in the South African organisational context.

Conclusion

In this chapter, the empirical study made an important contribution by providing insight of how person−centered characteristics are likely to influence career satisfaction in career construction theory approaches to career counselling and career development in the South African organisational context. The chapter, through analysing survey data from professional women in employee and senior managerial levels showed that career satisfaction levels are associated with person−centered characteristics within the career development theory. The findings provided organisations and career counsellors with knowledge for designing new and effective career development interventions to address the unique career needs of women. These organisational supportive measures could increase women's career satisfaction as they progress through different life/career stages. In this regard, the chapter provided empirical evidence of the role of career satisfaction in the women's career development in the contemporary work environment.

Summary

In summary, this chapter explored the influence of person−centered characteristics on the career satisfaction and retention of professional women in the career development context. The results from the study indicate that the core person −centered characteristics (race, job level and total monthly income) were significant predictors of career satisfaction, along with age, marital status, number of children and education level, indicating significant difference on the career satisfaction of professional women. Career counsellors and human resource practitioners must engage in career development practices that better match the unique career needs of professional women to ensure talent retention and satisfaction with careers.

Appendices

See Tables 12.1, 12.2, 12.3.

Table 12.1 Descriptive statistics and bivariate correlations

	Variables	M	SD	α	1	2	3	4	5	6	7
1	Age	–	–	–	–	–	–	–	–	–	–
2	Race	–	–	–	–	–	–	–	–	–	–
3	Marital status	–	–	–	–	–	–	–	–	–	–
4	Number of children	–	–	–	–	–	–	–	–	–	–
5	Job level	–	–	–	–	–	–	–	–	–	–
6	Monthly income	–	–	–	–	–	–	–	–	–	–
7	Education level	–	–		–	–	–	–	–	–	–
8	Overall career satisfaction	3.76	0.98	0.92	0.25***	0.19***	0.19***	0.16**	0.36***	0.28***	0.16**

Notes: N = 606. ***$p \leq 0.001$ **$p \leq 0.01$ *$p \leq 0.05$—statistically significant

Table 12.2 Results of the multiple regression of biographical variables and career satisfaction

Biographical variables	Career satisfaction	
	ß	*t*
Age	0.21	1.77
Race	0.21	2.49*
Marital status	−0.10	−1.03
Number of children	0.07	0.76
Job level	0.39	4.08***
Total monthly income	0.32	3.05**
Education level	0.03	0.25
Model info		
Fp	12.57***	
Adjusted R^2	0.13 ++	

Notes: N = 606. ***$p \leq 0.001$ **$p \leq 0.01$ *$p \leq 0.05$

Table 12.3 Biographical differences on career satisfaction

Biographical variable		N	Mean	(SD)	Mean differences	95% confidence limits		*F*	df	*p*	Cohen's d
						Lower	Upper				
Age								4.65	3	0.01	
	45–60 yrs 25–44 yrs	64 476	4.08 3.70	0.76 0.99	0.38	0.048	0.711			0.05	0.38 +
Race								11.40	3	0.000	
	White Indian	361 66	3.93 3.55	0.84 1.13	0.38	0.055	0.706			0.05	0.34 +
	White African	361 119	3.93 3.38	0.84 1.09	0.54	0.284	0.798			0.05	0.50 ++
	Coloured African	40 119	3.90 3.38	1.01 1.09	0.52	0.071	0.959			0.05	0.48 +
Marital status								8.70	3	0.000	
	Divorced/ Separated Single	23 172	4.05 3.45	0.92 1.10	0.60	0.0529	1.153			0.05	0.55 ++
	Married Single	392 172	3.88 3.45	0.90 1.10	0.43	0.201	0.654			0.05	0.39 +
Number of children								4.35	5	0.01	
	2 1	159 132	4.04 3.64	0.83 1.02	0.40	0.076	0.724			0.05	0.39 +
	2 0	159 252	4.04 3.61	0.83 1.00	0.43	0.147	0.705				0.43 +
Job level								18.11	5	0.000	
	Executive Manager	38 162	4.35 3.69	0.70 1.00	0.66	0.184	1.128			0.05	0.66 ++
	Executive Employee	38 207	4.35 3.36	0.70 1.03	0.98	0.522	1.45			0.05	0.95 +++
	Director Manager	55 162	4.27 3.69	0.72 1.00	0.57	0.166	0.983			0.05	0.57 ++
	Director Employee	55 207	4.27 3.36	0.72 1.03	0.90	0.505	1.299			0.05	0.87 +++
	Senior-manager Manager	117 162	4.09 3.69	0.73 1.00	0.40	0.082	0.717			0.05	0.40 +

(continued)

Table 12.3 (continued)

Biographical variable		N	Mean	(SD)	Mean differences	95% confidence limits		*F*	df	*p*	Cohen's d
						Lower	Upper				
	Senior-manager Employee		4.09 3.36	0.73 1.03	0.73	0.424	1.030			0.05	0.71 ++
	Manager Employee	162 207	3.69 3.36	1.00 1.03	0.33	0.053	0.602			0.05	0.32 +
Total monthly income								11.02	5	0.000	
	R50 000 and over R30 000–R39 999	229 123	4.04 3.65	0.83 0.94	0.39	0.093	0.689			0.05	0.41 +
	R50 000 and over R20 000–R29 999	229 81	4.04 3.41	0.83 0.98	0.63	0.287	0.976			0.05	0.64 ++
	R50 000 and over R15 000–R19 999	229 25	4.04 3.31	0.83 1.19	0.73	0.169	1.290			0.05	0.61 +++
	R50 000 and over Less than R15 000	229 26	4.04 3.08	0.83 1.04	0.96	0.414	1.515			0.05	0.92 +++
	R40 000–R49 999 R20 000–R29 999	103 81	3.86 3.41	0.98 0.98	0.45	0.058	0.849			0.05	0.46 +
	R40 000–R49 999 Less than R15 000	103 26	3.86 3.08	0.98 1.04	0.79	0.202	1.371			0.05	0.76 ++
Education level								5.57	4	0.01	
	Master's Degree	98 112	3.97 3.40	0.91 1.09	0.57	0.205	0.934			0.05	0.52 ++
	Honours Degree	327 112	3.82 3.40	0.94 1.09	0.42	0.127	0.704			0.05	0.39 +

Notes: N = 606. *** $p \leq 0.001$ ** $p \leq 0.01$ *$p \leq 0.05$. *d* = Cohen's practical effect size (+ *d* < 0.20 *(small practical effect size)*; + + *d* > 0.50 < 0.80 *(medium practical effect size)* +++ *d* > 0.80 *(large practical effect size)*

References

Amdurer, E., Boyatzis, R. E., Saatcioglu, A., Smith, M. L., & Taylor, S. N. (2014). Long term impact of emotional, social and cognitive intelligence competencies and GMAT on career and life satisfaction and career success. *Frontiers in Psychology, 5,* 1–15. https://doi.org/10.3389/fpsyg.2014.01447.

Bakan, I., & Buyukbese, T. (2013). The relationship between employees' income level and employee job satisfaction: An empirical study. *International Journal of Business and Social Science, 4*(7), 18–25.

Baruch, Y. (2004). Transforming careers: From linear to multidirectional career paths: Organisational and individual perspective. *Career Development International, 9*(1), 58–73. https://doi.org/10.1108/13620430410518147.

Baruch, Y. (2006). Career development in organisations and beyond: Balancing traditional and contemporary viewpoints. *Human Resource Management Review, 16,* 125–138. https://doi.org/10.1016/j.hrmr.2006.03.002.

Briscoe, J. P., & Hall, D. T. (2006). The interplay of boundaryless and protean careers: Combinations and implications. *Journal of Vocational Behavior, 69,* 4–18. https://doi.org/10.1016/j.jvb.2005.09.002.

Bronfenbrenner, U. (1977). Toward an experimental ecology of human development. *American Psychologist, 32,* 513–531. https://doi.org/10.1037/0003-066X.32.7.513.

Brown, J. (2016, March). Black CAs still a rare breed. Retrieved from http://city-press.news24.com/Business/black-cas-still-a-rare-breed-20160330.

Burke, R. J. (2005). Backlash in the Workplace. *Women in Management Review, 20*(3), 165–176.

Business Report. (2017). Women lag in senior roles. Retrieved from https://www.iol.co.za/business-report/careers/womensday-women-lag-in-senior-roles-8094125.

Business Women's Association. (2012). South African women in leadership census 2012. Retrieved from http://www.genderlinks.org.za/article/south-africa-businesswomens-association-of-south-africa-set-to-release-women-in-leadership-census-2012-06-04.

Cabrera, E. F. (2009). Protean organizations: Reshaping work and careers to retain female talent. *Career Development International, 14*(2), 186–201. https://doi.org/10.1108/13620430910950773.

Callanan, G. A. (2003). What price career success? *Career Development International, 8*(3), 126–133. https://doi.org/10.1108/13620430310471032.

Chin, W. S., & Rasdi, R. M. (2014). Protean career development: Exploring the individuals, organizational and job-related factors. *Asian Social Science, 10*(21), 203–215. https://doi.org/10.5539/as.v10n21p203.

Chu, F., Ye, L., & Guo, M. (2015). Research on the evaluation indicators of skilled employees' career success based on grounded theory. *Journal of Industrial Engineering and Management, 8*(2), 554–566. https://doi.org/10.3926/jiem.1396.

Chou, W, C, G., Fosh, P., & Foster, D. (2005). Female mangers in Taiwan: Opportunities and barriers in changing times. *Asia Pacific Business Review, 11*(2), 213−231.

Coetzee, M. (2017). Graduates' psycho-social career preoccupations and employability capacities in the work context. In M. Tomlinson & L. Holmes (Eds.), *Graduate employability in context: Research theory and debate* (pp. 295−315). London: Palgrave Macmillan.

Coogan, P. A., & Chen, C. P. (2007). Career development and counselling for women: Connecting theories to practice. *Counselling Psychology Quarterly, 20*(2), 191–204. https://doi.org/10.1080/09515070701391171.

Cook, E. P., Heppner, M. J., & O'Brien, K. M. (2002). Career development of women of color and white women: Assumptions, conceptualization, and interventions from an ecological perspective. *The Career Development Quarterly, 50,* 291–304. https://doi.org/10.1002/j.2161-0045.2002.tb00574.x.

Cook, E. P., Heppner, M. J., & O'Brien, K. M. (2005). Multicultural and gender influences in women's career development: An ecological perspective. *Journal of Multicultural Counseling and Development, 33,* 165–179. https://doi.org/10.1002/j.2161-1912.2005.tb00014.

Dai, L., & Song, F. (2016). Subjective career success: A literature review and prospect. *Journal of Human Resource and Sustainability Studies, 4,* 238–242. https://doi.org/10.4236/hrss.2016.43026.

Deemer, E. D., Thoman, D. B., Chase, J. P., & Smith, J. L. (2014). Feeling the threat: Stereotypes threat as a contextual barrier to women's science career choice intentions. *Journal of Career Development, 41*(2), 141–158. https://doi.org/10.1177/0894845313483003.

De Vos, A., De Hauw, S., & Van der Heijden, B. I. J. M. (2011). Competency development and career success: The mediating role of employability. *Journal of Vocational Behavior, 79,* 438–447. https://doi.org/10.1016/j.jvb.2011.05.010.

Doubell, M., & Struwig, M. (2014). Factors influencing the career success of professional and business women in South Africa. *South African Journal of Economics Management and Sciences, 17*(5), 531–543. https://doi.org/10.4102/sajems.v17i5.514.

Du Toit, D., & Coetzee, M. (2012). Exploring the perceived career success of staff in a South African science and engineering company. *Journal of Psychology in Africa, 22*(1), 96–105. https://doi.org/10.1080/14330237.2012.10874526.

Evers, A., & Sieverding, M. (2013). Why do highly qualified women (still) earn less? Gender differences in long-term predictors of career success. *Psychology of Women Quarterly, 38*(1), 93–106. https://doi.org/10.1177/0361684313498071.

Fleisher, C., Khapova, S. N., & Jansen, P. G. W. (2014). Effects of employees' career competencies development on their organizations: Does satisfaction matter? *Career Development International, 19*(6). https://doi.org/10.1108/cdi-12-2013-0150, ISSN: 1362–0436.

Faupel-Badger, J. M., Nelson, D. E., & Izmirlian, G. (2017). Career satisfaction and perceived salary competitiveness among individuals who completed postdoctoral research training in cancer preventions. *PLoS ONE, 12*(1), 1–13. https://doi.org/10.1371/journal.pone.0169859.

Fouad, N. A., & Byars-Winston, A. M. (2005). Cultural context of career choice: Meta-analysis of race/ethnicity differences. *The Career Development Quarterly, 53,* 223–233.

Gerli, F., Bonesso, S., & Pizzi, C. (2015). Boundaryless career and career success: The impact of emotional and social competencies. *Frontiers in Psychology, 6,* 1304. https://doi.org/10.3389/fpsyg.2015.01304.

Grala, L. (2013). Women changing the business landscape in South Africa. Retrieved from http://www.gaaaccounting.com/women-changing-the-business-landscape-in-south-africa/.

Greenhaus, J. H., Parasuraman, S., & Wormley, W. M. (1990). Effects of race on organizational experiences, job performance evaluations, and career outcomes. *Academy of Management journal, 33,* 64–86. https://doi.org/10.2307/256352

Greenhaus, J. H., Callanan, G. A., & Godshalk, V. M. (2010). *Career management* (4th ed.). New York, NY: Sage.

Greenhaus, J. H., & Kossek, E. E. (2014). The contemporary career: Work-home perspective. *Annual Review of Organisational Psychology and Organisational Behaviour, 1,* 361–388. https://doi.org/10.1146/annurev-orgpsych-031413-091324.

Gu, Q., & Su, Y. (2016). How does objective career success affect subjective career success? The moderating role of self-awareness. *Journal of Human Resource and Sustainability Studies, 4,* 227–237. https://doi.org/10.4236/jhrss.2016.43025.

Hall, D. T. (2013). Protean careers in the 21st century. In K. Inkson & M. L. Savickas (Eds.), *Career studies, Vol. 1. Foundations of career studies* (pp. 245–254). London: Sage.

Hall, D. T., & Chandler, D. E. (2005). Psychological success: When the career is a calling. *Journal of Organisational Behavior, 26,* 155–176. https://doi.org/10.1002/job.301.

Heslin, P. A. (2003). Self-and other-referent criteria of career success. *Journal of Career Assessment, 11*(3), 262–286. https://doi.org/10.1177/1069072703254500.

Jackson, D., & Wilton, N. (2016). Career management attitudes among business undergraduates. *Australian Journal of Career Development, 25*(1), 7–22. https://doi.org/10.1177/1038416215604002.

Judge, T. A., Cable, D. M., Boudreau, J. W., & Bretz, R. D., Jr. (1995). An empirical investigation of the predictors of executive career success. *Personnel Psychology, 48,* 485–519. https://doi.org/10.1111/j.1744-6570.1995.tb01767.x.

Karavardar, G. (2014). Career commitment, subjective career success and career satisfaction in the context of hazelnut processing industry in Giresun/Turkey. *International Journal of Business and Management, 9*(6), 98–105. https://doi.org/10.5539/ijbm.v9n6p98.

Kelly, S., & Breslin, J. (2010). *Women's rights in the Middle East and North Africa: Progress amid resistance*. New York, NY: Freedom House/Rowman & Littlefield.

Kirkbesoglu, E., & Ozder, E. H. (2015). The effect of organizational performance on the relationship between organizational support and career satisfaction: An application on insurance industry. *Journal of Management Research, 7*(3), 35–50. https://doi.org/10.5296/jmr.v7i3.7094.

Koekemoer, E. (2014). An exploratory study on factors influencing the career success of management employees. *South African Journal of Industrial Psychology, 40*(2), 1–10. https://doi.org/10.4102/sajip.v40i2.1204.

Lee, M. D., Kossek, E. E., Hall, D. T., & Litrico, J. (2011). Entangled strands: A process perspective on the evolution of careers in the context of personal, family, work, and community. *Human Relations, 64*(12), 1532–1553. https://doi.org/10.1177/0018726711424622.

Leigh, J. P., Tancredi, D. J., & Kravitz, R. L. (2009). Physician career satisfaction with specialties. *BioMed Central Health Services Research, 9*(166), 1–12. https://doi.org/10.1186/1472-6963-9-166.

Linge, T. (2015). Social-family issues as barriers to career advancement: The perception of women employees in Kenya. *International Journal of Business and Social Research, 5*(4), 52–57.

Mainiero, L. A., & Sullivan, S. E. (2005). Kaleidoscope careers: An alternative explanation for the "opt-out" revolution. *The Academy of Management Executive, 19*(1), 106–123.

Mainiero, L. A., & Sullivan, S. E. (2006). *The opt-out revolt: Why people are leaving companies to create kaleidoscope careers*. Mountain View, CA: Davies-Black

Mayrhofer, W., Meyer, M., Schiffinger, M., & Schmidt, A. (2008). The influence of family responsibilities, career fields and gender on career success. *Journal of Managerial Psychology, 23*(3), 292–323. https://doi.org/10.1108/02683940810861392.

Miles, P. C. (2013). Why do educated, successful women leave the workforce? *American International Journal of Social Science, 2*(2), 1–12.

Moore, D. (2011). What makes them happy? Comparing working and non-working men and women in typical and atypical occupations. In M. Cortini, G. Tanucci, & E. Morin (Eds.), *Boundaryless careers and occupational well-being* (pp. 57–88). Hampshire: Palgrave Macmillan.

Napasri, T., & Yukongdi, V. (2015). A study of Thai female executives: Perceived barriers to career advancement. *Review of Integrative Business and Economics, 4*(3), 108–120.

O'Neil, D. A., Hopkins, M. M., & Bilimoria, D. (2008). Women's careers at the start of the 21st century: Patterns and paradoxes. *Journal of Business Ethics, 80,* 727–743. https://doi.org/10.1007/s10551-007-9465-6.

Pachulicz, S., Schmitt, N., & Kuljanin, G. (2008). A model of career success: A longitudinal study of emergency physicians. *Journal of Vocational Behavior, 73,* 242–253. https://doi.org/10.1016/j.jvb.2008.05.003.

Patton, W. (2013). Understanding women's working lives. In W. Patton (Ed.), *Conceptualising women's working lives: Moving the boundaries of discourse* (Vol. 5, pp. 3–22). Rotterdam: Sense.

Patton, W., & McMahon, M. (2014). *Career development and systems theory: Connecting theory and practice* (3rd ed.). Rotterdam: Sense.

Payne, B. K., Blackwell, B., & Collins, S. C. (2010). Education and career satisfaction: Examining the specifics of the relationship among criminal justice graduates. *Journal of Police and Criminal Psychology, 25*(2), 105–112. https://doi.org/10.1007/s11896-009-9058-7.

Peterson, N. B., Friedman, R. H., Ash, A. S., Franco, S., & Carr, P. L. (2004). Faculty self-reported experience with racial and ethnic discrimination in academic medicine. *Journal of General Internal Medicine, 19,* 259–265.

Public Works Committee. (2013). Annual reports 2012/2013. Pretoria: Council for the Built Environment & Agrément. Retrieved from http://www.cbe.org.za/content/images/CBE_AR_2012_WEB1F6C.pdf.

Republic of South Africa. (2014). Employment Equity Amendment Act, No.47, 2013. Government Gazette, 583, (37238). Retrieved from http://www.labour.gov.za/DOL/downloads/legislation/acts/employment-equity/eea_amend2014.pdf/view.

Rowe, T., & Crafford, A. (2003). A study of barriers to career advancement for professional women in investment banking. *South African Journal for Human Resource, 1*(2), 21–27. https://doi.org/10.4102/sajhrm.v1i2.9.

Shepherd, D. L. (2017). Gender, self-concept and mathematics and science performance of South African grade 9 students. Stellenbosch Economic Working Papers, Stellenbosch, South Africa. Retrieved from https://www.ekon.sun.ac.za/wpapers/2017/wp112017/wp112017.pdf.

Shrestha, P. (2016). Barriers for women in career advancement in the hospitality industry: A review of literature. MBA Student Scholarship. Paper 52. Retrieved from http://scholarsarchive.jwu.edu/mba_student/52.

Sirgy, M. J. (2012). *The psychology of quality of life: Hedonic well-being, life satisfaction, and eudaimonia*. London: Springer.

Snyder, K. (2011). *A study of motherhood and perceived career satisfaction of women in student affairs*. Higher Education Ph.D. Dissertations. 43. Retrieved from http://scholarworks.bgsu.edu/he_diss/43.

Srikanth, P. B., & Israel, D. (2012). Career commitment and career success: Mediating role of career satisfaction. *The Indian Journal of Industrial Relations, 48*(1), 137–149.

Sullivan, S. E., & Mainiero, L. (2008). Using the Kaleidoscope career model to understand the changing patterns of women's careers: Designing HRD programs that attract and retain women. *Advances in Developing Human Resources, 10*(1), 32–49. https://doi.org/10.1177/1523422307310110.

Super, D. E. (1990). A life-span, life-space approach to career development. In D. Brown, L. Brooks, & Associates (Eds.), *Career choice and development: Applying contemporary theories to practice* (2nd ed., pp. 197–261). San Francisco, CA: Jossey-Bass.

Waters, L., Briscoe, J., Hall, D. T., & Wang, L. (2014). Protean career attitudes during unemployment and reemployment: A longitudinal perspective. *Journal of Vocational Behavior, 84,* 405–419. https://doi.org/10.1016/j.jvb.2014.03.003.

Yap, M., Cukier, W., Holmes, M. R., & Hannan, C.-A. (2010). Career satisfaction: A look behind the races. *Industrial Relations, 65*(4), 584–608.

Young, L., Milner, M., Edmunds, D., Pentsil, G., & Broman, M. (2014). The tenuous relationship between salary and satisfaction. *Journal of Behavioral Studies in Business, 7,* 1–9.

Ndayiziveyi Takawira (Ph.D. in Psychology) is a professionally registered Psychologist (cat. Industrial) with the Health Professions Council of South Africa (HPCSA) and a professional human resource practitioner with the South African Board for People Practices (SABPP). She is also currently a lecturer in the Department of Human Resource Management at Unisa and lectures in Human Resource Maintenance and Retention at undergraduate level since 2009. She has co-published a number of articles in accredited journals.

Chapter 13
Encouraging Older People to Continue Participating in Civil Society Organizations: A Systematic Review and Conceptual Framework

Rodrigo Serrat, Feliciano Villar and Montserrat Celdrán

Abstract The participation of older people in civil society organizations has received considerable attention in recent years due to its potential for contributing to the health and well-being of the individuals concerned and also for creating social and economic benefits for the community. However, much of the previous literature has focused on human and social capital predictors of participation and on individuals' motivations for joining organizations or the barriers to their entry; far less attention has been paid to the reasons why people stop participating once they have begun. The study of this issue is fundamental for the sustainability of organizations in the future, as it will allow the design of strategies to promote continued participation among older people. In this chapter, we revise the literature on factors associated with the retention of older people in civil society organizations. We propose a conceptual framework to understand these factors, which classifies them as means-related, motives-related, or organizational and opportunity context-related. The implications for retention theory and practice are discussed in the light of the results.

Keywords Civil society organizations · Retention of older people
Organizational sustainability · Ageing workforce

Introduction

With the progressive aging of the population, there is an increasing global awareness of the need to keep older people active and engaged within their communities. This concern is reflected in numerous policy recommendations at local, national, and international levels (United Nations 2002; WHO 2002). The participation of older people in civil society organizations promotes their health and

---

R. Serrat (✉) · F. Villar · M. Celdrán
University of Barcelona, Barcelona, Spain
e-mail: rserrat@ub.edu

M. Coetzee et al. (eds.), *Psychology of Retention*,
https://doi.org/10.1007/978-3-319-98920-4_13

well-being and also contributes to strengthening communities and developing social capital (Anderson et al. 2014; Gonzales et al. 2015). Similarly, participatory democracy approaches to public participation support the active inclusion of ordinary citizens in decision-making processes within civil society organizations (Fung and Wright 2001).

In recent years, an increasing number of studies have addressed the issue of older people's participation in civil society organizations. These studies could be broadly classified using a process model in which either (a) antecedents; (b) outcomes; or (c) experiences of participation are taken into account (Musick and Wilson 2008; Wilson 2012). Studies on antecedents focus on the factors that boost or facilitate seniors' participation. At present, this is by far the most developed line of research in this area, and focuses on the effects of factors such as socio-economic and social capital resources (Serrat et al. 2015; Warburton and Stirling 2007), or personality variables (Serrat et al. 2017; Warburton et al. 2001). Among antecedents, a considerable amount of research has also been carried out on older people's motivations for joining civil society organizations (Petriwskyj et al. 2014; Serrat and Villar 2016) and to a lesser extent on barriers to their participation (Petriwskyj et al. 2017), including some systematic reviews (Principi et al. 2012; Petriwskyj and Warburton 2007).

The second line of inquiry focuses on the outcomes of elders' participation in these organizations. This line of research addresses the potential benefits to individuals of this type of participation in terms of health, well-being, and mortality risk. Participation in civil society organizations has been associated with better physical and mental health (Kishimoto et al. 2013; Lum and Lightfoot 2005), higher scores on different measures of well-being (Kahana et al. 2013; Serrat et al. 2017; Son and Wilson 2012), and lower risk of mortality (Harris and Thoresen 2005; Okun et al. 2013). Several systematic reviews have also been conducted (Anderson et al. 2014; Cattan et al. 2011; Jenkinson et al. 2013).

Finally, the third line of research, which has received much less attention from scholars (Celdrán et al. 2017; Wilson 2012), addresses the experience of participating itself. A key aspect of this experience is its dynamics, defined as the process whereby people move in and out of participation. A number of studies have addressed the problem of retention: that is, the factors that explain why older people continue or stop participating in civil society organizations once they have begun (Morrow-Howell 2010). This line of research is fundamental for the sustainability of organizations in the future, as it may allow the design of strategies to ensure older people's continued commitment to their organizations. However, the evidence regarding the retention of older people in civil society organizations remains disperse, and no attempt has been made to develop a conceptual framework for understanding the factors that drive retention in this specific type of participation. A framework of this kind may also identify potential practices and policy measures to increase the retention of older participants. This chapter has the following objectives:

Objectives of the Chapter

- O1: To identify and classify factors associated with the retention of older participants in civil society organizations.
- O2: To identify empirically-based measures for promoting retention of older participants in civil society organizations.

Research Design

We conducted a systematic review of the literature on older people's retention in civil society organizations. The papers reviewed were obtained by searching Psycinfo, Sociological Abstracts, Web of Science, and Scopus prior to June 2017 using the search terms (*Ageing* OR *Aging* OR *Aged* OR *Old age* OR *older people* OR *older persons* OR *older adults* OR *seniors* OR *senior citizens* OR *elder** OR *later life* OR *third age*) AND (all the combinations between *civic* OR *civil* OR *citizen** OR *political* AND *participation* OR *engagement* OR *involvement,* AND *volunteering*). The searches were limited to peer-reviewed papers published in English.

Data were extracted in two phases. In the first phase, titles and abstracts were scanned applying the following set of inclusion criteria: (1) the paper's main focus was on civic participation; (2) the paper's main focus was on older adults (+50) or their comparison with younger cohorts. Papers with a broader focus or not focused on older adults were therefore excluded from the review. In the second phase, the full text of the remaining papers was scanned and a second set of inclusion criteria was applied: (3) the paper explicitly addressed issues of retention; (4) the paper was based on empirical data.

We content-analyzed the papers included in the review with the objective of identifying and classifying factors associated with retention. This process was conducted independently by authors 1 and 2, who read the papers, identified the retention factors mentioned, and grouped these factors into categories and subcategories based on the similarity of their content. Interrater agreement after discussion of discrepancies was 93%. To increase the validity of the results, the third author of the chapter—who was not involved in the content analysis—carried out a peer-debriefing process. This process, as described by Creswell and Miller (2000), consists of reviewing the category system and challenging researchers' explicit and implicit assumptions through regular group discussion meetings.

Findings

After the exclusion of duplicate references, the initial search revealed 1,083 papers (see Fig. 13.1). Screening of titles and abstracts (1st phase) resulted in the exclusion of 643 papers which were not focused on civic participation or had a broader focus (n = 378), or which were not focused on older adults (+50) or their comparison with younger cohorts (n = 265). The full text scanning of the remaining 440 papers (2nd phase) resulted in the final selection of 34 papers meeting the second set of inclusion criteria, after the exclusion of 402 papers which did not explicitly address issues of retention and four papers which were not based on empirical data.

The papers included were published between 1989 and 2017, although most of them (n = 31) were published after 2000, and half (n = 17) were published after 2010. There was a clear hegemony of studies using US samples (n = 20), followed at some distance by studies using Australian (n = 4), Chinese (n = 2), Spanish (n = 2), and UK (n = 2) samples. Other countries and regions of the globe were clearly underrepresented. Only one paper was based on a transnational comparison, in this case between European countries (see Table 13.1).

With regard to the methodological approach, most studies used a quantitative design (n = 26). There were very few qualitative (n = 6) or mixed-methods (n = 2)

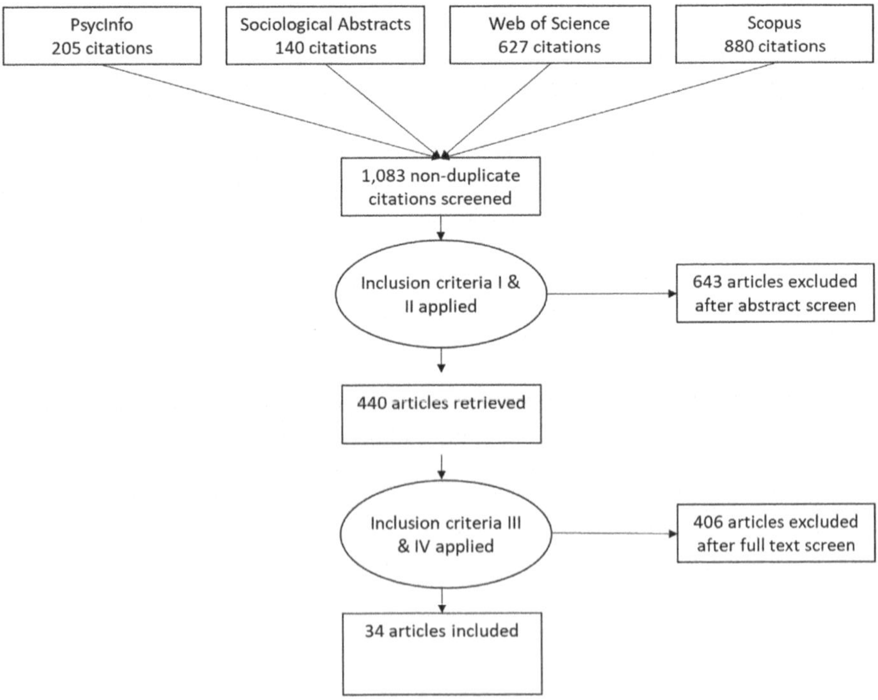

Fig. 13.1 Flow chart systematic review

Table 13.1 Characteristics and factor associated with retention identified in the studies included in the review (N = 34)

Study	Location	Sample	Design	Type of organization	Factors associated with retention		
					Means	Motives	Organizational/ opportunity context
Morrow-Howell and Mui (1989)	United States	Primary data, N = 83, age range not specified (M = 65 years old)	Cross-sectional	Volunteering (social/ community service)	X		X
Okun and Eisenberg (1992)	United States	Primary data, N = 242, age range: 55–79	Cross-sectional	Volunteering (social/ community service)		X	X
Kuehne and Sears (1993)	United States	Primary data, N = 19, age range: 58–77	Cross-sectional	Volunteering (health)		X	
Warburton et al. (2001)	Australia	Primary data, N = 236, age range: 65–74	Cross-sectional	Volunteering (diverse)	X	X	
Mehta and yunong (2004)	China	Primary data, N = 120, 50 years old and over	Cross-sectional	Volunteering (not specified)	X	X	
Cheung et al. (2006)	China	Primary data, N = 318, age range: 60–91	Cross-sectional	Volunteering (not specified)	X	X	
Martinez et al. (2006)	United States	Primary data, N = 443, age range: 42–93	Longitudinal	Volunteering (educational service)	X		
Adler (2007)	United States	Primary data, N = 125, 60 years old and over	Cross-sectional	Advocacy organizations	X		
Celdrán and Villar (2007)	Spain	Primary data, N = 88, 55 years old and over	Cross-sectional	Volunteering (diverse)		X	
Li (2007)	United States		Longitudinal		X		

(continued)

Table 13.1 (continued)

Study	Location	Sample	Design	Type of organization	Factors associated with retention		
					Means	Motives	Organizational/ opportunity context
		Secondary data (Americans' Changing Lives Study), N = 1,731, age range: 50–99		Volunteering (not specified)			
Lie and Baines (2007)	United Kingdom	Primary data, N = 76, 55 years old and over	Cross-sectional	Volunteering (social/ community service)		X	X
Warburton et al. (2007)	Australia	Primary data, N = 106, 60 years old and over	Cross-sectional	Advocacy organizations	X		X
Grano et al. (2008)	Italy	Primary data, N = 615, age range: 60–90	Longitudinal	Volunteering (diverse)		X	X
Butrica et al. (2009)	United States	Secondary data (Health and Retirement Study), N = 7,207, 55 years old and over	Longitudinal	Volunteering (not specified)	X	X	
Hong et al. (2009)	United States	Primary data, N = 51, not specified	Cross-sectional	Volunteering (diverse)			X
Tang et al. (2009a)	United States	Primary data, N = 374, age range: 60–90	Cross-sectional	Volunteering (diverse)			X
Tang et al. (2009b)	United States	Primary data, N = 401, age range: 51–90	Cross-sectional	Volunteering (diverse)			X
Hank and Erlinghagen (2010)	Europe (comparative)	Secondary data (Survey of Health, Ageing, and Retirement), N = 18,057, 50 years old and over	Longitudinal	Volunteering (not specified)	X		X

(continued)

Table 13.1 (continued)

Study	Location	Sample	Design	Type of organization	Factors associated with retention		
					Means	Motives	Organizational/ opportunity context
Mukherjee (2010)	United States	Primary data, N = 9, age range: 55–64	Cross-sectional	Volunteering (virtual)	X	X	X
Tang et al. (2010)	United States	Primary data, N = 207, age range: 56–89	Longitudinal	Volunteering (diverse)	X	X	X
Harlow-Rosentraub et al. (2011)	United States	Primary data, N = 1,347, 17 years old and over	Longitudinal	Volunteering (health)	X		X
McNamara and Gonzales (2011)	United States	Secondary data (Health and Retirement Study), N = 4,526, age range: 50–80 years old	Longitudinal	Volunteering (not specified)	X		
Mukherjee (2011)	United States	Primary data, N = 22, age range: 53–67	Cross-sectional	Volunteering (virtual)	X		X
Claxton-Oldfield et al. (2012)	United Kingdom	Primary data, N = 162, age range: 17–84	Cross-sectional	Volunteering (health)		X	
McBride et al. (2012)	United States	Primary data, N = 208, 50 years old and over	Cross-sectional	Volunteering (educational service)			X
Arinze Onyia et al. (2015)	Nigeria	Primary data, N = 284, age range: 21–79	Cross-sectional	Volunteering (health)	X		
Cheek et al. (2015)	United States	Primary data, N = 57, 50 years old and over	Cross-sectional	Volunteering (religious)		X	
Devaney et al. (2015)	Ireland	Primary data, N = 34, 55 years old and over	Cross-sectional	Volunteering (educational service)		X	

(continued)

Table 13.1 (continued)

Study	Location	Sample	Design	Type of organization	Factors associated with retention		
					Means	Motives	Organizational/ opportunity context
Ulsperger et al. (2015)	United States	Primary data, N = 10, 64 years old and over	Cross-sectional	Volunteering (social/ community service)	X		X
Okun et al. (2016)	United States	Secondary data (Americans' Changing Lives Study), N = 340, 65 years old and over	Longitudinal	Volunteering (not specified)	X		
Ramsey et al. (2016)	United States	Primary data, N = 298, 60 years old and over	Longitudinal	Volunteering (educational service)			X
Petriwskyj (2014)	Australia	Primary data, N = 332, age range: 55–90	Cross-sectional	Local government	X	X	X
Serrat et al. (2017)	Spain	Primary data, N = 192, age range: 65–86	Cross-sectional	Political organizations	X	X	X
Wilson et al. (2017)	Australia	Primary data, N = 76, age range: 18–85	Cross-sectional	Volunteering (not specified)		X	X

designs. As for ample size more than half of the studies reviewed (n = 18) used medium-sized samples (n = 106–615), eleven used small samples (n $\leq$ 88), and only a few (n = 5) larges samples (n $\geq$ 1,347). Finally, most papers were cross-sectional (n = 24), and thus provided a snapshot of the factors associated with retention among older adults. Of the 10 longitudinal studies identified, half were based on secondary data (Health and Retirement Study; Survey of Health, Ageing, and Retirement; American Changing Lives Survey) and half on primary data.

Regarding the type of organizations analyzed, most studies focused on older adults' participation in volunteer groups (n = 30), including educational, health, social and community, and religious organizations. Among them, six studies focused on programs whose target population was older people themselves, and five on intergenerational programs such as Experience Corps (the subject of three studies). Studies addressing other types of civil society organizations were far less frequent; they included research on older people's participation in advocacy organizations (n = 2), local government (n = 1), and political organizations (n = 1).

The results of the content analysis identified three main factors associated with older people's retention in civil society organizations: means-related, motives-related, and organizational and opportunity context-related factors (see Table 13.2).

Means-Related Factors

Means-related factors reflect the availability of individual resources that are deemed necessary for participation, such as civic skills, time or health. Participants' level of education was positively associated with longer involvement in civil society organizations (Butrica et al. 2009; Hank and Erlinghagen 2010), although one study found the opposite relationship (Martinez et al. 2006). Possessing specific skills that are considered essential for a volunteering role, such as computer skills in the case of virtual volunteering (Mukherjee 2010, 2011), have also been associated with continued participation. Also, age itself was negatively associated with retention (Serrat et al. 2017; Warburton et al. 2001).

Another reason for withdrawing was the loss of personal resources such as the experience of physical or mental health problems (Adler et al. 2007; Tang et al. 2010), or decreased availability, due to having to care for a close relative whose health deteriorates (McNamara and Gonzales 2011; Morrow-Howell and Mui 1989). In the opposite direction, the improvement in participants' health as a consequence of volunteering was identified as a reason to stay engaged (Mehta and Yunong 2004).

The loss of free time for participating due to work (Warburton et al. 2001) or other productive activities commitments (Arinze-Onyia et al. 2015; Morrow-Howell and Mui 1989) was also a reason for withdrawing. McNamara and Gonzales (2011) found that full-time employees who managed to reduce their

Table 13.2 Categories and frequencies of the factors associated with older people's retention in civil society organizations (N = 34)

Categories	n
Means-related factors	20
Educational level	
Specific skills needed for participating	
Age	
Physical or mental health problems	
Taking care of relatives	
Work or other productive activities commitments	
Transportation problems	
Financial constraints	
Length of participation	
Time committed to participation	
Motives-related factors	17
Perception of usefulness	
Satisfaction with the work carried out in the organization	
Fulfillment of participants' motives	
Loss of motivation	
Prioritize more important or enjoyable activities	
Organizational and opportunity context-related factors	16
Wide range of choices for participating	
Personal control over one's work	
Flexibility regarding roles and time committed to the organization	
Training opportunities	
Stipends	
Ongoing support and communication	
Recognition of participants' skills and service	
Specification of participants' roles, duties and rights	
Opportunities for social interaction	
Opportunities for inter and multigenerational contacts	
Organizational management problems	
Participants' problems with clients of the organization	
Social support and reinforcement	
Residential relocation	
Community attachment	
Church's attendance	
Government policies	
Familial systems/Welfare state regimes	

Note The sum of categories' frequency may be greater than 34 because some papers included more than one category working hours were more likely to continue participating. Transportation problems (Warburton et al. 2001) and financial constraints (Tang et al. 2010), including the loss of stipends for participation (Harlow-Rosentraub et al. 2011; Ulsperger et al. 2015), were associated with lower rates of retention. Interestingly, length of participation (Butrica et al. 2009; Okun et al. 2016) and time dedicated to participation (McNamara and Gonzales 2011) were positively associated with retention, probably due to an increase in personal resources and competences (Kuehne and Sears 1993).

Motives-Related Factors

Motives-related factors were mentioned by a number of studies which associated older people's perceptions, attitudes and motivations towards participation with their continuation (Petriwskyj et al. 2017). A body of research, for instance, shows that participants' perception of usefulness (Grano et al. 2008; Wilson et al. 2017) and their satisfaction with the work carried out in the organization (Cheung et al. 2006; Lie and Baines 2007) were positively associated with retention. Perceiving participation as part of one's identity (Cheek et al. 2015) or a sense of belonging to a larger organization (Lie and Baines 2007) were also reasons for staying engaged.

Both altruistic and self-oriented motives have been associated with retention. "Making a difference in the lives of others" (Cheek et al. 2015, p. 192), was found as a reason to stay (Claxton-Oldfield et al. 2012; Mukherjee 2010), whereas fulfillment of self-oriented motives included keeping or maintaining friends made at service or learning new things (Cheek et al. 2015; Lie and Baines 2007). Indeed, fulfillment of participants' motives by matching them with the experiences they have while engaged, rather than the motives per se, may influence certain participants' decisions to continue or to leave (Cheung et al. 2006; Okun and Eisenberg 1992).

Finally, participants' loss of motivation has been highlighted as a reason for leaving (Serrat et al. 2017; Tang et al. 2010). Some participants mention boredom (Celdrán and Villar 2007), while others stop participating in order to prioritize other activities which have become more important or enjoyable in their lives (Tang et al. 2010; Warburton et al. 2001).

Organizational and Opportunity Context-Related Factors

Several studies associated certain organizational and contextual factors with the retention of older people in civil society organizations. Regarding organizational factors, or what Hong et al. (2009) called "institutional capacity", research has shown that measures oriented to improve participants' decision-making capacity, such as offering a wide range of choices for participating (Mukherjee 2010;

Warburton et al. 2007), providing personal control over one's work (Grano et al. 2008), involving participants in organizational decisions (Devaney et al. 2015), or flexibility with regard to participants' roles and the time they commit to the organization (Tang et al. 2009a; Warburton et al. 2007) were all factors associated with retention.

A second set of factors within this category relates to what organizations offer participants. For instance, training opportunities (Hong et al. 2009; Ulsperger et al. 2015), stipends (Hong et al. 2009; Tang et al. 2009a, 2010), ongoing support and communication (Morrow-Howell and Mui 1989; Mukherjee 2011), recognition of participants' skills and their service to the organization (Devaney et al. 2015; McBride et al. 2012), a clear specification of participants' roles, duties and rights (Morrow-Howell et al. 2009; Wilson et al. 2017), opportunities for social interaction within and outside the organization (Hong et al. 2009; Wilson et al. 2017), or opportunities for inter and multigenerational contacts (Harlow-Rosentraub et al. 2011; Warburton et al. 2007) were also positively associated with retention. In contrast, organizational management problems (Morrow-Howell and Mui 1989; Warburton et al. 2007) as well as participants' problems with clients (Morrow-Howell and Mui 1989; Ulsperger et al. 2015) were all identified as reasons for leaving.

Contextual factors affecting retention operated at the micro, meso and macro level. At the micro level, social support and reinforcement were positively associated with retention (Cheung et al. 2006; Okun and Eisenberg 1992). In contrast, residential relocation was identified as a reason for leaving (Butrica et al. 2009). At the meso level, factors such as community attachment (Harlow-Rosentraub et al. 2011) or church attendance (McNamara and Gonzales 2011) were positively associated with retention. Finally, macro level factors such as government policies (Warburton et al. 2007), family systems, or welfare state regimes (Hank and Erlinghagen 2010) were also associated with older people's retention in civil society organizations.

Discussion

The first objective of this chapter was to propose a conceptual framework for attempting to understand the factors associated with the retention of older participants in civil society organizations. To do so, we carried out a systematic review of the literature. This review identified 34 peer-reviewed papers focusing on this issue, most of them published in the last 15 years. The figures indicate the growing (though still relatively new) interest in the topic.

On the basis of a content analysis of the papers included, we built an initial conceptual framework of the factors associated with older people's retention in civil society organizations. This framework classified factors as means-related, motives-related, and organizational and opportunity context-related. Means-related factors reflect the availability (or loss) of resources that are considered necessary for participation, such as time, education, health, or income. Motives-related factors include participants' perceptions, attitudes, and motivations towards participation, such as their perceptions of its usefulness or their own satisfaction. Finally, organizational and opportunity context-related factors reflect a wide range of organizational and socio-cultural factors that affect older people's decisions to continue their participation.

In this chapter we bring together the rather dispersed literature on older people's retention in civil society organizations and provide a useful conceptual framework for understanding what drives retention in this specific type of participation. Our systematic review also suggests the need for more studies on this topic. Specifically, at least four key areas are in need of further development.

First, we need to understand how socio-demographic diversity impacts on retention. In other words, we need to move on from identifying factors associated with retention to examining how these factors interact with individuals' socio-demographic characteristics. For instance, Serrat et al. (2017) showed that organizational and opportunity context-related factors may be more salient for younger elders than for their older peers, probably because they are less certain of how aging may affect their opportunities for participation; similarly, with regard to retention, Tang et al. (2010) stressed that means-related factors, and particularly incentives, may exert a greater influence on lower-income Americans than on their higher income peers. However, although the efforts to understand these interactions have increased in recent years (Petriwskyj et al. 2017), much of the research is still in its early stages.

Second, most research on retention has focused on older people's participation in volunteer groups, and has thus neglected other types of civil society organizations. Factors driving retention are strongly shaped by the specific characteristics of the type of organization considered. Serrat et al. (2017), for instance, showed that certain reasons for leaving that older volunteers did not report, such as feeling that the organization has changed its mission or philosophy, were important for those participating in political organizations. So, we need to look beyond the limits of volunteering organizations to consider how retention operates in a wider range of civil society organizations. Even inside the field of volunteering, Celdrán and Villar (2007) identified striking differences in the factors affecting retention among different types of organizations. This variable, therefore, needs to be taken into account in any analysis of older people's retention rates.

Third, most of the studies of older people's retention in civil society organizations are from English-speaking countries, notably the US and Australia. Other regions of the globe are clearly underrepresented. Civic participation is highly influenced by the socio-historical context; considering where and when participation occurs is key to understanding why some older participants may decide to leave their organizations or continue to participate. Thus, there is a clear need for more research in non-English-speaking regions, and also for cross-cultural studies comparing factors associated with older people's retention in civil society organizations across countries. To our knowledge, the only study of this issue carried out from a cross-cultural perspective is the one by Hank and Erlinghagen (2010), but they considered volunteering only at the European level.

Finally, there is a clear problem of measurement. Most studies used ad hoc questionnaires to assess retention, thus impeding therefore the comparability of results. Thus, the development of a standardized questionnaire that takes into account the results from previous research and the conceptual framework we propose in this chapter may be a desirable goal for future research. To date, the only attempt in this direction is the study by Hong et al. (2009), who developed a questionnaire to measure what they called 'institutional capacity'. However, this instrument addresses only one dimension (organizational and opportunity context-related) of the three we have identified in our conceptual framework. Thus, the development of an instrument measuring retention across the three categories identified in this chapter is now necessary.

Implications for Retention Theory and Practice

The second objective of this chapter was to identify empirically-based measures for increasing the rates of retention of older participants in civil society organizations. These measures can be defined using the initial conceptual framework proposed in this chapter, which classifies factors associated with retention as a) means-related, b) motives-related, and c) organizational and opportunity context-related.

Measures addressing means-related factors that can encourage continued participation among older people include the following. First, organizations must pay attention to older people's diversity and provide opportunities for participants with diverse backgrounds and skills (Warburton et al. 2007). Second, adapting the tasks and allowing less-time intensive forms of participation may be a way to retain older participants with disabilities or in poor health, or those with care commitments or those engaged in other productive activities (McNamara and Gonzales 2011; Warburton et al. 2001). Third, ride-share opportunities may be appropriate for those experiencing transport problems or who live in rural areas (Adler et al. 2007), and ways to allow virtual or home-based participation should be explored (Mukherjee 2010; Tang et al. 2010). Finally, measures such as free or inexpensive meals (Adler et al. 2007), transport stipends (Kuehne and Sears 1993), or economic stipends (Tang et al. 2010) may help to keep those with financial constraints engaged with the organization.

The second set of measures impact on motives-related factors. In general, research shows that in order to keep older people participating for longer periods, organizations need to match the experiences, activities and tasks assigned to them with their motives, interests and expectations (Butrica et al. 2009; Okun and Eisenberg 1992). This implies paying attention to the wide range of motives that could keep participants engaged—not just altruistic motives but also self-oriented ones such as learning new things and meeting new friends (Cheek et al. 2015; Cheung et al. 2006; Lie and Baines 2007).

Finally, measures to address organizational and opportunity context-related factors should seek to improve participants' capacity for decision-making and increase the range of the activities on offer. For instance, widening the range of choices for participating (Mukherjee 2010; Warburton et al. 2007), providing personal control over one's work (Grano et al. 2008), and involving participants in decisions (Devaney et al. 2015) may help to increase their engagement in organizational aspects, while providing training (Hong et al. 2009; Morrow-Howell and Mui 1989) and ongoing support and communication (Mukherjee 2011; Tang et al. 2010), and recognizing participants' skills and service (Devaney et al. 2015; Tang et al. 2009b) are useful ways to expand the range of opportunities offered and, as a result, increase retention rates.

Summary

In today's ageing societies, older people have an increasingly important role to play in civic organizations. Many studies have sought to determine factors that promote their involvement, and the barriers that hamper or impede it. However, factors influencing retention have not received comparable attention. The present chapter highlights the variety of these retention factors, which range from means-related to motives-related and organizational and opportunity context-related. We have tried to show how taking these factors into account and implementing appropriate organizational managing policies is key to maintaining older participants' satisfaction and commitment and to making the most of the scarce resources available to these civic organizations.

Acknowledgements This study was funded by the Spanish Ministry of Economy, Industry and Competitiveness (grant PSI2016-77864-R).

Rodrigo Serrat was supported by a Postdoctoral Fellowship by the University of Barcelona in collaboration with "La Caixa" Bank Foundation.

We want to thank Jordi Tremosa Armengol, librarian at the University of Barcelona (Mundet Campus), who provided invaluable help with the systematic review of the literature.

References (*Papers included in the systematic review)

*Adler, G., Schwartz, J., & Kuskowski, M. (2007). An exploration study of older adults' participation in civic action. *Clinical Gerontologist*, *31*(2), 65–75. https://doi.org/10.1300/J018v31n02.

Anderson, N. D., Damianakis, T., Kröger, E., Wagner, L. M., Dawson, D. R., Binns, M. A., Bernstein, S., Caspi, E., Cook, S. L. (2014). The benefits associated with volunteering among seniors: A critical review and recommendations for future research. *Psychological Bulletin*, *140*(6), 1505–1533. https://doi.org/10.1037/a0037610.

*Arinze-Onyia, S. U., Modebe, I., Aguwa, E. N., & Nwobodo, E. (2015). Assessment of knowledge and factors that may predict willingness to volunteerism : A pilot study of community directed distributors in Anambra state. *Nigerian Journal of Clinical Practice*, *18* (1), 61–67. https://doi.org/10.4103/1119-3077.146981.

*Butrica, B. A., Johnson, R. W., & Zedlewski, S. R. (2009). Volunteer dynamics of older americans. *Journals of Gerontology: Series B Psychological Sciences and Social Sciences*, *64* (5), 644–655. https://doi.org/10.1093/geronb/gbn042.

Cattan, M., Hogg, E., & Hardill, I. (2011). Improving quality of life in ageing populations: what can volunteering do? *Maturitas, 70*(4), 328–332. https://doi.org/10.1016/j.maturitas.2011.08.010.

Celdrán, M., Serrat, R., Villar, F., Pinazo, S., & Solé, C. (2017). The experiences of retired managers acting as volunteers in an entrepreneurial mentoring organization. *Journal of Population Ageing*. https://doi.org/10.1007/s12062-017-9210-6.

*Celdrán, M., & Villar, F. (2007). Volunteering among older Spanish adults: Does the type of organization matter? *Educational Gerontology*, *33*(3), 237–251. https://doi.org/10.1080/03601270601161181.

*Cheek, C., Piercy, K. W., & Grainger, S. (2015). Leaving Home: How older adults prepare for intensive volunteering. *Journal of Applied Gerontology*, 34(2), 181–198. https://doi.org/10.1177/0733464813480268.

*Cheung, F. Y., Tang, C. S., & Yan, E. C. (2006). Factors influencing intention to continue volunteering: A study of older Chinese in Hong Kong. *Journal of Social Service Research*, *32* (4), 193–209. https://doi.org/10.1300/J079v32n04.

*Claxton-Oldfield, S., Claxton-Oldfield, J., Paulovic, S., & Wasylkin, L. (2012). A study of the motivations of British hospice volunteers. *American Journal of Hospice and Palliative Medicine*, *30*(6), 579–586. https://doi.org/10.1177/1049909112463117.

Creswell, J. W., & Miller, D. L. (2000). Determining validity in qualitative inquiry. *Theory into Practice, 39*(3), 37–41. https://doi.org/10.1207/s15430421tip3903.

*Devaney, C., Kearns, N., Fives, A., Canavan, J., Lyons, R., & Eaton, P. (2015). Recruiting and retaining older adult volunteers: implications for practice. *Journal of Nonprofit and Public Sector Marketing*, *27*(4), 331–350. https://doi.org/10.1080/10495142.2015.1015373.

Fung, A., & Wright, E. O. (2001). Deepening democracy: Innovations in empowered participatory governance. *Politics and Society, 29*(1), 5–41. https://doi.org/10.1521/siso.2006.70.4.566.

Gonzales, E., Matz-Costa, C., & Morrow-Howell, N. (2015). Increasing the opportunities for the productive engagement of older adults: A response to population aging. *The Gerontologist, 55* (2), 252–261. https://doi.org/10.1093/geront/gnu176.

*Grano, C., Lucidi, F., Zelli, A., & Violani, C. (2008). Motives and determinants of volunteering in older adults: An integrated model. *International Journal of Aging and Human Development*, *67*(4), 305–326. https://doi.org/10.2190/AG.67.4.b.

*Hank, K., & Erlinghagen, M. (2010). Dynamics of volunteering in older Europeans. *The Gerontologist*, *50*(2), 170–178. https://doi.org/10.1093/geront/gnp122.

*Harlow-Rosentraub, K., Wilson, L. B., & Swindell, D. (2011). Multigenerational approaches to civic engagement: Findings from a panel study. *Journal of Intergenerational Relationships*, *9* (2), 146–160. https://doi.org/10.1080/15350770.2011.567917.

Harris, A. H. S., & Thoresen, C. E. (2005). Volunteering is associated with delayed mortality in older people: Analysis of the Longitudinal Study of Aging. *Journal of Health Psychology, 10* (6), 739–752. https://doi.org/10.1177/1359105305057310.

*Hong, S.-I., Morrow-Howell, N., Tang, F., & Hinterlong, J. (2009). Engaging Older Adults in Volunteering: Conceptualizing and measuring institutional capacity. *Nonprofit and Voluntary Sector Quarterly*, *38*(2), 200–219.

Jenkinson, C. E., Dickens, A. P., Jones, K., Thompson-Coon, J., Taylor, R. S., Rogers, M., … Richards, S. H. (2013). Is volunteering a public health intervention? A systematic review and meta-analysis of the health and survival of volunteers. BMC Public Health, 13(1), 773. https://doi.org/10.1186/1471-2458-13-773.

Kahana, E., Bhatta, T., Lovegreen, L. D., Kahana, B., & Midlarsky, E. (2013). Altruism, helping, and volunteering: Pathways to well-being in late life. *Journal of Aging and Health, 25*(201), 159–187. https://doi.org/10.1177/0898264312469665.

Kishimoto, Y., Suzuki, E., Iwase, T., Doi, H., & Takao, S. (2013). Group involvement and self-rated health among the Japanese elderly: An examination of bonding and bridging social capital. *BMC Public Health, 13,* 1189. https://doi.org/10.1186/1471-2458-13-1189.

*Kuehne, V. S., & Sears, H.A. (1993). Beyond the call of duty: Older volunteers committed to children and families. *Journal of Applied Gerontology, 12*(4), 425–438. https://doi.org/10.1177/073346489301200402.

*Li, Y. (2007). Recovering from spousal bereavement in later life: does volunteer participation play a role? *The Journals of Gerontology: Series B, Psychological Sciences and Social Sciences, 62*(4), S257–66. https://doi.org/10.1093/geronb/62.4.S257.

*Lie, M., & Baines, S. (2007). Making sense of organizational change: Voices of older volunteers. *Voluntas, 18*(3), 225–240. https://doi.org/10.1007/s11266-007-9043-7.

Lum, T., & Lightfoot, E. (2005). The effects of volunteering on the physical and mental health of older people. *Research on Aging, 27*(1), 31–55. https://doi.org/10.1177/0164027504271349.

*Martinez, I. L., Frick, K., Glass, T. A., Carlson, M., Tanner, E., Ricks, M., & Fried, L. P. (2006). Engaging older adults in high impact volunteering that enhances health: Recruitment and retention in the experience Corps® Baltimore. *Journal of Urban Health, 83*(5), 941–953. https://doi.org/10.1007/s11524-006-9058-1.

*McBride, A. M., Greenfield, J. C., Morrow-Howell, N., Lee, Y. S., & McCrary, S. (2012). Engaging older adult volunteers in national service. *Social Work Research, 36*(2), 101–112. https://doi.org/10.1093/swr/svs017.

*McNamara, T. K., & Gonzales, E. (2011). Volunteer transitions among older adults: The role of human, social, and cultural capital in later life. *Journals of Gerontology: Series B Psychological Sciences and Social Sciences, 66 B*(4), 490–501. https://doi.org/10.1093/geronb/gbr055.

*Mehta, K. K., & Yunong, H. (2004). A Cross-National Study of Senior Volunteerism in Two Non-Governmental Organizations in Singapore and P.R. China. *Hallym International Journal of Aging, 6*(2), 157–173. https://doi.org/10.2190/BXCU-1AEK-Y4HH-15K9.

Morrow-Howell, N. (2010). Volunteering in later life: Research frontiers. *Journal of Gerontology: Social Sciences, 65B*(4), 461–469. https://doi.org/10.1093/geronb/gbq024.Advance.

Morrow-Howell, N., Hong, S. I., & Tang, F. (2009). Who benefits from volunteering? *Variations in perceived benefits. Gerontologist, 49*(1), 91–102. https://doi.org/10.1093/geront/gnp007.

*Morrow-Howell, N., & Mui, A. (1989). Elderly Volunteers: Reasons for Initiating and Terminating Service. *Journal of Gerontological Social Work, 13*(3/4), 21–34. https://doi.org/10.1300/J083V13N03_03.

*Mukherjee, D. (2010). An exploratory study of older adults' engagement with virtual volunteerism. *Journal of Technology in Human Services, 28*(3), 188–196. https://doi.org/10.1080/15228835.2010.508368.

*Mukherjee, D. (2011). Participation of Older Adults in Virtual Volunteering: A Qualitative Analysis. *Ageing International, 36*(2), 253–266. https://doi.org/10.1007/s12126-010-9088-6.

Musick, M., & Wilson, J. (2008). *Volunteers: A social profile*. Bloomington: Indiana University Press.

*Okun, M. A., & Eisenberg, N. (1992). Motives and intent to continue organizational volunteering among residents of a retirement community area. *Journal of Community Psychology, 20*(3), 183–187. https://doi.org/10.1002/1520-6629.

*Okun, M. A., Infurna, F. J., & Hutchinson, I. (2016). Are Volunteer Satisfaction and Enjoyment Related to Cessation of Volunteering by Older Adults? *Journals of Gerontology - Series B Psychological Sciences and Social Sciences, 71*(3), 439–444. https://doi.org/10.1093/geronb/gbu159.

Okun, M. A., Yeung, E. W., & Brown, S. (2013). Volunteering by older adults and risk of mortality: A meta-analysis. *Psychology and Aging, 28*(2), 564–577. https://doi.org/10.1037/a0031519.

*Petriwskyj, A., Serrat, R., Warburton, J., Everingham, J., & Cuthill, M. (2017). Barriers to older people's participation in local governance: The impact of diversity. *Educational Gerontology, 43*(5), 259–275. https://doi.org/10.1080/03601277.2017.1293391.

Petriwskyj, A., & Warburton, J. (2007). Motivations and barriers to volunteering by seniors: A critical review of the literature. *The International Journal of Volunteer Administration, 24*(6), 3–25.

Petriwskyj, A., Warburton, J., Everingham, J., & Cuthill, M. (2014). Seniors' motivations for participation in local governance: Evidence from an Australian study. *Local Government Studies, 40*(2), 240–263. https://doi.org/10.1080/03003930.2013.790812.

Principi, A., Chiatti, C., Lamura, G., & Frerichs, F. (2012). The engagement of older people in civil society organizations. *Educational Gerontology, 38*(2), 83–106. https://doi.org/10.1080/03601277.2010.515898.

*Ramsey, C. M., Parisi, J. M., Rebok, G. W., Gross, A., Tanner, E. K., Carlson, M. C. et al. (2016). Attendance and retention of older adults in school-based volunteer activities: The role of school climate. *Journal of Intergenerational Relationships, 14*(1), 27–42. https://doi.org/10.1080/15350770.2016.1138274.

*Serrat, R., Petriwskyj, A., Villar, F., & Warburton, J. (2017). Barriers to the retention of older participants in political organisations: Evidence from Spain. *Ageing and Society, 37*(3), 581–606. https://doi.org/10.1017/S0144686X15001361.

Serrat, R., & Villar, F. (2016). Older people's motivations to engage in political organizations: Evidence from a Catalan study. *VOLUNTAS: International Journal of Voluntary and Nonprofit Organizations, 27*(3), 1385–1402. https://doi.org/10.1007/s11266-016-9710-7.

Serrat, R., Villar, F., & Celdrán, M. (2015). Factors associated with Spanish older people's membership in political organizations: the role of active aging activities. *European Journal of Ageing, 12*(3), 239–247. https://doi.org/10.1007/s10433-015-0341-4.

Serrat, R., Villar, F., Giuliani, M., & Zacarés, J. (2017a). Older people's participation in political organizations: The role of generativity and its impact on well-being. *Educational Gerontology, 43*(3), 128–138. https://doi.org/10.1080/03601277.2016.1269541.

Serrat, R., Villar, F., Warburton, J., & Petriwskyj, A. (2017b). Generativity and political participation in old age: A mixed method study of Spanish elders involved in political organisations. *Journal of Adult Development, 24*(3), 163–176. https://doi.org/10.1007/s10804-016-9255-4.

Son, J., & Wilson, J. (2012). Volunteer work and hedonic, eudemonic, and social well-being. *Sociological Forum, 27*(3), 658–681. https://doi.org/10.1111/j.1573-7861.2012.01340.x.

*Tang, F., Morrow-Howell, N., & Choi, E. (2010). Why do older adult volunteers stop volunteering? *Ageing and Society, 30*(5), 859–878. https://doi.org/10.1017/S0144686X10000140.

*Tang, F., Morrow-Howell, N., & Hong, S. (2009a). Inclusion of diverse older populations in volunteering: The importance of Institutional Facilitation. *Nonprofit and Voluntary Sector Quarterly, 38*(5), 810–827. https://doi.org/10.1177/0899764008320195.

*Tang, F., Morrow-Howell, N., & Hong, S. (2009b). Institutional facilitation in sustained volunteering among older adult volunteers. *Social Work Research, 33*(3), 172–182. https://doi.org/10.1093/swr/33.3.172.

*Ulsperger, J. S., Robertson, H., & Ulsperger, K. (2015). Senior companion program volunteers: exploring experiences, transformative rituals, and recruitment/retention issues senior companion program volunteers: exploring experiences, *20*(9), 1458–1475.

United Nations. (2002). *Madrid international plan of action on ageing*. Madrid.

*Warburton, J., Paynter, J., & Petriwskyj, A. (2007). Volunteering as a productive aging activity: Incentives and barriers to volunteering by Australian seniors. *Journal of Applied Gerontology, 26*(4), 333–354. https://doi.org/10.1177/0733464807304568.

Warburton, J., & Stirling, C. (2007). Factors affecting volunteering among older rural and city dwelling adults in Australia. *Educational Gerontology, 33*(1), 37–41. https://doi.org/10.1080/03601270600846824.

*Warburton, J., Terry, D. J., Rosenman, L. S., & Shapiro, M. (2001). Differences between older volunteers and nonvolunteers: Attitudinal, normative, and control beliefs. *Research on Aging, 23*(5), 586–605.
WHO. (2002). *Active ageing: A policy framework*. Madrid.
Wilson, J. (2012). Volunteerism research: A review essay. *Nonprofit and Voluntary Sector Quarterly, 41*(2), 176–212. https://doi.org/10.1177/0899764011434558.
*Wilson, M., Mirchandani, D., & Shenouda, R. (2017). Older-person volunteering in rural and regional Australia: Recruitment, retention, and health benefits. *Educational Gerontology, 43*(3), 139–146. https://doi.org/10.1080/03601277.2016.1269546.

Rodrigo Serrat (Ph.D.) is a postdoctoral researcher at the Department of Cognition, Development, and Educational Psychology of the University of Barcelona, Spain. His research focuses on civic participation in later life, with particular focus on issues of inclusion and diversity.

Feliciano Villar (Ph.D.) is tenured lecturer and researcher at the Department of Cognition, Development, and Educational Psychology of the University of Barcelona, Spain. His research interests are focused on generative concerns in the second half of life and the contributions of older people to their communities and families.

Montserrat Celdrán (Ph.D.) is an associate professor at the Department of Cognition, Development and Educational Psychology of the Universitat de Barcelona, Spain. Her research interests are focused on active ageing and social participation, volunteerism, grandparenthood, and dementia.

Part V
Organisational–Individual Relationship: Psychological Contract

Overview and Insights

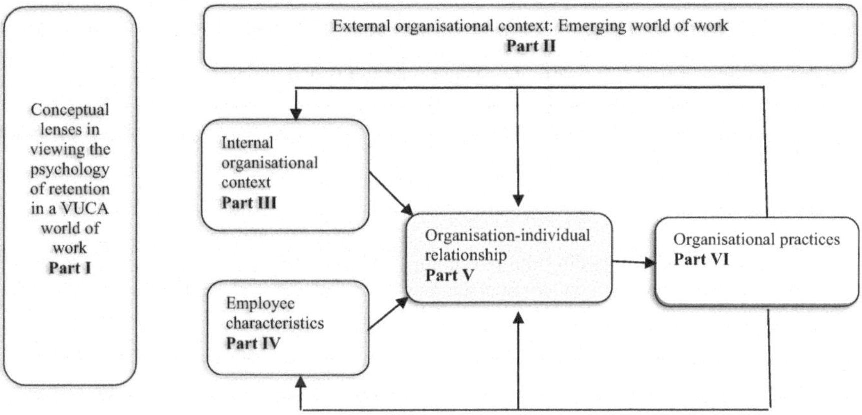

Towards an integrated conceptual framework for the psychology of retention

Part V, *Organisational–Individual Relationship: Psychological Contract*, comprises three chapters that illustrate the role of the psychological contract in the psychology of retention. Linking back to the external organisational context (VUCA and digital landscape; see Part II) influencing the psychology of retention, Part V highlights the psychological contract needs of the millennials who are digital natives.

Overview

In Chap. 14, *Millennial and Psychological Contract: Social Constructivist Approach*, Ade Irma Anggraeni makes a compelling case for adopting a social constructivist approach in designing career development support interventions for the retention of millennial workers. Based on a sound literature review, the author argues that millennial workers tend to like collaborative work environments and social interaction. Facilitating social, collaborative learning practices may help to manage psychological contracts in the context of millennial workers, especially in encouraging their participation and contribution as a form of self-esteem fulfilment and self-actualization. The chapter presents practical implications of millennial worker collective activity in developing millennial worker knowledge, especially related to the organizational efforts in building a learning culture. The author provides mentoring guidelines for career development based on millennial worker characteristics.

Chapter 15, *Knowing Me is the Key: Implications of Anticipatory Psychological Contract for Millennials' Retention* by Nada Zupan, Katarina Katja Mihelič and Darija Aleksić, describes millennial talents as an important source of competitive advantage in an increasingly digitalized and globalized business environment. The chapter makes a valuable contribution to the retention research literature by exploring through a quantitative survey millennials' employment expectations with the anticipatory psychological contract in two under-investigated contexts—Central and Eastern Europe and East Asia. In a second study, the authors also identified potential psychological contract breach situations for a Slovenian sample when comparing students' and employers' expectations. The authors propose relevant retention strategies and practices for young talent retention.

In Chap. 16, *Managing Diversity in Talent Retention: Implications of Psychological Contract, Career Preoccupations and Retention Factors*, Alda Deas reflects on the implications of diversity on the retention of talented employees. The chapter focuses on race, gender, generational cohorts, marital status, job level and employment level as important precursors for the psychological contract, psychosocial career preoccupations and retention factors. Drawing from an empirical study involving a sample of academic and support staff employees from a higher education institution in South Africa (N = 579), the chapter highlights that employees' diverse biographical characteristics may influence their psychological contract and psychosocial career preoccupations. Organisational retention strategies may benefit from the study findings by considering the unique needs of diverse groups of employees.

Key Insights

Relatively little is known regarding the psychology of retaining the younger generation of millennials. Part V contributes to a better understanding of millennials' expectations at work and their retention especially.

Practice Guidelines

The author of Chap. 14 suggests a constructivist approach in developing interventions for millennials to develop their career resilience through learning as part of their career development and growth. Career development programmes need to be based on the specific skills that employees need to build for maintaining work quality and performance improvements. The use of information technology and social approaches in mentoring, coaching, performance assessment, training and career development support is emphasized for millennials. The authors of Chap. 15 demonstrate the importance of analysing psychological contracts, and more specifically the anticipatory psychological contracts to better understand millennials' expectations at work and their retention. The authors highlight inter alia practices such as assessing perceptions of career development obligations to identify perceptions of psychological contract violations. The research highlights that in developing talent management practices, national and socio-economic contexts should be considered as they both affect the formation of expectations. In Chap. 16, the author demonstrates the importance of conducting surveys that assess the differing career development needs and psychological contract expectations of diverse groups of employees, including generational cohorts as these influence their satisfaction with retention practices.

Research Gaps
Chapter 14 highlights the need for research on the psychological contract needs of millennials who are digital natives and which influences the psychology of retaining them. The authors of Chap. 15 emphasize additional research on the antecedents and mechanisms that lead to the turnover intentions and actual turnover of millennial talent because little is known about the psychology of retaining this younger generation of employees. In Chap. 16, the author recommends further research on the links between employees' psychological contract, psychosocial career preoccupations and retention factors in diverse occupational settings.

Chapter 14
Millennial and Psychological Contract: Social Constructivist Approach

Ade Irma Anggraeni

Abstract The psychological contract as a manifestation of employment relationship needs to touch the motivational aspect of employees in line with the increasingly intense competition in recruiting and maintaining the talented worker, especially the millenial generation that currently occupies the largest portion of the workforce. Work characteristics and values of the millennial generation affect the dynamics of psychological contract management that has become more focused on flexibility and employability skill development. Millenial workers—motivated to develop professional competence—tend to like collaborative work environments. Based on the social constructivist paradigm, organizations can facilitate learning process of millennial workers through social interaction. The process of sharing knowledge becomes the focus of millenial workers in order to improve decision-making ability, problem solving and communication building. The social constructivist approach becomes relevant in managing psychological contracts in the context of millennial workers, especially in encouraging their participation and contribution as a form of self-esteem fulfillment and self-actualization. This chapter presents practical implications of millenial worker collective activity in developing millennial worker knowledge, especially related to the organizational efforts in building learning culture. In addition, human resource practitioners are expected to be able to gain a valuable guidance in devising strategies to maintain millenial workers by focusing on building professional and social competence. There are also mentoring guidelines for career development based on millenial worker characteristics.

Keywords Millenial workers · Psychological contract · Retention
Employment relationship · Learning culture · HR practices · Career development
Social constructivism

A. I. Anggraeni (✉)
Jenderal Soedirman University, Purwokerto, Indonesia
e-mail: aianggraeni.psdie.undip@gmail.com

M. Coetzee et al. (eds.), *Psychology of Retention*,
https://doi.org/10.1007/978-3-319-98920-4_14

Introduction

Research in the field of employment relationship emphasizes that human resource management does not just stop at the practical adoption of HR management practices without considering the dynamics of aspirations and employee expectations. Therefore, some written agreements and HR management practices require supporting components to be well internalized and achieve their primary goal of directing employee attitudes and behaviors in a harmonious atmosphere. The latest developments in the field of employment relationship concludes that successful organization building competitive advantage through human resources have a tendency to follow up the agreements and the written policies in the form of psychological contract (Hughes 2008).

Psychological contract is also an important concern for the organization as the competition gets deeper in recruiting and retaining talented employees. In the competition for high-skilled employees, psychological contracts are used as an employer branding that can provide a foundation for talented employees in interpreting employee value proposition (O'Donohue 2009). To build employer branding, the management of psychological contract needs to consider improving and developing talented employees who can add value to the organization (Rosethorn 2009).

There is a substantial change in the management of employment relationships. In the past, companies emphasized more on providing assurance to employees to work until retirement in the company. Past employee relationships were also identical with the rewards that tend to be based on equity, and incremental benefit adjustment (Chambel and Fotinha 2009). But this strategy creates problems especially when the company plans to expand and move massively to achieve more optimal performance and competitiveness. These rewards and benefits cause serious problems because employees are not motivated to build competence within the organization (Bittner and Schipper 2014). This condition causes the organization and employees tend to move in different directions so that at a certain point, the company does not have competent human resources to run its business. This strategy is also potentially incompatible with the demographic characteristics of the labor force that comes with different expectations. Certainly, it is really different to the previous generation. If the previous generations were more motivated on working guarantees to retirement, the characteristics of the current millennials generation tend to be more mobile and they are very unique in terms of the combination of orientation toward high career achievement as a form of self actualization and the necessities of work in the environment conducive work (Moore et al. 2015).

Psychological contract as a strategy for retaining employees needs to consider the generation change component. (Strauss and Howe 1991). Today, the millennials occupy the largest proportion of the global workforce. This generation needs special attention because their expectations and needs are very different to the previous one (Deloitte 2014). The characteristics of the millennial generation that consider themselves as a privileged resource within the organization raises expectations.

They expect that the organization need to treat them differently (Lancaster and Stillman 2010). The millennial generations have a high self-esteem because the social environment and family believe that these generations will achieve success. It needs to understand that the characteristics of millennial generation in the workplace also aim to build an effective communication. This generation is team-oriented because they grow up with peers, through collaborative learning in group learning systems. The dominant characteristic of these generations is high achievers because they process with high educational standards (Ferri-Reed 2013).

The millennials are also the generation of technology users and they are fast response in following the development of technology and social media (Taylor 2014; Winograd and Hais 2011). As this generation is very close to technology, they believe that working with social media can boost the work productivity, especially for speeding up the work processes, becoming more organized as well as building more active working relationships.

Developing Millenials Careers Through Psychological Contract

In the context of talented employee management, psychological contract plays a role in encouraging employees to develop sustainable knowledge-sharing capabilities (O'Neill and Adya 2007). Employees who are committed to their personal career development, tend to be proactive in sharing knowledge to improve the work professionalism. Chen (2014) affirmed that the importance of building a psychological contract can provide space for career development and employee retention. In line with that, Dhanpat and Parumasur's research (2014) concluded that the effectiveness of psychological contract is determined by its strategic components. This becomes relevant that the organization needs to design the factors that can grab the millennials' interest. This generation has an expectation that their workplace provides an opportunity to contribute to the success of the organization, to have a quality training and education program, harmonious superior-subordinate relationships, challenging work experience and open communication (Lynch 2008). So, the strategic components developed by organization in managing the millennials need to focus on the massive use of technology, the development of work-to-live mentality, regular feedback, the development of collaborative activities in daily routines and the opportunities to engage in community at the work place (Vincent 2012).

Psychological contract has wide scope covering throughout the process of recruitment to career development for the employees within the organization. The career development programs are run and socialized by the organization fairly and transparently in the perception by employees to build positive employees relationships. Furthermore, the flexible work programs organized by organization in the perception by employees as an organization's effort provide a conducive working environment for employees so that they can balance the time between work and personal life (Vos and Freese 2011). It becomes so important because the millennials seek a workplace that is challenging, solid leadership, non-traditional work schedules and friendly organizational culture (Raines 2002). It deals with the study results of Pyoria et al. (2017) on the work orientation of millennials, it can be concluded that this generation puts family life and pleasure as a priority. It means that in the effort to manage millennials in the workplace, it is necessary to consider the work-life balance components. This study also discusses the work commitments of millennials. The results conclude that this generation is committed to the work that they are interested in. The characteristics of this generation have a tendency to switch jobs, but still in same work fields for the purpose of gaining the work experience in the field of interest.

Psychological contract is an approach used by the organization to maintain the spirit, commitment and performance of employees in the face of increasingly dynamic business demands. Intensive socialization is an organizational effort to prepare and assist employees to face the process of organizational transformation (Vos and Freese 2011). Socialization is also considered by new employees as a proactive effort of the organization in creating a conducive working environment (Tomprou and Nikolau 2011). In the context of change, the millennials would like to work in the environments that encourage collaboration rather than competition (Gutfreund 2014). This generation also has a goal of working on innovative activities and the achievement of social missions (Walsh 2015). Therefore, the process of organizational change is interpreted by the millennials as an opportunity to build a collaboration which aims to harmonize the dynamics of organizational motion that demands creativity and personal goals that want to contribute to a better social life.

Psychological contract is an employees' belief about the organization's proactive efforts in understanding and facilitating the needs and expectations of employees. Expectations become the basis for employees in contributing and otherwise the organization need to manage employee expectations through a fair exchange mechanism. Employees will work effectively when there is fairness between what the organization will give and what employees should give to the organization. For that reason, a psychological relationship should be capable of creating emotions that lead to the attitudes and positive behavior of employees. This relationship can harmonize the relationship between the employees and the organization (Armstrong 2009). This relationship helps the organization in predicting the output that employees can provide. In the context of millennial generation management, it should be a major concern as this generation has the belief that their opinions are worth listening to. This generation also has high confidence that they are able to achieve success (Vanmeter et al. 2013). The millennials seek flexibility in the workplace. They are an independent generation and prioritize moral responsibility to make a difference in the workplace. They are also a generation that puts forward smart and fast working patterns, tends to be multitaksing and wants clear direction and standards (Caraher 2015).

The results of Freese et al. (2011) concluded that the effectiveness of the psychological contract is determined by the competence development and the employees' development within the organization. This condition makes employees feel that the organization they work with, can fulfill their expectations for talent development. The employees are motivated to develop themselves when the demands of work require them to maximize all their capabilities. Herriot et al. (1997) argued that the components of work can motivate employees to master and develop their skills. The research conducted by Corder and Ronnie (2017) concluded that psychological contract affects employee motivation, especially on the aspects that involve support, flexibility and direction. The study has found that employees have expectations about openness in communication and involvement in decision making. The psychological contract components that are considered important by employees also relate to the opportunities to improve professionalism through training. A various and challenging work design can encourage employees to master new skills to meet job demands. It deals with the expectations of the millennial generation that wants flexible working time and professionalism development (Sujansky and Ferri-Reed 2010; Lancaster and Stillman 2010; Riccardi et al. 2014).

Career Development Approach as the Strategy of the Millenials Retention

One of the career theories is the Self Concept Theory of Career Development by (Super 1980) based on the dynamic interaction between mental development, experience, environmental characteristics and stimulation in shaping career development. This theory was developed further by Savickas (2002) and he argued that career development is strongly influenced by the social environment and relationships affect each other between the individuals and their environment. In order to develop a career, the individuals need to work to meet the existing standards in the environment and be accepted by their social environment (Leung and Chen 2007).

Career is interpreted as the series of behaviors and habits related to the work of a person throughout his life (Hall 1996). To develop a career, one needs the ability and knowledge to respond to work challenges and constantly learn to improve the personal qualities, be able to adapt to the environmental changes and remain focused in achieving superior performance to achieve the organizational goals (Collard et al. 1996). The ability to adapt and grow in a dynamic work environment embodies career development. It is built by a career management process and it involves an interaction between the individual and the work environment by engaging the risk-taking with the wisest consideration and can be built by every employee (London 1983).

Career development studies began to develop in the late 1990s as concluded by Bernard (1996) that everyone can develop a career by increasing optimism and opening up to sharing possibilities. The concept of career resilience is a new paradigm in the study of employment relationships. In the old paradigm, organization provides a clear work. It is a status as a member of the organization and long-term employment guarantees. In return, employees are required to work hard, be loyal and perform well. Nevertheless, the view has quite radically changed along with the phenomenon of free trade, the process of industrial engineering, downsizing and the development of information technology. The employees are no longer to focus on long-term job security, but the ability of the organization to provide career development for the employees. So, the employees' competency and skills can always keep up with the demands of the labor market (Kristof-Brown 1996).

There is a supporting literature revealed by Latack (1984) who divided the dimensions of career resilience into six dimensions: adaptability, individual assessment toward the outcomes, individual beliefs toward his ability, independence, risk-taking and tolerance to uncertainty and workplace pressures. The ideas of Luthar et al. (2000) interpreted the career resilience as a dynamic development process of individual, not just personal characteristics so that anyone can master the ability.

Concerning the concept of career resilience, the existence of millennials in the workplace poses some challenges but also positively impacts the organization. The millennials are the generation that has a high tolerance for changes. The career development programs of millennials need to be designed to optimize their capabilities and engagement in changing situations and ensure that their best contribution impacts on improving their careers. This is because these generations want a work environment that values their self-development and gives them the opportunities to learn new things (Gilbert 2011). The millennials look for workplaces that are able to provide challenges in employment and professional development skills. These necessities should be addressed by the organization with a focus on providing feedback toward the achievement of performance as the millennials retaining strategy (Park and Gursoy 2012). Specifically, it is necessary to include the management initiatives of knowledge and the teamwork in the millennials' planning careers to increase their involvement. The implementation of this strategy requires a leadership role as a partner in the millennium planning process. The process of meeting the employees' expectations and the organization occurs in this process. The organization needs to provide a clear guidance in helping the millennials to design their career paths. Thompson and Gregory (2012) asserted that millennials will be loyal to the organization if they are given the opportunities to develop their abilities and relationships with other members of the organization.

London and Mone (1987) concluded that individual who has career resilience, is able to control the situations, to take risks under the uncetainty conditions, to tolerate in confusing situations, to have confidence that they are capable of achieving goals, to be independent, to be adaptable in environmental changes, and able to work together with other organization members. Furthermore, Collard et al. (1996) developed the concept of career resilience to six characteristics including the ability to understand the personal potentials, to orientate adding values to the work, to focus on the future, to dedicate themselves engaging in learning process, to be flexible and able to build cooperation network in organization.

One's career resilience is determined by two aspects: the personal aspect and the aspect of the work environment. In the context of work environment, career resilience is obtained through the organizational support in the form of constructive feedback and the opportunities to work autonomously. Career resilience also becomes a practical study in counseling programs in various organizations. This concept is used in the career development process so that the organization builds the work environments and the relationships that are able to encourage the employees' career resilience. Generally, the organization has adopted a career resilience model in four stages. First, the organization actively explains this concept in the form of employee professionalism development policy. Second, the organization determines a career counseling process to build employees' understanding of the personal value and expectations of employees in the workplace. Third, the organization helps employees to identify and face challenges in achieving the desired career through an understanding of employee intrinsic motivation. Fourth, the organization builds communities for employees so they can develop themselves together (Rickwood 2002).

The application of career development theory in organization does not only rely on the individual independence in building career. Byster (1988) concluded that although the individual is the primary architect in building his career, the individual also needs a help to find the personal value and the expectations in the work. The organization also needs to provide supports so that the employees can meet changes in the organization. It deals with Kerka (1993) who believes that a clear and real information about the concerned work is a major component that can encourage employees to be more capable to do the job.

London (1983) built the dimensions of career resilience into three domains: self-manageability, risk-taking and connectivity. Self-managing ability is divided into sub domains. They are self-esteem ability, ability to work autonomously, adaptability, self-control, desire to get achievement, initiative, creative, have personal work standard and progress orientation. Furthermore, courage to risk-taking is divided into sub domains. They include the ability to tolerate the uncertainty. Connectivity components include the ability to establish relationships for career development and the necessity of acceptance by colleagues and leaders.

King (2003) explained that there are seven aspects about career resilience. They are not easily giving up in the face of difficult situations, persistent in pursuing career goals, able to control the situation, remain responsible for completing work in uncertain conditions, taking risks, responsible for career planning personally, avoid to get more boss' attention for self-advantage.

The concept of career resilience evolves as the business environment changes. The processes, patterns and technologies adopted by the organization give a new perspective on career concepts (Bridges 1995; Cascio 1995; Kotter 1995). In addition, the increasingly flat organizational structure and design and organizational tendencies to delegate non-core business creates new challenges and opportunities for the employees to develop their careers (Hammer and Champy 1994; Meyer 1996; Handy 1988). These changes have an impact on human resource management so that the organization needs to focus more on identifying the intellectual and learning needs within the organization (Kiechel 1993; Birchall and Lyons 1995). Starting from the understanding of the changes above, Fourie and Vuuren (1998) elaborates the concept of career resilience into three dimensions: self-belief, independence and willingness to accept a change.

Based on the changes in the business environment, Bryant (1995) thought about the needs for organization to focus on building the employee resilience. The organization needs to direct the positive behavior of the employees so that they can be optimistic and able to interact with the work environment quickly and efficiently. This opinion confirms an expert opinion, Conner (1992). He concluded that the individual who has career resilience, can assimilate to the new working conditions.

Millennials are the generation that seeks to find the organization that is able to meet their expectations. This generation is known to be very career-oriented and has high career ambitions. (Kong et al. 2015). This generation also has a strong work ethic and high learning skills so it requires a work environment that can provide a consistent feedback and support. To retain the millennials, the organization needs to encourage them to determine career paths clearly and find some ways to develop the millennial employee skills toward the top performers. The main concern of the millennials is the rapid development of performance even in an environment of rapidly organizational change. The millennials require challenges of work. It deals with the expectations of millennials who tend to love the career progress that comes from acquiring new professional skills. It deals with Bannon's et al. (2011) explanation that the millenials presence at work—with its uniqueness, talents and abilities—are capable of significantly changing the work environment. Maxwell (2013) asserted that if the organization commits to retaining millennial employees, the organization needs to build the millennials to be ready for jobs that can drive and guide them to maximize their skill sets.

Building Career Resilience Through Learning: A Social Constructivist Approach

The constructivist existence in the learning process begins with criticism of the rigid behavior and focuses only on the intrapersonal aspect (Mayer 1996). Individual acquires knowledge and learning not exclusively but through the role of active learner and interaction with the social environment (Vygotsky 1978). Thus, learning in a constructivist view emphasizes the social interaction aspect as a stimulus for individual cognitive development. Social constructivist is a realistic approach that emphasizes learning activities in a highly contextual and specific community (Woolfolk 2004). Learning in a social constructivist view involves a process of personal and social development that performs a function as a whole community. Thus, knowledge is a new understanding formed by the situation in the community. There is a collective subjectivity derived from the participation and contribution of each member of the community that is real and original (Davydov and Kerr 1995).

In constructivist paradigms, individual builds knowledge through interaction and interpretation of the social environment. It is seen from the socio-cultural context, the practice and value that exist in a community directly or indirectly guides the individual to establish a cognitive system (Vygotsky 1978). The learning process in the organization involves individual and groups to do planning, discussing and solving problems (Sawchuk 2003). Planning, negotiating and building status in a working relationship reflect the real experiences and they just happen. The learning process also occurs when the employees internalize the values of the organization and identify themselves both individually and socially. This situation is called flying and grounding (Fenwick 2008) which deal with the concept of situational learning. In this process, the employees do not learn about the technical aspects of the work but they give more focus actively influencing each other's existing knowledge and values through a participatory process (Billet 2004).

The millennials are also accustomed to the situational learning to find the real experiences and problems in their work. Roehling et al. (2011) suggested that the participatory learning of the millennials aims to make the learning process more active, resulting in a deeper understanding of the learned material and encourages the sharing of perspectives. The concept of situational learning was firstly introduced by Resnick (1987) who tried to bridge the theoretical learning knowledge into the real world. The situational learning firstly was developed in the literature on adult education and subsequently adopted by Marsick and Watkins (1999) in the organizational context by formulating two types of learning: informal and incidental. A research conducted by Enos et al. (2003), the learning process in organization mostly occurs in informal situations and it is a part of daily work activities. This type of informal learning occurs through the interaction among the members of the organization in the most obvious conditions. This is what distinguishes from formal organizational learning. Roehling et al. (2011) suggested that the participatory learning tends to be warmer and more informal, thus encouraging the millennials to improve self-efficacy. This method of learning also encourages the millennials to explore ideas, risks and creativity to understand the decision choices (Blashki et al. 2007). This generation is interested in displaying learning outcomes in practical aspects especially when they face new roles (Broadbridge et al. 2007).

In the perspective of learning as an effort to develop ideas and knowledge, Sawchuk (2003) concluded that learning is a series of analysis of an object to understand the actual conditions and possibilities that can be developed to produce new knowledge or solutions and then it can be applied in a system. This process does not occur linearly, but simultaneously it involves the individual goals, abilities and perspectives (Engestrom 2001). Wright's research (2003) on software development companies concluded that the process of interaction and employee engagement enable the development of new skills. Employees involvement involves two things: procedural involvement related to work and conceptual engagement related to value and organization expectations (Gott 1989).

In a socio-cultural perspective, the real experience allows an individual to gain new skills through social interaction with the other members of the organization and participate in collective activities (Lave and Wenger 1991). The research conducted by Cahoon (1995) concluded that most of the learning processes in organization occurs in daily work practices and social interaction contributes more to the development of new employee skills than formal job training. Furthermore (Billet 1995) concluded that the participation of an individual with other members of the organization through the authentic experiences provides an opportunity for the employees to understand the organizational goals, develop skills and have a constructive connectivities to the job they have.

Billet's research (2001) on companies with various industry backgrounds such as mining, transportation, distribution, services, manufacturing and the public sector concluded that situational learning can be applied in all areas of industry. Job activities involve a set of practices and learning processes that can strengthen, improve and develop new knowledge when employees participate in the work (Billet 2004). This confirms the opinion of Eraut (2004) which explained that the development of cognitive and reflective skills of employees is obtained through the problem solving in the work. In the context of applying new knowledge, the situational learning processes help millennials to interpret a big-picture into an applicative knowledge. This process allows the millennials to gain hands-on experience in solving a problem. It deals with the opinion of Weiler (2005) that the millennials want the process of obtaining efficient information for subsequent application in the work.

In the context of human capital management, intellectuality, information and knowledge are important aspects in driving business success in an era of knowledge-based economic progress. For that, the learning process becomes an important aspect in achieving the organizational goals (Mezirow 1991). Designing long-term vision and strategy requires an understanding of the learning objectives in the organization and how learners (employees) can improve career resilience to add value to the work relationships. Neesham (2007) argued that there are five competencies that can be mastered by employees in the learning process. First is the personal ability that has been attached to the individual before joining and playing its role in the organization. This competency is obtained through single competence learning experience. The second competence is the ability to run the various roles in the organization obtained through the multiple competences learning experience. The third competence is flexibility and adaptability. The next competence is the ability to transform personal knowledge into the organizational knowledge capital and it is built through the interactive and collective experiences. The last competence is the ability to combine individual and group learning objectives with the organizational learning goals to achieve the business success and it is gained through the innovative-progressive experiences.

Single competence learning experience is special and the competence of the employees is technically appropriate in the field of expertise and job qualification. Furthermore, the competencies gained through multipe competence learning experience do not only focus on the job description but they are relevant to the organization's long-term needs. The situational-adaptive learning experience aims to build employee competencies to adapt and keep performing optimally in a business competition environment by focusing on a strong vision and risk-taking courage.

The social constructivist approach emphasizes new ways of thinking in dealing with old problems through coordination processes (Hosking and Bass 2001). In relation to the presence of generations in the workplace, social consturctivist-based learning becomes relevant. This is why the millennials love learning through a group work, team projects and collaborations that aim at sharing knowledge and ideas (Murphy 2012). This generation loves a learning experience that can contribute to career enhancement. The learning experience makes the learning process more active which is proved by a deeper understanding of the learning materials being worked on and encouraging the development process of sharing perspectives (Roehling et al. 2011). The interactive-partisipative learning process encourages the millennials to generate the conclusions independently. This process encourages the exploration of ideas, consideration of risk and creativity in an informal and warm atmosphere (Blashki et al. 2007). The characteristics of millennial generation in the workplace are demonstrated by the use of communication methods and information-based social media search (Young and Hinesly 2014). However, the typical millennial characteristics that work multitasking and want to display their best performance requires a casual work environment and minimal bureaucracy. The millennials are determined to be able to contribute more to the organization and prefer doing the challenging work to working the rigid work environment. This generation tends to desire a career in a work environment that implies flexibility and makes rooms for them to perform the philanthropic and voluntary activities (Taylor 2014).

Implications: Mentoring the Millennials for Retention

Rousseau and Schalk (2000) concluded that psychological contract affects the improvement of employees' ability. In this study it is explained that the organization needs to focus on efforts to understand and meet the needs of employees in terms of career development within the organization. The career development programs designed by the organization need to be based on the specific skills that employees need to build in order to maintain the work quality and the performance improvements. This opinion deals with the conclusion of Stevens and Campion's (1994) research that organization needs to adopt new paradigms in human resource management from the attributes related to employee personalities to the attributes related to employee knowledge, skill and abilities. The current working environment demands employees' ability to work together and collaborate so that employee career development program must include the development of interpersonal competencies such as team-ability and negotiation skills (Mannering 2002; Tractenberg et al. 2002).

A research conducted by Aichinger and Barnes (2010) on employee expectations concluded that the reason of employees choose to work in an institution is due to fulfill their expectations to improve the ability to work together and collaborate in a team. This finding deals with Diplari and Dimou's (2010) study which concluded that psychological contract of the employees' development in the form of experimental learning enhance the employees' managerial skills including time management, team-building skills and leadership. The results of this study deal with the findings of Callaghan et al. (2010) which concluded that psychological contract focuse on a fair employee development program and it enhances the ability of employees to work together. In the context of millennial generation management in the workplace, this becomes relevant. The millennials are individuals who need guidance, direction, certainty and feedback in performing the task. They also expect appreciation, passion and access in return for their success (Hershatter and Epstein 2010). This generation tends to be multitasking, has a high curiosity, a desire to be unique and authentic, independent thinking and freedom in making choices. The millennials love the work atmosphere that can provide an intellectual stimulation and work together in a team (Smith 2000). For that, the organization needs to provide the challenging assignments and opportunities to collaborate.

The findings of Busby and Gibson (2010) also showed evidence that career development program has an effect toward the development of teamwork skills. Confirming the previous findings on the relationship between career development and employee positive behavior, the results of Osibanjo et al. (2014) concluded that career development contributes to the improvement of employees' critical skills that can add a value to the organization. The psychological contract relates to the organizational efforts to prepare employees for any changes that occur within the organization. If it is not properly managed, the changes will cause a resistance. However, if it is managed and anticipated well, the changes in the organization will have an opportunity to improve the employees' critical skills (Harigopal 2006). The psychological contract plays a role in giving assurance to employees that the process of the organizational transformation in order to meet the needs and the expectations of both parties. They are the organization and the employees that grow together, along with the business growth. Therefore, in the process of the organizational transformation, the role of psychological contract becomes important in describing and socializing the organizational change programs, so that the implementation of change is same with the achieved objectives.

In an increasingly dynamic business environment, change is an aspect that continually needs to be adapted by employees. Cope (2009) stated that organizational transformation shapes the knowledge and strategic capabilities of employees. The organizational transformation also encourages employees to get out of the comfort zone and work to develop the creativity of employees so that they can adapt in the dynamics of the work environment (Chocqueel-Mangan 2011). The employees who understand that change positively impact both themselves and organization tends to see and follow up on opportunities to collaborate and work together in team to stay in the flow of change (Miller 2011).

Related to the organizational change, the millennials are the generation that has optimism and high expectations about the future of the organization (Hershatter and Epstein 2010). These generations tend to be willing to follow rules, respect the values of organizational social responsibility, have high social awareness, and expect that the organization has high ethical and moral standards (Sonier 2012). It causes that the millenials have a concern and interest to be involved in achieving the mission and the goals of the organization (Hershatter and Epstein 2010). The organization can retain the millennials by considering these characteristics. Establishing the value conformity between the organization and the employees can encourage the millennials to move in changing situations. The organization that is able to create the value conformity will be able to move the employees to contribute more in achieving the success of the organization.

As part of the efforts to build the harmonious employment relationships, psychological contracts needs to give the employees confidence that the organization where they work with are able to create a conducive working environment to enhance their knowledge and skills. The opinion supports Schwepker and Good (2007) research which concluded that a conducive work environment encourages employees to be more proactive and add value to the organization. For that reason, the millennial retention strategies need to focus on encouraging them to design the career goals, to plan the career success and to provide the feedback for achieving the subsequent career goals (Seibert et al. 2013). In the early stages, the organization needs to design challenging positions and jobs to be achieved by the millennials. Such achievements require a mastery of technical, social and managerial knowledge to improve job satisfaction (O'Shea et al. 2014). Organization can also increase the millennials involvement by rewarding achievements when they are able to build teams and through training as a process of organizing the organization (Mayfield and Mayfield 2014). The millennials will feel more appreciated if they are given the opportunity to improve their skills and be given more challenging responsibilities (Ruys 2013). They will also be satisfied with their work if their completion of duties can facilitate their need for the achievement of personal work goals with the organizational support (Hakanen and Schaufeli 2012).

In addition to building a conducive working environment and productive working relationships, the organization also need to build a climate that can encourage an effective communication. The current phenomenon shows that the position of managers is largely dominated by baby boomers generation. For the current middle managers positions are dominated by the employees of X generation, while the demographic characteristics of employees who occupy the position of new entry are dominated by the millennial generation. The differences of these characteristics affect the pattern of communication. The organization can do some programs that can bridge the pattern of inter-generational communication for example routinely sharing experience in informal and fun discussion. The organization needs to foster a stronger relationship and information sharing within the organization. Practically, the organization can build a climate that can encourage cooperation by optimizing the process of transfer of knowledge through the workshop activities and the optimization of social media system.

The millennials love the work environments that provide mentorship, rewarding for innovative activities and teamwork (Gilbert 2011). This generation also enjoys the work environment that gives them the authority to complete work, provides opportunities in job rotation and assignments that allow them to collaborate with others outside the organization (Lyons and Kuron 2013). In terms of building employment relationships, the organization can increase the level of engagement of the millennials through a reverse mentoring program that allows the young employees to train the senior managers in technology and social media. Instead, the senior managers can train the millennials about organizational experience and knowledge (Mayfield and Mayfield 2014). This program is not only a bridge in building intergenerational communication and building social capital, but also helping the millennials to grow as leaders.

The organization needs to focus on encouraging the employees especially their involvement in providing innovative advices for the organizational progress. In the era of talent war, the organization needs to find lots of breakthrough in order to maintain the knowledge worker through clear talent development programs as a strong employee value proposition base. The implemented talent development programs need to emphasize to ideal positions that directly relate to business development. The development programs are no longer done similarly and yet they increasingly lead to the needs of each employee. The organization needs to seriously focus on developing talents that support the employees to achieve the capabilities they need including the technical capabilities, professional managerial and leadership. The organization can adopt the blended learning methods that combine the classical learning-based and online learning (Budiharseno 2017). To achieve an optimal learning outcome, it is necessary to set up a learning team that serves to design and organize some training for the employees.

In order to encourage the employees' involvement to provide innovative suggestions, the organization needs to provide the decision-making opportunities. The organization (HR department) needs to design policies that facilitate the employees to be more flexible in making decisions regarding the implementation of operational roles and managerial roles, starting from designing step to execution. The organization also needs to encourage the employees' productivity through the performance assessment based on information technology. It is used as a basis for office automation and employee self-service development. The employees' productivity can also be enhanced by achievement awards, considering the employee expectations especially to the aspects of recognition and self-actualization. The millenials are the generation that wants treatments that can make them feel appreciated and supported. Related to the mentoring programs, the organization needs to focus on non-traditional approaches and based on the use of technology. The mentoring can start by involving the millennials in solving problems and implementing the worthy opinions to do. This method is able to evoke feelings as part of the organization and create a sense of informality (Zemke et al. 2013).

Summary

This chapter presents the development of research in the field of psychological contract as a strategy in managing millennial generation, reviewed from the perspective of social constructivist. This section describes the typical characteristics of millennial generations that need to be considered in designing the effective psychological contracts. One of the strategic aspects of the psychological contracts implementation is related to an understanding of millennial expectations on career development within organizations. Career development is the basis for building the capabilities and resilience of millennial employees in order to give their best contribution to the organization. It can be built by adopting a social constructivist perspective that focuses on aspects of social interaction in the learning process that are capable of encouraging the increasing knowledge, abilities and employee participation of millennials. At the end of this chapter discusses about the mentoring programs that need to be included in the psychological contracts implementation as an effort to retain millennial employees.

References

Aichinger, J., & Barnes, L. (2010). Accounting employee expectation and the psychological contract. *Global Review of Accounting and Finance, 1*(1), 189–202.

Armstrong, M. (2009). *Armstrong's handbook of human resource management practice*. London: Kogan Page.

Bannon, S., Ford, K., & Meltzer, L. (2011). Understanding millennials in the workplace. *The CPA Journal, 81*(11), 61–65.

Bernard, B. (1996). From research to practice: The foundation of the resiliency paradigm. In: *Resiliency in action* (pp. 7–11).

Billet, S. (1995). Workplace learning: It's potential and limitations. *Education and Training, 37* (4), 20–27.

Billet, S. (2001). *Learning in the workplace: Strategies for effective practices*. Sydney: Allen & Unwin.

Billet, S. (2004). Co-participation at work: Learning through work and throughout lives. *Studies in the Education of Adults, 36*(2), 190–205.

Birchall, D., & Lyons, L. (1995). *Creating tommorow's organization: Unlocking the benefits of the future work*. London: Pitman.

Bittner, J. V., & Schipper, J. (2014). Motivational effects and age differences of gamification in product advertising. *Journal of Consumer Marketing, 31*(5), 391–400.

Blashki, K., Nichol, S., Jia, D., & Prompramote, S. (2007). The future is old: Immersive learning with generation Y engineering students. *European Journal of Engineering Education, 32*(4), 409–420.

Bridges, W. (1995). *Jobshift: How to prosper in a workplace without jobs*. London: Nicholas Brealey.

Broadbridge, A. M., Maxwell, G. A., & Ogden, S. M. (2007). Experiences, perceptions and expectations of retail employment for generation Y. *Career Development International, 12*(6), 523–544.

Busby, G., & Gibson, P. (2010). Tourism and hospitality internship experiences overseas: A British perspective. *Journal of Hospitality, Leisure, Sport and Tourism Education, 9*(1), 4–12.

Bryant, P. C. (1995). Predictive validity and test-retest reliability of a measure of resilience. Master's thesis, Georgia Institute of Technology, Atlanta.

Budiharseno, R. S. (2017). Factors affecting online buying behavior on g-market site among international students in busan: A qualitative research. *Arthatama: Journal of Business Management and Accounting, 1*(1), 1–5.

Byster, D. (1988). A critique of career self-reliance. *Career Planning and Adult Development Journal*, 17–27.

Cahoon, B. B. (1995). *Computer skill learning in the workplace: A comparative case study*. Doctoral dissertation, Univeristy of Georgia, Athens, GA.

Callaghan, V., Shen, L., Gardner, M., Shen, R., & Wang, M. (2010). A mixed reality approach to hybrid learning in mixed culture environments. In F. L. Wang, J. Fong, & R. Kwan (Eds.), *Handbook of research on hybrid learning models: Advanced tools, technologies and applications* (pp. 260–283). Hershey, PA: IGI Global.

Caraher, L. (2015). *Millennials and management: The essential guide to making it work at work*. Brookline, MA: Bibliomotion.

Cascio, W. F. (1995). Whither industrial and organizational psychology in changing world of work? *American Psychologist, 50*(11), 928–939.

Chambel, M. J., & Fotinha, R. (2009). Contingencies of contingent employment: psychological contract, job insecurity and employability of contracted workers. *Journal of Work and Organizational Psychology, 25*(3), 207–217.

Chen, M. (2014). The effect of training on employee retention, In: *International Conference on Global Economy, Commerce and Service Science*. Amsterdam: Atlantis Press.

Chocqueel-Mangan, J. (2011). Managing transition. *Training Journal*, 57–61.

Collard, B., Epperheimer, J. W., & Saign, D. (1996). *Career resilience in changing workplace*. ERIC Clearinghouse on Adult, Career, and Vocational Education.

Conner, D. R. (1992). *Managing at the speed of change*. New York: Villard Books.

Cope, J. (2009). Adapt to survive and thrive. *British Journal of Administrative Management, 68,* 26.

Corder, E., & Ronnie, L. (2017). The role of the psychological contract in the motivation of nurses. *Leadership in Health Services, 31*(1), 62–76.

Davydov, V. V., & Kerr, S. T. (1995). The influence of L. S Vygotsky on education theory, research and practice. *Educational Researcher, 25*(3), 12–21.

Deloitte. (2014). *Big demands and high expectations*. Retrieved from https://www2.deloitte.com/content/dam/Deloitte/global/Documents/About-Deloitte/gx-dttl-2014-millennial-survey-report.pdf.

Dhanpat, N., & Parumasur, S. B. (2014). Re-establishing the psychological contract as precusor to employee retention. *Problems and Perspectives in Management, 12*(4), 78–90.

Diplari, A., & Dimou, I. (2010). Public tourism education and training in Greece: A study of necessity for educational restructuring. *Industry and Higher Education, 24*(2), 115–120.

Engestrom, Y. (2001). Expansive learning at work: Toward an activity theoretical reconceptualization. *Journal of Educational and Work, 14*(1), 133–156.

Enos, M. D., Kehrhahn, M. T., & Bell, A. (2003). Informal learning and the transfer of learning: How managers develop proficiency. *Human Resource Development Quarterly, 14*(4), 369–387.

Eraut, M. (2004). The practice of reflection. *Learning in Health and Social Care, 3*(2), 47–52.

Ferri-Reed, J. (2013). Onboarding strategies to supercharge millennial employees. *The Journal for Quality and Participation, 36,* 32–33.

Fenwick, T. (2008). Understanding relations of individual-collective learning in work: A review of research. *Management Learning, 39*(3), 227–243.

Fourie, C., & Vuuren, L. J. V. (1998). Defining and measuring career resilience. *Journal of Industrial Psychology, 24*(3), 52–59.

Freese, C., Schalk, R., & Croon, M. (2011). The impact of organizational change on psychological contract: A longitudinal study. *Personnel Review, 40*(4), 404–422.

Gilbert, J. (2011). The millennials: A new generation of employees, new set of engagement policies. *Ivey Business Journal, 75*(5), 26–29.

Gott, S. (1989). Apprenticeship instruction for real-world tasks: The co-ordination of procedures, mental models, and strategies. In E. Z. Rothhopf (Ed.), *Review of research in education*. American Educational Research Association: Washington, D.C.

Gutfreund, J. (2014). What millennials want in the workplace (and why you should start giving it to them). Forbes. Retrieved January 13, 2014, from https://www.forbes.com/sites/robasghar/2014/01/13/what-millennials-want-in-the-workplace-and-why-you-should-start-giving-it-to-them/.

Hakanen, J. J., & Schaufeli, W. B. (2012). Do burnout and work engagement predict depressive symptoms and life satisfaction? A three-wave seven-year prospective study. *Journal of Affective Disorders, 141*(2–3), 415–424.

Hall, D. T. (1996). Protean careers of the 21st century. *Academy of Management Executives, 10*(4), 8–16.

Hammer, M., & Champy, J. (1994). *Re-engineering the corporation: A Manifest for business revolution*. New York: Brealey.

Handy, C. (1988). *The age of unreason*. Boston: Harvard Business School.

Harigopal, K. (2006). *Management of organizational change: Leveraging transformation* (2nd ed.). New Delhi: Response Books.

Herriot, P., Manning, W. E. G., & Kidd, J. M. (1997). The content of the psychological contract. *British Journal of Management, 8*, 151–162.

Hershatter, A., & Epstein, M. (2010). Millennials and the world of work: An organization and management perspective. *Journal of Business and Psychology, 25*(2), 211–223.

Hosking, D. M., & Bass, A. (2001). constructing changes in relational processes: Introducing a social constructionist approach to change work. *Career Development International, 6*(7), 348–360.

Hughes, J. C. (2008). Human resource management in the hospitality industry. In B. Brotherton, & R. C. Woods (Eds.), *The sage handbook of hospitality management* (pp. 273–302). London: Sage.

Kerka, S. (1993). *Career education for a global economy* (ERIC Digest). Colombus: The Ohio State University, Eric Clearinghouse on Adult, Career and Vocational Education. (Eric Document Reproduction Service No. ED 355457).

Kiechel, W. (1993). How will we work in the year 2000. *Fortune, 127*(10), 38–52.

King, Z. (2003). New or traditional careers? A study of UK graduates preferences. *Human Resource Management Journal, 3*, 5–26.

Kong, H., Wang, S., & Fu, X. (2015). Meeting career expectation: Can it enhance job satisfaction of generation Y? *International Journal of Contemporary Hospitality Management, 27*(1), 147–168.

Kotter, J. P. (1995). *The new rules: How to succed in today's postcorporate world*. New York: Free Press.

Kristof-Brown, A. L. (1996). Person-organizational fit: An Integrative review of its conceptualizations, measurements, and implications. *Personnel Psychology, 49*, 1–49.

Lancaster, L. C., & Stillman, D. (2010). *The M-factor: How the millennial generation is rocking the workplace*. New York: HarperCollins.

Latack, J. C. (1984). Career transitions within organizations: An explanatory study of work, nonwork, and coping strategies. *Organizational Behavior and Human Performance, 34*, 296–322.

Lave, J., & Wenger, E. (1991). *Situated learning: Legitimate peripheral participation*. New York: Cambridge University Press.

Leung, A. S.-M., & Chen, P. W. (2007). Developing counseling psychology in chinese communities in Asia: Indigenous, multicultural, and cross-cultural considerations. *The Counseling Psychologist, 37*(7), 944–966.

London, M. & Mone, E. M. (1987). *Career management and survival in the workplace*. San Fransisco: Jossey-Bass.

London, M. (1983). Career Motivation of full and part time workers in mid and late career. *Academy of Management Review, 8*, 620–630.
Luthar, S., Cicchetti, D., & Becker, B. (2000). The construct of resilience: A critical evaluation and guidelines for future work. *Child Development, 71*(3), 573–575.
Lynch, A. J. (2008). ROI on generation Y employees: Best practice human capital management of generation Y. *Knoxville Chamber*, 1–23.
Lyons, S., & Kuron, L. (2013). Generational differences in the workplace: A review of the evidence and directions for future research. *Journal of Organizational Behavior, 35*, 139–157.
Mannering, K. (2002). *Staying ahead at work*. Mumbai, India: Jaico.
Marsick, V., & Watkins, E. (1999). Envisioning new organisations for learning. In Bould, D. & Garrick, J. (Eds.), Understanding learning at work. London: Routledge.
Maxwell, J. A. (2013). *Qualitative research design: An interactive approach* (3rd ed.). Thousand Oaks, CA: Sage.
Mayer, R. E. (1996). History of instructional psychology. In E. De Corte, & F. E. Weinert (Eds.), *International encyclopaedia of developmental and instructional psychology* (pp 29–33). Pergamon Press.
Mayfield, J. R., & Mayfield, M. R. (2014). Step by step to better performance: Organizational-citizenship behavior can transform employees and the workplace. *Human Resource Management International Digest, 22*(4), 36–39.
Meyer, T. (1996). *Competencies: Currency fot the 21st century*. Randburg: Knowledge Resouces.
Mezirow, J. (1991). *Transformative dimensions in adult learning*. San Fransisco: Jossey-Bass.
Miller, J. (2011). How to Achieve lasting change. *Training Journal*, 58–62.
Moore, S., Grunberg, L., & Krause, A. J. (2015). Generational differences in workplace expectations: A comparison of production and profesional workers. *Current Psychology, 34*(2), 346–362.
Murphy, W. M. (2012). Reverse mentoring at work: Fostering cross-generational learning and developing millennial leaders. *Human Resource Management, 51*(4), 549–574.
Neesham, C. (2007). Authentic learning in business organizations: Opportunities and challenges. *Management and Marketing, 2*(4), 35–42.
O'Donohue, W. (2009). Linking psychological contract type and power distance orientation to exit, voice, loyalty and neglect behavior. In: *Proceeding of the British Academy of Management Conference*. Retrieved from https://research-repository.griffith.edu.au/bitstream/handle/10072/40616/68157_1.pdf.
O'Neill, B. S., & Adya, M. (2007). Knowledge sharing and the psychological contract: Managing knowledge workers across different stages of employment. *Journal of Managerial Psychology, 22*(4), 411–436.
O'Shea, D., Monaghan, S., & Ritchie, T. D. (2014). Early career attitudes and satisfaction during recession. *Journal of Managerial Psychology, 29*, 226–245.
Osibanjo, A. O., Oyewunmi, A. E., & Ojo, S. I. (2014). Career Development as a determinant of organizational growth: Modelling the relationship between these constructs in the nigerian banking industry. *American International Journal of Social Science, 3*(7), 67–76.
Park, J., & Gursoy, D. (2012). Generation effects on work engagement among U.S. hotel employees. *International Journal of Hospitality Management, 31*, 1195–1202.
Pyoria, P., Ojala, S., Saari, T., & Jarvinen, K. M. (2017). The millennial generation: A new breed of labour? *Sage Open, 7*(1), 1–14. https://doi.org/10.1177/2158244017697158.
Raines, C. (2002). Managing Millennials generations at work. Retrieved June 2016, from http://www.generationsatwork.com/articles/millennials.htm.
Resnick, L. (1987). Learning in school and out. *Educational Researcher, 16*(9), 13–20.
Riccardi, M. J., Jenkins, D., & Strawn, T. (2014). Mentoring in the workplace: Millennials demand a new approach. *Business Strategies*.
Rickwood, R. R. (2002). *Enabling high-risk clients: Exploring a career resiliency model*. Canada: British Columbia.
Roehling, P. V., Vander Kooi, T. L., Dykema, S., Quisenberry, B., & Vandlen, C. (2011). Engaging the millennial generation in class discussions. *College Teaching, 59*(1), 1–6.

Rosethorn, H. (2009). *The employer brand: Keeping the faith with the deal*. Farnham: Gower Publishing.
Rousseau, D. M. & Schalk, R. (2000). *Psychological contracts in employment: Cross-national perspectives*. Thousand Oaks: Sage.
Ruys, J. (2013). *Leadership behaviors and workplace factors millennial workers find important for job satisfaction*. Doctoral dissertation, Retrieved from ProQuest Dissertations and Theses database. (UMI No. 3573678).
Savickas, M. L. (2002). Career construction: A developmental theory of vocational behavior. In Brown, D. (Ed.), *Career development and counseling: putting theory and research to work*. Hoboken: Wiley.
Sawchuk, P. H. (2003). Informal learning as a speech-exchange system: implications for knowledge production, power and social transformation. *Discourse and Society, 14*(3), 291–307.
Schwepker, C. H., & Good, D. J. (2007). Sales management's influence on employment and training in developing an ethical sales force. *Journal Personal Selling Sales Manage, 27*(4), 325–339.
Seibert, S. E., Kraimer, M. L., Holtom, B. C., & Pierotti, A. J. (2013). Even the best laid plans sometimes go askew: Career self-management processes, career shocks, and the decision to pursue graduate education. *Journal of Applied Psychology, 98*(1), 169–182.
Smith, P. J. (2000). Flexible delivery and apprentice training: Preferences, problems and challenges. *Journal of Vocational Education and Training: The Vocational Aspect of Education, 52*(3), 483–502.
Stevens, M., & Campion, M. (1994). The knowledge, skill and ability requirements for teamwork: Implications for human resource management. *Journal of Management, 20*, 503–530.
Sonier, D. (2012). Gen xers and millennials still want work-life balance. *Healthcare Design, 12*(2), 20–22.
Strauss, W., & Howe, N. (1991). *Generations: The history of America's future, 1584 to 2069*. New York: Quill/William Morrow.
Sujansky, J. G., & Ferri-Reed, J. (2010). Motivate your millennial employees. *Supervision, 71*(4), 13–15.
Super, D. E. (1980). A life-span, life-space approach to career development. *Journal of Vocational Behavior, 16*, 282–298.
Taylor, P. (2014). *The next America*. New York: Public Affairs.
Thompson, C., & Gregory, J. B. (2012). Managing millennials: A Framework for improving attraction, motivation, and retention. *The Psychologist-Manager Journal, 15*(4), 237–246.
Tomprou, M., & Nikolau, I. (2011). Model of psychological creation upon organizational entry. *Career Developmental International, 16*(4), 342–363.
Tractenberg, L., Steumer, J., & Zolingen, S. (2002). Career counseling in the emerging psot-industrial society. *International Journal for Education and Vocational Guidance, 2*, 5–99.
Vanmeter, R. A., Grisaffe, D. B., Chonko, L. B., & Roberts, J. A. (2013). Generation Y's ethical ideology and its potential workplace implications. *Journal of Business Ethics, 117*(1), 93–109.
Vincent, E. (2012). Generation gaps in the workplace: Making friends with technology and millennials. *American Medical Writers Association Journal, 27*(3), 144.
Vos, A. D., & Freese, C. (2011). Sensemaking during organizational entry: Changes in newcomer information seeking and the relationship with psychological contract fulfillment. *Journal of Occupational and Organizational Psychology, 84*, 288–314.
Vygotsky, L. (1978). *Mind in society*. Cambridge: Harvard University Press.
Walsh, D. (2015). Millennials in the workplace: For employers, words to the wise from the Y's. *Crain's Detroit Business, 30*(13), 11–16.
Weiler, A. (2005). Information-seeking behavior in generation Y students: Motivation, critical thinking, and learning theory. *Journal of Academic Librarianship, 31*(1), 46–53.
Winograd, M., & Hais, M. D. (2011). *Millennial momentum: How a new generation is remaking America*. Piscataway: Rutgers University Press.
Woolfolk, A. (2004). *Educational psychology* (9th ed.). London: Allyn and Bacon.

Wright, P. A. (2003). *The human resource-firm performance relationship: Methodological and theoretical challenges, a guide to the human impact of modern working practices*. London: Wiley.

Young, A. M., & Hinesly, M. (2014). Infographics as a business communication tool: An empirical investigation of user preference, comprehension and efficiency. Retrieved January 12, 2014, from SSRN https://ssrn.com/abstract=2548559 or http://dx.doi.org/10.2139/ssrn.2548559.

Zemke, R., Raines, C., & Filipczak, B. (2013). *Generations at work: Managing the clash of boomers, genxers, and genyers in the workplace* (2nd ed.). New York: Amacom.

Ade Ima Anggraeni (PhD) is a faculty member at Jenderal Soedirman University, Purwokerto, Central Java, Indonesia. Her research focuses on employment relations, psychological contract, talent development and career resilience. She has presented numerous articles at national and international conferences and published several articles in reputable international journals.

Chapter 15
Knowing Me is the Key: Implications of Anticipatory Psychological Contract for Millennials' Retention

Nada Zupan, Katarina Katja Mihelič and Darija Aleksić

Abstract Millennial talents are an important source of competitive advantage in an increasingly digitalized and globalized business environment. However, many employers report challenges related to attracting, managing and especially retaining young talents. Often, individual preferences and needs are not known and(or) sufficiently considered, which creates tensions and increases the risk of losing young talents. We explore Millennials' employment expectations with the anticipatory psychological contract in two under investigated contexts—Central and Eastern Europe and East Asia. A quantitative research design is used to analyse the features of anticipatory psychological contract, employing samples of undergraduate business students. Findings reveal that Millennials prefer balanced types of anticipatory psychological contract for both employee and employer obligations, followed by relational and transactional types. The analysis uncovered certain regional differences as well. In addition, potential psychological contract breach situations are identified for a Slovenian sample when comparing students' and employers' expectations. Based on these insights we propose relevant retention strategies and practices for young talent retention.

Keywords Anticipatory psychological contracts · Employment expectations
Millennials · Psychological contract breach · Talent retention
Central and Eastern Europe · East Asia

Introduction

How to keep employees engaged and interested in staying in the company has become a pervasive issue for HR professionals, managers, and leaders. Specifically, in recent years, interest has grown in terms of how to retain the youngest employees, often referred to as Millennials. These young talents with unique values,

N. Zupan (✉) · K. K. Mihelič · D. Aleksić
Faculty of Economics, University of Ljubljana, Ljubljana, Slovenia
e-mail: nada.zupan@ef.uni-lj.si

M. Coetzee et al. (eds.), *Psychology of Retention*,
https://doi.org/10.1007/978-3-319-98920-4_15

beliefs and expectations, are changing existing HR practices. Many suggest that due to their distinct characteristics Millennials need a special consideration with regard to talent management models used by their employers (e.g. McCracken et al. 2016; Festing and Schäfer 2014). Stereotypically, Millennials are characterized as disloyal, difficult to work with, entitled, and individualistic. Unlike previous generations, they put much less emphasis on work and more on hobbies and leisure time. Born in times of increased globalization and digital transformation, they are not afraid of changes. They have witnessed that job stability and working for a single employer in the entire working life are becoming outdated. They appreciate varied and challenging tasks and they build their career based on their personal development and not loyalty to an employer. We see these characterizations in popular press and everyday discussions. Nevertheless, academic research about Millennials at work both confirms and disputes some of these claims (e.g. Twenge 2010; Cogin 2012; Becton et al. 2014; Kuron et al. 2015; Stewart et al. 2017). This confusion about who the Millennials are and what they want is calling for further and more theory-based research.

Millennials' expectations regarding employment can be approached with a psychological contract (PC) perspective, which has proven to be a useful concept for researching talent management (Gallardo-Gallardo et al. 2015), and particularly talent retention (Festing and Schäfer 2014; D'Amato and Herzfeld 2008). A PC is usually referred to as employee and employer perceptions regarding their mutual employment obligations (Rousseau 1995), they are subjective and implicit. Many studies show that a breach of the PCs leads to lower employee satisfaction and commitment as well as higher turnover intentions (Zhao et al. 2007). Therefore, it is important to study PCs to understand and manage employee expectations regarding the employment relationship. In addition, anticipatory psychological contracts (APC), which refer to individuals' pre-employment beliefs about expected employee and future employer obligations, provide useful insights into young talents' expectations (e.g. De Vos et al. 2009). Although they are often based on incomplete information (Sherman and Morely 2015) and naïve (Dulac et al. 2008), entrants into labour market use APCs to evaluate relationship with prospective employers (Sherman and Morley 2015). As such, APCs have important implications for talent management, especially for recruitment and retention.

Thus far, most of what is known about Millennials comes from studies conducted in developed and mostly Western countries, while researchers rarely address other geographical contexts. In addition, extant studies on APC focus mostly on what prospective employees expect and the employers' perspective has been largely neglected. The main objective of this chapter is to deepen our understanding about expectations that Millennials have about their future work and employment relationship and how those might affect their retention. Thus, we intend to complement the existing literature by addressing the following research questions: (1) What are the features of Millennials' APC in transitional countries in Central and Eastern Europe (CEE) and East Asia (EA)?, (2) What are the differences among Millennials, in regards to APC, employment preferences, demographics and geographical location?, and (3) What are the potential risks for psychological contract breach and increased turnover intentions once Millennials get their first employment? In order to answer these questions, a quantitative research design was used. The data for the first study were collected from Millennials in two CEE (Slovenia and Poland) and EA countries (China and South Korea), addressing the first two research questions. Additionally, employers' data were collected in Slovenia on their perception of PCs for Millennials for the second study to answer the third research question.

In what follows, we describe the theoretical background regarding Millennials at work and retention challenges faced by employers. The last theoretical part focuses on establishing the link between PC, PC breach and turnover intensions. Next, we present results of both studies, followed by a discussion and practical implications for retention management.

Theoretical Background

Millennials and Work

Because Millennials are changing the nature of relationships and ways of working in organizations, academic interest in their characteristics has grown over the years. Unlike previous generations, Millennials have embraced the "work to live" philosophy of life (Johnson and Johnson 2010), as evident from a lower work centrality (Smola and Sutton 2002; Twenge et al. 2010) and a desire for more leisure time and work-life balance (Kuron et al. 2015). Overall, research finds that Millennials are more extrinsically motivated (Twenge et al. 2010). A recent empirical study confirms that they perceive as the most important extrinsic work values, such as work-life balance, salary, job security, but intrinsic values such as achievement, interesting work and advancement are also important to them (Kuron et al. 2015). Especially learning, development and advancement have been identified among top work values for Millennials (Lyons and Kuron 2014; Zupan et al. 2015), but it seems their wish to enhance professional skills through training and mentoring is often linked to a desire to be flexible and remain marketable (Holden and Harte 2004; Cennamo and Gardner 2008). While they are willing to invest effort in their work and demonstrate excellent performance, at the same time they want much in return, and quickly (Winter and Jackson 2016). Another important thing they look for in a potential employer is a meaningful and fulfilling job (Ng et al. 2010).

According to recent research, young Millennials prefer organizations that stress a socially responsible culture and a work environment characterized by collegiality (Kuron et al. 2015). They want to get involved in decision-making (Luscombe et al. 2013). Millennials have different communication patterns and feel most comfortable using text-based or computer-mediated communication (Pearson et al. 2010). They are self-centred and stubborn and want to climb the hierarchical ladder quickly. In fact, seeking opportunities for fast career advancement is Millennials' high priority thus confirming that they are ambitious (Ng et al. 2010). They also expect investments of their employers into career management (Kong et al. 2015).

In terms of relationships at work, they want a greater level of support from managers (Ng et al. 2010), the development and maintenance of high-quality work relationships (Kong et al. 2015), they appreciate feedback (Graen and Schiemann 2013) and praise (Shaw and Fairhurst 2008). They do not want to be micromanaged (Broadbridge et al. 2007), although they may seek detailed instructions on how to complete their tasks (Hershatter and Epstein 2010). They tend to challenge authority (Gursoy et al. 2013) and prefer their managers to be open and positive (Broadbridge et al. 2007).

Challenges for Retaining Millennials

Millennials are the fastest-growing segment of the workforce, with a prediction that they will comprise 35% of workforce by 2020 (Manpower Group 2016). They possess the talent and the intellect to achieve their goals; thereby Millennials will most likely be one of the greatest assets of organizations in the future (McCracken et al. 2016). The challenge regarding retention mostly stems in the fact that Millennials are known to be rather disloyal to the organization and appear to be prone to switching jobs and/or careers (Gursoy et al. 2008; Thompson and Gregory 2012). Job mobility is a new normal for them (Lyons et al. 2015), indicating that changing jobs every few years does not represent a burden but rather a challenge and an opportunity to learn something new. According to the Pew Research Centre (2010), nearly 60% of employed Millennials have already changed jobs at least once in their careers, indicating that they do not plan to stay at the same organization throughout their career. Many organizations are unable to retain these young professional, thereby losing resources due to unwanted turnover of Millennials and lost productivity (Smith and Galbraith 2012; Sujansky and Ferri-Reed 2009).

It seems that because Millennials are the newest employees in the workforce, employers do not have enough experience with managing these young talents (Campione 2015). Namely, organizations are mostly failing to create work environment that leverages the potential of Millennials but does not alienate the rest of the workforce (Spiro 2006; Winter and Jackson 2016).

These young talents have high expectations with regard to the organizations they want to work for, particularly involving the importance of working conditions (e.g., autonomy, social involvement), opportunities (e.g., career advancement), and flexibility (e.g., providing the freedom to maintain a better balance between work and personal goals) organizations can offer (Ng et al. 2010; Twenge et al. 2010). Millennials also value fairness, equitable treatment and honoring any promises made to employees and are prone to leave the job if they do not get it (Luscombe et al. 2013). According to Park and Gursoy (2012), young generations who are highly engaged in work activities will be more satisfied with their job and will thereby show less turnover intention than older generations. Similarly, Thompson and Gregory (2012) argue that "Millennials expect organizations to continually re-engage them and remind them why they should stay" (p. 240).

Scholars argue that Millennials value job security less then members of previous generations (Hart 2006) and some studies report lack of loyalty and work ethic (Del Campo et al. 2011; Cogin 2012). Yet, there is recent evidence that shows that uncertainty in economy and fewer job opportunities have caused Millenials to desire greater stability (Deloitte 2017). Compared to previous years, the percentage of Millennials who expect to leave the employing company in the coming two years was in 2016 substantially lower, potentially indicating an increase in loyalty.

Psychological Contract Breach as a Framework to Study Retention of Millennials

Scholars use psychological contract perspective to study talent management (Höglund 2012; Rodwell et al. 2015) and retention (Festing and Schäfer 2014; Blomme et al. 2010; de Vos and Meganck 2008; Kraak et al. 2017). It is a particularly useful concept to study retention due to the established link between the breach of psychological contract and employee attitudes, including job satisfaction, commitment and turnover intentions (Robinson and Morrison 2000; Zhao et al. 2007; Dulac et al. 2008; Tekleab et al. 2013). For retention management, existing PC studies focus on how employees perceive employer's obligations regarding pay, job security, personal development etc. PCs are usually classified along two dimensions, transactional and relational, but Rousseau (2000) added the balanced type to reflect changes in the employment relationships and labour market, such as the need for flexibility, new forms of work, knowledge economy, and globalization. Transactional PCs are short-term, narrow with regard to tasks and responsibilities, and mostly materialistically-oriented. Relational PCs are based on loyalty and stability and build relationships beyond economic exchange. Balanced PCs are dynamic and open-ended employment arrangements that include both the economic success of the firm and employee opportunities to develop career advantages inside organization and externally. Research suggests that relational PCs are positively and transactional PCs negatively related to work outcomes and attitudes (Zhao et al. 2007). Thus, transactional PCs increase turnover intentions.

For retention, the next important concept is a breach of the PC. It occurs with the employee's recognition that the employer has not fulfilled one or more obligations (Morrison and Robinson 1997). Following the logic of the social exchange and the norm of reciprocity, when employees perceive that a breach occurs they respond with negative feelings and behaviours (Taylor and Tekleab 2004). Employees may perceive a breach of PC as a negative event at work (Zhao et al. 2007) and develop feelings of anger and betrayal that turn breach into perceived violation of the PC

(Robinson and Morrison 2000). PC breach and/or violation are important concepts explaining negative employee attitudes and outcomes, including turnover (Zhao et al. 2007; Conway and Briner 2005).

Research has confirmed that young people without much working experience enter the employment relationship with high and less realistic expectations (De Vos et al. 2003; Thomas and Anderson 1998). According to the life span theory, they are also less capable to manage disappointments at work due to lower ability to regulate emotions (Heckhausen et al. 2010). Therefore, a PC breach/violation seems to be more harmful to younger employees than to older ones (Bal and Smit 2012). D'Amato and Herzfeldt (2008) summary of research findings on generational differences confirm that the young are keener on moving to a good opportunity elsewhere if their expectations are not met with current employer. Bal et al. (2008) performed a meta-analysis of the research on PC breach and job attitudes with age as a moderator. They confirmed that PC breach leads to higher intentions to leave and especially younger workers may respond to contract breaches by becoming less attached to the organization. Bloome et al. (2010) also found that the younger the respondents, the less committed they were to their organization and the more likely they were to leave if they perceived the breach of PC. In their study, job content appeared to be the most significant predictor of the intention to leave, followed to a much lesser extent by promotion opportunities and salary.

Study 1: Insights into Millennials' APC: An Empirical Analysis

Methodology

To answer our first two research questions regarding the characteristics of APC, we used a quantitative research design. Data were collected from April to September 2015 by using a convenience sample of undergraduate business students. The relevance of a student sample for predicting expectations at work has been confirmed by Taris et al. (2006) and Luscombe et al. (2013) who have not discovered any significant differences between students and those employed belonging to the same age cohort (Generation Y in their studies). Our sample includes countries for which there is little data on APC: Slovenia, Poland, China, and South Korea. To ensure comparability of the data, the survey was conducted in leading business schools that have international quality accreditations or strong international ties: University of Ljubljana in Slovenia, University of Warsaw in Poland, Shanghai University of International Business and Economics, Beijing Foreign Studies University, and Southwestern University of Finance and Economics (Chengdu) in China, and Chonnam National University (Gwangju) and Kyungpook National University (Daegu) in South Korea.

The questionnaires were administered in the local language after a typical translation—back translation procedure for Slovenian, Polish, Mandarin, and Korean. In each country, we had the country representative researchers who were responsible for distribution of the survey to target participants. In Slovenia, an Internet-based survey was used and in South Korea, Internet-based survey was supplemented by a paper version, while Polish and Chinese students were offered only a paper version of survey. The decision to use different types of survey for collecting data was based on the experiences of the country representative in terms of administering surveys and getting adequate response rates among students. The student participation was voluntary and anonymous.

The aim of the study was to get an insight into students' attitudes and their views of employers. Thus, Rousseau's (2008) PCI—Psychological Contract Inventory—was used to measure the expectations regarding employee and employer obligations. Besides the typical transactional and relational types of PC, this inventory includes a balanced type of PC, which reflects changes in the labour market and fits well with the characteristics of Millennials. The expectations are grouped in seven dimensions and three types of PCs: transactional (short-term and narrow dimensions), relational (loyalty and stability dimensions) and balanced (development, performance and external marketability dimensions). Each dimension features four items and each item is scored on a 5-point scale from 1-not at all to 5-to a great extent. Since we explored APC of students, they were asked to what extent they expect to make the listed obligations to their future employer and to what extent they expect their future employer to make the listed obligations to them. We calculated aggregate means for PC types and dimensions as proposed by the author of the instrument. In addition, students were also asked about the following employment preferences regarding: company size (small, medium, large), sector (public, private), entrepreneurial orientation (i.e. owning a company as opposed to working for someone else), and type of job (expert, managerial).

Results

Altogether, 953 Millennials responded to the survey; 166 questionnaires were excluded from further analysis due to missing values. The final sample consisted of 180 respondents in Slovenia, 209 in Poland, 177 in China and 221 in South Korea. Thus, in the present study, we employ a sample that consists of 787 Millennials, who are pursuing business education. In terms of demographic characteristics of the respondents, 41% of are male and 59% female, most of respondents were born from 1992 and 1994. As indicated above, the data were gathered from business students in four selected countries, two from Central and Eastern Europe (i.e. Slovenia and Poland) and two from East Asia (i.e. China and South Korea). 52% of respondents in the sample belong to the CE European sample, while 48% comprise the East Asian sample.

In terms of future employment preferences, 22% of respondents would prefer to work in a small company, 50% in a medium-sized and 28% in a large company. We also inquired about the preferred type of job. Specifically, 51% of Millennials prefer an expert job, and 49% executive/leadership position. Further, 55% would prefer to have their own company (self-employed), while 45% prefer working in an existing company. In terms of sector, 29% would prefer being employed in a public and 71% in private sector.

In answering the first research question, we look into the dimensions of APC based on two perspectives. The first one includes Millennials' perceptions of what is a future employer obliged to offer them (i.e. employer obligations), while the second one contains Millennials' views of what commitments they are willing to make to a potential employer (i.e. employee obligations). In both instances, we asked respondents to consider potential employers, as they were pursuing education at the time and will only enter the labour market in the future.

In Table 15.1, we report the average values of seven dimensions of obligations, employers' and employees' respectively. Findings reveal that Millennials prefer balanced types of APC for both employee and employer obligations, followed by relational and transactional. For employee obligations, all three dimensions of the balanced APC got a higher average score than other relational and transactional dimensions. The highest score of 4.21 is for the dimension development, which included four items: *seeking out developmental opportunities that enhance my value to this employer, building skills to increase my value to this organization, making myself increasingly valuable to my employer and actively seeking internal opportunities for training and development*. Interestingly, the second highest score (3.89) is for the dimension external marketability, which includes *building skills and seeking assignments to increase employability, developing contacts outside the organization and increasing visibility on the market*. Performance support dimension is the third highest score and it pertains to willingness to accept more demanding performance standards and challenges. Within the relational type APC, loyalty scored higher (3.48) than stability (3.05). Loyalty is described by *protecting company image, commitment, care and sacrifice for the organization*, and stability *by remaining with this organization for a long time or indefinitely, continuing to work here and making no plans to work anywhere else*. The least difference between the scores for dimensions is within the transactional type of APC, both short-term (2.85) and narrow (2.76) scored below 3, indicating that students mostly do not expect to quit/leave whenever they want and have no future obligations to this employer, or have narrowly defined tasks and responsibilities.

For employer obligations, which with the exception of stability mirrors the obligations for employees, development again got the highest score (4.19) of all dimensions, but the second highest is stability (4.05). Stability includes four items: *secure employment, wages and benefits I can count on, steady employment, and stable benefits for employees' families*. The third highest score is for performance support (3.91), followed by external marketability (3.69). Again, score for both transactional dimensions are close or below 3, with short-term scoring the lowest (2.48) and narrow (3.03).

Table 15.1 Comparing students' expectations regarding employee and employer obligations

Types of PCs	Dimensions of PC	Employee obligations		Employer obligations	
		Mean	*St. dev.*	*Mean*	*St. dev.*
Transactional		2.81	(0.64)	2.76	(0.59)
	Short-term	2.85	(0.87)	2.48	(0.74)
	Narrow	2.76	(0.76)	3.03	(0.77)
Relational		3.27	(0.53)	3.79	(0.74)
	Loyalty	3.48	(0.71)	3.55	(0.85)
	Stability	3.05	(0.71)	4.05	(0.82)
Balanced		3.95	(0.51)	3.93	(0.71)
	Performance support	3.75	(0.63)	3.91	(0.78)
	Development	4.21	(0.61)	4.19	(0.76)
	External marketability	3.89	(0.75)	3.69	(0.91)

[a]N = 787

The second research question entailed the differences among Millennials in regards to APC, employment preferences, gender and geographical location. First, we investigated the differences between male and female Millennials and found that their assessments of obligations of potential employers differ only in one APC dimension. Specifically, for the short-term dimension, there are significant differences between males and females, with the score being lower for females ($M = 2.44$), meaning that the employers' obligations related to short-term dimension with a mostly materialistic focus are more important for males ($M = 2.51$) then they are for females ($t = -1.204$; $p = 0.038$). In addition, male and female Millennials expectations differ only regarding the employers' obligations for the transactional type of APC ($t = -1.736$; $p = 0.055$). Women expect this type more as an element of their employment relationship ($M = 2.792$ for female; $M = 2.71$ for male). We further checked the gender differences in regards to employment preferences (Table 15.2). The only marginally significant difference was in the sector ($t = -2.714$; $p = 0.109$).

To further explore the potential differences among Millennials regarding their APC and employment preferences, we conducted a two-step cluster analysis. In terms of geographical location, we grouped responses in two categories, merging data from Poland and Slovenia in one group (termed Europe) and joining data for Chinese and Korean respondents, which represents another group (termed Asia). The analysis of the sample data identified two relatively equally-sized clusters of young talents, one comprising 50.1% (394) and the other one 49.9% (392) respondents. The ration of largest to smallest cluster was acceptable at 1.01. We used the following 8 variables: psychological contract types, geographical location, employment preferences (i.e. public/private sector, company size, entrepreneurial tendencies, type of job).

Table 15.2 Gender differences in employment preferences

Gender	Company size			Sector		Entrepreneurial orientation		Type of job	
	Small (%)	Medium (%)	Large (%)	Public (%)	Private (%)	Someone else's (%)	Self-employed (%)	Expert (%)	Managerial (%)
Male	24	46	30	34	66	45	55	51	49
Female	20	52	28	29	71	44	56	49	51

Based upon the analysis two distinct clusters of Millennials were revealed (Table 15.3). We termed the first cluster the EA cluster and the second one the CEE cluster. Interesting differences were uncovered with regard to the types of psychological contract regarding employer obligations and employment characteristics. Specifically, we find that Millennials in EA have a strong tendency for balanced psychological contracts, followed by a relational contract. The average values for these two types are high and lie at 4.06 and 4.03 respectively. The elements of transactional contract received the least recognition in the EA as well as the CEE cluster and the average scores were practically identical, demonstrating that short-term and narrow obligations in terms of limited involvement and little training are not desired and expected. The CEE cluster differs from the EA one in terms of relatively lower average scores attributed to balanced (3.80) and relational types (3.56).

Finally, while the two clusters are similar in the fact that respondents in CEE as well as EA tend to prefer working in a medium sized company, differences were observed in other preferences, one of them being the lower preference of CEE Millennials for working in public sector as opposed to EA Millennials. While CE Europeans are practically unanimous in their preference to work in private sector, in EA only about a half of respondents prefer this option to public sector work. Two thirds of respondents in CEE would prefer an executive position, while two thirds of EA respondents are more keen on expert positions. A preference for an entrepreneurial career was indicated by 69% of CEE and 58% of EA Millennials.

Study 2: Insights into a Potential Breach of PC for Millennials—The Example of Slovenia

Methodology

To explore the third research question, which considered the potential risks for psychological contract breach for Millennials, we report results from a supplemental study, conducted in one of the countries, Slovenia. In order to identify possible elements of APC where a breach could occur due to differences in expected mutual obligations, data were gathered from employers in Slovenia.[1] Again, the PC Inventory questionnaire by Rousseau (2008) was used for employers as one part of a broader study on talent management. A convenience sample was used in order to target companies that are active on the labor market. Through partnership with one of the leading private employment agencies, which distributed the questionnaire among their customers, responses from HR managers in 101 companies were collected. The final sample therefore consists of mostly private

[1]Quantitative data were collected by two master students at University of Ljubljana, Slovenia as a part of their graduation thesis.

Table 15.3 Results of cluster analysis

Preference and type of APC	Cluster 1 (CEE)	Cluster 2 (EA)
Prefer to work in private sector (in %)	97.4	55.3
Ideal career type (as % of all career types)	Managerial (64.8)	Expert (64.2)
Prefer to have entrepreneurial career (in %)	69.1	58.6
Preferred company size (as % of all firms)	Medium (58.4)	Medium (40.9)
Relational (employer) (scale: 1–5)[a]	Below average (3.56)	Above average (4.03)
Balanced (employer) (scale: 1–5)[b]	Below average (3.80)	Average (4.06)
Transactional (employer) (scale: 1–5)[c]	Average (2.75)	Above average (2.76)

Note [a]mean equals to 3.80, [b]mean equals to 3.93, [c]mean equals to 2.76

sector companies (81%), about half of them are considered large employers by Slovenian standards (over 250 employees), 28% medium (from 50 to 249 employees) and 10% each small (10–49 employees) and micro companies (up to 9 employees). Data was gathered from January to February 2017.

Results

When we compare HR managers' and students' opinions regarding employer and employee obligations, we observe some differences when looking at PC dimensions (Table 15.4). For both, HR managers and students, development got a score slightly above 4 for both employee and employer obligations and it is thus the highest scored dimension overall. For these expectations regarding development, it also seems that there is good agreement both between and within groups. However, if we look at individual items, HR managers expect more with regard to learning as employee obligation and students with promotion and development opportunities as employer's obligation. The biggest differences between HRM managers and students expectations are for the dimension external marketability. While students expect that building on external marketability is a strong element of employer obligations (mean score of 4.02), HR managers do not (mean score of 2.98). Students also expect the employer to build employee external marketability much more than HR managers see it as an employer obligation. Quite the opposite are the results for performance support, where HR managers expect high performance and constant striving to increase it to be an obligation for both employees and employers much more than students do (the highest score for dimensions from HR managers 4.16 for employer and 4.00 for employee obligations, while scores for students are 3.59 for both obligations).

For relational dimensions, scores are rather similar for stability, but for loyalty HR managers score much higher than students. Among four items in this dimension, it is the care for company's reputation, which contributes the most to this difference for employee obligations. Protecting company's image is the most

Table 15.4 Comparing HR managers' and students' expectations regarding employee and employer obligations

		Employee obligations		Employer obligations	
		HR managers	Students	HR managers	Students
Short-term	*Mean*	2.34	2.91	2.29	2.46
	St. dev.	(1.15)	(0.97)	(1.15)	(0.29)
Narrow	*Mean*	2.35	2.92	2.29	2.77
	St. dev.	(0.94)	(0.63)	(0.93)	(0.62)
Loyalty	*Mean*	3.64	3.04	3.72	3.09
	St. dev.	(0.89)	(0.58)	(0.93)	(0.61)
Stability	*Mean*	3.41	3.30	4.06	3.95
	St. dev.	(0.98)	(0.67)	(0.95)	(0.84)
Performance	*Mean*	4.00	3.59	4.16	3.59
	St. dev.	(0.78)	(0.60)	(0.83)	(0.66)
Development	*Mean*	4.14	4.15	4.08	4.13
	St. dev.	(0.77)	(0.64)	(0.88)	(0.81)
External marketability	*Mean*	2.98	4.02	3.39	3.77
	St. dev.	(1.05)	(0.78)	(1.07)	(0.93)

important obligation for HR managers (score 4.43). For employer obligations, the difference stems from students' lower evaluation of obligations for personal concerns and well-being of employees. Within the four items for the stability dimension, it seems that while HR managers see secure employment and wages as stronger obligation, students perceive benefits for the family to be important.

For both transactional dimensions (short-term and narrow), students' expectations are higher than HR managers' for employer and employee obligations are. A more detailed look at items in each dimension shows that students expect employers more to have a job for them only for a short period of time and only as long as they need them. In addition, they expect employees to be more free to leave the job when they desire and without any future obligations. For the narrow dimension, students expect employee and employer obligations to be more characterized by only limited involvement in the organization and a limited set of duties.

If only employer obligations for all items are considered, we can identify potential PC breach situations (Fig. 15.1) which could lead to higher turnover intentions. Out of seven items with a possibility for unmet employee expectations, there are all four items from the dimension external marketability; students expect employers to offer to them opportunities and contacts for potential work outside the organization and to develop externally marketable skills. Students also expect opportunities for promotion, development within the firm, and family benefits to a larger extent than employers are expected to provide them. A risk of the potential breach of PC leading to violation and possible turnover is higher because most of these seven items rank among the top expectations of the students from their employer.

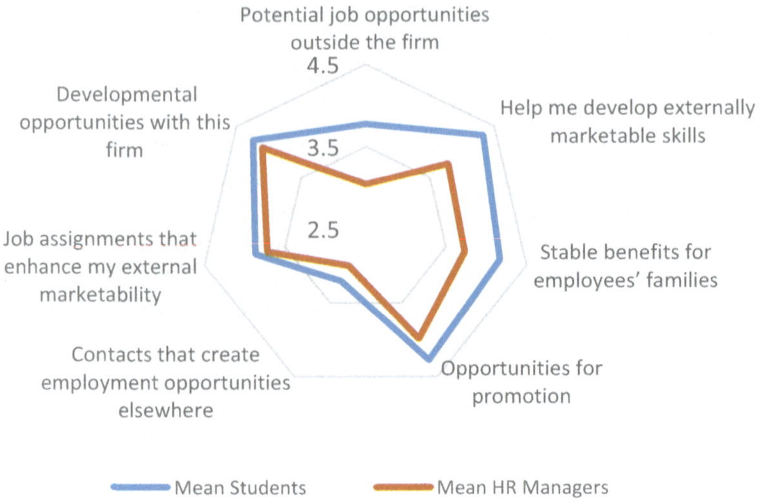

Fig. 15.1 Items with the largest difference between what students expect from employers and what employers offer

Discussion, Limitations and Suggestions for Future Research

In order to solve challenges pertaining to retention of young talents, it is important to understand their employment expectations and our study offers several insights in this regard with important implications for talent retention. In the first study, we analysed the APC and employment preferences of undergraduate students from leading business schools in two CEE countries (Slovenia and Poland) and two EA countries (China and South Korea). Results show that the preferred type of APC for Millennials in these four countries is the balanced one, followed by the relational and the transactional as the last one. These holds true for both employee and employer obligations, although the difference between the scores for balanced and relational type is larger for employee (0.48) than employer (0.14) obligations. The difference can be attributed to relatively lower score for external marketability and higher for stability for employer compared to employee obligations. Results are somewhat surprising as some previous research suggested that Millennials would prefer more transactional than relational PCs (e.g. Bal and Kooij 2011). Since transactional PCs are linked to higher turnover intentions, our results could be somewhat encouraging regarding Millennials' retention.

Overall, results demonstrate relatively high expectations regarding balanced and relational dimensions of APC. Detected high expectations are confirming some previous studies (Ng et al. 2010). Yet, high expectations could pose a challenge from the retention management perspective. Winter and Jackson (2016) report that employers see these high expectations as unrealistic and the main reason for higher turnover as they cannot be met by employers. Some managers even talked about excessive and unhealthy expectations implying a mismatch with realities of employment relationships. The challenge of meeting high expectations can be also depicted from the results of our second study on comparing Millennials and HR managers' expectations regarding employer obligations.

Additional insights can be drawn from analysing PC dimensions. Based on our results, performance support scores are relatively low compared to other dimensions, possibly indicating lower work centrality mentioned by other studies (e.g. Twenge 2010). However, lower work centrality is supposedly linked to more transactional contracts (Bal and Kooij 2011) which scored significantly lower than relational and balanced in our sample. This may suggest that in developing employment expectations, lower work centrality is offset with Millennials' strong ambition and needs for advancement and development. In addition, stability has a relatively high score among APC dimensions for employer obligations. This could be a sign that Millennials are not necessarily having inherently strong turnover intentions. However, willingness to stay in the company may decrease if their expectations are not met (Campione 2015). Even more worrisome are highly expressed expectations regarding external marketability (especially for employee obligations). Combined with the fact that stability is much more expected from employers than is seen as an employee obligation by Millennials, these indicate the risk of undesired turnover. High scores of both development and external marketability suggest that their own development is important to Millennials, but also with the goal to increase their employability as was suggested by previous research (Holden and Harte 2004; Cennamo and Gardner 2008). It confirms that Millennials are not so attached to the organization but rather pursue their career aspirations wherever they find good opportunities (Luscombe et al. 2013; Blomme et al. 2010).

Cluster analysis shows that EA students have higher expectations than CEE students, which could reflect both differences in cultures and socio-economic context. Namely, EA culture is known to be more collectivistic (House et al. 2004) and is based on Confucianism, hence it is characterized by loyalty, relationship building, the importance of learning and work ethics (Ralston et al. 1997; Cooke et al. 2014). Another source of variation could lie in the economic and labour market conditions in observed countries. Compared to China and South Korea, both Poland and Slovenia have witnessed stronger effects of the financial and economic crises, with slower economic growth and higher youth unemployment (World Bank n.d.), which may have contributed to lower expectations (Zupan et al. 2017). Due to limited space we have presented only a cluster analysis for geographical regions and gender differences. Nevertheless, descriptive statistics for our sample show that there is some variability in responses with regard to expectations and employment preferences, which implies caution regarding overgeneralization or even worse, stereotyping when dealing with individuals.

In the second study, we combined student and employer components of PC for Slovenia in order to identify potential PC breach situations. Our second study, which compares Millennials' and employers' expectations, confirms that employers may not be willing or able to meet some of the Millennials' expectations, especially with regard to external marketability, development and promotion and stable benefits for the family. On the other hand, a relatively big gap between both sides regarding performance support, marketability and loyalty expectations could pose a provocative question. Namely, should employers in Slovenia even wish to employ Millennials who are more focused on their own development and employability than on what they will contribute to their employers in terms of performance and loyalty. However, employers may have a little choice since Millennials entering the labour market constitute the largest pool of candidates. It is also worth mentioning, that Slovenian sample seems to be standing out compared to other three countries in our study with regard to relatively low scores of performance support and loyalty, suggesting that national culture and context matters in order to explain PC components (Thomas et al. 2003).

We have presented some notable contributions to understanding APC of Millennials in general and with regard to retention. However, the present research is not without limitations. The first one concerns the selected samples. While we obtained samples from two countries in CEE and two in EA, we cannot assume that these are representative countries for each of the respective regions. Therefore, in order to make generalizations, future research could systematically explore the APC in different countries of the two regions. This could further increase understanding of the characteristics of Millennials from non-Western countries which are under-represented in current academic literature. In addition, when doing cross-national research on APC, more attention should be devoted to the socio-economic context of countries (e.g. economic growth, labour market indicators) as it may play a significant role in APC formation and the level of importance ascribed to different PC dimensions (De Hauw and De Vos 2010; Eilam-Shamir and Yaakobi 2014). In this regard it would be interesting to investigate how PC expectations change depending on favourable and less favourable economic circumstances.

Second, while our analysis tested for potential differences in APC based on employment preferences, other variables need to be considered. For example, future research could uncover how personality factors affect the prominence of certain APC dimension. Further, contextual variables deserve more attention as well. Here, we recommend that cultural characteristics (e.g. national values) and perceived economic situation and certain economic indicators, could provide more information regarding the more and less important dimensions and types.

The third limitation concerns the sample of Study 2, which is based on an example from a single country, Slovenia. While the results concerning potential breach are informative, we need further analyses on other samples that are larger in size to verify the relationships. It may also be expected that the reasons for potential breach and reactions to the breach would differ across national and geographical contexts, so these variables should be included in future studies as well. Another important venue for future research is to include measures for a PC breach and reactions to it for both future and newly employed Millennials from different countries and organizations, thereby controlling for organizational and country specific factors that may have influenced our results.

Finally, in this study we used an established measure of Psychological contracts, yet, it may be useful to consider updating the dimensions and including novel expectations that fit more to the desires and ambitions of the current young generation. Due to their unique characteristics, we recommend that researchers develop a PC questionnaire specifically for the Milennial employees. A new PC inventory for Millennials would therefore measure expectations that are typical for this cohort. For example, the PC inventory by Rousseau (2008) which was used for this research, does not examine issues related to work-life balance, social meaningfulness, and work environment which are very important to this group of talents. Similarly, in the existing questionnaires used in other APC studies there are no items related to marketability or employability, which are relevant for Millennials.

Future research should also examine how Millennials' characteristic shape their expectations regarding the employer obligations. In order to manage these high expectations, it is crucial that we understand the factors that influence APC. Furthermore, comparative studies of APC and PC of Millennial newly employed would shed more light on how PC are formed and changed over time. In addition, a mixed methods research could provide more in-depth insights into understanding PC formation and differences stemming from demographics and national culture and socio-economic context.

Implications for Retention Theory and Practice

Managers and HR professionals need to be well aware of what Millennials expect, desire and find challenging at work, if they want to retain them in respective organizations. However, Zhao (2006) found that organizations underestimate the expectations of graduates and their impact on outcomes and behaviour. Based on our study, we suggest that APC could be a useful tool to improve existing understanding of Millennials' expectations. By adjusting their talent and retention management strategies and practices accordingly, they will be more successful in retaining the young talents. It seems that employers are not realizing this opportunity and they have not yet adjusted their approach and talent management to Millennials. For example, of 101 companies in our Slovenian sample (study 2), only 26% responded that they use tailored HR practices for Millennials. In addition, better understanding could lead to better fulfilment and organizations could benefit from their young talents' increased engagement and performance as well as lower turnover intentions. including paying attention to individual needs and expectations as suggested by Thunissen (2016) and offering I-deals (Rousseau et al. 2006), However, Millennials' expectations may prove to be in many instances too high, therefore an important action from employers is required already with early recruitment HR practices when cooperating with universities and students (e.g. company presentations, projects and internships). Thereby, employers can influence APC to be more realistic and thus reduce the risk of psychological contract breach upon employing young talents.

Next, as an expectations lowering procedure (Buckley et al. 2002), discussion about expectations and PC should be part of the recruitment process in order to clarify these expectations on both sides. Realistic job preview is a useful tool for lowering expectations and has a positive effect on reduced turnover (Baur et al. 2014). A realistic job preview needs to be followed by realistic promises regarding PC elements, especially with regard to development and promotion. Our study shows that a lot of Millennials, especially in CEE, prefers a managerial over professional/expert career. If it unclear from the beginning how long could it possibly take and what needs to be done to get to a managerial position, the risk of a perceived breach of the PC is higher. High promises and overly favourable descriptions of what to expect are often made just to attract Millennials (Tekleab et al. 2013), but this can easily backfire since they are sensitive to not being treated fairly or to their employers not keeping promises (Luscombe et al. 2013). By knowing APC of business students, i.e. the way young talents perceive their future obligations towards employers on the one hand and employers' obligations on the other, employers can develop such talent management practices, which speak to Millennials' values. In addition to recruiters, managers have an important role in shaping more realistic expectations (Rousseau 1995) through implementing HR practices, including on-boarding, managing performance, rewarding, mentoring and developing newcomers. If properly implemented, these reduce the risk of turnover and can turn challenges into opportunities (Stewart et al. 2017).

Despite the above, some HR practitioners may oversimplify their approach to managing Millennials and focus their retention efforts exclusively on pay raises and promotional opportunities. However, these may not necessarily serve as remedies for retaining Millennials. Our study indicates that pay and promotion are expected from employers to a lesser degree than personal development and performance support. Pay may attract Millennials initially, but Campione (2015) found its weaker significance relative to other factors for retention purposes. However, while it may not be the most important, pay is also not trivial. Lub et al. (2016) found that if Millennials perceive that their pay is not fair it would increase their intentions to leave.

As evident from our research, there is some variability among Millennials and if employers devote effort to find a good match, they could reduce the risk of losing young talents too quickly. By knowing similarities and differences in APC, employers can decide on the level of individualization of the employment relationship needed to retain young talent. By doing so they can avoid the negative consequences of I-deals, which may create tensions among co-workers due to preferential treatment and could add too much complexity to HRM systems (Rousseau et al. 2006).

Finally, variability in APC dimension and item scores suggests that a PC breach has to be understood as a multidimensional construct (Kraak et al. 2017). Therefore, elements of the PC should be identified where Millenials would actually feel PC violation, which would lead to increased turnover intentions. For example, Lub et al. (2016) found that for Millennials the fulfilment of career development obligations have a stronger impact on work outcomes compared to other generations.

If such incentives are provided, it may be expected that they enhance affective commitment. However, in their study the predictive value of development for turnover intentions was weak, so it seems that Millennials would still change employer if they considered the employment there to be a better opportunity.

In conclusion, the topic of managing Millennial talents is relatively new and although the challenges of retention are often cited, not enough is known about antecedents and mechanism that lead to turnover intentions and actual turnover. An analysis of psychological contracts, and more specifically the anticipatory psychological contracts that were the focus of this study, contributes to a better understanding of Millennials' expectations at work and their retention. By taking into consideration the expectations that are formed at the pre-employment stage, employers could take an active role early on (during university years) to (1), make those expectations realistic and (2) to adjust their talent management, HR practices and management/leadership styles to the preferences of Millennials to reduce the risk of a psychological contract breach. As results suggest, Millennials are thinking about their development mostly in terms of employability and might use early years of employment more as a catalyst for their future careers rather than contributing to current employers. Employers could thus capture the potential of young talents only through properly implemented and potentially individualized talent management practices. In addition, while there are similarities among Millennials around the world, our research affirms that there are also some notable differences, national and contextual specifics should be considered.

Summary

In order to address challenges related to Millennials' retention, it is important to recognize their preferences regarding employment expectations and employer-employee relationships. The concept of anticipatory psychological contracts (APC) provides a rich understanding of young talents' expectations, comprising both the obligations the young have of themselves as potential employees and of employers. The present research found that the preferred type of APC for Millennials in Central and Eastern Europe (CEE) and East Asia (EA) is the balanced one, with results indicating high scores for development and external marketability dimensions. Regarding the second, relational type, the score is considerably higher for employer than employee obligations, showing that Millennials expect more stability and loyalty than they are willing to give. The transactional type is least preferred, indicating that Millennials may not be inherently prone to turnover. Rather, Millennials are most focused on their personal development to increase employability and could be loyal only if they get what they expect from employers. If not, they would capitalize on their external marketability and search for opportunities elsewhere. That the above mentioned second scenario is likely to occur can be inferred from the identified potential breach of psychological contract, specifically when comparing APC dimensions perceived by Millennials and their potential employers. To retain young talents, it is important for employers to make Millennials' expectations more realistic via pre-recruitment activities. Then they should discuss PC elements during recruitment and provide realistic job previews. Once Millennials are employed, employers should develop and implement tailored talent management practices to effectively respond to their needs and expectations. Moreover, in developing talent management practices, national and socio-economic contexts should be considered as they both affect the formation of expectations.

Acknowledgements The authors would like to thank our research colleagues for their contribution to data collection and helping us understand country/region specific results: Matej Černe, Robert Kaše, Matevž Rašković, Katarzyna Dziewanovska, Lorne Hwang, Seong-Do Cho, Ilsang Ko. Also, special thanks to Martin Virag and Katja Podrepšek for their efforts to collect data from employers in Slovenia. The development of theoretical framework and literature review was supported by European Union's Horizon 2020 research and innovation programme under the Marie Skłodowska-Curie grant agreement No 734824.

References

Bal, P. M., & Kooij, D. (2011). The relations between work centrality, psychological contracts, and job attitudes: The influence of age. *European Journal of Work and Organizational Psychology, 20*(4), 497–523.

Bal, M. P., & Smit, P. (2012). The older the better! *Career Development International, 17*(1), 6–24.

Bal, M. P., De Lange, A. H., Jansen, P. G. W., & Van Der Velde, M. E. G. (2008). Psychological contract breach and job attitudes: A meta-analysis of age as a moderator. *Journal of Vocational Behavior, 72*(1), 143–158.

Baur, J. E., Buckley, M. R., Bagdasarov, Z., & Dharmasiri, A. (2014). A historical approach to realistic job previews: An exploration into their origins, evolution, and recommendations for the future. *Journal of Management History, 20*(2), 200–223.

Becton, J. B., Walker, H. J., & Jones-Farmer, A. (2014). Generational differences in workplace behavior. *Journal of Applied Social Psychology, 44*(3), 175–189.

Blomme, R. J., van Rheede, A., & Tromp, D. M. (2010). The use of the psychological contract to explain turnover intentions in the hospitality industry: A research study on the impact of gender on the turnover intentions of highly educated employees. *The International Journal of Human Resource Management, 21*(1), 144–162.

Broadbridge, A. M., Maxwell, G. A., & Ogden, S. M. (2007). 13_2_30: Experiences, perceptions and expectations of retail employment for generation Y. *Career Development International, 12*(6), 523–544.

Buckley, M. R., Mobbs, T. A., Mendoza, J. L., Novicevic, M. M., Carraher, S. M., & Beu, D. S. (2002). Implementing realistic job previews and expectation-lowering procedures: A field experiment. *Journal of Vocational Behavior, 61*(2), 263–278.

Campione, W. A. (2015). Corporate offerings: Why aren't millennials staying? *The Journal of Applied Business and Economics, 17*(4), 60–75.

Cennamo, L., & Gardner, D. (2008). Generational differences in work values, outcomes and personorganisation values fit. *Journal of Managerial Psychology, 23*(4), 891–906.

Cogin, J. (2012). Are generational differences in work values fact or fiction? Multi-country evidence and implications. *The International Journal of Human Resource Management, 23*(11), 2268–2294.

Conway, N., & Briner, R. B. (2005). *Understanding psychological contracts at work. A critical evaluation of theory and research*. Oxford, United Kingdom: Oxford University Press.

Cooke, F. L., Saini, D. S., & Wang, J. (2014). Talent management in China and India: A comparison of management perceptions and human resource practices. *Journal of World Business, 49*(2), 225–235.

D'Amato, A., & Herzfeldt, R. (2008). Learning orientation, organizational commitment and talent retention across generations. *Journal of Managerial Psychology, 23*(8), 929–953.

Del Campo, R. G., Haggerty, L. A., Haney, M. J., & Knippel, L. A. (2011). *Managing the multi-generational workforce*. Surrey, United Kingdom: Gower.

De Hauw, S., & De Vos, A. (2010). Millennials' career perspective and psychological contract expectations: Does the recession lead to lowered expectations? *Journal of Business Psychology, 25*(2), 293–302.

Deloitte. (2017). *The Deloitte Millennial Survey 2017*. Retrieved May 6, 2017, from https://www2.deloitte.com/global/en/pages/about-deloitte/articles/millennialsurvey.html.

De Vos, A., Buyens, D., & Schalk, R. (2003). Psychological contract development during organizational socialization: Adaptation to reality and the role of reciprocity. *Journal of Organizational Behaviour, 24*(5), 537–559.

De Vos, A., & Meganck, A. (2008). What HR managers do versus what employees value: Exploring both parties' views on retention management from a psychological contract perspective. *Personnel Review, 38*(1), 45–60.

De Vos, A., De Stobbeleir, K., & Meganck, A. (2009). The relationship between career-related antecedents and graduates' anticipatory psychological contracts. *Journal of Business and Psychology, 24*(3), 289–298.

Dulac, T., Coyle-Shapiro, J. A. M., Henderson, D. J., & Wayne, S. J. (2008). Not all responses to breach are the same: The interconnection of social exchange and psychological contract processes in organizations. *Academy of Management Journal, 51*(6), 1079–1098.

Eilam-Shamir, G., & Yaakobi, E. (2014). Effects of early employment experiences on anticipated psychological contracts. *Personnel Review, 43*(4), 893–912.

Festing, M., & Schäfer, L. (2014). Generational challenges to talent management: A framework for talent retention based on the psychological-contract perspective. *Journal of World Business, 49*(2), 262–271.

Gallardo-Gallardo, E., Nijs, S., Dries, N., & Gallo, P. (2015). Towards an understanding of talent management as a phenomenon-driven field using bibliometric and content analysis. *Human Resource Management Review, 25*(3), 264–279.

Graen, G. B., & Schiemann, W. A. (2013). Leadership-motivated excellence theory: An extension of LMX. *Journal of managerial psychology, 28*(5), 452–469.

Gursoy, D., Maier, T., & Chi, C. (2008). Generational differences: An examination of work valuesand generational gaps in the hospitality workforce. *International Journal of Hospitality Management, 27*(3), 448–458.

Gursoy, D., Chi, C. G. Q., & Karadag, E. (2013). Generational differences in work values and attitudes among frontline and service contact employees. *International Journal of Hospitality Management, 32*(1), 40–48.

Hart, S. M. (2006). Generational diversity: Impact on recruitment and retention of registered nurses. *Journal of Nursing Administration, 36*(1), 10–12.

Heckhausen, J., Wrosch, C., & Schulz, R. (2010). A motivational theory of life-span development. *Psychological Review, 117*(1), 32–60.

Hershatter, A., & Epstein, M. (2010). millennials and the world of work: An organization and management perspective. *Journal of Business and Psychology, 25*(2), 211–223.

Holden, R., & Harte, V. (2004). New graduate engagement with 'professional development'. *Journal of European Industrial Training, 28*(2/3/4), 272–282.

Höglund, M. (2012). Quid pro quo? Examining talent management through the lens of psychological contracts. *Personnel Review, 41*(2), 126–142.

House, R. J., Hanges, P. J., Javidan, M., Dorfman, P. W., & Gupta, V. (2004). *Culture, leadership, and organizations: The GLOBE study of 62 societies*. Thousand Oaks, CA: Sage.

Johnson, M., & Johnson, L. (2010). *Generations Inc: From boomers to linksters–managing the friction between generations at work*. New York: AMACOM.

Kong, H., Wang, S., & Fu, X. (2015). Meeting career expectation: Can it enhance job satisfaction of generation Y? *International Journal of Contemporary Hospitality Management, 27*(1), 147–168.

Kraak, J. M., Lunardo, R., Herrbach, O., & Durrieu, F. (2017). Promises to employees matter, self-identity too: Effects of psychological contract breach and older worker identity on violation and turnover intentions. *Journal of Business Research, 70*(1), 108–111.

Kuron, L. K., Lyons, S. T., Schweitzer, L., & Ng, E. S. (2015). Millennials' work values: Differences across the school to work transition. *Personnel Review, 44*(6), 991–1009.

Lub, X. D., Bal, M. P., Blomme, R. J., & Schalk, R. (2016). One job, one deal...or not: Do generations respond differently to psychological contract fulfillment? *The International Journal of Human Resource Management, 27*(6), 653–680.

Luscombe, J., Lewis, I., & Biggs, H. C. (2013). Essential elements for recruitment and retention: Generation Y. *Education + Training, 55*(3), 272–290.

Lyons, S. T., Schweitzer, L., & Ng, E. S. (2015). How have careers changed? An investigation of changing career patterns across four generations. *Journal of Managerial Psychology, 30*(1), 8–21.

Lyons, S., & Kuron, L. (2014). Generational differences in the workplace: A review of the evidence and directions for future research. *Journal of Organisational Behaviour, 35*(S1), S139–S157.

Manpower Group. (2016). *Millennial careers: 2020 vision; facts, figures and practical advice*. Retrieved December 12, 2017, from http://www.manpowergroup.com/wps/wcm/connect/660ebf65-144c-489e-975c-9f838294c237/MillennialsPaper1_2020Vision_lo.pdf?MOD=AJPERES.

McCracken, M., Currie, D., & Harrison, J. (2016). Understanding graduate recruitment, development and retention for the enhancement of talent management: Sharpening "the edge" of graduate talent. *International Journal of Human Resource Management, 27*(22), 2727–2752.

Morrison, E. W., & Robinson, S. L. (1997). When employees feel betrayed: A model of how psychological contract violation develops. *Academy of Management Review, 22*(1), 226–256.

Ng, E. S., Schweitzer, L., & Lyons, S. T. (2010). New generation, great expectations: A field study of the millennial generation. *Journal of Business and Psychology, 25*(2), 281–292.

Park, J., & Gursoy, D. (2012). Generation effects on work engagement among US hotel employees. *International Journal of Hospitality Management, 31*(4), 1195–1202.

Pearson, J. C., Carmon, A., Tobola, C., & Fowler, M. (2010). Motives for communication: Why the millennial generation uses electronic devices. *Journal of the Communication, Speech & Theatre Association of North Dakota, 22*(1), 45–55.

Pew Research Center. (2010). *Millennials: A portrait of generation next*. Retrieved on November 4, 2017, from http://www.pewresearch.org/topics/millennials/.

Ralston, D. A., Holt, D. H., Terpstra, R. H., & Yu, K. C. (1997). The impact of national culture and economic ideology on managerial work values: A study of the United States, Russia, Japan, and China. *Journal of International Business Studies, 28*(1), 177–207.

Robinson, S. L., & Morrison, E. W. (2000). The development of psychological contract breach and violation: A longitudinal study. *Journal of Organizational Behavior, 21*(5), 525–546.

Rodwell, J., Ellershaw, J., & Flower, R. (2015). Fulfill psychological contract promises to manage in demand employees. *Personnel Review, 44*(5), 689–701.

Rousseau, D. M. (1995). *Psychological contracts in organizations: Understanding written and unwritten agreements*. Thousand Oaks: Sage.

Rousseau, D. M. (2000). *Psychological contract inventory technical report.* Pittsburgh, PA: Carnegie Mellon University.

Rousseau, D. M. (2008). *Psychological contract inventory, employee and employer obligations.* Pittsburgh: The Heinz School, Carnegie Mellon University.

Rousseau, D. M., Ho, V. T., & Greenberg, J. (2006). I-deals: Idiosyncratic terms in employment relationships. *Academy of Management Review, 31*(4), 977–994.

Shaw, S., & Fairhurst, D. (2008). Engaging a new generation of graduates. *Education + Training, 50*(5), 366–378.

Sherman, U. P., & Morley, M. J. (2015). On the formation of the psychological contract: A schema theory perspective. *Group and Organization Management, 40*(2), 160–192.

Smith, S. D., & Galbraith, Q. (2012). Motivating millennials: Improving practices in recruiting, retaining, and motivating younger library staff. *The Journal of Academic Librarianship, 38*(3), 135–144.

Smola, K. W., & Sutton, C. D. (2002). Generational differences: Revisiting generational work values for the new millennium. *Journal of Organizational Behavior, 23*(4), 363–382.

Spiro, C. (2006). Generation Y in the workplace. *Defense AT&l, 35*(6), 16–19.

Stewart, J. S., Oliver, E. G., Cravens, K. S., & Oishi, S. (2017). Managing millennials: Embracing generational differences. *Business Horizons, 60*(1), 45–54.

Sujansky, J., & Ferri-Reed, J. (2009). *Keeping the Millennials: Why companies are losing billions in turnover to this generation-and what to do about it.* Hoboken: Wiley.

Taylor, M. S., & Tekleab, A. G. (2004). Taking stock of psychological contract research: Assessing progress, addressing troublesome issues, and setting research priorities. In J. A. Coyle-Shapiro, L. M. Shore, M. S. Taylor, & L. E. Tetrick (Eds.), *The employment relationship: Examining contextual and psychological perspectives* (pp. 253–283). Oxford: Oxford University Press.

Tekleab, A., Orvis, K., & Taylor, M. (2013). Deleterious consequences of change in newcomers' employer-based psychological contract obligations. *Journal of Business and Psychology, 28* (3), 361–374.

Taris, T. W., Feij, J. A., & Capel, S. (2006). Great expectations—and what comes of it: The effects of unmet expectations on work motivation and outcomes among newcomers. *International Journal of Selection and Assessment, 14*(3), 256–268.

Thomas, D. C., Au, K., & Ravlin, E. C. (2003). Cultural variation and the psychological contract. *Journal of Organizational Behavior, 24*(4), 451–471.

Thomas, H. D. C., & Anderson, N. (1998). Changes in newcomers' psychological contracts during organizational socialization: A study of recruits entering the British Army. *Journal of Organizational Behavior, 19*(S1), S745–S767.

Thompson, C., & Gregory, J. B. (2012). Managing millennials: A framework for improving attraction, motivation, and retention. *The Psychologist-Manager Journal, 15*(4), 237–246.

Thunnissen, M. (2016). Talent management: For what, how and how well? An empirical exploration of talent management in practice. *Employee Relations, 38*(1), 57–72.

Twenge, J. M. (2010). A review of the empirical evidence on generational differences in work attitudes. *Journal of Business Psychology, 25*(2), 201–210.

Twenge, J. M., Campbell, S. M., Hoffman, B. J., & Lance, C. E. (2010). Generational differences in work values: Leisure and extrinsic values increasing, social and intrinsic values decreasing. *Journal of Management, 36*(5), 1117.

Winter, R. P., & Jackson, B. A. (2016). Work values preferences of generation Y: Performance relationship insights in the Australian public service. *The International Journal of Human Resource Management, 27*(17), 1997–2015.

World Bank. (n.d.). GDP per capita growth (annual %). Retrieved December 17, 2017, from http://data.worldbank.org/indicator.

Zhao, H. (2006). Expectations of recruiters and applicants in large cities of China. *Journal of Managerial Psychology, 21*(5), 459–475.

Zhao, H., Wayne, S. J., Glibkowsky, B. C., & Bravo, J. (2007). The impact of psychological contract breach on work-related outcomes: A meta-analysis. *Personnel Psychology, 60*(3), 647–680.

Zupan, N., Kase, R., Raskovic, M., Yao, K., & Wang, C. (2015). Getting ready for the young generation to join the workforce: A comparative analysis of the work values of Chinese and Slovenian business students. *Journal of East European Management Studies, 20*(2), 174–201.

Zupan, N., Dziewanowska, K., & Pearce, A. (2017). Wanting it all: The challenges of managing young talent in transition economies. *Baltic Journal of Management, 12*(1), 63–85.

Nada Zupan (PhD) is Full Professor of Management at the Faculty of Economics, Universtity of Ljubljana, Slovenia. Her main research interests include strategic HRM, human capital and competencies, talent management, performance management and compensation. She is actively involved in management training programs and consulting projects as she likes to combine theory and practice. She has published over 40 articles and monographs. She is an active member Slovenian Human Resource Association and she led the project to develop Slovenian HR Standards.

Katarina Katja Mihelič is Associate Professor of management at the Faculty of Economics, University of Ljubljana, Slovenia. Her main research interests lie in the area of work-family interface, (un)ethical behavior, engagement, and values. She regularly attends international conferences in the areas of management and organizational psychology. Her research has been published in SSCI-ranked international journals.

Darija Aleksić is Assistant Professor at the Faculty of Economics, University of Ljubljana, Slovenia, major Management and Organization. Her research interests include unethical behavior, workaholism, organizational behavior, motivation and creativity. She is also a co-founder of Slovenian Society for Business Ethics and Ethical leadership and a member of the expert council of the association. She actively participates in domestic (scientific and expert) and international conferences in the field of management.

Chapter 16
Managing Diversity in Talent Retention: Implications of Psychological Contract, Career Preoccupations and Retention Factors

Alda Deas

Abstract The contemporary employment relationship is faced with various challenges because of aspects such as globalization, international competition, the brain drain and technological advances, making the retention of diverse and multicultural employees more challenging. This chapter provides valuable knowledge into the role of different biographical characteristics on the psychological contract, psychosocial career preoccupations and retention factors of employees. A sample of academic and support staff employees form a higher education institution in South Africa (N = 579) participated in this study. The empirical results indicated that there were significant differences for the biographical characteristics gender, race, generational cohorts, marital status, job level and employment status and the psychological contract, psychosocial career preoccupations and retention factors. This chapter adds new insights into the psychological contract and career development theories that could potentially enlighten industrial and organisational psychologists in the retention of diverse and multicultural employees.

Keywords Psychological contract · Psychosocial career preoccupations
Retention · Diversity · Careers · Expectations

Introduction

Talent retention is at present a major concern and complex matter for many organisations across the globe (Shore 2013; Tladinyane et al. 2013). Organisations are in a constant battle to attract and retain a sufficient supply of talented employees from the labour market in this continuously changing, globalised environment (Allui and Sahni 2016). Organisations are realising that, in order to accomplish a competitive advantage, their

---

A. Deas (✉)
Department of Human Resource Management, University of South Africa,
Pretoria, South Africa
e-mail: deasaj@unisa.ac.za

M. Coetzee et al. (eds.), *Psychology of Retention*,
https://doi.org/10.1007/978-3-319-98920-4_16

key strategic focus should be on the retention of knowledgeable and talented employees (Akhtar et al. 2015; Heinen and O'Neill 2004; Bersin 2008; Holbeche 2009).

The Society for Human Resource Management (SHRM) reported that, in 2016, 46% of human resource managers considered employee turnover as their key concern, a significant increase from 25% in 2013 (Lee et al. 2017; SHRM 2016). The retention strategies of organisations are therefore important as turnover of key employees could have adverse effects on the organisation (Allui and Sahni 2016). According to previous research, the success of retention management does not only depend on the development of effective human resources practices, but similarly on managing the expectations of employees regarding these practices (Al-Emadi et al. 2015; De Vos and Meganck 2009).

These expectations can be managed through the psychological contract and psychosocial career preoccupations of employees. Research over the past decade has supported the function of the psychological contract and employee expectations in regulating employees' work lives and relationships (O'Meara et al. 2016) and provided an additional comprehensive framework towards understanding employee retention (De Vos and Meganck 2009). Research has also shown that unfulfilled career expectations may have an impact on the retention of valued employees (Lam and de Campos 2015).

Furthermore, due to the persistent turnover of talent, organisations should focus their retention strategies on retaining any kind of talent, including younger and older employees, women and ethnic minorities (Ariss et al. 2013; Festing and Schäfer 2014), resulting in a more diverse workforce. Research has shown that organisations with no appreciation of diversity, will experience a decline in productivity together with the adverse effects of high turnover and the subsequent costs for replacing employees (Greer and Virick 2008; Hsiao et al. 2015; Van der Walt and Du Plessis 2010). Diversity management refers to the efforts of organisations to actively recruit, retain and support work relationships between diverse employees (Donnelley 2015; Miller and Rowney 1999; Uys 2003). According to Singh and Selvarajan (2013), prioritising diversity management will have a significant effect on the actions and attitudes of employees as well as employee turnover and retention.

The focus of this chapter is therefore to determine how the psychological contract, psychosocial career preoccupations and satisfaction with retention factors differ among employees with different biographical characteristics such as gender, race, generational cohorts, marital status, job level and employment status.

Theoretical Background

Psychological Contract

The psychological contract can be referred to as an employee's perceptions, which is shaped by the organisation, regarding the conditions of an exchange agreement relating to that employee and the organisation (Rousseau 1995). Given the subjective nature of the psychological contract, employees can develop the perception that their employer has some obligations towards them, and they, in turn have some obligations towards their employer (Persson and Wasieleski 2015). The content of the psychological contract therefore includes specific items that the employee experiences as the employer's obligations towards him/her (Bordia et al. 2015; Rousseau 1995). It is therefore important for organisations to understand and manage employee expectations to consequently fulfil its obligations in terms of the psychological contract (Festing and Schäfer 2014).

Employees evaluate the performance of the psychological contract with the onset of the exchange relationship (Bordia et al. 2015; Morrison and Robinson 1997). A fulfilled psychological contract results in increased trust and reciprocal benefits for both parties to the exchange relationship (Li et al. 2016). However, breach of the psychological contract occurs when an employee perceives that the organisation has failed to deliver on certain promises or expectations (Morrison and Robinson 1997; Rayton et al. 2015).

Mediating the relationship between psychological contract fulfilment or breach and behavioural factors such as intention to leave and commitment are the notions of fairness and trust (Clinton and Guest 2004; Guest 2004). The notions of fairness and trust refers to the state of the psychological contract (Guest 2004; Van der Vaart et al. 2013). Thus, where the psychological contract concentrates on the mutual expectations and obligations between the parties in the employment relationship, the state of the psychological contract explores whether these expectations and obligations were fulfilled, whether they were perceived as fair and its consequences on trust (Guest 2004; Guest and Conway 2002; Van der Vaart et al. 2013). The state of the psychological contract are found to be a significant precursor of employee attitudes and behaviour, elaborating on the differences explained through the content of the psychological contract (Guest 1998; Van der Vaart et al. 2013).

Psychosocial Career Preoccupations

Coetzee (2014, 2015a, b) defined psychosocial career preoccupations as an individual's psychological state which is based on career concerns and that are at the forefront of his/her thoughts at a specific point in time. These concerns normally includes matters relating to vocational developmental tasks of adaptability that an individual encounter during a career life cycle which are significant in the career life story (Coetzee 2015a; Savickas 2005; Sharf 2010). Savickas's career construction theory (Savickas 1997, 2002, 2005) are responsible for a deeper understanding of vocational development relating to a contextual viewpoint of vocational development through the life-span (Duffy et al. 2015). At the core of this theory is the concept of adaptability—the psychosocial process in terms of the predisposition of an individual to manage change and transitions (Maree 2016; Savickas 2013).

The contemporary career is however emerging into a career that is less organised (Arthur and Rousseau 1996; Zhou et al. 2016), characterised by a series of lifelong

Table 16.1 Psychosocial career preoccupations

Dimension	Psychosocial career preoccupations
Career establishment preoccupations	Fitting into a group, career and economic steadiness and security, creating prospects for self-expression and personal growth and development, and progressing in one's career in the current organisation
Career adaptation preoccupations	Employability-related fears about adjusting to fluctuating circumstances that might include career changes and adjusting one's interests, talents and competencies to fit opportunities in the employment market
Work/life adjustment preoccupations	Settling down, reducing one's workload and reaching greater synchronisation between one's work and personal life, possibly extracting oneself from remunerated employment

decisions, changes and amendments (Coetzee 2015b; Savickas 2013). Consequently, individuals now have the propensity to predict and adapt to the constant career moves and role changes (Cook and Maree 2016; Hartung 2007). Coetzee (2015a) identified additional career preoccupations that are not associated to careers or age, which may be important in the career-life stories of adults and the outcome of career experiences in a troubled economy and an unpredictable employment market. These career preoccupations can be divided into three principle dimensions of psychosocial career preoccupations (Coetzee 2014, 2015a, b). An overview of these preoccupations is provided in Table 16.1.

Retention Factors

Döckel (2003) identified seven critical retention factors, namely compensation, job characteristics, training and development opportunities, supervisor support, career opportunities, work/life balance and commitment. Organisations should take cognisance of these retention factors in their efforts to retain talented employees (Coetzee et al. 2015; Döckel et al. 2006; Van Dyk and Coetzee 2012) as it can be considered as significant human resource practices effecting both turnover intention and employee retention (Coetzee and Stoltz 2015).

Compensation can be viewed as one of the most important factors for retaining employees (Ibidunni et al. 2016; Kakar et al. 2015) and refers to the competitiveness of an organisation's salary packages, its policy on remuneration and salary increases (Döckel 2003; Van Dyk et al. 2013).

Job characteristics relate to the positive features of a job such as challenging and wide-ranging tasks, opportunities to participate in tasks with expert employees, freedom, flexibility and the capacity to pursue interesting tasks (Döckel 2003; Coetzee et al. 2015; Van Dyk et al. 2013). The specific characteristics of a job may also increase employee retention and organisational commitment as a result of employees' experience that their contributions are significant and that their capabilities are increasing (Döckel 2003).

Another retention factor proven to have a positive effect on employee retention is supervisor support (Allen et al. 2003; Bergiel et al. 2009; George 2015; Van Dyk et al. 2013; Van Dyk and Coetzee 2012) and refers to the feedback and recognition that a supervisor provides to an employee (Van Dyk and Coetzee 2012).

Career opportunities refer to the degree to which employees are provided opportunities to develop their careers within an organisation (Aruna and Anitha 2015; Presbitero et al. 2016). According to previous research, career opportunities is more significant than other rewards and the most significant predictor of retention (Döckel et al. 2006; Kochanski and Ledford 2001) and a lack of career opportunities contributes significantly to employee turnover (Presbitero et al. 2016).

Work/life balance can be described as employees' perception that a satisfactory balance between their personal life and work schedule exist, including the minimum conflict between the various roles they have to fulfil in terms of personal and work life (Döckel 2003; Presbitero et al. 2016). Research has indicated that organisations with work/life policies such as parental leave, flexible working hours, support with childcare and information concerning childcare, will have increased organisational commitment and significantly lower turnover intentions (Döckel et al. 2006; Grover and Crooker 1995; Presbitero et al. 2016).

Organisational commitment refers to employees' psychological state in terms of their connection with the objectives and values of the organisation, which influences their decision to remain with the organisation (Allen and Meyer 1991; Santosh and Muthiah 2016). Singh and Gupta (2015) argues that knowledge-driven organisations should take cognisance of employees' organisational commitment as it is an important factor in retaining knowledge employees.

The psychological contract and retention factors are both constructs that have been researched widely in the retention context. Le Roux and Rothmann (2013) however postulate that there exist a gap in the research investigating the impact of different biographical variables, such as gender, age and tenure on the direct and indirect relationship between the psychological contract and turnover intentions. Research relating to the dimensions of psychosocial career preoccupations is, however, particularly limited in the South African workplace context, specifically in terms of retention outcomes (Coetzee 2015a). The role of employees' biographical characteristics (i.e. gender, race, generational cohorts, marital status, job level and employment level) in explaining the psychological contract, psychosocial career preoccupations and retention factors is not clear. Understanding how the psychological contract, psychosocial career preoccupations and satisfaction with retention factors may differ between employees with different biographical characteristics may contribute to inform retention practices concerned with the diverse and multicultural workforce.

Method

Employees and Procedure

A purposive sample of academic and support staff employees (N = 579) of a higher education institution in South Africa was involved in the study. Data were collected through an online survey and participation was voluntary and anonymous. The sample was represented by black African (52%) and white (38.2%) employees and males (63%) and females (37%) either married (59%) or single (29%). The sample comprised predominantly of generation X (44%) employees aged between 36 and 55 years (58%), mostly in the establishment/maintenance stage of their careers. The employees were represented by permanent (83%), academic (38.3%) employees. Permission to conduct the survey and ethical clearance was provided by the higher education institution.

Measures

Biographical questionnaire. Gender, race, generational cohorts, marital status, employment status and job level were included in the biographical questionnaire.

Psychological contract. The 44-item psychological contract questionnaire (PQ), developed by de Cuyper, van der Heijden and de Witte (2011), was used to assess employer obligations (15 items; e.g. Has your organisation promised or committed itself to providing you with a job that is challenging?), employee obligations (16 items; e.g. Have you promised or committed yourself to showing loyalty to your organisation?), satisfaction with the psychological contract (6 items; e.g. I feel happy) and the state of the psychological contract (7 items; e.g. Do you feel that organisational changes are implemented fairly in your organisation?). For both employer and employee obligations, a 6-point Likert-type scale was used to capture responses (0 = no, the promise has not been made; 1 = yes, but promise has not been kept at all; 6 = yes, promise fully kept). Satisfaction with the psychological contract and state of the psychological contract were measured using a 5-point Likert-type scale (1 = strongly agree; 5 = strongly agree). Van der Vaart, Linde, and Cockeran (2013) reported high reliability for employer obligations ($\alpha = 0.94$), employee obligations ($\alpha = 0.93$), and state of the psychological contract ($\alpha = 0.90$). Snyman (2014) reported a high Cronbach's alpha coefficient for the satisfaction with the psychological contract ($\alpha = 0.70$).

Psychosocial career preoccupations. The 24-item psychosocial career preoccupations scale (PCPS), developed by Coetzee (2014), was used to measure employees' career preoccupations in terms of career establishment preoccupations (13 items; e.g. To what extent are you concerned about having a full-time job?), career adaption preoccupations (5 items; e.g. To what extent are you concerned about how your concept of your interests, talents and capabilities fits with the changes in the employment market?) and work/life adjustment preoccupations (6-items; e.g. To what extent are you concerned about withdrawing from paid employment altogether?). A 5-point Likert-type scale was used to capture responses (1 = not concerned; 5 = extremely concerned). Coetzee (2014) reported high internal consistency reliability in the PCPS with Cronbach's alpha coefficients ranging between 0.72 and 0.95. Construct validity was confirmed through bi-variate correlations ranging between $r \geq 0.53 \leq 0.66$ ($p = 0.00$).

Retention factors. The 35-item retention factor questionnaire (RFMS) was developed by Döckel (2003) to measure the participant's satisfaction with certain retention factors within an organisation and includes compensation (13 items; e.g. My benefits package), job satisfaction (4 items; e.g. The job requires me to use a number of complex or high level skills), training and development opportunities (6 items; e.g. This organisation provides me with job-specific training), supervisor support (6 items; e.g. I feel undervalued by my supervisor), career opportunities (6 items; e.g. My chances for being promoted are good), work/life balance (4 items; e.g. I often feel that there is too much work to do), and commitment (3 items; e.g. How would you rate your chances of still working at this organisation a year from now?). A 6-point Likert-type scale was used to capture responses for all the sub-scales (1 = strongly dissatisfied; 6 = strongly satisfied) except commitment (1 = chances are very low; 6 = chances are very good). Döckel (2003) confirmed construct validity of the RFMS and Döckel et al. (2006) reported internal consistency reliability for compensation ($\alpha = 0.90$), job satisfaction ($\alpha = 0.41$), training ($\alpha = 0.83$), supervisor support ($\alpha = 0.90$), career opportunities ($\alpha = 0.76$), work/life balance ($\alpha = 0.87$) and commitment ($\alpha = 0.89$).

Statistical Analysis

The Kolmogorov-Smirnov (KS) test was utilised to determine whether the data were normally distributed. The KS test indicated that non-parametric tests should be utilised in order to determine the significant mean differences. The Kruskal-Wallis *H* test was used to determine the significant mean differences between the sub-scales of the psychological contract, psychosocial career preoccupations and retention factors. The Kruskal-Wallis *H* test is a non-parametric method that is performed when the dependant variable is either interval/ratio scale or ordinal and is performed by comparing the rank totals of multiple independent groups (Rovia et al. 2013). A significance level of $p \leq 0.05$ indicates that the test are significant and valid. In order to examine the effect size of the mean differences Cohen's *d* is used. The effect sizes of Cohen's *d* are suggested as follow: $d = 0.02$; small effect; $d = 0.05$; medium effect; $d = 0.08$; large effect (Gravetter et al. 2016).

Results

Correlations

Table 16.2 indicates the descriptive statistics and correlations of all the subscales and the biographical characteristics. Overall, the results indicated significant correlations between the biographical variables and the subscales of the RFMS scale, the PCPS scale and the PQ scale, with practical effect sizes ranging between small and medium.

Significant Differences in Biographical Characteristics

As indicated in Table 16.3, the Kruskal-Wallis tests for the biographical characteristics presented significant differences in terms of the subscales.

Retention Factors

For compensation, males ($M = 4.18$; $SD = 1.25$; $d = 0.21$, small practical effect) scored significantly higher than their female counterparts ($M = 3.90$; $SD = 1.29$) and permanent employees scored significantly higher than contract employees ($M = 3.47$; $SD = 1.33$; $d = 0.44$, small practical effect).

For job characteristics, administrative employees ($M = 4.10$; $SD = 0.99$) scored significantly lower than academic employees ($M = 4.61$; $SD = 0.93$; $d = 0.53$, moderate practical effect) and permanent employees ($M = 4.28$; $SD = 0.99$) scored significantly lower than contract employees ($M = 4.67$; $SD = 1.33$; $d = 0.30$, small practical effect).

For career opportunities, white employees ($M = 2.09$; $SD = 0.89$) scored significantly lower than Black employees ($M = 3.55$; $SD = 1.18$; $d = 0.61$, moderate practical effect) and generation Y ($M = 3.56$; $SD = 1.05$; $d = 0.40$, small practical effect) scored significantly higher than Generation X ($M = 3.40$; $SD = 1.16$) and Baby Boomers ($M = 3.02$; $SD = 1.06$). Married employees ($M = 3.16$; $SD = 1.09$; $d = 0.30$, small practical effect) scored significantly lower than single/divorced employees ($M = 3.52$; $SD = 1.16$). Administrative employees ($M = 3.45$; $SD = 1.18$) scored significantly higher than academic employees ($M = 3.25$; $SD = 1.04$; $d = 0.19$, small practical effect), and permanent employees ($M = 3.24$; $SD = 1.11$) scored significantly lower than contract employees ($M = 3.59$; $SD = 1.23$; $d = 0.24$, small practical effect).

In terms of work/life balance, white employees ($M = 2.96$; $SD = 1.52$) scored significantly lower than Black employees ($M = 4.07$; $SD = 1.45$; $d = 0.73$, moderate practical effect). Generation Y ($M = 3.98$; $SD = 1.42$; $d = 0.34$, small

Table 16.2 Descriptive statistics and bivariate correlations

Variables	Means	*SD*	α	CR	AVE's	Age	Generational cohorts	Gender	Race	Marital status	Job level	Employment status
1. Compensation	4.08	0.95	0.95	0.95	0.62	0.06	0.06	−0.11**	0.06	0.05	0.01**	−0.22***
2. Job characteristics	4.35	0.51	0.47	0.47	0.22	0.06	0.06	0.07	0.04	0.03	0.12**	0.14***
3. Training and development opportunities	3.94	0.89	0.87	0.87	0.54	−0.01	−0.02	−0.00	−0.02	−0.05	0.03	0.02
4. Supervisor support	3.88	0.79	0.77	0.77	0.41	−0.03	−0.04	0.03	−0.08	−0.01	0.04	0.15***
5. Career opportunities	3.30	0.73	0.74	0.74	0.35	−0.14***	−0.16***	0.02	−0.30***	−0.12**	−0.12**	0.09*
6. Work/life balance	3.62	0.90	0.89	0.89	0.69	−0.18***	−0.17***	−0.01	−0.37***	−0.14***	−0.18***	0.14***
7. Organisational commitment	4.70	0.84	0.85	0.85	0.67	0.12**	0.13**	−0.10*	0.07	0.04	0.04	−0.05
8. RFMS overall scale						−0.02	−0.03	−0.05	−0.11*	−0.03	0.03	−0.01
9. Career establishment preoccupations	3.54	0.94	0.94	0.94	0.57	−0.27***	−0.29***	−0.08*	−0.29***	−0.06	−0.18***	0.14***
10. Career adaptation preoccupations	2.83	0.90	0.90	0.90	0.66	−0.27***	−0.29***	−0.06	−0.33***	−0.12**	−0.19***	0.01
11. Work/life adjustment preoccupations	3.05	0.78	0.77	0.77	0.38	−0.17***	−0.19***	−0.07	−0.17***	−0.03	−0.09*	0.09*
12. PCPS overall scale						−0.27***	−0.29***	−0.08*	−0.30***	−0.07	−0.18***	0.11**
13. Employer obligations	2.97	1.00	0.93	0.93	0.47	−0.01	−0.01	0.02	−0.05	−0.02	0.06	0.02
14. Employee obligations	5.07	0.82	0.91	0.93	0.47	0.01	0.02	−0.06	−0.07	0.02	0.05	−0.01
15. Satisfaction with psychological contract	3.05	0.46	−0.25	0.01	0.57	0.03	0.02	−0.05	0.09*	0.03	0.06	−0.08
16. State of psychological contract	2.96	1.00	0.89	0.88	0.54	−0.06	−0.06	−0.05	−0.16***	−0.03	0.00	0.12**
17. PQ Overall scale						−0.01	−0.01	−0.03	−0.09*	−0.00	0.07	0.03

Notes N = 579. $^{***}p \leq 0.001$ $^{**}p \leq 0.01$ $^{*}p \leq 0.05$

practical effect) scored significantly higher than Generation X ($M = 3.72$; $SD = 1.58$) and Baby Boomers ($M = 3.28$; $SD = 1.62$). Academic employees scored significantly lower than administrative employees ($M = 4.15$; $SD = 1.44$; $d = 0.75$, moderate practical effect) and permanent employees ($M = 3.51$; $SD = 1.57$) scored significantly lower than contract employees ($M = 4.26$; $SD = 1.45$; $d = 0.37$, small practical effect).

For organisational commitment females ($M = 4.52$; $SD = 1.40$) scored significantly lower than males ($M = 4.80$; $SD = 1.37$; $d = 0.24$, small practical effect) and white employees ($M = 4.87$; $SD = 1.33$) scored significantly higher than Black employees ($M = 4.58$; $SD = 1.42$; $d = 0.24$, small practical effect). Baby Boomers ($M = 4.90$; $SD = 1.36$; $d = 0.35$, small practical effect) scored significantly higher than Generation X ($M = 4.71$; $SD = 1.37$) and Generation Y ($M = 4.36$; $SD = 1.44$).

Psychosocial Career Preoccupations

In the case of the career preoccupations variables white employees scored significantly lower than Black employees on all three variables: career establishment preoccupations (Whites: $M = 3.20$; $SD = 1.01$; Blacks: $M = 3.78$; $SD = 1.04$; $d = 0.62$, moderate practical effect); career adaptation preoccupations (Whites: $M = 2.36$; $SD = 1.02$; Blacks: $M = 3.15$; $SD = 1.19$; $d = 0.68$, moderate practical effect); and work/life adjustment preoccupations (Whites: $M = 2.86$; $SD = 0.94$; Blacks: $M = 3.19$; $SD = 0.97$; $d = 0.35$, small practical effect size).

Generation Y ($M = 3.77$; $SD = 1.06$; 0.62, moderate practical effect) scored significantly higher than Generation X ($M = 3.76$; $SD = 0.98$) and the Baby Boomers ($M = 3.11$; $SD = 1.06$) in terms of the career establishment preoccupation. Generation Y ($M = 3.07$; $SD = 1.20$) and Generation X ($M = 3.07$; $SD = 1.20$) scored significantly higher than the Baby Boomers ($M = 2.37$; $SD = 1.10$; d = 0.60, moderate practical effect) on the career adaptation preoccupation. Likewise, Generation Y ($M = 3.20$; $SD = 0.96$) and Generation X ($M = 3.20$; $SD = 0.93$) scored significantly higher than the Baby Boomers ($M = 2.76$; $SD = 0.98$; $d = 0.43$, small practical effect) on the work/life adjustment preoccupation.

Married employees ($M = 3.43$; $SD = 1.06$; $d = 0.27$, small practical effect) scored significantly lower than single/divorced employees ($M = 3.69$; $SD = 1.08$). Married employees ($M = 2.67$; $SD = 1.17$; $d = 0.34$, small practical effect) scored significantly lower for career adaptation preoccupations than single/divorced employees ($M = 3.07$; $SD = 1.19$). As to work/life adjustment preoccupations, married employees ($M = 2.97$; $SD = 0.98$; $d = 0.18$, small practical effect) scored significantly lower than single/divorced employees.

Administrative employees ($M = 3.74$; $SD = 1.04$) scored significantly higher on career establishment preoccupations than academic employees ($M = 3.43$; $SD = 1.02$; $d = 0.35$, small practical effect) while the latter ($M = 3.13$; $SD = 1.22$)

Table 16.3 Biographical differences on the psychological contract, psychosocial career preoccupations and retention factors

Biographical variable		N	Mean	SD	Chi-Square	Cohen's *d*
Gender						
Compensation	Females Males	216 363	3.90 4.18	1.29 1.25	6.45	0.21**
Organisational commitment	Females Males	216 363	4.52 4.80	1.40 1.37	7.91	0.24**
Race						
Career opportunities	White Black (African, coloured, Indian)	221 348	2.90 3.55	0.89 1.18	48.61	0.61***
Work/life balance	White Black (African, coloured, Indian)	221 348	2.96 4.07	1.52 1.45	66.59	0.73***
Organisational commitment	White Black (African, coloured, Indian)	221 348	4.87 4.58	1.33 1.42	7.68	0.24**
Career establishment preoccupations	White Black (African, coloured, Indian)	221 348	3.20 3.78	1.01 1.04	49.89	0.62***
Career adaptation preoccupations	White Black (African, coloured, Indian)	221 348	2.36 3.15	1.02 1.19	58.88	0.68***
Work/life adjustment preoccupations	White Black (African, coloured, Indian)	221 348	2.86 3.19	0.94 3.19	16.55	0.35***
Satisfaction with the psychological contract	White Black (African, coloured, Indian)	221 348	3.12 3.01	0.43 0.48	9.98	0.27**
State of the psychological contract	White Black (African, coloured, Indian)	221 348	2.79 3.07	0.89 1.05	12.36	0.30***
Generational cohorts						
Career opportunities	Baby Boomers Generation X Generation Y	199 253 125	3.02 3.40 3.56	1.06 1.16 1.05	22.20	0.40***
Work/life balance	Baby Boomers Generation X Generation Y	199 253 125	3.28 3.72 3.98	1.62 1.58 1.42	15.85	0.34***
Organisational commitment	Baby Boomers Generation X Generation Y	199 253 125	4.90 4.71 4.36	1.36 1.37 1.44	17.31	0.35***
Career establishment preoccupations	Baby Boomers Generation X Generation Y	199 253 125	3.11 3.76 3.77	1.06 0.98 1.06	51.20	0.62***
Career adaptation preoccupations	Baby Boomers Generation X Generation Y	199 253 125	2.37 3.07 3.07	1.10 1.20 1.20	47.45	0.60***

(continued)

Table 16.3 (continued)

Biographical variable		N	Mean	SD	Chi-Square	Cohen's *d*
Work/life adjustment preoccupations	Baby Boomers	199	2.76	0.98	25.16	0.43***
	Generation X	253	3.20	0.93		
	Generation Y	125	3.20	0.96		
Employee obligations	Baby Boomers	199	5.05	0.85	10.83	0.28**
	Generation X	253	5.15	0.81		
	Generation Y	125	4.92	0.80		
Marital status						
Career opportunities	Married	340	3.16	1.09	12.68	0.30***
	Single/Divorced	219	3.52	1.16		
Career establishment preoccupations	Married	340	3.43	1.06	9.89	0.27**
	Single/Divorced	219	3.69	1.08		
Career adaptation preoccupations	Married	340	2.67	1.17	15.79	0.34***
	Single/Divorced	219	3.07	1.19		
Work/life adjustment preoccupations	Married	340	2.97	0.98	4.38	0.18*
	Single/Divorced	219	3.16	0.96		
Job level						
Job characteristics	Academic	221	4.61	0.93	28.05	0.53***
	Administrative	214	4.10	0.99		
Career opportunities	Academic	221	3.25	1.04	3.99	0.19*
	Administrative	214	3.45	1.18		
Work/life balance	Academic	221	3.04	1.55	53.16	0.75***
	Administrative	214	4.15	1.44		
Career establishment preoccupations	Academic	221	3.43	1.02	13.15	0.35***
	Administrative	214	3.74	1.04		
Career adaptation preoccupations	Academic	221	2.56	1.08	20.79	0.45***
	Administrative	214	3.13	1.22		
Employer obligations	Academic	221	3.05	0.98	4.02	0.19*
	Administrative	214	2.87	1.04		
Employment status						
Compensation	Contract	97	3.47	1.33	26.81	0.44***
	Permanent	478	4.21	1.22		
Job characteristics	Contract	97	4.67	1.33	12.35	0.30***
	Permanent	478	4.28	0.99		
Supervisor support	Contract	97	4.34	1.19	15.31	0.33***
	Permanent	478	3.79	1.23		
Career opportunities	Contract	97	3.59	1.23	7.48	0.24**
	Permanent	478	3.24	1.11		
Work/life balance	Contract	97	4.26	1.45	18.62	0.37***
	Permanent	478	3.51	1.57		
Career establishment preoccupations	Contract	97	3.86	1.10	15.54	0.33***
	Permanent	478	3.47	1.05		
Work/life adjustment preoccupations	Contract	97	3.22	1.02	4.35	0.17*
	Permanent	478	3.01	0.96		
Satisfaction with the psychological contract	Contract	97	2.96	0.49	6.18	0.21*
	Permanent	478	3.07	0.46		
State of the psychological contract	Contract	97	3.27	1.02	11.31	0.28***
	Permanent	478	2.90	0.98		

Notes N = 579. $^{***}p \leq 0.001$ $^{**}p \leq 0.01$ $^{*}p \leq 0.05$

also scored significantly higher than academic employees ($M = 2.56$; $SD = 1.08$; $d = 0.45$, small practical effect) on career adaptation preoccupations.

Permanent employees ($M = 3.47$; $SD = 1.05$) scored significantly lower than contract employees ($M = 3.86$; $SD = 1.10$; $d = 0.33$, small practical effect) on career establishment preoccupations. In addition, permanent employees ($M = 3.01$: $SD = 0.96$) scored significantly lower than contract employees ($M = 3.22$; $SD = 1.02$; $d = 0.17$, small practical effect) on work/life adjustment preoccupations.

Psychological Contract

Academic employees ($M = 3.05$; $SD = 0.98$) scored significantly higher than administrative employees ($M = 2.87$; $SD = 1.04$; $d = 0.19$, small practical effect) for employer obligations.

Generation X ($M = 5.15$; $SD = 0.81$; $d = 0.28$, small practical effect) scored significantly higher than the Baby Boomers ($M = 5.05$; $SD = 0.85$) and Generation Y ($M = 4.92$; $SD = 0.80$) for employee obligations.

For satisfaction with the psychological contract, white employees ($M = 3.12$; $SD = 0.43$) scored significantly higher than Black employees ($M = 3.01$; $SD = 0.97$; $d = 0.35$, small practical effect). Permanent employees ($M = 3.07$; $SD = 0.46$) scored significantly higher than contract employees ($M = 2.96$; $SD = 0.49$; $d = 0.21$, small practical effect).

For the state of the psychological contract, Black employees ($M = 3.07$; $SD = 1.05$) scored significantly higher than white employees ($M = 2.79$; $SD = 0.89$; $d = 0.30$, small practical effect. Contract employees ($M = 3.27$; $SD = 1.02$) scored significantly higher than permanent employees ($M = 2.90$; $SD = 0.98$; $d = 0.28$, small practical effect).

Discussion

The research presented in this chapter explored the differences in biographical characteristics in terms of the psychological contract, psychosocial career preoccupations and satisfaction with retention factors. The results highlighted gender, race, generational cohorts, marital status, job level and employment level as biographical characteristics that significantly differ in terms of the psychological contract, psychosocial career preoccupations and satisfaction with retention factors (Deas 2017).

Gender. Males were found to be more concerned about compensation than females; whereas females were found to be less committed to an organisation than males. Previous research found that male employees were more concerned about extrinsic job factors including fringe benefits and higher salaries (Bellou 2009;

Metcalfe 1993). Jena (2015) revealed that females indicated less organisational commitment than males.

Race. In terms of race, white employees were found to be less concerned about career opportunities and work/life balance than black employees. Similarly, Hofhuis et al. (2014) proposed that employees from the minority group will present greater dissatisfaction in terms of career opportunities as a predictor of turnover intentions than the majority group. For the underrepresented minority employees, work/life balance policies are progressively becoming more essential in the recruitment and retention of this group of employees (Castaneda et al. 2015). Black employees were found to be less committed to the organisation than white employees. Gonzalez and Denisi (2009) found that male employees from the minority racial group in an organisation indicated lower organisational commitment than the majority racial group.

In terms of the psychosocial career preoccupations, the results revealed that black employees were more concerned about their career development in the organisation than their white counterparts. Previous research has consistently shown that employees from minority groups believe that racial discrimination will prevent them from accomplishing their desired career outcomes (Haynes et al. 2015; McWhirter 1997). For the psychological contract, it was found that black employees were less satisfied with their psychological contract than white employees. Wöcke and Sutherland (2008) also pointed out that African employees where satisfied the least regarding the fulfilment of employers' obligations. Black employees were also found to perceive their psychological contract as more fair and just than white employees. It is possible that white employees have found that employment equity practices create disruptions in the relational components of their psychological contract with their employer (Wöcke and Sutherland 2008).

Generational cohorts. The results revealed that Generation Y employees were more likely to be satisfied with career opportunities and work/life balance than employees from the Generation X and Baby Boomer cohorts. Previous research have found that Generation Y employees favour stimulating jobs that offer them opportunities to improve their long-term career development (de Cooman and Dries 2012; Guillot-Soulez and Soulez 2014; Hite and McDonald 2012). Generation Y employees are also more prone to demand work/life balance through all their careers stages (McDonald and Hite 2008; Ng et al. 2010). Baby Boomers were also found to be more committed to the organisation. A study among nurses similarly revealed that Baby Boomer employees were significantly more committed to their organisation than employees from Generation X and Y (Brunetto et al. 2012; Nelson 2012).

For the psychosocial career preoccupations, it was found that Generation Y employees were more concerned with establishing their careers than employees from the Generation X and Baby Boomers cohorts. This result was expected as employees from Generation Y includes the age group of individuals who recently joined the employment market and are currently establishing themselves in their careers. Baby Boomers showed less concern in terms of advancing in their careers and work/life adjustment than Generation X and Y employees. The significant differences observed among the three generational cohorts may suggest that the career preoccupations in the current study might be generation-related. This is in contrast to the findings of Coetzee's (2015a) study, which revealed that career preoccupations were not age-related. The results of the present study do, however, support the opinion that career preoccupations were not narrowed down to a specific generational cohort only (Coetzee 2015a; Mahoney 1987).

In terms of the psychological contract, Generation X employees perceived that they have fulfilled their promises to their employers more than employees from Generation Y and Baby Boomers. This finding is in contrast with Bal and Kooij's (2011), who found that Generation X employees showed less transactional and relational obligations than Baby Boomer employees.

Marital status. The results indicated that married employees were less likely to be satisfied with career opportunities than single/divorced employees. Mubarak et al. (2012) argues that marital status, as a biographical variable, has an effect on retention factors. Additionally, research have shown that job satisfaction appears to increase with progressive life stages and amid married academics (Ryan et al. 2012). Single/divorced employees were found to be more concerned about their career development than married employees. Marital and family obligations interrupts the career development of women and work/life balance conflicts often emerge for women employees (Blomme et al. 2010).

Job level. Administrative employees were found to be less satisfied with job characteristics than academic employees. Barkhuizen and Rothmann (2008) found that job characteristics were a stressor that had a significant effect on affective commitment of academic employees in higher educational institutions. The results also found that administrative employees were likely to be more satisfied with work/life balance than academic employees. Barkhuizen and Rothmann's (2008), however, found that academic employees experienced high levels of anxiety as a result of trying to attain a work/life balance. Academic employees were found to be less concerned with preoccupations related to establishing and adapting to their careers than administrative employees. This could be attributed to the fact that, in general, administrative employees do not have clear, well-defined paths in terms of their career development (Renkema et al. 2009). For the psychological contract, administrative employees experienced that the organisation has made and fulfilled less promises than the academic employees. In contrast, Shen (2010) revealed that academic employees' sense of fulfilment of the psychological contract was low, as 17 of 21 employer obligations scored low.

Employment level. The results indicated that permanent employees were less likely to be concerned with job characteristics, supervisor support, career opportunities and work/life balance as retention factors than contracted employees. Similarly, Jafri (2014) suggested that contracted employees expected more from the organisation in terms of job content and supervisor support. Permanent employees were found to be more satisfied with compensation than contracted employee. In contrast, Unsal-Akbiyik (2014) found no statistically significant differences between permanent and contract employees' perceptions regarding remuneration practices in their organisations. It was also found that contracted employees were less likely to be satisfied with their psychological contract than permanent employees. De Jong et al. (2009) however found that permanent employees experienced less fulfilled obligations, and were therefore less satisfied with their psychological contract. Permanent employees were furthermore found to be less likely to experience their psychological contract as fair and just than contract employees. Correspondingly, De Jong et al. (2009) found contracted employees experience relatively fair and good exchanges in terms of fulfilment of the psychological contract.

Implications for Retention Practices

Rousseau's (1995) theory on the psychological contract and Coetzee's (2014) psychosocial career preoccupations framework has proven to be useful tools in the retention of employees. This chapter provided a deeper understanding on how employees' diverse biographical characteristics may influence their psychological contract and psychosocial career preoccupations. Human resource practitioners could use this information in order to develop retention strategies specifically for diverse employees. Organisations should acknowledge that diverse employees will have different expectations in terms of the psychological contract and therefore they should manage these different expectations of diverse employees accordingly. Organisations should also realise that the career concerns and preoccupations of a diverse group of employees will also vary from employee to employee due to their biographical characteristics. Employees with different biographical characteristics are also satisfied with different retention factors. Organisations should take cognisance of this when they develop human resource practices and policies. Future research might have possible outcomes such as creating awareness of the fact that employees have different psychological contracts and preoccupations in terms of their careers. In order to fulfil the expectations of employees in terms of their psychological contracts and their careers, they should be treated appropriately in terms of their biographical characteristics. There is a need for further research on the psychological contract, psychosocial career preoccupations and retention factors, specifically in the diverse South African context.

Summary

This chapter reflected on the implications of diversity on the retention of talented employees. More specifically, this chapter focused on race, gender, generational cohorts, marital status, job level and employment level as important precursors for the psychological contract, psychosocial career preoccupations and retention factors. It is concluded that human resource practitioners should consider these biographical differences when developing retention management strategies for talented employees.

References

Akhtar, C. S., Aamir, A., Khurshid, M. A., Abro, M. Q., & Hussain, J. (2015). Total rewards and retention: case study of higher education institutions in Pakistan. *Procedia—Social and Behavioural Sciences, 210*(2015), 251—259.

Allen, D. G., Shore, L. M., & Griffeth, R. W. (2003). The role of perceived organizational support and supportive human resource practices in the turnover process. *Journal of Management, 29,* 99–118.

Allen, N. J., & Meyer, J. P. (1991). A three-component conceptualization of organisational commitment. *Human Resource Management Review, 1*(1), 61–98.

Allui, A., & Shani, J. (2016). Strategic human resource management in higher education institutions: empirical evidence from Saudi. *Procedia-Social and Behavioral Sciences, 235,* 361–371.

Al-Emadi, A. A. Q., Schwabenland, C., & Wei, Q. (2015). The vital role of employee retention in Human Resource Management: A literature review. *The IUP Journal of Organizational Behavior, XIV*(3), 7–32.

Ariss, A. A., Vassilopoulou, J., Özbilgin, M. F., & Game, A. (2013). Understanding career experiences of skilled minority ethnic workers in France and Germany. *The International Journal of Human Resource Management, 24*(6), 1236–1256.

Arthur, M. B., & Rousseau, D. M. (1996). The boundaryless career: A new employment principle for a new organizational era. *General Information, 43,* 732–736.

Aruna, M., & Anitha, J. (2015). Employee retention enablers: Generation Y employees. *SCMS Journal of Indian Management, 12*(3), 94–103.

Bal, P. M., & Kooij, D. (2011). The relations between work centrality, psychological contracts, and job attitudes: The influence of age. *European Journal of Work and Organizational Psychology, 20*(4), 497–523.

Barkhuizen, N., & Rothmann, S. (2008). Occupational stress of academic staff in South African higher education institutions. *South African Journal of Psychology, 38*(2), 321–336.

Bellou, V. (2009). Profiling the desirable psychological contract for different groups of employees: Evidence from Greece. *The International Journal of Human Resource Management, 20*(4), 810–830.

Bergiel, B. E., Nguyen, V. Q., Clenney, B. F., & Taylor, G. S. (2009). Human resource practices, job embeddedness and intention to quit. *Management Research News, 32*(3), 205–219.

Bersin, J. (2008). The business impact of talent management. *Banking Strategies, 84*(5), 6.

Blomme, R. J., Van Rheede, A., & Tromp, D. M. (2010). The use of the psychological contract to explain turnover intentions in the hospitality industry: a research study on the impact of gender on the turnover intentions of highly educated employees. *The International Journal of Human Resource Management, 21*(1), 144–162.

Bordia, S., Bordia, P., & Restubog, S. L. D. (2015). Promises from afar: A model of international student psychological contract in business education. *Studies in Higher Education, 40*(2), 212–232.

Brunetto, Y., Farr-Wharton, R., & Shacklock, K. (2012). Communication, training, well-being, and commitment across nurse generations. *Nursing Outlook, 60*(1), 7–15.

Castaneda, M., Zambrana, R. E., Marsh, K., Vega, W., Becerra, R., & Perez, D. J. (2015). Role of institutional climate on underrepresented faculty perceptions and decision making in use of work-family policies. *Family Relations, 64,* 711–725.

Clinton, M., & Guest, D. (2004). Fulfilment of the psychological contract and related work attitudes. In *Proceedings of the Occupational Psychology Conference of the British Psychological Society* (pp. 60–64), Stratford.

Coetzee, M. (2014). *Exploratory factor analysis of the career preoccupations scale: A preliminary analysis of its reliability and construct validity (Unpublished research report).* Pretoria: University of South Africa.

Coetzee, M. (2015a). Employees' psychosocial career preoccupations in relation to their work-related commitment. *South African Business Review, 19*(3), 30–47.

Coetzee, M. (2015b). Adaptive behaviour in the workplace: Psycho-social career preoccupations and openness to technological change. In V. Martin (Ed.), *Career development: Theories, practices and challenges* (pp. in press). New York: Nova Science.

Coetzee, M., Oosthuizen, R. M., & Stoltz, E. (2015). Psychosocial employability attributes as predictors of staff satisfaction with retention factors. *South African Journal of Psychology,* 1–12.

Coetzee, M., & Stoltz, E. (2015). Employee's satisfaction with the retention factors: Exploring the role of career adaptability. *Journal of Vocational behavior, 59,* 83-91

Cook, A., & Maree, J. G. (2016). Efficacy of using career and self-construction to help learners manage career-related transitions. *South African Journal of Education, 36*(1), 1–11.

Deas, A. J. (2017). *Constructing a psychological retention profile for diverse generational groups in the higher educational environment.* (Unpublished doctoral thesis). Pretoria: University of South Africa.

De Cooman, R., & Dries, N. (2012). Attracting Generation Y: How work values predict organizational attraction in graduating students in Belgium. In E. Ng, S. T. Lyons, & L. Schweitzer (Eds.), *Managing the new workforce: International perspectives on the millennial generation.* Northampton, MA: Edward Elgar.

De Cuyper, N., Van der Heijden, B. I., & De Witte, H. (2011). Associations between perceived employability, employee well-being, and its contribution to organizational success: A matter of psychological contracts? *The International Journal of Human Resource Management, 22*(7), 1486–1503.

De Jong, J., Schalk, R., & de Cuyper, N. (2009). Balanced versus unbalanced psychological contracts in temporary and permanent employment: Associations with employee attitudes. *Management and Organisational Review, 5*(3), 329–351.

De Vos, A., & Meganck, A. (2009). What HR managers do versus what employees value: Exploring both parties' views on retention management from a psychological contract perspective. *Personnel Review, 38*(1), 45–60.

Döckel, A. (2003). *The effect of retention factors on organisational commitment: an investigation of high technology employees (Unpublished MCom dissertation).* South Africa: University of Pretoria.

Döckel, A., Basson, J. S., & Coetzee, M. (2006). The effect of retention factors on organisational commitment: An investigation of high technology employees. *SA Journal of Human Resource Management, 4*(2), 20–28.

Donnelley, R. (2015). Tensions and challenges in the management of diversity and inclusion in IT services multinationals in India. *Human Resource Management, 54*(2), 199–215.

Duffy, R. D., Douglass, R. P., & Autin, K. L. (2015). Career adaptability and academic satisfaction: Examining work volition and self-efficacy as mediators. *Journal of Vocational Behavior, 90,* 46–54.

Festing, M., & Schäfer, L. (2014). Generational challenges to talent management: A framework for talent retention based on the psychological-contract perspective. *Journal of World Business, 49,* 262–271.

George, C. (2015). Retaining professional workers: What makes them stay? *Employee Relations, 37*(1), 102–121.

Gonzalez, J. A., & Denisi, A. S. (2009). Cross-level effects of demography and diversity climate on organizational attachment and firm effectiveness. *Journal of Organizational Behavior, 30,* 21–40.

Gravetter, F. J., Wallnau, L. B., & Forzano, L.-A. B. (2016). *Essentials of statistics for the behavioral sciences.* Belmont, CA: Cengage Learning.

Greer, C. R., & Virick, M. (2008). Diverse succession planning: Lessons from the industry leaders. *Human Resource Management, 47*(2), 351–367.

Grover, S. L., & Crooker, K. J. (1995). Who appreciates family-responsive human resources policies: The impact of family-friendly policies on the organisational attachment of parent and non-parents. *Personnel Psychology, 48*(2), 271–289.

Guest, D. E. (1998). Is the psychological contract worth taking seriously? *Journal of Organizational Behavior*, 649–664.

Guest, D. E. (2004). The psychology of the employment relationship: An analysis based on the psychological contract. *Applied Psychology: An International Review, 53,* 541–555.

Guest, D. E., & Conway, N. (2002). Communicating the psychological contract: An employer perspective. *Human Resource Management Journal, 12,* 22–38.

Guillot-Soulez, C., & Soulez, S. (2014). On the heterogeneity of Generation Y job preferences. *Employee Relations, 36*(4), 319–332.

Hartung, P. J. (2007). Career construction: principles and practice. In K. Maree (Ed.), *Shaping the story: A guide to facilitating narrative career counselling*. Van Schaik: Pretoria.

Haynes, N., Jacobson, S. K., & Wald, D. M. (2015). A life-cycle analysis of minority underrepresentation in natural resource fields. *Wildlife Society Bulletin, 39*(2), 228–238.

Heinen, J. S., & O'Neill, C. (2004). Managing talent to maximise performance. *Employment Relations Today, 31*(2), 67–82.

Hite, L. M., & McDonald, K. S. (2012). Career counselling for millennials: Practitioners' perspectives. In E. Ng, S. T. Lyons, & L. Schweitzer (Eds.), *Managing the new workforce: International*. Northampton, MA: Edward Elgar.

Hofhuis, J., Van der Zee, K. I., & Otten, S. (2014). Comparing antecedents of voluntary job turnover among majority and minority employees. *Equality, Diversity and Inclusion: An International Journal, 33*(8), 735–749.

Holbeche, L. (2009). *Aligning human resources and business strategy* (2nd ed.). Oxford: Elsevier.

Hsiao, A., Auld, C., & Ma, E. (2015). Perceived organizational diversity and employee behavior. *International Journal of Hospitality Management, 48*(2015), 102–112.

Ibidunni, S., Osibanjo, O., Adeniji, A., Salau, O., & Falola, H. (2016). Talent retention and organizational performance: A competitive positioning in Nigerian Banking Sector. *Periodica Polytechnica Social and Management Sciences, 24*(1), 1–13.

Jafri, H. (2014). Study on psychological contract of faculties of Royal University of Bhutan. *KIIT Journal of Management, 10*(II), 21–32.

Jena, R. K. (2015). An assessment of demographic factors affecting organizational commitment among shift workers in India. *Journal of Contemporary Management Issues, 20*(1), 59–77.

Kakar, P., Raziq, A., & Khan, F. (2015). Impact of human resource management practices on employee retention: a case of banking sector in Quetta Balochistan. *Journal of Management Info, 5*(1), 97–119.

Kochanski, J., & Ledford, G. (2001). How to keep me: Retaining technical professionals. *Research Technology Management, 44*(3), 31–38.

Lam, A., & De Campos, A. (2015). Content to be sad or runaway apprentice? The psychological contract and career agency of young scientists in the entrepreneurial university. *Human Relations, 68*(5), 811–841.

Lee, T. W., Hom, P., Eberly, M., & Li, J. (2017). Managing employee retention and turnover with 21st century ideas. *Organizational Dynamics, 2017,* 1–11.

Le Roux, C. H., & Rothmann, S. (2013). Contractual relations between employers and employees in an HEI: Individual and organizational outcomes. *South African Journal of Higher Education, 27*(4), 252–274.

Li, J., Wong, I. A., & Kim, W. G. (2016). Effects of psychological contract breach on attitudes and performance: The moderating role of competitive climate. *International Journal of Hospitality Management, 55,* 1–10.

Mahoney, D. J. (1987). An exploration of the construct validity of a measure of adult vocational maturity (Doctoral dissertation). *Teacher's College, Columbia University. Dissertation Abstracts International, 61,* 2–14.

Maree, J. G. (2016). Career construction counseling with a mid-career black man. *The Career Development Quarterly, 64,* 20–34.

McDonald, K. S., & Hite, L. M. (2008). The next generation of career success: Implications for HRD. *Advances in Developing Human Resources, 10,* 86–103.

McWhirter, E. H. (1997). Perceived barriers to education and careers: Ethnic and gender differences. *Journal of Vocational Behavior, 50,* 124–140.
Metcalfe, A. (1993). Women in management: Organizational socialization and assessment practices that prevent career advancement. *International Journal of Selection and Assessment, 1*(2), 68–83.
Miller, G. E., & Rowney, J. L. A. (1999). Workplace diversity management in a multicultural society. *Women in Management Review, 14*(8).
Morrison, E. W., & Robinson, S. L. (1997). When employees feel betrayed: A model of how psychological contract violation occurs. *Academy of Management Review, 22*(1), 226–256.
Mubarak, R. Z., Wahab, Z., & Khan, N. R. (2012). Faculty retention in higher education institutions of Pakistan. *Journal of Theories and Research in Education, 7*(2), 65–78.
Nelson, S. A. (2012). Affective commitment of generational cohorts of Brazilian nurses. *International Journal of Manpower, 33*(7), 804–821.
Ng, E. S. W., Schweitzer, L., & Lyons, S. T. (2010). New generation, great expectations: A field study of the millennial generation. *Journal of Business and Psychology, 25,* 281–292.
O'Meara, K., Bennet, J. C., & Neihaus, E. (2016). Left unsaid: The role of work expectations and psychological contrats in faculty careers and departure. *The Review of Higher Education, 39* (2), 269–297.
Persson, S., & Wasieleski, D. (2015). The seasons of the psychological contract: Overcoming the silent transformations of the employer-employee relationship. *Human Resource Management Review, 25,* 368–383.
Presbitero, A., Roxas, B., & Chadee, D. (2016). Looking beyond HRM practices in enhancing employee retention in BPOs: Focus on employee-organisation value fit. *The International Journal of Human Resource Management, 27*(6), 635–652.
Rayton, B. A., Brammer, S. J., & Millington, A. I. (2015). Corporate social performance and the psychological contract. *Group and Organizational Management, 40*(3), 353–377.
Renkema, A., Schaap, H., & Van Dellen, T. (2009). Development intention of support staff in an academic organization in The Netherlands. *Career Development International, 14*(1), 69–86.
Rousseau, D. M. (1995). *Psychological contracts in organizations: Understanding written and unwritten agreements*. Thousand Oaks: Sage.
Rovai, A. P., Baker, J. D., & Ponton, M. K. (2013). *Social science research design and statistics: A practitioner's guide to research methods and IBM SPSS*. Chesapeake: Watertree Press.
Ryan, J. F., Healy, R., & Sullivan, J. (2012). Oh, won't you stay? Predictors of faculty intent to leave a public research university. *Higher Education, 63,* 421–473.
Santosh, B. R., & Muthiah, K. (2016). An empirical study on the organizational commitment of repatriated female employees. *IUP Journal of Management Research, XV*(4), 7–21.
Savickas, M. L. (1997). Career adaptability: An integrative construct for life-span, life-space theory. *The Career Development Quarterly, 45,* 247–259.
Savickas, M. L. (2002). Career construction: A developmental theory of vocational behaviour. In D. Brown & Associate (Eds.), *Career choice and development* (pp. 149–205) (4th ed.). San Francisco: Jossey-Bass.
Savickas, M. L. (2005). The theory and practice of career construction. In R. W. Lent & S. D. Brown (Eds.), *Career development and counselling: Putting theory and research to work* (2nd ed.). Hoboken: Wiley.
Savickas, M. L. (2013). Life design: A paradigm for career intervention in the 21st century. *Journal of Counselling & Development, 90,* 13–19.
Sharf, R. S. (2010). *Applying career development theory to counseling* (5th ed.). Belmont: Cengage Learning.
Shen, J. (2010). University academics' psychological contracts and their fulfilment. *Journal of Management Development, 29*(6), 575–591.
Shore, B. (2013). Improving employee retention in a South Korean high growth organization: Do western strategies apply? *The Journal of Global Business Issues, 7*(2), 1–8.

Singh, A., & Gupta, B. (2015). Job involvement, organizational commitment, professional commitment, and team commitment: A study of generational diversity. *Benchmarking, 22*(6), 1192–1211.

Singh, B., & Selvarajan, T. T. (2013). Is it spillover or compensation? Effects of community and organizational diversity climates on race differentiated employee intent to stay. *Journal of Business Ethics, 115*(2), 259–269.

Snyman, A. M. (2014). *The effect of employment equity legislation on the psychological contract in a tertiary institution (Master's thesis).* Pretoria: University of Pretoria.

Society of Human Resource Management. (2016). *SHRM Survey Findings: Influencing workplace culture through employee recognition and other efforts.*

Tladinyane, R. T., Coetzee, M., & Masenge, A. (2013). Psychological career meta-capacities in relation to employees' retention-related dispositions. *Southern African Business Review, 17*(2), 140–163.

Unsal-Akbiyik, B. S. (2014). The mediating role of human resource management practices on affective commitment and type of contract. *Journal of Social Sciences, VII, I*(1), 72–86.

Uys, I. (2003). Diversity management: Reasons and challenges. *Politeia, 22*(3), 30–48.

Van der Vaart, L., Linde, B., & Cockeran, M. (2013). The state of the psychological contract and employees' intention to leave: The mediating role of employee well-being. *South African Journal of Psychology, 43*(3), 356–369.

Van der Walt, S., & Du Plessis, T. (2010). Age diversity and the aging librarian in academic libraries in South Africa. *South African Journal of Libraries and Information Science, 76*(1), 1–10.

Van Dyk, J., & Coetzee, M. (2012). Retention factors in relation to organisational commitment in medical and information technology services. *South African Journal of Human Resource Management, 10*(2), 1–11.

Van Dyk, J., Coetzee, M., & Takawira, N. (2013). Satisfaction with retention factors as predictors of the job embeddedness of medical and information technology services staff. *Southern African Business Review, 17*(1), 57–75.

Wöcke A., & Sutherland, M. (2008). The impact of employment equity regulations on psychological contracts in South Africa. *The International Journal of Human Resource Management, 19*(4), 528–542.

Zhou, W., Guan, Y., Xin, L., Mak, M. C. K., & Deng, Y. (2016). Career success criteria and locus of control as indicators of adaptive readiness in the career adaptation model. *Journal of Vocational Behavior, 94,* 124–130.

Alda Deas (PhD) is a lecturer in Labour Relations Management at the Department of Human Resource Management at the University of South Africa (Unisa), South Africa. She is registered with the South African Board of People Practices (SABPP) as a human resource practitioner.

Part VI
Organisational Practices

Overview and Insights

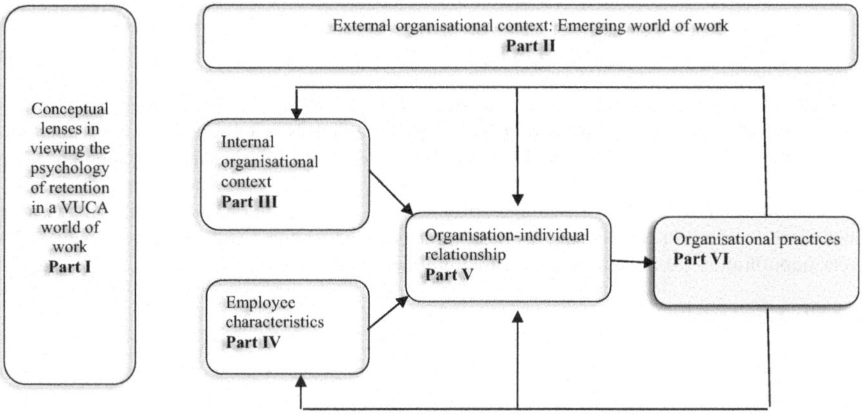

Towards an integrated conceptual framework for the psychology of retention

Part VI, *Organisational Practices*, comprises four chapters that address work ethics, mentoring and reward solutions as important practices in the psychology of retention.

Part VI: Overview

In Chap. 17, *Ethical Context in Relation to Employee Commitment in a Developing Country Setting,* Jeremy Mitonga-Monga addresses an under-researched theme in the retention space, namely work ethics. Drawing from a cross-sectional quantitative study among a sample of N = 839 in a railway organisation in the Democratic Republic of Congo (DRC), the author shows that perceived work ethics culture and work ethics climate variables predict employees' levels of affective, continuance and normative commitment. The author makes a convincing case for establishing comprehensive ethical standards, good ethical role models, adequate resources and working conditions that enable ethical actions, as well as cultivating a work ethic that supports common organisational values to enhance employees' loyalty or commitment to the organisation and extend their job tenure. The chapter makes a valuable contribution to the retention research literature by positioning work ethics in the retention space.

In Chap. 18, *Tap the Experienced to Care for the Inexperienced: Millennial Employees' Retention Challenge? Mentoring is the Solution*, Mohammad Faraz Naim continues with the discussion on the unique career development support needs of millennial workers (see Part V). Based on a sound review of the research literature, the author explores the role of mentoring as an organisational practice in influencing employee positive work-related behaviours that benefit the retention of millennial workers. The chapter contributes a conceptual framework for workplace mentoring that facilitates personal learning and affective commitment, which in turn reduces the turnover intentions of millennial employees.

In Chap. 19, *Reward Solutions to Retention Questions*, Mark Bussin argues that in the volatile, uncertain, complex, ambiguous (VUCA) landscape, conventional reward procedures, plans and strategies are no longer sufficient for talent retention. The chapter makes a valuable contribution to the retention literature by outlining the reward strategies and remuneration factors that are linked to greater retention of talent as well as the latest developments and trends associated with these strategies. The author cautions that although remuneration is important as a retention strategy, it should not be considered in isolation. The author proposes the application of a holistic approach involving a total rewards strategy that includes both monetary and non-monetary rewards to ensure an attractive workplace and to drive the attraction and retention of the employees. The chapter provides a practical guide on how to design a world-class reward strategy and apply it in the retention context.

Chapter 20 by Calvin Mzwenhlanhla Mabaso, *Total Rewards as a Psychosocial Factor Influencing Talent Retention*, builds on Chap. 19 by showing how total rewards as psychosocial factors influence talent's choice to join, remain and leave an organisation from the theoretical lens of expectancy theory. Drawing from a cross-sectional quantitative study among a sample of N = 262 academics in a South African university context, the chapter shows that compensation, benefits, performance management, work-life balance, recognition, and talent development and career opportunities all have a positive effect on talent retention.

Part VI: Key Insights

Part VI highlights key insights regarding organisational practices such as work ethics, mentoring and a total rewards strategy, all of which broaden insight regarding the psychology of retention.

Practice Guidelines

The author of Chap. 17 demonstrates the importance of conducting surveys to establish perceptions of work ethics as part of a retention strategy. Practices that support employees' commitment to the organisation may include creating conditions (a work ethics culture) that foster perceptions that the organisation embraces comprehensive ethical standards, positive ethical conditions and values, transparency, opportunities to discuss ethical issues, reinforcement of ethical behaviour and sanctionability. In Chap. 18, the author emphasises the importance of formal mentoring programmes for millennials to address their need for continuous learning and growth and to enhance their affective commitment towards the organisation.

The author of Chap. 19 makes a convincing case for adopting a total rewards strategy in retaining talent. It is argued that in terms of understanding the psychology of retention, a total rewards strategy should include both monetary and non-monetary rewards to ensure an attractive workplace and to drive the attraction and retention of the employees. Organisational practices relating to the following components of the total rewards strategy should be considered: compensation/remuneration, benefits; work-life effectiveness/balance; recognition; performance management; and talent development programmes and interventions to develop skills and abilities and promote career growth. Chapter 20 continues to provide important insight into the role of a total rewards strategy in retention practices. The author reiterates that retention practices should address the total rewards elements of compensation, benefits, performance management, work-life balance, recognition, and talent development and career opportunities. The author recommends that rewards specialists develop fair and equitable rewards packages to attract and retain talent.

Research Gaps

Work ethics in the retention space is under-researched. The author of Chap. 17 recommends studies on how the work ethics culture components of clarity, congruency of supervisor, congruency of management, feasibility, supportability, discussability, transparency and sanctionability, as well as the elements of a work ethics climate, namely caring, law and code, rules, independence and instrumental, affect employees' job satisfaction, motivation and organisational citizenship behaviour. More needs to be known about the moderating effect of ethical leadership and other influencing variables, such as gender, age, education and tenure. Longitudinal studies should establish the causal relationships between these variables. Qualitative studies which explore the meaning of ethical behaviour are recommended with the view to enhance understanding of work ethics in the psychology of retention.

The author of Chap. 18 reiterates continued research on the psychology of retaining millennials as young talent. Research on mentoring as an organisational practice is emphasised, especially research to examine different forms of mentoring, including group mentoring, peer mentoring and e-mentoring in the context of millennial employees. The author argues that there is also a need to develop a scale for personal learning and turnover intentions from the perspective of millennial employees. In Chaps. 19 and 20, the authors argue for continued research on the link between the components of the total rewards strategy and retention factors in diverse occupational contexts.

Chapter 17
Ethical Context in Relation to Employee Commitment in a Developing Country Setting

Jeremy Mitonga-Monga

Abstract This chapter examines the relationship between perceived ethical context and employee commitment. The convenience sample of employees (n = 839; males = 68%; females = 32%) consisted of permanent employees in a railway organisation in the Democratic Republic of Congo (DRC). The research constructs were measured using the corporate ethical virtues questionnaire (CEVQ), the ethical climate questionnaire (ECQ) and the organisational commitment scale (OCS). Standardised multiple regressions were calculated to predict employee commitment through work ethics culture and work ethics climate. The results indicate that the perceived work ethics culture and work ethics climate variables predict employees' level of commitment. Using the data from a very large organisation in a developing country, the results are generalised to human resource management. Interpretations are formulated about how organisational leaders who facilitate ethical values in building a work ethics culture and a work ethics climate can significantly decrease turnover intention and increase the level of commitment towards collaboration among organisation members.

Keywords Ethics organisational context · Work ethics culture
Work ethics climate · Employee commitment · Democratic Republic of Congo

Introduction

Organisations are increasingly seeking ways to curb malpractice, mismanagement, unethical behaviour and corruption (Ruiz-Polomino and Martinez-Cañas 2014), and given the effects of the 2008 global financial downturn (Balakrisnan et al. 2016), Volkswagen's scandal involving unethical practices, corruption and fraud (Zhakypova 2016) and the bribery and corruption uncovered at FIFA (Mansouri 2016) scholars and practitioners are likely to keep monitoring this development

J. Mitonga-Monga (✉)
University of Johannesburg, Johannesburg, South Africa
e-mail: jeremym@uj.ac.za

M. Coetzee et al. (eds.), *Psychology of Retention*,
https://doi.org/10.1007/978-3-319-98920-4_17

closely (Trevino and Nelson 2010). While the positive effects of upholding ethics and values are well known (Mitonga-Monga and Cilliers 2015), there is still a paucity of research on how ethics in an organisational context can help businesses to achieve excellence in moral and technical terms, as well as in shaping employees' job responses, attitudes and behaviours. This study focuses on ethics organisational context (Victor and Cullen 1988), which is one of the variables that are increasingly associated with ethical decision-making in the workplace. Ethical context refers to the prevailing perceptions of norms, procedures and ethical policies within an organisation (Bedi et al. 2015). Researchers have used two related frameworks to represent an ethical context in organisations: work ethics climate (Victor and Cullen 1988) and work ethics culture (Treviño and Nelson 2010). A previous study by Hollingsworth and Valentine (2015) found that the variables of work ethics culture and work ethics climate relate positively to employees' intention to engage in ethical practices and increase their willingness to report unethical behaviour.

In line with the call from Kaptein (2008), Mitonga-Monga and Cilliers (2015) and Victor and Cullen (1988) and others, the purpose of this study is to examine the extent to which variables of work ethics culture and work ethics climate are strongly associated with employees' level of commitment. Although the variables of work ethics culture and work ethics climate (Treviño and Nelson 2010) have frequently been studied for their relationship to work-related outcomes such as satisfaction, organisational citizenship behaviour and work engagement (Mitonga-Monga and Cilliers 2015), few studies have explored their relationship to employees' commitment (Huhtala and Feldt 2016). Employee commitment is an important construct to study in relation to ethics organisational context because, given its psychological and attitudinal nature, it is likely to reduce turnover and absenteeism in the organisation (Gould-Williams and Davies 2005). Losing talented employees causes severe losses in terms of productivity, creativity, efficiency and profit (Lin and Liu 2017). Mitonga-Monga and Cilliers (2016) note that positive work attitudes depend on employees' perceptions of how organisational culture, climate and values of the employing organisation. For instance, Huhtala and Feldt (2016) contend that an organisation that treats its employees well, maintains a good reputation and upholds ethical values can produce positive work responses in its employees, indicating a good person-organisation fit. Yet even though researchers suggest that employees wish to work for an ethical organisation (Novelskaite and Pucetaite 2014), there is a dearth of concrete empirical scrutiny to support this claim. Therefore, this chapter will contribute to the field of work ethics culture, work ethics climate and employee commitment and retention by examining the association between the variables of work ethics culture, work ethics climate and employee commitment in a railway organisation in the DRC.

In the following sections we will discuss the DRC work context, theoretical framework and hypotheses, methodological aspects and results of the study.

The DRC Work Context

The DRC is seen as an emerging and developing country with vast mineral and natural wealth (gold, copper, diamonds, forests and agricultural) and a huge political and economic potential (Mitonga-Monga and Cilliers 2016). Despite its natural resources, the DRC remains one of the poorest countries globally, mainly because of political and economic crises, ineffective leadership, unemployment, lack of a culture of accountability, corruption and a high level of unethical behaviour (Gilpin and Boor 2012). All these factors have resulted in the country's being ranked below 7% in all six indicators, with the lowest scores on government effectiveness, rule of law, political crisis and control of accountability (Mitonga-Monga and Cilliers 2015). It seems that persistent political instability has and still is affecting all sectors of the society. This includes the transport industry, in terms of a lack of good infrastructure and reliable railroads, locomotives, rail beds and commuter services. According to Mitonga-Monga and Cilliers (2015), efforts by the World Bank and African Development Bank to address engineering and human resources issues (e.g. transformation of most of the reportedly corrupt entities into ethical organisations) have been largely unsuccessful because of the high level of unethical behaviour and lack of good governance and culture of accountability.

Next we will discuss the theoretical framework and hypotheses of this study.

Theoretical Framework and Hypotheses

Work Ethics Culture

"Work ethics culture" is perceived as the ethical quality of a work environment and is defined as the shared values, norms and beliefs that can encourage ethical behaviour (Kaptein 2008; Treviño and Weaver 2003; Mitonga-Monga and Cilliers 2015). One of the classic theories of business ethics is virtue ethics (Huhtala and Feltd 2016; Kaptein 2008), according to which virtues nurture an intrinsic motivation that has a positive impact on individuals' behaviour and attitudes (Solomon 2004; Huhtala and Feldt 2016). A fundamental aspect of ethical virtues is that moral values and beliefs are desirable goods in themselves and the realisation of these virtues results in individual satisfaction and loyalty. Thus organisations that embrace corporate ethical virtues can encourage employees to flourish and produce quality work (Ciula 2004; Huhtala and Feldt 2016). From the virtues theory, Kaptein (2008) developed the corporate ethical virtues questionnaire, which comprises the following key components:

- *Clarity.* This refers to the extent to which an organisation sets clear and comprehensive ethical standards and normative expectations for employees.

- *Congruency of supervisor* and *congruency of management*. These refer to the extent to which managers are good ethical role models and act with integrity and respect.
- *Feasibility*. This refers to the extent to which top management provides workers with appropriate resources and practical conditions that facilitate ethical action.
- *Supportability*. This refers to the extent to which individuals share, support, trust and are committed to the common organisational ethical values and beliefs.
- *Transparency*. This refers to the extent to which the organisation makes visible both good behaviour and wrongdoing and its consequences.
- *Discussability*. This refers to the extent to which an organisation provides opportunities/a forum to raise and discuss ethical issues.
- *Sanctionability*. This refers to the extent to which an organisation reinforces ethical behaviour by rewarding ethical employees and punishing wrongdoers.

Together, these virtues constitute the ethical features of an organisational culture, which promotes ethical behaviour (Kaptein 2008). Previous research by Mitonga-Monga and Cilliers (2015) indicates that work ethics culture relates positively to employees' well-being and commitment to the organisation, resulting in a lower level of intention to quit. According to Huhtala and Feldt (2016), the multidimensional CEV model is crucial in that it permits us to examine whether various virtues are associated with certain work-related outcomes. It is our purpose to examine whether some of these virtues are less significant than others in ensuring a good employee–employer fit, since this can have positive consequences when assigning resources in the organisation. These ethical virtues should also be taken into consideration and prioritised when developing employee-retention strategies for an organisation. Based on the above-mentioned discussion, we can hypothesise that a work ethic culture will be positively associated with employee commitment.

Next we will discuss the theory related to a work ethics climate.

Work Ethics Climate

The "work ethics climate" is perceived as a cluster of prescribed climate elements reflecting the organisational procedures, policies and practices that have moral consequences (Al-Omari 2013; Martin and Cullen 2006; Victor and Cullen 1988). Practically, the work ethics climate of an organisation is a shared perception among organisational members of how ethical concerns are addressed and what defines "ethical behaviour". The literature review identifies the following five key elements of a work ethics climate:

- *Caring*. This refers to individual employees' perception that their organisation fosters a positive and ethically caring atmosphere that enhances their well-being.

- *Law and code.* This reflects the principal ethical criteria in an organisation. These criteria require that workers adhere to the codes of practice and regulations of their respective professions or other affiliated bodies.
- *Rules.* This refers to the extent to which employees accept the rules and code of conduct determined by the organisation.
- *Independence.* This refers to the extent to which individual employees act according to their own personal moral beliefs, based on a set of well-considered principles.
- *Instrumental.* This refers to the extent to which individual employees believe that decisions are made that serve the organisation's interests or provide personal benefits.

Together, these elements of the work ethics climate comprise the ethical elements of organisational procedures and policies that influence employees' attitudes and behaviour (Mitonga-Monga and Cilliers 2015). Previous studies by Lin and Liu (2016) and Treviño et al. (1998) indicate that these different elements of a work ethics climate have proven to have positive effects on organisational outcomes such as job satisfaction, commitment and reduced employee turnover intention. Although the empirical evidence pertaining to the association between the work ethics climate and employee commitment is clear (Treviño et al. 1998), there is still a need to research this in developing country settings (Al-Omari 2013; Valentine et al. 2011). Based on the aforementioned reasoning and previous studies, we hypothesise that a work ethics climate will indeed be associated with employee commitment in developing countries.

Next we will discuss the theory related to employee commitment.

Employee Commitment

Nationwide, organisations are increasingly seeking to develop loyal workers in an effort to increase performance and productivity and reduce employee turnover and absenteeism, while improving individual employees' psychological attachment to the organisation (Gould-Williams and Davis 2005; Mitonga-Monga and Cilliers 2016) The concept of employee commitment has captured the attention of both practitioners and scholars (Meyer and Allen 1997). According to Mullins (2013), research on employees' commitment to the organisation, as well as antecedents and outcomes of this commitment, has been studied extensively. Employees who are committed are loyal to the organisation and extend their membership in the organisation (Mitonga-Monga and Cilliers 2016). "Employee commitment" refers to an employee's belief in and enthusiasm for working according to the goals and values of the organisation (Allen and Meyer 1996; Mitonga-Monga and Cilliers 2016; Mowday et al. 2013). From the literature, we can see that employee commitment comprises the following three components:

- *Affective commitment*. This reflects the extent of workers' emotional attachment to, identification with and involvement in the organisation. Individual employees with a high level of affective commitment stay in the organisation or extend their membership within it because they *want* to.
- *Continuance commitment*. This reflects the extent to which employees examine whether the costs of leaving the organisation are greater than the costs of staying. Employees who regard the costs of leaving the organisation as greater than the costs of staying remain in the organisation because they *need* to.
- *Normative commitment*. This represents the employees' sense of obligation to an organisation. Individual employees with a high level of normative commitment extend their membership within the organisation because they feel they *ought* to.

According to Morrow (2011) most studies show that the development of organisational commitment is based on the belief in social exchange theory. Specifically, the organisation is encouraged to create a good working environment for its members, who, in turn, demonstrate their loyalty and psychological attachment to their employer. Furthermore, according to the social exchange view, if employees notice that their organisation has positive policies, regulations and procedures (Mitonga-Monga and Cilliers 2016), employees will develop an implicit obligation to reciprocate by forming an affective, emotional bond with the organisation (Lee et al. 2016). In other words, if employees perceive that there are clear procedures, policies and regulations in an organisation, they may feel a sense of obligation to stay with the organisation (Mitonga-Monga and Cilliers 2015). A previous study by Vakola and Nikolaou (2005) found that employee commitment was positively related to organisational citizenship behaviour and lower employee absenteeism and turnover. In the next section we will discuss the relationship between ethics organisational context variables and employee commitment.

The Relationship Between Ethics Organisational Context Variables and Employee Commitment

Based on previous research (Huhtala and Feldt 2016; Vakola and Nikolaou 2005; Treviño et al. 1998), there is reason to believe that an ethical context of organisations will effect some positive work-related outcomes, mostly in terms of employees' attitudinal responses to the organisation. For instance, work ethics culture and work ethics climate arguably strengthen employees' level of commitment and reduce their turnover intention (Hashish 2017; Huhtala and Feldt 2016; Mayer 2014). Research indicates that employees and organisations are negatively affected when commitment is low (Mitonga-Monga and Cilliers 2016) and that both benefit when commitment is high (Mitonga-Monga and Flotman 2017). Employee commitment is connected with increased performance (Huhtala and Feldt 2016), job satisfaction (Mitonga-Monga et al. 2016) and organisational citizenship behaviour (Vakola and Nikolaou 2005), as well as less absenteeism (Mowday et al. 2013) and employee turnover (Valentine et al. 2011). Both work ethics culture and climate may boost employees' level of psychological attachment to the organisation (Arnaud and Schminke 2012). Individual employees might show loyalty to their employer if the organisation has positive ethical practices and a good reputation (Huhtala and Feldt 2016). Mayer (2014) found that work ethics culture was positively related to employees' commitment. Kish-Gephart, Harrison and Treviño (2010) found that the work ethics climate was significantly related to employees' job satisfaction, commitment and organisational citizenship behaviours. Although previous studies have shown a link between the above-mentioned constructs (Huhtala and Feldt 2016; Ruiz-Palomino and Martinez-Canas 2014), there seems to be a dearth of research examining the extent to which work ethics culture and work ethical climate relate to employees' commitment in developing country settings, such as the DRC.

Purpose, Research Question and Contribution

The purpose of this chapter is to investigate the relationship between employees' perception of their ethical context variables (work ethics culture and work ethics climate and their level of commitment in a railway organisation in the DRC. The research question that supports this study is formulated as follows: How do the variables of work ethics culture and work ethics climate relate to employees' commitment to an organisation in the DRC? This chapter makes a valuable contribution to both the theory and practice. Firstly, it contributes to theoretical debate in the disciplines of organisational behaviour, business ethics, industrial and organisational psychology and human resource management concerning the association between ethical context variables (work ethics culture and work ethics climate) and employee commitment. Secondly, on a practical level, this chapter makes recommendations for leadership and human resource management practitioners for the retention of staff in a developing country setting.

Method

Participants and Setting

This study employed a quantitative research approach, following a cross-sectional survey design (Tabachnick and Fidell 2013), with respondents drawn from permanently employed employees in the selected railway organisation in the DRC. A convenience sample ($n = 839$; males = 68%; females = 32%) was used, reflecting the following characteristics: A total of 63.1% of the participants were

Table 17.1 Descriptive statistics: Mean, standard deviations and Cronbach alpha coefficients

Variables	Mean	Stand. Dev	Α
Overall work ethics culture	4.04	0.51	0.97
Clarity	3.63	0.57	0.88
Congruency of supervisor	4.01	0.68	0.84
Congruency of management	4.05	0.64	0.79
Feasibility	4.42	0.82	0.68
Supportability	4.05	0.66	0.83
Transparency	4.02	0.68	0.87
Discussability	4.07	0.60	0.88
Sanctionability	4.10	0.63	0.89
Overall work ethics climate	4.04	0.55	0.95
Caring	4.02	0.60	0.91
Law and code	4.08	0.64	0.88
Rules	4.03	0.66	0.81
Independence	3.98	0.85	0.86
Instrumental	4.12	0.60	0.81
Overall employee commitment	4.09	0.54	0.94
Affective commitment	4.07	0.55	0.86
Continuance commitment	4.08	0.65	0.88
Normative commitment	4.13	0.59	0.88

aged between 26 and 40 years; 42.1% were unmarried; 66% had honours degrees; and 38% had been employed in the organisation for between 6 and 10 years. The demographical characteristics of the sample are included in Table 17.1

Measuring Instruments

The participants completed a biographical and demographical survey. They also completed the measurement instruments for work ethics culture, work ethics climate and organisational commitment, which are described next.

*__Corporate ethical virtue questionnaire__ (CEVQ: Kaptein 2008). This is a 58-item self-reported measure scored on a five-point Likert scale (where 1 = strongly disagree and 5 = strongly agree). It measures the organisation's ethical virtues across eight dimensions: *Clarity.* "My organisation makes it sufficiently clear to me how I should conduct myself appropriately towards others within the organisation." *Congruency of supervisor.* "My supervisor sets a good example in terms of ethical behaviour." *Congruency of management.* "The board and senior management would never authorise unethical or illegal conduct to meet business goals." *Feasibility.* "In my job, I am sometimes put under pressure to break the rules." *Supportability.* "In my immediate working environment, everyone takes the existing norms and standards seriously." *Transparency.* "If a colleague does something that is not permitted, my manager will find out about it." *Discussability.* "In my immediate working environment, reports of unethical conduct are handled with caution." *Sanctionability.* "In my immediate working environment, employees will be disciplined if they behave unethically."

The internal consistency (Cronbach alpha) scores from the CEVQ reported in a previous study ranged from 0.93 to 0.96 (Kaptein 2008). In the current study, scores from the CEVQ obtained reliability coefficients ranging from 0.83 to 0.90.

The ethical climate questionnaire (ECQ: Victor and Cullen 1988) consisted of 26 items scored on a five-point Likert scale (where 1 = strongly disagree and 5 = strongly agree). It measures the work ethics climate according to the following five dimensions: *Caring.* "The most important concern is the good of all the people in the organisation as a whole." *Law and code.* "In my organisation, the law or ethical code of a person's profession is the major consideration." *Rules.* "Successful people in this organisation go by the book." *Independence.* "In this organisation, people are expected to follow their own personal moral beliefs." *Instrumental* "Employees are working for their own interests."

Previous research reported an internal consistency (Cronbach alpha) ranging between 0.60 and 0.80 (Victor and Cullen 1998). In the current study, scores from the ECQ obtained Cronbach alpha coefficients (internal consistency) ranging from 0.81 to 0.90.

Organisational commitment scale (OCS: Meyer and Allen 1991). This is a 24-item self-report measure scored on a five-point Likert scale (where 1 = strongly disagree and 5 = strongly agree). It measures the employees' organisational commitment across three dimensions: *Affective commitment.* "I think I could easily become as attached to another organisation as I am to this one." *Continuance commitment.* "I feel that I have too few options to consider leaving this organisation." *Normative commitment.* "This organisation deserves my loyalty." The internal consistency (Cronbach alpha) of scores from the OCS reported in a previous study ranged from 0.75 to 0.79 (Meyer and Allen 1997). In the current study, scores from the OCS obtained reliability coefficients ranging from 0.81 to 0.94.

Research Procedure

Ethical clearance to conduct the research was obtained from the University of South Africa's Ethics Research Review Committee and the management of the railway organisation in the DRC. A cover letter was used to explain the purpose of the study, the measurement procedure and the researchers' adherence to ethical aspects pertaining to voluntary participation, anonymity and confidentiality. The measurement instruments were translated from English to French and then back-translated into English by a linguistic expert from the University of Pretoria. All three measurements were compiled into a booklet and distributed to the entire population. Eventually, 839 usable completed questionnaires were returned.

Statistical Analysis

The data were analysed using the Statistical Package for Social Sciences (SPSS), version 24 for Windows software (SPSS 2017). The descriptive statistics, correlational analysis and hierarchical regression analysis were used to analyse the data. At the first level, the descriptive statistics were used to calculate the mean standard deviations and Cronbach alpha coefficients. At the second level, correlational analysis was used to examine the relationship between work ethics culture, work ethics climate and employee commitment. The researchers decided to set the statistical significance cut-off value at the 95% confidence interval level ($p \leq 0.05$) (Hair et al. 2010). Hierarchical regression was performed to determine whether or not work ethics culture (CEVQ) and work ethics climate (ECQ) act as predictors of employees' organisational commitment (OCS). In order to counter the probability of Type I errors, the researcher decided to set the significance value at a 95% confidence interval level ($p \leq 0.05$). R^2 was used to test the predictive power of work ethics culture and work ethics climate (independent variables) on employees' organisational commitment (dependent variable). R^2 changes were calculated with the F-test. A significant F-value for change in the R^2 meant that the variables added significantly to improving the prediction (Tabachnick and Fidell 2013).

Results

Descriptive Analysis

In terms of the CEVQ (work ethics culture) variables, sanctionability obtained the highest mean score (M = 4.10; SD = 0.63), followed by discussability (M = 4.07; SD = 0.60), congruency of management (M = 4.05; SD = 0.64), supportability (M = 4.05; SD = 0.66), overall work ethics culture (M = 4.04; SD = 0.51), transparency (M = 4.02; SD = 0.68) and congruency of supervisor (M = 4.01; SD = 0.68). The lowest mean scores were obtained in clarity (M = 3.63; SD = 0.57) and feasibility (M = 3.42; SD = 0.83). In terms of the ECQ (work ethics climate) variables, instrumental obtained the highest mean score (M = 4.12; SD = 0.60), followed by law and code (M = 4.08; SD = 0.64), overall work ethics climate (M = 4.04; SD = 55), rules (M = 4.03; SD = 0.66) and caring (M = 4.02; SD = 0.60). The lowest mean score was obtained for independence (M = 3.98; SD = 0.85). In terms of the OCS (employee commitment) variables, normative commitment obtained the highest mean score (M = 4.13; SD = 59), followed by overall employee commitment (M = 4.09; SD = 0.54), continuance commitment (M = 4.08; SD = 0.65) and affective commitment (M = 4.04; SD = 0.55). All three components indicated a relatively high level of OCS in the sample.

Correlational Analysis

Table 17.2 shows that CEVQ and ECQ were significantly related to OCS. The results in this table show the significant correlation coefficients identified between the CEVQ, ECQ and OCS variables. The correlations range from $r \geq 0.18$ (small practical effect size) to $r \geq 0.88$ (large practical effect size). These results show that the zero-order correlations are below the threshold level of concern ($r \geq 0.90$) of multicollinearity (Hair et al. 2010).

Overall, work ethics culture, clarity, congruency of supervisor, congruency of management, feasibility, supportability, transparency, discussability, sanctionability, work ethics climate, caring, law and code, rules, independence and instrumental were positively and significantly related to overall employee commitment, affective commitment, continuance commitment and normative commitment (the p-values ranged between $p \leq 0.001$ and $p \leq 0.005$).

Standardised Multiple Regressions

Table 17.3 shows the results for the standardised multiple regressions.

In the **first equation**, the congruency of management, sanctionability, law and code, instrumental, caring and rules variables produced a significant regression model ($F_{(13;826)} = 86.59$), accounting for 58.1% (*$R^2 = 0.58$; $P \leq 0.001$*; large practical effect) of variance in affective commitment, more specifically congruency of management ($\beta = 0.21$; $p \leq 0.001$), law and code ($\beta = 0.14$; $p \leq 0.001$), instrumental ($\beta = 0.14$; $p \leq 0.001$), sanctionability ($\beta = 0.13$; $p \leq 0.001$), caring ($\beta = 0.12$; $p \leq 0.001$), rules ($\beta = 0.09$; $p \leq 0.001$) and feasibility ($\beta = 0.07$; p 0.001), contributing significantly towards explaining the proportion of variance in the OCS affective commitment variable.

In the **second equation**, the congruency of supervisor, caring, supportability, instrumental, sanctionability, transparency, discussability and independence variables produced a significant regression model ($F_{(13;826)} = 120.28$), accounting for 65.5% (*$R^2 = 0.66$; $P \leq 0.001$*; large practical effect) of variance in continuance commitment, more specifically congruency of supervisor ($\beta = 0.25$; $p \leq 0.001$), caring ($\beta = 0.25$; $p \leq 0.001$), supportability ($\beta = 0.12$; $p \leq 0.001$), instrumental ($\beta = 0.14$; $p \leq 0.001$), sanctionability ($\beta = 0.13$; $p \leq 0.001$), transparency ($\beta = 0.12$; $p \leq 0.001$) discussability ($\beta = 0.11$; $p \leq 0.001$) and independence

Table 17.2 Correlations among variables

Variables	1	2	3	4	5	6	7	8	9
Overall work ethics culture	1								
Clarity	0.86***	1							
Congruency of supervisor	0.88***	0.76***	1						
Congruency of management	0.76***	0.61***	0.69***	1					
Feasibility	0.50***	0.36**	0.41**	0.35**	1				
Supportability	0.82***	0.66***	0.70***	0.65***	0.38**	1			
Transparency	0.84***	0.76***	0.73***	0.61***	0.41**	0.74***	1		
Discussability	0.85***	0.67***	0.71***	0.57***	0.28*	0.65***	0.75***	1	
Sanctionability	0.78***	0.65***	0.64***	0.56***	0.27*	0.56***	0.61***	0.66***	1
Overall work ethics climate	0.71***	0.76***	0.65***	0.62***	0.34**	0.65***	0.69***	0.69***	0.69***
Caring	0.56***	0.67***	0.52***	0.55***	0.29*	0.59***	0.63***	0.63***	0.61***
Law and code	0.69***	0.65***	0.64***	0.42**	0.56***	0.54***	0.62***	0.61***	0.61***
Rules	0.64***	0.57***	0.58***	0.52***	0.18*	0.47**	0.44**	0.47**	0.52***
Independence	0.79***	0.59***	0.74***	0.53***	0.30**	0.57***	0.59***	0.57***	0.62***
Instrumental	0.68***	0.46**	0.62***	0.65***	0.30**	0.50***	0.55***	0.57***	0.55***
Overall employee commitment	0.73***	0.60***	0.71***	0.56***	0.24*	0.65***	0.67***	0.71***	0.66***
Affective commitment	0.71***	0.58***	0.66***	0.55***	0.28*	0.56***	0.60***	0.59***	0.61***
Continuance commitment	0.65***	0.63***	0.60***	0.58***	0.30**	0.62***	0.60***	0.66***	0.64***
Normative commitmenNormative commitmentt	0.56***	059***	0.57***	0.58***	0.31**	0.57***	0.64***	0.68***	0.59***

(continued)

Table 17.2 (continued)

Variables	10	11	12	13	14	15	16	17	18	19	
Overall work ethics culture											
Clarity											
Congruency of supervisor											
Congruency of management											
Feasibility											
Supportability											
Transparency											
Discussability											
Sanctionability											
Overall work ethics climate	1										
Caring	0.82***		1								
Law and code	0.74***		0.62***	1							
Rules	0.76***		0.61***	0.65***	1						
Independence	0.72***		0.75***	0.56***	0.51***	1					
Instrumental	0.75***		0.55***	0.57***	0.52***	0.56***	1				
Overall employee commitment	0.78***		0.73***	0.67***	0.58***	0.67***	0.56***	1			
Affective commitment	0.73***		0.61***	0.63***	0.55***	0.57***	0.64***	0.65***	1		
Continuance commitment	0.79***		0.70***	0.62***	0.57***	0.66***	0.57***	0.58***	0.76***	1	
Normative commitment	0.71***		0.64***	0.61***	0.52***	0.63***	0.66***	0.59***	0.79***	0.71***	1

Note N = 839; *$p < 0.05$—statistically significant. **$p < 0.01$—statistically significant. ***$p < 0.001$—statistically significant. Correlation values $r \leq 0.29$ are practically significant (small effect). Correlation values $r \geq 0.30 \leq 0.49$ are practically significant (medium effect). Correlation values $r \geq 0.50$ are practically significant (large effect)

Table 17.3 Multiple regressions analysis: Work ethics culture and work ethics climate as predictors of employee commitment

Variables	Model 1 affective commitment			Model 2 continuance commitment			Model 3 normative commitment		
	B	*β*	*t*	*B*	*β*	*t*	*B*	*β*	*t*
(Constant)	0.96		7.48***	0.27		1.91	0.67		4.858***
Clarity	−0.00	−0.02	−0.479	0.00	−0.00	−0.054	−0.01	−0.08	−2.076
Congruency of supervisor	0.00	0.03	0.655	0.04	0.25	6.29***	0.03	0.17	3.829***
Congruency of management	0.04	0.21	5.98***	−0.01	−0.04	−1.34	0.03	0.13	3.939***
Feasibility	0.01	−0.07	2.77*	0.01	0.05	2.06	−0.00	0.01	0.256
Supportability	0.00	0.03	0.707	0.03	0.16	4.58***	−0.01	−0.03	−0.807
Transparency	0.01	0.08	1.81	0.02	0.12	3.03**	0.02	0.12	2.78**
Discussability	0.00	0.03	0.835	0.01	0.11	3.04**	0.03	0.27	6.80***
Sanctionability	0.01	0.13	3.57***	0.02	0.13	3.98***	−0.01	−0.07	−1.89
Caring	0.01	0.12	2.86**	0.02	0.25	6.59***	0.01	0.21	5.05***
Law and code	0.02	0.14	3.65***	0.01	0.05	1.49	0.00	0.00	0.038
Rules	0.02	0.09	2.65**	−0.01	−0.03	−0.85	0.01	0.04	1.20
Independence	0.00	0.03	0.700	0.02	0.10	2.95**	0.01	0.04	1.05
Instrumental	0.02	0.14	4.03***	0.03	0.14	4.58***	0.02	0.12	3.53***
F (13;826) = 86.59[c] R = 0.581 R^2 = 0.575 +++ ΔR^2 = 0.581				F (13;826) = 120.28[c] R = 0.658 R^2 = 0.655 +++ ΔR^2 = 0.658			F (13;826) = 91.26 R = 0.594 R^2 = 0.587 +++ ΔR^2 = 0.594		

Note N = 839; $^{*}p < 0.05$, $^{**}p < 0.01$, $^{***}p < 0.001$

($\beta = 0.10$; $p \leq 0.001$), contributing significantly towards explaining the proportion of variance in the OCS continuance commitment variable.

In the **third equation**, the discussability, caring, congruency of supervisor, congruency of management, transparency and instrumental variables produced a significant regression model ($F_{(13;826)} = 91.26$), accounting for 58.7% (*$R^2 = 0.59$; $P \leq 0.001$*; large practical effect) of variance in normative commitment, more specifically discussability ($\beta = 0.27$; $p \leq 0.001$), caring ($\beta = 0.21$; $p \leq 0.001$), congruency of supervisor ($\beta = 0.17$; $p \leq 0.001$), congruency of management ($\beta = 0.13$; $p \leq 0.001$), transparency ($\beta = 0.12$; $p \leq 0.001$) and instrumental ($\beta = 0.12$; $p \leq 0.001$), contributing significantly towards explaining the proportion of variance in the OCS normative commitment variable.

Discussion

The objective of this study was to examine whether ethical context variables (work ethics culture and work ethics climate) influence employees' organisational commitment in a railway organisation in the DRC. Overall, the results of our study support that work ethics culture and work ethics climate influences affective, continuance and normative commitment variables. This makes a valuable contribution to the scarce empirical findings on this relationship (Huhtala and Feldt 2016; Ruiz-Palomino and Martinez-Canas 2014). These findings mirror those of Huhtala and Feldt (2016) and Lin and Liu (2016), who also found that work ethics culture and work ethics climate related to certain organisational outcomes (i.e. job satisfaction, commitment and a reduction in turnover intention among workers).

The results suggest that work ethics culture relates to affective, continuance and normative commitment variables. This can be explained by the fact that when employees perceive the existence of comprehensive ethical standards, good ethical role models, adequate resources and working conditions that enable ethical actions, as well as support of and commitment to common organisational values, they are likely to be loyal to the organisation and extend their job tenure. Moreover, if employees feel that there are opportunities/forums to raise and discuss ethical issues and that ethical behaviour is reinforced by rewarding ethical behaviour and punishing wrongdoing, these employees are likely to be committed to the organisation. These findings corroborate those by Huhtala and Feldt (2016) and Meyer and Allen (1987), who found that an ethics culture has the potential to help fulfil employees' psychological needs and increase their satisfaction with the organisation and their competence in their work-role, which are key in promoting affective commitment.

The results suggest that a work ethics climate relates to affective, continuance and normative commitment variables. This can be explained by the fact that when employees perceive positive policies, practices and procedures in an organisation, the reward of ethical conduct and support for ethical standards, they are likely to feel psychologically attached to the organisation and identify with the organisation's goals. These findings concur with that of Kish-Gephart, Harrison and Treviño

(2010) and Lin and Liu (2017), who found that employees are more committed to their organisations when their ethical values match those of the organisation.

The findings of this study indicate that work ethics culture and work ethics climate can positively predict employees' organisational commitment in terms of affective, continuance and normative commitment variables. This implies that employees who prefer their organisation to encourage moral values and actions and who desire their organisation to enforce positive ethical policies, procedures and regulations, are likely to be loyal and feel emotionally attached to the organisation (indicative of a high level of commitment).

These findings can be explained by the fact that work ethics culture and work ethics climate are characterised by shared values, norms, beliefs, policies and practices that can stimulate employees' attitudes and behaviour, which, in turn, contribute to a decrease in turnover intention (Huhtala and Feldt 2016; Mitonga-Monga and Flotman 2017; Valentine et al. 2011).

Implications for Employee Retention Strategies

These results have important implications for managers and human resource practitioners in terms of retention strategies in the railway organisation concerned. Organisations with a high level of employee commitment and a reputation for upholding ethical conduct seem to attract skilled workers who are willing to stay with the organisation for a long time and contribute to its productivity. This gives such organisations a competitive advantage and a greater chance of survival in the turbulent business environment.

Consequently, managers should consider enhancing employees' perceptions that the organisation embraces comprehensive ethical standards, positive ethical conditions and values, transparency, opportunities to discuss ethical issues, reinforcement of ethical behaviour and sanctionability, since all these aspects would increase employees' organisational commitment. In other words, if managers wish to promote affective, continuance and normative commitment among their employees, they should create and develop a positive ethical work environment that is characterised by a sound code of conduct and positive policies, rules and procedures, particularly those related to compensation. Ethics in the work context is an important issue for managers to address, since previous studies have confirmed that work ethics culture and work ethics climate are important predictors of work engagement (Mitonga-Monga and Cilliers 2015) and employees' intention to stay with the organisation (Zehir et al. 2012). Managers should also set a good example for their employees to follow and should treat employees with respect. These efforts will likely increase the perceptions among employees of sound work ethics, thus resulting in an increase in positive work outcomes, such as a decrease in turnover intention (Lau et al. 2017).

Human resource practitioners, as the custodians of training and development in organisations, should not underestimate the influence of formal and informal ethics training. Training managers should organise ethics-related courses and follow-up sessions to ensure both learning and application of ethics in the work context. Warren et al. (2014) provide a two-year ethics training programme after a single session of ethics training. This has had sustained, positive effects on identified indicators of work ethics culture and climate in the form of observed ethical behaviour, intentions to behave ethically, perceptions of organisational efficacy in managing ethical behaviour and normative structures. Top management, managers and human resource practitioners must also be seen to behave ethically and consistently, while dealing firmly with unethical behaviour in the workplace. They will thus create a positive work environment that will stimulate ethical behaviour and discourage unethical behaviour, which, in turn can stimulate positive work responses, such as decreased turnover intention and absenteeism (Kaptein 2016; Tapscott and Ticoll 2003).

Limitations of the Study

This study had a few limitations. Firstly, as the study adopted a cross-sectional research design, information was provided only about goals at a specific point in time. Common methods bias may have existed, as self-reported measures were used for the predictors and outcome variables. Social desirability bias may also have occurred. Secondly, the sample consisted of employees working in a single organisation, so the results could not be generalised to other organisations. In future, researchers could study how the work ethics culture components of clarity, congruency of supervisor, congruency of management, feasibility, supportability, discussability, transparency and sanctionability, as well as the elements of a work ethics climate, namely caring, law and code, rules, independence and instrumental, affect employees' job satisfaction, motivation and organisational citizenship behaviour. As work ethics culture and work ethics climate describe the code of conduct and the atmosphere in an organisation (Mitonga-Monga and Cilliers 2016; Schneider et al. 2013), future researchers could consider investigating the moderating effect of ethical leadership and other influencing variables, such as gender, age, education and tenure, and then establish the causal relationships between these variables. Future researchers could also endeavour to conduct qualitative studies, which could explore the meaning of ethical behaviour with a view to enhancing our understanding of this phenomenon.

Conclusion and Implications for Retention Practice

This chapter examined how ethical context variables (work ethics culture and work ethics climate) influence employees' affective, continuance and normative commitment in a railway organisation in the DRC. With a view to identifying positive mechanisms and factors that may affect employees' commitment and decrease turnover intention, work ethics culture and work ethics climate are regarded as organisational resources in the hands of managers and human resources practitioners. It is likely that congruency between employees' values and morals and those of the organisation will result in greater employee commitment and will increase employees' psychological attachment to the organisation, which is essential to decrease their turnover intention and extend their job tenure.

From a practitioner's perspective, ethical values, policies, procedures and practices should be understood as an organisational resource that can stimulate or activate a positive, motivational process among workers. When organisations and managers invest in ethical aspects, it can contribute to increased job satisfaction, organisational citizenship behaviour, increased commitment and decreased turnover intention among employees. Based on the results of this study, organisations should pay more attention to their reward and punitive systems, which should help to retain highly committed workers. When employees believe that their organisation acts ethically, they are more likely to identify with, invest time and energy in and be psychologically and emotionally attached to the organisation. This has beneficial outcomes, such as low absenteeism and low turnover intention.

Summary

This chapter reviewed ethical context and employee commitment as important aspects of staff retention. Work ethics culture and work ethics climate are all factors of ethics organizational context that symbolize positive norms, procedures and ethical policies within the organization. Work ethics culture and work ethics climate are organisation's resources that drive employee's job response and psychological attachment. The Democratic Republic of Congo work context, ethical context trends, political and economic crises, ineffective leadership, unethical behavior and lack of a culture of accountability present unique challenges that must be consider when the planning the retention strategies.

Enforcing work ethics culture and work ethics climate would strengthen workers' psychological attachment, loyalty and their intention to stay. The method, results, discussions, and implications for employee retention strategies were discussed. The limitations were discussed with reference to the empirical study and the conclusion of the chapter was then provided. Finally, ethical context (work ethics culture and work ethics climate) are important factors in business ethics and human resources management, with new trends developing continuously. We can expect favourable ethical work environment, strong rewards, punitive systems and positive culture of accountability could help to retain highly committed employees and lead to beneficial outcomes such as low absenteeism and low turnover intention pertinent normative key elements.

References

Allen, N. J., & Meyer, J. P. (1996). Affective, continuance, and normative commitment to the organization: An examination of construct validity. *Journal of Vocational Behaviour, 49*(3), 252–276.

Al-Omari, A. A. (2013). The perceived organisational ethical climate in Hashemite University. *Asia-Pacific Education Resources, 23*(3), 273–279.

Arnaud, A., & Schminke, M. (2012). The ethical climate and context of organisations: A comprehensive model. *Organisation Science, 23*(6), 1767–1780.

Balakrishnan, K., Watts, R. L., & Zuo, L. (2016). The effect of accounting conservatism on corporate investment during the global financial crisis. *Journal of Business Finance and Accounting, 43*(6), 513–542.

Bedi, A., Alpaslan, C.M. & Green, S. (2015). A meta-analytic review of ethical leadership outcomes and moderators. *Journal of Business Ethics, 128*(1), 1–20.

Ciula, J. B. (2004). *Ethics, the heart of leadership*. Westport, CT: Quorum.

Gilpin, R., & Boor, B. (2012). Instability in the DRC: United states institute of peace. Retrieved December 9, 2017, from http://www.usip.org/publications/instability-in-the-drc.

Gould-Williams, J., & Davis, F. (2005). Using social exchange theory to predict the effects of human resource management practices on employee outcomes. *Public Management Review, 7*(1), 1–24.

Hair, J. F., Black, W. C., Babin, B. J., & Anderson, R. E. (2010). *Multivariate data analysis: A global perspective* (7th ed.). Upper Sadler River, NJ: Pearson.

Hashish, E. A. A. (2017). Relationship between ethical work climate and nurses' perception of organisational support, commitment, job satisfaction and turnover intent. *Journal of Nursing Ethics, 24*(2), 152–166.

Hollingsworth, D., & Valentine, S. (2015). The moderating effect of perceived organisational ethical context on employees' ethical issue recognition and ethical judgement. *Journal of Business Ethics, 128,* 457–466.

Huhtala, M., & Feldt, T. (2016). The path from ethical organisational culture to employee commitment: Mediating role of value congruence and work engagement. *Scandinavian Journal of Work and Organisational Psychology, 1*(1), 1–14.

Kaptein, M. (2008). Developing and testing a measure for the ethical culture of organisations: The corporate ethical virtues model. *Journal of Organisational Behaviour, 29,* 923–947.

Kaptein, M. (2016). When organisations are too good: Applying Aristotle's doctrine of the mean to the corporate ethical virtues model. *Business Ethics: A European Review, 2*(15), 1–12.

Kish-Gephart, J. J., Harrison, D. A., & Treviño, L. K. (2010). Bad apples, bad cases, and bad barrels: Meta-analytic evidence about source of unethical decisions at work. *Journal of Applied Psychology, 95,* 791–799.

Lau, P. Y. Y., Tong, J. L. Y. T., Lien, B. Y. H., Hsu, Y. C., & Chong, C. L. (2017). Ethical work climate, employee commitment and proactive customer service performance: Test of the mediating effects of organisational politics. *Journal of Retailing and Consumer Services, 35*(2), 20–26.

Lee, J. F., Chiang, F. F. T., Van Esch, E., & Cai, Z. (2016). Why and when organisational culture fosters affective commitment among knowledge workers: The mediating role of perceived psychological contract fulfilment and moderating role of organisational tenure. *The International Journal of Human Resource Management, 139,* 1–30.

Lin, C.-P., & Liu, M.-L. (2017). Examining the effects of corporate social responsibility and ethical leadership on turnover intention. *Personnel Review, 46*(3), 526–550.

Lin, Y. T., & Liu, N. C. (2016). High performance work systems and organisational service performance: The role of different organisational climate. *International Journal of Hospitality Management, 55*(4), 118–128.

Martin, K. D., & Cullen, J. B. (2006). Continuities and extension of ethical climate theory: A meta-analysis review. *Journal of Business Ethics, 90*(4), 293–606.

Mansouri, N. (2016). A case study of Volkswagen unethical practice in diesel emission test. *International Journal of Science and Engineering Applications, 5*(4), 211–216.
Mayer, D. M. (2014). A review of the literature on ethical climate and culture. In Schneider, B & Barbera, K. M. (Eds.) *The Oxford handbook of organisational climate and culture* (pp 415–442). Oxford University Press.
Meyer, J. P., & Allen, N. J. (1987). A longitudinal analysis of early development and consequences of organisational commitment. *Canadian Journal of Behavioural Science, 19,* 199–215.
Meyer, J. P., & Allen, N. J. (1991). A three-component conceptualization of organizational commitment. *Human Resource Management Review, 1*(1), 61–89.
Meyer, J. P., & Allen, N. J. (1997). *Commitment in the workplace: Theory, research and application*. Thousand Oaks, CA: Sage.
Mitonga-Monga, J., & Cilliers, F. (2015). Ethics culture and ethics climate in relation to employee engagement in a developing country setting. *Journal of Psychology in Africa, 25*(3), 242–249.
Mitonga-Monga, J., & Cilliers, F. (2016). Perceived ethical leadership: Its moderating influence on employees' organisational commitment and organisational citizenship behaviours. *Journal of Psychology in Africa, 26*(1), 35–42.
Mitonga-Monga, J., Flotman, A. P., & Cilliers, F. (2016). Workplace ethics culture and work engagement: The mediating effect of ethical leadership in a developing world context. *Journal of Psychology in Africa, 26*(4), 326–333.
Mitonga-Monga, J., & Flotman, A. P. (2017). Gender and work ethics culture as predictors of employees' organisational commitment. *Journal of Contemporary Management, 14*(1), 270–290.
Morrow, P. C. (2011). Managing organisational commitment: Insights from longitudinal research. *Journal of Vocational Behaviour, 79*(1), 18–35.
Mowday, R. T., Porter, L. W., & Steers, R. M. (2013). *Employee–organization linkages: The psychology of commitment, absenteeism, and turnover*. London: Academic Press.
Mullins, L. (2013). *Management and organizational behaviour* (10th ed.). London: Pearson.
Novelskaite, A., & Pucetaite, R. (2014). Validation of data collection instrument for measurement of ethical organisational culture in Lithuanian organisations. *Economics and Management, 19,* 290–299.
Ruiz-Palomino, P., & Martinez-Cañas, R. (2014). Ethical culture and ethical intent, and organisational citizenship behaviour: The moderating and mediating role of person-organisational fit. *Journal of Business Ethics, 120,* 173–188.
Schneider, B., Ehrhart, M. G., & Macey, W. H. (2013). Organisational climate and culture. *Annual Review of Psychology, 64,* 361–388.
SPSS. (2017). *SPSS for the social sciences*. Chicago.
Solomon, R. C. (2004). Aristotle, ethics and business organisation. *Organisation Studies, 25,* 1025–1043.
Tabachnick, B. G., & Fidell, L. S. (2013). *Using multivariate statistics* (6th ed.). Boston, MA: Pearson.
Tapscott, D., & Ticoll, D. (2003). *The naked corporation: How the age of transparency will revolutionize business*. New York, NY: Free Press.
Treviño, K. L., Butterfield, K. D., & McCabe, D. L. (1998). The ethical context in organisations: Influence on employee attitudes and behaviours. *Business Ethics Quarterly, 8*(1), 447–476.
Treviño, L. K., & Nelson, K. A. (2010). *Managing business ethics* (5th ed.). London: Wiley.
Treviño, L. K., & Weaver, G. R. (2003). *Managing ethics in business organisations: Social scientific perspectives*. Stanford: Stanford University Press.
Valentine, S., Godkin, L., Fleischman, G. M., & Kidwell, R. (2011). Corporate ethical values, group creativity, job satisfaction and turnover intention: The impact of work context on work response. *Journal of Business Ethics, 98*(3), 353–372.
Vakola, M., & Nikolaou, L. (2005). Attitudes towards organizational change: What is the role of employees' stress and commitment? *Employee Relations, 27*(2), 160–174.

Victor, B., & Cullen, J. B. (1988). The organisational bases of ethical work climates. *Administrative Science Quarterly, 33,* 101–125.

Victor, B., & Cullen, J. B. (1998). A theory and measure of ethical climate in organizations. In W. C. Frederick & L. E. Preston (Eds.), *Business ethics: Research issues and empirical studies* (pp. 77–97). Greenwich: JAI Press.

Warren, D. E., Gaspar, J. P., & Laufer, W. S. (2014). Is formal ethics training merely cosmetic? A study of ethics training and ethical organisational culture. *Business Ethics Quarterly, 24*(1), 85–117.

Zehir, C., Müceldili, B., & Zehir, S. (2012). The moderating effects of ethical climate on the relationship between job satisfaction and organisational commitment: Evidence from large companies in Turkey. *Procedia-Social and Behavioural Sciences, 58*(12), 734–743.

Zhakypova, A. (2016). Dissecting corporate sustainability reporting: VW emission scandal case: VW and corporate sustainability reporting. Retrieved December 20, 2017, from https://nature.berkeley.edu/classes/es196/projects/.

Jeremy Mitonga-Monga (DCom) is a Post-doctorate Research Fellow in the Department of Industrial Psychology and People Management at the University of Johannesburg, South Africa. He has more than 8 years' experience in teaching and research. His research interests include ethical behaviour, culture, climate, leadership, and employee retention and research methodology. He has published various articles in accredited journals and has presented papers and posters at national and international conferences.

Chapter 18
Tap the Experienced to Care for the Inexperienced: Millennial Employees' Retention Challenge? Mentoring is the Solution

Mohammad Faraz Naim

Abstract The primary objective of this chapter is to explore the role of mentoring in the talent retention of Millennial employees. Grounded on social exchange and social learning perspectives, this chapter develops a conceptual framework to reduce turnover intentions of Millennial employees. The conceptual framework suggests that workplace mentoring facilitates personal learning, contributing to affective commitment, which in turn, reduces turnover intentions of Millennila employees. The framework is significant for academics and practitioners. It provides useful insights to assist management in bolstering the retention of Millennial employees. This chapter contributes to the literature on mentoring, affective commitment, and turnover intentions. This is also one of the first study that addresses mentoring and talent retention from a generational perspective. Organizations therefore, should integrate mentoring into the talent management strategy to develop and retain Millennial employees. Limitations and future direction of research are outlined thereafter.

Keywords Mentoring · Millennials · Generation Y · Personal learning
Competency · Affective commitment · Turnover intentions · Retention
Talent retention

Introduction

In contemporary dynamic, turbulent. and ever-competitive environment, firms worldwide are facing a major challenge to develop and retain high potential employees (Schuler et al. 2011; Tarique and Schuler 2010). The unprecedented

M. F. Naim (✉)
School of Business, University of Petroleum & Energy Studies,
Dehradun, India
e-mail: mfaraznaim@yahoo.com

M. Coetzee et al. (eds.), *Psychology of Retention*,
https://doi.org/10.1007/978-3-319-98920-4_18

influx of Millennial employees into the workforce has catalysed the growing workforce mobility and diversity, which further contribute to the talent management challenge. As a result, three different Generations are working simultaneously, namely, Baby boomers (1946–1960), Generation X (1961–1980) and Millennials (1981–2000) (Naim and Lenka 2018, in press). Notably, members of these generations are reported to exhibit idiosyncratic work values and preferences (Ng et al. 2010). Of these, Millennial employees needs most attention as they are the future face of the workforce. To an estimate, they will constitute roughly fifty percent of workfoce population by 2020 (Saxena and Jain 2012). However, they are shown to be less loyal towards their employer and frequently hop jobs to explore advancement and developmental opportunities (Cennamo and Gardner 2008; Ng et al. 2010). A recent study by Deloitte found that nearly one-third Millennial workers are planning to leave their employer (Talent Edge 2020 2011).

This is largely attributed to their strong preference for continuous learning and development avenues (Terjesen et al. 2007). In addition, learning and development help improve employees' retention and motivation (Cook and Macaulay 2009). Thus, it is imperative that HR policies should emphasize on learning and development and therefore, organizations must invest in learning and developemnt. Besides, one of the main attributes that Millennials seeks is a supportive environment wherein managers facilitate mentoring and follow an inclusive style of management and offer creative freedom and decision-making powers (Lowe et al. 2008).

This distinctive needs render HRM practices as ineffective to appeal Millennial employees. Therefore, there is a need to formulate generation-specific approach to manage Millennial employees. In so doing, we propose mentoring to be an ideal initiative to induce personal learning of Millennial employees through dissemination of work-related knowledge, insights, and experiences. Mentoring facilitates employee development by offering valuable support and opportunities of competency development to inexperienced Millennial employees. Further, studies reveal that mentoring is an ideal intervention to develop Millennial members and also suggested to be studied for retaining them (Holt et al. 2012; Stahno and Yang 2014; Weyland 2011). We analyze psychological profile of Millennial members by capturing their idiosyncratic work-related values and preferences in the context of talent management. Grounded on social exchange perspective, when Millennial employees realize their career growth and employability skill enhancement, they develop a sense of affective commitment to the organization, which in turn, translates to lowering the turnover intentions. On this backdrop, this article aims to map a social-exchange based conceptual framework that examines the relationship between mentoring and Millennial employees' turnover intentions. This article responds to call for unraveling the underlying mechanism of the effect of mentoring relationships on individual employees' attitudinal outcomes (Hezlett and Gibson 2007).

The major contribution of this paper is that we contribute to the literature on mentoring and employee attitudinal outcomes from a Generational perspective. In so doing, grounded on psychological-contract theory, we incorporated mentoring, personal learning, leading to affective commitment and finally, reduced turnover intention. The paper is structured as follows; first section highlights the review of literature on Millennial employees' profile and mentoring, second section presents the conceptual framework along with propositions. It is followed by discussion and implications for practice, and future scope of research.

Literature Review

Millennials' Description

Millennials are otherwise termed as Generation Y. The name 'Generation Y' is first appeared in the literature in a US magazine Advertising Age in 1993 to denote the last generation of the twentieth century. Although there is no consistency in the literature with regard to birth years of Millennial cohort, most authors have used 1981–2000 as the time-frame for this Generation. They represent the most recent entrants to the workforce globally.

Literature reveals that Millennials are inherently different in workplace values and behavior from its predecessors (Naim and Lenka 2017b; Ng et al. 2010). This is largely due to changing socio-demographic factors and unique life events that Millennial employees have witnessed during their developmental times. Their formative years are characterized by a fast-paced, instant world catalyzed by the technological revolution, economic liberalization and knowledge-based economy. They are raised in a technologically advanced era; hence they are techno-savvy and most adept users of technology (Lowe et al. 2008). However, despite their techno-savvy nature, Millennial employees crave meaning and fulfillment in their work. They seek challenge and variety in the work to overcome monotony. In general, Millennial members have strong social tendencies i.e. they value relationship building with supervisors and peers (Twenge 2010). They enjoy working in collaborative environments as they have grown up working in teams on projects at school and college. Moreover, they are entrepreneurial by nature and display high expectations from organizations regarding support for innovation, risk-taking, autonomy, intrinsic rewards and the challenging nature of work This has given them the name 'High maintenance generation' (Martin 2005).

Besides, they desire a flat hierarchy where they can get access to senior leadership in organizations. They are repotted to display a preference for an inclusive style of management; and supportive and approachable supervisors, who act as mentors and treat them as individual partners (Lowe et al. 2008). They prefer orderly work environments and dislike ambiguity of any kind i.e. desire well-defined roles and clear expectations. They prefer open and honest communication with open sharing of ideas. In addition, they crave quick promotions and immediate performance feedback. This 'impatience to succeed' attitude reflects the sense of immediacy, which is the product of their hyper-connected lifestyle achieved through use of instant technologies. Millennial employees value timely recognition for their accomplishments and consistent feedback makes it possible. Regular feedback opens avenues for taking corrective measures to rectify the mistake and develop skills and knowledge (Lowe et al. 2008; Martin 2005; Naim 2014).

They are reported to have the dispositional characteristics particularly, a high growth need, learning-orientation, a need for achievement, self-actualisation and self-esteem. As a result, they place high value on nurturing and supportive work environment, where they foresee avenues of development (Terjesen et al. 2007). Further, extant research reveals that Millennial employees crave mentoring (Cunningham 2007). This explains their quest for continuous learning in order to make a positive impact on the organizational leadership and to stay self-marketable in the talent market (Cennamo and Gardner 2008). Therefore, organisations committed to invest in their development appeal highly to Millennial employees.

Mentoring

Over the years, mentoring has been the subject of widespread academic interest; as such different scholars have defined mentoring through their own conceptualization. However, most definitions are derived from Kram's (1985) seminal work on mentoring. Mentoring is a developmental relationship between a more experienced or skilled mentor and a less experienced or less skilled protégée whereby both benefit from the relationship (Johnson and Ridley 2015; Kram 1985). It is a process where a more experienced member of the organisation called mentor guides and assists the development of skills and abilities of a less experienced member called mentee. In other words, it is a developmental relationship wherein people help people; by means of counseling, teaching, advising, instructing and guiding. Bozeman and Feeney (2007) define mentoring as "a process for the informal transmission of knowledge, social capital and psychosocial support perceived by the recipient as relevant to work, career, or professional development" (p. 731). It involves informal communication, usually face-to-face occurring over time "between someone perceived to have greater relevant knowledge, wisdom, or experience (the mentor) and a person who is perceived to have less (the protégé)" (p. 731).

Kram (1985) identified a two-dimensional concept of mentoring, Vocational (career support) and psycho-social (social support). Career support function includes making challenging assignments, promoting job related behaviors, fostering career development, enhancing their sense of competence through mentor functions of exposure, sponsorship, visibility, protection and challenging assignments. Exposure, sponsorship and visibility provide public support to mentee. To do so, mentor offers guidance and direction towards developmental avenues such as lateral moves within organizations, role-hopping, new learning opportunities through stretch roles. While by introducing mentees to significant senior employees of the organizations, mentor enhances their network and recognition thereby increasing exposure and visibility. Besides, protection involves the mentor shields the mentee in situations of high risks of failure which might limit their career progress. Challenging assignments support career development by providing opportunities to learn from new roles and responsibilities. Psychosocial support function serves to develop a sense of belongingness, professional identity and effectiveness. Mentor serves a source of social support and offers friendship, acceptance, confirmation, counseling and role modeling. Friendship leads to positive experiences and allows them to be at ease with a senior employee. Acceptance and confirmation build a sense of positive self-regard among mentees. Counseling support promotes positive self-views through self-exploration. Kram (1985). Role modeling helps mentees to identify with the mentor and providing the opportunity for the mentee to observe others and learn from their actions, particularly in relationship to the application of personal values in work settings and strategic tactics used to address problems. Thus, career support improves mentees' professional lives whereas psychosocial support improves personal lives. However, further studies conceptualized role modeling as a distinct mentoring function (Johnson and Ridley 2015; Scandura and Ragins 1993).

The extant literature on mentoring mainly focuses on its beneficial outcomes such as greater career satisfaction and commitment, lower turnover intentions, increased, compensation and promotions, self-confidence and career development of mentees; personal satisfaction of mentorand higher organizational performance (Craig et al. 2013; DeCastro et al. 2014; Kammeyer-Mueller and Judge 2008; Kirchmeyer 2005; Kram 1985). Also mentoring has been shown to improve job involvement, engagement and affective commitment of employees through satisfaction of need for belonging and acceptance (Allen and Meyer 1990; Lynn Stallworth 2003; Payne and Huffman 2005). However, this study opens new vistas on exploring mentoring effect on mentee affective commitment and turnover intentions via personal learning. On this backdrop, mentoring is an ideal intervention to support Millennial expectations by providing informational and emotional support and satisfying their higher order needs of self-esteem and self-actualisation. The subsequent section discusses the theoretical underpinnings of the role of mentoring to retain Millennial employees.

Conceptual Framework and Propositions

This study presents a conceptual framework for Millennial retention through the lens of Social Exchange theory (SET). This theory purports that all social relationships are formed, sustained or severed based on the perceived cost benefit analysis. It suggests that when an individual receives something beneficial in a relationship with the other one, it develops a sense of reciprocity. As a result, the individual on the receiving end reciprocates in order to repay the received benefit (Emerson 1976). Therefore, in response to received benefits from others, employees

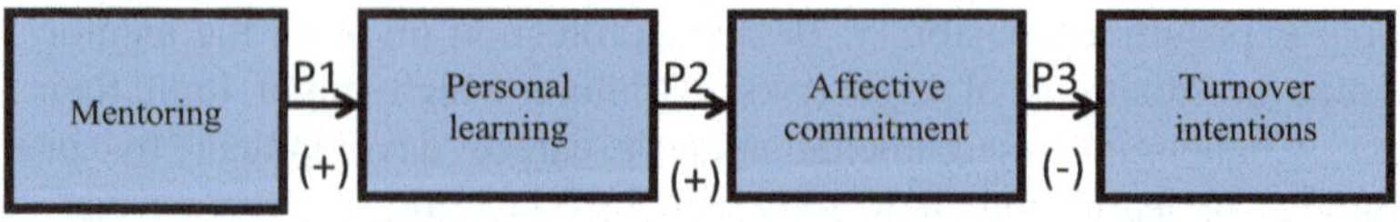

Fig. 18.1 The Conceptual framework

tend to oblige by exhibiting positive psychological responses, including commitment and turnover intentions (Eisenberger et al. 1990) (Fig. 18.1).

Mentoring and Personal Learning

Personal learning is defined as "knowledge acquisition, skills or competencies contributing to individual development, including interpersonal competencies of self-reflection, self-disclosure, active listening, empathy, and feedback. Such development invokes a greater understanding of oneself as increasingly connected to others" (Kram 1996, p. 140). In broad terms, it encompasses two facets: job-related learning defined as "understanding about the interdependence or connectedness of one's job to others"; and personal skill development defined as "acquisition of new skills and abilities that enable better working relationships" (Lankau and Scandura 2002, p. 6). Job-related learning involves acquiring technical knowledge, understanding of work context, business kills, and procedural information about the organization. While, personal skill development involves interpersonal skills, self-efficacy, self-perception, self-confidence, and self-direction. Stated differently, job-related learning has important implications for professional development and career success, while, personal skill development promotes personal growth and competency enrichment. Consequently, personable learning is indispensable for Millennial employees to succeed in their career.

Mentoring is a learning intervention involving pairing of an experienced mentor to a novice mentee. It also helps them navigate the learning curve for professional growth and enable development of new professional relationships within the organization (Dow 2014). More importantly, "mentoring influences advancement of protégés by developing their social skills, serving as contacts with the social system and sending signals of ability, reputation and organizational" (Kirchmeyer 2005: p. 641). In context of Millennial employees, mentoring is more significant as they lack experience, however are ambitious and eager to learn and develop. Millennial employees enter the workforce with enthusiasm, energy and expectations; yet require consistent support, guidance, and feedback to ascend the career ladder. Therefore, mentoring is a vital HR intervention harnessing mentor's knowledge and extensive experience, for overall development of Millennial employees by facilitating their competency building (Naim and Lenka 2017a). To achieve this purpose, mentor would often assign challenging tasks to mentees to create learning opportunities, assist in goal setting, provide career guidance by depicting clear picture about their career, support the advancement of job position, expand their networks, help in resolving task-related problems and provide developmental feedback (Eby et al. 2015; Johnson and Ridley 2015). It involves consistent interaction with mentees and sharing of insights, experiences, tried-and-tested best work practices and mishaps or failures. In particular, such interactions between mentor and mentee involve dialogue and enquiry as mentees ask questions and knowledge interflow from mentor results in informal learning opportunities (Gong, Chen and Yang 2014; Hamburg 2013). This leads to development of social and personal competencies such as networking, internal locus of control, self-efficacy, self-confidence, achievement motivation, risk-taking, interpersonal skills, negotiation, persuasion, interpretation, initiative taking, collaborative potential and leadership competencies such as self-management (Eddy et al. 2003; Stead 2005). Further, knowledge transfer achieved through mentoring in itself facilitates competency development as Millennial mentees learn and acquire organizational knowledge, in turn fostering professional competencies such as technical skills (product or process related, customer relationship skills, client management, project management), managerial skills, organization-specific norms, strategic thinking, decision making, opportunity identification (Browne-Ferrigno and Muth 2004; Ehrich et al. 2004; Naim and Lenka 2016b). Furthermore, mentoring builds a culture of organizational learning and knowledge creation and sharing and in turn, creates a learning organization (Hamburg 2013; Karkoulian et al. 2008). It hastens the process of tacit knowledge sharing by allowing mentees to have an easier access to internal experts. Thus, it enables discovery of tacit knowledge of mentors which otherwise, is difficult to explore. It is also positively linked to talent development and leadership development by influencing competency enhancement in mentees (Eddy et al. 2003; Gannon and Maher 2012). In addition, mentoring creates an environment of trust, support and belongingness. It gives employees an outlet to voice their concerns by encouraging self-expression, dialogue and inquiry, in turn, reinforcing social competencies.

Further, considering Millennial employees' quest for continuous learning and development, mentoring will have a profound positive influence on their perception of personal learning. In similar vein, it can be proposed that Millennial employees are more likely to perceive personal learning within the organisation that practice mentoring. Thus, there is a positive relationship between mentoring and personal learning. Thus, we propose

Proposition 1 Participation in mentoring program is positively related to Millennial employees' perception of personal learning.

Personal Learning and Affective Commitment

Affective commitment is one of the widely studied constructs in positive organizational psycholog. It is significant for this study due to the emotional reactions employees may experience in response to perceived learning. Affective commitment is denned as "an affective or emotional attachment to the organization such that the strongly committed individual identifies with, is involved in, and enjoys membership in, the organization" (Allen and Meyer 1990, p. 2). It acts as a binding force and affectively committed employees want to remain employed with the same organization. In this study, we focus on how affective commitment arises from personal learning and development achieved through mentoring.

Organisations offering developmental opportunities to enhance employees' competencies, earn a sense of emotional bonding, resulting in feeling of affective commitment. In particular, personal learning and development of employees is one of the most significant factors influencing their turnover intentions (Chikumbi 2012). This factor is most relevant to Millennial employees who harbor an ambition to succeed and have learning goal orientation; hence they are more likely to participate in developmental initiatives (Aryee et al. 1999). Likewise, there is compelling evidence in the literature that mentoring is positively related to affective organizational commitment, and in turn, negatively predicts turnover intentions (Joo 2010; Payne and Huffman 2005; Lapointe and Vandenberghe 2016; Reid et al. 2008; Stahl et al. 2009). This is consistent with Affective events theory, which states that affective work events result in affective reactions, which in turn, shape employees' work attitudes and behaviors (Weiss and Cropanzano 1996). In this vein, personal learning achieved through mentoring is also an affective experience, which Generation rate affective reactions in the form of affective commitment. This is supported by Lynn Stallworth (2003) who noted, "mentoring relationships fit the definition of affective commitment antecedents as work experiences 'that satisfy employees' needs to feel comfortable in their relationship with the organization and to feel competent in the work-role' (Allen and Meyer 1990, p. 4)" (p. 407). Moreover, when an organisation exhibits care and concern for employees and offer avenues for development in a compelling Employee value proposition, it satisfies their higher order needs of self-esteem and self-actualisation and generates reciprocal positive outcome such as affective commitment. Therefore, we assume that mentoring facilitates perceived learning of Millennial employees, which results in generating an emotional connect with the organization. Thus, we propose:

Proposition 2 Millennial employees' perception of personal learning is positively related to their affective commitment with the organization.

Affective Commitment and Turnover Intentions

In accordance with the theory of reasoned action (TRA), intentions are the best predictors of actual human behavior (Ajzen and Fishbein 1980). However, there is lack of consistency in the literature on what determines such intentions. Although, predictors of turnover intentions have been the subject of considerable attention in academic domain, stull there is little research done in the context of Millennial employees' turnover intentions. The extant literature reports several factors for these intentions including perceived stress, management support, commitment, job satisfaction, job characteristics, justice, and organization culture (Griffeth et al. 2000; Maertz et al. 2007). However, in accordance with their distinct psychological contract, Millennial strongly values learning and career development and has no room for job security and life-time employment, therefore drivers of above-noted turnover are irrelevant (Sonnenberg et al. 2011; Twenge 2010). The effective fulfillment of psychological contract through learning and development is indispensable to evoke reduced turnover intentions among Millennial employees.

In broad terms, turnover intentions is an employees' perceived desirability to terminate his/her relationship with the employer. It can also be viewed as the individual s intention to voluntary quit the organization (Fox and Fallon 2003). It is a complex psychological process constituted by a sequence of thinking of quitting, intentions to search, intention to leave, and finally quitting (Mobley et al. 1979). Hence, turnover intention is the last cognitive step employees make in the voluntary turnover process and considered to be the stongest factor influencing the turnover decision (Fox and Fallon 2003; Mathieu and Zajac 1990).

For Millennials, access to learning and development opportunities is the most critical factor to reduce their turnover intention (Ng et al. 2010). In other words, when the organisation offers developmental opportunities to enhance employees' personal learning by developing their personal, social and professional competencies, it exhibits organziation's care and concern for employees' wellbeing. This nurtures a sense of realisation of emotional belonging; leading to building affective commitment, which in turn results in reducing turnover intentions.

Furthermore, provision of learning can be a strategy to retain talent (Cole 1999), as Millennial employees have a strong learning orientation; there will be a profound impact on their affective commitment. This affective commitment mediates the influence of such events on employee attitudes and behaviors, including turnover intentions (Stahl et al. 2009). Hence, we expect a significant positive influence of perceived personal learning on affective commitment leading to reduced turnover intentions of Millennial employees. In addition, organisational commitment is shown to be a strong determinant of turnover intentions, particularly affective commitment (Joo 2010). Likewise, another study reports a mediating role of affective commitment on relationship of between mentoring with turnover intention (Payne and Huffman 2005). Thus, we propose:

Proposition 3 Development of affective commitment is negatively related to Millennial employees' turnover intentions.

Discussion and Implications for Retention Practice

In the present turbulent environment, talent retention has become a significant challenge for organisations. In particular, Millennial employees, by their inherent nature are more prone to job-switching. The extant research reports that employees with high need for growth and achievement, have ambition to succeed and are more inclined towards mentoring (Aryee et al. 1999). In similar vein, Millennial employees want to upgrade their skills to remain employable and sought-after in the talent market and they do not want to be deemed ignorant and failures. Therefore, Millennial employees crave mentoring and continuous learning (Cunningham 2007). In this vein, organization's human resource practices including mentoring are likely to result in stimulating affective commitment of these employees, which then influence their turnover intentions (Bawa and Jantan 2005).

This chapter sought to explore mentoring to retain Millennial employees. To achieve this, the study presents a conceptual framework to link constructs namely mentoring, perceived learning, affective commitment, and turnover intentions. This study is based on the underlying principle of social exchange theory to explore this phenomenon. The extant literature provides support to the notion that mentoring has a negative relationship with turnover intentions (Kammeyer-Mueller and Judge 2008; Kram 1985; Lankau and Scandura 2002; Payne and Huffman 2005). The research however is scarce on how mentoring influences employees' turnover intentions and hence further exploration is required (Hezlett and Gibson 2007). This paper fills this gap by examining the role of mentoring in facilitating personal learning of Millennial employees thereby satisfying their their higher order needs (self-worth, self-development, recognition, feedback, and socialization) resulting in affective commitment and ultimately lowering their turnover intentions (Naim and Lenka 2016a).

As such, it is consistent with social learning theory, which states that individuals learn in a social context via interactions with others (Bandura 1977). People also learn by observing other people through role modeling called vicarious learning. In mentoring relationships, mentees learn from their mentors through interacting with and observing them, whereby mentors act as role models. This theory explains how mentoring facilitates personal learning. Mentors provide challenging assignments to mentees to improve their personal or professional competencies. Through friendship, counseling and acceptance the mentor also helps the mentee′ develop the sense of professional competence (Kram 1985). In line with this theory, mentoring provides an opportunity for mastery experience, vicarious experience (i.e. observing mentors being role models)and verbal persuasion (e.g., encouragement and feedback) to mentees. Therefore, mentees are offered learning opportunities and support, which in turn improve their absorptive capacity i.e. their ability and motivation to learn. This results in learning behavior and acquisition of competencies. In this view, perceived learning is an outcome of mentoring received. Thus, the more mentoring functions mentees receive, the more competencies they develop, resulting in perception of personal learning. Moreover, social interactions between mentor and mentees further enhance learning behaviors, ultimately leading to expansion of competencies namely personal, social, and professional.

The present day organisations are relying on their employees more than ever. The conceptual framework of this study showed that organisations need to nurture mentoring to foster learning in the organisation. The perception of learning and competency development in Millennial employees will give them increased assurance of a more profitable future with the organisation. This in turn will result into positive psychological responses leading to reducing their turnover intentions. The present study has significant implications that extend to both industry and academia. From an industry standpoint, the study offers insights on Millennial needs and motivators. Managers gain the understanding on how members of Millennial cohort are inherently different from more experienced employees, which facilitate developing suitable policies. In addition, HR managers can fine-tune their retention strategy for Millennial employees. The insights will encourage them in adopting mentoring to expand Millennials' competencies, not only to reap dividends of improved organizational performance and competitive edge but also to boost retention rates. To achieve contextual operationalization of this framework, organization must be cognizant of national and regional culture. However, it is applicable and valid across the national boundaries including US, Europe, and Asian countries, as Millennial members, form across the globe are shown to be oriented towards learning and development, and career advancement opportunities (Ng et al. 2010; Holt et al. 2012; Cooke et al. 2014). More importantly, in today's mutigenerational workforce, mentoring has become even more beneficial as it fosters healthy relationships resulting in workplace harmony.

From an academic standpoint, this study contributes to the literature on linkage between mentoring and turnover intentions. To the best of our knowledge, so far no academic work examines mentoring in context of Millennial employees' turnover intentions. In other words, this paper is first of its kind to examine mentoring effect on affective commitment and turnover intentions through satisfaction of cognitive or developmental needs of Millennial mentees via personal learning. This study will help close the gap between mentoring relationships and how it relates to Millenials' attitudinal outcomes such as turnover intentions.

Limitations and Future Scope

Despite its academic and managerial implications, the study being theoretical in nature has some limitations. The article is grounded on a literature review and secondary data. Future work should conduct the empirical validation of the proposed conceptual framework. Mentoring acts as an enabler of personal learning in the framework; however future study may add to this stream by incorporating other enablers such as learning climate, job satisfaction, knowledge sharing culture, supportive leadership to reduce Millennial turnover intentions The framework is designed for Millennial cohort irrespective of national culture's effects on

Millennials' chracteristics. It will be prudent, therefore to explore the competencies required to be developed in country-specific Millennial employees. In this vein, investigating workplace needs and values of Millennials from emerging economies will be a notable contribution (Fang 2010). Personal learning is the central element of the framework; however various competency types such as generic, technical, functional or social competencies are not differentiated. Therefore future studies should acknowledge the specific competencies held valuable by Millennial employees.

The framework may or may not be effective in context of other Generational groups such as Generation X or Baby boomers. This can be evaluated in future work through a comparative analysis using heterogeneous sample form different generations. Meanwhile, we have to acknowledge that other measures, such as gender, trust, and organizational structure may have moderating effect on outcome variables. Moreover, research should continue to examine different forms of mentoring, including group mentoring, peer mentoring and e-mentoring in the context of Millennial employees. In this vein, examine the most effective mentoring forms from both Millennial employees' and management's perspective Finally, there is a need to develop a scale for personal learning, and turnover intentions from the perspective of Millennial employees as most available scales are developed in different context.

Summary

This study was embarked upon investigating the impact of mentoring on Millennial employees' turnover intentions. In this line, this chapter proposed a framework explaining the relationship between mentoring and Millennial employees' turnover intentions through personal learning and affective commitment. This study has highlighted the impact of how mentoring can influence an employees' turnover intentions, especially of young employees. Importantly, this research provides organizations with guidelines on how practicing mentoring can influence employee positive work-related behaviors.

Acknowledgements I would like to thank my parents for their continuous blessings and unconditional support. Last, but not the least, all praise to Al-Kareem for keeping me motivated throughout.

References

Ajzen, I., & Fishbein, M. (1980). Understanding attitudes and predicting social behavior. Englewood-Cliffs, NJ, USA: Prentice-Hall.

Allen, N. J., & Meyer, J. P. (1990). The measurement and antecedents of affective, continuance and normative commitment to the organization. *Journal of Occupational Psychology, 63*(1), 1–18.

Aryee, S., Lo, S., & Kang, I. L. (1999). Antecedents of early career stage mentoring among Chinese employees. *Journal of Organisational Behavior, 20*(5), 563–576.

Bandura, A. (1977). *Social learning theory*. Englewood Cliffs, NJ: Prentice-Hall.

Bawa, M. A., & Jantan, M. (2005). Human resource practices as determinants of employee turnover: An empirical investigation. *Asian Academy of Management Journal, 10*(2), 69–80.

Bozeman, B., & Feeney, M. K. (2007). Toward a useful theory of mentoring a conceptual analysis and critique. *Administration and Society, 39*(6), 719–739.

Browne-Ferrigno, T., & Muth, R. (2004). Leadership mentoring in clinical practice: Role socialization, professional development and capacity building. *Educational Administration Quarterly, 40*(4), 468–494.

Cennamo, L., & Gardner, D. (2008). Generational differences in work values, outcomes and person-organisation values fit. *Journal of Managerial Psychology, 23*(8), 891–906.

Chikumbi, C. N. L. (2012). *An investigation of talent management and staff retention at the bank of Zambia*. Doctoral dissertation.

Cole, J. (1999). The art of wooing generation Xers. *HR Focus, 76*(911), 7–8.

Cook, S., & Macaulay, S. (2009, September). Talent management. *Training Journal*.

Cooke, F. L., Saini, D. S., & Wang, J. (2014). Talent management in China and India: A comparison of management perceptions and human resource practices. *Journal of World Business, 49*(2), 225–235.

Craig, C. A., Allen, M. W., Reid, M. F., Riemenschneider, C. K., & Armstrong, D. J. (2013). The impact of career mentoring and psychosocial mentoring on affective organizational commitment, job involvement, and turnover intention. *Administration and Society, 45*(8), 949–973.

Cunningham, S. (2007). Managing the Millennials. Best's review. *Oldwick, 107*(11), 67–110.

DeCastro, R., Griffith, K. A., Ubel, P. A., Stewart, A., & Jagsi, R. (2014). Mentoring and the career satisfaction of male and female academic medical faculty. *Academic Medicine: Journal of the Association of American Medical Colleges, 89*(2), 301.

Dow, R. S. (2014). Leadership responsibility in mentoring organization newcomers. *Journal of Management Policy and Practice, 15*(1), 104.

Eby, L. T., Butts, M. M., Hoffman, B. J., & Sauer, J. B. (2015). Cross–lagged relations between mentoring received from supervisors and employee OCBs: Disentangling causal direction and identifying boundary conditions. *Journal of Applied Psychology, 100,* 1275–1285.

Eddy, E., Tannenbaum, S., Alliger, G., D'Abate, C., & Givens, S. (2003). Mentoring in industry: The top 10 issues when building and supporting a mentoring program. Presented in S. Tannenbaum (Chair), Ensuring Employee Development on the Job. Symposium presented at the 2003 meeting of the Society of Industrial and Organizational Psychology, Orlando, Florida.

Ehrich, L. C., Hansford, B., & Tennent, L. (2004). Formal mentoring programs in education and other professions: A review of the literature. *Educational Administration Quarterly, 40*(4), 518–540.

Eisenberger, R., Fasolo, P., & Davis-LaMastro, V. (1990). Perceived organisational support and employee diligence, generation, commitment and innovation. *Journal of Applied Psychology, 73*(1), 51–59.

Emerson, R. M. (1976). Social exchange theory. *Annual Review of Sociology, 2,* 335–362.

Fang, T. (2010). Asian management research needs more self-confidence: Reflection on Hofstede (2007) and beyond. *Asia Pacific Journal of Management, 27,* 155–170.

Fox, S. R., & Fallon, B. J. (2003, January). Modelling the effect of work/life balance on job satisfaction and turnover intentions. *Australian Journal of Psychology, 55,* 123–124.

Gannon, J. M., & Maher, A. (2012). Developing tomorrow's talent: the case of an undergraduate mentoring programme. *Education + Training, 54*(6), 440–455.

Gong, R., Chen, S. Y., & Yang, M. L. (2014). Career outcome of employees: The mediating effect of mentoring. *Social Behavior and Personality: An International Journal, 42*(3), 487–501.

Griffeth, R. W., Hom, P. W., & Gaertner, S. (2000). A meta-analysis of antecedents and correlates of employee turnover: Update, moderator tests, and research implications for the next millennium. *Journal of Management, 26,* 463–488.

Hamburg, I. (2013). Facilitating learning and knowledge transfer through mentoring. In *CSEDU* (pp. 219–222).
Hezlett, S. A., & Gibson, S. K. (2007). Linking mentoring and social capital: Implications for career and organization development. *Advances in Developing Human Resources, 9*(3), 384–411.
Holt, S., Marques, J., & Way, D. (2012). Bracing for the millennial workforce: Looking for ways to inspire Generation Y. *Journal of Leadership, Accountability and Ethics, 9*(6), 81.
Johnson, W. B., & Ridley, C. R. (2015). *The elements of mentoring*. Macmillan.
Joo, B. K. B. (2010). Organizational commitment for knowledge workers: The roles of perceived organizational learning culture, leader–member exchange quality, and turnover intention. *Human Resource Development Quarterly, 21*(1), 69–85.
Kammeyer-Mueller, J. D., & Judge, T. A. (2008). A quantitative review of mentoring research: Test of a model. *Journal of Vocational Behavior, 72*(3), 269–283.
Karkoulian, S., Halawi, L. A., & McCarthy, R. V. (2008). Knowledge management formal and informal mentoring: An empirical investigation in Lebanese banks. *The Learning Organization, 15*(5), 409–420.
Kirchmeyer, C. (2005). The effects of mentoring on academic careers over time: Testing performance and political perspectives. *Human Relations, 58*(5), 637–660.
Kram, K. (1985). *Mentoring at work: Developmental relationships in organisational life*. University Press of America.
Kram, K. E. (1996). A relational approach to career development. In D. Hall & Associates (Eds.), *The career is dead—Long live the career* (pp. 132–157). San Francisco: Jossey-Bass.
Lankau, M. J., & Scandura, T. A. (2002). An investigation of personal learning in mentoring relationships: Content, antecedents and consequences. *Academy of Management Journal, 45* (4), 779–790.
Lapointe, É., & Vandenberghe, C. (2016). Supervisory mentoring and employee affective commitment and turnover: The critical role of contextual factors. *Journal of Vocational Behavior*.
Lowe, D., Levitt, K. J., & Wilson, T. (2008), Solutions for retaining Generation Y employees in the workplace. *Business Renaissance Quarterly, 3*(3).
Lynn Stallworth, H. (2003). Mentoring, organizational commitment and intentions to leave public accounting. *Managerial Auditing Journal, 18*(5), 405–418.
Maertz, C. P., Griffeth, R. W., Campbell, N. S., & Allen, D. G. (2007). The effects of perceived organizational support and perceived supervisor support on employee turnover. *Journal of Organizational Behavior, 28*(8), 1059–1075.
Mathieu, J. E., & Zajac, D. M. (1990). A review and meta-analysis of the antecedents, correlates, and consequences of organizational commitment. *Psychological Bulletin, 108*(2), 171.
Martin, C. A. (2005). From high maintenance to high productivity, What managers need to know about Generation Y. *Industrial and Commercial Training, 37*(1), 39–44.
Mobley, W. H., Griffeth, R. W., Hand, H. H., & Meglino, B. M. (1979). Review and concept analysis of the employee turnover process. *Psychological Bulletin, 14*, 224–247.
Naim, M. F. (2014). Leveraging social media for Generation Y retention. *European Journal of Business and Management, 6*(23), 173–179.
Naim, M. F., & Lenka, U. (2016a). Knowledge sharing as an intervention for Generation Y employees' intention to stay. *Industrial and Commercial Training, 48*(3), 142–148.
Naim, M. F., & Lenka, U. (2016b). Mentoring, social media, and Generation Y employees' intention to stay: Towards a conceptual model. *International Journal of Business System and Research, 11*(1/2), 28–43.
Naim, M. F., & Lenka, U. (2017a). How does mentoring contribute to Gen Y employees' intention to stay? *An Indian Perspective, 13*(2), 314–335.
Naim, M. F., & Lenka, U. (2017b). Investigating the impact of social media on Gen Y employees' engagement: An Indian perspective. *International Journal of Human Capital and Information Technology professionals, 8*(3), 29–48.

Naim, M. F. & Lenka, U. (2018, in press). Development and retention of Generation Y employees: a conceptual framework. *Employee relations* (n/a, n/a).
Ng, E. S., Schweitzer, L., & Lyons, S. T. (2010). New generation, great expectations: A field study of the millennial generation. *Journal of Business and Psychology, 25*(2), 281–292.
Payne, S. C., & Huffman, A. H. (2005). A longitudinal examination of the influence of mentoring on organizational commitment and turnover. *Academy of Management Journal, 48*(1), 158–168.
Reid, M. F., Allen, M. W., Riemenschneider, C. K., & Armstrong, D. J. (2008). The role of mentoring and supervisor support for state IT employees' affective organizational commitment. *Review of Public Personnel Administration, 28*(1), 60–78.
Saxena, P., & Jain, R. (2012). Managing career aspirations of generation Y at work place. *International Journal of Advanced Research in Computer Science and Software Engineering, 2* (7), 114–118.
Scandura, T. A., & Ragins, B. R. (1993). The effects of sex and gender role orientation on mentorship in male-dominated occupation. *Journal of Vocational Behavior, 43*(3), 251–265.
Scheible, A. C. F., & Bastos, A. V. B. (2014). Analyzing the impacts of commitment and entrenchment on behavioral intentions.*Universitas Psychologica, 13*(1), 109–119.
Schuler, R. S., Jackson, S. E., & Tarique, I. (2011). Global talent management and global talent challenges: Strategic opportunities for IHRM. *Journal of World Business, 46*(4), 506–516.
Sonnenberg, M., Koene, B., & Paauwe, J. (2011). Balancing HRM: The psychological contract of employees. *Personnel Review, 40*(6), 664–683.
Stahl, G. K., Chua, C. H., Caligiuri, P., Cerdin, J. L., & Taniguchi, M. (2009). Predictors of turnover intentions in learning-driven and demand-driven international assignments: The role of repatriation concerns, satisfaction with company support, and perceived career advancement opportunities. *Human Resource Management, 48*(1), 89–109.
Stahno, J. & Yang, J. (2014). *Are there any best practices for developing Gen Y/Young professionals*? Unpublished thesis. Retrieved May 4, 2017, from http://digitalcommons.ilr.cornell.edu/student/53/.
Stead, V. (2005). Mentoring: a model for leadership development? *International Journal of Training and Development, 9*(3), 170–184.
Talent. Edge "2020" (2011). *Blueprints for the new normal.* Raport Deloitte.
Tarique, I., & Schuler, R. S. (2010). Global talent management: Literature review, integrative framework, and suggestions for further research. *Journal of world business, 45*(2), 122–133.
Terjesen, S., Vinnicombe, S., & Freeman, C. (2007). Attracting Generation Y graduates: Organisational attributes, likelihood to apply and sex differences. *Career Development International, 12*(6), 504–522.
Twenge, J. M. (2010). A review of the empirical evidence on generational differences in work attitudes. *Journal of Business and Psychology, 25*(2), 201–210.
Weiss, H. M., & Cropanzano, R. (1996). Affective events theory: A theoretical discussion of the structure, causes and consequences of affective experiences at work.
Weyland, A. (2011). Engagement and talent management of Gen Y. *Industrial and commercial training, 43*(7), 439–445.

Mohammad Faraz Naim (Ph.D.) is presently working as Assistant Professor at UPES, Dehradun, India. His research interest includes talent management, HR technology and knowledge management. He has published research articles in peer-reviewed journals of International repute. He is also continuously involved in presenting research papers in International Conferences. He is the recipient of Young Research Award at 14th HUSOC Conference, Dubai.

Chapter 19
Reward Solutions to Retention Questions

Mark Bussin

Abstract Over the last few years, organisations have had difficulty facing a changing financial setting that has challenged conventional reward procedures and plans. A complete understanding of reward packages is needed including both the intrinsic and extrinsic factors that impact total reward. These factors have a key impact on performance, job satisfaction and the retention of high calibre talent; all of which contribute to organisation effectiveness. More specifically, research has shown that the different types of rewards employers offer to employees affect the recruitment and retention of top talent. Few businesses realise just how much employee turnover impacts their bottom line. Reward strategy is one of the least understood elements of retention strategies, yet one of the most frequently used. This chapter will cover the trends in remuneration options linked to staff retention.

Keywords Reward · Remuneration · Compensation · Total rewards
Job performance · Recruitment · Retention · Intrinsic rewards · Extrinsic rewards
Reward strategy

Introduction

Organisations are facing an increase in pressure to remain competitive. Apart from revenue and market pressure, the competition for top talent is significant. It is essential that organisations determine the most efficient and effective means for attracting, recruiting and retaining this talent. What is clear is that conventional reward procedures, plans and strategies are no longer sufficient. To adapt to a volatile, dynamic business environment organisations must consistently evaluate and adapt attraction and retention strategies.

Remuneration is one of the most concrete, significant and commonly used mechanisms in talent management. What should be noted, however, is that

M. Bussin (✉)
Gordon Institute of Business Science, University of Pretoria, Pretoria, South Africa
e-mail: drbussin@mweb.co.za; drmarkbussin@gmail.com

M. Coetzee et al. (eds.), *Psychology of Retention*,
https://doi.org/10.1007/978-3-319-98920-4_19

remuneration does not follow a 'one-size-fits-all' approach, nor is it a retention strategy that is successful in isolation. To be successful and sustainable, remuneration must be located within a broader reward and talent management strategy. This chapter outlines the reward strategies and remuneration factors that are linked to greater retention of talent as well as the latest developments and trends associated with these strategies.

Key Talent is Essential for Business Productivity and Sustainability

Key talent is fundamental to the success of any organisation. These people fill critical roles, are high performers, or have high potential. They are also the staff who become the organisations' leaders, increasing an organisation's sustainability and longevity. During times of economic recovery or low growth organisations depend on this key talent as it is necessary to compete aggressively for profitability, viability and sustainability.

Globalisation and increasing economic development have created a workplace where the demand for talent far exceeds the supply (Ready and Conger 2007). Employee turnover rates are increasing (Smit et al. 2015), and consequently, employee retention has become a topic of great importance (Ibidunni et al. 2016). This is not surprising as talented employees are the basis of organisational performance and growth (Ibidunni et al. 2016) and replacing them is costly.

Losing key talent costs the organisation more than the average employee as their contribution is exponentially greater than others (Masango and Mpofu 2013). Estimates of how much the loss of talent costs companies ranges from 90 to 200% of annual salary, and the cost of replacement ranges from 50 to 60% of annual salary. These direct costs don't include the opportunity costs of bringing a new employee up to speed (Neese 2016). The intellectual capacity, expertise, business processes and relationships that accompany employees are of the highest value to organisations (Byerly 2012). Employee turnover, therefore, has a large impact on an organisation's expenses (Ratna and Chawla 2012). Leaving an organisation, an employee takes with them organisational knowledge, experience gained from the organisation and even customers (Ratna and Chawla 2012). Employee retention is a topic of concern for most organisations today (Tladinyane et al. 2013).

Not only is staff turnover expensive, finding replacement skills can be a difficult task. Knowledge workers are specifically in great demand and with an individual skills base, these workers are highly mobile. They have the intellectual clout, ability and opportunity to follow attractive opportunities and offers as they arise (Schlechter et al. 2014a, b). This leaves employers in a challenging situation.

Remuneration as a Factor in Retaining Talent

Future Workplace (Schwabel 2016) found that improving retention is a critical priority for 87% of employers. Remuneration is one—albeit significant—factor in retaining key talent. Organisations are finding that traditional remuneration procedures and plans are no longer effective as drivers of retention for talent. Key talent is able to negotiate higher remuneration, understands comparative salary bands, and is able to interview outside the workplace with ease.

Although remuneration impacts retention for all employees including talent, it should not be considered in isolation. The impact of leadership and management on retention is critical, and sometimes even when remuneration is highly favourable, it is not sufficient to drive retention where leadership is poor. Botha et al. (2011) note that many organisations are now developing specially designed retention mechanisms, including new reward practices.

The Problem—The Place of Reward in an Effective Retention Strategy

There is no comprehensive understanding of the efficacy, motivation and retention value behind reward packages. Reward packages need to be understood both as a whole, and as part of the intrinsic and extrinsic factors that accompany them. This has implications for their successful implementation and the ability of organisations to recruit and retain talented employees. This chapter outlines research on reward strategies that have been found to be successful in attracting and retaining key talent. The role of remuneration within retention strategy is thus clarified and can be applied to the design of future reward strategies and packages.

Conceptualising Retention and Engagement

Employee retention refers to how an organisation dissuades employees from leaving using policies and practices (Hong et al. 2012). It includes efforts to encourage and entice employees to remain at the organisation such as rewarding for desirable performance, offering a healthy and stable working environment, and the provision of other benefits. Schwabel (2016) argues that as much as 25% of the "stay decision"—to remain with a company—relates to remuneration.

The definition of "retain" has two meanings: "to hold or keep in possession" and "to engage the services of". The traditional focus in many HR practices has been to hold or keep rather than to engage a service. High-value employees and those with "hot" skills want to be "engaged" and not "kept". Organisations need to shift their thinking and focus on what they need to do to help these employees become fully engaged in the organisation. Perhaps the focus then is to engage people for as long as possible, rather than trying to retain them for as long as possible. An innovative retention strategy and an organisation reward strategy would certainly aid this process.

Engagement is linked to better organisational outcomes, increased performance, customer satisfaction, employee satisfaction, and reduced turnover. When almost a third of an employee's life is spent at work, it is essential that they are effective and engaged. The consequences of not being engaged are far reaching for the organisation's performance and the wellbeing of the individual (Hoole and Hotz 2016).

Employee engagement is currently at an all-time low globally. Hoole and Hotz (2016) cite statistics that up to 80% of employees are disengaged, that South African employees are amongst the most disengaged, and that 43% of employees consider leaving their jobs. Hoole and Hotz (2016) also found a significant, positive relationship between total rewards and work engagement, proving that effective total reward packages are instrumental in increasing engagement and therefore retention.

Factors Impacting Retention

Döckel's Retention Factor Framework outlines six retention factors that impact employee retention: compensation (this is synonymous with remuneration), characteristics of the job, supervisory support, training and development opportunities, work-life balance as well as career opportunities (Döckel et al. 2006) (Fig. 19.1).

Compensation: Compensation is often considered the most important factor (Ibidunni et al. 2016) and affects the willingness of employees to remain in a job (Armstrong 2003). Abiodun et al. (2012) argue that the degree of job satisfaction experienced by employees as well as their willingness to remain at an organisation largely depends on the reward system and compensation packages offered by the organisation. And in fact, Döckel et al. (2006), Ibidunni et al. (2016); Schaubroeck et al. (1994) and other researchers have found a relationship between salary, fair compensation and commitment.

Organisations need to choose the most appropriate way to reward the employee to achieve the optimal results (Falola et al. 2014). This can include monetary and non-monetary rewards (Roy 2015). Monetary rewards include:

- salary
- incentive payments and salary add-ons
- profit sharing, and
- bonuses.

Non-monetary rewards are indirect financial rewards received (Schlechter et al. 2015).

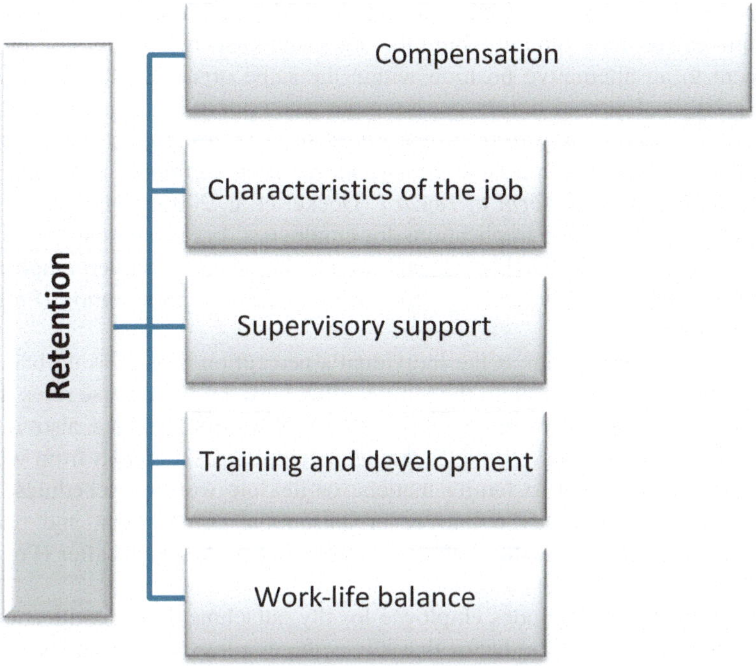

Fig. 19.1 Summary of Döckel's retention factor framework

Characteristics of the job: Positive characteristics lead to better retention, and include having a wide range of work tasks, interesting tasks, assignments that are challenging, more desirable team members or co-workers, flexibility and freedom (Coetzee et al. 2015). These job characteristics influence the perceived competence of employees, and increase the perceived meaning of the work, which then leads to enhanced organisational commitment and retention (Döckel 2003).

Training and development: Training and development are linked to advancement opportunities and continuous employee growth, effectiveness and efficiency (Mubarak et al. 2012; Presbitero et al. 2016). These opportunities foster a sense of value for employees through the perception that the organisation is prepared to invest in them, leading to an increase in attachment to the organisation, with rising organisational commitment (Van Dyk et al. 2013). Organisations that offer training and development programmes are found to secure retention, have higher profitability and increased employee commitment, satisfaction and productivity (Presbitero et al. 2016).

Supervisory support: This includes the recognition and feedback that supervisors afford their employees (Döckel et al. 2006), which increases employees' loyalty to the organisation (Van Dyk and Coetzee 2012).

Career Opportunities: These are the opportunities linked to career development where the opportunities in career goals match employees' job requirements

(Roy 2015). They consist of internal and external career options. Internal career opportunities are those offered within the organisation such as promotion or lateral movement to an alternative position within the same organisation (Van Dyk and Coetzee 2012). External career opportunities are opportunities in an alternative organisation. ***Career opportunities are found to have the highest retention predictability*** (Döckel et al. 2006). ***Furthermore, they influence retention more strongly than any other form of reward*** (Döckel et al. 2006). The lack of career opportunities has negative implications for employees' organisational commitment (Van Dyk and Coetzee 2012). Organisations that place a larger emphasis on practicing career development are those with higher retention ratios (Presbitero et al. 2016).

Work-Life balance: This is the individual's perception of a pleasing balance of work life and personal life, with the least conflict between the diverse roles that the individual must fulfil (Presbitero et al. 2016). Work-life balance also includes policies such as family leave policies that allow employees to depart from work for certain periods to attend to family matters; or flexible working schedules. These practices all lead to higher employee organisational commitment and retention (Döckel et al. 2006). Work-life balance is becoming more sought after (Presbitero et al. 2016).

Commitment: This includes employee loyalty, attachment or identification with an organisation and it is the factor that aligns the employees' feelings and actions with the goals and purpose of the organisation (Singh and Gupta 2015). It ultimately influences retention.

Nienaber (2010) describes a Total Rewards Strategy that includes a mix of financial and non-financial rewards encapsulating similar retention factors to Döckel's Retention Factor Framework, but expanding on the nature of compensation. Figure 19.2 from Nienaber elaborates on these rewards and how together they present a holistic view of total reward.

It is clear that remuneration plays a key role in retention, but that it is not the most important driver of retention, and that it is best included in a broader total rewards strategy to promote retention.

Reward and Retention Strategies are not One-Size-Fits-All

There is no ideal or universal reward strategy that drives retention for all employees. Instead there are a multitude of factors that impact the perceived value of both reward and retention strategies. This perceived value varies between employees and even within employees at different stages of their lives and careers. Some of these factors are discussed below.

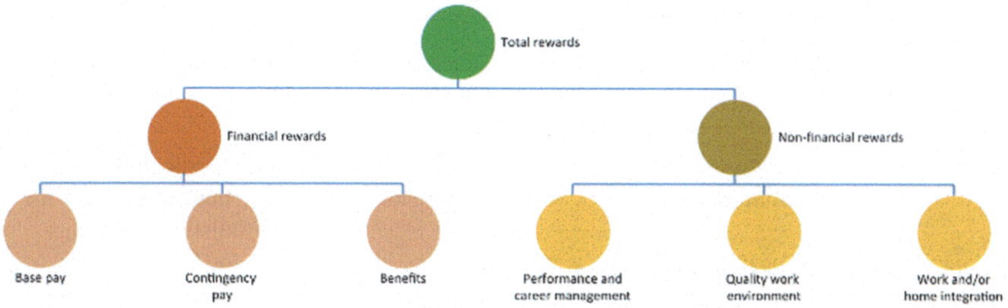

Base pay	**Performance and career management**
Monthly salary	Monthly communication sessions with management on business progress
Merit increases linked to personal performance	Constructive and honest feedback on performance
Merit increases linked to inflation not personal performance	Opportunities to rotate and experience different types of jobs
The ability to structure remuneration according to personal needs	Growth opportunities, learning and development
	Bursaries for tertiary qualifications
	Coaching and mentoring
	Formal and informal recognition
	Control over own work methods
	Career path planning aligned with personal goals and interests
	Challenging job that tests abilities
	Accountable for job outputs
	International secondments
Contingency pay	**Quality work environment**
Annual performance bonus	Good relationship with colleagues
Shares/share options	Comfortable working environment
Bonus allocations linked to personal performance	On-site fitness centre, restaurant, medical centre and convenience store
Bonus allocations linked to the team performance	Personal safety and security in the workplace
	Quality of co-workers in the team
	Management encourage team performance
Benefits	**Work–home integration**
Medical aid	Flexible working hours
Retirement & disability	Employer provides holiday programmes for children
Study leave	Subsidy for financially dependent parents
Sabbatical leave	Ability to log into the employer's network from home
Dedicated parking bay	Laptop and 3G card are required to perform optimally
Subsidised tuition for children	Phased in return to work after maternity/paternity leave
Financial assistance to buy a house	

Fig. 19.2 Nienaber's (2010) total reward preference model (author's own compilation)

Characteristics of Employees—Generational Diversity

Each generation has different values and reward preferences that predispose the effect they will have on motivation and retention (Stone and Deadrick 2015). These preferences should be recognised and applied according to each of the groups, and should be used to attract employees from each generation (Singh and Gupta 2015). Generational Cohort Theory advocates using a different approach for each generation in the workforce as individuals carry their uniqueness to the workplace with differences in workplace performance, motivation and communication (Pant and Vijaya 2015).

Farr-Wharton et al. (2012) specify four generational cohorts, but this chapter focuses on the three most common in the workplace today: Baby Boomers, Generation X and Generation Y. Table 19.1 describes the factors that impact commitment across these three generations.

Table 19.1 Factors impacting commitment across generations

	Baby boomers 52–70 years old	Generation X 37–51 years old	Generation Y 17–36 years old
Reward	Internal benefits over external rewards	Compensation in monetary form	Internal benefits have more value, but high regard for materialistic belongings
Characteristics of the job	Job design, lower stress	Freedom and challenges to remain stimulated	Job rotation and enrichment
Training and development	Perceived as part of continuous development and purpose	Continual training	Multi-media and development programmes
Supervisory support	Bureaucratic leadership	Bureaucratic leadership	Valued very highly; seek honest, consistent feedback with support and compliments
Career opportunities			Note they are unpredictable; will move easily. Offer activities important for career advancement
Work-life balance	Flexi-time, job-sharing, condensed work-week, part-time work, long-term leave, career breaks and telecommuting	Family time	Opt for work-life balance when given the option of deciding between jobs

Summarised from Gamage et al. (2014); Michael (2014); Aruna and Anitha (2015); Earl and Taylor (2015).

The highest guarantee of organisational commitment is work environment, training and development and supervisory support. Bussin and Van Rooy (2014) found that rewards that are non-monetary in nature establish higher value among every generation.

Context Impacts the Effectiveness of Reward Packages

The downside of the various reward and retention strategies organisations use is that a dedicated focus on remuneration as a tool may have the perverse incentive of driving up pay costs. It is important to implement employee engagement strategies that focus on the various elements of reward, as well as both the intrinsic and extrinsic reward offerings.

Table 19.2 Top 10 drivers of attraction, engagement and retention in **Europe**

	Attraction drivers	Engagement drivers	Retention drivers
1	Work/life balance	Senior management interest in employees	Manager inspires enthusiasm for work
2	Recognition for work	Ability to improve skills	Career advancement opportunities
3	Career advancement opportunities	Senior management to demonstrate values	Company reputation as a good employer
4	Challenging work	Challenging work	*Fair and consistent pay determination*
5	*Competitive pay*	Decision-making authority	Intention of working after retirement in another field
6	Learning/development opportunities	Company reputation as a good employer	Decision-making authority
7	Job autonomy	Ability to influence company decisions	Overall work environment
8	Variety of work	Company focus on customer satisfaction	Intention of working after retirement to stay active
9	Pay rises linked to individual performance	*Fair and consistent pay determination*	Manager provides access to learning opportunities
10	Company reputation as a good employer	Overall work environment	Senior management demonstrates values

Towers Perrin carried out research in the United States and across six countries in Europe. They asked both groups questions on a variety of workplace factors in their organisation—practices, processes, culture, leadership style, and development opportunities. In effect, they probed all the key elements typically seen to be the drivers of workforce behaviour. They found a "top 10" list of drivers of attraction, retention and engagement (Tables 19.2 and 19.3). There are clear geographical differences, which again emphasises the necessity for customising reward strategies to the location and composition of the workplace. For instance, 'competitive pay' fell at the number 5 driver in attracting staff in Europe, but at number 2 in the US. As a retention factor, pay fell at number 4 in Europe, but number 6 in the US.

Research by Willyerd (2014) at SAP found that most employees value monetary rewards in the workplace with competitive compensation (65%), bonuses and merit-based rewards (55%) and retirement plans (45%) rated highest.

Context thus plays a key role in determining the reward mix and perceived value of remuneration in relation to retention strategies. It is important to research and investigate the nature of the workplace and workforce before designing a reward strategy.

Table 19.3 Top 10 drivers attraction, engagement and retention in the **United States of America**

	Attraction drivers	Engagement drivers	Retention drivers
1	Competitive healthcare benefits	Senior management interest in employees	Career advancement opportunities
2	*Competitive pay*	Challenging work	Retention of high-calibre people
3	Work/life balance	Decision-making authority	Overall work environment
4	Competitive retirement Benefits	Company focus on customer satisfaction	Ability to improve skills
5	Career advancement opportunities	Career advancement opportunities	Resources to get job done
6	Challenging work	Company reputation as a good employer	*Competitive pay*
7	Calibre of co-workers	Collaboration with co-workers	Clear goals from manager
8	Pay rises linked to individual performance	Resources to get job done	Challenging work
9	Recognition for work	Ability to influence company decisions	Manager inspires enthusiasm for work
10	Company reputation as a good employer	Senior management vision	Overall satisfaction with Benefits

Developing a World-Class Reward Strategy

Reward strategies are not one-size-fits-all—the characteristics of the organisation and what its employees value must be considered. While a diverse group of employees may all value different reward components, the organisation must balance these demands to create a strategy that is suitable to balance the capability and resources of the organisation against the retention and attraction drivers of employees. This balancing act needs to consider that reward is only one component of a reward strategy and should be considered alongside other offerings from the organisation (such as flexi-time, secondments, rotations, training and so forth). Financial rewards themselves also take many forms. The sections below list the primary considerations of which to be aware when designing a reward strategy.

Developing a Reward Strategy—Remuneration

Reward strategies are developed to support the achievement of business goals. The reward strategy leads to the policies and processes which drive the strategy and the actual components of the strategy are determined by what is important to the business and its employees. It is essential to find a solution that supports the needs and values of both the business and the employees. And, as mentioned above, remuneration is only one part of a comprehensive reward package, although it remains a significant one (Armstrong 2014; Gross and Edelsten 2006). A total reward strategy should include both monetary and non-monetary rewards to ensure an attractive workplace, and to drive the attraction and retention of employees.

Monetary components of a retention strategy can include one or more of the following elements, and depend on the composition of the workplace and what is valued:

- **Sign-on payment/Retention payment**: occurs when an employee joins an organisation. Practices differ somewhat, but the two most common approaches are: Pay the bonus on day one, and the employee repays if he or she leaves within a period of time, often one to three years. Promise the payment in, say, two to three years, on condition that the employee stays and accomplishes certain performance targets.
- **Rolling or banking of incentives earned**: This is a popular approach for non-listed organisations that do not offer long term incentives in the form of shares or share equivalents because of its ease and efficacy. Typically, organisations will target a salary to variable pay (VP) ratio based on salary surveys and niche benchmarking.
- **Short-term incentives (STIs)**: The global trend for the past ten years has been to ratchet up the variable pay portion in the reward package. This links the very large salary bill to how the business performs. These incentives are usually able to motivate and retain over the period of the incentive plan typically up to 12 months.
- **Long-term incentives (LTIs)**: This vehicle is still an important one to retain employees for a longer period. It is essential to balance short-term and long-term incentives so employees remain motivated over the long-term and do not only chase short term goals.
- **Deferred remuneration**: A more recent trend has been for companies to defer a portion of the STI to a future date linked to continued employment of the employee. These incentives are meant to incentivise the employee for longer than the short-term, without the onerous requirements of longer term strategies. Holding periods post vesting of long term incentives create the same result but over a period of up to 3 years post vesting of the LTIs.
- **Post-retirement benefits**: This approach is better for employees close to retirement. The organisation typically continues to pay into the retirement and medical funds for a period after the person has retired.

Developing a Reward Strategy—Intrinsic Rewards

In the past reward strategies focused almost entirely on financial remuneration. Research has shown that this view is simplistic, and that engagement and motivation are driven by more than financial reward. Hoole and Hotz (2016) assert that both intrinsic and extrinsic rewards are important. These are defined as follows:

- Intrinsic rewards are focused more on actual performance of the job and the inherent nature of the work itself. These types of rewards can include growth opportunities, status, a sense of accomplishment, recognition and acknowledgement, challenge, autonomy and responsibility
- Extrinsic rewards, the more traditional form of rewards, include elements such as pay, job security, benefits, promotions, salary increases and bonuses.

Total reward strategies must include both intrinsic and extrinsic rewards. Focusing just on intrinsic rewards makes it hard for the organisation to attract employees and demonstrate its competitiveness in the industry. For instance, Schlechter et al. (2014a, b) found that high remuneration is the most significant driver of attraction, followed by benefits and then variable pay. But focusing just on extrinsic rewards leads to people focusing only on monetary gain rather than the actual work itself. When talent is in high demand, an over-reliance on extrinsic rewards leads to job-hopping as there is little else to motivate an employee to stay in their current organisation. A balance between extrinsic and intrinsic reward is required.

Developing a Reward Strategy—The Link to Strategy, Values and Culture (The WorldatWork Total Rewards Model)

WorldatWork (2015) developed a total rewards model to show the link that must be made to the organisation's strategy, values and culture while also considering the context in which the strategy is located (including market practices, trends in remuneration, diversity of employee base and best practices) (Fig. 19.3).

WorldatWork (2015) lists the six parts of an organisations reward strategy as the following:

Compensation/Remuneration: This includes the 'business as usual' pay that an employee receives from the organisation for the time and effort they put in. It can include fixed pay or variable pay (see Sect. Implications for Retention Theory and Practice for types of remuneration).

Benefits: Benefits are over and above pay that organisations provide. These can include programmes such as health and medical benefits, income protection, savings and retirement. All these have a financial benefit for employees without a direct payment. They also provide the addition of increasing engagement and motivation and loyalty to the organisation as they provide security.

Work-Life Effectiveness: These are the organisations' practices, policies and programs that support and motivate employees to be successful at work and home.

Recognition: Recognition systems can be formal, but can also be more informal and run through teams or managers. More formally, these are programmes that show recognition for specific positive performances, increased effort, or behaviours and can range from a written acknowledgment, time off or a small 'bonus' or cash

Fig. 19.3 Total Rewards Model (WorldatWork, 2015) Contents © 2018. Reprinted with permission from WorldatWork. Content is licensed for use by purchaser only. No part of this article may be reproduced, excerpted or redistributed in any form without express written permission from WorldatWork. www.worldatwork.org

reward. It's important that the behaviour, effort and performance are linked to the organisation's goals.

Performance Management: It is essential to link the expectations of the organisation in terms of what it will take to achieve its goals, to the actions and goals of the individual employee. In this way, performance can be managed, and employees are clear on what behaviour and performance will be rewarded. This not only leads to increased motivation but also continuous adaption of performance to goals.

Talent Development: Being able to develop skills and abilities is not only linked to motivation and engagement, but also has a positive benefit to the organisation.

While the components of the WorldatWork Total Rewards Strategy are not highly differentiated to other models, what does distinguish this model is the strong link to business strategy and organisational culture. Using this framework instigates an investigation and understanding of both the external and internal environments.

Developing a Reward Strategy—Flexibility

There is an increasing trend for employees to want to customise their reward packages. Some younger employees would prefer a lower pension benefit and greater take-home pay. Other employees want a greater STI based on performance, or more time-off, or an opportunity to contribute to socially relevant programmes of work. The alternatives are endless. It is unrealistic and unaffordable to allow each employee to customise their reward strategy. Many large organisations rely on the size of their employee base to negotiate and secure preferential rates for medical, pension and other benefits. These preferential rates would not be possible if employees were allowed to opt-in or out on an ad hoc basis.

This has resulted in a low level of flexibility in reward strategy and components. For example, many employees are forced to join a specific medical aid or pension fund if they want to work at an organisation. While this has been accepted without much question in the past, younger generations and key talent are starting to challenge these norms. Organisations can no longer turn a blind eye to these challenges if they want to drive attraction and retention of talent.

It is difficult to find a good balance between customised benefits/rewards and free choice while still realising the benefits of an organisational reward strategy. When designing a total rewards strategy, the notion of flexibility must be considered. One alternative is to segment employees and customise offerings to each segment which are more aligned to their needs and value drivers. This allows for a degree of defined customisation which is more palatable than a 'take-it-or-leave-it', uni-dimensional approach.

Developing a Reward Strategy—Design

To develop an appropriate reward strategy for an organisation, the following design principles are useful to consider (adapted from the components of reward strategies in high performance organisations by de Waal and Jansen 2011):

Align to values and performance: It is important to use any performance-related pay to also communicate the organisation values, critical success factors and how people are expected to contribute. It is essential that employees understand the link between reward and performance of the individual, their teams and the business strategy. Research has shown that there is a relationship between the pay and incentives received by employees and the long-term success of the organisation. Aligning rewards to team performance increases team performance.

Ensure buy-in: Involve employees in the design of reward processes. This could be in the form of surveys or interviews. Employees must be able to relate the intention and fairness of reward strategies to themselves.

Communication: Communicate reward innovations to employees to ensure efficacy as well maintain buy-in and therefore retention.

Training: linked to the above, provide training to everyone on the application and implications of the reward policies and practices.

Reward package design and composition:

- Include both input (competence) and output (results) in performance reviews, which then link to reward allocations. Make these as clear and objective as possible.
- Introduce robust broad-band pay structures where employees can also develop laterally, take up secondments and participate in job rotations.
- Develop team reward systems which support flexible work practices, multi-skilling and team work.
- Consider pay-for-contribution rather than job duty adherence or service. Remuneration or a pay reward can be linked to a specific contribution that is made, rather than a reward such as a "13th cheque".
- Introduce gain-sharing, profit sharing or any bonus scheme that shares the added value of employee efforts.

Conclusion and Implications for Retention Practice

Money is not the only or even the most important way to motivate and retain employees. Total Reward Strategies include both monetary and non-monetary rewards and research shows that the mix of these rewards is where the magic lies. There is no formula that can be applied to ensure the best reward strategy where retention is a proven outcome. Instead, an understanding of external and internal context is a critical lever of success. Remuneration is the most commonly used factor when organisations strive to attract and retain talent; but it is also the least understood.

This chapter has looked at the link between reward and the retention of talent. It has outlined a framework to develop a Total Rewards Strategy, the considerations to make when developing this strategy, and the types of rewards which can be used.

The primary implication for retention is the insight that although remuneration impacts retention for all employees, it should not be considered in isolation. To successfully retain employees, organisations need to balance intrinsic and extrinsic rewards and focus on engaging people for as long as possible, rather than trying to retain them for as long as possible. In the modern workplace where the demand for talent is far greater than the supply, it is essential to make every effort to retain top talent. Remuneration is key, but a Total Rewards Strategy is required to ensure a balanced and customised solution.

The main components of a total reward strategy include:

Compensation/Remuneration: including fixed and/or variable pay.

Benefits: including programmes such as health and medical benefits, income protection, savings and retirement.

Work-Life Effectiveness/Balance: including organisations' practices, policies and programs that support and motivate employees to be successful at work and home.

Recognition: including formal and informal programmes designed to acknowledge and reward positive performance and behaviour.

Performance Management: including systems to define, measure and assess performance and behaviour against clearly defined goals and objectives.

Talent Development: including programmes and interventions to develop skills and abilities and promote career growth.

There are a number of factors that impact the reward mix that best promotes retention. Two fundamental factors explored include generational mix and context. There is no one size-fits-all formula for determining the best reward mix and it has been suggested that organisations make every effort to engage with their employees and better understand their circumstances and needs before determining the reward mix.

A practical guide on how to design a world class reward strategy is included in the chapter. It is argued that a total rewards strategy should include both monetary and non-monetary rewards to ensure an attractive workplace, and to drive the attraction and retention of employees. Factors to consider include:

Remuneration: monetary reward strategies are developed to support the achievement of business goals.

Intrinsic rewards: strategies focused more on the actual performance of the job and the inherent nature of the work itself.

Link to the organisation's strategy, values and culture: also considering the context in which the strategy is located (including market practices, trends in remuneration, diversity of employee base and best practices).

Flexibility: the need to address the trend/desire for employees to want to customise their reward packages.

Formulation of Reward Design Principles: including the alignment to values and performance, ensuring employee buy-in, communicating reward innovations and training.

In conclusion, the relationship between reward and retention is strong, but reward alone is not sufficient to ensure retention.

Summary

The retention of employees is widely acknowledged as a critical strategy to ensure the avoidance of recruitment and replacement costs. In addition, as talent becomes a currency that is increasingly scarce, mobile and expensive, organisations that are able to promote retention will command a competitive advantage. Remuneration is a commonly used strategy to drive retention and while it is undoubtedly an important part of any retention strategy, this chapter has shown the need for a holistic application of a total rewards strategy.

References

Armstrong, M. (2003). *Strategic human resources management: A guide to action*. UK: KoganPage.

Armstrong, M. (2014). *A handbook of personnel management practice* (13th ed.). Cambridge, UK: Cambridge University Press.

Aruna, M., & Anitha, J. (2015). Employee retention enablers: Generation y employees. *SCMS Journal of Indian Management, 12*(3), 94–103.

Botha, A., Bussin, M., & De Swardt, L. (2011). An employer brand predictive model for talent attraction and retention. *SA Journal of Human Resource Management, 9*(1), 1–12.

Bussin, M., & Van Rooy, D. J. (2014). Total reward strategy for a multi-generational workforce in a financial institution. *SA Journal of Human Resource Management, 12*(1), 1–11.

Byerly, B. (2012). Measuring the impact of employee loss. *Performance Improvement, 51*(5), 40–47.

Coetzee, M., Oosthuizen, R. M., & Stoltz, E. (2015). Psychosocial employability attributes as predictors of staff satisfaction with retention factors. *South African Journal of Psychology*, 1–12.

De Waal, A., & Jansen, P. (2011). *The bonus as hygiene factor: The role of reward systems in the high performance organisation*. Presented during the 3rd European Reward Management Conference 2011, 1–2 December 2011.

Döckel, A. (2003). *The effect of retention factors on organisational commitment: An investigation of high technology employees* (Unpublished M.Com dissertation). University of Pretoria, South Africa.

Döckel, A., Basson, J. S., & Coetzee, M. (2006). The effect of retention factors on organisational commitment: An investigation of high technology employees. *SA Journal of Human Resource Management, 4*(2), 20–28.

Earl, C., & Taylor, P. (2015). Is workplace flexibility good policy? Evaluating the efficacy of age management strategies of older women workers. *Work, Aging and Retirement, 1*(2), 214–226.

Falola, H. O., Ibidunni, A. S., & Olokundun, A. M. (2014). Incentives packages and employees' attitudes to work: a study of selected government parastatals in Ogun State, South-West, Nigeria. *International Journal of Research in Business and Social Science, 3*(1), 2147–4478.

Farr-Wharton, R., Brunetto, Y., & Shacklock, K. (2012). Communication, training, well-being and commitment across nurse generations. *Nursing Outlook, 60,* 7–15.

Gamage, H. R., Sailikitha, T., Karamchandani, J., Gowda, K., & Tong, X. X. (2014, November). *Three generations and their work life balance: Are we balancing work and life or adjusting life for work?* Paper presented at the International Conference on Emerging Economics (ICEE), Bali. Retrieved from http://researchonline.jcu.edu.au/36770/1/36770%20Gamage%20et%20al%20%202014.pdf.

Gross, S. E., & Edelsten, M. (2006). Paying the price of global expansion. *Workspan, 09*(06), 42–46.

Hong, E. N., Hao, L. Z., Kumar, R., Ramendran, C., & Kadiresan, V. (2012). An effectiveness of human resource management practices on employee retention in institute of higher learning: A regression analysis. *International Journal of Business Research and Management, 3*(2), 60–79.

Hoole, C., & Hotz, G. (2016). The impact of a total reward system of work engagement. *SA Journal of Industrial Psychology, 42*(1), a1317. https://doi.org/10.4102/sajip.v42i1.1317.

Ibidunni, S., Osibanjo, O., Adeniji, A., Salau, O., & Falola, H. (2016). Talent retention and organizational performance: A competitive positioning in Nigerian Banking Sector. *Periodica Polytechnica Social and Management Sciences, 24*(1), 1–13.

Masango, R. S., & Mpofu, M. (2013). Staff retention in higher education institutions: A case of selected South African universities. *Journal of Public Administration, 48*(4.1), 883–896.

Michael, T. (2014). *A comparative study of intrinsic motivational triggers for generation X and generation Y members.* ProQuest Dissertations & Theses Global. (1625969974). Retrieved from http://0-search.proquest.com.oasis.unisa.ac.za/docview/1625969974?accountid=14648.

Mubarak, R. Z., Wahab, Z., & Khan, N. R. (2012). Faculty retention in higher education institutions of Pakistan. *Journal of Theories and Research in Education, 7*(2), 65–78.

Neese, B. (2016). *The hidden cost of employee turnover.* Retrieved from https://online.alvernia.edu/cost-employee-turnover/.

Nienaber, R. (2010). *The relationship between personality types and reward preferences. Doctor of Commerce dissertation*. Johannesburg: University of Johannesburg.

Pant, J. J., & Vijaya, V. (2015). Challenges in diversity management: A case study of MediHealth systems. *South Asian Journal of Management, 22*(1), 159–186.

Presbitero, A., Roxas, B., & Chadee, D. (2016). Looking beyond HRM practices in enhancing employee retention in BPOs: Focus on employee-organisation value fit. *The International Journal of Human Resource Management, 27*(6), 635–652.

Ratna, R., & Chawla, S. (2012). Key factors of retention and retention strategies in telecom sector. *Sona Global Management Review, 6*(3), 35–46.

Ready, D. A., & Conger, J. A. (2007). Talent factory. *Harvard Business Review, 85*(6), 69–77.

Roy, B. (2015). A study on employee retention factors in the Indian banking industry: An empirical study. *International Journal of Advance Research in Computer Science and Management Studies, 3*(3), 346–352.

Schaubroeck, J., May, D. R., & Brown, F. W. (1994). Procedural justice explanations and employee reactions to economic hardship: A field experiment. *Journal of Applied Psychology, 79,* 455–460.

Schlechter, A., Faught, C., & Bussin. M. (2014a). Total Rewards: A study of artisan attraction and retention within a South African context. *SA Journal of Human Resource Management/SA Tydskrif vir Menslikehulbron bestuur, 12*(1), Art # 648, 15 p, https://doi.org/10.4102/sajhrm.v12i1.648.

Schlechter, A., Hung, A., & Bussin, M. (2014b). Understanding talent attraction: The influence of financial rewards elements on perceived job attractiveness. *SA Journal of Human Resource Management, 12*(1), 13. https://doi.org/10.4102/sajhrm.v12i1.647.

Schlechter, A., Thompson, N. C., & Bussin, M. (2015). Attractiveness of non-financial rewards for prospective knowledge workers: An experimental investigation. *Employee Relations, 37*(3), 274–295.

Schwabel, D. (2016). *What Employers Will Worry About in 2017*. Fortune. Retrieved from http://fortune.com/2016/12/28/employers-2017-employee-retention-unemployment/.

Singh, A., & Gupta, B. (2015). Job involvement, organizational commitment, professional commitment, and team commitment: A study of generational diversity. *Benchmarking, 22*(6), 1192–1211.

Smit, W., Stanz, K., & Bussin, M. (2015). Retention preferences and the relationship between total rewards, perceived organisational support and perceived supervisor support. *SA Journal of Human Resource Management, 13*(1), 1–13.

Stone, D. L., & Deadrick, D. L. (2015). Challenges and opportunities affecting the future of human resource management. *Human Resource Management Review, 25*, 139–145.

Tladinyane, R. T., Coetzee, M., & Masenge, A. (2013). Psychological career meta-capacities in relation to employees' retention-related dispositions. *Southern African Business Review, 17*(2), 140–163.

Van Dyk, J., & Coetzee, M. (2012). Retention factors in relation to organisational commitment in medical and information technology services. *South African Journal of Human Resource Management, 10*(2), 1–11.

Van Dyk, J., Coetzee, M., & Takawira, N. (2013). Satisfaction with retention factors as predictors of the job embeddedness of medical and information technology services staff. *Southern African Business Review, 17*(1), 57–75.

Willyerd, K. (2014). What high performers want at work. *Harvard Business Review*. Retrieved November 18, 2014, from www.hbr.org.

WorldatWork. (2015). *The WorldatWork handbook of compensation, benefits & total rewards*. Hoboken, NJ: John Wiley & Sons Inc.

Mark Bussin (DCom) is the Chairperson of 21st Century, a specialist reward consultancy. He has reward experience with many multinational companies across all industry sectors, and is viewed as a thought leader in the HR, remuneration and performance arena. He serves on, and advises, numerous boards, remuneration and audit committees on executive remuneration, strategy and board performance. He has published or presented over 400 articles and papers. He has appeared on television and radio, and in the press, giving expert views on remuneration, performance related pay and management. Mark is a guest lecturer at several universities and supervises masters' dissertations and doctoral theses in the reward area. He is the past President of SARA (South African Reward Association) and past Commissioner for the Remuneration of Public Office Bearers in the Presidency.

Chapter 20
Total Rewards as a Psychosocial Factor Influencing Talent Retention

Calvin Mzwenhlanhla Mabaso

Abstract The retention of people who possess talent and are highly qualified is a major concern for contemporary organisations who are operating in a competitive environment (Neininger et al. J Vocat Behav 76:567–579, 2010). Remaining in a competitive environment entails special endeavours to retain talent for the long-standing strength of an organisation. The retention of skilled workers can be a vital edge or advantage for any organisation (Mullins Management and organisational behaviour, Prentice Hall, London, 2005; Ngozwana and Rugimbana Afr J Bus Manag 5:1524–1527, 2010; Armstrong 2015). Ultimately, retention of talent has an important part in maintaining the overall organisational performance. Most organisations realise the importance of embracing total rewards as the best strategy to retain key talent. Therefore, this chapter will focus on total rewards as a means for retention-related dispositions that will ensure valuable employees remain in the organisation. Exploring total rewards as psychosocial factors that influence talent's choice to join, remain and leave an organisation has become crucial in the light of changes in organisations. The study employed semi-structured questionnaire using 262 participants to unearth the influence of total rewards on talent retention.

Introduction

Higher education institutions is seen as the center for knowledge and contribue to the economy of the country. Talent retention in higher education institution is therefore critical. Erasmus et al. (2015) affirm that, within higher education institutions, talent retention of highly qualified workforce is considered a major challenge due to the pull factors of private sector institutions or other higher education institutions that can afford to offer further benefits. Robyn and du Preez (2013) attest that employee retention is a presently an global problem facing businesses and particularly among academic staff in higher education institutions. Boshoff

C. M. Mabaso (✉)
College of Business and Economics, University of Johannesburg, Johannesburg, South Africa
e-mail: calvinm@uj.ac.za

M. Coetzee et al. (eds.), *Psychology of Retention*,
https://doi.org/10.1007/978-3-319-98920-4_20

et al. (2002) as well as Grobler and De Bruyn (2011) observe the recent war for talent and labour turnover, which is challenging to organisations when their employees quit to join other organisations. Pienaar and Bester (2006) warn organisations to pay attention to retention of talent where economic feasibility and existence rest on scarce skills. Bidisha and Mukulesh (2013) state that employee retention refers to keeping employees in their present jobs and inspiring them to continue working for the organisation for lengthier periods. Ultimately, Mita et al. (2014) attests that talent retention is a method implemented by an organisation to sustain an operative labor force and, at the same time, meet operational requirements.

Workforce Planning state that talent retention is an organized determination to generate an atmosphere that motivates staff to continue working by implementing practices and policies that address employees' various needs. The South African Board for People Practices's (2012) study revealed that 32% of South African organisations do not concern themselves with the talent retention phenomenon, while 46% of these organisations indicated that talent retention as major concern. It is evident that, for organisations to remain competitive, talent retention strategies need to be in place. To accomplish a competitive advantage organisations rely on expertise from employees while maintaining quality to safeguard continued performance (Harvey 2009; Reiche 2007). Cardy and Lengnick-Hall (2011) support that, if highly qualified employees are not kept in their positions, this will affect both operations and strategies. In this regard, employees should be the most vital asset for an organisation. Therefore, special care should be given to retain such assets. Additionally, retaining talented and excellence centered employees turns out to be the top strategic policy for organisations (Heinan and O'Neill 2004; Holbeche 2009). However, studies confirms that organisations adopt numerous policies and procedures to retain talent (Samuel and Chipunza 2009; Holland et al. 2007; Hom et al. 2008).

Khan et al. (2014) state that organisations are using different human resource practices in order to increase retention levels. Haider et al. (2015) noted the significance for organisations to develop atmosphere that encourages employees to remain longer in their organisations. Organisations should also pay attention to the costs associated with employee turnover, which is typically two and a half times greater than the salary of an individual (Haider et al. 2015). Talent retention entails measures through which employees are encouraged to remain longer in the organisation. As a means of achieving this, it is critical for an organisation to recognize what attracts employees and what keeps good employees. Employees are the sole reason for organisation existence (Wisnefski 2008; Rasli et al. 2014). Therefore, it is essential to retain talented employees for the survival of the organisation and a competitive advantage.

Objectives of the Study

If employees are not retained within the organisation, it tends to show higher turnover which makes organisations face more financial costs in regard to recruiting, training, and the development of new employees. It is believed that the cost of hiring new talent and training is two and a half times higher than their individual salary. Thus, the main objective of this study is to evaluate the influences of psychosocial factors on talent retention.

Theoretical Background

The current study adopted Vroom's (1964) expectancy theory as a framework. Vroom's study (1964) is of the view that individuals' perception of effort is correlated with levels of performance. This theory confirms that there is a correlation between these variables, performance–outcome expectancy, or instrumentality. Employees expect that their individual efforts in the workplace will result in rewards based on their performance. Khan and Mufti (2012) demonstrate that employees expect rewards in exchange for effort they put in on the job. Khan and Mufti (2012) explain that the self-belief in skills is called expectancy, the belief that performance will bring rewards is referred to as instrumentality, while the value placed on the reward is described as the valence. Valence means that employees will be inspired when they are compensated with rewards they value. In addition, instrumentality shows that employees' performance will result in rewards and motivation. People differ regarding what they value. For example, to some employees, pay has more value than other rewards whereas to others, more intrinsic rewards such as recognition and achievement are significant.

Talent Retention

Retention is significant for employees since it impacts costs on two dimensions. The Corporate Leadership Council (2004) differentiates direct and indirect expenditure that result from costs associated with retention. Direct expenditure over labour turnover (recruitment expenses, low productivity, training and development, and lost opportunity costs) and indirect expenditure, which includes employee engagement. Scott et al. (2012) affirm that retention of vital talent is critical for organisations that ought to achieve a competitive advantage. Talent retention entails the attraction and maintenance of highly qualified talent in organisations (Swanepoel et al. 2014). Additionally, it remains the task of an organisation to enhance the skills of newly appointed employees in order to attain organisational goals.

Scholars in the remuneration field show that the key aspect that keeps employees longer in their present job can be achieved through competitive remuneration systems (Kwenin et al. 2013). Terera and Ngirande (2014) confirm a positive relationship between rewards and talent retention. Findings of Terera and Ngirande (2014) are in agreement with other studies which posit the importance of rewards on talent retention. Taylor et al. (2006) concur that remuneration influences job satisfaction and is regarded as a major contributor to retention. Remuneration is a predictor for organisational commitment and intention to stay in organisation. Financial rewards play a vital role in talent retention (Chew and Chan 2008).

Hausknect et al. (2009) explains that policies and procedures implemented by the organisation are crucial to prevent the loss of talented workers throughout the organisation. Browell (2003) states that employee retention focuses on preventing the organisations talented workforce from being exposed to its major competitors in order to preserve them. Talented employees are essentially employees that contribute significantly to the organisations success and are thus crucial assets. Their position within the organisation create a large competitive advantage. It is highly important that organisations create strategies that focus on retaining their talented workforce by motivating employees to stay in their positions for long time periods. The retention of talented employees can been seen as a costly process, however, it is important in making sure the organisations is as competitive as possible. Human capital maintenance is costly but extremely important. Talent retention is also referred to as employee retention (Okioga 2012). Netswera et al. (2005) state that the retention process is centred around employee satisfaction by providing them with reasons to stay in their position and thus creating deeper organisational commitment. Hong et al. (2012) explain that no matter the size of the organisation, there should be a deep focus on employee satisfaction. A competitive advantage is one of the many benefits of retaining talented employees.

Significance of Talent Retention

Attaining talent retention depends on employing organisational culture which is employee driven and recognises talent as the most important asset (Chikumbi 2011). Top management should drive this culture to retain talent. Recruitment, training, and development can also act as the talent retention strategy which will enable the organisation to attain a competitive advantage. Customer satisfaction increases sales, promotes working relationships, improves employee-manager relationships, and enables valuable success planning which is fostered by employee retention. Inability to retain key talent is costly in any kind of business format.

Total Rewards

Armstrong and Murlis (2007) state that total rewards encompasses things that fall outside of the traditional means of reward such as salary increases and benefits. In addition, rewards include aspects that are not cash based such as furthering their position of responsibility within the organisation, learning opportunities and an increase in the value of the work environment itself. Gross and Friedman (2004) affirm that total rewards refers to the total sum of remunerations that the employer passes on to the employee. A total package would provide compensation in the form of benefits and career focused opportunities. Career opportunities refer to any means that would allow the employee to further themselves within their line of work. Similarly, Kantor and Kao (2004) claim that total rewards refer to compensation and benefits that are sometimes tangible elements such as employee development which focuses on how employees are given opportunities to develop and learn more skills. In higher education institutions, objectives of reward include, but are not limited to, attracting and retaining staff of high quality and potential (HESA 2014).

World at Work (2015) proposes a total rewards model with six essential elements, they are discussed in detail below (Boswell et al. 2011). These elements are strong predictors of both job satisfaction and the commitment to an organisation. Makhuzeni and Barkhuizen (2015) reported the importance of implementing total rewards in schools and recommended this to Department education for consideration. However, World at Work (2007) attests that by adopting a total rewards strategy, organisations can improve their recruitment and talent retention. Additionally, there is an increase of organisations lacking key productivity and talent factors. Recruitment and retention issues rely heavily on a good total rewards strategy. A total rewards strategy can assist in meeting the needs of employees and thus encouraging them to contribute more to the organisation (World at Work 2007).

Elements of Total Rewards

Snelgar et al. (2013) argue that a key factor to employee commitment within higher education is remuneration. Nujjoo and Meyer (2012) suggest that all South African organisations should recognize the value of intrinsic rewards within their reward management strategies. Financial rewards focus largely on reward management. Employees should be receiving a balanced reward system which is a mixture of financial and non-financial rewards (Shields 2007). The following are components of total rewards:

Compensation as Element of Total Rewards

World at Work (2015) explains that compensation is essentially monetary reward given to an employee based on the amount of time, effort, and skill they put into their work. This refers to both fixed income in the form of salary as well as variables such as bonuses. Swanepoel et al. (2014) refer to compensation as being financial and non-financial extrinsic rewards that employer provides in return for the time, skill, and job fulfilment of the employee in terms of organisational goals. Absar et al. (2010) contend that compensating employees is one of the main functions of the human resource department. In regard to attracting, retaining, and motivating employees, compensation is a central function. Ray and Ray (2011) state that compensation is vital due to the fact that it is the main motivating factor for most employees. Compensation, or total compensation, is "the total of all rewards provided to employees in return for their services" (Phonsanam 2010: 6). De Bruyn (2014) observes that, within higher education institutions, it is clear that fair remuneration results in benefits for both the organization and its employees. The employee is afforded a better state of living while the institution is allowed the benefit of retaining talented and qualified staff.

Benefits as Element of Total Rewards

World at Work (2007) states that benefits are an added supplement to the cash compensation employees receive for their work. This refers to things such as retirement plans, job security, and income protection which all basically serve to provide a safety net for employees and their families. Employee benefits are essentially schemes that serve to benefit the employee, put in place by the employer. All of these benfits are provided as well as regular pay and make up the total rewards package (Armstrong 2012). Nazir et al. (2013) conducted a study within higher education institutions, their study reveals a high positive correlation between fringe benefits, job satisfaction, and organisational commitment in higher education institutions. Similarly, Yamoah's (2013) study shows that academic staff were not satisfied with fringe benefits offered to them. However, this study (Yamoah 2013) adds that satisfaction with fringe benefits will allow academic staff to remain longer within higher education institutions.

Work-Life Balance as Element of Total Rewards

World at Work (2007) states that work-life programmes are intended and introduced as policies enabling employees to reach a better work-life balance. Furthermore, World at Work (2007) mentions that work life practices are means to enable individuals to balance their work life and home. Rumpel and Medcof (2006) argue that a balance for the time spent at work and at home is included in the work environment. For instance, flexible working is one of the most important aspects of a balanced life. According to Maphanga (2014), organisations need to come to the realisation that people are their most valuable assets, upon realising this they will put a greater emphasis on allowing for employees to balance their work and home lives. An equilibrium is achieved when an employee can find a balance between work life and personal life (Lockwood 2003).

Recognition as an Element of Total Rewards

World at Work (2007) states that any attention or acknowledgment given to an employee's actions, efforts, behaviour, or performance is referred to as recognition. There is an intrinsic psychological need within every employee to have their achievements recognized, in doing so employers reinforce behaviours that contribute to organisational success. Additionally, Kwenin et al. (2013) states that recognition is directly correlated to employee retention. There is a need from employees to receive recognition on top of financial reward.

Performance Management as Element of Total Rewards

Brudan (2010) states that the task of establishing, monitoring and achieving personal and organisational goals is directly corelated to performance management. Verbeeten (2008) claims that performance management also includes the task or defining goals and selecting strategies to chieve them, as well as assigning decision making rights, and measuring and rewarding performance. Soni (2003) articulates that there is only a temporary increase in performance from employees that have been praised or rewarded. Shikongo (2011) suggests that a proper performance system should be implemented in order to assess overall performance and reward employees accordingly. This will serve both to reward those that are already working hard as well as to encourage poor performers to essentially work harder for the promise of further reward.

Talent Development and Career Opportunities as Element of Total Rewards

World at Work (2007) state that talent development allows for the honing of skills as well as an opportunity to correct any pitfalls in an employee's performance. It also benefits the organisation by instilling its employees with skills that will ultimately help achieve organisational goals. Development is a tool that furthers employees' abilities to perform as well as instilling in leaders the ability to further the organisations people skills. Further, World at Work (2007) defines development as an opportunity for employees to learn and grow within the organisation. Bernadin and Russell (2013) claims career advancement opportunities are essentially crucial motivators in regard to Herzberg's theory. Akhtar et al. (2015) state that a lack of development and promotion opportunities can lead to academics leaving higher education institutions and that pay doesn't necessarily have to be the key factor in their departure.

Research Hypothesis

Thus, an established hypothesis based on the above literature is:

H_1: Total rewards elements would have a positive and significant relationship with talent retention.

Research Design and Methodology

This study took into account a quantitative research method using the survey research design. The quantitative method was appropriate as it enables the researcher to examine influence of total rewards on talent retention.

Research Approach

The study implemented a quantitative research design. Babbie (2007) defines research design as a set of decisions regarding what topic is to be studied among what population with what research methods for what purpose, research design is the process of focusing your perspective for the purposes of a particular study.

Research Participants

The study implemented a survey to collect data. The study used a sample of 262 academics from the institution of higher learning in South Africa. The study employed a probability sampling using systematic sampling method. This was the

Table 20.1 Demographic profile of respondents (N = 262)

Variable	Categories	N	%
Gender	Male	100	38
	Female	162	62
Age	18–29	79	30
	30–45	102	39
	46–64	76	29
	65+	5	2
Race	African	201	77
	Indian	14	5
	White	39	15
	Coloured	8	3
Tenure	0–1 year	42	16
	1–4 years	67	26
	5–7 years	78	30
	7–15 years	75	29
Qualification	Honours degree	53	20
	Master's degree	77	29
	Ph.D.	8	3
	B.Tech	80	31
	M.Tech	37	14
	D.Tech	7	3
Rank	Lecturer	226	86
	Senior lecturer	20	8
	Head of department	12	5
	Professor	4	2

Source Authors' compilation from survey data

most applicable method in terms of participant recruitment. Each university gave consent and confirmed their participation. Permission to conduct research was granted by both institutions. The characteristics of each respondent are depicted in Table 20.1. A breakdown of the demographic profile of respondents (Table 20.1) shows that 38% (n = 100) of the respondents were male, whereas 62% (n = 162) were female. Through the collection of all the respondents ages it was revealed that the lost number (39%; n = 102) were aged between 30 and 45 years. Additionally, 31% (n = 80) of the respondents had a B-Tech degree. Racially, Africans (77%; n = 201) accounted for most of the respondents. In regard to position held, the biggest group of respondents (86%; n = 226) were lecturers, followed by senior lecturers (8%; n = 20), with professors (2%; n = 4) accounting for the least number of respondents.

Data Collection Method

According to Maree (2017), face to face, postal, personal, telephone, group, and computer assisted survey methods can be used to collect data. In this study, a structure questionnaire was used as a method of collecting data using a personal method. The method chosen is relatively cheap, offers greater anonymity since there is no face-to-face interaction between respondents, easy to administer, and respondents can complete the questionnaire at a convenient time. The sample respondents were also easily accessible to the researcher.

Measuring Instrument

The study used a questionnaire as a measuring instrument. The Total Rewards Model taken from the World at Work publication (2015) was utilized in the construction and of the questionnaire that was distributed to respondents. The total rewards questionnaire was designed to measure specific performance dimension, recognition, talent development, and career opportunities for academic staff. The retention scale was adapted from the study of Theron et al. (2014). Both these instruments are based on the five Likert rating scale. The respondents were asked to indicate the extent of their agreement or disagreement with the statements on a scale of one to five. On this scale, one would mean that they strongly disagreed and five that they strongly agreed with the statement provided.

Reliability and Validity of the Study

The validation of the usefulness of a research instrument is vital. The validity and reliability of this study's research tool was assessed, as proposed by Alumran et al. (2012). Cronbach's alpha values for the scale were as follows: total rewards ($\alpha = 0.822$) and retention ($\alpha = 0.932$). It was concluded that each of these instruments measured high on internal consistency; therefore, data analysis was possible.

Data Analysis

The assistance of the Statistical Package for the Social Sciences (SPSS version 23.0) was used to analyse data. Initially, demographic data of the subjects, frequencies, and the scores of the overall work-related factors as well as measures of central tendency were established. Internal consistency estimates were formulated using Cronbach's alpha coefficients. Following this, a series of multivariate statistical procedures that included exploratory factor analysis, Pearson correlation analysis, and linear regression were computed on all the variables in order to ascertain the relationship between variables. The required level of significance (p) was set at 0.01.

Results

Correlation Matrix for the Study Variables

Table 20.2 presents correlation matrix for the three-factor model with performance management, talent development, career opportunities, and job satisfaction.

It is demonstrated how variables are connected to one another through the process of correlation. Creative Research Systems (2009) states the correlation between variables but fails to show which correlation is strongest or most reliable. In order to answer the first research objective, to determine the relationship between total rewards and talent retention, the correlation between total rewards and talent retention is illustrated in Table 20.2. Pearson correlation computed to determine the relationship among variables (total rewards and talent retention). Pearson correlation indicates a positive strong relationship between total rewards elements:

- Compensation ($r = 0.652$, $p < 0.01$); Benefits ($r = 108$, $p < 0.01$); work-life balance ($r = 0.211$, $p < 0.01$); performance management ($r = 741$, $p < 0.01$); recognition ($r = 591$, $p < 0.01$); talent development and career opportunities ($r = 652$, $p < 0.01$)

Table 20.2 Pearson correlations

		Talent retention	Coefficient of determination (R^2)
Talent retention	Pearson correlation	1	
Compensation	Pearson correlation	0.652**	0.4251
	Sig. (2-tailed)	0.000**	
Benefits	Pearson correlation	0.108	0.0117
	Sig. (2-tailed)	0.184	
Work-life balance	Pearson correlation	0.211	0.0445
	Sig. (2-tailed)	0.009**	
Performance management	Pearson correlation	0.741	0.5491
	Sig. (2-tailed)	0.000**	
Recognition	Pearson correlation	0.591**	0.345
	Sig. (2-tailed)	0.000	
Talent development and career opportunities	Pearson correlation	0.652**	0.4251
	Sig. (2-tailed)	0.000**	

** = Statistically significant at the 1% level ($p < 0.01$)

Table 20.3 The model statistics using stepwise regression

Model	R	R Square	Change statistics		Durbin-Watson
			F Change	Sig. F Change	
5	0.826[e]	0.682	6.595	0.011	1.730

e. Predictors: (Constant), performance management, recognition, benefits, compensation talent development and career opportunities, work-life balance

Therefore, the hypothesis is accepted. Pallant (2010) explains that how associated the variables are depends heavily on the size of the negative or positive correlation value. Small relationships are indicated by values ranging from 0.10 to 0.29, medium relationships are values from 0.30 to 0.49, and a value of 0.5 to 1.0 shows that there is a strong relationship between variables. This means that total rewards elements have a positive effect on talent retention. Therefore, these results confirm the research objective. The results obtained, which indicate a positive relationship between study variables, dimensions of the instruments were assessed using multiple regression analysis. Table 20.3 presents the results. These factors were all interval variables and this research wishes to determine their influence on talent retention. Thus, retention of talent will serve as the outcome variable and dependent variables (total rewards) as predictors. In this way one will be able to determine which one of the factors is the best predictor of employee retention. The equation for determining the various values is:

$$Y_i = (b_0 + b_1X_1 + b_2X_2 + \ldots b_nX_n) + \varepsilon_i$$

where Y_i is the outcome variable (Employee retention), b_0 is the constant, b_1 is the coefficient of the first predictor (X_1), b_2 is the coefficient of the second predictor (X_2), b_n is the coefficient of the nth predictor (X_n) and ε_i is the error (Field 2009). Thus, using the dependent factors developed one could write:

$$FGH(2.0) = b_0 + b_1FB + b_2FC2.0 + b_3FD2.0 + b_4FE + b_5FF2.0 + \varepsilon.$$

Stepwise, regression was used where the programme searches for the predictor (from the five available ones) that best predicts the outcome variable. If this predictor significantly improves the ability of the model to predict the outcome, then the predictor is retained in the model and the programme searches for a second predictor (Field 2009). In this way, SPSS identified five models, of which the fifth model was retained for this research. The model statistics are provided in Table 20.3. The R^2 value of model 5 indicates that when total rewards elements are used as these predictors explain predictors then 68.2% of the variance in the outcome variable (talent retention). The change in F is also significant and the ANOVA table also indicated that model 5 was a significant fit, F specifically: [F (5,147) = 63.18; p = 0.000]. The Durbin-Watson statistic was close to 2.0 and hence the assumption of errors in the regression being independent was also met.

Table 20.4 Coefficients of the regression model

Independent variables	Standardized beta coefficients	t	Sig.
Recognition	0.286	5.474	0.000*
Performance management	0.317	3.897	0.000*
Compensation	0.348	5.973	0.000*
Benefits	0.178	2.926	0.004*
Talent development and career opportunities	0.276	3.894	0.000*
Work-life balance	0.099	2.075	0.040

*Statistically significant at $P < 0.05$

Cohen et al. (2011) suggested that r square greater than 0.5 indicates a strong model fit. Therefore, these results confirm that total rewards have a greater influence on talent retention. The next step is the contribution each independent variables makes on the prediction of talent retention, this was evaluated and is delineated in Table 20.4. The model coefficients as generated for Model 5 by SPSS using stepwise regression are displayed in Table 20.4.

Of greatest importance in Table 20.4 are the Beta (β) values or standardised coefficients as they denote the deviations that the outcome (talent retention) shall be altered as a result of a single standard deviation and this will change the prediction (Field 2009). These Beta values indicate the importance of the predictors in the model. These results outlined in Table 20.4 suggest that compensation ($\beta = 0.348$), benefits ($\beta = 0.178$), performance management ($\beta = 0.317$), work-life balance ($\beta = 0.099$), recognition ($\beta = 0.286$), and talent development and career opportunities ($\beta = 0.276$) all have a statistically positive effect on talent retention. In terms of the largest beta coefficients recorded, compensation and performance management seem to make the strongest contribution to explaining talent retention. The t values of the independent variables are greater than 0.107. Ndungu (2017) states that values greater than 0.107 indicates a strong impact of the predicting quality of the coefficient.

Discussion

Previous studies have indicated that talent retention can be attained by using total rewards as a strategy (Armstrong and Stephens 2006; Cao et al. 2013, Akhtar et al. 2015). Theron et al. (2014) conducted a study that revealed that the majority of academics were most likely to leave because of the following reasons: dissatisfaction with financial compensation, discontent with career development opportunities, and a lack of promotional opportunities. These results echo previous results that show a lack of proper reward systems could lead to an intention to leave among employees (HESA 2011; Ngobeni and Bezuidenhout 2011). Additionally, Haider et al. (2015) attest that compensation and training as well as development and career opportunities are strong predictors of employee retention. Employees that are trained and qualified will be likely to switch to other organisations if they are not properly compensated. Suresh and Krishnaraj (2015) suggest that there is a growing need to retain talented and high performing staff members by implementing performance management and career planning strategies. Approaches to increase the level of retention include compensation packages and total rewards. These approaches can also be used as retention strategies. Each organisation must analyse which employees need to be retained and why they should be retained. They must employ methods that encourage these employees to be loyal, stay with the organisation, as well as remain committed and productive (Suresh and Krishnaraj 2015).

Umamaheswari and Krishnan (2016) also find that employee retention has a definitive relationship with training and development. Mehta and Kurbetti (2014) affirm that in order to improve talent retention, development and training opportunities, compensation and benefits, and a work-life balance should be in place. Additionally, performance management can also be used effectively in order to enhance talent retention in organisations. Makhuzeni and Barkhuizen (2015) shows that elements of total rewards (compensation, performance management, career development) were not correctly implemented in schools and as a result, teachers were considering leaving the organisation were they worked due to few rewards. However, teachers were satisfied with benefits and work-life balance. Mubarak et al. (2012) state that academics will remain within their institutions longer if they are well rewarded. Academics inspired by academic policies, funding for research, and a scheduled compensation package. Gakure et al. (2013) study revealed a lack of competitive reward system which propelled academics to leave their higher education institutions. Additionally, academics indicated they were not satisfied with the recognition they received. Bayissa and Zewedie (2010) confirm that reward systems had a common theme of excluding recognition for exceptional performance. Makondo (2014) attests to the significance of higher education institutions to have properly qualified talent in order to improve research capabilities. It is suggested that higher education institutions be proactive enough to manage their attraction and retention strategies in ways to enhance their strategic positioning.

Implications for Retention Practice

Total rewards elements are strategic to the organisation's goals and thus should be able to ensure employee satisfaction and retention. The current study found that total rewards had a positive impact on employee retention. Since efforts are directed towards the achievement of organisational goals, and this relies heavily on total rewards, the management should enhance proper implementation of total rewards in order to increase talent retention.

In conclusion, an organisation's, success, productivity, branding, and competitiveness, are all reliant on the employees within the institution and thus, said employees should receive recognition and be valued based on their work. A culture of high performance within and organisation is heavily influenced by the amount of recognition given to employees. Rewards packages that fulfil monetary needs of employees as well as their material wants are correlated closely to retention. Employees are expectant of their employers to properly compensate them for their work. The job of management within higher education institutions is to make sure they have developed a fair, equitable, and free of bias remuneration package that serves to attract the best candidates for the job as well as retain them. Said remuneration package is considered to be one of the most important factors in keeping employees. To remain competitive and attract the best employees, an organisation must be prepared to pay salaries that are equal to or more than what their competitors are paying. The opportunity for promotion and other relating factors are considered to be equally important in order to stop employees seeking work elsewhere. Success within the institution should be something clearly outlined to employees. Recognition plays the largest role when referring to strategies that encourage a high performance work environment and thus, employees who complete effective work should receive acknowledgement. Management can use results of this study and develop reward strategies to ensure talent retention, this will ensure a talent pool that can contribute to the overall performance of the organisation.

Summary

In this chapter, credible relationship between psychosocial factors and talent retention has been indicated. The presence of total rewards in organisations has assure the retention of talent. Furthermore, employees expect that their employers provide them with rewards that they value not what management value. A clear description of retention drivers has been discussed. The rewards specialists have to develop a fair and equitable rewards packages to attract and retain talent. The suggested rewards discussed in this chapter can also be used for development of talent retention strategies in contemporary world of work. The possible rewards preference and talent retention can be further researched since various rewards capable of keeping talent in organisations.

References

Absar, M. M. N., Azim, M. T., Balasundaram, N., & Akhter, S. (2010). Impact of human resources practices on job satisfaction: Evidence from manufacturing firms in Bangladesh. *Economic Sciences Series, 62*(2), 31–42.

Akhtar, C. S., Aamir, A., Khurshid, M. A., Abro, M. M. Q., & Hussain, J. (2015). Total rewards and retention: Case study of higher education institutions in Pakistan. *Procedia-Social and Behavioral Sciences, 210*, 251–259.

Alumran, A., Hou, X., & Hurst, C. (2012). Validity and reliability of instruments designed to measure factors influencing the overuse of antibiotics. *Journal of Infection and Public Health, 5,* 221–232.

Armstrong, M., & Murlis, H. (2007). *Reward management: A handbook of remuneration strategy and practice*. (Revised 5th ed). London: Kogan Page Limited.

Armstrong, M. (2012). *Armstrong's handbook of reward management practice*. London: Kogan Page.

Armstrong, M. (2015). *Armstrong's handbook of reward management practice, improving performance through rewards*. London: Kogan Page.

Armstrong, M., & Stephens, T. (2006). *A handbook of employee reward management and practice*. United Kingdom: Kogan Page Ltd.

Babbie, E. (2007). Conducting qualitative field research. In *The practice of social research* (11th ed.). United State of America: Thomson Wadsworth.

Bayissa, W., & Zewdie, S. (2010). Academic staff reward system: A case of Jimma University. *Ethiopian Journal of Education and Science, 6*(1), 13–27.

Bernadin, H. J., & Russel, J. E. (2013). *Human resource management: An experiential approach* (International ed.). McGraw Hill: New York.

Bidisha, L. D., & Mukulesh, B. (2013). Employee retention: A review of literature. *Journal of Business and Management, 14,* 8–16.

Boshoff, A. B., Van Wyk, R., Hoole, C., & Owen, J. H. (2002). The prediction of intention to quit by means of biographic variables, work commitment, role strain and psychological climate. *Management Dynamics, 11*(4), 14–28.

Boswell, W. R., Cook, A. L., Horner, M. T., Payne, S. C., & Shaub, M. K. (2011). The relative influence of total rewards elements on attraction, motivation and retention. *World at Work Journal, 20*(1), 1–45.

Browell, S. (2003). *Employee retention in a week*. London: Hodder and Stoughton.

Brudan, A. (2010). Rediscovering performance management: systems, learning and integration. *Measuring Business Excellence, 14*(1), 109–123.

Cao, Z., Chen, J., & Song, Y. (2013). Does total rewards reduce the core employees' turnover intentions? *International Journal of Business and Management, 8*(20), 62–75.

Cardy, R. L., & Lengnick-Hall, M. L. (2011). Will they stay or will they go? Exploring a customer-oriented approach to employee retention. *Journal of Business and Psychology, 26,* 213–217.

Chew, J., & Chan, C. C. A. (2008). Human resource practices, organisational commitment and intention to stay. *International Journal of Manpower, 29*(6), 503–522.

Chikumbi, C. N. L. (2011). *An investigation of talent management and employee retention at the bank of Zambia*. Unpublished doctoral dissertation, Nelson Mandela Metropolitan University.

Cohen, L., Manion, L., & Morrison, K. (2011). *Research methods in education*. London: Routledge.

Corporate Leadership Council. (2004). *The effort dividend–driving employee performance and retention through engagement*. Washington DC: Corporate Executive Board.

Creative Research System. (2009). Retrieved November 10, 2017 from http://www.surveysystem.com/contact.htm.

De Bruyn, M. (2014). *Job satisfaction of staff member at two faculties of an academic instittution*. Unpublished Masters Dissertation. University of Johannesburg.

Erasmus, B. J., Grobler, A., & Van Niekerk, M. (2015). Employee retention in a higher education institution: An organisational development perspective. *Progressio: South African Journal for Open and Distance Learning Practice, 37*(2), 33–63.

Field, A. (2009). *Discovering statistics using SPSS*. London: Sage.

Gakure, R. W., Kamau, A. W., & Waititu, A. G. (2013). Reward systems as determinant of talent management in Public Universities in Kenya. *Journal of Humanities and Social Sciences, 18*(2), 41–47.

Grobler, P. A., & De Bruyn, A. J. (2011). Flexible work practices (FWP)–an effective instrument in the retention of talent: A survey selected JSE-listed companies. *South African Journal of Business Management, 42*(4), 63–78.

Gross, S. E., & Friedman, H. M. (2004). Creating an effective total rewards strategy: Holistic approach better supports business success. *Benefits Quarterly, 20*(3), 7–12.

Haider, M., Aamir, A., Akhtar, S. S., Yusoff, R. B. M., Malik, O. M., Arif, A., et al. (2015). The impact of human resource practices on employee retention in Telecom Sector. *International Journal of Economics and Financial Issues, 2*(2), 63–69.

Harvey, D. (2009). Talent strategy is vital. Personnel Today, June 23, 13.

Hausknect, J. P., Rodda, J., & Howard, M. J. (2009). Targeted employee retention: Performance-based and job-related differences in reported reasons for staying. *Human Resource Management, 48*(2), 269–288.

HESA. (2011). *A generation of growth: Proposal for a national programme to develop the next generation of academics for South African higher education*. Pretoria: University of South Africa.

Higher Education South Africa (HESA). (2014). Strategic framework for universities South Africa, 2015 – 2019. Online. Available at http://www.universitiessa.ac.za/sites/www.universitiessa.ac.za/files/Strategic%20Framework%20for%20Universities%20South%20Africa,%202015-2019.pdf.

Heinen, J. S., & O'Neill, C. (2004). Managing talent to maximize performance. *Employment Relations Today, 31*(2), 67–82.

Holbeche, L. (2009). *Aligning human resources and business strategy*. London: Routledge.

Holland, P., Sheenan, C., & De Cieri, H. (2007). Attracting and retaining talent: Exploring human resources development trends in Australia. *Human Resource Development International, 10*(3), 247–262.

Hom, P. W., Roberson, L., & Ellis, A. D. (2008). Challenging conventional wisdom about who quits: Revelations from Corporate America. *Journal of Applied Psychology, 93,* 1–34.

Hong, E. N. C., Hao, L. Z., Kumar, R., Ramedran, C., & Kadiresan, V. (2012). An effectiveness of human resource management practices on employee retention in institute of higher learning: A regression analysis. *International Journal of Business Research and Management, 3*(2), 60–79.

Kantor, R., & Kao, T. (2004). Total rewards: Clarity from the confusion and chaos. *World at Work Journal, 13*(3), 7–15.

Khan, F., Yusoff, R. M., & Khan, A. (2014). Effect of human resource practices on job satisfaction in Pakistan. *Sains Humanika, 1*(1), 5.

Khan, W., & Mufti, E. O. (2012). Effect of compensation on motivating employees in public and private banks of Peshawar. *Journal of Basic and Applied Scientific Research, 2*(5), 4616–4623.

Kwenin, D. O., Muathe, S., & Nzulwa, R. (2013). The influence of employee rewards, human resource policies and job satisfaction on the retention of employees in Vodafone Ghana Limited. *European Journal of Business and Management, 5*(12), 13–20.

Lockwood, N. (2003). *Work-life balance: Challenges and solutions*. Society for Human Resource Management.

Makhuzeni, B., & Barkhuizen, N. E. (2015). The effect of a total rewards strategy on school teachers' retention. *South African Journal of Human Resource Management, 13*(1), 1–10.

Makondo, L. (2014). Academics attraction and retention trends at a South African University. *Journal of Sociology, 5*(2), 169–177.

Maphanga, C. H. (2014). *The relationship between manager support, work-life balance and talent retention in a South African utility organisation*. Unpublished Master's Dissertation. University of Pretoria. Pretoria.

Maree, K. (2017). *First steps in research*. Pretoria: Van Schaik Publishers.

Mehta, M., & Kurbetti, A. (2014). Study on employee retention and commitment. *International Journal of Advance Research in Computer Science and Management Studies, 2*(2), 154–164.

Mita, M., Aarti, K., & Ravneeta, D. (2014). Study on employee retention and commitment. *International Journal of Advance Research in Computer Science and Management Studies, 2,* 154–164.

Mubarak, R. Z., Wahab, Z., & Khan, N. R. (2012). Faculty retention in higher education institutions of Pakistan. *Journal of Theories and Research in Education, 7*(2), 65–78.

Mullins, L. J. (2005). *Management and organisational behaviour* (7th ed.). Prentice Hall: London.

Nazir, T., Khan, S. R., Shah, S. F. H., & Zaman, K. (2013). Impact of rewards and compensation on job satisfaction: Public and private universities of UK. *Middle-East Journal of Scientific Research*, 394–403.

Ndungu, D. N. (2017). The effects of rewards and recognition on employee performance in public educational institutions: A case of Kenyatta University, Kenya. *Global Journal of Management and Business Research: Administration and Management, 17*(1), 43–68.

Netswera, F., Rankhumise, E., & Mavundla, T. (2005). Employee retention factors for South African higher education institutions: A case study. *South African Journal of Human Resource Management, 3*(2), 36–40.

Neininger, A., Lehmann-Willenbrock, N., Kauffeld, S., & Henschel, A. (2010). Effects of team and organizational commitment–A longitudinal study. *Journal of Vocational Behavior, 76*(3), 567–579.

Ngobeni, E. K., & Bezuidenhout, A. (2011). Engaging employees for improved retention at a higher education institution in South Africa. *African Journal of Business Management, 5*(23), 9961–9970.

Ngozwana, K., & Rugimbana, R. (2010). Assessment of talent retention strategies: The case of a large South African company (CSA). *African Journal of Business Management, 5*(5), 1524–1527.

Nujjoo, A., & Meyer, I. (2012). The relative importance of different types of rewards for employee motivation and commitment in South Africa. *South African Journal of Human Resource Management, 10*(2), 1–10.

Okioga, C. K. (2012). The contribution of a developed Reward system on employee Retention; a case of Kisii Bottlers Limited: Kenya. *European Journal of Business and Management, 16*(4), 1–14.

Pallant, J. (2010). *SPSS survival manual: A step-by-step guide to data analysis using the SPSS program* (4th ed.). New York: McGraw Hill.

Phonsanam, S. T. (2010). *Total compensation practices and their relationship to hospitality employee retention*. Unpublished Master of Science Dissertation, University of Nevada, Las Vegas.

Pienaar, C., & Bester, C. (2006). Typical career dilemmas of academic employee during the early career phase within a changing South African higher education institution. *South African Journal of Education, 26*(4), 581–594.

Rasli, A. M., Norhalim, N., Kowang, T. O., & Qureshi, M. I. (2014). Applying managerial competencies to overcome business constraints from small technology-based firms in Malaysia. *Journal of Management Info, 3*(1), 99–121.

Ray, S., & Ray, I. A. (2011). Human resource management practices and its effect on employees' job satisfaction: A study on selected small and medium sized iron and steel firms in India. *Public Policy and Administration Research, 1*(1), 22–31.

Reiche, S. (2007). The effect of international staffing practices on subsidiary staff retention in multinational corporations. *The International Journal of Human Resource Management, 18*(4), 523–536.

Robyn, A., & Du Preez, R. (2013). Intention to quit amongst Generation Y academics in higher education. *South African Journal of Industrial Psychology, 39*(1), 1–14.

Rumpel, S., & Medcof, J. W. (2006). Total rewards: Good fit for tech workers. *Research Technology Management*, 27–35.

Samuel, M. O., & Chipunza, C. (2009). Employee retention and turnover: Using motivational variables as a Panacea. *African Journal of Business Management, 3*(8), 410–415.

Scott, K. D., McMullen, T. D., Royal, M. (2012). Retention of key talent and the role of rewards. *World at Work Journal, 21*(4), 58–70.

Shields, J. (2007). *Managing employee performance and reward concepts, practices, strategies*. New York: Cambridge University Press.

Shikongo, J. N. (2011). *Staff attraction and retention: A model for a Namibian State*. M-Tech dissertation, Cape Peninsula University of Technology, Cape Town.

Snelgar, R. J., Renard, M., & Venter, D. (2013). An empirical study of the reward preferences of South African employees. *SA Journal of Human Resource Management, 11*(1), 1–14.

Soni, T. J. (2003). *The relationship between the big five personality dimensions and job satisfaction in a petro-chemical organization*. Unpublished Master's dissertation, North-West University.

South African Board for People Practices. (2012). HR Survey 2012. 4th Update. Randburg: Knowres.

Suresh, L., & Krishnaraj, R. (2015). A study on the importance of employee retention in pharmaceutical sector in India. *International Journal Pharmaceutical Science Review and Research, 32*(1), 108–111.

Swanepoel, B. J., Erasmus, B. J., Schenk, H. W., & Tshilongamulenzhe, T. (2014). *South African human resource management: theory and practice* (4th ed.). Cape Town: Juta.

Taylor, L. J., Murphy, B., & Price, W. (2006). Goldratt's thinking process applied to employee retention. *Business Process Management Journal, 12*(5), 646–670.

Terera, S. R., & Ngirande, H. (2014). The impact of rewards on job satisfaction and employee retention. *Mediterranean Journal of Social Sciences, 5*(1), 481–487.

Theron, M., Barkhuizen, N., & Du Plessis, Y. (2014). Managing the academic talent void: Investigating factors in academic turnover and retention in South Africa. *Journal of Industrial Psychology, 40*(1), 1–14.

Umamaheswari, S., & Krishnan, J. (2013). Work force retention: Role of work environment, organisation commitment, supervisor support and training and development in ceramic sanitary ware industries in India. *Journal of Industrial Engineering and Management, 9*(3), 612–633.

Verbeeten, F. H. (2008). Performance management practices in public sector organizations: Impact on performance. *Accounting, Auditing and Accountability Journal, 21*(3), 427–454.

Vroom, V. H. (1964). *Work and motivation*. San Francisco, CA: Jossey-Bass.

Wisnefski, M. (2008). Employee retention in the new millennium. *Business Services, 16*(3), 465–507.

World at Work. (2007). World at Work total rewards model: A framework for strategies to attract, motivate and retain employees. http://www.worldatwork.org/pub/total_rewards_brochure.pdf.

World at Work. (2015). Total rewards model a framework for strategies to attract, motivate and retain employees. http://www.worldatwork.org/waw/adimLink?id=28330.

Yamoah, E. E. (2013). Reward systems and teachers' performance: Evidence from Ghana. *Canadian Social Science, 9*(5), 57.

Calvin Mzwenhlanhla Mabaso (PhD) is currently employed as a Lecturer and Undergraduate Qualification Leader in the Department of Industrial Psychology and People Management at the University of Johannesburg, South Africa. His research focuses primarily on talent retention and total rewards, other focus include organisational commitment, job satisfaction and employee socialisaton. He has written numerous papers at national and international level. He is also registered with South African Board of People Practice (SABPP) as an HR Professional. He is also an accredited assessor and moderator with ETDPSETA.

Conclusion: Theory, Practices and Research in Support of an Integrated Conceptual Framework for the Psychology of Retention

The chapter contributions in the various parts of the book present elements of an integrated conceptual framework for understanding the psychology of retention. In summary, the various elements of the conceptual framework seem to highlight the following guidelines for retention practice:

- Develop a working knowledge of how theory such as Job Demands-Resources, Conservation of Resources theory, Self-determination theory, Broaden-and Build theory and Expectancy theory deepen understanding of the dynamics of the psychology of retention, including the dynamic interplay between individuals, their retention behaviour, and the organisational/environmental context.
- Utilising empirically validated scales as diagnostic and intervention frameworks (e.g. Flow@Work model) for measuring the impact of employees' engagement and psychological work immersion on business performance. Ultimately, retention practices should benefit both the individual and organisation.
- Develop a working knowledge of the influence of the external organisational context on the psychology of retention, including the emerging world of work in a VUCA and digital landscape with the changing psychological contract needs and expectations of especially young talent (e.g. Millennials).
- Practices that consider the impact of the fourth industrial revolution and employee value proposition (EVP) on the psychology of retention.
- Surveys to assess how engaging or disengaging employees view their working conditions and job characteristics in their organisations in terms of JRs and JDs.
- Surveying the engagement experiences of employees in the processes of sourcing and recruiting, pre-boarding, onboarding (orientation and initial training), compensation and benefits, ongoing learning and development, ongoing engagement, communication, and community involvement, rewards and recognition, performance planning, feedback, and review, career advancement, and retirement, termination, or resignation.

M. Coetzee et al. (eds.), *Psychology of Retention*,
https://doi.org/10.1007/978-3-319-98920-4

- Interventions to grow and develop those personal dispositional factors that will result in optimally functioning individuals who possess competencies and skills to effectively and systematically deal with job challenges and hindrances (JDs).
- Measures and interventions to enhance the job embeddedness and self-regulatory capacities of employees.
- Measures and interventions to assess perceptions of the psychological contract (expectations, obligations and violations) for diverse groups of employees.
- Interventions that address the unique and diverse needs (i.e. person-job fit, career development support, social interaction, mentoring, psychological needs satisfaction, wellbeing, rewards and remuneration) of various socio-demographic groups.
- Practices that help create ethical, supportive and intrinsic motivational environments.
- Implement a total rewards strategy that align to important organisational practices (i.e. compensation, benefits, performance management, work-life balance, recognition, and talent development and career opportunities) that support the psychology of retention.

In general, the chapter contributions provided evidence-based practice guidelines supported by empirical research. However, the psychology of retention remains an important area of inquiry and more research is needed to understand the psychology of retention in the VUCA and digital landscape. Millennials as young talent remain under-researched in this landscape and more research in various organisational, occupational and cultural contexts are needed. The measures and frameworks presented in the various chapters stem mostly from cross-sectional research in specific cultural settings, and longitudinal studies in various organisational and cultural contexts are needed to establish cause-effect links between constructs and the manifestation of retention factors among employees from diverse socio-demographic and cultural backgrounds. Some of the chapters illustrated the application of frameworks, measures and interventions in real-life case settings. Evaluation research is required to test the effectiveness and long term impact of different interventions on talent retention and business performance. More empirical evidence is required on how the external environmental factors, internal organisational context factors, employee characteristics, organisation-individual relationship and organisational practices influence the experiences, perceptions and engagement and retention of employees.

Index

A
Advancement opportunities, 12, 20, 24, 86, 208, 211, 246, 389, 399, 403, 404, 422
Anticipatory psychological contract, 307
Attraction-Selection-Attraction paradigm (ASA), 98

B
Benefits, 36, 42, 49, 66, 69, 70, 78–81, 88, 98, 102, 106, 108, 110, 111, 172, 192–194, 208, 209, 211–213, 216, 229, 254, 263, 264, 288, 314, 319, 322, 333, 337, 343, 361, 383, 397, 402, 404–406, 408, 410, 415, 418–420, 422, 425–428, 435, 436
Branding, 59, 66, 288, 428
Broaden-and build theory, 157, 159, 160, 435

C
Career adaptability, 183, 185, 186, 188–190, 192–195, 223–227, 231–237
Career development, 172, 184, 186, 188, 194, 204, 209, 211, 212, 214, 216, 224, 226, 229–237, 243–245, 247–249, 252–255, 287, 289, 291–293, 297, 298, 301, 324, 331, 344, 345, 382, 383, 387, 399, 400, 427, 428, 436
Career opportunities, 7, 119, 123, 127–129, 229, 252, 334, 335, 337–339, 341, 342, 344, 345, 398–400, 402, 419, 424–428, 436
Career satisfaction, 185, 236, 243, 244, 246–257, 383
Characteristics of the job, 8, 398, 399, 402
Civil society organizations, 180, 263–265, 271–276
Climate, 8, 13, 41, 62, 98, 121, 150, 171, 172, 299, 357, 358, 360–374, 389
Collaboration, 23, 42, 61, 67, 70, 71, 76, 82, 109, 290, 357, 404
Collaborative work environments, 287
Commitment, 8, 11, 39–44, 60, 62, 66, 80, 97, 99, 104, 105, 108, 110, 121, 124, 140, 150, 157, 160, 162, 163, 166–173, 185, 188, 190–192, 194, 205, 207, 224, 227–229, 231, 232, 264, 277, 290, 308, 311, 314, 325, 333, 334, 337, 345, 357, 358, 360–374, 379, 380, 383–390, 398–402, 419
Compensation, 11, 66, 69, 80, 208, 209, 211, 212, 229, 334, 337–339, 341–343, 345, 372, 383, 398, 400, 402, 403, 406, 410, 419, 420, 425–428, 435, 436
Conceptual framework, 263, 264, 274–276, 379–381, 383, 384, 388, 389, 435
Conservation Of Resources theory (COR), 21, 101, 104–108, 111, 112
Contextual factors, 5–8, 12, 15, 18–21, 24, 93, 152, 216, 273, 274
Contract breach, 11, 12, 20, 24
Counter-productive work behaviors, 104
Culture, 41, 45–47, 55, 56, 58, 61, 62, 64–68, 71, 77, 79, 81, 82, 84–86, 88, 98, 100, 102, 163, 171, 290, 309, 321–323, 358–360, 371, 374, 385, 387, 389, 403, 406, 408, 410, 418, 429

D
Digital 2020 mind-set, 59
Digital disruption, 55, 56, 58, 64, 68, 71
Digital transformation, 55, 57, 61, 68–72, 308

M. Coetzee et al. (eds.), *Psychology of Retention*,
https://doi.org/10.1007/978-3-319-98920-4

Digital workforce, 55, 56, 60, 61, 64
Distal contextual (environmental) factors, 5–8, 24
Diversity, 59, 61, 85, 86, 210, 214–216, 224, 275, 276, 332, 346, 380, 406, 410
Dual process framework, 6, 19, 24

E
Embeddedness, 95–112, 436
Embeddedness foci, 101, 103–105, 110
Emotional intelligence, 157, 159, 160, 162–164, 169, 184, 232
Employability attributes, 180, 181, 183, 186–189, 194, 223, 225, 226, 231–233, 235–237
Employee engagement, 14, 56, 60, 64–66, 77, 206, 295, 398, 402, 417
Employee Value Proposition (EVP), 54, 66, 75, 78–89, 288, 300, 386, 435
Employment expectations, 307, 320, 321, 325
Enabling environment, 42–45
Entrepreneurial culture, 77
Expectancy theory, 417, 435

F
Factors
  environmental, 5–7, 12, 15, 19, 24, 44, 436
  job and career, 343
  psychological, 119, 128, 158, 184
  push and pull, 23, 24
  retention, 110, 192, 223, 224, 229, 233, 234, 236, 237, 265, 277, 331, 332, 334, 335, 337, 341, 343, 345, 346, 398, 400, 403, 436
Feedback, 7, 37, 42, 44–46, 69, 130, 139, 140, 143, 151, 153, 172, 209, 211, 229, 234, 235, 289, 292–294, 298, 299, 310, 335, 381, 382, 384, 385, 388, 399, 402, 435
Financial wellness, 84, 86, 87
Flourishing, 152, 157, 159, 160, 162, 164, 166–169
Flow@Work Model, 35, 36, 38–41, 44, 46, 49, 50, 435
Fourth Industrial revolution, 35, 36, 435

G
Generational cohorts, 180, 181, 206–208, 211, 212, 214–216, 284, 331, 332, 335, 336, 339, 341, 343–346, 401
Generational Cohort Theory, 401
Generational diversity, 401
Goal achievement, 41, 42, 44
Growth opportunities, 13, 20, 24, 406

H
Hardiness, 157, 159, 160, 162–164, 166–172
Human capital, 48, 55, 58, 65, 68, 77, 82–84, 158, 296, 418

I
Idiosyncratic work values and preferences, 380
Individual congruence, 37, 41, 44–46
Individual dispositions, 5, 6, 15, 20
Intention to leave, 22, 121, 137–141, 145–153, 186, 312, 333, 387, 427
Intrinsic rewards, 381, 405, 406, 410, 417, 419

J
Job Demands – Resources (JD-R) model, 5–8, 10, 19, 21, 22, 24, 92, 123, 124, 128, 129
Job embeddedness theory, 95, 108, 109, 111
Job insecurity, 14, 20, 24, 159

K
Knowledge economy, 36, 40, 42, 43, 49, 77, 311

L
Leadership, 15, 21, 45, 46, 48, 57, 58, 61, 64, 66, 79, 84, 85, 87, 138–140, 157, 171–173, 207, 208, 212, 254, 290, 292, 298, 300, 314, 325, 359, 363, 373, 374, 381, 382, 385, 389, 397, 402, 403, 417
Learning culture, 287
Lifelong learning, 35, 36, 59

M
Manager effectiveness, 37, 41, 45
Meaningful work, 35, 36, 86, 170, 172, 208–211, 213
Meaning of work, 15, 18, 20, 24
Mentoring, 172, 236, 254, 287, 297, 300, 301, 309, 324, 379–390, 436
Millenial workers, 287
Millennials, 98, 102, 111, 203, 204, 206, 208, 210–216, 288–290, 292, 294–301, 307–311, 313–315, 317, 320–326, 380, 381, 387, 389, 390, 435, 436
Mobile workforce, 35, 36, 76
Motivation, 17, 39–44, 99, 103, 106, 110, 123, 138–140, 152, 153, 158, 170, 172, 188,

205, 212, 272, 273, 291, 293, 359, 373, 380, 385, 388, 397, 401, 405, 406, 408, 417
Multigenerational diversity, 203, 204
Multi-generational workforce, 35, 36, 77, 203–205, 211, 213, 214

N
Nomadic employees, 77

O
Obligations, 11, 122, 245, 307, 308, 311, 313–315, 317–321, 323–325, 333, 336, 339, 342–346, 436
Occupational groups, 92, 93, 119, 125, 129–131, 181, 243
Older people, 263–265, 271–277
Organisational commitment, 9, 138, 183, 185, 188–190, 192–195, 223–225, 227–229, 231–237, 334, 335, 339–341, 344, 357, 362, 364–366, 371, 372, 387, 399, 400, 402, 418, 420
Organisational effectiveness, 38, 43, 44, 77
Organisational loyalty, 77
Organisational performance, 42, 43, 172, 396, 415
Organizational citizenship behaviors, 99, 104

P
People effectiveness, 38–40, 43–46, 48
Perceived External Prestige (PEP), 10, 11, 20
Perceived organisational support, 8, 9, 20, 24, 44
Performance management, 11, 45, 77, 172, 407, 410, 421, 425–428, 436
Person−centered characteristics, 243, 244, 247–249, 252–255
Personal agency, 6, 18, 20, 24
Personal attributes, 183, 184, 186, 187, 189, 190–195, 225
Personal resources, 6, 16–20, 23, 24, 157, 159, 160, 162, 170, 271, 273
Person-job fit, 119–121, 126–131, 436
Positive psychology, 37–39
Principal support, 137, 139–141, 145–152
Professional women, 243, 244, 248, 249, 252–255
Proximate contextual factors, 5–7, 12, 20
Psychological contract, 11, 78, 79, 85, 86, 207, 287–291, 297, 298, 301, 308, 311, 313, 315, 317, 326, 331–333, 335–337, 339, 341–346, 387, 435, 436
Psychological contract breach, 11, 307, 309, 311, 317, 323, 325
Psychological need satisfaction, 137–141, 143, 145–147, 149–153
Psychological wellbeing resources, 157
Psychological work immersion, 35–37, 39–41, 43, 44, 46, 48, 49, 435
Psychosocial career preoccupations, 331–337, 341, 343, 344, 346

R
Reasons for leaving, 274, 275
Recognition, 44–46, 69, 106, 130, 208, 209, 229, 272, 274, 300, 311, 317, 335, 382, 388, 399, 403, 404, 406, 410, 417, 421, 424–429, 435, 436
Remuneration, 12, 79, 83, 119, 121, 126–130, 229, 233, 234, 334, 345, 395–398, 400, 402, 403, 405, 406, 409–411, 418–420, 429, 436
Retention Factor Framework, 398–400
Reward Design Principles, 411
Reward package design, 409
Rewards strategy (total), 400, 408, 410, 411, 419, 436

S
Self-actualisation, 38, 383, 386
Self-Determination Theory (SDT), 17, 38, 92, 138, 141, 150, 152, 435
Self-esteem, 15, 157–160, 162–164, 166–169, 183, 184, 186, 188–195, 233, 289, 293, 382, 383
Self-esteem fulfillment, 287
Self-regulation theory, 17
Sense-making, 15, 20, 24
Social capital, 97, 106–108, 111, 121, 263, 264, 300
Social competence, 287
Social connection, 67
Social constructivist approach, 287, 294, 297
Social interaction, 130, 193, 272, 274, 287, 294–296, 301, 436
Social media literacy, 59
Societal norms regarding work, 15
Strategic connection, 41, 42, 44–46
Supervisory support, 9, 398, 399, 402
Support, 7–9, 11, 49, 61, 87, 88, 104, 106–108, 110, 123, 126, 128–130, 138–141, 143, 145, 147, 149–153, 159, 162, 169, 171, 172, 186, 190, 194, 211, 224, 225, 229, 231–233, 235, 253, 254, 264, 272, 274,

277, 291, 293, 294, 299, 300, 310, 314, 315, 318, 321, 322, 324, 331, 332, 334–337, 339, 342, 345, 358, 360, 371, 380–385, 387, 388, 402, 404, 406, 409, 410, 416, 436
Sustainable organisation, 36, 77

T
Talent development, 67, 291, 300, 385, 408, 410, 421, 424–427, 436
Talent management, 45, 66, 203–205, 211, 213–216, 308, 311, 317, 323–326, 379, 380, 395, 396
Talent recruitment, 203, 204, 418
Talent retention, 6, 22, 24, 35–37, 46, 49, 87, 88, 189, 194, 205, 211–216, 230, 231, 236, 255, 307, 308, 320, 331, 379, 388, 415–419, 422, 425–429
Task identity, 10, 20, 24
Task significance, 42
Team climate, 8, 11, 20, 24
Team effectiveness, 43–45, 72
Technological innovation, 35, 36, 58
Total rewards, 45, 398, 400, 406–408, 410, 411, 415, 419, 420, 422, 424–429, 436
Training and development, 229, 230, 235, 314, 334, 337, 339, 372, 398, 399, 402, 417, 428
Turnover contagion, 98
Turnover intentions, 5, 12, 21, 22, 43, 98, 100, 104, 105, 153, 157, 170–172, 308, 309, 311, 319–321, 323–325, 335, 344, 379, 380, 383, 384, 386–390

V
Valued work outcomes, 16
Values, 9, 16, 38, 39, 67, 70, 72, 79, 85, 86, 88, 98, 101, 104, 121, 122, 139, 140, 144, 152, 165, 167, 185, 186, 204, 206–208, 210–216, 227, 244–246, 248, 287, 292, 295, 298, 307, 309, 313, 314, 317, 322, 324, 335, 357–361, 367–369, 371, 372, 374, 380, 381, 383, 387, 390, 401, 403, 404, 406, 409–411, 424, 426, 427
VUCA landscape, 76, 88

W
Wellbeing attributes, 157, 159, 160, 162, 165, 167–170, 173
Work engagement, 6, 7, 9, 12, 16, 17, 21, 22, 36, 39–44, 124, 130, 137, 138, 140, 141, 143–145, 149–153, 157, 159, 160, 162–164, 167, 169–172, 358, 372, 398
Work ethics, 321, 357, 358, 360–374
Work ethics culture, 357–360, 362–364, 366–374
Work−family balance, 244
Work goals, 7, 8, 16, 299
Work-life effectiveness, 354, 406, 410
Work load, 9, 20
Workplace analytics, 68, 70, 72
Workplace bullying, 157–162, 164, 165, 168–173
Work-role identification, 16

The manufacturer's authorised representative in the EU is Springer Nature Customer Service Centre GmbH, Europaplatz 3, 69115 Heidelberg, Germany. If you have any concerns regarding our products, please contact ProductSafety@springernature.com

Printed and bound by CPI Group (UK) Ltd, Croydon, CR0 4YY
05/10/2026
02228139-0017